T0211505

Lecture Notes in Artificial Intelligence 10318

Subseries of Lecture Notes in Computer Science

More information about this series at http://www.springer.com/series/1244

Jorge Gracia · Francis Bond
John P. McCrae · Paul Buitelaar
Christian Chiarcos · Sebastian Hellmann (Eds.)

Language, Data, and Knowledge

First International Conference, LDK 2017
Galway, Ireland, June 19–20, 2017
Proceedings

Editors
Jorge Gracia
Universidad Politécnica de Madrid
Madrid
Spain

Francis Bond
Nanyang Technological University
Singapore
Singapore

John P. McCrae
Insight Centre for Data Analytics
National University of Ireland, Galway
Galway
Ireland

Paul Buitelaar
Insight Centre for Data Analytics
National University of Ireland
Galway
Ireland

Christian Chiarcos
Goethe-University Frankfurt
Frankfurt
Germany

Sebastian Hellmann
University of Leipzig
Leipzig
Germany

ISSN 0302-9743 ISSN 1611-3349 (electronic)
Lecture Notes in Artificial Intelligence
ISBN 978-3-319-59887-1 ISBN 978-3-319-59888-8 (eBook)
DOI 10.1007/978-3-319-59888-8

Library of Congress Control Number: 2017942992

LNCS Sublibrary: SL7 – Artificial Intelligence

Printed on acid-free paper

This Springer imprint is published by Springer Nature
The registered company is Springer International Publishing AG
The registered company address is: Gewerbestrasse 11, 6330 Cham, Switzerland

Preface

Welcome to Galway for the first international conference on Language, Data and Knowledge (LDK 2017). It is hosted by the Insight Centre for Data Analytics at the National University of Ireland, Galway.

This the first of a new biennial conference series on Language, Data and Knowledge (LDK) which aims to bring together researchers from across disciplines concerned with the acquisition, curation and use of language data in the context of data science and knowledge-based applications. With the advent of the Web and digital technologies, an ever increasing amount of language data is now available across application areas and industry sectors, including social media, digital archives, company records, etc. The efficient and meaningful exploitation of this data in scientific and commercial innovation is at the core of data science research, employing NLP and machine learning methods as well as semantic technologies based on knowledge graphs.

Language data is of increasing importance to machine learning-based approaches in NLP, Linked Data and Semantic Web research and applications that depend on linguistic and semantic annotation with lexical, terminological and ontological resources, manual alignment across language or other human-assigned labels. The acquisition, provenance, representation, maintenance, usability, quality as well as legal, organizational and infrastructure aspects of language data are therefore rapidly becoming major areas of research that are at the focus of the conference.

Knowledge graphs are an active field of research concerned with the extraction, integration, maintenance and use of semantic representations of language data in combination with semantically or otherwise structured data, numerical data and multimodal data among others. Knowledge graph research builds on the exploitation and extension of lexical, terminological and ontological resources, information and knowledge extraction, entity linking, ontology learning, ontology alignment, semantic text similarity, Linked Data and other Semantic Web technologies. The construction and use of knowledge graphs from language data, possibly and ideally in the context of other types of data, is a further specific focus of the conference.

A further focus of the conference is the combined use and exploitation of language data and knowledge graphs in data science-based approaches to use cases in industry, including biomedical applications, as well as use cases in humanities and social sciences.

The LDK conferences have been initiated by a consortium of researchers from the Insight Centre for Data Analytics, InfAI (University Leipzig) and Wolfgang Goethe University and a Scientific Committee of leading researchers in Natural Language Processing, Linked Data and Semantic Web, Language Resources and Digital Humanities. LDK is endorsed by several international organisations: DBpedia, ACL SIGANN, Global Wordnet Association, CLARIN and Big Data Value Association (BDVA).

There were a total of 68 submissions reviewed, of which 15 were accepted as full papers (one was subsequently withdrawn) and 19 as short papers (an acceptance rate of 50%).

Reviewing was single blind (due to the difficulty in making language resources anonymous). There were at least 3 reviews per paper, with an average of 3.7. Papers came from all over the world.

A successful conference is the result of many people's efforts and contributions. The papers included in the program are the results of our participants' contributions as well as the insightful reviews from the program committee members. Besides the oral and poster paper presentations, the program is enriched by the keynote and invited speakers: Dr. Chris Welty, Senior Research Scientist at Google in New York, and an Endowed Professor of Cognitive Systems at the VU University, Amsterdam; Kathleen R. McKeown, Henry and Gertrude Rothschild Professor of Computer Science and Director of the Institute for Data Sciences and Engineering at Columbia University; Antal van den Bosch, director of the Meertens Institute in Amsterdam and Professor of Language and Speech Technology at the Centre for Language Studies at Radboud University, Nijmegen, the Netherlands; and Graham Isaac of the Irish Department at NUI Galway. On behalf of the program committee, we express our thanks to them all.

We would like to thank the scientific advisory committee for their guidance, and the local organizing committee led by Dr John P. McCrae and Dr Paul Buitelaar, for their great work in ensuring the success of this conference.

Finally, we wish that you will all enjoy the conference presentations, discussions, and exchanges between old and new friends at the beautiful harbor city of Galway.

April 2017

Jorge Gracia
Francis Bond

Organisation

Paul Buitelaar	Insight Centre for Data Analytics, NUI Galway, Ireland
Christian Chiarcos	Goethe Universität Frankfurt, Germany
Sebastian Hellmann	InfAI, Universität Leipzig, Germany
John P. McCrae	Insight Centre for Data Analytics, NUI Galway, Ireland

Scientific Advisory Committee

Pushpak Bhattacharyya	IITP, India
Francis Bond	Nanyang Technological University, Singapore
Key-Sun Choi	KAIST, South Korea
Philipp Cimiano	Bielefeld University, Germany
Edward Curry	Insight Centre for Data Analytics, NUI Galway, Ireland
Franciska de Jong	Utrecht University, The Netherlands
Thierry Declerck	DFKI GmbH, Saarland University, Germany
Tatjana Gornostaja	Tilde, Latvia
Jorge Gracia	Universidad Politécnica de Madrid, Spain
Nancy Ide	Vassar College, USA
Eric Nyberg	Carnegie Mellon University, USA
Felix Sasaki	DFKI GmbH, W3C Fellow, Germany
Karin Verspoor	University of Melbourne, Australia

Program Chairs

Francis Bond	Nanyang Technological University, Singapore
Jorge Gracia	Universidad Politécnica de Madrid, Spain

Program Committee

Nitish Aggarwal	IBM Watson, USA
Guadalupe Aguado	Universidad Politécnica de Madrid, Spain
Sören Auer	University of Bonn, Germany
Caroline Barrière	Computer Research Institute of Montreal, Canada
Núria Bel	Universitat Pompeu Fabra, Spain
Pushpak Bhattacharyya	IITP, India
Francis Bond	Nanyang Technological University, Singapore
Claire Bonial	U.S. Army Research Lab, USA
Carmen Brando	Institut National de L'Information Géographique et Forestière, France
Nicoletta Calzolari	ILC-CNR, Italy
Steve Cassidy	Macquarie University, Australia

Damir Cavar	Indiana University, USA
Key-Sun Choi	KAIST, South Korea
Philipp Cimiano	Bielefeld University, Germany
Kevin B. Cohen	University of Colorado School of Medicine, USA
Edward Curry	Insight Centre for Data Analytics, NUI Galway, Ireland
Brian Davis	Insight Centre for Data Analytics, NUI Galway, Ireland
Thierry Declerck	DFKI GmbH, Saarland University, Germany
Franciska de Jong	Utrecht University, The Netherlands
Gerard de Melo	Rutgers University, USA
Dongpo Deng	Institute of Information Science, Academia Sinica, Taiwan
Alexis Dimitriadis	Universiteit Utrecht, The Netherlands
Richard Eckart de Castilho	Technische Universität Darmstadt, Germany
Agata Filipowska	Poznan University of Economics, Poland
André Freitas	University of Passau, Germany
Francesca Frontini	Université Paul Valéry Montpellier, France
Elena González-Blanco García	Universidad Nacional de Educación a Distancia, Madrid, Spain
Jeff Good	University at Buffalo, USA
Tatjana Gornostaja	Tilde, Latvia
Dagmar Gromann	IIIA-CSIC, Barcelona, Spain
Yoshihiko Hayashi	Waseda University, Japan
Graeme Hirst	University of Toronto, Canada
Nancy Ide	Vassar College, USA
Hitoshi Isahara	Toyohashi University of Technology, Japan
Clement Jonquet	University of Montpellier, France
Fahad Khan	ILC-CNR, Italy
Bettina Klimek	Leipzig University AKSW, Germany
Roman Klinger	University of Stuttgart, Germany
Seiji Koide	Ontolonomy, LLC, Japan
Dimitris Kontokostas	Leipzig University AKSW, Germany
Vanessa Lopez	IBM Europe, Ireland
Monica Monachini	Consiglio Nazionale delle Ricerche, Italy
Elena Montiel	Universidad Politécnica de Madrid, Spain
Steven Moran	University of Zürich, Switzerland
Luis Morgado Da Costa	Nanyang Technical University, Singapore
Andrea Moro	Microsoft, UK
Hatem Mousselly Sergieh	Darmstadt University, Germany
Yohei Murakami	Kyoto University, Japan
Roberto Navigli	Sapienza University of Rome, Italy
Petya Osenova	Bulgarian Academy of Sciences, Sofia, Bulgaria
Maciej Piasecki	Wroclaw University of Technology, Poland
Simone Ponzetto	University of Mannheim, Germany
Laurette Pretorius	UNISA, South Africa
Nils Reiter	University of Stuttgart, Germany
Mariano Rico	Universidad Politécnica de Madrid, Spain

Martin Riedl	University of Hamburg, Germany
Víctor Rodríguez-Doncel	Universidad Politécnica de Madrid, Spain
Harald Sack	FIZ Karlsruhe, Leibniz Center for Information Infrastructure, Germany
Felix Sasaki	DFKI GmbH, W3C Fellow, Germany
Agata Savary	University of Tours, France
Andrea Schalley	Griffith University, Australia
Sabine Schulte im Walde	University of Stuttgart, Germany
Gilles Sérasset	Grenobles Alpes University, France
Kiril Simov	Bulgarian Academy of Sciences, Sofia, Bulgaria
Milena Slavcheva	JRC-Brussels, Belgium
Armando Stellato	University of Rome, Tor Vergata, Italy
Marko Tadić	University of Zagreb, Croatia
Hideaki Takeda	National Institute of Informatics, Japan
Ricardo Usbeck	Leipzig University AKSW, Germany
Marieke van Erp	Vrije Universiteit Amsterdam, The Netherlands
Marc Verhagen	Brandeis University, USA
Karin Verspoor	University of Melbourne, Australia
Cristina Vertan	University of Hamburg, Germany
Marta Villegas	Universitat Autònoma de Barcelona, Spain
Piek Vossen	Vrije Universiteit Amsterdam, The Netherlands
Sebastian Walter	Bielefeld University, Germany
Ulli Waltinger	Siemens AG, Germany
Eveline Wandl-Vogt	Austrian Academy of Science, Austria
Haofen Wang	East China University of Science and Technology, China
Krzysztof Wecel	Poznan University of Economics, Poland
Masaharu Yoshioka	Hokkaido University, Japan

Contents

An Evaluation Dataset for Linked Data Profiling

Andrejs Abele(✉), John P. McCrae, and Paul Buitelaar

Insight Centre for Data Analytics, National University of Ireland, Galway,
IDA Business Park, Lower Dangan, Galway, Ireland
{andrejs.abele,john.mccrea,paul.buitelaar}@insight-centre.org

Abstract. Since the beginning of the Linked Open Data initiative, the number of published Linked Data datasets has gradually increased. However, the reuse of datasets is hindered by a lack of descriptive and reliable metadata about the nature of the data, such as their topic coverage. Manual curation of metadata is however costly and hard to maintain, because of which we advocate a Linked Data profiling approach that will be able to automatically extract topics from datasets as metadata. One of the main challenges in developing this is the lack of evaluation data, i.e. manually curated metadata (topics) for datasets. In this paper we describe such an evaluation dataset and the framework that enabled its creation.

Keywords: Linked Data · Linked Data profiling · Topic extraction · Metadata · Evaluation dataset

1 Introduction

With the emergence of the Web of Data, in particular Linked Open Data (LOD), the amount of machine readable Linked Data (LD) datasets has rapidly increased. However, reuse of these datasets is hindered by a lack of descriptive and reliable metadata about the nature of the data, such as their topic coverage. Manual curation of metadata is however costly and hard to maintain, because of which we advocate a Linked Data profiling approach that will be able to automatically extract topics from datasets as metadata. There have been recent attempts to automatically create qualitative descriptions of LD datasets, such as by Fetahu et al. [7], but research in Linked Data profiling to date has largely been stymied by the unavailability of evaluation datasets.

Apart from the lack of metadata describing datasets, there is incomplete classification of existing metadata. Currently, the most widely used topic classification was introduced by the Linked Open Data cloud diagram [9]. This classification contains 9 topics (domains): Government, Publications, Life sciences, User-generated content, Cross-domain, Media, Geographic, Social web, Linguistics. In contrast, the "Linguistic Linked Open Data Cloud" [1] focuses only on linguistic data and provides two types of classification, i.e., by dataset type and by dataset license. Obviously, these classifications are very broad and do not, for

J. Gracia et al. (Eds.): LDK 2017, LNAI 10318, pp. 1–9, 2017.
DOI: 10.1007/978-3-319-59888-8_1

example, support use cases where users are looking for more specific or similar datasets.

Our goal is, by extracting and analyzing topics from all datasets on the LOD cloud, to create an extended hierarchical topic classification for use in subsequent LD dataset classification. In this paper, we describe an important first step towards achieving this goal, consisting of the development of an evaluation dataset for topic extraction from LD datasets.

The rest of this paper is structured as follows: Sect. 2 describes our approach in creating the evaluation dataset, whereas Sect. 3 describes the dataset itself, followed by some conclusions of our work in Sect. 4.

2 Topic Extraction from Linked Data

In this section we describe our approach for topic extraction from Linked Data, which is leveraged for the construction of the evaluation dataset. A graphical representation of the framework is provided in Fig. 1. In this diagram, we show all steps of the process that are performed for each of the datasets (in the LOD cloud) in the plate labelled "D". We also show the external datasets, especially DBpedia [4], which is a knowledge base that provides relations about entities and is used to generate the topic classification hierarchy. We also compile a term database that contains statistics about extracted n-grams (unigram, bigram, trigram) from LOD datasets, i.e., term frequency and inverse dataset term frequency. Before the extraction of n-grams, all literal text was transformed to lower-case, and all standard English stop words[1] and HTML keywords (e.g., http, https, string, font, family, style, size, width, html) were removed.

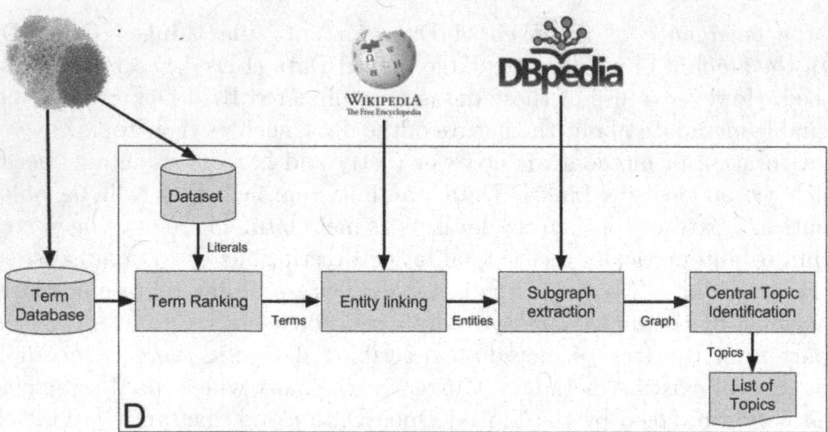

Fig. 1. Linked Data dataset extraction framework

[1] http://ir.dcs.gla.ac.uk/resources/linguistic_utils/stop_words.

2.1 Term Ranking

Our approach relies on the assumption that top ranked terms from a dataset provide enough information and it is not required to create statistics based on the whole textual context (all literals) of the dataset. For this reason we have implemented multiple ranking approaches, where the user can choose which ranking algorithm to use, or use aggregated top results from all ranking methods.

Term Frequency is a basic approach to identify term importance in a dataset, which provides good results on LD datasets as literals mostly contain nouns and if a noun often appears in the dataset, it is important.

Term Probability uses additional information that is collected while processing all datasets. To identify terms that frequently occur not only in the analysed dataset but also in other datasets, we aggregate the term occurrence over all processed datasets and calculate the probability that the term occurs in this dataset:

$$TP_d(x) = \frac{TF_d(x)}{\sum_{d'}^{D} TF_{d'}(x)} \tag{1}$$

where d is a given dataset and D is the collection of all processed datasets. $TF_d(x)$ is the frequency of term, x, in dataset, d, and $TP_d(x)$ is the probability that term, x, will occur in dataset, d. The higher the probability, the more important the term is to the dataset.

Term Frequency–Inverse Document Frequency is the most popular approach and is commonly used in the field of information retrieval and text mining. To calculate TF-IDF [3] we use the following formula:

$$TFIDF_d(x) = TF_d(x) \times IDF(x) \tag{2}$$

where $IDF(x)$ is inverse document frequency:

$$IDF(x) = log\frac{1 + n_D}{1 + DF_D(x)} \tag{3}$$

where n_D is the number of processed datasets, $DF_D(x)$ is number of datasets that contain term x.

Pointwise Mutual Information is a measure of association used in information theory and statistics, and we modified it to identify the most important terms in a dataset.

$$PMI(x) = log\frac{P_{xd}}{PX(x)} \times n_D \tag{4}$$

$$P_{xd} = \frac{TF_d(x)}{n_d} \tag{5}$$

where n_d is size of dataset d.

$$PX_x = \sum_{d}^{D} P_{xd} \tag{6}$$

2.2 Entity Linking

Once the top terms have been identified they are linked to DBpedia, for which we used an existing library: Yahoo Fast Entity Linker Core [5,6]. This library performs query segmentation and entity linking to a target reference Knowledge Base (Wikipedia[2]). It is tailored towards query entity linking and meant for short text fragments in general, which is appropriate for our application as we also deal with short text fragments in the form of LD literals. DBpedia uses the same id's for entities as Wikipedia for articles, for this reason Wikipedia articles can be directly linked to DBpedia entities and their categories.

2.3 Subgraph Extraction

After the entities have been identified, we select the top most frequent and extract them together with their surrounding entities. We use a local DBpedia SPARQL endpoint and programmatically use two *SPARQL Queries*. First, the query searches for objects that are connected to the *entity* by the properties `skos:broader` or `dc:subject`, filtering out all objects that are not URIs. In the next step, we filter out those URIs that are not linked to DBpedia, as we cannot guarantee that external links will be resolvable.

```
"select distinct ?P ?O where {
VALUES ?P {<http://www.w3.org/2004/02/skos/core#broader>
       <http://purl.org/dc/terms/subject> }
<"+entity+"> ?P ?O
FILTER ( ISIRI(?O) ) }"
```

The second query retrieves objects (entities) that are connected to our original *entity* and filters out all objects that are not URIs and are not linked to DBpedia.

```
"select distinct ?OO ?P ?O where {
VALUES ?P {<http://www.w3.org/2004/02/skos/core#broader>
         <http://purl.org/dc/terms/subject> }
<"+entity+"> <http://purl.org/dc/terms/subject> ?OO .
?OO ?P ?O FILTER ( ISIRI(?O) )   }"
```

To reduce the amount of irrelevant data, we remove certain types of entities e.g.:

- http://dbpedia.org/resource/Template
- http://dbpedia.org/ontology/wikiPageWikiLink
- http://dbpedia.org/ontology/language

Once all the entities from the queries are connected they form a small graph (DBpedia subgraph) that covers all topics in the given dataset.

---
[2] https://en.wikipedia.org.

2.4 Central Topic Identification

Similarly to Term Ranking, we implemented multiple graph centrality algorithms to identify central topics:

Betweenness [2] is a centrality measure of a node within a graph. A node is important if it facilitates the flow of information between other nodes in the graph. The betweenness centrality is strongly biased towards nodes with high degree or nodes that are central in large local groups of nodes.

Degree centrality represents the number of edges that a node has.

EigenVector is a centrality measure that represents a node's influence in a network. It assigns relative scores to all nodes in the network based on the idea that connections to high-scoring nodes provide higher score.

PageRank [8] is a measure similar to EigenVector that calculates influence of a node based on its connection to other influential nodes.

Closeness is a centrality measure that represents the average length between the node and all other nodes in the graph.

3 Evaluation Dataset

The requirements for a Linked Data topic extraction evaluation dataset are as follows: consist of accessible LD datasets that contain textual data (literals) and for each dataset provide a list of relevant topics associated with it. An example of the evaluation dataset is shown in Table 1

Table 1. Evaluation dataset example

Dataset name	Topic list
education-data-gov-uk	Education, School, United_Kingdom
olia	Linguistics, Ontology_(information_science)
nobelprizes	Awards, Nobel_Prize, Royal_Swedish_Academy_of_Sciences

3.1 Dataset Collection

We wanted to use known datasets, so annotators could easier annotate them. For this reason we downloaded all 570 datasets that are present in the LOD Cloud Diagram 2014 [10]. When we attempted to download these using information present at DataHub[3], only 245 were reachable by using our automated crawler.[4]

[3] https://datahub.io/.

[4] On 07.06.2016.

3.2 Dataset Filtering

For annotators to be able to annotate the dataset, they require background information about the dataset, for which reason we excluded 70 datasets that did not contain any metadata (not even a link to the data publisher). Furthermore, for any topic extraction system to be able to process a dataset, the dataset has to contain textual data (literals). 34 datasets did not contain any literals. After excluding all datasets that did not comply with our requirements we obtained a collection of 141 datasets for our evaluation dataset construction.

3.3 Candidate Topic Extraction

To provide annotators with a reasonable amount of topics to select from for every dataset, we processed the datasets using the approach described in Sect. 2. As mentioned in Sect. 2.1, our approach provides multiple term ranking options. For this reason and to remove any bias towards one of the ranking methods, we selected the top results from all methods. When we performed Central Topic Identification, we collected top results using each centrality measure to remove bias towards one of the algorithms, as described in Sect. 2.4.

After collecting all possible topics for each dataset, a domain expert who is knowledgeable in LOD domains, reviewed the data to further narrow down the topic options for the annotators. The domain expert, after reviewing the output of the framework, excluded multiple datasets for the following reasons: (1) datasets with text literals in a language other than English (our approach only supports the analysis of English text) (2) datasets that cover multiple domains (making it challenging for annotators to come to an agreement). The domain expert further limited the number of possible topic options for each dataset, where the number can be from nine to fourteen topics per dataset. In Table 2 we show 3 of the processed datasets and their description. As shown, these datasets cover diverse domains.

Table 2. List of datasets

Dataset	Description
clean-energy-data-reegle	Linked Clean Energy Data (reegle.info) Comprehensive set of linked clean energy data
nobelprizes	Nobel Prizes Linked Open Data about every Nobel Prize since 1901, including information about the Nobel Prizes, the Nobel Laureates and related documentation.
statistics-data-gov-uk	Statistics.data.gov.uk Linked data about administrative areas used within UK government official statistics

3.4 Survey Creation

For each annotator to be able to perform their task, they require a list of topics for each dataset, as well as a description of the dataset. For some of the datasets

Nobel Prizes

Linked Open Data about every Nobel Prize since 1901, including information about the Nobel Prizes, the Nobel Laureates and related documentation.

- Robert_B._Laughlin
- Torsten_Wiesel
- Ernest_Rutherford
- Awards
- Nobel_laureates_in_Physics
- American_Nobel_laureates
- Dennis_Gabor
- Tomas_Lindahl
- Nobel_Prize
- Christiaan_Eijkman
- Medicine
- Physiology
- Royal_Swedish_Academy_of_Sciences

Fig. 2. LimeSurvey question form example

there is sufficient description in Datahub.io (e.g., nobelprizes), but there are many that do not have any descriptions (e.g., dws-group). For these datasets we went to the publisher's homepage and manually extracted the description for the dataset.

To publish and manage the survey, we used LimeSurvey[5], an open source tool. Annotators could select up to 10 topics for each dataset, and they can see only one dataset at a time. In Fig. 2 it is shown how a question looks like in the LimeSurvey system.

3.5 Dataset Description

After evaluating the results, we kept only those topics where from 10 annotators at least 6 agreed, which was chosen to balance the number of topics extracted with the overall accuracy of the annotation. In Fig. 3 we can see that only for 13 topics all annotators came to a full consensus, and for 91 topics they agreed that the topics do not belong to the dataset. Figure 4 shows the number of topics in each dataset, where 6 or more annotators reached a consensus about the topic. As can be seen, there is 1 dataset (dataset 27) that has 0 topics. This dataset is about "Ontos News Portal". From 13 possible topics, the highest consensus was reached for the topic "News_media", but it was only by 5 annotators and it is below our threshold. The full evaluation dataset in TSV format can be found here[6]. The full survey data in TSV format can be found here[7].

[5] https://www.limesurvey.org.

[6] https://nuig.insight-centre.org/unlp/evaluationdataset-tsv/.

[7] http://nuig.insight-centre.org/unlp/datasetsurveydata-csv/.

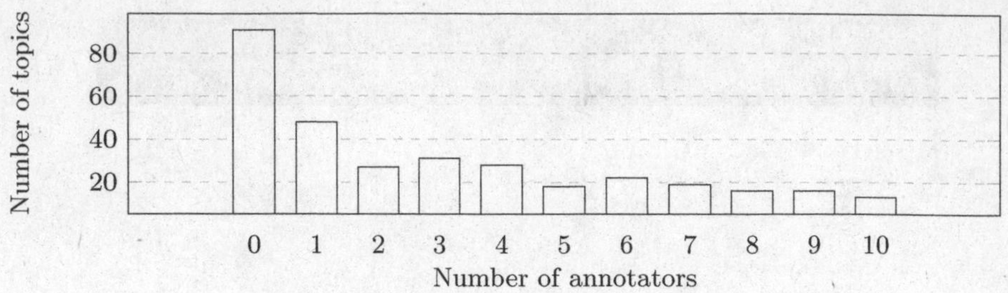

Fig. 3. Number of topics selected by certain number of annotators

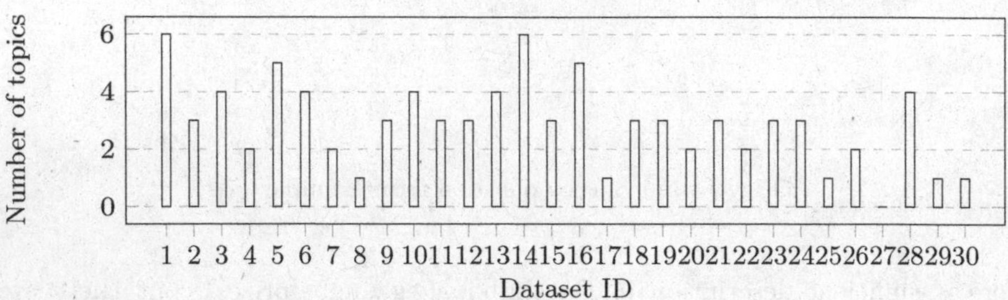

Fig. 4. Number of topics for each dataset in the evaluated dataset

4 Conclusion

We have constructed an evaluation dataset for Linked Data profiling by applying a topic extraction approach that links extracted topics to categories drawn from the DBpedia hierarchy. The assignment of topics to datasets had a high degree of agreement among human annotators, which makes it a good benchmark for automatic Linked Data profiling approaches. The evaluation dataset will enable us also to define a more fine-grained topic classification for Linked Data, which will be important for further uptake and automatic use by data consumers. Current categorizations, such as used for the LOD cloud diagram [9], are very high-level and are not organized hierarchically.

Acknowledgements. This work was supported by Science Foundation Ireland under grant number SFI/12/RC/2289 (Insight) and by the European Union under grant number H2020-644632 (MixedEmotions).

References

1. Chiarcos, C., Hellmann, S., Nordhoff, S.: Linking linguistic resources: examples from the open linguistics working group. In: Chiarcos, C., Nordhoff, S., Hellmann, S. (eds.) Linked Data in Linguistics: Representing Language Data and Metadata, pp. 201–216. Springer, Heidelberg (2012)

2. Freeman, L.C.: A set of measures of centrality based on betweenness. Sociometry **40**, 35–41 (1977)
3. Salton, G., McGill, M.J.: Introduction to Modern Information Retrieval, pp. 402–403. McGraw-Hill, New York (1983). ISBN 0-07-054484-0
4. Auer, S., Bizer, C., Kobilarov, G., Lehmann, J., Cyganiak, R., Ives, Z.: DBpedia: a nucleus for a web of open data. In: Aberer, K., et al. (eds.) ASWC/ISWC - 2007. LNCS, vol. 4825, pp. 722–735. Springer, Heidelberg (2007). doi:10.1007/978-3-540-76298-0_52
5. Blanco, R., Ottaviano, G., Meij, E.: Fast and space-efficient entity linking for queries. In: Proceedings of the Eighth ACM International Conference on Web Search and Data Mining, pp. 179–188. ACM (2015)
6. Pappu, A., Blanco, R., Mehdad, Y., Stent, A., Thadani, K.: Lightweight multilingual entity extraction and linking. In: Proceedings of the Tenth ACM International Conference on Web Search and Data Mining, pp. 365–374. ACM (2017)
7. Fetahu, B., Dietze, S., Pereira Nunes, B., Antonio Casanova, M., Taibi, D., Nejdl, W.: A scalable approach for efficiently generating structured dataset topic profiles. In: Presutti, V., d'Amato, C., Gandon, F., d'Aquin, M., Staab, S., Tordai, A. (eds.) ESWC 2014. LNCS, vol. 8465, pp. 519–534. Springer, Cham (2014). doi:10.1007/978-3-319-07443-6_35
8. Page, L., Brin, S., Motwani, R., Winograd, T.: The PageRank Citation Ranking: Bringing Order to the Web. Technical report, Stanford InfoLab (1999). http://ilpubs.stanford.edu:8090/422/
9. Abele, A., McCrae, J.P., Buitelaar, P., Jentzsch, A., Cyganiak, R.: Linked Open Data cloud diagram 2017. http://lod-cloud.net/
10. Schmachtenberg, M., Bizer, C., Paulheim, H.: State of the LOD Cloud 2014. Data and Web Science Group, University of Mannheim, 30 August 2014

Personal Research Agents on the Web of Linked Open Data

Bahar Sateli and René Witte(✉)

Semantic Software Lab, Department of Computer Science and Software Engineering, Concordia University, Montréal, QC, Canada
{sateli,witte}@semanticsoftware.info

Abstract. We introduce the concept of *Personal Research Agents* as semantics-based entities, capable of helping researchers who have to deal with the overwhelming amount of scientific literature to carry out their daily tasks. We demonstrate how a confluence of state-of-the-art techniques from the Semantic Web and Natural Language Processing domains can realize a proactive agent that can offer *personalized* services to researchers in retrieval and understanding of scientific literature, based on their background knowledge, interests and tasks. The agent's knowledge base is populated with knowledge automatically extracted from scientific literature of a given domain using text mining techniques and represented in Linked Open Data (LOD) compliant format. Personalization is achieved through automated user profiling, based on a user's publications. We implemented these ideas in an open source framework and demonstrate its applicability based on a corpus of open access computer science articles.

1 Introduction

"Good morning, Prof. Smith. I found one new publication matching your areas of interest with a contribution that you have not seen before. Would you like to read a summary now?"—Would not it be nice if we all had personal research agents that work around-the-clock, continuously scanning novel research publications and other scholarly communications; agents who know about our daily tasks (reading, reviewing, writing proposals, planning experiments, learning), our interests, even the state of our knowledge in a specific domain, and who can recommend focused information to us? In recent years, the increasing need for an enrichment of scientific literature with semantic metadata has sparked a new series of initiatives in research and development of innovative ways for enhanced scientific dissemination, referred to as *Semantic Publishing* [1]. A recent user survey of scientists, conducted in the context of the *Dr Inventor* EU project [2], revealed that researchers spend almost half of their time locating and reading scientific literature in order to compare their work with other relevant works, highlighting the significant potential for automated support in this area. Semantic publishing aims at making scientific knowledge accessible to both humans and

J. Gracia et al. (Eds.): LDK 2017, LNAI 10318, pp. 10–25, 2017.
DOI: 10.1007/978-3-319-59888-8_2

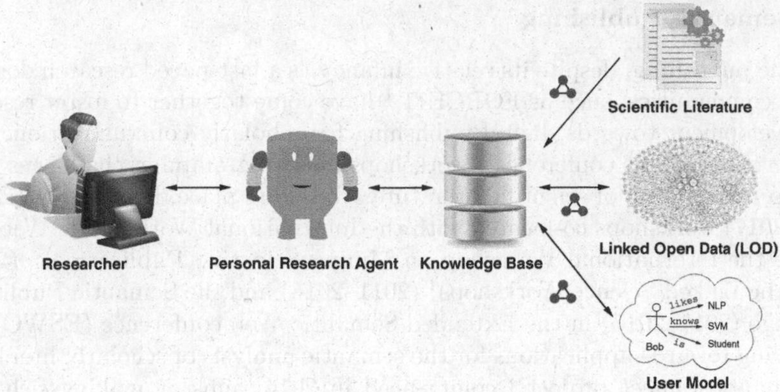

Fig. 1. A high-level overview of our proposed personal research agents

machines, by adding semantic annotations to scholarly content. These annotations are added to research objects, like documents, using special markup with formally defined meanings, in order to explicitly mark their structure (e.g., different sections of an article), as well as their *semantics* (e.g., a publication's contributions, methods, or application domains). However, despite these promises of better knowledge access [3,4], the manual annotation of existing research literature remains prohibitively expensive for a wide-spread adoption.

In this paper, we investigate how close we are today to the vision of intelligent research agents. Specifically, we build on our previous works in automated text analysis of research articles for their rhetorical structure [5] and the construction of semantic user profiles [6]. Our novel contribution here is the definition of *semantic research agents,* based on Linked Open Data (LOD) principles [7], which are capable of supporting their users through an automatically constructed knowledge base. We analyze the requirements of different user groups for such a personal research agent and formulate services that can satisfy these requirements. The services are then formalized in form of queries against a knowledge base, as shown in Fig. 1. We applied our method on a corpus of 100 open access articles from the *PeerJ Computer Science* journal. All our tools are available as open source software and we published the complete datasets in a GitHub repository at https://github.com/SemanticSoftwareLab/Supplements-LDK2017.

2 Literature Review

As mentioned in the introduction, our work is grounded in ideas from the field of semantic publishing, which we review in the following subsection. Work in intelligent agents specifically for the scientific domain is discussed in Sect. 2.2.

2.1 Semantic Publishing

Semantic publishing, despite its relative infancy, is a fast-paced research domain. Several communities, such as FORCE11,[1] have come together to foster research and development towards digital publishing for scholarly communication. Academic events such as conferences, workshops and programming challenges dedicated to text mining of scientific literature are taking place, like the SAVE-SD[2] (2015–2017) workshops co-located with the International World Wide Web conference, the International Workshop on Mining Scientific Publications[3] (2011–2017), the Linked Science Workshops[4] (2011–2015) and the Semantic Publishing Challenge (2014–2017) in the Extended Semantic Web conference (ESWC).

Moving towards applications for the semantic analysis of scholarly literature, the Semantic Lancet project,[5] commenced in 2014, aims at making rich data about scholarly publications available as linked open data [8]. Specifically, the Semantic Lancet project goals are *(i)* to extract structured information from scholarly articles, and *(ii)* to provide a publicly-available triplestore from the extracted results, upon which a series of value-added services, such as a "*data browser*" or "*abstract finder*" can be implemented.

Semantic Scholar[6] was developed in 2015 by researchers at the Allen Institute for Artificial Intelligence, as an intelligent search engine to "*cut through the clutter*" when finding computer science literature. Semantic Scholar uses machine learning techniques to find key phrases and citation information from articles and show relevant and "*impactful*" articles by allowing users to filter them using automatically generated facets, like authors or venues.

2.2 Intelligent Scholarly Agents

While intelligent agents and agent-based techniques have a long history in AI, concrete implementations that demonstrate working agents in the domain of science have only started to emerge in recent years.

O'Donoghue et al. [9] introduce a four-level hierarchy of computational processes for sustainable, computationally creative systems that can produce "*new ideas in the form of knowledge or artefacts that represent that knowledge.*" They demonstrate two applications in the Computer Graphics domain that given an input and a goal, can produce *creative* artefacts and processes.

An interesting position paper by Kuhn [10] proposed the concept of "*science bots*" as a model for the future of scientific computation. Kuhn's bots are autonomous entities that can perform programmed tasks on scholarly data and publish the results. He makes an example of "*a bot [that] could apply text mining to extract relations from the abstracts... and publish the results*", for example as

[1] FORCE11, http://www.force11.org.
[2] SAVE-SD workshops, http://cs.unibo.it/save-sd/.
[3] WOSP workshops, https://wosp.core.ac.uk/jcdl2017/.
[4] LISC workshops, http://linkedscience.org/events/.
[5] Semantic Lancet Project http://www.semanticlancet.eu.
[6] Semantic Scholar, https://www.semanticscholar.org/.

nanopublications, while "*another one could infer new facts from existing nanopublications by applying specified rules or heuristics*" [10]. Kuhn argues that the bots' contributions can then be evaluated in a de-centralized way by employing a reputation system, in which humans and other bots can verify the reliability and trustworthiness of the initial bot's output.

Dr Inventor [11] is a European Commission's Seventh Framework-funded (EU FP7) project[7] that aims at creating a "*personal research assistant, utilizing machine-empowered search and computation... [to help researchers] by assessing the novelty of research ideas and suggestions of new concepts and workflows.*" The project has received more than 2.6 million Euros and involves multiple university and research institutions from Germany, Spain, Ireland, UK, and Czech Republic. Interestingly, they conducted a survey of researchers [12] on their habits in reading and finding research articles that outlined finding, reading and comparing the rhetorics of different articles with their research goals as the most difficult and time-consuming tasks, which we target to facilitate in this paper.

2.3 Discussion

The retrieval of scientific documents is by now well-supported through numerous Internet search engines, bibliographic databases, and scientific social networks. However, so far there are no tools available that support researchers in some concrete tasks *after* they have retrieved a set of documents (such as, triage, writing a literature review, learning a topic, summarizing a paper). Thus, this is the main goal we want to address with our personal research agents. Albeit very similar in its outlook to create personal research assistants, the focus of the *Dr Inventor* project is to "*promote scientific creativity by utilising web-based research objects*", specifically for researchers in the Computer Graphics domain. To the best of our knowledge, none of the analysis pipelines developed in that project are available under open source licenses, which is an important contribution of our work.

3 Realizing Personal Research Agents

What distinguishes a personal research agent from other semantic scholarly tools is the ability to construct a flexible, semantically-rich representation of its environment, which can be queried, inferred on and interlinked with external knowledge available on the web of LOD. The three fundamental concepts we need to model in an agent's knowledge base are *(i)* scholarly documents, *(ii)* users with various backgrounds and information needs, and *(iii)* tasks that the agent is capable of conducting. In this section, we elaborate on how we can automatically construct and exploit such a knowledge base, such that the agent can provide various scholarly services.

[7] Dr Inventor Project, http://drinventor.eu.

3.1 Semantic Modeling of Scientific Literature

Scholarly documents are published in various formats (e.g., PDF, HTML) and typesettings (e.g., ACM, LNCS) optimized for human-reading. In contrast, the agent – as a machine – maintains a different representation of documents in its knowledge base. In our approach, we use the plain-text of documents to extract specific entities that can help the agent to understand their meaning.

Table 1. Terms from linked open vocabularies for semantic agent modeling

LOV term	Modeled concept
bibo:Document	A class that represents scholarly documents
doco:Sentence	A class that represents sentences in a document
sro:RhetoricalElement	A class used to classify sentences containing a rhetorical entity, e.g., a *contribution* or *claim*
pubo:LinkedNamedEntity	A class to represent document topics, which are linked to their corresponding LOD resource
cnt:chars	A property to store the verbatim content of entities as they appeared in the document
pubo:hasAnnotation	A property to relate annotations (e.g., named entities) to documents
pubo:containsNE	A property to relate rhetorical and named entities in a document
oa:start & oa:end	A property to show the start and end offsets of entities in a document's text
um:User	A class to represent scholar users
c:Competency	A class to represent authors' competence topics (LOD resources) in their publications
c:CompetenceRecord	A class to record the metadata of authors' competences (e.g., provenance, LOD resource)
um:hasCompetencyRecord	A property to assign a competence record to the user
c:competenceFor	A property to represent the relation between a competence record and the competence topic

um: http://intelleo.eu/ontologies/user-model/ns/
cnt: http://www.w3.org/2011/content#
pubo: http://lod.semanticsoftware.info/pubo/pubo#
oa: http://www.w3.org/ns/oa/
bibo: http://purl.org/ontology/bibo/
c: http://intelleo.eu/ontologies/competences/ns/
sro: http://salt.semanticauthoring.org/ontologies/sro#
rdf: http://www.w3.org/1999/02/22-rdf-syntax-ns#
rdfs: http://www.w3.org/2000/01/rdf-schema#
doco: http://purl.org/ontology/bibo/

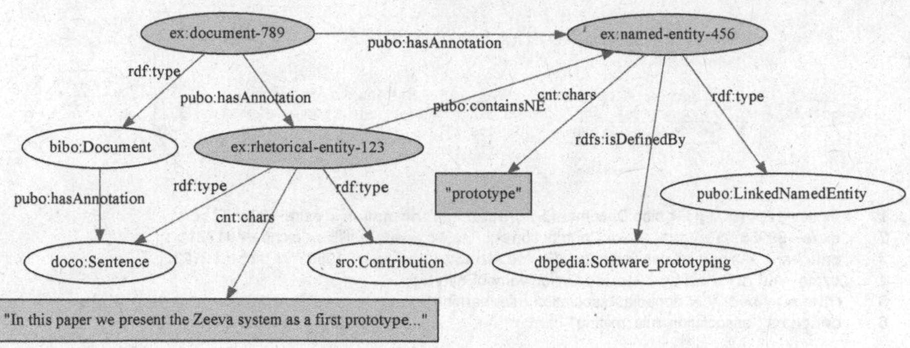

Fig. 2. Agent's model of relations between documents and topics using RDF

Design. The agent's knowledge base is populated with information extracted from input documents using our approach described in [5]. Our workflow transforms scholarly articles to semantic triples using a text mining pipeline. The generated triples contain various structural and semantic elements. Structural entities encompass mostly the bibliographical metadata, such as title and authorship, while the semantic entities are concerned with the *meaning* of the document. The meaning of a document is modeled as a set of selected sentences highlighting its authors contributions (rhetorics). As we demonstrated previously in [5], the collective set of topics mentioned within these rhetorical zones can be used to model the meaning of an article. Figure 2 shows the vocabularies used to model documents in the agent's knowledge base. We use a selected set of vocabularies from BIBO, DOCO, SRO and PUBO ontologies, as explained in Table 1. The shaded resources in Fig. 2 are example instances of the agent's document schema.

Implementation. Our agent's knowledge base is populated with document entities using our text mining pipeline described in [5]. Developed based on the GATE framework [13], it accepts (English) articles in PDF or XML formats and stores the generated triples in a TDB-based[8] triple store. It uses GATE's ANNIE plugin [13] to pre-process the documents. To extract the rhetorical entities (REs), documents are analyzed by our Rhetector[9] plugin that can classify each sentence into one of Claims, Contributions or *neither* categories (with 0.73 F-measure [5]). Document's topics (in form of linked named entities) are spotted using the LODtagger[10] plugin that acts as a wrapper for the DBpedia Spotlight [14] named entity recognition service. Every mention of a topic (named entity) is tagged with a semantic type and linked to its corresponding LOD resource using a uniform resource identifier (URI). In contrast to REs that span over one or more

[8] Apache Jena TDB, https://jena.apache.org/documentation/tdb/.
[9] Rhetector, http://www.semanticsoftware.info/rhetector.
[10] LODtagger, http://www.semanticsoftware.info/lodtagger.

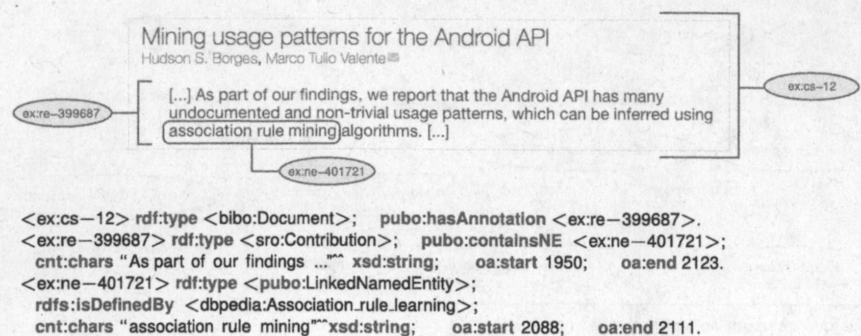
Mining usage patterns for the Android API
Hudson S. Borges, Marco Tulio Valente
[...] As part of our findings, we report that the Android API has many undocumented and non-trivial usage patterns, which can be inferred using association rule mining algorithms. [...]
ex:re–399687
ex:cs–12
ex:ne–401721
1 <ex:cs–12> rdf:type <bibo:Document>; pubo:hasAnnotation <ex:re–399687>.
2 <ex:re–399687> rdf:type <sro:Contribution>; pubo:containsNE <ex:ne–401721>;
3 cnt:chars "As part of our findings ..."^^ xsd:string; oa:start 1950; oa:end 2123.
4 <ex:ne–401721> rdf:type <pubo:LinkedNamedEntity>;
5 rdfs:isDefinedBy <dbpedia:Association_rule_learning>;
6 cnt:chars "association rule mining"^^xsd:string; oa:start 2088; oa:end 2111.

Fig. 3. Example triples (bottom) generated from a document's sentence (top)

sentences, NEs are nouns and noun phrases. Finally, all extracted (RE and NE) entities are stored in the knowledge base, using our LODeXporter[11] component.

Example. To demonstrate how a document is represented in the agent's knowledge base, we chose a random document from the dataset in our supplementary materials and analyzed it with our text mining pipeline [5]. Figure 3 shows an excerpt of the resulting triples in Turtle syntax. The namespaces shown in the listing can be resolved using Table 1. Line 1 of the listing represents the document (doi:10.7717/peerj-cs.12) in the knowledge base, along with a rhetorical entity (sentence) that was found in its text. Lines 2–3 and 4–6, respectively, model the rhetorical entity classified as a sro:Contribution and one of the named entities (topics) mentioned in the sentence, i.e., <dbpedia:Association_rule_learning>. The corresponding sentence from the original document is shown in Fig. 3 (top).

3.2 Semantic Modeling of Scholarly Users

While most modern information retrieval tools can help users to semantically expand or restrict a set of result documents, the personalized aspect of research agents provides for value-added features, like showing a ranked list of documents, based on how *relevant* or *novel* they are for a user. It can also be used to help a user, like a student, to understand previously unseen topics when reading them. This, in turn, requires the agent to have a detailed model of a user's context, in particular for background knowledge (what the user already knows) and the task at hand (what information is needed right now). In our agent's design, we store these information in so-called *scholarly user profiles.*

Design. Our semantic representation of user profiles is inspired by the IntelLEO framework[12] for modeling learning contexts. The idea here is to record the background knowledge of a scholar as a set of *competences*. User's competences are

[11] LODeXporter, http://www.semanticsoftware.info/lodexporter.
[12] IntelLEO framework, https://www.intelleo.eu/ontologies/learning-context/spec/.

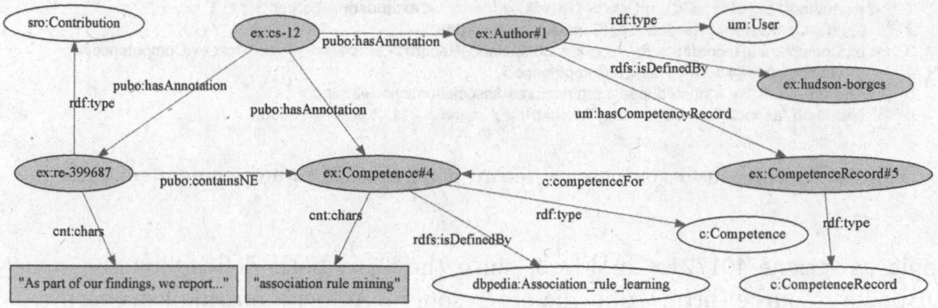

Fig. 4. An RDF graph representing a user profile in the agent's model

defined using a *competence record* that stores the metadata of how and where it was inferred from (e.g., a sentence in a document), as well as a *competence topic* that specifies the relevant entity (e.g., 'LOD'). Constructing user profiles requires collecting user information over an extended period of time and suffers from the *cold-start* problem, where not enough information about the user is available at the beginning to make meaningful recommendations. Since asking users to populate their user profiles with potentially thousands of topics that they know about or are interested in is impractical, we bootstrap users' profiles using their publication history [6]. For each user, we process his publicly available publications to automatically extract his relevant competences. Note that such a model follows a closed-world assumption, i.e., if a topic is not available in a user's profile, the agent will consider it as novel or unknown to the user. Figure 4 shows the agent's user profile schema with shaded nodes as instances.

Implementation. The assumption in our user modeling is that, if a user has authored a publication on a topic, the user is most likely competent in that topic to various degrees. Therefore, using our approach in [6], for each user we analyze their publications with our text mining pipeline. We customized the text mining pipeline, such that the topics (named entities) within the rhetorical zones of a user's publications are stored as his competences, along with their term frequency using a selected set of terms from the IntelLEO ontology.

Example. We generated a user profile for the first author shown in Fig. 3 as an example. An excerpt of the generated profile is listed in Fig. 5. Line 1 and 3, respectively, model the author and his competence record. Lines 4–6 describe his competence in '*association rule learning*', because it was mentioned in his publication. An advantage of modeling topics as LOD named entities is that *(i)* user profile competence topics can be integrated with the agent's modeling of documents, and *(ii)* if authors use different surface forms of the same topic (e.g., ARL instead of association rule mining), they can be resolved to the same semantics. In this example, resource <ex:Competence#4> represent the same

```
<ex:Author#1> rdf:type <um:User> ; rdfs:isDefinedBy <ex:hudson-borges> ;
  um:hasCompetencyRecord <ex:CompetenceRecord#5> .
<ex:CompetenceRecord#5> rdf:type <c:CompetenceRecord> ; c:competenceFor <ex:Competence#4> .
<ex:Competence#4> rdf:type <c:Competence> ;
  rdfs:isDefinedBy <http://dbpedia.org/resource/Association_rule_learning> ;
  cnt:chars "association rule mining"^^xsd:string ;  oa:end 2111 ; oa:start 2088 .
```

Fig. 5. Example user competence record generated from a document sentence

topic as <ex:ne-401721> in Fig. 3, since they are both defined by the same DBpedia resource (http://dbpedia.org/resource/Association_rule_learning).

3.3 Semantic Modeling of Agent's Tasks

We now introduce our new model for a semantic description of the workflow between a scholar and his personal research agent. While document models and user profiles in the knowledge base are populated as the user interacts with his agent, the metadata and services of the agent are mostly modeled up-front and may be extended throughout the agent's lifecycle. A formal semantic description of tasks facilitates consistent implementation of the agent's services and allows for composing new services by combining various tasks that an agent can perform.

Our Personal Research Agent Vocabulary (PRAV)[13] is an adaptation of the Lifecycle Schema,[14] which was originally designed to model the lifecycle of any resource throughout a transition. Following the best practices of LOD design [7], we tried to re-use existing linked open vocabularies to the extent possible.

Design. An agent's work unit is a *Task* assigned to it by a user. Tasks are aggregated into *Task Groups* and can be composed in an ordered sequence. While tasks are essentially conceptual entities with properties, such as a description or status, the underlying computations are instances of the *Action* class. Whereas tasks are designed by the agent developers for a specific goal, actions are generic operations, like querying the knowledge base or crawling a repository. In the process, actions can consume, produce or modify *artifacts*. In this paper, we restrict our agent's design to analyze scholarly literature (e.g., journal articles or conference proceedings) as artifacts. Figure 6 shows our agent's task schema, as well as example instances. For example, a literature review task group shown in the model is divided between two consequent tasks: *(i)* finding all rhetorical entities from documents mentioning a topic, and *(ii)* given a user profile, re-ranking the result documents based on how interesting they are for the user. As seen in the agent's schema, certain actions like <ex:ranking_action> need access to the knowledge available both within documents and a user's competence records.

---

[13] Personal Research Agent Vocabulary, http://lod.semanticsoftware.info/prav/prav#.
[14] Lifecycle Schema, http://vocab.org/lifecycle/schema#.

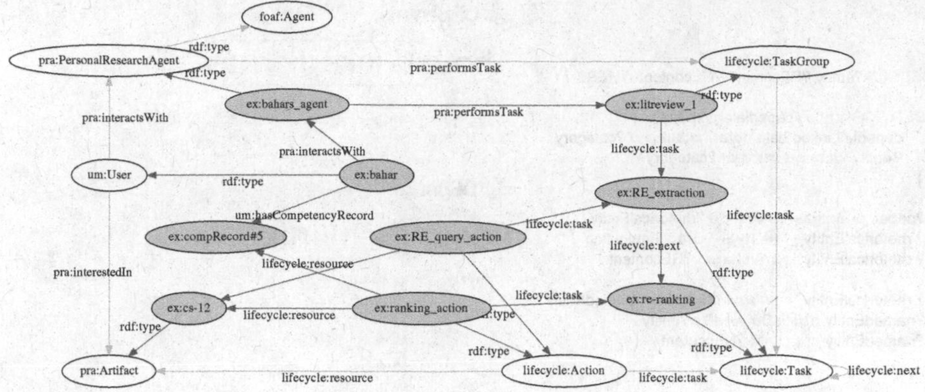

Fig. 6. Example literature review task modeling using the agent's task model

Implementation. As a concrete implementation of our agent's tasks, we defined three semantic scholarly services and formulated them as a set of queries. The queries are hand-crafted and implemented using SPARQL syntax. There are two types of queries in our design: *(i)* queries looking for *concepts*, like finding all things of type <bibo:Document> in the knowledge base, and *(ii)* queries that can be parameterized, such as finding all Contribution sentences mentioning '*linked open data*'. Wherever the required knowledge does not readily exist in the agent's knowledge base, but may be available on the web of LOD, we incorporated federated queries to integrate additional information from external resources. In particular, we query the DBpedia ontology[15] through its SPARQL endpoint.

Example. As part of our contribution, we define a number of research-related semantic services and demonstrate how our personal research agent can offer them to a user. The services described below by no means form an exhaustive list – a multitude of other services can be provided to users by exploiting the agent's knowledge base, simply by virtue of defining additional queries.

S1: Summarizing Relevant Articles. Our agent can help researchers in finding and reading scientific literature, by showing only parts that are interesting for a task, like a literature review. One way of obtaining such a summary is by listing all Contributions or Claim sentences from the document mentioning specific topics. This way, users can examine the rhetorical zones of a document prior to deciding whether they need to read the full-text paper. Figure 7 shows the agent's query that can retrieve such results from its knowledge base. Note that since the topics in the knowledge base are essentially LOD resources, by traversing the LOD cloud, our agent can expand the user-provided topics and bring in topics that are semantically related entities from external sources, thus

[15] DBpedia Ontology, http://wiki.dbpedia.org/services-resources/ontology.

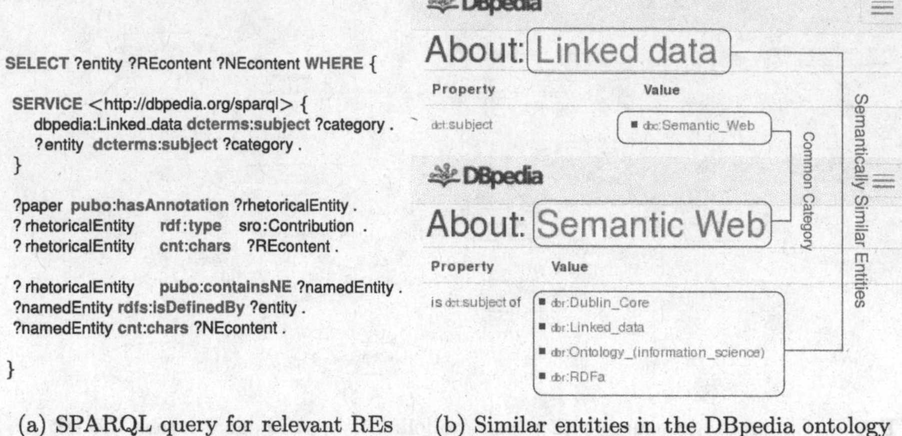
SELECT ?entity ?REcontent ?NEcontent WHERE {
SERVICE <http://dbpedia.org/sparql> {
dbpedia:Linked_data dcterms:subject ?category .
?entity dcterms:subject ?category .
}
?paper pubo:hasAnnotation ?rhetoricalEntity .
? rhetoricalEntity rdf:type sro:Contribution .
? rhetoricalEntity cnt:chars ?REcontent .
? rhetoricalEntity pubo:containsNE ?namedEntity .
?namedEntity rdfs:isDefinedBy ?entity .
?namedEntity cnt:chars ?NEcontent .
}
DBpedia
About: Linked data
Property
Value
dct:subject
dbc:Semantic_Web
DBpedia
About: Semantic Web
Property
Value
is dct:subject of
dbr:Dublin_Core
dbr:Linked_data
dbr:Ontology_(information_science)
dbr:RDFa
Common Category
Semantically Similar Entities

(a) SPARQL query for relevant REs (b) Similar entities in the DBpedia ontology

Fig. 7. Agent's query to find semantically relevant topics for query expansion

showing a broadened set of relevant documents that may not directly mention the user topics but contain similar entities. In this case, we defined semantic similarity between two resources as being under the same DBpedia category, as shown in Fig. 7b.

S2: Curating a Personalized Reading List. To demonstrate the personalization aspect of our research agent, we formulated a query that can integrate a user profile in order to re-rank a set of documents retrieved from a service like *Summarization* (S1). The idea here is that the number of matching topics (i.e., named entities in a document and competence topics in a user profile) can be used as a means to rank a document in terms of its *interestingness* for the user. Figure 8 shows how the agent calculates the total number of matching topics in the contribution sentences of document <ex:cs-78> and user <ex:hudson-borges>' competence records from his profile, by examining their matching LOD URIs. By incorporating the semantic expansion of topics using the query shown in Fig. 7a, the agent can also find topics that may not be mentioned in the user competence record, but fall under the same category in the DBpedia ontology.

S3: Filling the Knowledge Gap of Learners. Another task to demonstrate the advantage of using personal research agents is to offer contextual help to users, for example, when reading a document. The goal of this service is to provide the user with a brief explanation of terms that he is not familiar with as the user is reading the article. Here the agent interprets *new* topics as named entities that do not exist in his knowledge model of the user's competences. The SPARQL query shown in Fig. 9 allows the agent to detect these previously unseen topics in a document and retrieve a brief description from the DBpedia knowledge base.

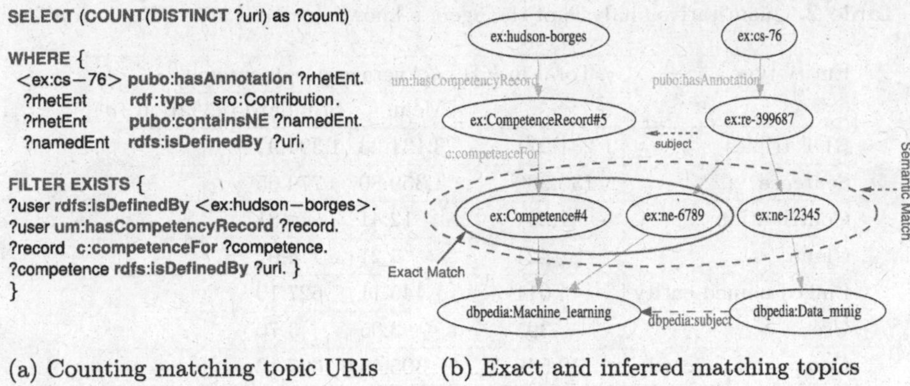

(a) Counting matching topic URIs (b) Exact and inferred matching topics

Fig. 8. Counting the number of common topics between a paper and user profile

4 Experiments

As a concrete application of our personal research agent, we performed a number of experiments using a set of open access articles from a computer science journal.

4.1 Dataset

We downloaded a subset of articles from the computer science edition of *PeerJ Computer Science* journal. The dataset contains 100 articles with an average length of 23.25 pages. Since additional metadata is available in the PeerJ XML article format, for each document we retrieved its corresponding XML file and

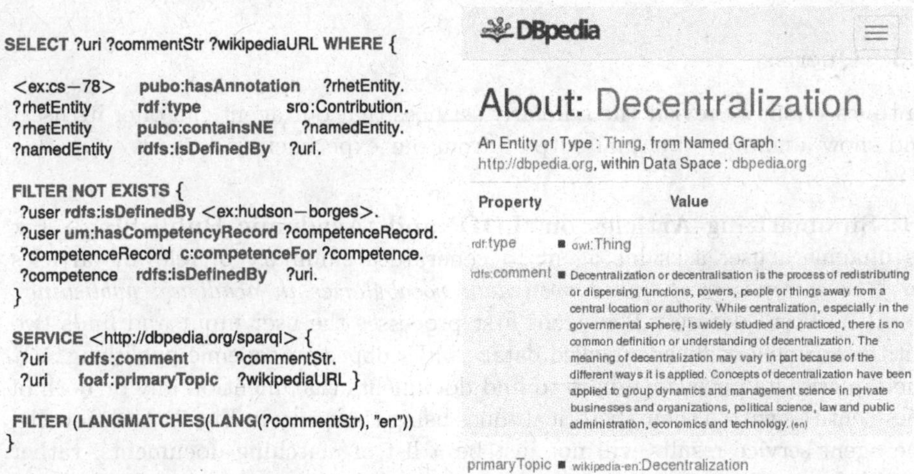

(a) Federated query for external knowledge (b) Available information from DBpedia

Fig. 9. Agent's query for topics in the document that are unknown to the user

Table 2. Quantitative analysis of the agent's knowledge base after population

Entity type	#Total in KB	#Average per document	
		Mean	Standard deviation (σ)
RDF triples	1,281,971	3,131.93	1,394.92
Sentence	135,980	1,359.80	779.65
Contribution	1,241	12.41	16.81
Claim	421	4.21	4.07
Linked named entity	144,611	1,446.11	627.10
User	395	3.95	3.70
Competence record	30,545	305.45	627.12

processed them with the text mining pipelines for document analysis and user profile construction, described in Sects. 3.1 and 3.2, respectively.

4.2 Knowledge Base

We populated a TDB-based knowledge base with the text mining pipelines' output, resulting in a total of 1,281,971 RDF triples. The complete processing time for the analysis of the documents and their authors' competences took 16.05 min on a MacBook Pro 2.5 GHz Intel Core i7 with 16 GB memory, with DBpedia Spotlight taking up to 55% of the processing time. For each author of the dataset documents, we populated a user profile with competence records extracted from their corresponding documents' rhetorical zones. User profile triples are merged with the document models through common named entity URIs. Table 2 shows a quantitative analysis of the agent's knowledge base.

4.3 Queries

In this section, we revisit the scholarly services that our agent can offer its users and show a number of actual outputs from our experiment's dataset.

S1: Summarizing Articles on 'LOD' and 'Academic Publishing'. Let us imagine a user asks his agent to generate a summary of relevant articles on "*the integration of linked open data vocabularies in academic publishing*" from the PeerJ dataset. The agent first processes the user input and finds two entities, namely, <dbpedia:Linked_data> and <dbpedia:Academic_publishing>. It then queries its knowledge base to find documents that mention any or both of these entities within their rhetorical zones using the query in Fig. 7. Additionally, the agent service results will not just be a list of matching documents, rather it will determine sentences of the documents the user needs to read. Figure 10 shows an example output produced by the agent for this query.

Documents matching dbpedia:Linked_data and dbpedia:Academic_publishing:
Document ID: http://example.com/papers/cs-78
Title: Decentralized provenance-aware publishing with nanopublications (Tobias Kuhn et al.)
Matched Entities:
• dbpedia:Linked_data *Inferred matches:* dbpedia:Ontology_(information_science), dbpedia:Semantic_Web, dbpedia:Controlled_vocabulary,...
• dbpedia:Academic_publishing *Inferred matches:* dbpedia:Proceedings, dbpedia:Literature_review, dbpedia:Open_access, ...
Selected Snippets to Read:
"We show how this approach allows researchers to publish, retrieve, verify, and recombine datasets of nanopublications in a reliable and trustworthy manner, and we argue that this architecture could [...] serve the Semantic Web in general."

Fig. 10. The agent's output assisting a researcher in a literature review task

S2: A Personalized Reading List from S1 Output. Using the agent's service in the previous section, our user receives 34 articles in the PeerJ dataset that matches either <dbpedia:Linked_Data>, <dbpedia:Academic_publishing>, or both, as well as any semantically relevant entities to his query terms. Next, he asks the agent to personalize his results according to their *interestingness*. Here, the agent assumes an article is interesting for a user, if there are matching named entities both in an article and in the users' profile. The agent then sorts the results from the first service based on the total number of common topics between each article and the users profile competences, in descending order, as retrieved by the SPARQL query shown in Fig. 8. We show an example output in Fig. 11.

S3: Suggesting Background Knowledge During Reading Tasks. While our user is reading an article from his personalized list, whenever he encounters a new topic, the agent can retrieve a brief description of the topic from available ontologies, point him to its reference Wikipedia page, or better, retrieve passages

Documents matching dbpedia:Linked_data and dbpedia:Academic_publishing:
1. Document ID: http://example.com/papers/cs-78
Title: A technology prototype system for rating therapist empathy from audio recordings in addiction [...] (Tobias Kuhn et al.)
Matching Interests in your profile:
dbpedia:Semantic_Web dbpedia:Data, dbpedia:Publishing, dbpedia:First-order_logic, dbpedia:Client-server_model, ...
2. Document ID: http://example.com/papers/cs-64
Title: Enriching scientific publications with interactive 3D PDF: an integrated toolbox for creating ready [...] (Axel Newe)
Matching Interests in your profile:
dbpedia:Academic_publishing, dbpedia:Document, dbpedia:Software, dbpedia:Portable_Document_Format, ...

Fig. 11. A personalized reading list with matching interests as explanation

Document ID: http://example.com/papers/cs-78
Title: A technology prototype system for rating therapist empathy from audio recordings in addiction [...] (Tobias Kuhn et al.)
Selected Snippets to Read:
• "In this article, we propose to design scientific data publishing as a web-based bottom-up process, without top-down [..]."
• "We argue that the centralized nature of existing data repositories is inconsistent with the decentralized manner in [..]."
Topics New to You:
• *Top-down and bottom-up design:* Top-down and bottom-up are both strategies of information processing and knowledge ordering, used in a variety of fields including [..]. *Source:* https://en.wikipedia.org/wiki/Top-down_and_bottom-up_design

Fig. 12. Personal agent assisting researchers in understanding unknown topics

from other documents in the knowledge base on how, e.g., a methodology is used in practice. For example, the agent can identify topics that the user does not know about (i.e., absent from his profile) and suggest background knowledge by executing the query shown in Fig. 9. We show an example output in Fig. 12.

5 Conclusion and Future Work

The amount of knowledge available in digital libraries is still increasing at a rapid pace. While finding and accessing scientific documents has become easier in recent years, thanks to various search engines and bibliographic services, the most labor-intensive tasks of reading and evaluating these search results still remains largely unsupported. In this paper, we proposed *personal research agents* that support their human users in knowledge-intensive, research-related activities.

While this idea been envisioned for more than a decade now, we examined the concrete support that can be realized with available technologies today: In our approach, we first transform scientific articles from natural language documents living in isolation into queryable knowledge bases with explicit semantics. Orthogonal to this, we formally model scientific users, their background knowledge, projects and tasks that they carry out in their day-to-day research activities. The synthesis of these individual knowledge bases then serves as the 'brain' of our personal research agents. With this approach, we can formulate a number of complex tasks performed daily by researchers, students, editors, or reviewers, in form of knowledge base queries. The presented ideas are fully implemented and our open source pipelines can be immediately deployed by anyone who wants to start running their own personal research agent. In future work, we will perform a number of user studies to examine how end users interact with their agents, and evaluate how they improve manually performed tasks in a scientific workflow.

References

1. Peroni, S.: Semantic Web Technologies and Legal Scholarly Publishing. Springer, Cham (2014)
2. Dr. Inventor: Promoting scientific creativity by utilising web-based research objects. Technical report, Program no. FP-ICT-2013.8.1, February 2014
3. Berners-Lee, T., Hendler, J.: Publishing on the semantic web. Nature **410**(6832), 1023–1024 (2001)
4. Shotton, D.: Semantic publishing: the coming revolution in scientific journal publishing. Learn. Publ. **22**(2), 85–94 (2009)
5. Sateli, B., Witte, R.: Semantic representation of scientific literature: bringing claims, contributions and named entities onto the Linked Open Data cloud. PeerJ Comput. Sci. **1**, e37 (2015)
6. Sateli, B., Löffler, F., König-Ries, B., Witte, R.: Semantic user profiles: learning scholars' competences by analyzing their publications. In: Gonzàlez-Beltrán, A., Osborne, F., Peroni, S. (eds.) SAVE-SD 2016. LNCS, vol. 9792, pp. 113–130. Springer, Cham (2016). doi:10.1007/978-3-319-53637-8_12
7. Heath, T., Bizer, C.: Linked data: evolving the web into a global data space. Synth. Lect. Semant. Web Theor. Technol. **1**, 1–136 (2011). Morgan & Claypool Publishers
8. Bagnacani, A., Ciancarini, P., Di Iorio, A., Nuzzolese, A.G., Peroni, S., Vitali, F.: The semantic lancet project: a linked open dataset for scholarly publishing. In: Lambrix, P., Hyvönen, E., Blomqvist, E., Presutti, V., Qi, G., Sattler, U., Ding, Y., Ghidini, C. (eds.) EKAW 2014. LNCS, vol. 8982, pp. 101–105. Springer, Cham (2015). doi:10.1007/978-3-319-17966-7_10
9. O'Donoghue, D.P., Power, J., O'Briain, S., Dong, F., Mooney, A., Hurley, D., Abgaz, Y., Markham, C.: Can a computationally creative system create itself? Creative artefacts and creative processes. In: 5th International Conference on Computational Creativity, Jožef Stefan Institute (2014)
10. Kuhn, T.: Science bots: a model for the future of scientific computation? In: Proceedings of the 24th International Conference on World Wide Web Companion, pp. 1061–1062 (2015)
11. Ronzano, F., Saggion, H.: Dr. Inventor framework: extracting structured information from scientific publications. In: Japkowicz, N., Matwin, S. (eds.) DS 2015. LNCS, vol. 9356, pp. 209–220. Springer, Cham (2015). doi:10.1007/978-3-319-24282-8_18
12. Chaudhry, E., Yang, X., You, L.: Promoting Scientific Creativity by Utilising Web-based Research Objects: Deliverable No. 2.1 User Requirement and Use Case Report (2014)
13. Cunningham, H., et al.: Text Processing with GATE (Version 6) (2011)
14. Mendes, P.N., Jakob, M., García-Silva, A., Bizer, C.: DBpedia spotlight: shedding light on the web of documents. In: Proceedings of the 7th International Conference on Semantic Systems, pp. 1–8. ACM (2011)

Hybrid Method for Stress Prediction Applied to GLAFF-IT, a Large-Scale Italian Lexicon

Basilio Calderone(✉), Matteo Pascoli, Franck Sajous, and Nabil Hathout

CLLE-ERSS (CNRS and Université de Toulouse 2), Maison de la Recherche - 5, Allées Antonio Machado, 31058 Toulouse Cedex 9, France
{basilio.calderone,matteo.pascoli,franck.sajous, nabil.hathout}@univ-tlse2.fr

Abstract. This paper presents a hybrid method for automatic stress prediction that we apply to GLAFF-IT, a large-scale Italian lexicon we extracted from GLAW-IT, a Machine-Readable Dictionary grounded on Wikizionario. Our approach combines heuristic rules and a logistic model trained on the words' sets of phonological features. This model reaches a 98.1% accuracy. The resulting resource is a large lexicon for the Italian language that we release under a free licence. It includes morphological and phonological information for each of its 457,702 entries. As of today, it is the only Italian lexicon featuring both large coverage and indication of stress position.

Keywords: Italian stress prediction · Phonological transcriptions · Free large-scale lexicon · Wiktionary · Wikizionario

1 Introduction

As a consequence of the expansion of corpus and data-driven approaches to language, lexical resources (LRs) are nowadays essential for quantitative and qualitative studies of the language. Despite the linguistic richness available in existing LRs (morphological, morpho-syntactic annotations, semantic relations, etc.), phonological information such as the phonemic transcriptions of lexical forms and stress markers, is often not reported by such resources. This lack is problematic for data-based phonological analysis of the language and for phonetic and prosodic studies. Phonologists are interested in the sounds that are distinctive in a given language and on the rules that govern these sounds. In this context, the availability of a phonological lexicon tagged with stress placement is a prior condition for any investigations in the phonological domain. Phonological and stress information are also necessary in psycholinguistics where researchers manipulate a large set of word properties in order to design experimental protocols. Moreover, phonological lexicons reporting word stress and prosodic information are crucial in language acquisition analysis [12] and in the study of word recognition [16]. In a more practical perspective, phonological lexicons may integrate with other modules in NLP applications as, for example, text-to-speech systems [7].

J. Gracia et al. (Eds.): LDK 2017, LNAI 10318, pp. 26–41, 2017.
DOI: 10.1007/978-3-319-59888-8_3

Most resources conceived for the Italian language do not provide any word stress information and, more generally, they do not report phonological transcriptions at all [3,4,14,17]. An exception is represented by PhonItalia [8], an Italian lexicon designed for researchers working in the psycholinguistic domain. Besides the orthographic forms and their lemmas, PhonItalia also reports the phonological encoding of words with the stress placement. Although the resource provides a comprehensive range of phonological and distributional information, its limited coverage (120,000 entries) constitutes a serious deterrent for its utilisation in quantitative/descriptive language analysis and for its exploitation in the NLP domain.

In this paper, we present a hybrid method for the prediction of Italian stress and we apply it to a large-scale morpho-phonological lexicon. Our method combines phonologically-motivated rules with a logistic regression model (henceforth *logit* model) for the automatic prediction of stressed/unstressed vowels. By exploiting this method we enrich s present in a large Italian lexicon, GLAFF-IT, with the word stress placement. Besides the lexical resource itself, a significant contribution of this work is the method we developed for stress prediction. Used here to complete the current version of the lexicon, the method will also prove useful in the future to generate the transcriptions and stress placements of the neologisms that are regularly added to Wikizionario (or potentially originating from other sources). The paper describes the creation of GLAFF-IT from a machine-readable dictionary that encodes the Wikizionario's micro- and macrostructure (Sect. 2). We present the lexicon and explain how we complete it with the missing forms by exploiting the systematic regularities of the Italian language regarding the orthography and the phonology. Section 3 focuses on the phonological transcriptions of GLAFF-IT and the problematic issue of Italian stress. In this section, we propose a hybrid method adopted for the stress assignment. The evaluation of the predictions and some conclusions are given in Sect. 4.

2 GLAFF-IT, a Large-Scale Italian Lexicon

2.1 GLAW-IT

In a previous paper [6], we introduced GLAW-IT, a free machine-readable dictionary (MRD) that encodes in a workable XML format the micro- and macrostructure of Wikizionario, the Italian edition of Wiktionary.[1] The method used to convert Wikizionario into GLAW-IT is similar to the conversion process from Wiktionnaire (the French language edition of Wiktionary) to GLAWI [10,15]. GLAW-IT contains all the lexical knowledge found in Wikizionario. Articles may include fields reporting etymologies, definitions, lemmas and inflected forms, lexical semantic and morphological relations, hyphenations, translations and phonological transcriptions. GLAW-IT does not report systematically all this kind of

[1] Available at: http://redac.univ-tlse2.fr/lexicons/glawit.html.

```
<article>
  <title>danno</title>
  <id>70444</id>
  <text>
    <etymology>
      <wiki>dal [[latino]] ''[[damnum]]''</wiki>
      <xml>dal <innerLink>latino</innerLink> <i><innerLink>damnum</innerLink></i></xml>
      <txt>dal latino damnum</txt>
    </etymology>
    <pos type="sost" lemma="1" m="1" sing="1">
      <paradigm>
        <inflection type="Ncmp" form="danni"/>
        <inflection type="Ncms" form="danno"/>
      </paradigm>
      <defs>
        <def>
          <gloss>
            <labels>
              <label type="term">diritto</label>
              <label type="term">economia</label>
            </labels>
            <wiki>{{term|diritto|it}}{{term|economia|it}} conseguenza di un'[[azione]]
                negativa subita</wiki>
            <txt>conseguenza di un'azione negativa subita</txt>
            <xml>conseguenza di un'<innerLink>azione</innerLink> negativa subita</xml>
          </gloss>
        </def>
        <def>
          <gloss>
            <labels> <label type="term">medicina</label> </labels>
            <wiki>{{Term|medicina|it}} ogni fenomeno patologico che modifichi l'organismo o l'[[efficienza]]
              di una parte del corpo</wiki>
            <txt>ogni fenomeno patologico che modifichi l'organismo o l'efficienza di una parte del corpo</txt>
            <xml>ogni fenomeno patologico che modifichi l'organismo o l'<innerLink>efficienza</innerLink>
              di una parte del corpo</xml>
          </gloss>
        </def>
      </defs>
    </pos>
    <pos type="verb" lemma="0">
      <defs>
        <def>
          <gloss>
            <wiki>terza persona plurale, indicativo presente di [[dare]]</wiki>
            <txt>terza persona plurale, indicativo presente di dare</txt>
            <xml>terza persona plurale, indicativo presente di <innerLink>dare</innerLink></xml>
          </gloss>
        </def>
      </defs>
      <inflectionInfos>
        <inflectedForm gracePOS="Vmip3p-" lemma="dare"/>
      </inflectionInfos>
    </pos>
    <section type="sill"> <item>dàn|no</item> </section>
    <section type="pron"> <item type="IPA">'da:nno</item> </section>
    <section type="sin">
      <item>danneggiamento</item>
      <item>rottura</item>
      <item>oltraggio</item>
      <item labels="medicina">male</item>
      <item labels="medicina">lesione</item>
      <item>svantaggio</item>
    </section>
    <section type="ant">
      <item>sistemazione</item>
      <item>risarcimento</item>
    </section>
    <section type="der">
      <item>dannare</item>
    </section>
  </text>
</article>
```

Fig. 1. General structure of the article *danno* in GLAW-IT

information. The basic unit of GLAW-IT is the wordform and when some homographs correspond to the same wordform, the article contains a separate POS section for each one of them. An example is reported in Fig. 1 for the entry *danno*, which is both the lemma (masculine singular) of *danno* 'damage' and the inflected forms (indicative present, 3rd person plural) of the verb *dare* 'to give'.

As we can see, the stress placement is reported independently in the hyphenation field (*dàn|no*) as well as in the phonological transcription (ˈdaːnno). It may also occur in only one of the two fields or be missing. Conceived as a general-purpose MRD, GLAW-IT is intended to be to used as such or as a starting point to tailor specific lexicons. In the section below, we explain how we derived GLAFF-IT (which stands for *Un Grande Lessico 'Tuttofare' dell'Italiano*, 'A Large Versatile Italian Lexicon') from GLAW-IT.

2.2 From GLAW-IT to GLAFF-IT

A first step in the creation of GLAFF-IT is filtering GLAW-IT by all the morphosyntactic and phonological tags and collecting all the inflected forms related to each lemma. In GLAW-IT, for a given lemma not all the inflected forms of the paradigm are present. This compels us to complete the missing forms by exploiting the systematic variations of Italian inflection with respect to each grammatical class. In particular, given some orthographic preconditions, certain inflected forms are totally predictable from other forms of the same paradigm. For example, for a particular set of missing nouns, we have generated the Plural Masculine forms from their Singular forms. Specifically, we have applied the general rule governing the alternation Masculine Singular/Masculine Plural for those nouns ending in *-o*, like *allomorfo* ('allomorph'), which change the last letter in *-i* for the Plural (Masculine) forms (*allomorfi*, 'allomorphs'). We report below the main deterministic inflection rules we implemented for the generation of the missing forms:

Nouns:

- lemma's Feminine Singular ending = *-a* → *-e* for the Feminine Plural, as in *casa* 'home' → *case* 'homes'
- lemma's Feminine Singular ending = *-e* → *-i* for the Feminine Plural, as in *siepe* 'hedge' → *siepi* 'hedges'
- lemma's Feminine Singular ending = *-ista* → *-iste* for the Feminine Plural, as in *rivista* 'magazine' → *riviste* 'magazines'

Adjectives:

- lemma's (Singular Masculine) ending = *-ico* → *-ici, -ica, -iche* respectively for the Masculine Plural, Feminine Singular and Plural, as in *magnifico* 'magnificent' → *magnifici, magnifica, magnifiche*
- lemma's (Singular Masculine) ending = *-go* or *-co* (but not *-ico*) → *-(c)(g)hi, -(c)(g)a, -(c)(g)he* respectively for the Masculine Plural, Feminine Singular and Plural, as in *metallico* 'metallic' → *metallici, metallica, metalliche*

Verbs:

- for the highly regular conjugation *-are*, we generate the missing verbal forms by adding regular inflectional suffixes to the stem base of the verb

Table 1. Size of GLAFF-IT: number of lemmas and forms

	lemmas	Forms		
		Initial	Generated	Total
Nouns	19,340	36,726	2,505	39,231
Adjectives	7,835	23,932	4,140	28,072
Verbs	7,552	351,604	36,200	387,804
Adverbs	2,593	2,595	0	2,595
Total	37,320	414,857	42,845	457,702

(which is always detectable). For example the Gerund and the Singular and Plural Present Participle of the verb *manipolare* 'to manipulate' are created by adding respectively *-ando*, *-ante* and *-anti* to the stem base *manipol*: *manipolando*, *manipolante* and *manipolanti*. When missing, we create 54 verbal forms of the paradigm by exploiting the regular inflectional suffixes of the Italian conjugation.

The aforementioned inflection rules enabled us to generate 42,845 new wordforms which are integrated into GLAFF-IT. Table 1 reports the number of lemmas extracted from GLAW-IT and the number of forms generated by the aforementioned rules. The current version of GLAFF-IT counts 37,320 lemmas for 457,702 wordforms and includes nouns, verbs, adjectives and adverbs.[2] Each entry of the lexicon includes a wordform, a tag in MULTEXT-GRACE format [13] specifying the main syntactic category and inflection features, a lemma and API phonological transcriptions with the stress placement when present in GLAW-IT. An extract of GLAFF-IT is reported in Fig. 2. This version has been converted into Lexical Markup Framework, as illustrated in Fig. 3.

```
...
danni|Ncmp|danno|'daːnni
danno|Ncms|danno|'danno
danno|Vmip3p-|dare|'danno
dannoso|Afpms-|dannoso|dann'oso
dannosa|Afpfs-|dannoso|dann'osa
dannose|Afpfp-|dannoso|dann'ose
...
```

Fig. 2. An extract of GLAFF-IT.

As is the case for the inflected forms, phonological information may be absent from GLAW-IT. The next section describes the automatic generation of missing phonological transcriptions and stress placements.

[2] GLAFF-IT is freely available at: http://redac.univ-tlse2.fr/lexicons/glaffit.html.

```
<lexicalEntry id="danno">
  <formSet>
    <lemmatizedForm>
      <orthography>danno</orthography>
      <grammaticalCategory>commonNoun</grammaticalCategory>
      <grammaticalGender>masculine</grammaticalGender>
      <pronunciation>'daːnno</pronunciation>
    </lemmatizedForm>
    <inflectedForm>
      <orthography>danno</orthography>
      <grammaticalNumber>singular</grammaticalNumber>
      <pronunciation>'daːnno</pronunciation>
    </inflectedForm>
    <inflectedForm>
      <orthography>danni</orthography>
      <grammaticalNumber>plural</grammaticalNumber>
      <pronunciation>'daːnni</pronunciation>
    </inflectedForm>
  </formSet>
</lexicalEntry>
<lexicalEntry id="dannoso">
  <formSet>
    <lemmatizedForm>
      <orthography>dannoso</orthography>
      <grammaticalCategory>adjective</grammaticalCategory>
      <pronunciation>daːnno'so</pronunciation>
    </lemmatizedForm>
    <inflectedForm>
      <orthography>dannoso</orthography>
      <grammaticalGender>masculine</grammaticalGender>
      <grammaticalNumber>singular</grammaticalNumber>
      <pronunciation>daːnno'so</pronunciation>
    </inflectedForm>
    <inflectedForm>
      <orthography>dannosi</orthography>
      <grammaticalGender>masculine</grammaticalGender>
      <grammaticalNumber>plural</grammaticalNumber>
      <pronunciation>daːnno'si</pronunciation>
    </inflectedForm>
    <inflectedForm>
      <orthography>dannosa</orthography>
      <grammaticalGender>feminine</grammaticalGender>
      <grammaticalNumber>singular</grammaticalNumber>
      <pronunciation>daːnno'sa</pronunciation>
    </inflectedForm>
    <inflectedForm>
      <orthography>dannose</orthography>
      <grammaticalGender>feminine</grammaticalGender>
      <grammaticalNumber>plural</grammaticalNumber>
      <pronunciation>daːnno'se</pronunciation>
    </inflectedForm>
  </formSet>
</lexicalEntry>
```

Fig. 3. Extract of GLAFF-IT in Lexical Markup Framework

3 The Problematic Italian Stress Issue

3.1 Phonological Transcriptions and Stress in GLAW-IT

Only 4.2% of GLAW-IT's wordforms (corresponding to 17,720 articles) include phonological transcriptions. 98.5% of these transcriptions also report stress placement. The stress information has been taken either from the phonological field or from the hyphenation field (cf. Sect. 2.1). Table 2 provides a breakdown with respect to the four grammatical classes.

Table 2. Number and percentage of phonological transcriptions with and without stress in GLAW-IT

	Total	Stressed	Without stress
Nouns	9,135 (23.28%)	8,983 (22.89%)	152 (0.38%)
Adjectives	4,227 (15.05%)	4,196 (14.94%)	31 (0.11%)
Verbs	4,165 (1.07%)	4,093 (1.05%)	72 (0.01%)
Adverbs	193 (7.43%)	188 (7.24%)	5 (0.19%)
Total	17,720	17,460	260

In order to assess GLAW-IT's phonological transcriptions, we compare them to those of PhonItalia. We first build the intersection of their entries, resulting in 66,371 orthographic forms (that corresponds to 15% of GLAW-IT and 57% of PhonItalia's vocabularies). The number of wordforms per POS contained in this intersection, as well as the proportion of forms having transcriptions and stress placements in GLAW-IT, are reported in Table 3.

Table 3. Intersection of GLAW-IT and PhonItalia.

	Wordforms	With phonological transcription in GLAW-IT		
		Total	With stress	Without stress
Nouns	18,315	6,626 (36.18%)	6,535 (35.68%)	91 (0.5%)
Adjectives	12,835	2,763 (21.53%)	2,744 (21.4%)	19 (0.1%)
Verbs	34,233	1,867 (5.45%)	1,823 (5.33%)	44 (0.13%)
Adverbs	988	154 (15.59%)	149 (15.08%)	5 (0.5%)
Total	66,371	11,410	11,251	159

We then compared the 11,410 shared entries in order to check the correspondence of their transcriptions and stress placements. The results of the comparison are given in Table 4: GLAW-IT and PhonItalia present a 87% agreement both for the transcriptions and the stress placement. The main differences stem from

Table 4. Agreement between GLAW-IT and PhonItalia with respect to the phonological transcriptions and the stress placement.

	Agreement between GLAW-IT and PhonItalia			
	# entries	Phonological transcription	# entries	Stress placement
Nouns	6,626	5,635 (85.05%)	6,535	5,585 (85.46%)
Adjectives	2,763	2,448 (88.59%)	2,744	2,442 (88.99%)
Verbs	1,867	1,697 (90.89%)	1,823	1,669 (91.55%)
Adverbs	154	137 (88.96%)	149	132 (88.59%)
Total	11,410	9,917 (86.91%)	11,251	9,828 (87.35%)

the inventory of phonems used by the two resources. For example, in the group of the nasal consonants, GLAW-IT marks the velar nasal /ŋ/ (as in <anche> 'also' /aŋke/), which is absent in PhonItalia (where <anche> is transcribed /anke/). In such a case, our comparison, based on the exact matching of phonemes, leads to a disagreement.

3.2 Automatic Generation of Phonological Transcriptions in GLAFF-IT

This section describes a method to generate phonological transcriptions from orthographic forms. We used this method to transcribe each wordform from GLAFF-IT when no transcription is given in GLAW-IT.

Knowing the pronunciation of an Italian word is enough to know its orthography (with very few exceptions, e.g. /kw/ in some words is written as <cu> - e.g. <cuore> 'heart' /kwɔre/ - instead of the more common <qu> - e.g. <quale> 'which' /kwale/). The opposite is not true in general: if most of the Italian graphemes are mapped one-to-one to phones, some cases do not allow automatic conversion. Here are some representative examples:

- a written <e> can be realised as /e/ or /ɛ/ when stressed. This distinction is crucial because it enables to differentiate homographic words having the same stress such as <pesca> = /pˈeska/ 'fishing' and /pˈɛska/ 'peach'
- a written <o> can be realised as /o/ (as in <asino> 'donkey' /azino/) or /ɔ/ when stressed (as in <rosa> 'rose' /rɔza/)
- a written <z> can be the voiced affricate /dz/ as in <zaino> 'backpack' /dzaino/ or unvoiced affricate /ts/ as in <canzone> 'song' /kantsone/
- a written <s>, intervocalic or after suffixes, can be realised as /s/ or /z/ as <casa> = /kasa/ 'home', <rosa> = /rɔza/ 'rose', <transatlantico> = /tranzˈatlantico/ 'transatlantic', <transiberiano> = /tranzˈsiberiano/ 'trans-Siberian')
- <j>, <y> and <w>, mostly found in loanwords (as in 'jazz', 'yacht', 'know-how'), can represent a wide range of phonemes: /j/, /dʒ/, /ʒ/, /i/, /v/, /w/, etc.

To set up a letter-to-phoneme mapping, henceforth *orth2phon*, we distinguished unambiguous from ambiguous cases:

Unambiguous cases. We adopted the conversion rules grapheme(s)-to-phoneme only for the unambiguous cases in which we distinguished transparent and opaque conditions. For example, some cases of transparent grapheme-to-phoneme mapping are given by <p> → /p/ (<pane> 'bread' /pane/), <l> → /l/ (<lino> 'linen' /lino/) or <t> → /t/ (<tutto> 'all' /tutto/). Less transparent cases of mapping are <gli> → /ʎ/ (<figlio> 'son' /fiʎʎo/) and <gli> → /gl/ (<siglare> 'to initial' /siglare/). Conversely, opaque cases need the orthographic context to be converted in phonemes. Opaque cases are for example <ch> → /k/ (<anche> 'also' /aŋke/), <q> → /k/ (<quadri> 'paintings' /kwadri/), <c> → /k/ (<casa> 'home' /casa/). In many cases the stressed vowel reported in the hyphenation information can be used for the disambiguation of some ambivalent phonemes such as <e> or <o> that are respectively realised as /ɛ/ and /ɔ/ when stressed.

Ambiguous cases. We encoded by a *ad hoc* capital letter all the cases which are not unambiguously convertible. For example, an intervocalic <s> may lead to the two different phonemes /s/ or /z/ and cannot be automatically predicted. We choose to encode such cases into capital letters (here, intervocalic <s> → S). We define eight different ambiguous cases: (1) E = /e/ or /ɛ/; (2) O = /o/ or /ɔ/; (3) I = /i/, /j/ or ∅; (4) U = /u/ or /w/; (5) S = /s/ or /z/; (6) Z = /ts/ or /dz/; (7) J = /j/ or /dʒ/; (8) W = /w/ or /v/

We first applied *orth2phon* to the entries from the intersection between GLAW-IT and PhonItalia described in Table 3. We then compared the agreement between the two resources on their phonological transcriptions and stress placements. As can be seen in the Table 5, the *orth2phon* coding increases GLAW-IT and PhonItalia's agreement on transcriptions from 86% (cf. Table 4) to 92% and the agreement on stress placement (from 86% to from 90%).

Table 5. Agreement between GLAW-IT+*orth2phon* and PhonItalia intersection.

	Agreement between GLAW-IT+*orth2phon* and PhonItalia			
	# entries	Phonological transcription	# entries	Stress placement
Nouns	6,626	6,056 (91.39%)	6,535	5,753 (88.03%)
Adjectives	2,763	2,581 (93.41%)	2,744	2,528 (92.12%)
Verbs	1,867	1,755 (94.00%)	1,823	1,669 (91.55%)
Adverbs	154	137 (88.96%)	149	132 (88.59%)
Total	11,410	10,529 (92.27%)	11,251	10,082 (89.60%)

Finally, the *orth2phon* method enabled us to generate all the phonological transcriptions missing from GLAFF-IT. In the next section we introduce our method for the prediction of the stress placement in the phonological transcriptions of GLAFF-IT.

3.3 A Hybrid Method for Stress Prediction in GLAFF-IT

Stress placement is lexically marked in Italian [1,11] and has a contrastive function: *capito* /'kapito/ 'I happen by' vs. *capito* /ka'pito/ 'understood' vs. *capitò* /kapi'to/ 'it happened'. This means that *a priori* the speaker should have a phonological knowledge of the word to pronounce it correctly (unless the stress is on the last vowel: in this case, the stress is orthographically marked as in *capitò*).

As Fig. 1 shows, GLAW-IT can report word stress information in two different sections: (a) in the phonological transcriptions and (b) in the hyphenation of the word in which the stressed vowel is orthographically marked. By gathering information from both these sections we collect 59,891 wordforms presenting a stress marker (Table 6). In this section, we present a hybrid method which allows us to complete the stress information for the remaining 397,812 wordforms of GLAFF-IT by combining heuristic rules and predictions performed by a *logit* model.

Heuristic Rules

In some known cases, stress placement in Italian is deterministic. We design a set of heuristic rules in order to predict words' stress in such situations:

- Stress position is generated for the words in which the stressed vowel is orthographically marked, as in <liquidità> 'liquidity' /likwidit'a/ or <avrò> 'I will have' /avr'o/.
- Bisyllabic words in which the last vowel is not graphically marked always have the stress on the first vowel, as <gonna> 'skirt' /g'ɔnna/ or <casa> 'home' /k'asa/.
- Some verbs with particular endings have regular stress patterns. For example, it is the case of the verbal ending /-v'amo/ which identifies the 1st person imperfect indicative as in <amavamo> 'we were loving' /amav'amo/ or the ending of 3rd person present conditional /-r'ɛbbero/ as in <amerebbero> '(they) would love' /amer'ɛbbero/. We distinguished 15 verbal endings (mostly coming from the subjunctive and conditional mood) exhibiting predictable stressed vowels.

By exploiting the heuristic rules, we determine the stress placement for 289,717 forms. Table 6 reports the details of this stress generation. This processing mainly involves the verbal entries (288,095 stress placements generated) and a limited number of nouns and adjectives. This fact is quite unsurprising, given that Italian stress is lexically marked and so the application of possible heuristics is highly constrained for nouns and adjectives.

Machine Learning

Stress prediction has been performed for the 108,095 remaining wordforms for which no heuristic rule has been applied. We use a model that has learned the phonological contexts for stressed and unstressed Italian vowels. Orthographic and phonological context-based approaches have been extensively used in the

Table 6. Number and percentage of the stress markers present in GLAW-IT and generated by heuristic rules.

	Initially stressed	Heuristic-generated	Total	Remaining to stress
Nouns	24,435 (62.28%)	1,072 (2.73%)	25,507 (65.01%)	13,724 (34.98%)
Adjectives	17,908 (63.79%)	507 (1.80%)	18,415 (65.59%)	9657 (34.40%)
Verbs	15,144 (3.90%)	288,095 (74.28%)	303,239 (78.19%)	84,565 (21.80%)
Adverbs	2,403 (92.60%)	43 (1.65%)	2446 (94.25%)	149 (5.74%)
Total	59,891 (13.80%)	289,717 (63.29%)	349,607 (76.38%)	108,095 (23.60%)

text-to-speech domain for stress detection [2,7] and for accenting unknown words in a specialised language [18]. The rationale behind our approach is that the exploitation of the phonological neighbourhood of a vowel helps estimate its probability of being stressed or unstressed.

We trained a feed-forward (one hidden layer) neural network, using a logistic activation function, encoding the phonological neighbourhoods of the unstressed and the stressed vowel (respectively 0 and 1). Such a method has been used successfully in similar settings for the syllabification of Italian words [5]. In our model, the representation of the input data was constituted by each vowel composing the word with its left and right phonological context. The Fig. 4 reports the representation for two Italian words, <decadere> 'to decay' /dekad'ere/ and <decidere> 'to decide' /detʃ'idere/. Although phonologically quite similar and with identical syllabic structure, the two words present different stress placement: on the third vowel for <decadere> and on the second for <decidere>. In the input representation, the binary response unstressed/stressed vowel (0/1) is mapped to the left (L) and right (R) phonological context of the vowels (which are in Focus position). Each context defines the phonemes occurring in a given position with respect to the vowel in Focus. For example, the L_1 and R_1 contexts indicate respectively the phonemes occupying the first position on the left and the first position on the right with reference to the Focus. There are as many rows as the number of vowels in the word. The number of contexts considered is determined by the phonological length of the words: the longest word imposes the final number of contexts that will be equal to its number of phonemes N - 1 for L and R. In our input representation, each phoneme is encoded as a set of binary features defining the place and the manner of articulation. Although some authors report a clear correlation between stress patterns and phonological similar words [9], our choice was largely motivated by phonological reasons, with the rationale of taking into account the specific phonemic nature of each phoneme according to a set of phonologically-based features. We distinguished 14 features for all the Italian phonemes:

1. Voicing (VO): marks that the phonemes is voiced - or not
2. Bilabial (BI): consonants articulated with both lips
3. Labiodentals (LD): consonants articulated with the lower lip and the upper teeth

ID	L_n	$L_{...}$	L_8	L_7	L_6	L_5	L_4	L_3	L_2	L_1	Focus	R_1	R_2	R_3	R_4	R_5	R_6	R_7	R_8	$R_{...}$	R_n	Out
1	#	#	#	#	#	#	#	#	#	d	e	k	a	d	e	r	e	#	#	#	#	→ 0
2	#	#	#	#	#	#	#	d	e	k	a	d	e	r	e	#	#	#	#	#	#	→ 0
3	#	#	#	#	#	d	e	k	a	d	e	r	e	#	#	#	#	#	#	#	#	→ 1
4	#	#	#	d	e	k	a	d	e	r	e	#	#	#	#	#	#	#	#	#	#	→ 0
1	#	#	#	#	#	#	#	#	#	d	e	tʃ	i	d	e	r	e	#	#	#	#	→ 0
2	#	#	#	#	#	#	#	d	e	tʃ	i	d	e	r	e	#	#	#	#	#	#	→ 1
3	#	#	#	#	#	d	e	tʃ	i	d	e	r	e	#	#	#	#	#	#	#	#	→ 0
4	#	#	#	d	e	tʃ	i	d	e	r	e	#	#	#	#	#	#	#	#	#	#	→ 0

Fig. 4. Input representation for two Italian words, <decadere> (/dekad'ere/) 'to decay' and <decidere> (/detʃ'idere/) 'to decide'.

4. Dental-alveolar (DA): consonants articulated with a flat tongue against the alveolar ridge and upper teeth
5. Palato-alveolar (PA): consonants articulated with the blade of the tongue behind the alveolar ridge
6. Palatal (PL): consonants articulated with the body of the tongue raised against the hard palate .
7. Velar (VE): consonants articulated with the back part of the tongue against the soft palate
8. Nasal (NA): consonants produced with a lowered velum, allowing air to escape freely through the nose
9. Stop (SP): consonants in which the vocal tract is blocked, so that all airflow ceases
10. Affricate (AF): consonants that begins as a stop and conclude with a sound of friction
11. Fricative (FR): consonants produced by the friction of breath in a narrow opening
12. Glides (GL): consonants which have is a sound that is phonetically similar to a vowel
13. Liquid (LQ): consonants produced when the tongue approaches a point of articulation within the mouth but does not come close enough to obstruct
14. Vowel (VW): marks that the phoneme is a vowel, without any specifications

Features 2 to 7 specify the place of articulation of the phonemes, while the manner is given by features 8–13. Feature 1 concerns voiced consonants and feature 14 marks the presence of a vowel. Table 7 reports the phonological feature encoding for the phonemes of the word <decadere> (/dekad'ere/) 'to decay'. Although the three phonemes /d/,/k/ and /r/ are different, they share common phonological features as, for example, *Stop* for /d/ and /k/ or *Voicing* and *Dental-alveolar* for /d/ and /r/.

We designed our test sets by sampling respectively 10,000 stressed wordforms from GLAFF-IT and absent from PhonItalia, and 10,000 stressed wordforms from PhonItalia and absent from GLAFF-IT. Our training dataset is composed of all the stressed wordforms reported in Table 6, excluding those used for the

Table 7. Phonological feature encoding for the phonemes of the word <decadere> (/dekad'ere/) 'to decay', see Table 4.

Phoneme	Phonological features													
	VO	*BI*	*LD*	*DA*	*PA*	*PL*	*VE*	*NA*	*SP*	*AF*	*FR*	*GL*	*LQ*	*VW*
d	1	0	0	1	0	0	0	0	1	0	0	0	0	0
e	0	0	0	0	0	0	0	0	0	0	0	0	0	1
k	0	0	0	0	0	0	1	0	1	0	0	0	0	0
a	0	0	0	0	0	0	0	0	0	0	0	0	0	1
r	1	0	0	1	0	0	0	0	0	0	0	0	1	0
e	0	0	0	0	0	0	0	0	0	0	0	0	0	1

test sets. We implemented different architectures for the model by varying the number of neurons of the hidden layer. For a set of architectures, POS information have also been considered as features in the input words. A detailed evaluation of the stress prediction output is reported in the next section.

4 Evaluation and Conclusions

We designed four architectures by varying the size of the hidden layer (5, 10, 20 and 40 neurons). For each architecture, we trained and evaluated two models, including or excluding the POS information of the word. In our approach, a word presents one (and only one) stressed vowel. During the testing phase, we identify the vowel in the word with the highest probability of being stressed: this vowel represents the stressed vowel and thus determines the stress position of the word. Selecting the vowel with the highest probability is computationally convenient because we do not have to identify the probability threshold for separating stressed and unstressed vowels. The Fig. 5 displays the behaviour of the four architectures by ROC curves with respect to the 10,000 GLAFF-IT test wordforms. The ROC curves show the trade-off between the true positive rate (sensitivity, y-axis) and the false positive rate (1 - specificity, x-axis). Sensitivity refers to the proportion of the stressed vowels whereas specificity refers to the proportion of the unstressed vowels. The closer the curve follows the left-hand border, from the origin of axes (0.0 and 0.0) to the top left corner (0.0 and 1.0) and then to the top right corner (1.0 and 1.0), the more accurate the classification. The 5- and 10-neuron models exhibit a substantial false positive rate for the test data, meaning that the model predicts unstressed vowels wrongly categorised as stressed. The 20- and 40-neuron models are very good at classifying with a nearly perfect separation between the stressed and the unstressed vowels. The POS information (dotted lines in Fig. 5) does not seem to significantly affect the prediction. The Table 8 reports the percentages of correct stress prediction for the 10,000 words of the two testing datasets. We observe that the POS information does not improve the prediction (in some cases models without

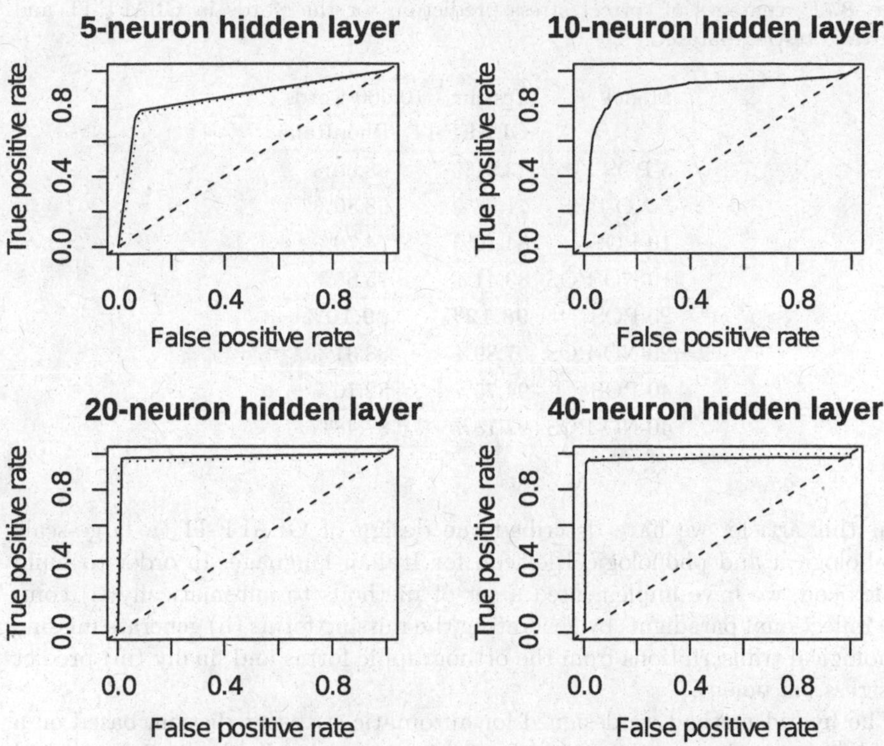

Fig. 5. ROC curves for the four architectures. Testing dataset: 10,000 stressed word-forms from GLAFF-IT. Solid lines represent models integrating POS information about the word, dotted lines represent models excluding this information.

POS information exhibit a better prediction than the models with POS). The grammatical class was a crucial factor for the applicability of the heuristic rules used to predict the stress placement. We can see here that this is not true the stress prediction by the *logit* model. The 20-neuron model with POS information performs the best prediction and reaches more than 98% of correct stress predicted. We also notice a difference in terms of stress prediction between the two testing sets: the evaluation performed against the PhonItalia test reaches 89.1% of correct predictions by the best model (20-POS). This difference can be explained by the nature of the two test sets. For instance, the PhonItalia test lists a great number of loanwords such as <fairplay>, <academy> or <mission> which have a phonotactic structure totally different from the words of the training dataset. Moreover, the PhonItalia test contains verbs with clitic pronouns as <mangiarlo> 'to eat it' or locative clitic as <andateci> 'you (2nd person plural) go there' which are totally absent from the training data.

Table 8. Percentages of correct stress prediction for the words in GLAFF-IT and PhonItalia testing dataset.

Model	Testing - 10,000 words	
	GLAFF-IT	PhonItalia
5-POS	73.31%	68.60%
5-NO-POS	71.87%	68.80%
10-POS	84.10%	74.70%
10-NO-POS	83.41%	75.65%
20-POS	**98.12%**	**89.10%**
20-NO-POS	97.89%	88.31%
40-POS	94.75%	82.10%
40-NO-POS	97.18%	87.48%

In this article, we have described the design of GLAFF-IT, a large-scale morphological and phonological lexicon for Italian language. In order to build this lexicon, we have implemented a set of methods to automatically (i) complete inflectional paradigms by generating the missing forms (ii) generate missing phonological transcriptions from the orthographic forms and finally (iii) predict the stress placement.

The hybrid method we designed for automatic stress prediction, based on a set of heuristic rules and the responses of a *logit* model, reliably predicts stressed and unstressed vowels. Applied to GLAFF-IT, it reaches an accuracy of 98.12%. To our knowledge, GLAFF-IT is the only free Italian lexicon featuring a large coverage (457,702 entries) and reporting phonological transcription with stress markings. Moreover, this model will be useful when updating the resource with the new entries regularly added to Wikizionario. Indeed, if contributors are prone to add new entries, they often neglect to provide inflectional and phonological information.

In the near future, we plan to add syllable boundaries to the phonological transcriptions of GLAFF-IT. Regarding the stress prediction, we intend to evaluate the adaptability of our model to other languages presenting variable stress placement. In a psycholinguistic perspective, the model's responses could be compared to the responses provided by speakers with respect to the same set of stimuli, in order to assess the possible correlation between speakers and automatic predictions.

References

1. Bafile, L.: Antepenultimate stress in italian and some related dialects: Metrical and prosodic aspects. Rivista di linguistica **11**(2), 201–229 (1999)
2. Behravan, H., Hautamäki, V., Siniscalchi, S.M., Kinnunen, T., Lee, C.H.: i-Vector modeling of speech attributes for automatic foreign accent recognition. IEEE/ACM Trans. Audio Speech Lang. Process. **24**(1), 29–41 (2016)

3. Bel, N., Busa, F., Calzolari, N., Gola, E., Lenci, A., Monachini, M., Ogonowski, A., Peters, I., Peters, W., Ruimy, N., Villegas, M., Zampolli, A.: SIMPLE: a general framework for the development of multilingual lexicons. In: Proceedings of the Ninth International Conference on Language Resources and Evaluation (LREC 2000), Athens, Greece (2000)
4. Bertinetto, P.M., Burani, C., Laudanna, A., Lucia Marconi, D.R., Rolando, C.: Corpus e Lessico di Frequenza dell'Italiano Scritto (CoLFIS) (2005). http://linguistica.sns.it/CoLFIS/Home.htm
5. Calderone, B., Bertinetto, P.M.: From phonotactics to syllables. a psychò - computational approach. In: 46th Annual Meeting of the Societas Linguistica Europaea, Split, Croatia (2013)
6. Calderone, B., Sajous, F., Hathout, N.: GLAW-IT: a free large Italian dictionary encoded in a fine-grained XML format. In: Proceedings of the 49th Annual Meeting of the Societas Linguistica Europaea (SLE 2016), Naples, Italy, pp. 43–45 (2016)
7. Dou, Q., Bergsma, S., Jiampojamarn, S., Kondrak, G.: A ranking approach to stress prediction for letter-to-phoneme conversion. In: Proceedings of the 47th Annual Meeting of the ACL, pp. 118–126. Association for Computational Linguistics, Suntec, Singapore (2009)
8. Goslin, J., Galluzzi, C., Romani, C.: PhonItalia: a phonological lexicon for Italian. Behav. Res. Methods **46**(3), 872–886 (2014)
9. Guion, S.G.: Knowledge of English word stress patterns in early and late Korean-English bilinguals. Stud. Second Lang. Acquisiti **27**, 503–533 (2005)
10. Hathout, N., Sajous, F.: Wiktionnaire's Wikicode GLAWIfied: a workable French machine-readable dictionary. In: Proceedings of the Tenth International Conference on Language Resources and Evaluation (LREC 2016), Portorož, Slovenia (2016)
11. Krämer, M.: The Phonology of Italian. Oxford University Press, Oxford (2009)
12. Peperkamp, S.: Lexical exceptions in stress systems: arguments from early language acquisition and adult speech perception. Language **80**(1), 98–126 (2004)
13. Rajman, M., Lecomte, J., Paroubek, P.: Grace GTR-3-2.1. Technical report, EPFL and INaLF (1997)
14. Roventini, A., Alonge, A., Calzolari, N., Magnini, B., Bertagna, F.: ItalWordNet: a large semantic database for Italian. In: Proceedings of the Ninth International Conference on Language Resources and Evaluation (LREC 2000), Athens, Greece, pp. 783–790 (2000)
15. Sajous, F., Hathout, N.: GLAWI, a free XML-encoded machine-readable dictionary built from the French Wiktionary. In: Proceedings of the of the eLex 2015 Conference, Herstmonceux, England, pp. 405–426 (2015)
16. Slowiaczek, L.M.: Stress and context in auditory word recognition. J. Psycholinguist. Res. **20**(6), 465–481 (1991)
17. Talamo, L., Celata, C., Bertinetto, P.M.: derIvaTario: an annotated lexicon of Italian derivatives. Word Struct. **9**(1), 72–102 (2016)
18. Zweigenbaum, P., Grabar, N.: Accenting unknown words in a specialized language. In: Proceedings of the ACL 2002 Workshop on Natural Language Processing in the Biomedical Domain, Philadelphia, PA, pp. 21–28 (2002)

OnLiT: An Ontology for Linguistic Terminology

Bettina Klimek[1(✉)], John P. McCrae[2], Christian Lehmann[3], Christian Chiarcos[4], and Sebastian Hellmann[1]

[1] InfAI, University of Leipzig, Leipzig, Germany
{klimek,hellmann}@informatik.uni-leipzig.de
[2] Insight Centre for Data Analytics, National University of Ireland Galway, Galway, Ireland
john@mccr.ae
[3] University of Erfurt, Erfurt, Germany
christian.lehmann@uni-erfurt.de
[4] Applied Computational Linguistics, Goethe-University Frankfurt, Frankfurt, Germany
chiarcos@informatik.uni-frankfurt.de
http://aksw.org/Groups/KILT, https://www.insight-centre.org, http://www.christianlehmann.eu, http://acoli.informatik.uni-frankfurt.de

Abstract. Understanding the differences underlying the scope, usage and content of language data requires the provision of a clarifying terminological basis which is integrated in the metadata describing a particular language resource. While terminological resources such as the SIL Glossary of Linguistic Terms, ISOcat or the GOLD ontology provide a considerable amount of linguistic terms, their practical usage is limited to a look up of a defined term whose relation to other terms is unspecified or insufficient. Therefore, in this paper we propose an ontology for linguistic terminology, called OnLiT. It is a data model which can be used to represent linguistic terms and concepts in a semantically interrelated data structure and, thus, overcomes prevalent isolating definition-based term descriptions. OnLiT is based on the LiDo Glossary of Linguistic Terms and enables the creation of RDF datasets, that represent linguistic terms and their meanings within the whole or a subdomain of linguistics.

Keywords: Linguistic terminology · Linguistic linked data · LiDo database

1 Introduction

The research field of language data has evolved to encompass a multitude of interdisciplinary scientific areas that are all more or less closely bound to the central studies of linguistics. Understanding the differences underlying the scope, usage and content of language data provided by diciplines such as linguistics, computational linguistics, digital humanities or content analytics, requires the provision of a clarifying terminological basis which is integrated in the metadata describing a particular language resource. Moreover, the comparative use of resources

J. Gracia et al. (Eds.): LDK 2017, LNAI 10318, pp. 42–57, 2017.
DOI: 10.1007/978-3-319-59888-8_4

of different languages presupposes that they use the same conceptual framework and terminology. This demand for specifying linguistic terminology has been addressed mainly by linguists in creating look-up resources such as books, e.g. the lexicon of linguistics (Bußmann et al. 1996), online registries (e.g. ISOcat[1] (Kemps-Snijders et al. 2009), the SIL Glossary of Linguistic Terms[2] (Loos et al. 2004) and the CLARIN Concept Registry (Schuurman et al. 2016) or Web pages such as the online encyclopedia of linguistics[3].

While all these resources provide a considerable amount of linguistic terms, their practical usage is limited to a look up of a term whose relation to other terms is unspecified or too general. In this respect the available data resources of linguistic terminology fail to provide a meaningful representation of a linguistic term leaving it isolated within the whole domain of linguistic terminology. Retrieving more information about linguistic concepts necessitates reading their definitions and looking up further words that are contained in it, which might be also defined terms in the database. This procedure is not only time-consuming and impractical but also results in implicit and vague specifications of linguistic terms. This is the argument from the viewpoint of usability. However, maintenance of a consistent conceptual-terminological framework likewise requires that the relations among concepts be standardized and that, for each concept, the relevant relations be specified. A set of isolated terms cannot be kept consistent.

In this paper we propose an ontology for linguistic terminology, called OnLiT, as a data model which can be used to represent linguistic terms and concepts in a semantically interrelated structure. Every terminological dataset evolving from OnLiT will result in a data graph which is easy to navigate for human users, machine-processable for semantic applications and will serve the purpose of directly and indirectly interrelating linguistic terms and concepts throughout the whole dataset. The OnLiT model is based on the *Linguistic Documentation (LiDo) database* by Christian Lehmann[4,5], who established a relational network which represents linguistic terminology that defines and delimits a term by relating it to the linguistic concept it encodes and also by including a set of specifying conceptual relations (Lehmann 1996). What is more, the proposed model is independent of the particular language of the terms and thus allows integration of terminological networks in different languages and multilingual terminological networks. By transforming the structure of the LiDo relational database to RDF, the OnLiT data model aims to provide the following contributions:

- to enable a semantic search for linguistic terms and concepts,
- to provide unique reusable and citable identifiers for each data entry,

[1] http://www.isocat.org/.

[2] http://www-01.sil.org/linguistics/GlossaryOflinguisticTerms/.

[3] http://www.glottopedia.org.

[4] A browseable version of the database is available at: http://linguistik.uni-regensburg.de:8080/lido/Lido.

[5] Christian Lehmann is the data owner of LiDo and permitted to derive the OnLiT data model from it.

- to enable the creation of conceptually consistent terminological datasets that broadly interconnect and cover linguistic terms in a required linguistic (sub)domain,
- to establish the possibility for extending the data model and enriching an OnLiT dataset with external data,
- to allow free and open reuse of the OnLiT data model.

The remainder of the paper is structured as follows. Section 2 gives an overview of relevant related work. Following an outline of the LiDo database as basis for OnLiT in Sect. 3, the OnLiT data model is presented in Sect. 4.1. Further, the purpose, domain and requirements of OnLiT are presented in Sect. 4.2 and the modelled concepts, terms and the established relations between them are discussed in Sects. 4.3 and 4.4. Finally, in Section 5 the paper concludes giving a brief summary and a prospect of future work.

2 Related Work

An investigation of available datasets (excluding the LiDo database which is presented in Sect. 3) that contain models of representing linguistic terminology, resulted in two different types of data.

(i) Linguistic term bases that offer a term look-up via a Website: Resources such as the aforementioned ISOcat registry or SIL Glossary of Linguistic Terms (GLT) are mainly aimed at human users. Their underlying semantic structure is rather flat providing definitions and very unspecific superordinate and subordinate concept relations such as *is a* or *has kinds.* In the GLT, further, terms in a term entry can be traced by the user via established links. Navigating through ISOcat is harder since it provides a wide range of different "views" and "groups" which provide linguistic terminology in general but also specify linguistic terms in a specific language data model, e.g. the "STTS group" or "CLARIN group". In this regard such linguistic term bases have no underlying data model that represents linguistic terminology in an interrelating holistic structure. What is more, the arbitrary structure of the data models, which represent the linguistic term entries in alphabetical order (as in GLT) or according to linguistic views or linguistic data groups (as in ISOcat) is neither sufficient nor suitable for gaining comprehensive knowledge about a linguistic term in the domain of linguistics. A recent project, the CLARIN Concept Registry (Schuurman et al. 2016), has taken over the work of ISOcat and promises to define terms in a stricter manner, although still providing very limited structural and relational information.

(ii) Linguistic concepts represented as Linked Data ontology: In order to enable the description of linguistic data, formalized ontological models emerged within the realm of the Semantic Web. The most significant model for the scientific description of human language is the General Ontology for Linguistic Description (GOLD)[6] (Farrar and Langendoen 2003; Farrar 2010). It provides a taxonomy of nearly 600 linguistic concepts, which have been constructed from

[6] http://linguistics-ontology.org/gold-2010.owl.

the GLT, and formalizes 83 relations (i.e. 76 object properties and 7 data properties). GOLD has been designed to support Community-of-Practice Extensions (COPEs), meaning that it is a recommended upper model for ontologies of linguistic terminology that can define their concepts as sub-concepts of GOLD concepts (Farrar and Lewis 2007). This mechanism has been adopted by several ontology providers, e.g., (Wilcock 2007; Good et al. 2005; Goecke et al. 2005). In that usage and because the terms provided by the GLT have been transformed into concepts in GOLD, linguistic terms and concepts are not distinguished any more. The concepts are only defined within the domain of linguistic description but not in the more general domain of linguistics. In addition, the variety of object properties assigned to the concepts are very specific and interrelate mostly only two concepts, which leaves the majority of the concepts unrelated. The established relations are either too specific or too general to derive the meaning of a concept within the domain of linguistics, e.g. a "grapheme" concept is defined within the taxonomy as a "FormUnit" concept, which is a "LinguisticUnit" concept, which is an "Abstract" concept. It has no further relations to other concepts, e.g. to "Character", which only implicitly states in its `rdfs:comment` that it is "similar to grapheme". Also, it is unclear why the "Character" concept ist not also modelled as a subconcept of "FormUnit". These are solvable issues, however, the development of GOLD and the community process stopped in 2010. Despite the wealth of linguistic concepts in GOLD it would be a very inconcise model for linguistic terminology, due to the lack of terms relating to the concepts and due to the complexity of relations which is aimed at a subfield of descriptive linguistics but not at representing linguistic concepts in a more encompassing scope of the domain of linguistics.

These two primary kinds of sources for a model of linguistic terminology can be summarized as being either term-focussed or concept-focussed. A coherent model of linguistic terminology, however, presupposes explicitly establishing both linguistic concepts and terms and placing them into the whole domain of linguistics. To conclude, to our knowledge there is - with the exception of the LiDo database - no data model available that appropriately describes linguistic terminology as the domain of linguistic terms that encode linguistic concepts which are interrelated in a meaningful way.

3 The LiDo Glossary of Linguistic Terms as OnLiT Pioneer

The LiDo database[7] as it is available in its current form as a browsable glossary of linguistic terms has a thirty year old history. Christian Lehmann started to collect and systematize his terminological knowledge as a general comparative linguist by introducing a documentation system for linguistics in 1976 (Lehmann 1976). Twenty years later its technical implementation in 2006 resulted in the

[7] It has to be mentioned that LiDo encompasses also bibliographical data that is referenced to the terms. This bibliographic part of the dataset is, however, not focus of this paper and, hence, not further discussed.

LiDo Web frontend which is based on a relational database[8] that has been continuously updated and extended by Christian Lehmann ever since. To date, the LiDo term and concept data encompasses more than 4500 unique linguistic concepts and over 15000 terms, most of them in English, German, Spanish and Portuguese. Moreover, each concept is interrelated to at least one other concept which yields a coherent terminological data graph. Editing and curating this considerable data size is enabled by a manageable set of relations which fulfill the self-imposed requirement to explicitly express a direct relation between two linguistic concepts (Lehmann 1996). This is achieved by the two formal relations of coordination and subordination which generate an overall taxonomic and meronomic structure and 14 subrelations of those that permit a semantically specified interrelation of concepts. As a consequence, the data structure underlying the LiDo term and concept data inheres the following criteria which we see as essential for describing terminological data:

- explicit representation of concepts and terms as separate resources,
- meaningful interrelation of concept and term data,
- an easy to use and editable data structure.

Therefore, the underlying LiDo data structure does not only permit an appropriate representation of the domain of linguistic terminology but also implicitly contains an ontological modelling of the domain. These two aspects finally motivate the reuse of the LiDo model as a data basis for creating OnLiT.

4 The Ontology for Linguistic Terminology

4.1 Components of the OnLiT Model

The OnLiT vocabulary is freely available under the URL http://lido.linguistic-lod.org/onlit.rdf[9] and open for any kind of reuse under the CC BY 4.0 license[10]. As a Linked Data model which is based on the Web Ontology Language (OWL[11]), OnLiT consists of a hierarchy of conceptual classes which represent commonality among a variety of entities, i.e. the so-called instances, individuals or resources of a dataset. The semantics of entities within the ontology is formally defined by class usage restrictions that can hold between classes and are encoded within relations. Relations are formally expressed as object properties or as data properties.

An overview of the class modelling in OnLiT is given in Fig. 1 and a detailed view of the object property structure is provided in Fig. 2. For modelling the domain of linguistic terminology, the OnLiT vocabulary contains only

[8] This database is used to render the LiDo Website but not publicly available. The database was used in order to conduct the presented research.

[9] In case of unavailability: https://github.com/AKSW/lido2rdf/blob/master/OnLiT.owl.

[10] https://creativecommons.org/licenses/by/4.0.

[11] https://www.w3.org/OWL.

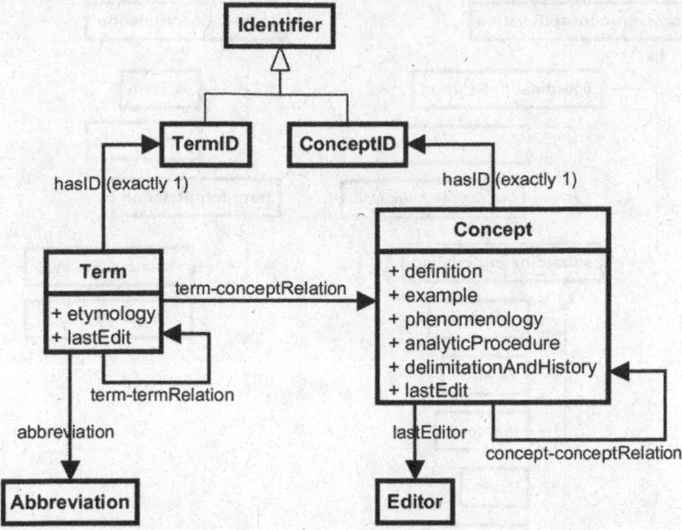

Fig. 1. Class diagram of the OnLiT model.

7 classes: `Concept`, `Term`, `Identifier` (with `ConceptID` and `TermID` as subclasses), `Abbreviation` and `Editor`. Only the first two are essential and should in any case contain instances (a more detailed presentation of their usage is given in Sect. 4.3). An `Concept` instance describes a language-independent mental entity which is encoded in different language-specific terms. As such concepts are cognitively defined as substantial meanings which are realized by a linguistic sign, which is then the term associated with the concept. In order to be able to identify and refer to such a mental (as opposed to the formal understanding of concepts as classes in OWL!) conceptual instance, it needs to be somehow denominated with a humanly readable name. This can be done by an arbitrary string identifier or by using the term expression that standardly encodes the concept in some language as, i.e., there could be a 'noun' `Concept` instance and a *noun* `Term` instance. The former, however, serves only as a conventionalized naming method[12] for a cognitive and language-independent meaning while the latter is a linguistic expression of the English language. This distinction is similar to the division of sense IDs which are associated to lexical entries in datasets such as WordNet[13]. The `Abbreviation` class is established, because linguistic terms can have various conventional abbreviations assigned. This is common practice in language description and might be, therefore, useful for some dataset creators. Meta-information provided by the `Identifier` and `Editor` classes are added for convenience, because they tend to be included in other dataset formats, such as tables and relational databases. These can be directly used in case already

[12] In the LiDo database Latin expressions are used to a large extent to denominate the concept entries.

[13] http://wordnet-rdf.princeton.edu.

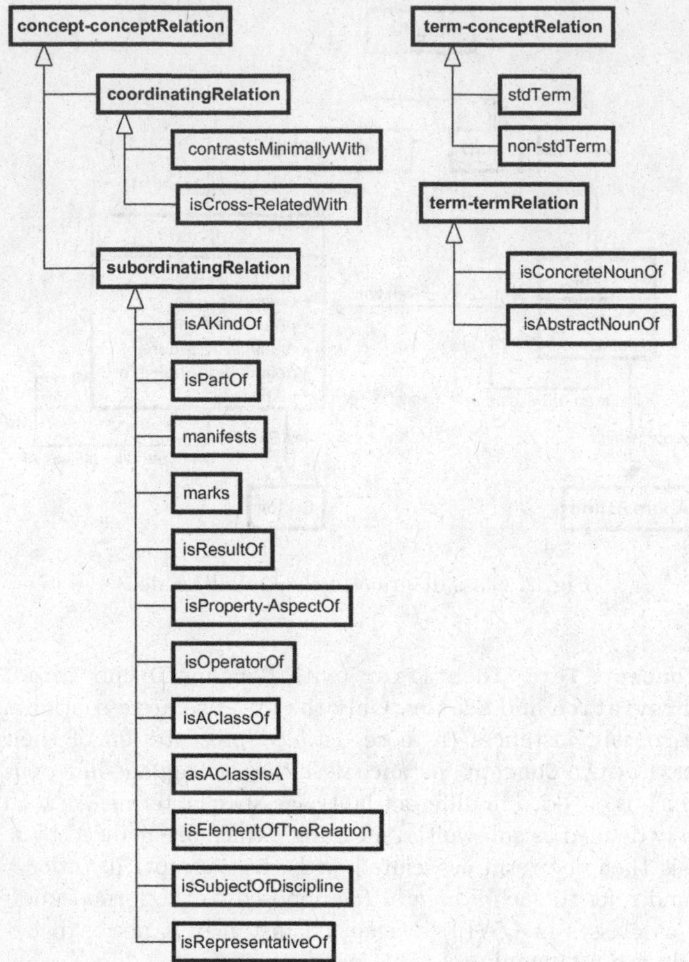

Fig. 2. Inheritance diagram of OnLiT object properties and subproperties.

existing datasets of linguistic terms in such formats shall be transferred into RDF with the OnLiT model. However, more fine-grained Linked Data vocabularies are available for representing the metadata of a dataset, e.g. DCMI terms[14] or PROV-O[15], which are easily integrable due to the interoperability of Linked Data vocabularies.

With regard to the relations, there are three main object properties established in OnLiT that interrelate instances of (1) terms with terms, (2) terms with concepts and (3) concepts with concepts. The `term-termRelation` property can be used to specify the relation between noun `Term` instances, on the one hand,

[14] http://dublincore.org/documents/dcmi-terms.
[15] https://www.w3.org/TR/prov-o.

and adjective and verb Term instances, on the other, in a dataset. That way adjective and verb terms can be included in a dataset if they are desired to be described as linguistic terms (cf. Sect. 4.3 below) and related to their corresponding noun Term resources[16] which are then interrelated to the respective Concept instance they encode. A term-conceptRelation is established in order to enable the assignment of the Term instance to its associated Concept instance. The most structuring are the concept-conceptRelation object properties. Because these are divided in the subproperties of coordinatingRelation and subordinatingRelation they add to the taxonomic and meronomic structure of the Concept data and therewith also of the Term data within an OnLiT dataset. The twelve subordinatingRelation subproperties are intended to establish a semantically more specific interrelation between concepts (a more detailed presentation of their usage is given in Sect. 4.4).

Overall the OnLiT model is of manageable size but yet provides sufficient explicitly modelled semantic interrelations to create a consistent dataset of linguistic terminology.

4.2 Purpose, Domain and Requirements of OnLiT

There are two main purposes pursued by the OnLiT model. First, it serves as the conceptual foundation for an RDF dataset of the LiDo Glossary of Linguistic Terms including the whole relational database of its Term and Concept data. Second, it provides users and creators of language data in general as well as the community of Linguistic Linked Open Data in particular with a means to easily set up and/or semantically interconnect various linguistic terminological datasets. Moreover, its basic properties are transferable to the definition of terminological datasets for other scientific disciplines.

The domain of linguistic terminology as represented by OnLiT is not restricted to a certain definition of *term*. Thus, any expression that needs to be described with OnLiT for theoretical or practical reasons can constitute a Term or Concept resource in an OnLiT dataset. As a consequence, even proper nouns denoting persons, e.g. *Noam Chomsky* or linguistically significant words of a language, e.g. the grammatical verb *be* can be entries in an OnLiT term base. In that respect Term entries in an OnLiT dataset are not limited to a narrow definition of *scientific term* as being a common noun (Kamlah and Lorenzen 1967). Rather, this definition is broadened to allow individuals' names, plain lexemes or even adjectives and verbs to be included as terminological entries. Given that OnLiT is based on the LiDo Glossary of Linguistic Terms, it meets the same criteria as outlined in Sect. 3. In addition to that and in contrast to the Lido data model, OnLiT is based on Semantic Web modelling principles. Due to that, OnLiT based datasets fulfill the requirements of semantic and structural interoperability which enable an easy reuse of data and further enrichment via interlinking to external data sources.

[16] This allows, for instance, to integrate the Term entries *homonymous* and *govern* and relate them to *homonymy* and *government*.

We assume that datasets evolving from the OnLiT model will add to the creation of a comprehensive terminological knowledge graph of the field of linguistics ranging from general and traditional linguistic terminology to the representation of newly evolving or very specifically used terms and concepts.

4.3 Linguistic Concepts and Terms

The `Term` and `Concept` classes constitute the essential classes of an OnLiT dataset since these contain the concept and term resources respectively. Two relations can be specified between them, which express that a `Term` resource is a standard or a non-standard term for a given concept. Their interrelations are illustrated in Fig. 3, which exemplifies the triples for the `Term` instance *noun* and the `Concept` instance 'nomen substantivum'. `Concept` resources are unique, since they are mental objects which are designated by a linguistic expression, i.e. the `Term` resource. As a consequence, there can be multiple `Term` resources related to a single `Concept` resource. Thus, there is also a *Substantiv* resource stated to be the standard German term and also a *Nennwort* resource to be a non-standard term for the `Concept` resource 'nomen substantivum'. This can be achieved by forming triples between `Term` and `Concept` resources via the two object properties `stdTerm` and `non-stdTerm`. This is the way of dealing with synonymous terms. For a homonymous term, the relation to one `Concept` resource is selected as `stdTerm`, and all the others are `non-stdTerm`. Each `Term` resource can use the property `stdTerm` for only one `Concept` resource, while it can be `non-stdTerm` for more `Concept` resources. For instance, the German term *Nomen* is standard for the concept 'nomen' and non-standard for the concept 'nomen substantivum'. Further, every `Term` resource should be explicitly assigned to a language. For that purpose the language identifiers of the lexvo vocabulary[17] are reused, because they provide a precise language assignment as well as machine-readability.

The `Concept` resources can be further specified for additional information by describing the definition, delimitation and history, analytic procedure, phenomenology and example(s) via the respective datatype properties (cf. Fig. 3). This information is provided by plain text and constitutes information a linguist might have documented about a certain linguistic concept and which should be included in the database. In fact, definition and examples are frequently found in terminological datasets (e.g. in GLT or ISOcat) and can be simply transferred to an OnLiT dataset by using these datatype properties. Even though information stated in such plain text literals is not directly machine-readable and, therefore, also not semantically explicit enough for automatic data processing, it is from a human data consumer perspective very insightful. Eventually, the definitions constitute indeed a useful information source that reveals information about a concept, that can be formally modelled. The definition of the 'nomen substantivum' `Concept` resource states that it is "a [...] part of speech", which can be formalized via a subordinating relation between the given `Concept` resource and another 'part of speech' `Concept` resource (this will be demonstrated in Sect. 4.4).

[17] http://www.lexvo.org.

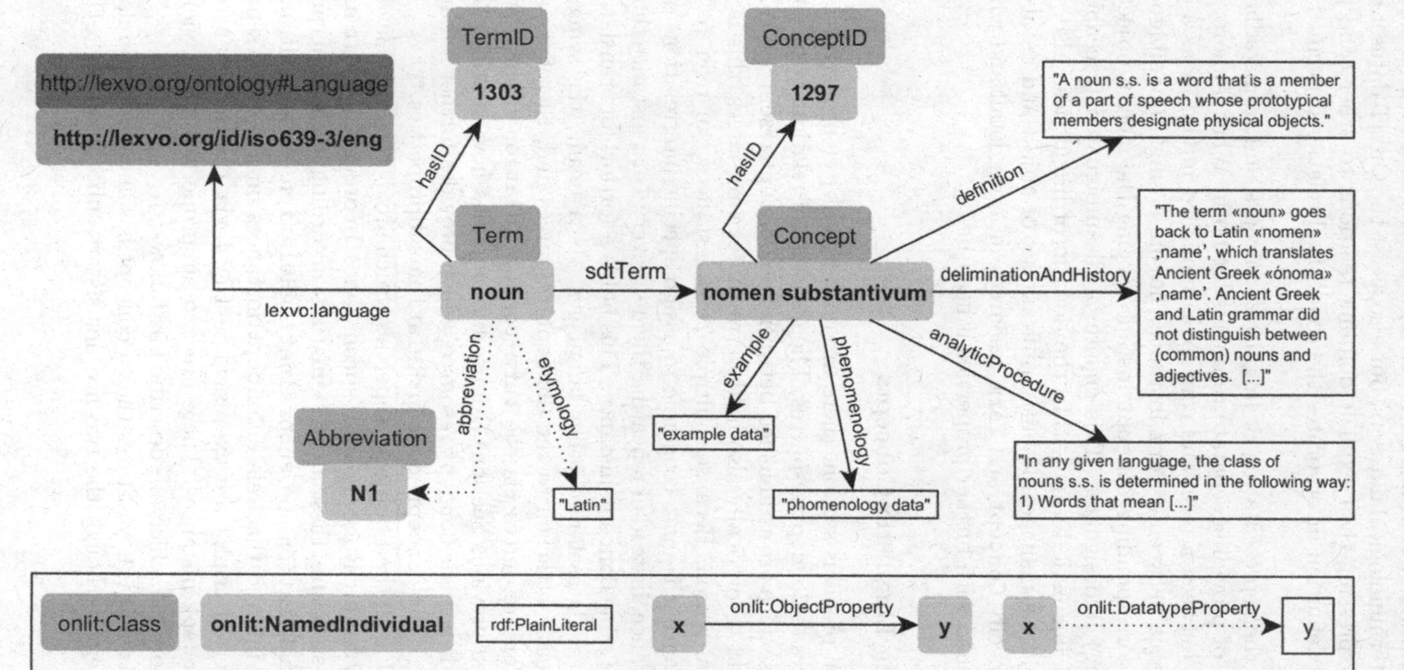

Fig. 3. Example modelling of the English `Term` instance *noun* and the `Concept` instance 'nomen substantivum' with OnLiT. (The exemplary data for both resources used here and in other parts of this paper can be consulted under the English "noun" entry in the LiDo database Web frontend: http://linguistik.uni-regensburg.de:8080/lido/Lido.)

Hence, textual information about linguistic concepts are not only most prevalent in already existing terminological datasets, but also assist the OnLiT dataset creators in formally expressing their explicit defining relations to other concepts. Conversely, a good definition incorporates the conceptual relations specified for the concept.

To summarize, the representation of linguistic concepts and terms adheres to the requirement of providing separate resources for both. What is more, the relation that holds between a term and concept is modelled in OnLiT as a one to one correspondence between a `Term` instance (having a single unambiguous meaning) and the corresponding `Concept` instance (being the mental object of that single meaning) it designates. This ensures a disambiguated traceability and clarification of linguistic terms within the domain of linguistics. Also, the OnLiT model provides a manageable but significant set of object and datatype properties which specify `Concept` and `Term` resources in more detail and which can be easily extended with further properties if need be.

4.4 Interrelating Linguistic Concepts

As presented in the previous section, there are only two object properties that relate `Term` resources to `Concept` resources. The majority of relations is specified in object properties which are established between two `Concept` resources. While these relations could theoretically also hold between `Term` resources, this is not done for a practical reason. Because multiple `Term` instances can refer to the same `Concept` instance it is more economic to assign specific interrelations once to the `Concept` instance, instead of repeating them on every `Term` instance that is associated with the same `Concept` instance. This holds a fortiori for translations of the terminological dataset into other languages. As a result, the semantic specification is directly attached to the `Concept` resources and, therefore, also indirectly to the `Term` resources via the `term-conceptRelation` subproperties (as described in the previous Section). Figure 4 exemplifies how multiple `Term` resources can encode a single `Concept` resource, which provides further semantic specification through the `concept-conceptRelation` subproperties.

As is shown in Fig. 2, the 14 object properties which are at the lowest level of the object property hierarchy are the most specific ones. In order to create a more general taxonomic structure, these are systematized according to the superproperties `coordinatingRelation` and `subordinatingRelation`. As a result, more statements can be inferred that relate `Concept` instances on a broader semantic level. Such inferred triples are expressed in Fig. 4 via the dashed arrows connecting the `Concept` instances. There are two subproperties which yield a coordinating relation and which are described as follows:

`x isCross-RelatedWith y`: States that a concept is somehow cross-related with another concept, although the two are not sisters subordinate to a third concept.

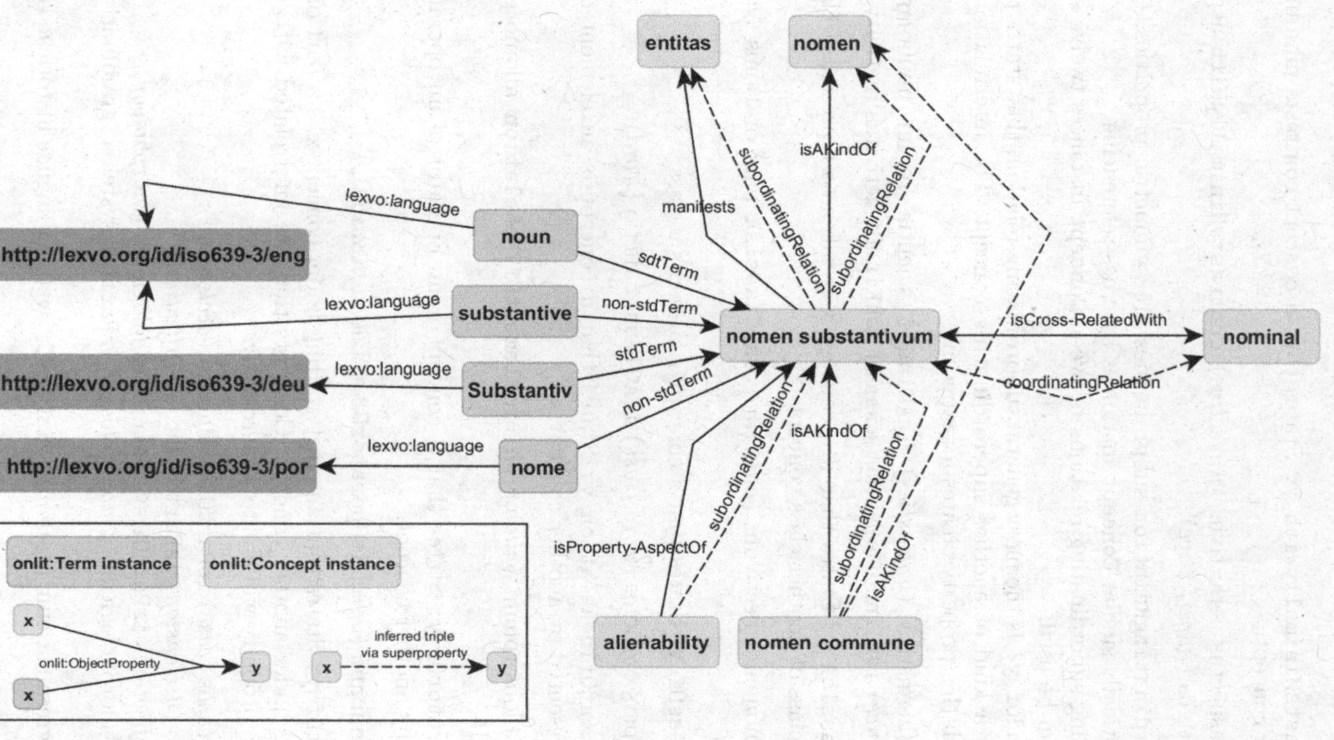

Fig. 4. Example modelling of the `Concept` instance 'nomen substantivum' with its interrelations to other concepts.

Example 1. nomen adjectivum (*adjective*)[18] `isCross-RelatedWith` attributum (*attribute*).

`x contrastsMinimallyWith y`: States that a concept contrasts minimally with another concept.

Example 2. aspectus perfectivus (*perfective*) `contrastsMinimallyWith` aspectus imperfectivus (*imperfective*).

The `coordinatingRelation` subproperties are symmetric properties, that group semantically similar `Concept` instances by cross-referencing.

For creating subordinating relations between `Concept` instances twelve subproperties can be used:

`x isAKindOf y`: Is the most general subordinating relation, that states that a concept is a kind of another superordinating concept. The interrelation of concepts with this property creates a taxonomy.

Example 3. linguistica (*linguistics*) `isAKindOf` scientia rerum humanarum (*human science*) `isAKindOf` scientia (science) `isAKindOf` activitas (activity).

`x asAClassIsA y`: States that if a concept x is taken to represent a class, this is a subclass of another class concept.

Example 4. nomen adjectivum (*adjective*) `asAClassIsA` pars orationis (*word class*).

`x isAClassOf y`: States that a concept represents a class.

Example 5. pars orationis (*word class*) `isAClassOf` dictio (*word*).

`x isElementOfTheRelation y`: States that a concept is an element of a relation represented by another concept.

Example 6. allomorphum (*allomorph*) `isElementOfTheRelation` allomorphia (*allomorphy*).

`x isOperatorOf y`: States that a concept is an operator of an operation represented by another concept.

Example 7. affixum (*affix*) `isOperatorOf` affixio (*affixation*).

`x isPartOf y`: States that an entity falling under concept x is a part of an entity falling under another concept. Concepts that are interrelated with this "part-whole" property will create a meronymy.

Example 8. casus (*case*) `isPartOf` declinatio (*declension*).
declinatio (*declension*) `isPartOf` flexio (*inflection*).
flexio (*inflection*) `isPartOf` systema morphologicum (*morphology*).
systema morphologicum (*morphology*) `isPartOf` systema grammaticum (*grammar*).
systema grammaticum (*grammar*) `isPartOf` systema linguae historicae (*language system*).

[18] For better comprehensibility the standard English `Term` instances corresponding to the given `Concept` instances are given in brackets.

`x isProperty-AspectOf y`: States that a concept represents a characteristic or possible aspect or property of its superordinate concept.

Example 9. arbitrarietas signi (*arbitrariness*) `isProperty-AspectOf` signum linguae (*linguistic sign*).

`x isRepresentativeOf y`: States that a person is a representative of a scientific discipline, movement or model.

Example 10. de Saussure (*de Saussure*) `isRepresentativeOf` schola Genavensis (*Geneva School*).

`x isResultOf y`: States that an entity falling under a concept is the result of an entity falling under another concept.

Example 11. vocabulum externum (*loan word*) `isResultOf` mutuatio (*borrowing*).

`x isSubjectOfDiscipline y`: States that a concept that represents some object (area) is the subject of a concept denoting the scientific discipline or a theory or model thereof.

Example 12. systema vocabulorum (*lexicon*) `isSubjectOfDiscipline` lexicologia (*lexicology*).

`x manifests y`: States that a concept denotes a grammatical or derivative category which manifests a concept that denotes a semantic, cognitive, communicative or functionally determined concept.

Example 13. tempus grammaticum (*tense*) `manifests` tempus (*time*).

`x marks y`: States that a concept represents a grammatical category which marks a grammatical relation or function represented by another concept.

Example 14. casus accusativus (*accusative*) `marks` objectum directum (*direct object*).

Figure 4 shows how the modelling of the `subordinatingRelation` property results in a taxonomic systematization of `Concept` instances. This allows for automatic reasoning over a dataset to yield insights such as 'nomen' is superordinate to 'nomen substantivum' which is superordinate to 'nomen commune' and, thus, 'nomen' is also superordinate to 'nomen commune'. This holds also for some of the subproperties, e.g. `isAKindOf` which is a transitive property ('nomen commune' `isAKindOf` 'nomen substantivum' and of 'nomen'). What is more, the 14 established object properties are all semantically more specific than a generic "see also" relation but general enough to be broadly applied to interrelate various (and ideally all) concepts. Especially relations such as `isOperatorOf` or `marks` play a central role in the domain of linguistic terminology. In that respect, a dataset modelled with OnLiT sets every linguistic term or concept in a meaningful interrelation to relevant other terms by placing it in a navigable and coherent context within the linguistic domain a dataset describes. Finally, relations such as `isAKindOf` and `isPartOf` are general across ontologies of any science and thus serve to integrate linguistic ontologies into an all-encompassing ontology.

5 Conclusion and Future Work

The OnLiT data model for representing terminological data of linguistic domains has been created as the ontological schema basis to transfer the currently relational database of the LiDo Glossary of Linguistic Terms into an RDF dataset in the future. Moreover, the OnLiT model constitutes a valuable contribution for users and creators of linguistic data. Due to the outlined benefits of the underlying Linked Data format, evolving terminological data will be interoparable, semantically and formally explicit as well as easy to reuse and extend. Moreover, OnLiT models linguistic terminology in a meaningful and structured way that goes beyond a single term definition. I.e. the additional subordinating and coordinating relations allow to derive coherent and specific insights and knowledge about the conceptualization of linguistic terms in a given language dataset. Therefore, it can benefit producers of language data in creating their own terminological dataset or in interrelating their data to an existing OnLiT dataset (e.g. the prospective LiDo RDF dataset). Furthermore, future work includes an interconnection of the OnLiT model with OntoLex[19], which will offer more possibilities of representing and integrating OnLiT `Term` and `Concept` resources within the domain of lexical language data.

Acknowledgements. This paper's research activities were partly supported and funded by grants from the EU's H2020 Programme ALIGNED (GA 644055) and the Federal Ministry for Economic Affairs and Energy of Germany (BMWi) for the Smart-DataWeb Project (GA-01MD15010B).

References

Bußmann, H., Trauth, G., Kazzazi, K.: Lexikon der Sprachwissenschaft. Taylor & Francis, London (1996)

Farrar, S.: General Ontology for Linguistic Description (GOLD). The LINGUIST List, Department of Linguistics, Indiana University (2010)

Farrar, S., Langendoen, D.T.: A linguistic ontology for the semantic web. GLOT Int. **7**, 97–100 (2003)

Farrar, S., Lewis, W.D.: The gold community of practice: an infrastructure for linguistic data on the web. Lang. Resour. Eval. **41**, 45–60 (2007)

Goecke, D., Lüngen, H., Sasaki, F., Witt, A., Farrar, S.: GOLD and discourse: domain- and community-specific extensions. In: Proceedings of the 2005 E-MELD-Workshop (2005)

Good, J., Cysouw, M., Albu, M., Bibiko, H.J.: Can GOLD "cope" with WALS? Retrofitting an ontology onto the world atlas of language structures. Max Planck Institute for Evolutionary Anthropology (2005)

Kamlah, W., Lorenzen, P.: Logische Propädeutik oder Vorschule des vernünftigen Redens. Bibliographisches Institut (B.I.-Hochschultaschenbücher 227/227a), Mannheim (1967)

[19] http://www.w3.org/ns/lemon/ontolex#.

Kemps-Snijders, M., Windhouwer, M., Wittenburg, P., Wright, S.E.: Isocat: remodelling metadata for language resources. Int. J. Metadata Semant. Ontol. **4**, 261–276 (2009)

Lehmann, C.: Um sistema de documentação para a lingüística. Instituto de Letras e Artes, Pontifícia Universidade Católica do RGS (1976)

Lehmann, C.: Linguistische Terminologie als relationales Netz. In: Knobloch, C., Schaeder, B. (eds.) Nomination-fachsprachlich und gemeinsprachlich, pp. 215–267. Springer, Wiesbaden (1996)

Loos, E.E., Anderson, S., Day, D.H., Jordan, P.C., Wingate, J.D.: Glossary of Linguistic Terms, vol. 29. SIL International, Dallas (2004)

Schuurman, I., Windhouwer, M., Ohren, O., Zeman, D.: CLARIN concept registry: the new semantic registry. In: Selected Papers from the CLARIN Annual Conference 2015, pp. 62–79. Linköping University Electronic Press (2016)

Wilcock, G.: An OWL ontology for HPSG. In: Proceedings of the 45th Annual Meeting of the ACL on Interactive Poster and Demonstration Sessions, pp. 169–172. Association for Computational Linguistics (2007)

Representing and Aligning Similar Relations: Parts and Wholes in isiZulu vs. English

C. Maria Keet(✉)

Department of Computer Science, University of Cape Town,
Cape Town, South Africa
mkeet@cs.uct.ac.za

Abstract. Ontology-enabled medical information systems are used in Sub-Saharan Africa, which require localisation of Semantic Web technologies, such as ontology verbalisation, yet keeping a link with the English language-based systems. In realising this, we zoom in on the part-whole relations that are ubiquitous in medical ontologies, and the isiZulu language. The analysis of part-whole relations in isiZulu revealed both 'underspecification'—therewith also challenging the transitivity claim—and three refinements cf. the list of common part-whole relations. This was first implemented for the monolingual scenario so that it generates structured natural language from an ontology in isiZulu. Two new natural language-independent correspondence patterns are proposed to solve non-1:1 object property alignments, which are subsequently used to align the part-whole taxonomies informed by the two languages.

1 Introduction

With the more widespread uptake of ontologies, localisation and internationalisation of existing ontologies, as well as *de novo* ontology development in a language other than English is becoming more commonplace. This brings afore a new set of problems in general regardless the natural language, as well as language-specific issues. In this paper, we zoom in on object properties, and part-whole relations in particular, and as other language isiZulu. isiZulu is a language in the Bantu language family that has about 12 million first language speakers and about 25 million people in South Africa can speak it. Tools with an isiZulu interface are being developed, such as the medical translation app mobilezulu[1] to assist doctors with the language barrier during consultations, and the Electronic Health Record system OpenMRS[2] is popular in Sub-Saharan Africa, which imports the medical ontology SNOMED CT [25]. Localisations of OpenMRS are under way[3], which, in turn, will assist with the automatic generation of patient summaries, so that they will adhere better to the treatment instructions [30]. Such 'intelligent' information systems require generation of natural language, with as minimum requirement to verbalise the ontology.

[1] mobilezulu.org.za.
[2] https://wiki.openmrs.org/display/projects/Home.
[3] https://www.transifex.com/openmrs/OpenMRS/.

J. Gracia et al. (Eds.): LDK 2017, LNAI 10318, pp. 58–73, 2017.
DOI: 10.1007/978-3-319-59888-8_5

To be able to realise this, the structured knowledge has to be localised and verbalised. It is well-known that medical and healthcare terminologies, such as SNOMED CT and the Foundational Model of Anatomy [21] are replete with part-whole relations, such as 'each heart is part of one human', 'operating team has as member at least one doctor', and 'HIV test is involved in a pre-natal checkup'. While the nouns (OWL classes) are fairly straightforward to translate and standardise, the relations (OWL object properties) are a different matter. It is known how to represent part-whole relations, notably the relatively wide uptake of the taxonomy of part-whole relations of [13], which is also popular in NLP (e.g., [26]). Recent efforts in finding verbalisation patterns for those part-whole relations to generate natural language sentences in isiZulu [14] focussed on the patterns, but essentially revealed that there are no 1:1 mappings between the identified part-whole relations in (the conceptualisation by people who speak as first/home language) isiZulu and English. This is further confounded by the issue that the 'has part' reading direction does not have a single word for it. The former issue brings afore the question *how to deal with non-1:1 mappings among object properties*, which, to the best of our knowledge, current multilingual models and tools do not have a solution for [3,6,8,12,17], though separation of ontology and natural language and lexicalisation [4] is obviously a good principle to start from.

The aim of this paper is to solve these two natural language-motivated problems, being non-1:1 alignments for object properties and absence of single reusable labels. We investigate this in detail for the demarcated, and well-researched, part-whole relations, and take as a use case the language isiZulu. First, a brief ontological analysis is carried out on the part-whole relations that were proposed for isiZulu natural language generation (NLG) in [14]. This revealed that there are both generalisations up to requiring parthood to be non-transitive, but also three refinements compared to the typical list of part-whole relations. Second, the engineering issues for the monolingual case are addressed and implemented for the ontology verbalisation algorithms of [14] with Owlready [15] as proof-of-concept. Third, this is extended to the multilingual case by proposing a refinement to the 'VAP' correspondence ontology design pattern, *HetOP*, and introducing a new pattern, *UnionOP*, so as to systematically handle non-1:1 object property alignments. This is then applied to aligning the taxonomy of part-whole relations to the part-whole relations informed by isiZulu.

In the remainder of the paper we describe related works in Sect. 2 and introduce the main contribution in Sect. 3 for the monolingual scenario and in Sect. 4 for the multilingual case. We discuss in Sect. 5 and conclude in Sect. 6.

2 Related Works

The contributions presented in the following sections draw in particular from related works on part-whole relations and from so-called "correspondence patterns" ontology design patterns, and a few relevant aspects of linguistic annotation models.

2.1 Part-Whole Relations

Part-whole relations have been investigated especially in the areas of Ontology (analytic philosophy), conceptual modelling, linguistics and NLP, notably [10,13,20,26,29,31]. Multiple types of part-whole relations have been proposed, which resulted in a fairly stable taxonomy of part-whole relations [13]. It distinguishes between 'real' parthood relations (mereology) and part-whole relations in natural language utterances only (meronymy). The primitive *part_of* relation in mereology is antisymmetric, reflexive, and transitive [27], whereas meronymic relations are not necessarily transitive and where 'part' is used loosely, such as in "a musician is part of [i.e., *member_of*] an orchestra". Similar to ideas discussed in [29], the part-whole relations taxonomy in [13] distinguishes relations also by the categories of the relata for their meaning and excludes certain undesirable inferences; e.g., involved-in is a parthood specifically among processes. This taxonomy (see Fig. 1) can be used with various different surface readings/labels, like using made of instead of constituted of or preferring has ingredient over stuff part. The set of relations themselves are not really contested. These relations have been proposed in research done by people from multiple countries and cultures who speak multiple natural languages, so one could assume a genericity or even universality of it.

Specific linguistically motivated analyses for languages other than English on their use of part-whole relations to confirm this are sparse. Vieu and Aurnague [29] focus on French, with an emphasis on parthood where the part has some particular function with respect to the whole, with "entities-as-a-lexical-type" for the Component Integral Whole parthood relation (s-part-of in Fig. 1). Thus, it remains within the same common set of recognised part-whole relations. To the best of our knowledge, no ontology research has been conducted on part-whole relations that is informed by a natural language in a family of languages other than Germanic or Italic. The works on mereology/meronymy in, notably, Arabic, Chinese, and Turkish focus on relation extraction, stating that they limit the extraction to the aforementioned typical set of part-whole relations or a subset thereof [1,5,32]. Upon further inspection, there are two noteworthily points. Cao et al. [5] did 'refine' constitution with an "Element-Object ... for convenient

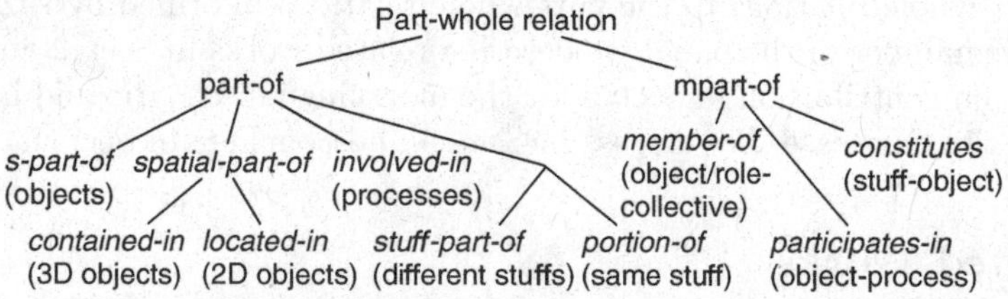

Fig. 1. Taxonomy of part-whole relations, based on [13], and informal description of their domain and range. The part-of branch is mereological parthood with transitivity; the mpart-of branch has relations that are non-transitive or intransitive.

verification"; e.g., calcium as part of milk. It Is unclear whether the authors assert this is a part-whole relation semantically or linguistically distinguishable from the others. Yıldız et al. [32] excluded the spatial part-whole relations, but 'constituted of' is distinguished from 'made of', with the former having a more built-type of flavour to it (examples of wholes given: system, program) and the latter more generic (examples of their wholes: questionnaire and public opinion). Finally, Keet and Khumalo [14] also started from the typical set of part-whole relations, but from a knowledge engineering and linguistic starting point and aimed at NLG, which resulted in some differences for isiZulu that we shall analyse in Sects. 3 and 4.

2.2 Correspondence Patterns And/Or Language Models

There are two principal ways to deal with language-motivated mismatches of object properties (relations): either they are conceptually different, are represented as such in the ontology, and then a possibly heterogeneous alignment has to be asserted, or the underlying conceptualisation is the same (or similar enough), which then is represented in the ontology with one object property, and the language differences are dealt with in a language model by means of a separate language annotation file. The former requires *correspondence patterns* to assert, e.g., subsumption between elements in the different ontologies, and more complex mappings. Pattern alignment, rather than 1:1 mappings between ontology vocabulary elements, has been proposed in [22] with ontology design patterns (ODPs) that includes property equivalence and subsumption axioms, and which later also included data property to object property transformation [23]. The online ODP catalogue[4] contains 13 alignment patterns, but is sparse for complex object property mappings. It lists three patterns that constitute one relevant alignment case, called the "Vocabulary Alignment Pattern: Sub property of an external Property", which we shall extend and formalise in Sect. 4.1.

Several language models have been proposed in recent years. To assess them on their potential applicability for isiZulu, we first need to illustrate some pertinent aspects of rendering an axiom with a part-whole relation in isiZulu. The main point here is not the whole process of verbalising an axiom, but rather the constituents that will have to be dealt with in a language model for annotations. Let us take 'has part' in isiZulu and the common axiom type $C \sqsubseteq \exists R.D$, as presented in [14]; the verbalisation *pattern* is:

$$\text{QCall}_{nc_x,pl}\,\text{W}_{nc_x,pl}\,\text{SC}_{nc_x,pl}\text{-CONJ-P}_{nc_y}\,\text{RC}_{nc_y}\text{-QC}_{nc_y}\text{-}dwa$$

where W: entity playing whole; P: entity that plays the part; CONJ: Conjunction (for enumerative-and; *na-*); SC: Subject Concord for conjugation; PC: Possessive Concord; RC: Relative Concord; QCall: quantitative concord for universal quantification; and QC: quantitative concord for existential quantification. The equivalent of 'All humans have as part some heart' is *bonke abantu <u>bane</u>nhliziyo*

[4] http://www.ontologydesignpatterns.org.

eyodwa, with 'has part' underlined: the SC *ba-* from noun class 2 (nc2)'s *abantu* (the W) and the phonologically conditioned CONJ *na* + *inhliziyo* = *nenhliziyo*. Therefore it generates *bane-* for 'has part' in this sentence. With W = orchestra' (nc5, SC = *a-*) and P = 'musician' (*isazi somnyuziki*), the 'has part' is *anesazi somnyuziki* and with W = 'computer' (nc5) and P = 'CPU' (*umqondo womshini*), the 'has part' results in *anomqondo womshini*. There are six different SCs for the plural noun classes and one CONJ that has three phonologically conditioned variants, hence, there are 6 * 3 = 18 strings all having the same meaning of 'has part'. Ontologically, this ought not to be put in an ontology as 18 different object properties with equivalences, for it is one conceptualisation with context-dependent surface realisations [12], not 18 different types of relation. If only one label is used, then there needs to be some annotation and rules to govern generating, or selecting, the right form. The other main complication is best illustrated with 'contained in' that uses phonologically conditioned locative affixes to verbalise this notion. For instance, *imvilophu* 'envelope' becomes *emvilophini*, so both reading directions ('contains' and 'contained in') do not have a single name or label that is reusable for all sentences. (The list of the relevant sections of the verbalisation patterns is included in the third column of Table 1.)

Language models proposed for the Semantic Web include *lemon* [18] and its smaller ontolex-lemon W3C submission, OLiA [6], and the model in [12]. LIME [8] complements *lemon* for metadata, and is therefore not further considered. OLiA's permanent URL (purl) is offline despite trying over several days. Therefore, we consider in some detail only *lemon* and the positionalist model in [12]. *Lemon* [18] is orthogonal to the ontology, where an IRI of the class, property, or individual has a lexical entry from the lexicon and it must have a canonical form. One can define syntactic behaviour such as a property's subject and object as `Argument` and annotate, e.g., the case (e.g:, genitive) in a `Frame`. This still requires a string for a lexical entry, not a stub for a system-generated identifier. For this to possibly work for multiple context-dependent labels for a relation, the `LexicalEntry` would need to be modified from `canonicalForm` and optional `altForms` into relating an identifier as lexical form with a concept description (in natural language at least), and optionally a `Form`.

The model in [12] also offers additional annotation options, such as for, among others, case, tense, and prepositions. However, that model represents object properties differently from OWL, which is then mapped to OWL. Instead of two properties, like an ex:teaches and ex:taught-by, there is one relationship, say *ex:teaching* with two roles, one for each participating entity (e.g., [*lecturer*] and [*course*]), alike UML's association ends. This construction can have multiple *relational expressions* attached to it, such as e.g., teaches, taught by, lectures etc. While this is ontologically preferable over *lemon*, it does not provide a solution for a property with no single label either, other than using an arbitrary string for the name of the relationship and linking it to a template or verbalisation pattern to generate the relational expressions.

Thus, no existing system or model can readily deal with unnamed or multiply named variants, and there are very limited object property mapping options.

3 Parts and Wholes in isiZulu NLG: The Monolingual Case

In order to be able to address the multilingual setting, some issues have to be resolved for the monolingual setting first. While there are non-trivial aspects for the verbalisation in isiZulu, such as deep prepositions [12], the main issue here is that *containment* and all types of whole-part relations do not have a stable surface realisation as they do in English, which in OWL ontologies typically are merged in the property's naming or labelling (e.g., has part). Hence, there is no readily available string to name the object property with. The second issue is which part-whole relations exist, and the consequences that follow from it. To address this, we first subject to a brief ontological analysis those part-whole relations that have been investigated for isiZulu NLG (Sect. 3.1), then propose how to handle the unnamed properties (Sect. 3.2), and finally describe how it has been implemented (Sect. 3.3).

3.1 Ontological Aspects of Part-Whole Relations in isiZulu

Structuring the verbalisation patterns of [14] by their linguistic realisations for 'part' and analysis on relata as reported therein, then a taxonomy emerges that is substantially different from Fig. 1, which is depicted in Fig. 2. This taxonomy with eight relations is preliminary, in that not all terms denoting 'parts' in isiZulu have been investigated yet. There are two points of note already, however: there are more refined distinctions in part-whole relations—for portions, participation, and constitution—and more coarse-grained ones to the extent that the distinction between mereology and meronymy-only does not exist. *Ingxenye* 'part of' is used for parthood, involvement, membership, stuff parts, participation of individual objects (vs. collectives), and containment. This is a mix of mereological and meronymic part-whole relations and, according to the linguist (L. Khumalo), there is no difference. This means that it can result in erroneous deductions, for different things can be chained together that should not. For instance, *ingxenye* is used for 'hand is part of the musician' (structural parthood) and for 'musician is part of the orchestra' (membership), but a derivation from this is incorrect ontologically, as the hand is not part of the orchestra. That is, *ingxenye* (the generic parthood) is not transitive. One could try to contest the universality of transitivity of parthood in that, unlike the examples discussed in [2,11,28], really no distinctions are being made in this case. However, before conceding to non-transitivity, there are four points to consider. First, by making parthood non-transitive, one also loses desirable deductions and it will not assist in resolving distinguishing desirable from undesirable deductions—which was a reason to have multiple part-whole relations in the first place. Second, to the best of our knowledge, no empirical investigation has been carried out into ascertaining how many desirable and undesirable deductions one loses/gains in an ontology by asserting, or not, transitivity on parthood. That is, there is no estimate of its practical importance. Third, a partial order, which parthood is,

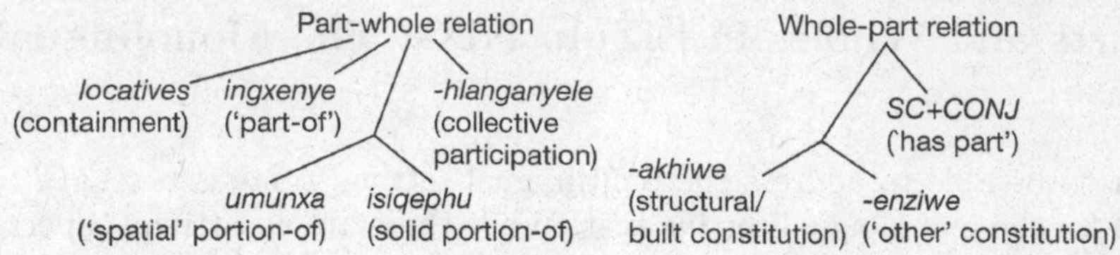

Fig. 2. Preliminary taxonomy based on the verbalisation patterns in [14].

does have the property of being transitive, both mathematically and ontologically. Fourth, there is no clear demarcation for pushing a tolerable little vs. too much, to shoe-horn the conceptualisation and language into the more widely used mereology vs. non/in-transitive distinction; e.g., *ilunga* is a 'member of an organisation' and *ilungu* is a 'council member' that, albeit having narrower meanings cf. *member_of*, might provide some wriggle room despite that it will not occur in text corpora like "member of" does in English.

The other aspect, refinement, has not been observed and investigated before, of which there are at least three cases. First, a difference is made between 'individual participation' and 'collective participation', as in a voter vs. the electorate participating in an election, and a doctor vs. an operating team participating in an operation. Depending on the foundational ontology (FO), this can be handled by the category of the participating objects—physical objects (e.g., a protein, human) or the roles they play (e.g., enzyme, voter) versus social agents (e.g., a company, electorate) as a minimum distinction. This would require all domain ontologies to adhere to some FO that contains this distinction. Whether this distinction can be pushed further ontologically, such as with Searle's collective intentions [24], remains to be investigated.

Second, there are special portions for space vs. for solid and solid-like objects, like between "the portion of the kitchen where the kitchen utensils are" vs. "the sample of blood is a portion of the blood of the human". This can be solved also by taking into account the FO categories the participating objects belong to. If it concerns essentially space and a portion thereof only, then *umunxa* should be used (whereas when the focus is the physical object and space secondary, then it is containment), and if it is any amount of matter and a part that is of the same type of matter, then it is *isiqephu* for 'portion'.

Third, there is a distinction between *-akh-* and *-enz-*, which bears some resemblance between 'constituted of', as in "a vase is constituted of clay" and the more generic 'made of', as in "a pill is made of starch", although they are generally treated equivalently in other works (e.g., [13] and references therein) other than, perhaps, in Turkish [32]. The *-akh-* verb root is used for 'built' or composed things, whereas *-enz-* is used for all other cases. At the time of writing, it is not clear how to distinguish computationally between the two, i.e., beyond the general desideratum for constitution relating a physical object to an amount of matter (stuff). This means that for the time being, it is up to the modellers to choose one correctly. Note also that *akhiwe* and *enziwe* are only used in the whole[object]-to-part[stuff] reading direction, not from part to whole.

3.2 Processing Unnamed Object Properties

We will now resolve handling relations that do not have a neat, single, label. Several options were explored, and we elaborate on two.

One can use an 'unnamed' object property in an axiom, provided the language supports declaring inverses and the property is named. OWL's `ObjectInverseOf` (Inv, for short) or `InverseObjectProperty` [19] can be used for that. Then, using Inv(partOf) amounts to hasPart; e.g., Human $\sqsubseteq \exists$Inv(partOf).Heart (or: Umuntu $\sqsubseteq$ $\exists$Inv(ingxenye).Inhliziyo). While the axioms require more effort to understand, this is not an issue with a natural language layer on top of it. A downside is that it still requires at least one name, which the containment relation does not have. Also, OWL 2 EL is popular for large medical terminologies and SNOMED CT is represented in OWL 2 EL, but this profile does not have inverses.

The second option is to 'squeeze' it somehow into OWL's vocabulary element naming options: (1) use some arbitrary label (possibly a system-generated identifier) and describe the intention in the object property's annotation, as *lemon* does not have an attribute for this either; (2) use the English term in the ontology, ignoring the localisation; or (3) use some abbreviation of the English term. The linguist consulted (L. Khumalo, UKZN) preferred the arbitrary string option and the annotation field to describe the type of relation. This option can be realised with the positionalist model of [12] and with modification of *lemon* [18], as described in Sect. 2.2, or without either. Because currently all verbalisation knowledge is encoded in the verbaliser already, including the noun class information and processing of the deep prepositions, the simple annotation was chosen as proof-of-concept, for the complex alignments are the eventual target.

3.3 Implementation

The investigated part-whole relations of isiZulu have been represented in an OWL ontology, `PWzu.owl`, that imports `DOLCEmini.owl`—a module of the OWL-ized DOLCE foundational ontology [16] (i.e., of DLP3971.zip)—so as to constrain the domain and range of each relation with relatively well-known and defined entities. The context-dependent (multi-label) relations have been given arbitrary names, which are listed in the 3rd column of Table 1. These labels are then linked to the applicable verbalisation pattern in the verbaliser.

To enable testing as well as taking a step toward applicability in one of the use case scenarios (healthcare), the ontology verbaliser in isiZulu has been extended to be able to process OWL files. A Python script was already developed that implements the verbalisation algorithms, which needed only to be linked to OWL, which was achieved the OWL API for Python, Owlready [15].

To test it, we represented in OWL all test cases of [14] and those from earlier works on ontology verbalisation in isiZulu, totalling to 82 logical axioms of which 41 with part-whole relations; the others include named class subsumption, disjointness, and negated object properties in existential restrictions. All files are available from http://www.meteck.org/files/geni/, as well as those files mentioned in the next section. An annotated screenshot is shown in Fig. 3.

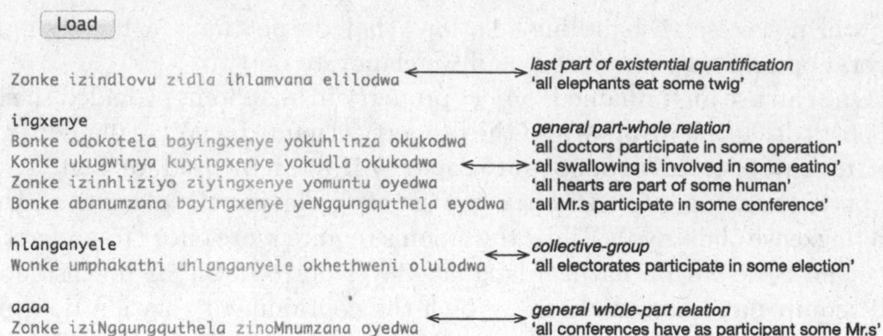

Fig. 3. Section of the GUI interface of the semantic web-enabled isiZulu verbaliser. Explanations were added on the right for clarification (not generated by the software). (Note: illustration was deemed more important than ontological precision.)

4 Parts and Wholes in a Multilingual Setting

The principal problem to address is the alignment of the commonly structured part-whole relations with those in isiZulu. This will be needed in practice with broader adoption of, notably, SNOMED CT in Sub-Saharan Africa for EHR and patient discharge notes tailored to one's language. To assist with maintainability, one would want to keep a link between the source ontology and the localised one. IT may also be used in the other direction, to relate local knowledge to other knowledge in the world, such as African architecture [9]. As can be readily observed from Fig. 1 vs. Fig. 2, this requires alignments that are not 1:1 mappings, hence, the need to resort to aligning *patterns*. This is described in Sect. 4.1 after which we apply it to the 'English↔isiZulu' part-whole relations in Sect. 4.2.

4.1 Non 1:1 Mappings for Object Properties

We will first extend and refine the "Vocabulary Alignment Pattern: Sub property of an external Property" of the aforementioned ODP catalogue, so that it can then also be used for the more general case of property subsumption and its domain and range. The extended version is shown in Fig. 4 for two arbitrary ontologies O_1 and O_2, where A, B, C, D are classes and R_1, R_2 object properties. For precision, we formalise the pattern as follows, assuming a Semantic Web setting with OWL [19] and in a similar way as in [7]. Because it is a pattern, its elements refer not to vocabulary elements of a particular ontology, but any, we use calligraphic letters to distinguish them from OWL classes in the ontology to be aligned.

- *alignment pattern name*: *HetOP*.
- *pattern elements*: $\mathcal{C}$, $\mathcal{D}$, $\mathcal{R}_1$ from O_1, $\mathcal{A}$, $\mathcal{B}$, $\mathcal{R}_2$ from O_2 where $\mathcal{C}, \mathcal{D} \in V_C \cup$ `owl:Thing`.

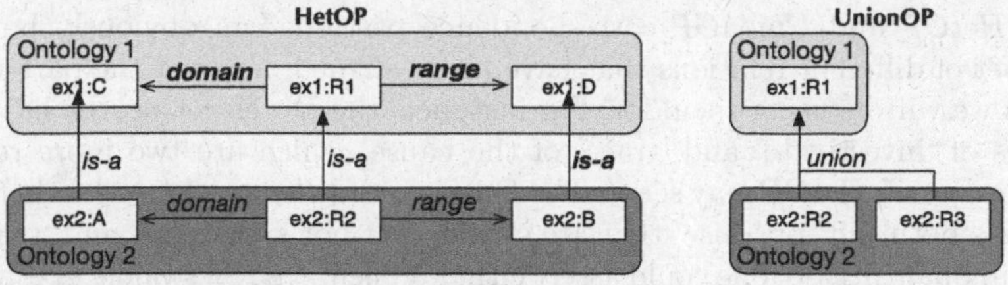

Fig. 4. Informal depiction of the *HetOP*, refining the VAP correspondence ODP (changes shown in bold face) and the new *UnionOP*.

- *alignment pattern contexts* (i.e., the fragment of interest):
  - *pattern* P_1 *in* O_1: $\exists \mathcal{R}_1.\mathcal{D} \sqsubseteq \mathcal{C}$, $\exists \mathcal{R}_1^-.\mathcal{C} \sqsubseteq \mathcal{D}$;
  - *pattern* P_2 *in* O_2: $\exists \mathcal{R}_2.\mathcal{B} \sqsubseteq \mathcal{A}$, $\exists \mathcal{R}_2^-.\mathcal{A} \sqsubseteq \mathcal{B}$.
- *Cross-ontology alignments*: $\mathcal{A} \sqsubseteq \mathcal{C}$ and $\mathcal{B} \sqsubseteq \mathcal{D}$ or $\mathcal{A} \equiv \mathcal{C}$ and $\mathcal{B} \sqsubseteq \mathcal{D}$ or $\mathcal{A} \sqsubseteq \mathcal{C}$ and $\mathcal{B} \equiv \mathcal{D}$, and $\mathcal{R}_2 \sqsubseteq \mathcal{R}_1$.
- *Global constraints* (to ensure the ontology does not become incoherent or inconsistent): $\mathcal{A} \sqcap \mathcal{C} \sqsubseteq \bot$ and $\mathcal{B} \sqcap \mathcal{D} \sqsubseteq \bot$ must NOT be asserted or derivable.

Note that `owl:Thing` as possible domain or range means that $\mathcal{R}_1$ thus may or may not have a user-defined domain and range declared. The three options for equivalence/subsumption (but not twice equivalence) follow the constraints for semantically correct role hierarchies as described in [13].

A second correspondence ODP for multilingual and heterogeneous alignments are where one ontology, and natural language, has one relation ($\mathcal{R}_1$) for which another language has two or more ($\mathcal{R}_i$ with $2 \leq i \leq n$). Aligning these differences can be accomplished systematically as follows.

- *alignment pattern name*: *UnionOP*.
- *pattern elements*: $\mathcal{R}_1$ from O_1, $\mathcal{R}_i$ with $2 \leq i \leq n$ from O_2.
- *alignment pattern contexts*:
  - *pattern* P_1 *in* O_1: $\mathcal{R}_1$;
  - *pattern* P_2 *in* O_2: $\mathcal{R}_i$.
- *Cross-ontology alignments*: $\mathcal{R}_2 \sqsubseteq \mathcal{R}', \ldots, \mathcal{R}_n \sqsubseteq \mathcal{R}'$, and $\mathcal{R}' \equiv \mathcal{R}_1$ or $\mathcal{R}' \sqsubseteq \mathcal{R}_1$, with $\mathcal{R}'$ in O_1.
- *Global constraints*: the context and cross-ontology alignments do not violate *HetOP*.

The cross-ontology alignment ought to have an additional union axiom, $\mathcal{R}' \sqsubseteq \mathcal{R}_2 \sqcup \ldots \sqcup \mathcal{R}_n$, but this type of axiom is beyond OWL 2 DL. While one could eliminate $\mathcal{R}'$ and use $\mathcal{R}_1$ directly, the auxiliary property reduces the number of inter-ontology links and therewith simplifies maintenance. Whether one asserts equivalence or subsumption between $\mathcal{R}'$ and $\mathcal{R}_1$ depends on (1) the confidence one has on the exhaustiveness of the refined object properties, (2) any conflicting domain or range axioms.

The *HetOP* and *UnionOP* correspondence patterns can obviously be used for any set of different relations that have to be aligned, not just the part-whole relations we will be using them for. For instance, the Dutch *naspeuren* has both meanings of 'investigate' and 'trace' of the cause, which are two more refined notions for which *HetOP* may serve. The Dutch verb *tillen* (and *levantar* in Spanish) means both 'lift' or 'raise' that are similar but not synonyms, and 'swindle' (*estafar* in Spanish). So, one could assert either a $\mathsf{tillen}_{sense1} \equiv \mathsf{swindle} \equiv \mathsf{estafar}$ if each language has its own ontology, or add one object property with those labels in an annotation file for a multilingual ontology, and $\mathsf{tillen}_{sense2} \equiv \mathsf{levantar}$ (one OWL object property) with $\mathsf{lift} \sqsubseteq \mathsf{tillen}_{sense2}$ and $\mathsf{raise} \sqsubseteq \mathsf{tillen}_{sense2}$ as object sub property assertions. A quick check for verbs—candidates for object properties—in dictionaries suggest many more such cases.

4.2 Aligning the Part-Whole Relations

The alignment between the two taxonomies was carried out manually in three stages. First, an informal alignment was carried out as a conceptualisation stage, so as to scope any issues, address naming and so on; the outcome of this informal alignment is included in Table 1. To ensure separation of concerns, the first column contains the name of the relationship, the second column lists a subset of the possible labels based on English that can be either syntactical differences or with terms that are generally used synonymously, and the third column contains the essential aspects of the isiZulu verbalisation patterns.

The second stage concerned the logical aspects and correspondence ODPs. For instance, *involvement* in the part-whole taxonomy has its domain and range restricted to DOLCE's Perdurant (rough ly: processes), so then the *HetOP* pattern has to hold for pw:involvedIn ⊑ pwzu:ingxenye, for the latter does not have domain and range restrictions. Aligning isiZulu's *space-portion*—i.e., umunxa in the 'part of' reading direction—with an instantiation of *HetOP* would result in an inconsistency if it were to be tried with pw:portionOf, for umunxa's domain and range are DOLCE's Region whereas that of *portion* is DOLCE's Amount of Matter, which are located in disjoint branches in DOLCE. For this reason, one also cannot use *UnionOP*, though one can assert that pw:portionOf ⊑ pwzu:portion-of, with pwzu:portion-of the $\mathcal{R}'$ of the *UnionOP* specification. The bridge axioms are, principally, as follows:

- Equivalence mappings: pw:part-whole ≡ pwzu:part-whole, pw:whole-part ≡ pwzu:whole-part, pw:containedIn ≡ pwzu:ffff;
- Subsumption mappings: pwzu:hlanganyele ⊑ pw:participatesIn, pw:portionOf ⊑ pwzu:portion-of, pwzu:isiqephu ⊑ pw:portionOf;
- *HetOP* alignments (only property subsumption axioms listed): pw:memberOf ⊑ pwzu:ingxenye, pw:involvedIn ⊑ pwzu:ingxenye, pw:sPartOf ⊑ pwzu:ingxenye, pw:stuffpartOf ⊑ pwzu:ingxenye.
- *UnionOP* alignments (all axioms listed): pwzu:akhiwe ⊑ pwzu:constitution, pwzu:enziwe ⊑ pwzu:constitution, pwzu:constitution ≡ pw:constitutedOf.

Table 1. Summarised and informal version of the alignments. P = part, W = whole, SC = subject concord, CONJ = conjunction, LOC = locative prefix, LOCSUF = locative suffix, EP = epenthetic, COP = copula; the patterns in column 3 omit the parts about quantifiers and pluralisation.

Relationship name	English surface realisations (notations and synonyms)	isiZulu part-whole patterns ("%": name in the OWL file)
Reading direction: from whole to part		
partwhole	has_part, hasPart, part, ...	SC+CONJ+P % 'aaaa'
involvement	involves, sub-process, ...	SC+CONJ+P % 'aaaa'
membership	has_member, member, ...	SC+CONJ+P % 'aaaa'
stuffpart	hasStuffPart, hasSubstuff, has_ingredient, ...	SC+CONJ+P % 'cccc'
ind-participation	has_participant, participant, ...	SC+CONJ+P % 'aaaa'
col-participation	has_participant, participant, ...	SC+CONJ+P % 'bbbb'
containment	contains	SC+CONJ+P %'aaaa'
space-portion	has_portion, portion, piece, ...	SC+CONJ+P % 'dddd'
solid-portion	has_portion, portion, piece, ...	SC+CONJ+P % 'eeee'
built-constitution	constituted_of, madeOf, ...	SC+akhiwe nga+P
constitution	constituted_of, madeOf, ...	SC+enziwe nga+P
Reading direction: from part to whole		
partwhole	part_of, isPartOf, ...	SC+COP+ingxenye ya+W
involvement	involvedIn, ...	SC+COP+ingxenye ya+W
membership	member_of, isMemberOf, ...	SC+COP+ingxenye ya+W
stuffpart	stuff_part_of, ingredientOf	SC+COP+ingxenye ya+W
ind-participation	participates_in, ...	SC+COP+ingxenye ya+W
col-participation	participates_in, ...	SC+hlanganyele LOC+W+LOCSUF
containment	contained_in, ...	SC+EP+LOC+W+LOCSUF %'ffff'
space-portion	portion-of, ...	SC+COP+umunxa wa+W
solid-portion	portion-of, ...	SC+COP+isiqephu sa+W

Third, this was implemented in order to verify that an alignment is indeed feasible such that it does not lead to contradictions or undesirable deductions in an ontology. To this end, we have taken the OWL file of the part-whole taxonomy, `PW.owl` and the new `PWzu.owl` with the isiZulu part-whole relations, and imported them into a new ontology that contains the aforementioned bridge axioms, `PWzuPWbridge.owl` (available from the aforementioned URL). There were no errors nor undesirable deductions.

5 Discussion

The solutions presented might appear specific to this scenario of part-whole relations. However, the solutions are generic for addressing 'unnamed' properties and, moreover, there are two new correspondence patterns for aligning object properties. It is also the first reported systematic assessment on, and, importantly, finding differences in, part-whole relations with respect to cultures with a language in a language family other than (Indo-)European.

The unintended 'byproduct' of attempting to verbalise part-whole relations in an ontology into isiZulu uncovered what may be considered different conceptualisations when one takes the category of domain and range as a desideratum to distinguish different part-whole relations. Given that there are a few papers that hint in a similar direction, such as the 'element-object' in Chinese [5], it suggests that there may be more generalisations and refinements in part-whole relations in other languages after all. A consequence of the differences in conceptualisation as perceived by amaZulu and their isiZulu language, was that transitivity does not hold for the main part-whole relation, *ingxenye*, when used as is. Transitivity is currently ignored in `PWzu.owl`, but that could be regained through the backdoor with the mappings to the part-whole relations taxonomy in `PW.owl`. It remains to be investigated how many 'interesting' deductions will be lost with the simple option and how much additional processing time the backdoor option would take.

While in hindsight the direction of the solution might be evident, it would have been useful to have had methodological guidance upfront. In particular, there were four possible cases that interfered with finding a solution: (1) same relationship with multilingual annotation vs. (2) different relationships, and (3) one 'base' ontology with possible alignments between annotations vs. (4) multiple localised ontologies with alignments between ontology vocabulary elements. For different relations, as in this case, one needs correspondence ODPs, as for multiple localised ontologies (though they are harder to maintain); for the same relation then annotations suffice, and for one base ontology with multiple language annotation models, perhaps annotation alignments will have to be devised.

Regarding the identified part-whole relations in isiZulu, we know there are more words used in prose to describe part-whole relations; e.g., *qukatha* 'containment' (roughly), *isididiyelo* 'ingredient' depending on how the whole came to be, and *ingqikithi* 'the essential part'. It remains to be seen whether they are synonyms or other refinements. A further point for investigation by linguists is that there may or may not be concept drift for the plurals of parts. A cursory check of *ingxenye* and its plural *izingxenye* in the 20 million-token isiZulu National Corpus (unpublished; pers. comm. L. Khumalo) indicated concept sameness in their use, but not *iminxa* (plural of *umunxa*) that relate abstract categories rather than spaces.

6 Conclusion

The analysis of part-whole relations in isiZulu revealed both 'underspecification' that complicates obtaining desirable deductions and three new refinements on part-whole relations for participation, spatial portions, and constitution. This was first implemented for the monolingual scenario that required a basic mechanism to deal with 'unnamed' object properties. It was shown to work to generate structured natural language from an ontology with isiZulu vocabulary to isiZulu sentences. The multilingual scenario required non-1:1 alignments between the common part-whole relations and those in isiZulu, for which two new correspondence patterns were introduced. These two patterns were used to align the part-whole relations. The patterns are specified such that they are natural language independent and thus can be used in aligning object properties in other ontologies as well.

Future research concerns a further analysis of part-whole relations in isiZulu and integrating the proof-of-concept tool with the model of [12].

Acknowledgments. This work is based on the research supported in part by the National Research Foundation of South Africa (Grant Number 93397). The author would like to thank M. Xakaza for assistance with tool development.

References

1. Al Zamil, M.G., Al-Radaideh, Q.: Automatic extraction of ontological relations from Arabic text. J. King Saud Univ. Comput. Inf. Sci. **26**(4), 462–472 (2014). Special issue on Arabic NLP
2. Barbier, F., Henderson-Sellers, B., Le Parc-Lacayrelle, A., Bruel, J.M.: Formalization of the whole-part relationship in the Unified Modelling Language. IEEE Trans. Softw. Eng. **29**(5), 459–470 (2003)
3. Bosca, A., Dragoni, M., Francescomarino, C.D., Ghidini, C.: Collaborative management of multilingual ontologies. In: Buitelaar, P., Cimiano, P. (eds.) Towards the Multilingual Semantic Web, pp. 175–192. Springer, Heidelberg (2014)
4. Buitelaar, P., Cimiano, P., Haase, P., Sintek, M.: Towards linguistically grounded ontologies. In: Aroyo, L., et al. (eds.) ESWC 2009. LNCS, vol. 5554, pp. 111–125. Springer, Heidelberg (2009). doi:10.1007/978-3-642-02121-3_12
5. Cao, X., Cao, C., Wang, S., Lu, H.: Extracting part-whole relations from unstructured Chinese corpus. In: Proceedings of FSKD 2008. IEEE Xplore (2008)
6. Chiarcos, C., Sukhareva, M.: OLiA - Ontologies of Linguistic Annotation. Semant. Web J. **6**(4), 379–386 (2015)
7. Fillottrani, P.R., Keet, C.M.: Patterns for heterogeneous TBox mappings to bridge different modelling decisions. In: Blomqvist, E., et al. (ed.) Proceedings of ESWC 2017. LNCS, vol. 10249. Springer, Heidelberg (2017, in press)
8. Fiorelli, M., Stellato, A., McCrae, J.P., Cimiano, P., Pazienza, M.T.: LIME: the metadata module for OntoLex. In: Gandon, F., Sabou, M., Sack, H., d'Amato, C., Cudré-Mauroux, P., Zimmermann, A. (eds.) ESWC 2015. LNCS, vol. 9088, pp. 321–336. Springer, Cham (2015). doi:10.1007/978-3-319-18818-8_20
9. Frescura, F., Myeza, J.: Illustrated Glossary of Southern African Architectural Terms. UKZN Press, Bilingual Glossary Series (2016)

10. Guizzardi, G.: Ontological foundations for structural conceptual models. Ph.D. thesis, University of Twente, The Netherlands. Telematica Instituut Fundamental Research Series No. 15 (2005)
11. Johansson, I.: On the transitivity of the parthood relation. In: Mulligan, K. (ed.) Relations and Predicates, pp. 161–181. Ontos Verlag, Frankfurt (2004)
12. Keet, C.M., Chirema, T.: A model for verbalising relations with roles in multiple languages. In: Blomqvist, E., Ciancarini, P., Poggi, F., Vitali, F. (eds.) EKAW 2016. LNCS (LNAI), vol. 10024, pp. 384–399. Springer, Cham (2016). doi:10.1007/978-3-319-49004-5_25
13. Keet, C.M., Artale, A.: Representing and reasoning over a taxonomy of part-whole relations. Appl. Ontol. **3**(1–2), 91–110 (2008)
14. Keet, C.M., Khumalo, L.: On the verbalization patterns of part-whole relations in isiZulu. In: Proceedings of INLG 2016, pp. 174–183, 5–8 September 2016. ACL, Edinburgh (2016)
15. Lamy, J.: Ontology-oriented programming for biomedical informatics. Stud. Health Technol. Inf. **221**, 64–68 (2016)
16. Masolo, C., Borgo, S., Gangemi, A., Guarino, N., Oltramari, A.: Ontology library. WonderWeb Deliverable D18, ver. 1.0, 31 December 2003 (2003). http://wonderweb.semanticweb.org
17. McCrae, J., Aguado-de Cea, G., Buitelaar, P., Cimiano, P., Declerck, T., Gómez-Pérez, A., Gracia, J., Hollink, L., Montiel-Ponsoda, E., Spohr, D., Wunner, T.: Interchanging lexical resources on the semantic web. Lang. Resour. Eval. **46**(4), 701–719 (2012)
18. McCrae, J., Aguado-de-Cea, G., Buitelaar, P., Cimiano, P., Declerck, T., Gómez-Pérez, A., Gracia, J., Hollink, L., Montiel-Ponsoda, E., Spohr, D., Wunner, T.: The Lemon Cookbook. Technical report, Monnet Project (2012)
19. Motik, B., Patel-Schneider, P.F., Parsia, B.: OWL 2 web ontology language structural specification and functional-style syntax. W3c recommendation, W3C (27 Oct 2009). http://www.w3.org/TR/owl2-syntax/
20. Motschnig-Pitrik, R., Kaasboll, J.: Part-whole relationship categories and their application in object-oriented analysis. IEEE Trans. Knowl. Data Eng. **11**(5), 779–797 (1999)
21. Rosse, C., Mejino Jr., J.L.V.: A reference ontology for biomedical informatics: the foundational model of anatomy. J. Biomed. Inf. **36**(6), 478–500 (2003)
22. Scharffe, F., Fensel, D.: Correspondence patterns for ontology alignment. In: Gangemi, A., Euzenat, J. (eds.) EKAW 2008. LNCS (LNAI), vol. 5268, pp. 83–92. Springer, Heidelberg (2008). doi:10.1007/978-3-540-87696-0_10
23. Scharffe, F., Zamazal, O., Fensel, D.: Ontology alignment design patterns. Knowl. Inf. Syst. **40**, 1–28 (2014)
24. Searle, J.R.: Collective intentions and actions. In: Cohen, P., Morgan, J., Pollak, M. (eds.) Intentions in Communication, pp. 401–415. MIT Press, Cambridge (1990)
25. Snomed, C.T.: http://www.ihtsdo.org/snomed-ct/. Accessed 27 Jan 2012
26. Tandon, N., Hariman, C., Urbani, J., Rohrbach, A., Rohrbach, M., Weikum, G.: Commonsense in parts: mining part-whole relations from the web and image tags. In: Proceedings of AAAI 2016, pp. 243–250. AAAI Press (2016)
27. Varzi, A.C.: Mereology. In: Zalta, E.N. (ed.) Stanford Encyclopedia of Philosophy. Stanford, fall 2004 edn (2004). http://plato.stanford.edu/archives/fall2004/entries/mereology/
28. Varzi, A.C.: A note on the transitivity of parthood. Appl. Ontol. **1**, 141–146 (2006)

29. Vieu, L., Aurnague, M.: Part-of relations, functionality and dependence. In: Aurnague, M., Hickmann, M., Vieu, L. (eds.) Categorization of Spatial Entities in Language and Cognition. John Benjamins, Amsterdam (2005)
30. Wilcox, L., Morris, D., Tan, D., Gatewood, J., Horvitz, E.: Characterising patient-friendly micro-explanations of medical events. In: Proceedings of CHI 2011, pp. 29–32. ACM (2011)
31. Winston, M., Chaffin, R., Herrmann, D.: A taxonomy of partwhole relations. Cogn. Sci. **11**(4), 417–444 (1987)
32. Yıldız, T., Diri, B., Yıldırım, S.: Acquisition of Turkish meronym based on classification of patterns. Pattern Anal. Appl. **19**(2), 495–507 (2016)

CoNLL-RDF: Linked Corpora Done in an NLP-Friendly Way

Christian Chiarcos(✉) and Christian Fäth

Goethe-University Frankfurt, Frankfurt, Germany
chiarcos@informatik.uni-frankfurt.de, faeth@em.uni-frankfurt.de
http://acoli.informatik.uni-frankfurt.de

Abstract. We introduce *CoNLL-RDF*, a direct rendering of the *CoNLL* format in *RDF*, accompanied by a formatter whose output mimicks CoNLL's original TSV-style layout. CoNLL-RDF represents a middle ground that accounts for the needs of NLP specialists (easy to read, easy to parse, close to conventional representations), but that also facilitates LLOD integration by applying off-the-shelf Semantic Web technology to CoNLL corpora and annotations. The CoNLL-RDF infrastructure is published as open source. We also provide SPARQL update scripts for selected use cases as described in this paper.

1 Motivation and Background

Representing NLP resources and linguistic annotations as Linked Data has become an established technique in the context of both the development of the Linguistic Linked Open Data (LLOD) cloud [6] and the advances on Knowledge Extraction in Artificial Intelligence, resp. their adaptation in different fields of practice, such as, e.g., Biomedical IE. Yet, current formalisms usually applied for the purpose [10,15,16] find limited resonance in the core NLP community: RDF serializations are often seen as needlessly complex, possible benefits of Linked Data for Natural Language Processing (and of standards in general) are not widely recognized yet,[1] and NLP specialists are used to work with established de-facto standards for most aspects of NLP.

The tradition of shared tasks organized by the Conference of Natural Language Learning (CoNLL)[2] helped to establish such task-specific de-facto standards for core aspects of NLP and corpus linguistics. While these formats were not generic, they are easy to parse (or at least, commonly known) and supported by many tools and corpora. An NLP researcher may thus rightfully ask why we should exceed beyond CoNLL if it is technically well supported, easy to process and established in existing workflows – given the complexity of the alternatives proposed.

---

[1] As summarized by Mark Johnson in his ACL-IJCLNP 2012 keynote on the future of computational linguistics, "[s]tandard data formats (...) I'm not sure these are important: if someone can use a parser, they can probably also write a Python wrapper" [12, slide 8].

[2] http://www.signll.org/conll.

J. Gracia et al. (Eds.): LDK 2017, LNAI 10318, pp. 74–88, 2017.
DOI: 10.1007/978-3-319-59888-8_6

We argue that there *is* added value in using RDF-based formalisms – namely in interoperability, interpretability, resource integration and infrastructural support [5], as well as eliminating the need for potentially error-prone transformations –, and that their apparent disadvantages can be compensated by establishing a middle ground between the CoNLL format family and RDF: *CoNLL-RDF* is a shallow, human-readable and easily processable, RDF compliant format which provides a compromise between established CoNLL representations used in NLP and more advanced and semantically well-defined formalisms brought forward in the context of Linguistic Linked Open Data [10,15,16]. CoNLL-RDF allows NLP researchers and engineers to seamlessly integrate corpus data with lexical resources, terminology bases and knowledge graphs.

We present the mapping of CoNLL to a lossless and isomorphic RDF representation and its canonical serialization. Taken together, both aspects, the RDF data model and the associated format conventions, define CoNLL-RDF. We describe infrastructure, use cases, related research and perspectives.

1.1 Turtle: A Human-Readable RDF Serialization

RDF data can be serialized in and losslessly converted between different standard formats – depending on the intended use. As such, Turtle provides a human readable instantiation [1]. It represents RDF statements (labeled edges in the graph) as triples of source node ("subject"), edge ("property"/"relation") and target ("object"), concluded with a dot.

```
<http://example.org/sbj>
    <http://www.w3.org/2000/01/rdf-schema#subClassOf>
        <http://example.org/SomeClass> .
<http://example.org/sbj><http://www.w3.org/2000/01/rdf-schema#label>"example"  .
<http://example.org/sbj> <http://www.w3.org/2000/01/rdf-schema#label> "Beispiel" .
```

Abbreviations are possible, e.g., using prefixes; also, if several triples refer to the same subject, the subject can be dropped if the triples are separated with ";". If they share the same subject and the same predicate, the objects can be enumerated in ","-separated sequences:

```
@prefix ex: <http://example.org/>
@prefix rdfs: <http://www.w3.org/2000/01/rdf-schema#>
ex:sbj rdfs:subClassOf  ex:SomeClass ;
      rdfs:label        "example", "Beispiel" .
```

Whitespaces are irrelevant in Turtle, and the format allows to provide explanatory comments following #. Turtle is an attractive representation formalism because of its close relationship with the SPARQL query language.[3] With basic understanding of Turtle, users of CoNLL-RDF can thus directly apply SPARQL and SPARQL end points for querying, storing and manipulating annotations. Because of its flexibility, compactness, and readability we decided to design CoNLL-RDF as a sublanguage of Turtle with additional serialization constraints.

[3] https://www.w3.org/TR/sparql11-overview.

1.2 The CoNLL Format Family

Most CoNLL shared tasks used variations of tab-separated columns as format for testing and evaluation with one word per line, annotations represented as column values in these various lines, sentences being separated by empty lines, and comments marked by #. Over time, different column separators were used (1999–2001, 2004–2005 spaces, 2002–2003 single space), but ultimately settled on tabulators (since 2006, CoNLL-X).

CoNLL-X (2006)[4] introduced dependency annotations with every word being identified by its position in the sentence (explicit `ID` column), pointing to its syntactic `HEAD`, with a particular dependency relation assigned to the word (abbreviated `EDGE` here). In addition, columns for word-level annotations of `LEMMA` and morphosyntactic features (`FEAT`) were added.

```
# ID WORD    LEMMA POS  POS2 FEAT                HEAD EDGE  HEAD2 EDGE2
  1  Cathy   Cathy N    N    eigen|ev|neut       2    su    _     _
  2  zag     zie   V    V    trans|ovt|1of2of3|ev 0   ROOT  _     _
  3  hen     hen   Pron Pron per|3|mv|datofacc   2    obj1  _     _
  4  wild    wild  Adj  Adj  attr|stell|onverv   5    mod   _     _
  5  zwaaien zwaai N    N    soort|mv|neut       2    vc    _     _
  6  .       .     Punc Punc punt                5    punct _     _
```

Shared tasks in 2008 and 2009 combined this format with annotations for semantic roles, with one *additional column per frame instance* found in the sentence. This is an important extension of the original TSV format, because it means a departure from the tabular data model: Within a corpus, sentences differ in the number of columns. Subsequent tasks introduced further additions, e.g. additional columns for document and document parts (`DOCID`, `PART`), speaker identification (`AUTHOR`), and word sense (`WSENSE`), as well as a column for co-indexing coreferential referring expressions (`COREF`) throughout the text.[5]

2 CoNLL-RDF: LLOD with NLP-friendly Flavor

CoNLL-RDF comprises the following components: A shallow and extensible RDF data model, its serialization(s), a core infrastructure for parsing, manipulating and formatting CoNLL (resp., CoNLL-RDF) and a library of exemplary SPARQL update scripts. It is designed to remain minimal, focusing on Un*x shell, but paving the way for more elaborate solutions in the future. In the following, we presume CoNLL to be represented by tab-separated values (TSV); we also concentrate in our presentation on the popular CoNLL-X format and its derivatives. We do, however, support all TSV dialects used for CoNLL Shared Tasks until 2015.

---

[4] http://ilk.uvt.nl/conll/.

[5] http://conll.cemantix.org/2011/data.html.

2.1 The CoNLL-RDF Data Model

The **original data model** of CoNLL is a sequence of variable-width tables, each representing a sentence, with rows in a fixed (sequential) order. Because of the variable width, CoNLL is not directly translatable to a relational database format, it is, however, conceptually close. Aiming for a light-weight and loss-less conversion of CoNLL to RDF, we roughly follow a trivial mapping approach comparable to R2RML [8]: Map rows to individuals, columns to properties, values to literals; cross-references (foreign keys) receive special treatment and are mapped to object properties.

In order to provide a generic converter of CoNLL data, we must not rely on a fixed set or order of columns. Instead, given a **user-provided list of column labels** at conversion time, we create a datatype property for each of them. These novel properties are assigned to a designated `conll` namespace and take literals as their values. In case these need to be transformed into object properties or the like, this can be easily implemented by SPARQL update. However, as most instantiations of the CoNLL format since 2006 comprise dependency annotations, the `HEAD` column must receive special treatment, and will *always* be converted to an object property. This convention enables special handling of intra-sentential cross-references and is suitable for, but not restricted to dependency syntax. For CoNLL RDF formatting, the surface form of a token is expected in a column with the label `WORD` (original terminology; since 2006 `FORM`), and labels for intrasentential relations defined in `HEAD` are drawn from the column `EDGE`. No additional a priori naming conventions apply within the CoNLL-RDF core infrastructure. Individual SPARQL update scripts, however, are usually defined with reference to specific CoNLL-RDF properties, imposing task-specific constraints on portability and applicability.

Unlike TSV, RDF is a conceptual model and does not impose any **sequential structure**. This is, however, necessary to represent words and sentences in linguistic corpora. For this purpose, we rely on NIF [10]:[6] Every word (a CoNLL row) is identified by its URI and defined as an instance of (`rdf:type` or `a`) `nif:Word`. Within a sentence, every word is connected to its successor by `nif:next`. Every newline-separated table is identified by a sentence URI and defined as `a nif:Sentence`. Every sentence is connected to its successor by `nif:nextSentence`. The sentence is implicitly identified with the virtual root of the syntactic annotation, hence, for every word that does not take another word as its `conll:HEAD`, we set `conll:HEAD` to the sentence URI.

For **generating URIs**, we identify sentences by their respective position in the data, starting with 1. Within a sentence, a word is identified either by its position (starting with 1) or by the value of its `ID` column, if provided. Following conventions of TIGER [2,13] the local name of the URI is formed

[6] For the sake of processability, we use only a minimal fragment of NIF. We do neither adopt its full semantic model nor its URI formation constraints; yet, it is possible to transform CoNLL-RDF to NIF using SPARQL update and to provide NIF-compliant URIs if information about the original spacing (which is not preserved in CoNLL) is provided externally.

by "s"+*SENTID*+"_"+*WORDID*, e.g., `s1_1` for the first word in the first sentence. Following conventions adopted for CoNLL dependency annotations, the word `ID` 0 is reserved for the (virtual root of the) sentence, identified here with the sentence itself, the corresponding local name of the first sentence is thus `s1_0`. The local name is concatenated with a user-provided base URI that identifies the corpus or document that the current CoNLL file represents.

For successfully working with CoNLL-RDF, it is not necessary that corpus **URIs resolve**; still, it can be beneficial to facilitate sustainability and reusability: Resolvable URIs allow references to CoNLL-RDF data provided at a particular location in the web of data, and content negotiation offers the possibility to distribute both CoNLL and CoNLL-RDF data over the same URL.

2.2 Parsing and Manipulating CoNLL-RDF

For the en-bloc conversion of CoNLL data we provide the JAVA class `CoNLL2RDF`. To facilitate processing data streams, the `CoNLLStreamExtractor` reads CoNLL from `stdin` and applies `CoNLL2RDF` sentence by sentence to return valid (albeit not canonically formatted) CoNLL-RDF.

When parsing CoNLL, every sentence is transformed into a `nif:Sentence`, every word as a `nif:Word`, and their order preserved by `nif:nextWord` resp. `nif:nextSentence`. As described above, every column is mapped to a datatype property in the `conll:` namespace and with a user-provided label as local name.

In addition to this mere conversion functionality, the `CoNLLStreamExtractor` supports data manipulation by means of SPARQL UPDATE statements. It takes as additional arguments a list of files containing SPARQL UPDATE statements, introduced by the flag `-u`. Every individual file represents a module, which can be stacked to form a processing pipeline. Successively, these SPARQL Updates are applied to the individual sentences, thereby rewriting the RDF graph. We also support iterated applications, marked by an integer that can follow the respective SPARQL file in curly brackets.

Finally, a SPARQL SELECT query can be applied to aggregate information from sentences and to produce a TSV table as output that may then be used for further evaluation, classifier training or database population. Without a SELECT query, the CoNLLStreamExtractor produces CoNLL-RDF as output.

2.3 CoNLL-RDF Syntax and Its Canonical Format

CoNLL-RDF is an extensible RDF vocabulary that can be serialized in any RDF format. Yet, to facilitate processability in NLP applications at a level comparable to the original CoNLL TSV format, it is accompanied with specifications for its canonical format: CoNLL-RDF syntax is a highly constrained subset of Turtle. However, these constraints represent layout conventions that the CoNLL-RDF formatter can enforce upon *any RDF data* from the `conll` namespace.

A document in **canonically formatted CoNLL-RDF** begins with a header that enlists all properties from the `conll` namespace used in the file. This header is a #-introduced comment, containing space-separated local names of properties meant to facilitate CoNLL-RDF parsing. It is not normative, but informational.

The header is followed by an empty line, then a block of PREFIX declarations that define the namespace mappings. The following typical prefixes will be assumed predefined for all examples in the text:

```
PREFIX nif: <http://persistence.uni-leipzig.org/nlp2rdf/ontologies/nif-core#>
PREFIX conll: <http://ufal.mff.cuni.cz/conll2009-st/task-description.html#>
PREFIX rdfs: <http://www.w3.org/2000/01/rdf-schema#>
PREFIX rdf:  <http://www.w3.org/1999/02/22-rdf-syntax-ns#>
PREFIX : <BASE_URI>                    # URI of the data source, provided by user
```

The prefixes are followed by the actual content of the corpus. Sentences within the corpus and words within a sentence are ordered sequentially. Sentences are separated by empty lines. The first line in a sentence refers to the sentence URI and defines it as a `nif:Sentence`. For all except the first sentence of a corpus, the first line is preceded by a `nif:nextSentence` statement marking its position.

The second line holds the first content word, defines it as a `nif:Word`, followed by its `conll:WORD`, then other annotations in desired order, finally concluded with a `nif:next` statement pointing to the next word in the sentence (if available). The relation between words and sentences is established via `conll:HEAD`. CoNLL-RDF uses the Turtle separator ";" to enumerate the annotations assigned to a particular `nif:Word`, and "," to enumerate multiple values for the same annotation. CoNLL-RDF follows CoNLL in that all triples referring to one `nif:Word` are written in one line, concluded with ".". An example of canonically formatted CoNLL-RDF is given in Fig. 1.

The resulting format adopts many basic CoNLL conventions (comments starting with #, sentences separated by empty lines, one token per line, strictly ordered fields) and others modified (annotations separated by ; and identified by property names rather than position). Most importantly, canonically formatted CoNLL-RDF can be as easily processed with low-level string manipulations as the original CoNLL format (see Sect. 3.5). Yet, it is still possible to process

```
# sent_id dev-s4/de
:s3_0 nif:nextSentence :s4_0 .
:s4_0 a nif:Sentence .
:s4_1 a nif:Word; conll:WORD "Nach"; conll:ID "1"; conll:LEMMA "nach"; conll:UPOS "AD
:s4_2 a nif:Word; conll:WORD "einem"; conll:ID "2";
    conll:LEMMA "ein"; conll:UPOS "DET"; conll:POS "ART";
    conll:FEAT "Case=Dat|Definite=Ind|Gender=Masc,Neut|Number=Sing|PronType=Art";
    conll:HEAD :s4_4; conll:EDGE "det"; nif:next :s4_3 .
:s4_3 a nif:Word; conll:WORD "viertel"; conll:ID "3"; conll:LEMMA "Viertel"; conll:UP
:s4_4 a nif:Word; conll:WORD "Jahr"; conll:ID "4"; conll:LEMMA "Jahr"; conll:UPOS "NO
:s4_5 a nif:Word; conll:WORD "hielt"; conll:ID "5"; conll:LEMMA "halten"; conll:UPOS
:s4_6 a nif:Word; conll:WORD "ich"; conll:ID "6"; conll:LEMMA "ich"; conll:UPOS "PRON
:s4_7 a nif:Word; conll:WORD "ein"; conll:ID "7"; conll:LEMMA "ein"; conll:UPOS "DET"
:s4_8 a nif:Word; conll:WORD "duftendes"; conll:ID "8"; conll:LEMMA "duftend"; conll:
:s4_9 a nif:Word; conll:WORD "Wunder"; conll:ID "9"; conll:LEMMA "Wunder"; conll:UPOS
:s4_10 a nif:Word; conll:WORD "in"; conll:ID "10"; conll:LEMMA "in"; conll:UPOS "ADP"
:s4_11 a nif:Word; conll:WORD "den"; conll:ID "11"; conll:LEMMA "der"; conll:UPOS "DE
:s4_12 a nif:Word; conll:WORD "Händen"; conll:ID "12"; conll:LEMMA "Hand"; conll:UPOS
:s4_13 a nif:Word; conll:WORD "."; conll:ID "13"; conll:LEMMA "."; conll:UPOS "PUNCT"
```

Fig. 1. CoNLL-RDF generated from the German UD corpus

CoNLL-RDF in any other RDF format or tool without losing semantic information. The canonical format can be easily restored using the provided API.

2.4 Serializing CoNLL-RDF

`CoNLLRDFFormatter` reads CoNLL-RDF data in any common RDF serialization from standard input and converts it to one of several advanced output options:

`-rdf` canonically formatted CoNLL-RDF output (= default).
`-debug` augment `-rdf` output with color-highlighting (on Un*x shells).
`-conll FIELD1[.. FIELDn]` generates CoNLL TSV output according to the columns (fields) in their given order.
`-sparqltsv` provided a custom SPARQL SELECT query, this also generates CoNLL TSV output.
`-grammar` linguistic visualization with special formatting for dependency syntax (`conll:HEAD`+`conll:EDGE`), see Fig. 2.
`-semantics` visualization of object properties and labels of `conll:WORD`s, with `conll:` properties removed; useful for visualizing extracted knowledge graphs.

Figure 1 illustrates canonically formatted CoNLL-RDF generated with `-rdf`, Fig. 2 illustrates the human-readable linearization produced with `-grammar`.

```
s4_1  . . . / case-- Nach       ID 1 LEMMA nach POS APPR UPOS ADP
s4_2  . . . / det--- einem      FEAT Case=Dat|Definite=Ind|Gender=Masc,Neut|Number=Sing|PronType=Art ID 2 LEMMA ein POS ART UPOS DET
s4_3  . . . / nummod viertel    FEAT NumType=Card ID 3 LEMMA Viertel POS ADJA UPOS NUM
s4_4  . . / nmod---- Jahr       FEAT Case=Dat|Gender=Masc,Neut|Number=Sing ID 4 LEMMA Jahr POS NN UPOS NOUN
s4_5  . \ root       hielt      FEAT Number=Sing|Person=1|VerbForm=Fin ID 5 LEMMA halten POS VVFIN UPOS VERB
s4_6  . . \ nsubj--- ich        FEAT Case=Nom|Number=Sing|Person=1|PronType=Prs ID 6 LEMMA ich POS PPER UPOS PRON
s4_7  . . . / det--- ein        FEAT Case=Acc|Definite=Ind|Gender=Masc,Neut|Number=Sing|PronType=Art ID 7 LEMMA ein POS ART UPOS DET
s4_8  . . . / amod-- duftendes  FEAT Case=Acc|Degree=Pos|Gender=Masc,Neut|Number=Sing ID 8 LEMMA duftend POS ADJA UPOS ADJ
s4_9  . . \ dobj---- Wunder     FEAT Case=Acc|Gender=Masc,Neut|Number=Sing ID 9 LEMMA Wunder POS NN UPOS NOUN
s4_10 . . . / case-- in         ID 10 LEMMA in POS APPR UPOS ADP
s4_11 . . . / det--- den        FEAT Case=Dat|Definite=Def|Number=Plur|PronType=Art ID 11 LEMMA der POS ART UPOS DET
s4_12 . . \ nmod---- Händen     FEAT Case=Dat|Number=Plur ID 12 LEMMA Hand POS NN UPOS NOUN
s4_13 . . \ punct--- .          ID 13 LEMMA . POS $. UPOS PUNCT
```

Fig. 2. Human-readable dependency visualization (`CoNLLRDFFormatter -grammar`)

3 Use Cases

A key feature of CoNLL-RDF is that comes with SPARQL 1.1 support, an easy, expressive and powerful mechanism for graph rewriting. Any piece of annotation can thus be transformed and enriched by pipelines of stacked, reusable SPARQL scripts. This modular approach offers a wide range of use cases. Here, we describe sample use cases of both core functionality and SPARQL-based enrichment operations. All examples are taken from the German UD corpus.[7] In future publications we plan to address SRL syntax with variable column width.

[7] https://github.com/UniversalDependencies/UD_German.

3.1 SPARQL Update Pipelines

Together with the core infrastructure for parsing, manipulating and formatting CoNLL, resp., CoNLL-RDF, we provide a library of SPARQL update scripts and a number of Un*x shell scripts that illustrate their usabilities for pipelines to manipulate, format and aggregate over CoNLL annotations for different NLP tasks.

As such, Fig. 3 shows a basic conversion pipeline for CoNLL-U files: (1) The `CoNLLStreamExtractor` reads CoNLL-U input from standard in, with base URI and CoNLL column labels as arguments (line 1–2). (2) A number of SPARQL update operations (details below) are called after `-u` (line 3–5). (3) The `CoNLLRDFFormatter` (line 7) produces canonically formatted CoNLL-RDF output (cf. Fig. 1). Alternative output options can be specified as arguments of the shell script and will be passed on to the `CoNLLRDFFormatter`.

```
1 java CoNLLStreamExtractor https://github.com/UniversalDependencies/UD_German# \
2                           ID WORD LEMMA UPOS POS FEAT HEAD EDGE DEPS MISC \
3                           -u sparql/link-UPOS.sparql \
4                              sparql/link-stanford-EDGE.sparql \
5                              sparql/gloss-de-to-en-DBnary.sparql \
6     | \
7 java CoNLLRDFFormatter $*
```

Fig. 3. Example pipeline script

3.2 Enriching a Corpus with Dictionary Glosses

Line 5 in Fig. 3 calls a SPARQL update script that illustrates enrichment of a corpus with information drawn at runtime from a remote dictionary in the LLOD cloud. One of the most important advantages of RDF and the semantic web standards is the possibility to easily integrate and aggregate such external information. DBnary [17] is a dictionary database covering 16 languages, applied here to heuristically generate English glosses from German lemmata:

```
PREFIX lemon: <http://lemon-model.net/lemon#>
PREFIX dbnary_deu:<http://kaiko.getalp.org/dbnary/deu/>
PREFIX dbnary:<http://kaiko.getalp.org/dbnary#>

INSERT { ?a conll:EN_GLOSS ?eng. }
WHERE { ?a conll:LEMMA ?lemma.
       SERVICE <http://kaiko.getalp.org/sparql> {
         SELECT ?lemma ?eng
         WHERE {
           GRAPH <http://kaiko.getalp.org/dbnary/eng> {
               ?tr dbnary:targetLanguage <http://lexvo.org/id/iso639-3/deu>.
               ?tr dbnary:writtenForm ?deTr.          FILTER(str(?deTr)=?lemma)
               ?tr dbnary:isTranslationOf/lemon:canonicalForm/lemon:writtenRep ?enTr.
               BIND(str(?enTr) AS ?eng)
           }
         } LIMIT 1
  }}
```

The nested SELECT query uses DBnary's SPARQL service to retrieve one English translation for each conll:LEMMA. Albeit the SPARQL updates appear relatively complex, they are easy to adapt. For example, they are portable to other resources as long as the same representation formalism is used. DBnary uses the lemon/Monnet [9] vocabulary and the query refers to the German lexvo:deu glosses in the English DBnary, but with minimal modifications on SERVICE and GRAPH (to point to the locations of other dictionaries), this script can be applied to *any* dictionary provided in this format via any SPARQL endpoint. An update to dictionaries using the more recent lemon/OntoLex model [7] requires similarly minimal adjustments on the vocabulary used.

3.3 Annotation Interpretation

Similarly to dictionaries, other LLOD resources can be integrated with corpus data and thus open new areas of application. In the context of pattern-based extraction, for example, one may want to develop patterns that are applicable to different part-of-speech (POS) tagsets. One strategy to achieve this is to translate POS tags into conceptual descriptions grounded in an external ontology. A SPARQL update script that performs this operation for the German data under consideration is called in Fig. 3, line 3 (and a similar one for dependency labels in line 4):

```
CREATE SILENT GRAPH <http://purl.org/olia/ud-pos-all.owl>;

# load OLiA Annotation Model for universal dependency POS tags
LOAD <http://purl.org/olia/ud-pos-all.owl> INTO GRAPH<http://purl.org/olia/ud-pos-all.owl>;

# load OLiA Linking Model for universal dependency POS tags
LOAD <http://purl.org/olia/ud-pos-all-link.rdf>
                                        INTO GRAPH <http://purl.org/olia/ud-pos-all.owl>;

PREFIX oliasys: <http://purl.org/olia/system.owl#>
INSERT { ?a a ?oliaConcept. }
WHERE {  ?a conll:UPOS ?pos.
        GRAPH <http://purl.org/olia/ud-pos-all.owl> {
          ?x oliasys:hasTag ?pos.
          ?x a ?concept.

          # complex property path to retrieve (possible) superclasses for ?x
          ?concept (rdfs:subClassOf|owl:equivalentClass|^owl:equivalentClass|
                    ((owl:intersectionOf|owl:unionOf)/rdf:rest*/rdf:first))*
                                                                ?oliaConcept.

          # limit results to concepts from http://purl.org/olia/olia.owl
          FILTER(strstarts(str(?oliaConcept), "http://purl.org/olia/olia.owl"))
         }};

DROP GRAPH <http://purl.org/olia/ud-pos-all.owl>
```

Similar to the dictionary lookup using SERVICE, the keyword LOAD allows to retrieve a terminological resource, and then to query it locally: These scripts match conll:UPOS values against tags as defined in the corresponding OLiA [3] annotation model, and then retrieve the OLiA Reference Model concepts with a complex property path that follows the a/rdfs:subClassOf* subsumption hierarchy (extended here to support owl:equivalentClass and set operations).

```
# sent_id dev-s4/de
:s3_0 nif:nextSentence :s4_0 .
:s4_0 a nif:Sentence .
:s4_1 a nif:Word, olia:Adposition; conll:WORD "Nach"; conll:EN_GLOSS "like"; conll:LEMMA "na
:s4_2 a nif:Word, olia:Determiner; conll:WORD "einem"; conll:EN_GLOSS "an"; conll:LEMMA "ein
:s4_3 a nif:Word, olia:Numeral; conll:WORD "viertel"; conll:EN_GLOSS "neighborhood"; conll:L
:s4_4 a nif:Word, olia:CommonNoun; conll:WORD "Jahr"; conll:EN_GLOSS "year"; conll:LEMMA "Ja
:s4_5 a nif:Word, olia:Verb; conll:WORD "hielt"; conll:EN_GLOSS "adhere"; conll:LEMMA "halte
:s4_6 a nif:Word, olia:Pronoun; conll:WORD "ich"; conll:EN_GLOSS "I"; conll:LEMMA "ich"; con
:s4_7 a nif:Word, olia:Determiner; conll:WORD "ein"; conll:EN_GLOSS "an"; conll:LEMMA "ein";
:s4_8 a nif:Word, olia:Adjective; conll:WORD "duftendes"; conll:EN_GLOSS "sweet"; conll:LEMM
:s4_9 a nif:Word, olia:CommonNoun;
        conll:WORD "Wunder";
        conll:EN_GLOSS "wonder";
        conll:LEMMA "Wunder";
        conll:UPOS "NOUN";
        nif:next :s4_10 .
:s4_10 a nif:Word, olia:Adposition; conll:WORD "in"; conll:EN_GLOSS "into"; conll:LEMMA "in"
:s4_11 a nif:Word, olia:Determiner; conll:WORD "den"; conll:EN_GLOSS "the"; conll:LEMMA "der
:s4_12 a nif:Word, olia:CommonNoun; conll:WORD "Händen"; conll:EN_GLOSS "hand"; conll:LEMMA
:s4_13 a nif:Word, olia:Punctuation; conll:WORD "."; conll:LEMMA "."; conll:UPOS "PUNCT"; co
```

Fig. 4. Sample output with OLiA POS-concepts and glosses from DBnary

After parsing the format specific string patterns in the `FEAT` column this approach can also be used for linking to OLiA features. Figure 4 shows sample output of the pipeline with DBnary glosses and OLiA parts-of-speech. One sentence has been expanded to multiple lines for better readability.

Such an annotation interoperability pipeline is relevant beyond NLP: The *Lin|gu|is|tik* portal recently extended the thesaurus-based indexing of linguistic literature to annotations of LLOD-native annotated corpora and other language resources [4]. CoNLL-RDF now allows extending the indexing to CoNLL corpora provided by the Universal Dependency community.

3.4 Generating TSV Output and Back-Transformation

With the flag `-conll`, followed by a list of column names (which are resolved to properties in the `conll:` namespaces), `CoNLLRDFFormatter` generates CoNLL output. This approach is particularly convenient to perform elementary operations such as dropping or switching columns in CoNLL annotations. Figure 5 shows the results of back-transformation. To generate problem-specific output, SPARQL update scripts may be applied to wrap this information in the corresponding `conll:` properties before exporting them via `-conll`. Alternatively, it is also possible to provide custom SPARQL SELECT queries after the flag `-sparqltsv` whose output will be formatted as TSV columns.

3.5 Preserving Low-Level Processability

One factor of the popularity of CoNLL formats has been that they can be very easily processed using regular expressions and built-in data structures. In fact, any stream of CoNLL data (without comments) can be transferred into a three-dimensional, ragged array by coupling three regular expressions to split sentences (`\n\n+`), words (`\n`) and columns (`\t`). This style of parsing requires less than 10 lines of code in any modern programming language and provides a data structure

```
# sent_id dev-s4/de
# ID    WORD     LEMMA    UPOS     POS FEAT     HEAD     EDGE     DEPS     MISC
1   Nach     nach     ADP APPR     _    4   case   _   _
2   einem    ein DET ART Case=Dat|Definite=Ind|Gender=Masc,Neut|Number=Sing|PronType=Art 4   det _   _
3   viertel Viertel NUM ADJA     NumType=Card     4    nummod   _   _
4   Jahr     Jahr     NOUN     NN   Case=Dat|Gender=Masc,Neut|Number=Sing    5    nmod    _   _
5   hielt    halten   VERB     VVFIN    Number=Sing|Person=1|VerbForm=Fin    0    root    _   _
6   ich ich PRON     PPER     Case=Nom|Number=Sing|Person=1|PronType=Prs   5    nsubj   _   _
7   ein ein DET ART Case=Acc|Definite=Ind|Gender=Masc,Neut|Number=Sing|PronType=Art 9   det _   _
8   duftendes   duftend ADJ ADJA    Case=Acc|Degree=Pos|Gender=Masc,Neut|Number=Sing    9   amod    _   _
9   Wunder   Wunder   NOUN     NN   Case=Acc|Gender=Masc,Neut|Number=Sing    5    dobj    _   _
10  in  in  ADP APPR     _    12   case   _   _
11  den der DET ART Case=Dat|Definite=Def|Number=Plur|PronType=Art  12  det _   _
12  Händen  Hand     NOUN     NN   Case=Dat|Number=Plur     5    nmod    _   _
13  .   .   PUNCT   $.   _    5    punct   _   _
```

Fig. 5. German UD corpus back-transformed from CoNLL-RDF

which can be effectively navigated.[8] With *canonically formatted* CoNLL-RDF, this advantage persists: sentence and word splitting remain identical; the different fields, however, should be parsed into a hash map (hashtable) rather than a plain array, using the following regular expression:

```
^([^\s]+)\s(.*\s)?([^\s]+)\s+([^;]+)(\s*;.*)?.$
   $1        $2      $3         $4      $5
 id (URI)          key/att    value
```

Handling annotations in a hashtable has the advantage of human-readable keys, and it also eliminates the threat of varying array dimensionality. Beyond this, however, CoNLL-RDF users can now benefit from other RDF technology, e.g., the availability of higher-level APIs, off-the-shelf data base solutions, and a standardized query language. In this way, canonically formatted CoNLL-RDF as produced by the `CoNLLRDFFormatter` provides a middle ground by providing both well-known low-level functionalities akin to that of CoNLL and higher-level technologies that come with using RDF standards.

4 Discussion and Related Research

The primary goal of CoNLL-RDF is to provide NLP-friendly and human readable text representations of CoNLL data that can be directly processed/combined with off-the-shelf Linked Data technology. CoNLL-RDF provides an RDF view on CoNLL corpora, yet it maintains the low-level processability of the original CoNLL. In this section we provide an overview over advantages and limitations in comparison to other RDF representations and processing options.

4.1 CoNLL/TSV Corpora in the Semantic Web

CoNLL-RDF is built on a minimal fragment of NIF to provide base datatypes, `nif:Word`, `nif:Sentence` and `nif:nextWord`, resp. `nif:nextSentence`. However, as mentioned above, we do not follow NIF URI formation principles nor its

[8] It should be noted that addressing elements in a ragged array requires great care, as it is not guaranteed that a given index exists for every sentence, e.g., in case of SRL annotations which differ in length per sentence. In this regard, hash maps are more permissive.

substring relations (e.g., `nif:referenceContext`, `nif:sentence` or `nif:word`). We deliberately omitted both characteristics (the actual core of NIF) because CoNLL words are not necessarily strings *in the original data*, but may also represent empty elements and exact character positions are not consistently represented in CoNLL. Such URIs, however, can be generated by SPARQL Update scripts if they de-tokenize, remove empty elements and recover the character offsets in the generated data. As evident from its name, NIF is, however, not focusing on the representation of corpora, but rather for use in NLP pipelines, its coverage of linguistic annotations is thus biased towards certain, frequent but less complex types of annotation. NIF is thus particularly well-suited for corpora with "simple" word-level, phrase-level and sentence-level annotations. It lacks support for representing annotation layers[9], non-branching syntactic nodes, empty elements (traces), labeled edges, conflicting tokenizations, semantic annotation, etc. It is well-suited for word-level NLP and entity linking.

The *Open Annotation (OA) Model* and the related *Web Annotation (WA)* specifications[10] were originally developed for expressing metadata about web content, but have occasionally been applied to represent bio-NLP annotations in text. OpenAnnotation relies on reification and uses a naming scheme which is intransparent from an NLP perspective. It is thus more verbose and less comprehensible than NIF. Given the verbose model and the (from a linguistic point of view) counterintuitive terminology (`hasTarget`, `hasBody`), it is doubtful whether it will be accepted widely in the NLP and language resource community. However, like NIF, also OA properties can be generated using SPARQL.

POWLA[11] is another vocabulary for modeling linguistically annotated corpora. Whereas NIF and OA have been grown in a bottom-up fashion and extended/adapted as needed, POWLA has been designed in a top-down perspective as a full-blown reconstruction of the ISO TC 37/SC4 LAF/GrAF model in RDF/OWL, specifically designed to facilitate corpus querying. Unlike NIF, POWLA can express arbitrarily complex annotations. Unlike OA, it is terminologically transparent. Similar to OA, it suffers from a certain degree of verbosity in comparison to NIF and has thus not widely applied yet.

All these ontological models have their own advantages and limitations but share one common feature: a complex interconnected structure and relatively rich semantics. In order to convert a generic CoNLL file to fit into one of these vocabularies considerable restructuring is required that must be specific for every individual CoNLL dialect. In comparison to these, CoNLL-RDF provides a low-level view on the data, highly generic and with shallow semantics isomorphic to that of the underlying CoNLL data, that may serve as an intermediate step towards generating NIF, OA or POWLA data, but that is already sufficient (and more comprehensible) for researchers accommodated with classical CoNLL.

---

[9] CoNLL-RDF provides a clear representation of annotation layers: CoNLL has been described as a 'hybrid standoff format' [11] in the sense that every column represents a self-contained annotation layer that refers to a common segmentation (tokens).

[10] http://www.openannotation.org/, https://www.w3.org/annotation/.

[11] http://purl.org/powla.

4.2 CoNLL-RDF and LOD Wrapping Frameworks

Several provider-side frameworks for the transformation and publication of tabular data in the Semantic Web exist. Among these, *RDB to RDF (R2RML)* and *RDB Direct Mapping (RDB-DM)*[12] are of particular importance. They do build, however, on relational databases rather than TSV data, and thus impose an additional level of complexity when it comes to the mere transformation and manipulation of tabular data.

Conceptually closer to CoNLL-RDF is *CSV2RDF*.[13] Partially grounded in RDB Direct Mapping, CSV2RDF formalizes the direct rendering of tabular data to RDF in a similar way as implemented here. A crucial difference, however, is that CSV2RDF regards tables as unstructured objects, meaning that it neither supports distinguishing individual sentences nor preserves the order of words. Another difference is that CoNLL data does not necessarily come as a fixed-width TSV table, but that SRL or discourse annotations lead to ragged arrays not supported by CSV2RDF.

4.3 CoNLL APIs

Another strand of related research is concerned with manipulating and visualizing CoNLL data. Unlike most of these tools (which are countless, but barely documented in the scientific literature), CoNLL-RDF is highly generic, it is applicable to *all* TSV formats ever used for a CoNLL Shared Task, as well as several other, related specifications, e.g., SketchEngine, Corpus Work Bench and TreeTagger. It focuses on processing one CoNLL file or stream at a time (no merging).

In comparison to popular APIs such as NLTK,[14] CoNLL-RDF is unique in that it introduces a very clear and transparent distinction between minimal core functionality (parsing, manipulation and formatting, implemented in JAVA) and advanced manipulations (e.g., interpreting annotations). Core functionality (parsing and formatting) already provides functionalities such as column dropping or reordering; more advanced manipulations, however, are *not* part of the core infrastructure but subject to an extensible and reusable repository of SPARQL UPDATE scripts and SELECT queries and thus portable across platforms, and highly reusable. In particular, SPARQL UPDATE operations can be stacked into modular pipelines – whose modules, however, can be re-used to apply to other data sources.

Thereby, it achieves a high degree of genericity that preserves its capabilities for low-level processing (as known from many APIs) but comes with native support by the rich infrastructure developed and maintained by the Semantic Web community.

---

[12] https://www.w3.org/TR/r2rml, https://www.w3.org/TR/rdb-direct-mapping.

[13] https://www.w3.org/TR/csv2rdf/.

[14] NLTK provides numerous corpus readers specialized for different CoNLL variants, cf. http://www.nltk.org/howto/corpus.html.

5 Summary and Outlook

We introduce CoNLL-RDF, comprising of the following components:

- an *extensible, shallow RDF vocabulary* grounded on existing LLOD specifications (NIF),
- its *canonical format* that facilitates low-level processability in a similar fashion as known from CoNLL,
- a *core infrastructure* for parsing, manipulating and formatting CoNLL-RDF,
- a library of *SPARQL Update scripts* to manipulate CoNLL-RDF, and
- *sample pipelines* illustrating their application to various use cases.

These are available under the Apache license 2.0 on our website.[15] In addition to this, we prepare the LLOD-edition of the Universal Dependency corpora [14, v.1.4, 47 languages, 12 mio tokens] using CoNLL-RDF.

For the moment, we anticipate four primary uses of CoNLL-RDF:

- off-the-shelf corpus infrastructure providing database, query language, APIs, web services, etc.,
- a new format to publish CoNLL-style corpora, still parseable with 10 lines of Python, but compliant with W3C standards and thus massively improved technical support,
- advanced manipulations of CoNLL data using the SPARQL modules,
- facilitated aggregation across distributed and local resources using resolvable URIs, federated search (`SERVICE`), and standardized access (`LOAD`).

Important for the practical application of CoNLL-RDF is to improve usability for researchers not too familiar with Semantic Web technologies. While developing SPARQL Update scripts will always require special expertise, their mere use, rearrangement and adaptation for NLP problems does not.

Even though it is very easy to employ existing SPARQL modules already with the command-line based approach taken here, identifying existing SPARQL modules is not a trivial task: With a growing number of SPARQL update scripts and endless possibilities to combine them, dependencies must be taken into account when developing stacked SPARQL pipelines. Fortunately, it is easy to automatically fetch their dependencies among data sources and SPARQL queries (by tracing URIs which are sought, deleted and/or inserted by a given SPARQL module), a convenient and user-oriented visualization of this information is, however, yet to be developed and a goal of active research.

Acknowledgments. The research of Christian Chiarcos was supported by the BMBF-funded Research Group 'Linked Open Dictionaries (LiODi)' (2015–2020). The research of Christian Fäth was conducted in the context of DFG-funded projects 'Virtuelle Fachbibliothek' (2015–2016) and 'Fachinformationsdienst Linguistik' (2017–2019).

[15] http://acoli.informatik.uni-frankfurt.de/resources.html.

References

1. Beckett, D., Berners-Lee, T., Prud'hommeaux, E., Carothers, G.: RDF 1.1 Turtle. (2014). https://www.w3.org/TR/turtle/
2. Brants, S., Hansen, S.: Developments in the TIGER annotation scheme and their realization in the corpus. In: LREC (2002)
3. Chiarcos, C., Sukhreva, M.: OLiA - Ontologies of Linguistic Annotation. Semant. Web J. **518**, 379–386 (2015)
4. Chiarcos, C., Fäth, C., Renner-Westermann, H., Abromeit, F., Dimitrova, V.: Lin|gu|is|tik: building the linguist's pathway to bibliographies, libraries, language resources and linked open data. In: Calzolari, N., Choukri, K., Declerck, T., Goggi, S., Grobelnik, M., Maegaard, B., Mariani, J., Mazo, H., Moreno, A., Odijk, J., Piperidis, S. (eds.) Proceedings of the Tenth International Conference on Language Resources and Evaluation (LREC 2016), European Language Resources Association (ELRA), Paris, France (May 2016)
5. Chiarcos, C., McCrae, J., Cimiano, P., Fellbaum, C.: Towards open data for linguistics: linguistic linked data. In: Oltramari, A., Vossen, P., Qin, L., Hovy, E. (eds.) New Trends of Research in Ontologies and Lexical Resources, pp. 7–25. Springer, Heidelberg (2013)
6. Chiarcos, C., Nordhoff, S., Hellmann, S.: Linked Data in Linguistics. Springer, Heidelberg (2012)
7. Cimiano, P., McCrae, J., Buitelaar, P.: Lexicon model for ontologies (2016). https://www.w3.org/2016/05/ontolex/
8. Das, S., Sundara, S., Cyganiak, R.: R2RML: RDB to RDF mapping language (2012). https://www.w3.org/TR/r2rml
9. Declerck, T., Buitelaar, P., Wunner, T., McCrae, J., Montiel-Ponsoda, E., de Cea, A.: Lemon: an ontology-lexicon model for the multilingual semantic web. In: W3C Workshop: The Multilingual Web - Where Are We? Madrid, Spain, October 2010
10. Hellmann, S., Lehmann, J., Auer, S., Brümmer, M.: Integrating NLP using linked data. In: Proceedings of 12th International Semantic Web Conference, 21–25 October 2013, Sydney, Australia (2013). http://persistence.uni-leipzig.org/nlp2rdf/
11. Ide, N., Chiarcos, C., Stede, M., Cassidy, S.: Designing annotation schemes: from model to representation. In: Ide, N., Pustejovsky, J. (eds.) Handbook of Linguistic Annotation: Text, Speech, and Language Technology. Springer, Dordrecht (2017, in press)
12. Johnson, M.: Computational linguistics. Where do we go from here? Invited talk at the 50th Annual Meeting of the Association of Computational Linguistics (ACL-IJCNLP 2012), Jeju, Korea (2012). http://web.science.mq.edu.au/mjohnson/papers/Johnson12next50.pdf. Accessed 13 July 2016
13. Lezius, W., Biesinger, H., Gerstenberger, C.: TigerXML quick reference guide (2002)
14. Nivre, J., Agić, Ž., Ahrenberg, L., et. al.: Universal dependencies 1.4 (2016). http://hdl.handle.net/11234/1-1827
15. Sanderson, R., Ciccarese, P., Van de Sompel, H.: Open annotation data model (2013). http://www.openannotation.org/spec/core
16. Sanderson, R., Ciccarese, P., Young, B.: Web annotation data model (2017). https://www.w3.org/TR/annotation-model
17. Sérasset, G.: DBnary: Wiktionary as a lemon-based multilingual lexical resource in RDF. Semant. Web J. 648 (2014). http://kaiko.getalp.org/about-dbnary/

LLODifying Linguistic Glosses

Christian Chiarcos(✉), Maxim Ionov, Monika Rind-Pawlowski, Christian Fäth, Jesse Wichers Schreur, and Irina Nevskaya

Goethe-Universität Frankfurt am Main, Frankfurt, Germany
{chiarcos,ionov,faeth,nevskaya}@em.uni-frankfurt.de,
{Rind-Pawlowski,Wichers-Schreur}@lingua.uni-frankfurt.de
http://www.acoli.informatik.uni-frankfurt.de/liodi/

Abstract. Interlinear glossed text (IGT) is a notation used in various fields of linguistics to provide readers with a way to understand the linguistic phenomena. We describe the representation of IGT data in RDF, the conversion from two popular tools, and their automated linking with resources from the Linguistic Linked Open Data (LLOD) cloud. We argue that such an LLOD edition of IGT data facilitates their reusability, their infrastructural support and their integration with external data sources.

Our converters are available under an open source license, two data sets will be published along with the final version of this paper. To our best knowledge, this is the first attempt to publish IGT data sets as Linguistic Linked Open Data we are aware of.

Keywords: Linguistic Linked Open Data (LLOD) · Interlinear Glossed Text (IGT) · Empirical linguistics · Data modeling

1 Background

Interlinear glossed text (IGT) is a notation frequently used in linguistics to provide readers with a way to understand the linguistic phenomena in languages they do not know. This notation provides a description for each morpheme of each word between the original text and translation, with one layer (line of text) for every level of description as in (1).

(1) bän söl-ir-ïm ora-nïn dil-n-dä ...
1sg say-aorist-1sg their-gen language-poss.3sg-loc ...
'I speak their language, ...' (Axiska corpus, cf. Sect. 2.2)

Here, we describe the publication of IGT data as a part of the Linguistic Linked Open Data (LLOD) cloud. Based on popular frameworks used for creating and exchanging IGT annotations, FLEx[1] and Toolbox,[2] and the structure of their

[1] http://fieldworks.sil.org/flex.
[2] http://www-01.sil.org/computing/toolbox.

J. Gracia et al. (Eds.): LDK 2017, LNAI 10318, pp. 89–103, 2017.
DOI: 10.1007/978-3-319-59888-8_7

respective formats, we propose a shallow RDF(S) data model and describe the conversion and linking of two representative data sets. The converters and data will be published under an open license with the final publication of this paper.

These data sets represent the first pieces of IGT data that will become available within the LLOD cloud. In order to do this, Toolbox and FLEx data are converted into an RDF representation *of their original data structures.* This shallow and direct conversion does not provide the rich semantics of more advanced vocabularies for language resources, but guarantees data structures that are transparent and familiar to their user community. The main contribution of this paper, however, are initial steps towards the development of an RDF vocabulary for IGT data. For this initial model, we follow strictly the structure of the original XML- and text-based formats of FLEx and Toolbox, in the longer perspective, these will represent the nucleus for developing an RDF-native data model that allows to generalize to other use cases in linguistics, as well.

Publishing interlinear glosses as LLOD facilitates their reusability and interoperability, demonstrated here for data from two representative tools. This can be partially achieved by the *linkability* inherent to the approach, i.e., the potential to integrate IGT data with external resources, e.g., to resolve abbreviations of grammatical categories against ontologies, or to link IGT data with existing dictionaries.

The research described in this paper is conducted as part of the BMBF-funded Research Group "Linked Open Dictionaries (LiODi)" (2015–2020) at the Goethe-Universität Frankfurt, Germany, and our activities focus on uses of Linked Data to facilitate the integration of data across different dictionaries, or between dictionaries and corpora. LiODi is a joint effort of the Applied Computational Linguistics (ACoLi) lab at the Institute of Computer Science and the Institute of Empirical Linguistics at Goethe University Frankfurt, Germany, with a focus on Turkic languages (pilot phase, 2015–2016), resp. languages of the Caucasus (main phase, 2017–2020) and selected contact languages.

One main type of data in the project are dictionaries [1], but IGT annotations are of particular relevance: The IGT tools addressed here (FLEx and Toolbox) provide a workflow that integrates dictionary (glossary) development with IGT annotation and grammar engineering: For a given expression, resp. its morphological segmentation, in a transcript, possible meanings are automatically looked up in an internal dictionary. If none can be found, the linguist manually assigns glosses, and these are then stored in the internal dictionary.

IGT data comes in different flavors, depending on the tools used for annotation (e.g., FLEx, Toolbox) or publication (e.g., Microsoft Word, LaTeX, PDF). One goal of our efforts is to provide them in an interoperable fashion, regardless of their original format. In the longer perspective, the RDF data and the vocabulary provided by us represent the basis to develop LLOD-native specifications that (a) generalize beyond these various source formats, and that (b) provide queriable and explicit links between IGT data, lexical and other linguistic resources. As argued in Sect. 6, popular RDF vocabularies currently applied to web annotation [2,3] or NLP pipelines for Semantic Web applications [4] are not directly appropriate to represent IGT data, so, instead, we build our efforts on established conventions in the scientific community that produces and uses this kind of data.

2 IGT Data

The *Leipzig Glossing Rules* [5] define a glossed example as a set of lines, each containing a representation or an analytic description of (a part of) the example. Every line has a particular type (or 'marker'), e.g.,

- The original orthography
- A morpheme-by-morpheme gloss
- A free translation into the description language

These are types of lines for (1), IGTs may, however, contain more information, for example, a phonetic transcription, etc.

An important aspect of IGTs is that lines tend to be positionally aligned: For example, word *dilndä* and its morpheme-by-morpheme gloss *language-poss.3sg-loc* refer to the same segment, more elaborate IGTs may also align morphemes with individual glosses, etc.

Considering morpheme-by-morpheme glosses, we cannot assume that there is a one-to-one correspondence between morpheme and grammatical value. In the Leipzig Rules, this is reflected by different separators, IGT tools such as Toolbox provide space-based subsegmentation and alignment.

Along with the segmentation issue, a second interoperability problem exists when it comes to the abbreviations (tags) used for glossing: Although there is a list of standard abbreviations for the grammatical categories in the rules, it is often extended or modified to reflect specifics of the language or theory adopted. In some cases even the definition of the grammatical categories varies across research teams and methodologies. This is often the case with the language description of less-studied languages. All these details increase variations between glosses produced by various researchers and thus decrease the reuse potential of collections of glossed texts drastically.

A third dimension of variation lies in differences of formats and tools used to produce and publish glosses in electronic form:

- Often, glosses are written with Office tools, primarily in word processing formats. The data produced this way is often disseminated as PDF, plagued by insufficient formalization, which practically leads to an inability to reuse this data.
- A second approach is glossing with tools originally developed for other annotation tasks, e.g., as ELAN or Exmaralda.[3]

[3] http://annotation.exmaralda.org/index.php?title=Advanced_Glossing.

- The third (and recommended) approach is to use tools developed specifically for creating and managing IGTs:Most widely known are Toolbox (formerly Shoebox)[4] and its successor FLEx;[5] both allow linguists to enter and store IGTs, perform analyses, and extract dictionaries.

As for data from the first group, [6] created an IGT mining service and provide their data in a structured XML form similar to the third group. As for the second group, these tools have wider application beyond IGTs (esp. multimedia annotation), and therefore their data structures are less transparent to the linguists that use them.

We thus focus on the third group: (1) We derive an initial RDF(S) vocabulary from the data structures of the XML-based export format of FLEx, illustrated for a small Megrelian corpus. (2) We demonstrate its applicability to Toolbox data from a corpus of Axiska (Meskhet).

2.1 Megrelian FLEx Data

Megrelian is a Kartvelian language spoken by approximately 500 000 people in Western Georgia. It is genealogically related to Georgian, the official language of the country.

The Megrelian data is a small FLEx corpus collected and processed by Jesse Wichers-Schreur in August 2016 during a short fieldwork stay in the village Orsantia. The data are translations from Georgian sentences, from three different speakers, recorded with a zoom recorder. The recorded files were transcribed in ELAN and exported into FLEx. The Megrelian corpus contains 5 889 tokens and 19 007 glossed morphemes but will be extended in subsequent fieldwork campaigns.

The goal of this effort is to document the specifics of the language contact situation Every speaker of Megrelian is bilingual and speaks Georgian from an early age onwards. Georgian is the language of bureaucracy, education and virtually all written communication. Hence, a lot of influence of this standard language on Megrelian is to be expected. However, this influence has not been studied yet, an automatically supported comparison with dictionaries of Georgian and historical contact languages may provide a quantitative basis for such an enterprise, and a LLOD edition of the Megrelian data together with its dictionary links will facilitate its subsequent reproducibility and transparency.

2.2 Axiska (Meskhet) Toolbox Data

The project "Interaction of Turkic Languages and Cultures in Post-Soviet Kazakhstan" (Irina Nevskaya and Claus Schönig; Volkswagen foundation, 2014–2017)) focused on the interaction of languages and cultures of 25 Turkic peoples in Kazakhstan. A nation-wide survey was carried out in Kazakhstan

[4] http://www-01.sil.org/computing/catalog/show_software.asp?id=79.

[5] http://fieldworks.sil.org/flex.

in order to collect information on self-identification, language use, the attitude towards education in the mother-tongue, the historic aspects of the settlement (such as deportation), interethnic relationships, the maintenance of the specific culture, and the role of religion. Speech samples of these Turkic languages were recorded and analyzed, focusing on oral literature and autobiographic narrations.

Axiska (Meskhet) is one of the Turkic languages in the scope of the project, spoken by a population that immigrated from Georgia in the 1940s. Their language contains a large number of loan words from an old layer, transmitted mainly via Persian and Georgian influence, as well as new layers of loan words in the 20th c., transmitted via Russian and Kazakh influence. The Axiska corpus contains 1,642 glossed sentences with 13,626 tokens and 21,104 glossed morphemes).

At the moment, the linguistic status of Axiska in relation to Azerbaijani and Turkish is debated, and it has been suggested that Axiska represents an intermediate state in a dialect continuum between both languages. Comparing this corpus data with dictionaries of Turkish, Turkish dialects, Osmanic Turkish, Azerbaijani and other varieties of Azeri may help to confirm this hypothesis. Using a Linked Data edition of the corpus glosses and morphemes can be directly linked with the lexical-semantic resources, thereby facilitating the scientific transparency and reproducibility of the comparison.

3 FLEx IGT ↦ RDF

Figure 1 shows selected glosses in the FLEx graphical user interface and Fig. 2 provides the corresponding fragment from the XML export for the word *koʒir* 'he saw'.

Info | Baseline | Gloss | Analyze | Tagging | Print View | Text Chart

1 Word	1	.	mužans			kingiǯin					išo ašo		koʒir			?ude	.
Morphemes	***		mu	žan	-s	ki-	no-	gi-	ǯin	-ə	išo	ašo	ko-	ʒir	-ə	?ude	
Lex. Gloss	***		what	time	DAT	AFF	PV	PV	look	S3SG	there	here	AFF	see	S3SG	house	

Free When he looked around, he saw the house.

Fig. 1. Megrelian IGT sample, FLEx print view

The FLEx distribution includes a (non-validating) XSD schema that illustrates the basic data structure of FLEx files, illustrated in Fig. 3. Although the schema is non-validating, we use it as a basis for FLEx concepts and properties. One characteristic is that the XML format clearly separates structures and annotations, the latter being kept in separate `item` elements whose `@type` carries the corresponding line type ('marker'). Another important characteristic (esp. in comparison to Toolbox) is that FLEx defines explicit datatypes for different types of segments and clarifies their nesting, we thus distinguish `paragraph`, `phrase`, `word` and `morph` – in Toolbox, such segmentation is implicitly expressed via spaces and indents.

```
<phrases>
  <phrase guid="6ddb5ab4-58b0-4a14-b0ba-de2a6ee50bd5" begin-time-offset="161450" e
    <item type="segnum" lang="en">1</item>
    <words>
      ...
      <word guid="d3fe4bf6-7150-4ab1-8346-dfae5a840930">
        <item type="txt" lang="xmf-Latn-GE-x-megrelia">koʒir</item>
        <morphemes>
          <morph type="prefix" guid="d7f713db-e8cf-11d3-9764-00c04f186933">
            <item type="txt" lang="xmf-Latn-GE-x-megrelia">ko-</item>
            <item type="gls" lang="en">AFF</item>
          </morph>
          <morph type="stem" guid="d7f713e8-e8cf-11d3-9764-00c04f186933">
            <item type="txt" lang="xmf-Latn-GE-x-megrelia">ʒir</item>
            <item type="gls" lang="en">see</item>
          </morph>
          <morph type="suffix" guid="d7f713dd-e8cf-11d3-9764-00c04f186933">
            <item type="txt" lang="xmf-Latn-GE-x-megrelia">-ə</item>
            <item type="gls" lang="en">S3SG</item>
          </morph>
        </morphemes>
      </word>
      ...
    </words>
    <item type="gls" lang="en">When he looked around, he saw the house.</item>
  </phrase>
</phrases>
```

Fig. 2. Megrelian IGT sample, FLEx XML export

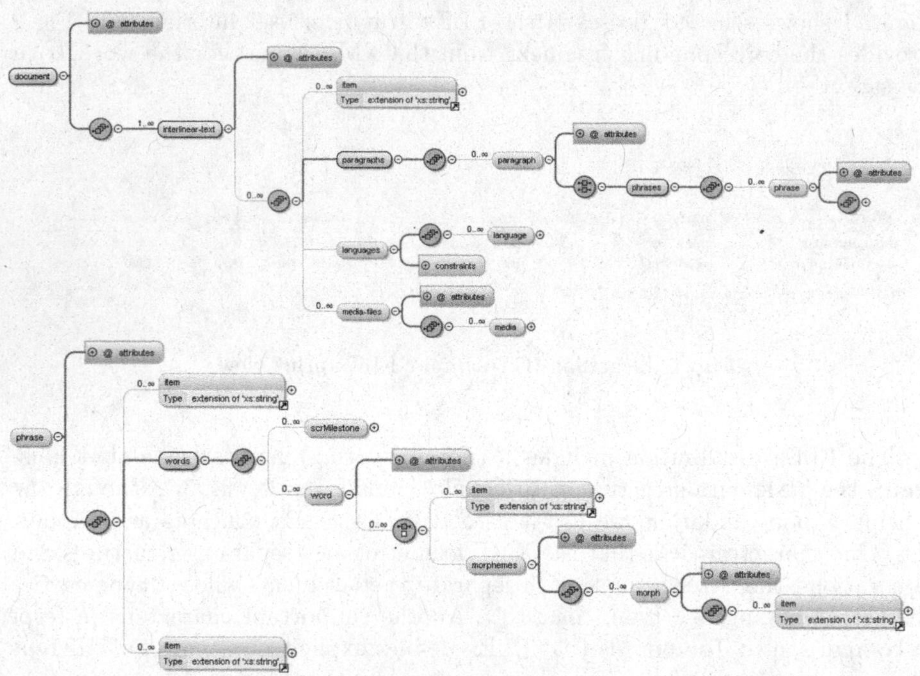

Fig. 3. Graphical visualization of the FLEx XSD schema (Oxygen)

The actual conversion is implemented with a simple XSLT script using the following procedure:

- Every XML element in FLEx IGT XML has an ID, we use this as the local name of the URI, the base URI is provided by the user at conversion time and should identify the original corpus. For FLEx concepts and properties, we use the FLEx IGT namespace http://fieldworks.sil.org/flex/interlinear/.
- Aggregators (`paragraphs`, `phrases`, `words`, `morphemes` aggregate multiple `paragraph`, `phrase`, `word`, `morph` elements, also cf. `languages` and `media-files` for `language` and `media`) and property wrappers (`item`) are omitted, their information is reorganized (see below). Language `constraints` are currently omitted.
- `media` and `language` with CDATA content *T* are captured as properties: *A* `flex:media`*T*, and *A* `flex:language` *T* for the closest non-omitted ancestor *A*.
- Every child *X* of an aggregator *X*`(eme)s` is connected with its following *X* sibling by the property `flex:next_`*X*.
- Every non-omitted element *X* is connected with its closest non-omitted ancestor by the property `flex:has_`*X*.
- If an aggregated element has a `@type` *X*, we define it as `rdf:type flex:`*X*.
- If an `item` has `@type` *X* and CDATA content *T*, we create a property *A* `flex:`*X* *T* for its parent *A*.
- If an `item` has CDATA content, we preserve the value of the attribute `@lang` content as the language type of the associated property.
- If an `item` has further attributes, the associated RDF property is reified and the item information attached to the `rdfs:Statement`.
- Every other attribute *a* is preserved as datatype property `flex:`*a* with its original value.

The result of the conversion process is illustrated in Fig. 4. Two aspects are to be noted: (1) This converter is generic in that it is not constrained to a fixed set of datatype properties (`item/@type`, line types, 'markers'). (2) We do *not* develop a novel data model for IGT – for which LLOD-native vocabularies are otherwise lacking –, but that we merely transpose the FLEx data model to the LLOD world by creating an isomorphic reconstruction of the FLEx data model in RDF(S). In both aspects, we do not provide explicit semantics, but rather mirror the structures in the original XML file as defined in the accompanying XSD schema. Such 'syntactically defined' semantics are, however, insufficient in terms of the Semantic Web. Nevertheless, the FLEx RDF data model represents a first, empirically grounded step to develop a full-fledged vocabulary for IGTs in the LLOD cloud.

Figure 5 illustrates the RDFS data model of the Megrelian corpus – with classes, their attributes (datatype properties) and object properties that can hold between them. Note that this schema is empirically deduced from the converted data, not pre-defined. It is expected to be exhaustive with respect to FLEx IGT concepts, but other corpora may introduce resource-specific properties not observed in our data.

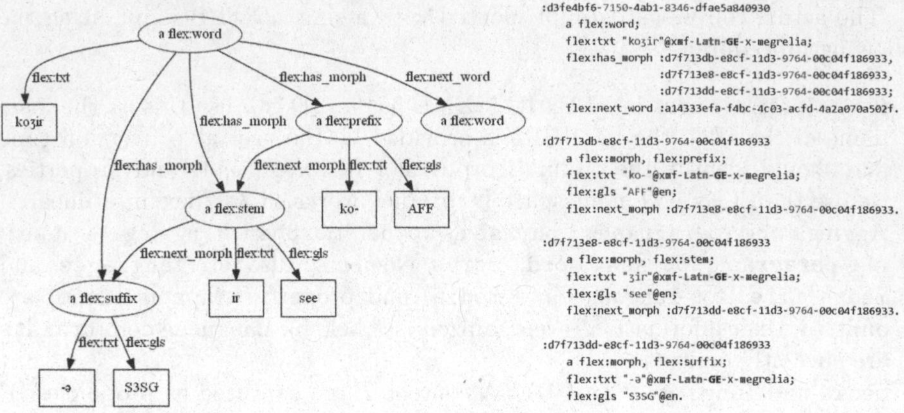

Fig. 4. Megrelian IGT sample, generated RDF graph

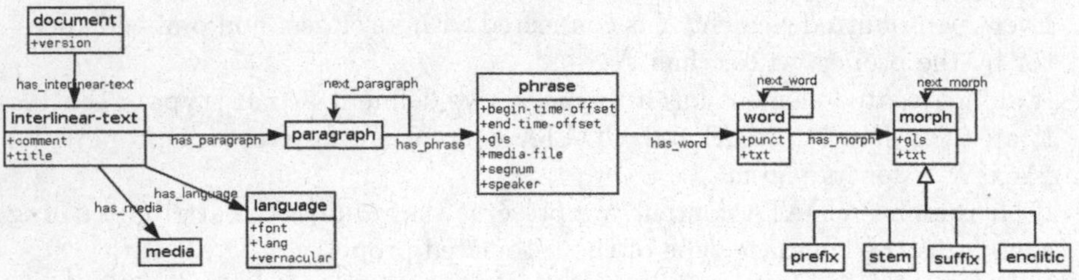

Fig. 5. RDF schema fragment for the Megrelian corpus

4 Toolbox IGT $\mapsto$ RDF

FLEx allows to import Toolbox IGT data, but differs from Toolbox in that it relies on predefined markers for different IGT lines. Importing from Toolbox, which is more flexible in this regard, thus requires a manual mapping from annotation-specific markers used in the original glosses and the FLEx identifiers. Such a mapping is, however, not always possible in a loss-less way, e.g., if problem-specific glossing layers are to be added that represent, for example, multiple orthographies (e.g., original non-Latin, transliterated into Latin alphabet, normalized/tonalized, internal scientific transcription, scientific transcription as required by a particular publisher). To preserve information which exceeds the capabilities of FLEx and to facilitate fully automated conversion of Toolbox data, we developed a second processing pipeline for converting Toolbox data directly (rather than via FLEx). We employ the FLEx data model, but as Toolbox is unrestricted in its markers, they (resp., the datatype properties generated from them) are kept apart in a separate `toolbox` namespace.

Internally, Toolbox uses a text-based format, with markers identifying different lines of IGT as well as metadata fields. Format and visualization in Toolbox is illustrated in Fig. 6. As a first glance, we recognize units of analysis that

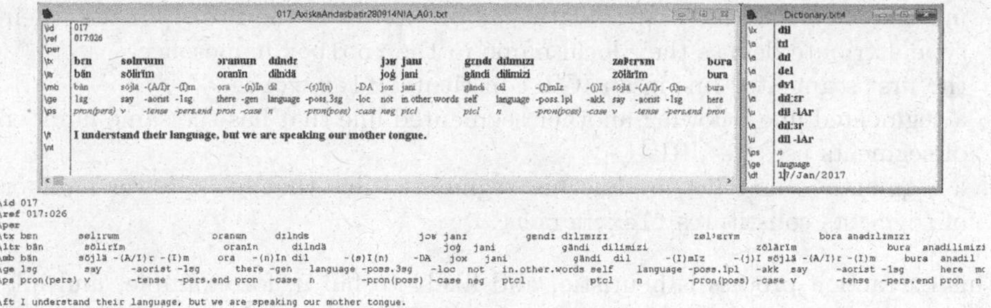

Fig. 6. Axiska sample data (Toolbox view and text format)

correspond to `flex:phrase` (i.e., one IGT, cf. `\ft`), `flex:word` ([multi-]columns containing orthographic words, cf. `\tx` and `\lt`), and `flex:morph` (columns aligned with the morphological segmentation, cf. `\mb`, `\ge` and `\ps`). A clear counterpart of `flex:paragraph` cannot be found, these are informally represented by IGT-like structures with special markers that occur *between* IGTs.

It should be noted that detecting layers and morph segmentation in Toolbox data can only be partially automatized, as it is not systematically formalized by the tool. Accordingly, our converter applies a number of heuristics, and extraction errors are possible. The flexibility of Toolbox poses three challenges, in particular:

(a) distinguish IGT markers (that constitute a IGT) and metadata markers (which apply to a document or parts of it),
(b) clarify which markers constitute a single IGT (empty lines may serve both as IGT separators but also occur within IGTs),
(c) capture alignment between different annotation layers (in Toolbox represented by 'exact' positioning using spaces)

As an approximative solution to (a) and (b), we provide the converter with an 'anchor' parameter that identifies the first and unique element in an IGT (normally, an identifier). Everything following it is considered part of the same IGT. All information preceding the first such 'anchor' marker is considered document metadata. Based on these conventions, paragraphs cannot be identified; in Toolbox data, we thus allow `flex:has_phrase` to hold directly between `flex:interlinear-glosses` and `flex:phrase`.

From Toolbox data, the alignment between word and morph segmentation can only be guessed,[6] as the 'exact' positioning using spaces is specific on the font. Using the number of space-separated segments per line, we apply the following heuristics:

- if a line contains multiple spaces, or if it precedes or follows another line with the same number of segments, it is a segmented line

[6] In fact, the FLEx importer also omits such data.

- unsegmented lines are cast as datatype properties of the `flex:phrase`, their type attribute defines their local name in the `toolbox` namespace
- the first segmented line in an IGT constitutes `flex:words`
- a segmented line following another segmented line that has the same number of segments uses its URIs
- a segmented line following another segmented line that has a lower number of segments constitutes `flex:morphs`

This extraction process is heuristic, and likely to fail if, for example, multiple whitespaces have been used in a comment. When extraction errors occur, it is recommended to check and to adjust the use of whitespaces in the original Toolbox data rather than to work the generated RDF data. In this way, the LLOD converter contributes to validating Toolbox data.

A subsequent problem pertains to the `flex:has_morph` property holding between `flex:words` and `flex:morphs`. As there is no principled way to align both layers automatically without enforcing additional constraints on markers, we formalize `toolbox:has_morph` as a direct relation between `flex:phrase` and `flex:morphs`. Subsequent, problem-specific processing, however, should replace this property with the regular `flex:has_morph` property. Technically, this can be implemented using SPARQL update scripts.

The revised FLEx data scheme as applied to the Axiska Toolbox data is shown in Fig. 7.[7] Despite minor systematic differences (different namespaces for datatype properties, omission of `flex:paragraph` in Toolbox, word-morph alignment in Toolbox), the basic data structures for both corpora resemble each other closely and will eventually lead to a common generalization: `toolbox:has_morph` and `flex:has_morph` refer to superstructures of morphemes, and are conceptually comparable (but not adequately represented by) `nif:subString`. The open set of Toolbox properties (markers), on the other hand, can be represented by means of property subsumption, with FLEx properties defining superproperties. In comparison to the mapping-based approach currently provided by the FLEx import (which may easily lead to data loss in the FLEx import if multiple Toolbox markers must be mapped to a single FLEx marker), this generalization is *lossless*—as neither the conversion from FLEx to Toolbox nor vice versa, thereby illustrating the added value of an RDF-based data model for IGT data in the current landscape of tools and infrastructures.

5 Resource Integration: Linking with Dictionaries

IGT annotation with FLEx or Toolbox is connected with maintenance of and reference to an internal dictionary. An important extension beyond FLEx is that an RDF edition of IGT data can also be easily integrate **externally provided** knowledge bases from the web of data. In particular, we may integrate further, externally provided dictionaries. Here, we employ DBnary [7] to facilitate the cross-linguistic interpretability of gloss labels. DBnary is an LLOD edition of

[7] The dotted lines are yet to be inferred from `toolbox:has_morph`.

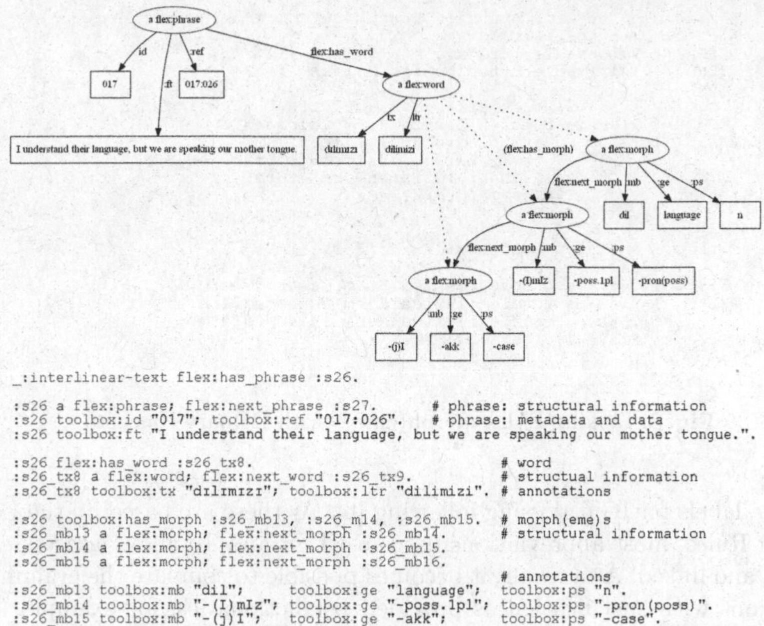


```
_:interlinear-text flex:has_phrase :s26.

:s26 a flex:phrase; flex:next_phrase :s27.      # phrase: structural information
:s26 toolbox:id "017"; toolbox:ref "017:026".   # phrase: metadata and data
:s26 toolbox:ft "I understand their language, but we are speaking our mother tongue.".

:s26 flex:has_word :s26_tx8.                              # word
:s26_tx8 a flex:word; flex:next_word :s26_tx9.            # structual information
:s26_tx8 toolbox:tx "dılımızı"; toolbox:ltr "dilimizi". # annotations

:s26 toolbox:has_morph :s26_mb13, :s26_m14, :s26_mb15.  # morph(eme)s
:s26_mb13 a flex:morph; flex:next_morph :s26_mb14.      # structural information
:s26_mb14 a flex:morph; flex:next_morph :s26_mb15.
:s26_mb15 a flex:morph; flex:next_morph :s26_mb16.
                                                         # annotations
:s26_mb13 toolbox:mb "dil";     toolbox:ge "language";  toolbox:ps "n".
:s26_mb14 toolbox:mb "-(I)mIz"; toolbox:ge "-poss.1pl"; toolbox:ps "-pron(poss)".
:s26_mb15 toolbox:mb "-(j)I";   toolbox:ge "-akk";      toolbox:ps "-case".
```

Fig. 7. RDF fragment for the Axiska IGT corpus

Wiktionary data for 16 languages, it provides definitions and – more importantly – translations. By linking the English gloss labels in our data that refer to lexical items with DBnary, we can thus easily lookup their translation in other languages. Glosses with different description languages can thus more easily compared with each other.

Figure 8 shows a SPARQL update script that links glossed FLEx concepts with the English DBnary via `ontolex:lexicalForm`.[8] While this update script requires a local copy of DBnary data, it should be noted that we can also access DBnary data *directly* via its SPARQL end point with the `SERVICE` keyword. In this way, it is also possible to provide external access to FLEx dictionaries (and corpus data), it will thus become possible to develop glosses and dictionaries in a distributed fashion, synchronized over shared dictionaries.

In the same way, we may also access other external resources. As an example, Ontologies for Linguistic Annotation [8, OLiA] represent a hub of annotation terminology in the LLOD cloud. Among other annotation schemes, they also

[8] As defined in the lemon/ontolex vocabulary, this implicitly casts **`flex:morphs`** as **`ontolex:Form`** (expected object of **`ontolex:lexicalForm`**). To satisfy the **`ontolex:Form`** definition, we may add **`flex:gls rdfs:subPropertyOf ontolex:representation`**. Note that the rendering of a gloss as a lexical entry mirrors the way glosses are treated in FLEx and Toolbox: During annotation, a dictionary comprising all glossed forms is created. In many cases, this dictionary (and the accompanying grammar) represents the main outcome of IGT annotation.

```
# preprocessing for Axiska: "translate" toolbox:ge to flex:gls
# as used in the FLex/Axiska data
INSERT { ?glossedTerm flex:gls    ?gloss }
WHERE  { ?glossedTerm toolbox:ge ?gloss };

# generate ontolex:lexicalForm links with DBnary lexical entries
INSERT { ?lexeme ontolex:lexicalForm ?glossedTerm }
WHERE  { ?glossedTerm flex:gls    ?gloss.
          GRAPH <http://kaiko.getalp.org/dbnary/eng> {
            ?lexeme dbnary:writtenForm ?form.
            FILTER(str(?form)=?gloss)
      }};

# remove ambiguous ontolex:lexicalForm links
# define ?glossedTerm as an ontolex:LexicalForm
DELETE { ?lexeme ontolex:lexicalForm ?glossedTerm. }
WHERE  { ?lexeme ontolex:lexicalForm ?glossedTerm.
         ?other  ontolex:lexicalForm ?glossedTerm.
         FILTER(?other!=?lexeme)
};
```

Fig. 8. Linking FLEx morph(eme)s with DBnary concepts

formalize labels for IGT glossing following [9]. As these are based on the Leipzig Glossing Rules, most abbreviations used in FLEx and Toolbox datasets can be resolved and linked. As a result, it becomes possible to compare the grammatical annotations with specification as provided by dictionaries, for example. These may also help disambiguating lexical forms, e.g., verbs and deverbal nouns in English (cf. *help* or *play*) and thus improve dictionary linking.

6 Summary and Discussion

We described an approach of representing interlinear glosses in RDF, the conversion of FLEx and Toolbox data, and we proposed an extensible FLEx-based RDFS vocabulary for IGT data. The converters described here are available from https://github.com/acoli-repo/LLODifier under an Apache 2.0 license. The IGT datasets for Axiska and Megrelian will be published with the final publication of this paper will be accompanied with the publication, until then, their linking with LLOD resources is being improved. Despite a considerable previous efforts towards this direction (see below), this is the first attempt to publish IGT data sets as Linguistic Linked Open Data we are aware of.

Our approach is based on a direct transformation of the highly popular XML-based data model of FLEx. The RDFS vocabulary derived in this fashion is semantically shallow, but represents a suitable basis for developing more advanced specifications and the semantic enrichment of IGT data with LLOD resources. We expect several benefits of an LLOD representation of IGT data: explicit, declarative and transparent linking with external dictionaries and terminology bases, the existence of off-the-shelf technology for querying, storing and manipulating RDF data, and the of RDFS and ontologies to formalize a data model that provides a loss-less generalization over the output of Toolbox and FLEx.

Although FLEx and Toolbox are normally considered as equivalent, conversion between them is neither lossless nor fully automated: Converting Toolbox data to FLEx requires a mapping of an unrestricted inventory of markers to a restricted inventory of markers; converting FLEx to Toolbox requires transforming nested data structures (`flex:word` and `flex:morph`) to space-aligned segments as well as recovering a highly complex structure of dependencies and configuration files which is laborsome and manual task. The FLEx-based IGT data model developed here, however, can be used to develop an RDF-native infrastructure for querying and evaluating data from both (and other) sources. While this is already possible with off-the-shelf RDF technology, it requires considerable experience with SPARQL. In order to develop a solution appropriate for field linguists, a user-friendly interface is yet to be designed. A natural choice in this regard is to develop a graphical query editor akin to the FLEx concordancer. Its queries, however, are internally translated to SPARQL and run against an RDF triple store. Yet, this is just one direction for future development.

Another direction is to elaborate on the relationship between FLEx data types and lemon/ontolex. The research described in this paper is conducted in the context on a project on "Linked Open Dictionaries". Among other aspects, it features the prototype of a comparative-linguistic workbench that implements a transitive search across multiple lexical resources, e.g., Chalkan > Russian > English > other Turkic.[9] This transitive search exploits the fact that the dictionaries employed all make use of (different variants of) lemon. Transitive search thus boils down to transitive property paths and can be easily implemented. With IGT data adherent to a lemon/ontolex-based vocabulary, it can be seamlessly added into the existing infrastructure.

A third direction is the development of the FLEx RDF(S) data model towards an LLOD-native vocabulary for IGTs. Such an effort must be cautiously aware of existing vocabularies and harmonized with related efforts. Although the predominant paradigm when developing novel tools for IGT annotation seems to continue to be XML (as, for example, in Xigt,[10] the toolset and native format of the ODIN project [6]), the RDF edition of IGTs data has been discussed early on [10]. For example, [11] "suggest that a unified RDF representation is well-suited for the creation of materials for local communities due to rapidly developing trends in data dissemination technology" and discuss this with application to ELAN, FLEx and Toolbox. To our best knowledge, no implementation nor RDF data has been published as results of these efforts, but nevertheless, the future development of the FLEx RDF specifications need to be coordinated with this community. In different branches of linguistics, similar efforts have begun. This includes TYTO, [12] a collaborative infrastructure for linguistic data grounded in Semantic Web technologies. At the moment, TYTO exists as a fully functional prototype, and it is populated with data comparable to that considered here, but has not been publicly released (A. Schalley – pers. comm., May 2016). Another relevant community effort is the Cross-Linguistic Linked Data (CLLD) platform [13] that provides LLOD editions of resources such as WALS and Glottolog. IGT data is a nat-

[9] http://dbserver.acoli.cs.uni-frankfurt.de:5000/search/?query=&originLang=&targetLang=trk.

[10] https://github.com/xigt/xigt/wiki.

ural extension to these data sets and its treatment has been discussed as an open issue, but seems to converge to a JSON variant of Xigt.[11] To our best knowledge, a common data model for IGT data in RDF is thus not in sight. The FLEx-based vocabulary introduced here represents an initial effort towards its creation.

RDF-native corpus formalisms represent another strand of related research. It should be noted, though, that the most popular vocabularies applied to represent linguistic annotations were originally developed for other aspects of metadata and data exchange in the Web of Data, in particular, approaches focusing on representing the output of natural language processing (NLP) tools for Semantic Web applications, and approaches to formalize metadata ('annotations') about web content. The NLP Interchange Format (NIF) is an RDF/OWL-based format that aims to achieve interoperability between tools, language resources and annotations [14]. It provides a URI scheme that identifies (sub-)strings in a particular reference context, and it comprises basic data structures for linguistic annotations such as `nif:Word`, `nif:Phrase` and `nif:Sentence` – all of which are subclasses of `nif:String`. However, NIF does not provide data structures required for IGTs such as annotation units below word level (morphs) or empty elements (zero pronouns, null morphemes). These could be modeled as `nif:String`, but they do not come with a predefined adjacency property (such as `nif:nextSentence` for `nif:Sentences`). Open Annotation (OA)/Web Annotation (WA) [2,3] was originally developed to represent textual descriptions ('annotations') to web content. OA/WA formalize the representation of annotations as reified `Annotation` properties that point from a body (= annotation value) to a target (= annotated string), can have a type and carry other annotations. While this can be employed for linguistic annotations, the string- ('target') based approach seems difficult when representing overlapping annotations with different segmentation granularity (morph vs. word), but also for the annotation of zero elements, be it elliptical pronouns (on the word level) or null morphology (on the morph(eme) level). Modelling IGTs with either NIF or OA/WA thus requires considerable conceptual work, potentially requiring a revision of the existing core specifications.

Neither of these established formalisms is thus adequate to provide a host vocabulary to which FLEx data structures can be added. A lesson to be learnt from the relative success of NIF and OA/WA is, however, that community standards are more likely to be applied if they follow the needs of their user community closely. Both have been developed in a bottom-up perspective and extended when needed (for their original use case, but not for IGTs). The RDF reconstruction of FLEx serves exactly this purpose, and represents a nucleus from which community-specific formalisms to represent IGT and related corpus formalisms adequately and transparently as Linked Open Data.

[11] https://github.com/glottobank/cldf/issues/10.

References

1. Abromeit, F., Chiarcos, C., Fäth, C., Ionov, M.: Linking the Tower of Babel: modelling a massive set of etymological dictionaries as RDF. In: McCrae, J., Chiarcos, C., Montiel Ponsoda, E., Declerck, T., Osenova, P., Hellmann, S. (eds.) Proceedings of the 5th Workshop on Linked Data in Linguistics (LDL-2016): Managing, Building and Using Linked Language Resources, Portoroz, Slovenia, 11–19 May 2016
2. Sanderson, R., Ciccarese, P., Van de Sompel, H.: Open annotation data model. Technical report, W3C Community Draft, 08 February 2013
3. Sanderson, R., Ciccarese, P., Young, B.: Web annotation data model. Technical report, W3C Recommendation, 23 February 2017
4. Hellmann, S., Lehmann, J., Auer, S., Brümmer, M.: Integrating NLP using linked data. In: Proceedings of 12th International Semantic Web Conference, Sydney, Australia, 21–25 October 2013. http://persistence.uni-leipzig.org/nlp.2rdf/
5. Comrie, B., Haspelmath, M., Bickel, B.: The Leipzig glossing rules: conventions for interlinear morpheme-by-morpheme glosses (2008). https://www.eva.mpg.de/lingua/pdf/Glossing-Rules.pdf
6. Lewis, W.D.: ODIN: a model for adapting and enriching legacy infrastructure. In: Second International Conference on e-Science and Grid Technologies (e-Science 2006), 4–6 December 2006, p. 137. IEEE Computer Society, Amsterdam (2006)
7. Sérasset, G.: DBnary: wiktionary as a lemon-based multilingual lexical resource in RDF. Semantic Web J. **648** (2014). http://kaiko.getalp.org/about-dbnary/
8. Chiarcos, C., Sukhareva, M.: OLiA - Ontologies of Linguistic Annotation. Semantic Web J. **518**, 379–386 (2015)
9. Dipper, S., Götze, M., Skopeteas, S.: Information structure in cross-linguistic corpora: annotation guidelines for phonology, morphology, syntax, semantics, and information structure. In: Interdisciplinary Studies on Information Structure (ISIS), Working papers of the SFB 632 7 (2007)
10. Poornima, S., Good, J.: Modeling and encoding traditional wordlists for machine applications. In: Proceedings of the 2010 Workshop on NLP and Linguistics: Finding the Common Ground, Uppsala, Sweden. Association for Computational Linguistics, 1–9 July 2010
11. Nakhimovsky, A., Good, J., Myers, T.: Interoperability of language documentation tools and materials for local communities. In: Digital Humanities (DH 2012), Hamburg, July 2012. http://www.dh2012.uni-hamburg.de/conference/programme/abstracts/interoperability-of-language-documentation-tools-and-materials-for-local-communities.1.html
12. Schalley, A.C.: Tyto - a collaborative research tool for linked linguistic data. In: Chiarcos, C., Nordhoff, S., Hellmann, S. (eds.) Linked Data in Linguistics, pp. 139–149. Springer, Heidelberg (2012)
13. Forkel, R.: The cross-linguistic linked data project. In: 3rd Workshop on Linked Data in Linguistics: Multilingual Knowledge Resources and Natural Language Processing, Reykjavik, Iceland, pp. 60–66, May 2014
14. Hellmann, S., Lehmann, J., Auer, S., Brümmer, M.: Integrating NLP using linked data. In: Alani, H., et al. (eds.) ISWC 2013. LNCS, vol. 8219, pp. 98–113. Springer, Heidelberg (2013). doi:10.1007/978-3-642-41338-4_7

A Semantic Frame-Based Similarity Metric for Characterizing Technological Capabilities

Scott Appling(✉) and Erica Briscoe

Georgia Institute of Technology, Atlanta, GA 30332, USA
{scott.appling,erica.briscoe}@gtri.gatech.edu
http://www.socialai.gatech.edu

Abstract. In this work we are motivated by the problem of representing technological *capabilities* that are present in text. We propose to use frames to capture the semantics around technologies and describe a new method, called FrameSim, that serves as a means of determining the similarity between these capabilities. We intentionally focus on a corpus built from informal media (e.g., news articles), which provides greater variability and an increased amount of suppositions about technologies' uses, deriving value from 'passive crowdsourcing'. Our evaluation shows that this semantic frame-based similarity metric preserves technology topic coherence, and we discuss how this method shows promise for improving conceptual search in scientific and technical writing.

Keywords: Frame semantics · Information retrieval · Semantic search

1 Introduction

Mining scientific literature has many potential payoffs, such as detecting emerging technology, making temporal predictions, and discovery [25]. Efforts toward fostering innovation include purposely incorporating creativity into scientific development, thus *technology intelligence* (also known as technology-forecasting, -watching, -monitoring, and horizon-scanning) is a process by through which potential alternatives and development pathways may be automatically identified [15]. Text mining tools stand to greatly improve our ability to readily extract information, discover significant relationships between scientific concepts, and to provide insight into how technologies may be used beyond their intended use. The application of NLP can aid researchers to understand how advances in one field may promote or accelerate innovation in complimentary areas (e.g. [22]); however, the complex nature of technological progress, with its many exogenous factors, make characterizing technological innovation based on textual sources a difficult endeavor. To address this challenge, bibliometric methods are often employed to organize and analyze large amounts of historical data to identify indicators or patterns that consistently point to technological significant breakthroughs, as through the use of approaches such as cluster and co-citation analysis [28]. Likewise, the analysis of patents has been shown as valuable in discovering indicators of notable innovations [1] and emerging technologies [4]. Utilizing

J. Gracia et al. (Eds.): LDK 2017, LNAI 10318, pp. 104–112, 2017.
DOI: 10.1007/978-3-319-59888-8_8

these traditional sources of scientific text, however, may also be problematic, as there is often used domain specific terminology and great variance across domains [3].

In this work we concentrate on the difficult problem of automatically processing text so as to characterize the *capabilities* that particular technologies provide. The motivation for our analysis on technology-related text intended for a broad audience (e.g., news articles) is multi-fold. First, most scientific text derives from traditional technical sources, i.e., journal publications, conference proceedings, and patents. While technically detailed, these texts are often written with heavy use of jargon and with a structure that adheres to the scientific method (e.g., as outlined in the method, analysis, and results sections of a journal paper), usually with little attention paid to the far-reaching *implications* of the resulting technology (though discussion sections will include more speculative content as to applications beyond those investigated). Second, these texts are written at the time when the scientific work has just been completed, where the implications for the science may not be fully understandable until it has propagated to other fields and applications. Third, technologies evolve, not only through scientific progress, but as they come to face with human creativity. Whereas a particular technology may be developed for a particular use, owners of that technology may create novel uses, either by necessity or through creative endeavors (e.g., the use of medical radiology equipment to map earthworm burrows [7]). Passive crowd-sourcing, which is characterized through the utilization of open content that has not been specifically solicited (e.g., [6]), has also been shown promising in previous work on predicting technology futures [5]. Though our corpus is focused on media-derived articles, we believe our method could easily be applied to traditional scientific writing. Much work on innovation and scientific discovery often centers on finding applications and capabilities from disparate fields, using methods such as Literature-Based Discovery [13], which could greatly benefit from improved natural language processing techniques.

Here, we explore how frame semantics can be effectively used for semantic search focused on identifying the capabilities of a particular technology or scientific product. We describe a novel process to calculate the similarity between technological capabilities by utilizing a path-based similarity method based on the frame structure identified in FrameNet [2,9]. We discuss the integration of path-based approaches with a structural contextual similarity metric, SimRank. Then we describe our evaluation using an annotated corpus containing technology capability statements and close with a discussion on the value of this and similar approaches for improving automated methods for technical intelligence.

2 Frame Semantics

Frame semantic approaches link lexical representations to conceptual schemas called 'frames' [8]. FrameNet, a frame semantic resource for English [2], is a manually constructed database based on Frame Semantics. A frame is evoked by a lexical unit (word) in a specific syntactic construction. For a construction, the frame uses the arguments of the sentence to fill frame-specific semantic roles called frame elements (FEs), which serve as binary role relations that relate a word or phrase to its role in a conceptual schema. For example, the phrase "it converts brain scans into music" would be parsed into the 'cause_change' frame with two FEs: 'agent' (that which causes the change) and the 'entity' (that which the agent causes to change).

2.1 Integrated Frame Semantic and Contextual Similarity

Several semantic similarity methods have been developed, many proving useful in various areas such as disambiguation [21] and image retrieval [23]. These approaches often fall into two groups: edge counting-based (or path-based) and information theory-based (or corpus-based) [14]. For the edge counting group, [20] showed that the minimum number of edges separating two concepts is a metric for measuring the conceptual distance between them using a tree-structured taxonomy.

Our approach falls in line with the edge-counting methodology, where we combine the taxonomic information available through FrameNet [9] with structure-based contextual information afforded by the evaluation of the usage of frames when describing particular technological capabilities. We model our path-based method on that of Wu and Palmer [29], using FrameNet instead of Wordnet [17]. For contextual information, we utilize the SimRank bipartite graph algorithm [11], which determines the similarity between two objects (documents, or in our study, statements) by considering recursively the similarity of neighbors, that is, by measuring the similarity of the structural context in which the frames occur, based on their relationships with other frames.

We discuss our method below, that we call FrameSim, which incorporates both frame semantic and contextual similarity information in producing similarity scores for pieces of text.

3 Calculating Frame Semantic Similarity

In the original SimRank formulation, the similarity matrix is initialized with an identity matrix. For FrameSim, we pre-compute frame-frame similarity scores to initialize the matrix with the method described below, using FrameNet as our taxonomy.

We utilize Wu and Palmer's metric which "takes the position of concepts c_1 and c_2 in the taxonomy relatively to the position of the most specific common concept $lcs(c_1, c_2)$ into account, though we could use other path-based similarity metrics as well. It assumes that the similarity between two concepts is the function of path length and depth in path-based measures" [16]. Let $lcs(c_1, c_2)$ refer to the lowest common subsumer of c_1 & c_2 and $depth(c_1, c_2)$ refer to the length of the path to concept c from the global root entity (with $depth(root) = 1$); and $len(c_1, c_2)$ refer to the length of the shortest path from concept c_1 to concept c_2 in the taxonomy.

The Wu and Palmer metric is defined as follows:

$$w(c_1, c_2) = \frac{2 * depth(lcs(c_1, c_2))}{len(c_1, c_2) + 2 * depth(lcs(c_1, c_2))} \tag{1}$$

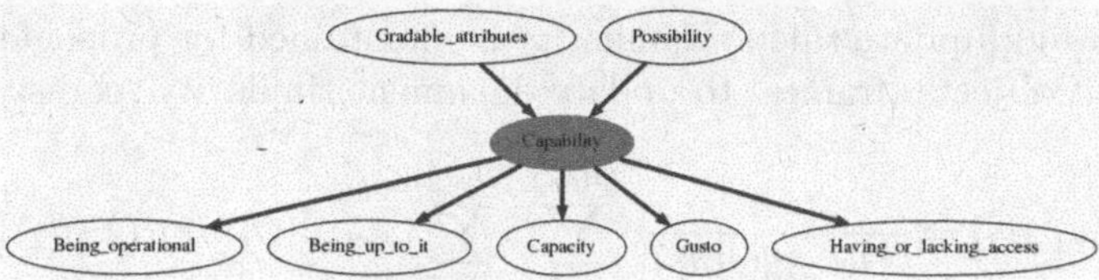

Fig. 1. Example: capability frame from FrameNet hierarchy using FrameGrapher.

In the case of Fig. 1[1] the value of $w(\text{'}BeingOperational\text{'}, \text{'}Capacity\text{'})$ would be 0.50.

For structure-based contextual similarity, we build off of the SimRank [11] approach[2], which computes a similarity matrix which represents the bipartite graph of the relationship between statements and frames, where x_{ij} is the similarity of statement/frame i with statement/frame j. The algorithm runs iteratively, propagating similarity information about frame similarity to update their statement-statement similarity scores.

Using the frame-frame similarity values calculated from the path-based similarity metric w previously discussed, we modify the identity matrix where $w(f_1, f_2)$ refers to the semantic similarity score between frames f_1 and f_2. During initialization, we only set off-diagonal semantic similarity scores for frame-frame items and not for statement-frame items, as there is no representation for document-frame similarity (Fig. 2).

$$\begin{bmatrix} 1\,0 \ldots\ldots & 0 \\ 0\,1\;\,0 & \ldots\;0 \\ \vdots\;\vdots\;\;\vdots & \ddots\;\vdots \\ 0\,0\;\,0 & \ldots\;1 \end{bmatrix} \begin{bmatrix} 1 & w(f_1,f_2) & w(f_1,f_3) & \ldots & w(f_1,f_n) \\ w(f_2,f_1) & 1 & w(f_2,f_3) & \ldots & w(f_2,f_n) \\ \vdots & \vdots & \vdots & \ddots & \vdots \\ w(f_n,f_1) & w(f_n,f_2) & w(f_n,f_3) & \ldots & 1 \end{bmatrix}$$

Fig. 2. The matrix on the left is the identity matrix originally used by SimRank and the right is the modified identity matrix to include FrameNet-based semantic similarity scores via a path-based metric.

[1] FrameGrapher is available at: https://framenet.icsi.berkeley.edu/fndrupal/FrameGrapher.

[2] While the description of SimRank refers to documents and objects, here we utilize statements and frames.

In this case, two modifications to the original SimRank are made:

- Modify the update rules to only push updates from the frames to the statement scores
- Compute the off-diagonal elements of the initial similarity matrix using the Wu and Palmer path-based similarity metric outlined in [29]

The following update rule for similarity is maintained for propagating information about objects (frames) to update document similarity scores:

$$s_1(d_1, d_2) = \frac{C_1}{|O(d_1)||O(d_2)|} \sum_{i=1}^{|O(d_1)|} \sum_{j=1}^{|O(d_2)|} s_{prev}(O_i(d_1), O_j(d_2)) \tag{2}$$

s_{prev} refers to the prior sim scores set using the initial matrix.

where s_1 is aggregate similarity of the out-neighbors (frames that documents point to), and $O(v)$ are the set out-neighbors.

Here, C is a constant between 0 and 1 that represents a'confidence level' meant to capture the reduced similarity between non identical items (following previous work, we set $C_1 = C_2 = 0.8$).

After convergence criteria is met, the resulting matrix then contains the pairwise similarity between each statement.

4 Corpus

While scientific publications and patent databases are fruitful sources of technology-related information, concentrating solely on these sources fails to take advantage of the human ability to integrate across sources and then consider the technology in combination with human creativity and likely contextual usage. An example target source is a 'tech trends' article that makes conclusions about the intended usage of a particular technology (e.g., "smartphones are overtaking traditional cameras for photography" [19]). Mass media science-related articles often summarize fields of work and, because they are intended for a less scientifically-oriented audience, frequently make summary statements that comprehensively point to the development or an effect of the science or technology being discussed. As such, this open-source text provides a rich source of analysis about the various ways that a technology may be used.

The corpus we developed to evaluate our model was derived from technology-focused articles downloaded from the website LiveScience. Using a web-based annotation framework, each of 1000 articles was annotated by evaluators to label the following elements:

- Technology topic: The technology under discussion in the text
- Capability statement(s): The phrases in the text that described any capabilities provided by that technology
- Maturity: The phrases in the text that described the maturity of the technology[3]

[3] This element is used in a study not discussed as part of this work, but included for completeness.

For example, given the phrase "Skype could be used to send orders to robots on the other side of the planet", the annotator would choose "Skype" as the technology topic and "could be used to send orders to robots" as the capability statement. Due to the complexity of normalizing capability phrases, two scientists familiar with the task went through and looked at the capability phrases that were annotated and deemed the agreement to be acceptable.

5 Evaluation

As a first step, we were interested if the statements that the annotators chose as expressing capabilities were aligned with a particular set of frames in FrameNet. Figure 3 depicts a histogram of the 10 most highly selected frames (as determined by using Semafor on the selected text).

We are interested if the labeled frames can be used to discriminate between technological capabilities. From our corpus, we selected 24 (annotator identified) capability statements about the three most frequently occurring technology topics: robots, displays, and batteries (also specified by annotators). We then calculated the SimFrame score between each statement and every other statement using the previously described method. A series of t-tests was then conducted to compare similarity scores among each of the three topics to every other topic. There were significant differences in the scores between within-topic similarity compared to cross-topic similarities: Battery (M = .1250, SD = .3333) to Display (M = .0149, SD = .0886), p = .042; Battery (M = .1250, SD = .3333) to Robotics (M = .0099, SD = .007), $p < .0005$; Display (M = .0149, SD = .0886) to Robotics (M = .0099, SD = .007), p = .001.

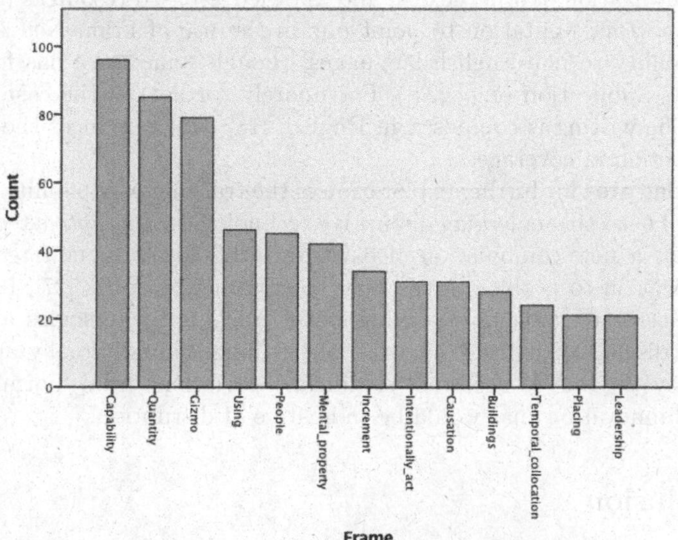

Fig. 3. Histogram of most common frames associated with the annotated technology capability statements in technology-related articles.

6 Discussion

The results from our evaluation showed that the use of a frame similarity metric effectively discriminates between disparate technologies. By concentrating on capabilities, we effectively limit the number of frames in consideration for similarity, which overcomes previously identified problems sparsity cause by frame variation (e.g., see [12] for another approach to overcome this problem.)

To fully leverage semantic capability similarity, we would want to wholly automate the capability detection and characterization process, so as to create a *capability search* function, wherein a user could specify "return all articles about technologies that provide adhesion". This would be valuable for providing the ability for conceptual search, especially in scientific domains where language between fields may exhibit a high level of variance. Here, it would benefit to utilize previous work centered on the summerization of scientific articles to identify the key concepts, such as through Argumentative Zoning, which classifies portions of text into categories (such as Aims, Background, etc.) [26]. These methods would be exceptionally useful to provide a high level direction to where the relevant parts of text about the particular technology under study may be found.

Though our results are promising, limitations of this study should be considered and addressed in future work. The current level of information that is used during similarity calculations is at the level of the frame when semantic frame comparisons are performed however these do not currently include the frame elements and the rich information contained within them. The current applicability of this method is affected by FrameNet's limited coverage and non-standard semantics. We intend future work focused on incorporating methods to increase utilization of other lexical and knowledge-based resources (e.g., [10]). Another important limitation to point out in the use of FrameNet is the limited applicability to non-English languages, though some work has focused on extending its application (e.g., [24]). Fortunately (or not, as the case may be), most scientific writing is composed in English [18], which reduces the potential impact reduction in coverage.

An exciting area for further exploration is the tracking of capability evolution as a means of detecting emerging disruptive technologies. *Disruptive* technologies can be either a new combination of existing technologies or new technologies whose application to problem areas may spur paradigm shifts [27], by altering usual product or technology capabilities. By tracking technologies along with how people discuss their uses (in text), either longitudinally or by application area, we may be able to ascertain significant deviations from 'normal use' or incremental innovation that would be indicative of disruption.

7 Conclusion

In this work, we proposed to use frames to capture the semantics around technologies that are discussed in text, concentrating specifically on the capabilities that they may afford. We propose FrameSim as a means of capturing both the structural and path-based similarity within text. Evaluation shows promise that this frame representation method may be combined with other text characterization methods to provide new capabilities for characterizing and searching scientific text.

Acknowledgement. This work was graciously funded by DTRA grant 1-15-1-0019.

References

1. Abraham, B.P., Moitra, S.D.: Innovation assessment through patent analysis. Technovation **21**(4), 245–252 (2001)
2. Baker, C.F., Fillmore, C.J., Lowe, J.B.: The Berkeley framenet project. In: Proceedings of the 36th Annual Meeting of the Association for Computational Linguistics and 17th International Conference on Computational Linguistics, ACL 1998, Association for Computational Linguistics, Stroudsburg, PA, USA, vol. 1, pp. 86–90 (1998). http://dx.doi.org/10.3115/980845.980860
3. Balla, M.I., Gandini, E., Nicolini, C.: Can bibliometric indicators assess science and technology? Cell Biochem. Biophys. **14**(1), 99–116 (1989)
4. Bengisu, M., Nekhili, R.: Forecasting emerging technologies with the aid of science and technology databases. Technol. Forecast. Soc. Chang. **73**(7), 835–844 (2006)
5. Briscoe, E.J., Appling, S., Schlosser, J.: Passive crowd sourcing for technology prediction. In: Agarwal, N., Xu, K., Osgood, N. (eds.) SBP 2015. LNCS, vol. 9021, pp. 264–269. Springer, Cham (2015). doi:10.1007/978-3-319-16268-3_28
6. Charalabidis, Y., Loukis, E.N., Androutsopoulou, A., Karkaletsis, V., Triantafillou, A.: Passive crowdsourcing in government using social media. Transform. Gov. People Process Policy **8**(2), 7–7 (2014)
7. Crumsey, J.M., Le Moine, J.M., Capowiez, Y., Goodsitt, M.M., Larson, S.C., Kling, G.W., Nadelhoffer, K.J.: Community-specific impacts of exotic earthworm invasions on soil carbon dynamics in a sandy temperate forest. Ecology **94**(12), 2827–2837 (2013)
8. Fillmore, C.J., Baker, C.F.: Frame semantics for text understanding. In: Proceedings of WordNet and Other Lexical Resources Workshop, NAACL (2001)
9. Fillmore, C.J., Baker, C.F., Sato, H.: The framenet database and software tools. In: LREC (2002)
10. Gangemi, A., Alam, M., Asprino, L., Presutti, V., Recupero, D.R.: Framester: a wide coverage linguistic linked data hub. In: Blomqvist, E., Ciancarini, P., Poggi, F., Vitali, F. (eds.) EKAW 2016. LNCS (LNAI), vol. 10024, pp. 239–254. Springer, Cham (2016). doi:10.1007/978-3-319-49004-5_16
11. Jeh, G., Widom, J.: Simrank: a measure of structural-context similarity. In: Proceedings of the Eighth ACM SIGKDD International Conference on Knowledge Discovery and Data Mining, pp. 538–543. ACM (2002)
12. Kim, H., Ren, X., Sun, Y., Wang, C., Han, J.: Semantic frame-based document representation for comparable corpora. In: 2013 IEEE 13th International Conference on Data Mining (ICDM), pp. 350–359. IEEE (2013)
13. Kostoff, R.N., Briggs, M.B., Solka, J.L., Rushenberg, R.L.: Literature-related discovery (LRD): methodology. Technol. Forecast. Soc. Chang. **75**(2), 186–202 (2008)
14. Li, Y., Bandar, Z.A., McLean, D.: An approach for measuring semantic similarity between words using multiple information sources. IEEE Trans. Knowl. Data Eng. **15**(4), 871–882 (2003)

15. Lichtenthaler, E.: Technological change and the technology intelligence process: a case study. J. Eng. Technol. Manag. **21**(4), 331–348 (2004)
16. Meng, L., Huang, R., Gu, J.: A review of semantic similarity measures in wordnet. Int. J. Hybrid Inf. Technol. **6**(1), 1–12 (2013)
17. Miller, G.A.: Wordnet: a lexical database for English. Commun. ACM **38**(11), 39–41 (1995)
18. Montgomery, S.L.: Does Science Need a Global Language?: English and the Future of Research. University of Chicago Press, Chicago (2013)
19. Poulter, S.: Do smartphones spell the end of the digital camera? Daily mail. http://www.dailymail.co.uk/sciencetech/article-2166220/Do-smartphones-spell-end-digital-camera-Sales-ordinary-device-plummet-30-years.html
20. Rada, R., Mili, H., Bicknell, E., Blettner, M.: Development and application of a metric on semantic nets. IEEE Trans. Syst. Man Cybern. **19**(1), 17–30 (1989)
21. Resnik, P.: Using information content to evaluate semantic similarity in a taxonomy. arXiv preprint cmp-lg/9511007 (1995)
22. Schultz, L., Joutz, F.: Methods for identifying emerging general purpose technologies: a case study of nanotechnologies. Scientometrics **85**(1), 155–170 (2010)
23. Smeulders, A.W., Worring, M., Santini, S., Gupta, A., Jain, R.: Content-based image retrieval at the end of the early years. IEEE Trans. Pattern Anal. Mach. Intell. **22**(12), 1349–1380 (2000)
24. Subirats, C., Petruck, M.: Surprise: Spanish framenet. In: Proceedings of CIL. vol. 17, p. 188 (2003)
25. Swanson, D., Smalheiser, N.: An interactive system for finding complementary literatures: a stimulus to scientific discovery. Artif. Intell. **91**(2), 183–203 (1997)
26. Teufel, S., Moens, M.: Summarizing scientific articles: experiments with relevance and rhetorical status. Comput. Linguist. **28**(4), 409–445 (2002)
27. Walsh, S.T., Linton, J.D.: Infrastructure for emergent industries based on discontinuous innovations. Eng. Manag. J. **12**(2), 23–32 (2000)
28. Watts, R.J., Porter, A.L., Newman, N.C.: Innovation forecasting using bibliometrics. Compet. Intell. Rev. **9**(4), 11–19 (1998)
29. Wu, Z., Palmer, M.: Verbs semantics and lexical selection. In: Proceedings of the 32nd Annual Meeting on Association for Computational Linguistics, ACL 1994, Association for Computational Linguistics, Stroudsburg, PA, USA, pp. 133–138 (1994). http://dx.doi.org/10.3115/981732.981751

Reassembling and Enriching the Life Stories in Printed Biographical Registers: Norssi High School Alumni on the Semantic Web

Eero Hyvönen[1,2(✉)], Petri Leskinen[1], Erkki Heino[1,2], Jouni Tuominen[1,2], and Laura Sirola[1]

[1] Semantic Computing Research Group (SeCo), Aalto University, Espoo, Finland
{eero.hyvonen,petri.leskinen,erkki.heino,jouni.tuominen, laura.sirola}@aalto.fi

[2] HELDIG – Helsinki Centre for Digital Humanities, University of Helsinki, Helsinki, Finland
http://seco.cs.aalto.fi
http://heldig.fi

Abstract. This paper presents the idea to enrich printed biographical person registers with linked data related to events that took place after the register was published. By transforming printed historical documents into structured data, semantic search to written texts can be provided for the reader. Even more importantly, life stories of historical persons can be extended based on data linking by extracting semantic structures from printed texts, and by combining this data with external datasets and data services. Such linking provides an enriched context for prosopographical research on people in the register, as well as an enhanced reading experience for anyone interested in reading the biographies. As a concrete case study, a register 1867–1992 of over 10 000 alumni of the prominent Finnish high school "Norssi" was transformed into RDF, was enriched by data linking, was published as a linked data service, and is provided to end users via a faceted search engine and browser for studying lives of historical persons and for prosopographical research.

1 Biographical Registers

Schools, professional guilds, scientific societies, and other person organizations regularly publish biographical registers of their members. Such registers provide a valuable source of information on personal data of groups of people. At the same time, social cohesion and self-esteem of people sharing e.g. common history, interests, or other aspects of life can be enhanced. To name a few examples in Finland, the government has regularly published the "State Calendar" (Suomen Valtiokalenteri)[1] of prominent Finnish officials, the historical Student Register (Ylioppilasmatrikkeli)[2] 1640–1852 of the University of Helsinki contains data

[1] https://www.valtiokalenteri.fi/.

[2] http://www.helsinki.fi/ylioppilasmatrikkeli/.

J. Gracia et al. (Eds.): LDK 2017, LNAI 10318, pp. 113–119, 2017.
DOI: 10.1007/978-3-319-59888-8_9

about 18 000 early academic persons in Finland, and there is a register of 73 100 engineers and architects in Finland[3], maintained by the labor union TEK since 1930's. Registers are usually created while the persons listed are still alive.

Such registers typically contain short biographical entries of people that belong to some group, with perhaps a photo attached. Traditionally, such registers have been published in print, making it difficult to keep the data up-to-date. When reading an old register, a recurring problem is to find out what happened to the persons after the register was published. For example, when reading one's old high school graduation register: what happened to the classmates afterwards?

This paper presents an overview of research underway, addressing the problem of transforming printed biographical registers into Linked Data, and enriching their contents using Named Entity Linking [2,3]. As a concrete case study, we consider the printed register "Norssit 1867–1992. Helsingin Norssin matrikkeli", a book of 708 pages, containing short bios of over 10 000 students and teachers of the prominent Finnish high school "Norssi", a training school of the University of Helsinki. This school celebrates its 150th anniversary in 2017, so this is a good moment to create an enriched look back at the history of its alumni.

2 Norssi Alumni on the Semantic Web

Extracting Structure from Text. The project started by digitizing the book at the Digitization Centre of the National Library of Finland. As a result, an OCR-version in XML of the book pages was obtained, including coordinates of detected images of persons. The data extracted was then transformed into RDF form, where each biographical entry was extracted from the OCR text. Also the photos of persons were extracted from the images of the book pages and linked with the bios. After this, a collection of regex rules and Python scripts were designed in order to (1) clean OCR errors in the data and to (2) extract various pieces of information from the short bios, such as the name of the person, birth place, hobbies, and relatives mentioned. An example of a short biograph in the book is depicted in Fig. 1. The extracted data was then uploaded into a SPARQL endpoint of the Linked Data Finland service[4] [5].

From a data linking viewpoint, the birthday and full name of the persons were known at this point, which could be used to enrich the data from several other datasets listed in Table 1. Links were created to Wikipedia, Wikidata, National Biography of Finland[5] and its Swedish complement BLF[6], BookSampo[7] Linked Data, CultureSampo[8] portal, WarSampo[9] portal, ULAN[10] authority register by

[3] https://fi.wikipedia.org/wiki/Tekniikan_akateemiset_ja_arkkitehdit_-matrikkeli.
[4] http://ldf.fi.
[5] http://www.kansallisbiografia.fi/english.
[6] http://www.sls.fi/sv/projekt/blf-biografiskt-lexikon-finland.
[7] http://www.kirjasampo.fi.
[8] http://www.kulttuurisampo.fi.
[9] http://sotasampo.fi/en/.
[10] http://www.getty.edu/research/tools/vocabularies/ulan/.

3216. Kuusi, Pekka Juhana. * Hki 9 VII 1917. Vh vakneuvos Aarne Juhana K ja Alli Maria Zidbäck. & I 40–55 Eeva Anneli Lumiala, II 55 FK Sirkka Saima Karolina Autio. Lapset Merja 42, Juha 44, Antti 46 †, Elina 48, Matti 57. – yo 35. – FK 45, VTT 56. – S Akat Raittiusliitto siht 45. Kansalaisryhti toiminnanj 45. Oy Alko Ab yleistark 46, apuljoht 49, jakelutoimen joht ja johtok jäs 52–71, johtok varapj ja pääJ varam 69–71, pääJ ja johtok pj 72–82. – Kansanedustaja 66–70, ulkoasvaliok pj 66–70. Sos- ja tervmin 71, pres valitsijam 68. HY sospol dos 62–82. Alkoholipolitiikan päätoim 49–72. Yhtyneet Kaivotalot Oy johtok vpj. Us komiteoiden pj ja jäs. Konventin pj 34. RUK 49 oppilask pj. Sosiaalipoliittinen yhd pj 63–69. SNS keskusjohtok jäs 67–84, Paasikivi-seuran varapj 70–84. S ja NL väl tiet-tekn yhttoimkomit pj 74–79. Väkijuomakysymyksen tutksäätiön rahavarainhoit. Oppikoulujen lausuntamest 34. valtion tiedonjulk palk 83. WSOY tunnustuspalk 83. – SVR K, SL K, VR 3, VR 4 tlk, VR 4, BKrR suurups. Ministeri 75. – Kapt. – Harr rationaalinen yhteiskuntapolitiikka. – † 25 V 1989. Isä 444, pojat 6242, 6444, 7691 veljet 2817, 3795, 3796.

Fig. 1. A short biographical entry in the register book Norssit 1867–1992

Table 1. Data sources linked to the Norssit register

Data source	Links	Description
Wikipedia	496	http://fi.wikipedia.org
Wikidata	501	http://www.wikidata.org
National Biography	136	National Biography of Finland
BLF	44	Biografiskt Lexikon för Finland
BookSampo	90	Finnish fiction literature on the Semantic Web service
CultureSampo	453	LOD from museums, archives, libraries, and media
WarSampo	353	Second World War LOD service and portal
ULAN	21	Union List of Artist Names Online
VIAF	135	Virtual International Authority Files
Geni	891	Family research and family tree data

The J. Paul Getty Trust, VIAF[11], and the genealogical data service Geni[12]. For entity linking to databases offering a SPARQL endpoint, the tool SPARQL ARPA[13] was used. In cases where the database provides a REST API, like Wikipedia or Geni.com, a special Python script was used. The script was used also in the case of BLF, where the data was available as a CSV formatted table.

[11] http://www.viaf.org.
[12] http://www.geni.com.
[13] http://seco.cs.aalto.fi/projects/dcert/.

For example, the RDF data corresponding to Fig. 1 is presented below (with long URIs and literal values shortened for brevity by using three periods):

```
@prefix schema: <http://schema.org/> .
@prefix registry: <http://ldf.fi/schema/person_registry/> .
@prefix dct:   <http://purl.org/dc/terms/> .
@prefix hobbies: <http://ldf.fi/hobbies> .
@prefix achievement: <http://ldf.fi/norssit/achievements/> .
@prefix bioc:  <http://ldf.fi/schema/bioc/> .
@prefix xsd:   <http://www.w3.org/2001/XMLSchema#> .
@prefix imagebank: <http://static.seco.cs.aalto.fi/norssit/images/profile/> .
@prefix skos:  <http://www.w3.org/2004/02/skos/core#> .
@prefix foaf:  <http://xmlns.com/foaf/0.1/> .
@prefix norssit: <http://ldf.fi/norssit/> .
norssit:norssi_3216  a              foaf:Person ;
        achievement:works          achievement:achievement_639 ;
        bioc:has_family_relation  [ a                  bioc:Brother ;
                                    bioc:inheres_in  norssit:norssi_3796 ] ;
        bioc:has_family_relation  [ a                  bioc:Son ;
                                    bioc:inheres_in  norssit:norssi_7691 ] ;
        bioc:has_family_relation  [ a                  bioc:Son ;
                                    bioc:inheres_in  norssit:norssi_6444 ] ;
        bioc:has_family_relation  [ a                  bioc:Son ;
                                    bioc:inheres_in  norssit:norssi_6242 ] ;
        bioc:has_family_relation  [ a                  bioc:Brother ;
                                    bioc:inheres_in  norssit:norssi_3795 ] ;
        bioc:has_family_relation  [ a                  bioc:Brother ;
                                    bioc:inheres_in  norssit:norssi_2817 ] ;
        bioc:has_family_relation  [ a                  bioc:Father ;
                                    bioc:inheres_in  norssit:norssi_444 ] ;
        norssit:genicom             <https://www.geni.com/people/...> ;
        norssit:kansallisbiografia  <http://www.kansallisbiografia...> ;
        norssit:kulsa               <http://www.seco.tkk.fi/...> ;
        norssit:kulttuurisampo      <http://www.kulttuurisampo.fi/...> ;
        norssit:wikidata            <https://www.wikidata.org/wiki/...> ;
        norssit:wikipedia           <https://fi.wikipedia.org/...> ;
        registry:birthPlace        "Helsinki"@fi ;
        registry:enrollmentYear    "1927"^^xsd:gYear ;
        registry:entryText         "3216. Kuusi, Pekka Juhana ... "@fi ;
        registry:matriculationYear "1935"^^xsd:gYear ;
        registry:pageImageURL       <http://static.seco.cs.aalto.fi/...> ;
        registry:pageNumber         271 ;
        dct:description            "Pekka Juhana Kuusi ...";
        schema:birthDate           "1917-07-09"^^xsd:date ;
        schema:birthPlace           <http://ldf.fi/places/Helsinki> ;
        schema:deathDate           "1989-05-25";
        schema:familyName          "Kuusi"@fi ;
        schema:gender               schema:Male ;
        schema:givenName           "Pekka Juhana"@fi ;
        schema:hobby                <http://ldf.fi/hobbies/...> ;
        schema:image                imagebank:3216.png .
```

Application Online. Based on the RDF data, a faceted search and browsing application[14] depicted in Fig. 2 was created using the SPARQL Faceter tool [6]. On the left, the first column contains the following facets: (1) Text search.

[14] http://www.norssit.fi/semweb.

Fig. 2. Faceted search for short biographies in the alumni register Norssit 1867–1992

(2) Links to the data sources listed in Table 1. (3) Family name. (4) Place of birth. (5) Year of enrollment. (6) Year of graduation. (7) Hobbies. Each box in the rows presents a person, containing the data related to the facets and the biograph. There are also links to the original text, the RDF data, and the book page of the register entry. By clicking on it, the page in the book from which the text comes from is shown. Especially interesting is the facet and column for links to other data sources. For example, by selecting WarSampo or Wikipedia, classmates with a history in the WarSampo Second Word War history portal or Wikipedia page can be filtered, and corresponding homepages on these external services be found. In this way, the reading experience of the end user can be extended substantially.

Prosopograhical Research. Furthermore, faceted search provides the end user with a means for filtering and studying subgroups of people in the register for prosopographical research, say persons having a Wikipedia page, born in the same area, having the same education or hobbies, etc. The upper bar of the application contains link buttons to two separate pages of visualizations that include, e.g., pie charts and histograms, based on Google charts. By making filtering selections on facets as in Fig. 2, the graphics are automatically updated accordingly. For example, a pie chart there depicts the distribution of the higher education degrees of the filtered alumni subgroup, a multi-bar histogram visualizes most common professions of the filtered persons as time goes by, and yet another graph shows the popularity of different universities and colleges chosen by the alumni after the high school.

3 Related Work and Discussion

Previous works of applying Linked Data technologies to biographical data include, e.g., [7], Biography.net[15] [8], and the Semantic National Biography of Finland [4]. The conference proceedings [1] includes several papers on bringing biographical data online, on analyzing biographies with computational methods, on group portraits and networks, and on visualizations. Complementing these works, the study of this paper focuses on extracting structure from printed biographical registers. Our work also emphasizes the idea of enriching the texts with external links to other biographical datasets, and on faceted search and browsing of biographical data for prosopographical studies. Our work continues, e.g., on developing new models of biographical data for prosopographical research, and on finalizing and evaluating the data linking process (precision and recall) and the demonstrator.

Our work is part of the Severi project[16], funded mainly by Tekes. Thanks to Vanhat Norssit for funding the digitization of the register and opening the data.

References

1. ter Braake, S., Fokkens, A., Sluijter, R., Declerck, T., Wandl-Vogt, E.: BD2015 Biographical Data in a Digital World 2015, CEUR Workshop Proceedings (2015). http://ceur-ws.org/Vol-1399/
2. Bunescu, R.C., Pasca, M.: Using Encyclopedic knowledge for named entity disambiguation. EACL **6**, 9–16 (2006)
3. Hachey, B., Radford, W., Nothman, J., Honnibal, M., Curran, J.R.: Evaluating entity linking with Wikipedia. Artif. Intell. **194**, 130–150 (2013)
4. Hyvönen, E., Alonen, M., Ikkala, E., Mäkelä, E.: Life stories as event-based linked data: case semantic national biography. In: Horridge, M., Rospocher, M., van Ossenbruggen, J. (eds.) Proceedings of ISWC 2014 Posters and Demonstrations Track, CEUR Workshop Proceedings, pp. 1–4 (2014). http://ceur-ws.org/Vol-1272/paper_5.pdf
5. Hyvönen, E., Tuominen, J., Alonen, M., Mäkelä, E.: Linked data Finland: a 7-star model and platform for publishing and re-using linked datasets. In: Presutti, V., Blomqvist, E., Troncy, R., Sack, H., Papadakis, I., Tordai, A. (eds.) ESWC 2014. LNCS, vol. 8798, pp. 226–230. Springer, Cham (2014). doi:10.1007/978-3-319-11955-7_24

[15] http://www.biographynet.nl.

[16] http://seco.cs.aalto.fi/projects/severi.

6. Koho, M., Heino, E., Hyvönen, E.: SPARQL Faceter–client-side faceted search based on SPARQL. In: Troncy, R., Verborgh, R., Nixon, L., Kurz, T., Schlegel, K., Sande, M.V. (eds.) Joint Proceedings of the 4th International Workshop on Linked Media and the 3rd Developers Hackshop, CEUR Workshop Proceedings (2016). http://ceur-ws.org/Vol-1615/semdevPaper5.pdf
7. Larson, R.: Bringing lives to light: biography in context. Final Project Report, University of Berkeley (2010). http://metadata.berkeley.edu/Biography_Final_Report.pdf
8. Ockeloen, N., Fokkens, A., ter Braake, S., Vossen, P., De Boer, V., Schreiber, G., Legêne, S.: BiographyNet: managing provenance at multiple levels and from different perspectives. In: Groth, P., van Erp, M., Kauppinen, T., Zhao, J., Keßler, C., Pouchard, L.C., Goble, C., Gil, Y., van Ossenbruggen, J. (eds.) Proceedings of the 3rd International Workshop on Linked Science, LISC 2013, pp. 59–71. CEUR Workshop Proceedings (2013). http://ceur-ws.org/Vol-1116/paper7.pdf

Named Entity Linking in a Complex Domain: Case Second World War History

Erkki Heino[1,2(✉)], Minna Tamper[1,2], Eetu Mäkelä[1,2], Petri Leskinen[1,2], Esko Ikkala[1,2], Jouni Tuominen[1,2], Mikko Koho[1,2], and Eero Hyvönen[1,2]

[1] Semantic Computing Research Group (SeCo), Aalto University, Espoo, Finland
{erkki.heino,minna.tamper,eetu.makela,petri.leskinen, esko.lkkala,jouni.tuominen,mikko.koho,eero.hyvonen}@aalto.fi

[2] HELDIG – Helsinki Centre for Digital Humanities, University of Helsinki, Helsinki, Finland
http://seco.cs.aalto.fi
http://heldig.fi

Abstract. This paper discusses the challenges of applying named entity linking in a rich, complex domain – specifically, the linking of (1) military units, (2) places and (3) people in the context of interlinked Second World War data. Multiple sub-scenarios are discussed in detail through concrete evaluations, analyzing the problems faced, and the solutions developed. A key contribution of this work is to highlight the heterogeneity of problems and approaches needed even inside a single domain, depending on both the source data as well as the target authority.

1 Introduction

This paper addresses entity linking [1,8] in a rich, complex, but focused environment. We extract links from textual data related to Second World War history against richly described linked data datasets on the places, people, events and army units mentioned therein. Here, problems arise due to the rapid and wide-ranging turbulence caused by the war. Structures of army units as well as the existence and roles of the people associated with them change rapidly, while geographical entities also change administrative jurisdiction. In addition, the people touched by war are a multitude from all ranks of society, causing further problems in for example disambiguation of homonymous people.

The primary contribution of this paper is in showing the individual deliberations and decisions taken to increase recall and precision in such a focused environment. On the other hand, while the individual tweaks are bound to the data, they do take place inside a pipeline that orients these considerations to a more general framework.

The context of this work is the WarSampo aggregated linked open dataset[1], which aims to provide richly interlinked data into the Second World War in Finland [11]. In total, the WarSampo dataset contains data of more than a dozen

[1] http://www.ldf.fi/dataset/warsa.

J. Gracia et al. (Eds.): LDK 2017, LNAI 10318, pp. 120–133, 2017.
DOI: 10.1007/978-3-319-59888-8_10

different types (e.g. casualty data, photographs, events, war diaries, and historical maps) from an even larger pool of sources (e.g. the National Archives, the Defense Forces, and scanned books). On top of the data, the WarSampo portal[2] serves multiple end user viewpoints. In the portal, persons, units, places, and events have homepages of their own, generated and linked to each other automatically based on the underlying Linked Open Data cloud. This rich interlinking allows one to e.g. move from the homepage of a war event to units and people participating in it, and to the photographs and articles depicting the persons, units, and places, or the event itself.

In order to create the links these functionalities are based on, different paths needed to be taken based on the type of source. This paper focuses on the datasets where the links to the actors, places and military units involved were described as free text, thus needing the application of Named Entity Linking (NEL) techniques [1,8]. These were as follows (examples translated from Finnish):

Events. Short descriptions of about 1000 events gathered from numerous sources such as timelines printed in books. Example: "Defense battles near Viipuri continued. Lieutenant general Öhquist gave colonel Kaila an order to occupy the main defense line of the 3rd Division at Patterimäki.", 1940-03-12

Photographs. Metadata, including captions, for a collection of some 160 000 wartime photographs from the Finnish Defense Forces. Example: "Field Marshal Mannerheim with his entourage at the headquarters of the 4th Division, negotiating with colonel Autti.", "Savujärvi" (place), 1943-06-22

Articles. Over 3300 articles from the Kansa Taisteli war remembrance magazine published by Sanoma Ltd. and the Sotamuisto association between 1957 and 1986 [21], each generally 2–5 pages of prose.

In the following, we will first present the reference datasets of places, people and military units against which these sources were linked. After that, the general pipeline used for linking will be shortly discussed, followed by detailed experiences and evaluations of linking each source against each type of data.

2 The WarSampo Reference Datasets

In creating a geospatial reference for WarSampo, the main source for trouble was the fact that at the end of the Second World War, Finland was forced to cede large areas of land to the Soviet Union. Fortunately, these changes happened only at the end of the war, so actual temporal reasoning over places [12] in this timeframe wasn't needed.

On the other hand, merely relying on a modern gazetteer wouldn't work. After the end of the war, the ceded areas have naturally not been included in any Finnish place registries, while in more general registries, they are referred to by their modern Russian names. Unrectified, this would cause major problems

[2] http://sotasampo.fi/en/.

to named entity linking of Finnish wartime material, as these areas, particularly the Karelia region, also happened to be the major arenas of action.

Thus, historical sources were used to create a snapshot of Finnish places covering the years 1939–44. Four sources were used: (1) the National Archives of Finland's map application data of 612 wartime municipalities,[3] (2) the Finnish Spatio-Temporal Ontology [12] describing Finnish municipalities in different times, (3) a dataset of Karelian map names (35 000 map names with coordinates and place types from the years 1922–44), and (4) the current Finnish Geographic Names Registry[4] (800 000 places) for places that had no reference source for the years 1939–44. In addition, some 450 historical map sheets from two atlases were rectified on modern maps, which makes it possible to examine the places on both modern and historical maps, without having to create explicit links between the place names and historical map sheets.

In contrast to the places, the actors participating in the war did change their status constantly. Thus, there was no way around a model that takes into account temporal changes. Accordingly, in WarSampo, the actor data model is an actor-event-model based on CIDOC CRM[5] [3]. According to CIDOC CRM, an event represents any change of status that divides the timeline into a period before and after the event, allowing for reconstructing the status of an actor at a certain moment by following these events through time.

Currently the actor data in WarSampo contains information on 99 000 people, collected semiautomatically from various sources: lists of generals and commanders, lists of recipients of honorary medals, the Finnish National Archives casualties database [14], the Finnish National Biography[6], Wikidata, and Wikipedia. Besides military personnel, 580 civil persons with political or cultural significance were included in WarSampo from the aforementioned sources due to their connections to other WarSampo data. The military unit data on the other hand consists of over 3000 Finnish army units, sourced mainly from War Diaries and Organization Cards.

Examples of events extracted from these sources into WarSampo are listed in Table 1. Following through such events, one can for example identify the rank and unit of a person at a particular date, as well as track their geographic position. However, due to gaps in the source data, exact dates are not available for all events. For example, a promotion event is created for all ranks mentioned in the sources, even if no specific date of attaining that rank is known.

For ease of use, all unit names as well as their abbreviations and nicknames are also repeated as alternate labels for the unit resources themselves. For people, their first and family names are given in separate properties, with known nicknames given as alternative labels.

---

[3] http://kronos.narc.fi/kartta/kartta.html.

[4] http://www.maanmittauslaitos.fi/en/digituotteet/geographic-names.

[5] http://cidoc-crm.org.

[6] http://www.kansallisbiografia.fi/english/.

Table 1. Event types and examples

Event type	Example
Unit formation	Troop founded as 24th Squadron (abbr. LLv 24)
Unit joining	Being part of flying regiment 2
Unit naming	Changing the name to 24th fighter Squadron (abbr. HLeLv 24)
Troop movement	Troop movement to Vesivehmaa and Selänpää
Unit dissolution	32nd Squadron was dissoluted in December 1944
Birth	Born at Pyhäjärvi, 1913
Person joining	Serving as commander in the 24th fighter Squadron, 1939
Promotion	Promotion to the rank of captain, 1941
Medal awarding	Awarded with the Mannerheim Cross of Liberty, 1942
Wounding	Simo Häyhä was wounded by an enemy sniper, 6th of March 1940
Disappearing	Disappearing of Onni Aaltonen at Äyräpää
Death	Died at Tampere, 2002
Battle	Aerial victory in Tainionkoski: enemy SB-2 shot down, 1939

3 Modular Architecture for Named Entity Linking

Named entity linking (NEL) [1,8] is the task of determining the identity of named entities mentioned in a text, by linking found named entity mentions to strongly identified entries in a structured knowledge base. In general, NEL consists of *named entity recognition (NER)*, followed by *named entity disambiguation (NED)* [8,16]. NER [6,19] recognizes the occurrence or mention of a named entity (e.g., names of persons, organizations, locations) in text, and NED [1,2,22] identifies which specific entity it is. A further refinement to this formulation is suggested by Hachey et al. [8], which divides NEL into *extraction*, *searching* and *disambiguation* steps.

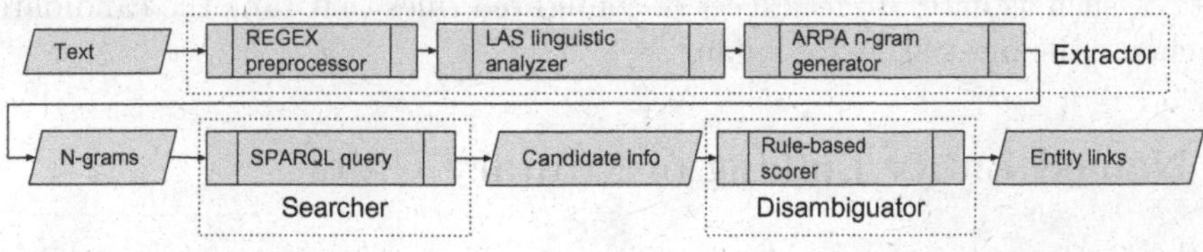

Fig. 1. The named entity linking architecture used

The system used for NEL linking in this paper is based on the ARPA modular configurable annotation architecture[7] [17], and can also be described using the framework presented above, as shown in Fig. 1.

[7] https://github.com/jiemakel/arpa/.

Here, the *extractor component* of the system further divides into a preprocessor, a linguistic analyzer and an n-gram generator. Of these, the preprocessor applies transformations based on a configurable battery of regular expressions in an attempt to regularize textual mentions. For example, unit and military rank abbreviations are standardized, and lists of people normalized to common form. In the case of the Kansa Taisteli magazines, this phase is also responsible for correcting recurring OCR errors found in the automatically extracted text.

As Finnish is a highly inflected language, where e.g. the noun for shop, "kauppa", can appear in a total of 2,253 different forms[8], candidate extraction heavily relies on linguistic analysis [15], whereby each word is annotated with morphological information, including the base or inflected form by which it appears in the reference datasets [18]. As the final part of this candidate extraction phase, the n-gram generator makes use of the linguistic information produced to craft n-grams [17]. Here, rules are used for example to filter candidates by part of speech, and inflectional information is applied to correctly format n-grams comprised of multiple parts or compound words (e.g. in Finnish the base form of "Helsingin varuskunnassa" ["in the garrison of Helsinki"] is "Helsingin varuskunta", where only the latter word is baseformed, and not "Helsinki varuskunta").

After candidate extraction, the *search component* is responsible for searching the reference datasets for potential strong identifiers for the candidates. As opposed to many systems relying on general-purpose knowledge bases or lexical resources such as Wikipedia [8,20] or WordNet [5], the ARPA architecture is tuned for utilizing configurable, domain specific vocabularies. For the WarSampo NEL task, this is important, as for example the Finnish Wikipedia lists only a limited amount of military units and personnel. Thus, in our pipeline, the searcher refers to custom SPARQL endpoints and queries defined for each entity type. These are then used both to retrieve candidates, as well as additional information such as ranks in the case of people.

Finally, given candidate identifiers, it is the job of the *disambiguator component* to rank and select from them. The disambiguator makes use of the information retrieved by the searcher, the original text, and any other data available regarding the text, such as dates, to feed a set of configured rules that rank the candidates and choose the most likely for linking.

4 Named Entity Linking of Military Units

Military unit mentions are generally quite unambiguous, so the main problem in their case was that they can be referred to by their full name, an abbreviation, or a nickname. An example of a photograph caption mentioning military units would be: "Kuvia Peiposten kylästä, jonka II/JR 8. ja 8./JR 8. ankaran taistelun jälkeen saarrostushyökkäyksellä valtasivat" ("Photographs from Peiposten village which II/JR 8 and 8./JR 8 took with an encircling attack after intense

[8] http://www.ling.helsinki.fi/~fkarlsso/genkau2.html.

battles"). Here, "II/JR 8" refers to the second battalion of the eight infantry regiment, and "8./JR 8" refers to the eight company of the same regiment.

As the actor ontology already contains the aliases for the units, only normalization of the mentions was needed. In addition, because of the unambiguous nature of military unit mentions, no disambiguation was needed when linking them – all candidates returned by the searcher were accepted.

The quality of the linking accomplished was evaluated by taking a random sample of the resources and checking the links that had been produced for those resources. For photographs the sample size was 100, and for events and magazine articles it was 50. The evaluation for each of the different links – i.e. military units, places, and people – was done by a single person, and the same sample sets were used for all link types. The evaluation method could be improved by having multiple people and/or a domain expert check the results.

For military units, the results of the evaluation are presented in Table 2. In the table, Target refers to the target data, N is the number of mentions, TP is the number of true positive matches and FP is the number of false positives, with P being the calculated precision. Because, in our approach, the recall of the method is maximally limited by the presence or absence of the entity in the reference data, two sets of numbers are reported for both false negatives as well as recall and the F_1 score. $FN_{ont.}$ is the number of entities that would have been available in the reference data but which the method missed, while $FN_{out.}$ is the number of entities outside the ontology. Accordingly, $R_{ont.}$ and $F1_{ont.}$ report recall and the F_1 score with regard to the reference data, while R_{all} and $F1_{all}$ is overall recall and F_1 score.

In relation to the Kansa Taisteli magazines, multiple versions of the data were tested. Here, the score for $\text{Magazines}_{orig.}$ relates to the data as it was received, which in this case means text automatically extracted from scanned images of the magazine using optical character recognition (OCR). $\text{Magazines}_{auto.}$ on the other hand reports results for a version in which the *extractor component* utilizes regular expressions to correct for commonly occurring OCR errors. Particularly, it was found that the OCR software often misread unit name abbreviations, rendering for example a 1 in them as an l, I or —, and a: as z. Given the particular context in which this happened, these were easy to correct using regex rules. Finally, Magazines_{clean} reports results for a manually cleaned up version.

Table 2. Precision and recall in linking of military units.

Target	N	TP	FP	P	$FN_{ont.}$	$FN_{out.}$	$R_{ont.}$	R_{all}	$F1_{ont.}$	$F1_{all}$
Photographs	9	7	0	1.00	0	2	1.00	0.78	1.00	0.88
Events	11	8	0	1.00	1	3	1.00	0.73	1.00	0.84
$\text{Magazines}_{orig.}$	133	73	16	0.82	24	36	0.75	0.55	0.78	0.59
$\text{Magazines}_{auto.}$	133	76	20	0.79	21	36	0.78	0.57	0.79	0.66
Magazines_{clean}	133	79	19	0.81	18	36	0.81	0.59	0.81	0.68

As can be seen from the table, precision was perfect for both events and photographs, and satisfactory for the magazines at around 80%. Here, their precision is hindered by problems in the original data which contained only a page level segmentation of the articles. Due to this, for example advertisements were not filtered away from the automatically extracted text, and articles not terminating on page boundaries caused entities to spill over from one article to the other, both increasing the number of false positives. When comparing the different versions of the magazine articles, one can see that OCR errors in the original data did cause significant problems for military unit recall. Of these, the automated cleanup using regular expressions in the extractor component was able to counter some, but not all.

The number of mentions in both the photographs and the events is quite low (9 and 11, respectively). This is because the samples taken were random, and only a portion of the somewhat short descriptions of events and photographs mention military units (or any named entities).

The low overall recall for units for the magazine articles (less than 60%) is mostly due to foreign units and units of the Finnish Civil War which are currently not available in the actor ontology.

5 Named Entity Linking of Places

Regarding the linking of places to the material, the most problematic part of the task was disambiguation. As stated before, the project had at its disposal both a temporally restricted snapshot of places relevant to the war period, as well as a general Finnish gazetteer to fall back upon. Together, these promised good recall, but as places are often very homonymous, both with regard to each other as well as family names, good precision could be difficult to attain. To ascertain the scope of the possible issues, a survey was done on the assembled place registries. The results of this are presented in Table 3, which shows the shares of unique place names by place type, both inside the type as well as overall.

Table 3. Unique place name portions in the place ontology

Place type	Total count	Portion unique	Portion unique inside type
Municipality	625	76%	99%
Town	50	54%	100%
Village	1544	59%	88%
Hypsographic feature	10864	66%	71%
Body of water	5553	63%	66%
Man-made feature	14362	40%	45%

Based on the table, it was decided that a simple priority list approach would be taken. In essence, the disambiguation process was as follows:

1. First, match against historic names of populated places in decreasing order of size inside the focus area of the war, as well as all Finnish municipalities regardless of location.
2. Then, match against other historic geographic names inside the focus area of the war.
3. Finally, match against contemporary modern place names in any source.

Additionally, a list of ca. 100 place names that were consistently confused with other words, such as “Pohjoinen” (north) and “Suomalainen” (Finnish), were excluded. In this simple approach, each place mention was disambiguated independently, and no other information was used.

Table 4 shows the evaluation results of the approach. In this evaluation, in cases where there is a village in a municipality with the same name, a link to the municipality was considered correct, even if this might have caused a loss of geographic precision.

Table 4. Precision and recall in place linking.

Target	N	TP	FP	P	$FN_{ont.}$	$FN_{out.}$	$R_{ont.}$	R_{all}	$F1_{ont.}$	$F1_{all}$
Photographs	92	54	16	0.77	17	21	0.76	0.59	0.77	0.67
Events	67	30	4	0.88	4	33	0.88	0.45	0.88	0.59
Magazines	411	182 + 1	113	0.62	107	122	0.63	0.44	0.62	0.52

In the photograph dataset place information for each photograph was available separately as a textual representation. Therefore, the problems of precision in that dataset reflect purely the ambiguity of place names. In the other datasets, place mentions had to be extracted from text, bringing about problems in e.g. interpreting family names of people as places.

As can be seen from the table, the simple priority list approach yielded acceptable, if not thrilling results in precision and recall within the place ontologies. Overall recall, however, was somewhat low because the place ontologies are still missing some extremely relevant places, such as the Karelian Isthmus. The better performance in linking events is due to these often referring to the major important places where coverage was better, in contrast to the photographs and articles that often also refer to much smaller places, where both ontology coverage is poorer, as well as homonymy problems more numerous. With regard to the different versions of the magazine articles, performance was nearly identical in this task – the only difference was the identification of one additional true positive for the manually cleaned up version of the data (yielding the 182 + 1 in the TP column of Table 4).

Examining the precision and recall more closely, one gets the notion that these were determined mostly by the ability of the disambiguator component to choose the correct place instance from available options – by making a bad choice, false positives rise by one diminishing precision, while false negatives also rise by one, diminishing recall. To further examine this hypothesis, a separate analysis was done on the magazine article corpus to identify the sources of false positive matches. The general breakdown of this analysis is presented in Table 5.

Table 5. A breakdown of place annotation false positives for semi-automatically cleaned magazine article texts.

Error type	Amount
Wrong place chosen with correct also available	32
Wrong place chosen, correct not in ontology	28
Person name misidentified as a place name	18
Other word misidentified as a place name	14
Noise from other articles	11
Noise from advertisements and other non-content	9
Total	113

As can be seen, indeed the most numerous type of error is where the system has not chosen the correct place even though it was available. This points towards needing more robust geographical disambiguation than the simple, local approach taken here. Luckily, this is a well-researched area, so ready choices for this are available for future work, e.g. [4,7,9,10].

On the other hand, in almost an equal number of cases, a wrong place has been chosen in a situation where the right place didn't exist in our domain ontology at all. For example, in the place ontologies the Karelia region itself is not identified as a geographic location, but instead there is a village, and a historical municipality in western Finland carrying the same name. This points towards the need for simply improving our gazetteer coverage.

The third category of false positives covers situations where a personal name was misidentified as a place name. This is a particularly hard problem for Finnish, because Finnish last names often originate from place names. Finally, also some other words were misidentified as places. For example, sometimes a sentence starts with a capitalized adjective such as Uupunut (tired in English) that could be confused with a village that has the same name.

To an extent, these two last categories could be further optimized for by tuning the configuration. For example, more aggressive filtering based on part of speech could be added, or further rules defined to try to guess whether a name refers to a person or a place [13].

In addition to these errors, a separate, significant source of false positives for the magazine articles arose from the fact that the articles were automatically segmented from raw OCR results. This in turn caused names appearing outside the article text, such as in other articles or advertisements, to sometimes be erroneously associated with the text under analysis.

6 Named Entity Linking of People

The person ontology of WarSampo contains a total of 99 483 people. As with places, the scope of disambiguation issues here was approximated by counting how many of them could be uniquely identified by various combinations of their names, as shown in Table 6.

Table 6. Examples of unique name portions in the person ontology

Part of name	Unique instances	Portion of unique person names
Family name	10 185	10.2%
Family name and any first name	50 553	50.8%
Full name	92 098	92.6%

As can be seen, basing linking on just family names for example would create huge problems for disambiguation. On one hand, requiring the full name including all first names would result in low recall as people are not often mentioned by their full name in the material. On the other hand, as discussed in the section on the actor ontology, the linking tool has rich contextual information at its disposal relating to the people – information on e.g. their ranks, awards, units, and deaths, often with attached dates. Thus, here a true effort was made to use as much of this information as possible in identifying the correct people from the material.

Accordingly, for people, the extractor has three tasks, designed to provide the further components with as much contextual information as possible. These are: rank normalization, list standardization, and handling pre-defined cases. First, ranks are normalized by replacing abbreviations and aliases by their proper names. Second, especially the photograph dataset contains lists of people in the form of "majors Jones, Smith, and Davis". In order to have the mentions in the format the searcher expects, lists like these were expanded to include the rank for each individual person: "major Jones, major Smith, major Davis". The expansions were done automatically using regular expressions. Lastly, identified important corner cases are handled: the spelling of specific names are adjusted to correspond to the person ontology, and other mentions which have been identified as resulting in an incorrect link or a missing link are amended to an unambiguous form.

The searcher then retrieves candidates based on the names and rank in mentions. As just the family name is considered too ambiguous for linking in general, a first name, initial, or rank is required in order for a mention to yield candidates. In addition to the candidates' names, the searcher retrieves their dates of birth and death, ranks, units they served in, and the sources where the information about the candidate originates. The positions of the candidates' ranks in the rank hierarchy are also fetched, as well as promotion dates.

The disambiguator then takes into account the names, ranks, lifespans, military units, and decorations of the candidates. As opposed to military unit and place linking where at least one of the candidates retrieved by the searcher was always selected for linking, the person disambiguator selects the top ranked candidate only if its score is above a specified threshold.

As a longer match is generally more specific, person candidates matching the longest piece of text are scored higher than those matching only a part of that text. The lifespan of the candidate is then compared to the date of the text. If the candidate has died before that date, the score is heavily reduced. On the other hand, the score of candidates that have died only a short while before the date are not reduced, as there are e.g. photographs depicting funerals.

Then, the ranks of the candidate are taken into account by comparing the rank mentioned in the surrounding text to the ranks of the candidate. As there are substantially more enlisted service personnel than there are high ranking officers, different ranks have different degrees of disambiguation power. For example, a reference to a general using their rank and family name is usually not ambiguous whereas a similar reference to a private is highly ambiguous. For this reason candidates were scored based on their rank: the higher the rank the better the score. The ranks of the candidates were also compared to the rank mentioned in the text, if any. If a rank was mentioned in the text but the candidate could not have had that rank at the time, the candidate's score is lowered. This includes soldiers who did not have such a rank, and those who were either only later promoted to that rank or already had a higher rank at the time. A reference to a person by their rank and family name was generally considered unambiguous enough to warrant a match in terms of the minimum threshold for scoring. However, as references to enlisted service personnel by their rank and family name are highly ambiguous without further information, a candidate matching, for example, "private Davis" would not receive enough points to result in a match unless the candidate scored highly in other aspects.

As initials are often used instead of the full first names of people in the texts, the format of the first names in a mention affects the candidates score. A full first name is better for disambiguation than an initial, and multiple initials is better than a single one.

A slight nod in the scoring is given to knights of the Mannerheim Cross (i.e. bearers of the Mannerheim Cross of Liberty), and people that were extracted from Wikipedia with the assumption that these people are well-known and are therefore more likely to be the correct match when the disambiguation is otherwise inconclusive. In case the surrounding text mentions the knighthood of the Mannerheim Cross, any candidates who are knights also receive a boost to their score.

The linked military units are also used when disambiguating people. If a unit has previously been identified in the text containing the person mention, candidates who have served in said unit receive additional points to their score. This was deemed possible based on the good recall and precision of the unit extraction itself.

In order to maximize recall, if multiple candidates received the same score that was also over the minimum threshold, all of them were selected rather than choosing one arbitrarily. This caused a dip in precision in some cases, where a mention of a kind generally considered unambiguous turned out to be ambiguous. For example, colonels are generally unambiguous but there are some with the same family name; in cases where there is no information by which to choose either, both are chosen. In the evaluated configuration, also an intermediate rank plus a family name were themselves deemed unique enough. However, this led to further false positives. Based on the evaluation, in later runs it could be beneficial to raise the bar in this regard to exclude linking based on just intermediate rank plus family name as well.

After all this, Table 7 shows the precision and recall attained. The results are shown only for photographs and events, as the magazine article evaluations are currently pending.

Table 7. Precision and recall in person linking.

Target	N	TP	FP	P	$FN_{ont.}$	$FN_{out.}$	$R_{ont.}$	R_{all}	$F1_{ont.}$	$F1_{all}$
Photographs	42	22	8	0.73	3	17	0.88	0.52	0.80	0.61
Events	34	26	0	1.00	7	1	0.79	0.76	0.88	0.87

The results show that in the case of people, attaining even comparable results to the unit and place linking required a much more complicated process of disambiguation. Recall dropped sharply in the case of photographs when people outside the ontology were taken into account, whereas the recall in events stayed almost the same. This is because the event descriptions mention mostly well-known people or high-ranking officers, whereas there are photographs of all kinds of people from Russian prisoners of war to small children. As further work, it would be interesting to investigate in more depth also here where exactly the disambiguation errors arise from. It would also be interesting to see if disambiguation could be improved by handling the entity linking as a group, and weighting more strongly those candidates who are known from background information to have links to each other.

7 Discussion

This paper discussed challenges encountered in NEL when applied to texts with mentions of military units, historical places, and person names. A key lesson learned during our work was that depending on the case, text, and data available, different approaches and methods are needed. For example, quite specific knowledge-based heuristics were needed in the case of the disambiguating military person names. Without resorting to such domain specific heuristics, the precision and recall would have remained unsatisfactorily low.

At the same time, there is an effort to encase such heuristics inside a common, configurable, modular pipeline. Of this pipeline, the language analysis, n-gram generation and search components[9] are currently the most well-developed [17], but also the preprocessing and disambiguation components have recently been made available as open source on GitHub[10].

Acknowledgements. Our work is funded by the Open Science and Research Initiative (http://openscience.fi/) of the Finnish Ministry of Education and Culture, the Finnish Cultural Foundation, and the Academy of Finland

References

1. Bunescu, R.C., Pasca, M.: Using encyclopedic knowledge for named entity disambiguation. In: EACL, vol. 6, pp. 9–16 (2006)
2. Cucerzan, S.: Large-scale named entity disambiguation based on Wikipedia data. In: EMNLP-CoNLL, vol. 7, pp. 708–716 (2007)
3. Doerr, M.: The CIDOC CRM - an ontological approach to semantic interoperability of metadata. AI Mag. **24**(3), 75–92 (2003)
4. Godoy, J., Atkinson, J., Rodriguez, A.: Geo-referencing with semi-automatic gazetteer expansion using lexico-syntactical patterns and co-reference analysis. Int. J. Geogr. Inf. Sci. **25**(1), 149–170 (2011). http://dx.doi.org/10.1080/13658816.2010.513981
5. Gracia, J., Mena, E.: Multiontology semantic disambiguation in unstructured web contexts. In: Proceedings of the 2009 K-CAP Workshop on Collective Knowledge Capturing and Representation, pp. 1–9 (2009)
6. Grishman, R., Sundheim, B.: Message understanding conference-6: a brief history. In: Coling, vol. 96, pp. 466–471 (1996)
7. Grover, C., Tobin, R., Byrne, K., Woollard, M., Reid, J., Dunn, S., Ball, J.: Use of the edinburgh geoparser for georeferencing digitized historical collections. Philos. Trans. R. Soc. Lond. A Math. Phys. Eng. Sci. **368**(1925), 3875–3889 (2010). http://rsta.royalsocietypublishing.org/content/368/1925/3875
8. Hachey, B., Radford, W., Nothman, J., Honnibal, M., Curran, J.R.: Evaluating entity linking with Wikipedia. Artif. Intell. **194**, 130–150 (2013). http://dx.doi.org/10.1016/j.artint.2012.04.005
9. Hoffart, J., Yosef, M.A., Bordino, I., Fürstenau, H., Pinkal, M., Spaniol, M., Taneva, B., Thater, S., Weikum, G.: Robust disambiguation of named entities in text. In: Proceedings of the Conference on Empirical Methods in Natural Language Processing, EMNLP 2011, Association for Computational Linguistics, Stroudsburg, PA, USA, pp. 782–792 (2011). http://dl.acm.org/citation.cfm?id=2145432.2145521
10. Hu, Y., Janowicz, K., Prasad, S.: Improving Wikipedia-based place name disambiguation in short texts using structured data from DBpedia. In: Proceedings of the 8th Workshop on Geographic Information Retrieval, GIR 2014, NY, USA, pp. 8:1–8:8 (2014). http://doi.acm.org/10.1145/2675354.2675356

[9] https://github.com/jiemakel/arpa/.

[10] https://github.com/SemanticComputing/python-arpa-linker, with the Warsampo configurations at https://github.com/SemanticComputing/warsa-linkers.

11. Hyvönen, E., Heino, E., Leskinen, P., Ikkala, E., Koho, M., Tamper, M., Tuominen, J., Mäkelä, E.: WarSampo Data Service and Semantic Portal for Publishing Linked Open Data About the Second World War History. In: Sack, H., Blomqvist, E., d'Aquin, M., Ghidini, C., Ponzetto, S.P., Lange, C. (eds.) ESWC 2016. LNCS, vol. 9678, pp. 758–773. Springer, Cham (2016). doi:10.1007/978-3-319-34129-3_46
12. Hyvönen, E., Tuominen, J., Kauppinen, T., Väätäinen, J.: Representing and utilizing changing historical places as an ontology time series. In: Ashish, N., Sheth, A. (eds.) Geospatial Semantics and Semantic Web: Foundations, Algorithms, and Applications. Springer, New York (2011)
13. Kettunen, K., Mäkelä, E., Kuokkala, J., Ruokolainen, T., Niemi, J.: Modern tools for old content - in search of named entities in a finnish ocred historical newspaper collection 1771–1910. In: Proceedings of LWDA 2016, September 2016
14. Koho, M., Hyvönen, E., Heino, E., Tuominen, J., Leskinen, P., Mäkelä, E.: Linked death - representing, publishing, and using second world war death records as linked open data. In: Sack, H., Rizzo, G., Steinmetz, N., Mladenić, D., Auer, S., Lange, C. (eds.) The Semantic Web: ESWC 2016 Satellite Events. Springer, Heidelberg (2016)
15. Löfberg, L., Archer, D., Piao, S., Rayson, P., McEnery, T., Varantola, K., Juntunen, J.P.: Porting an English semantic tagger to the finnish language. In: Proceedings of the Corpus Linguistics 2003 conference, pp. 457–464 (2003)
16. Mendes, P.N., Jakob, M., García-Silva, A., Bizer, C.: Dbpedia spotlight: shedding light on the web of documents. In: Proceedings of the 7th International Conference on Semantic Systems, pp. 1–8. ACM (2011)
17. Mäkelä, E.: Combining a REST Lexical Analysis Web Service with SPARQL for Mashup Semantic Annotation from Text. In: Presutti, V., Blomqvist, E., Troncy, R., Sack, H., Papadakis, I., Tordai, A. (eds.) ESWC 2014. LNCS, vol. 8798, pp. 424–428. Springer, Cham (2014). doi:10.1007/978-3-319-11955-7_60
18. Mäkelä, E.: LAS: an integrated language analysis tool for multiple languages. J. Open Source Softw. **1**(6), 2 (2016). http://dx.doi.org/10.21105/joss.00035
19. Nadeau, D., Sekine, S.: A survey of named entity recognition and classification. Lingvisticae Invest. **30**(1), 3–26 (2007)
20. Shen, W., Wang, J., Han, J.: Entity linking with a knowledge base: issues, techniques, and solutions. IEEE Trans. Knowl. Data Eng. **27**(2), 443–460 (2015)
21. The Association for Military History in Finland: Kansa taisteli lehdet 1957–1986 (2014). http://www.sshs.fi/sitenews/view/-/nid/92/ngid/1
22. Wentland, W., Knopp, J., Silberer, C., Hartung, M.: Building a multilingual lexical resource for named entity disambiguation, translation and transliteration. In: Proceedings of the Sixth International Conference on Language Resources and Evaluation, LREC 2008, European Language Resources Association (ELRA), Marrakech, Morocco, May 2008. http://www.lrec-conf.org/proceedings/lrec2008/

Using SWRL Rules to Model Noun Behaviour in Italian

Fahad Khan[1(✉)], Andrea Bellandi[1], Francesca Frontini[2], and Monica Monachini[1]

[1] Istituto di Linguistica Computazionale "A. Zampolli" - CNR, Pisa, Italy
{fahad.khan,andrea.bellandi,monica.monachini}@ilc.cnr.it
[2] Université Paul-Valéry Montpellier 3, Praxiling UMR 5267 CNRS - UPVM3, Montpellier, France
francesca.frontini@univ.montp3.fr

Abstract. In this article we describe our ongoing attempts to use the Semantic Web Rule Language (SWRL) to model the morphological layer of a wide-coverage Italian lexical resource, Parole-Simple-Clips (PSC); in this case that subset of PSC dealing with Italian noun morphology. After giving a brief introduction to SWRL and to Italian noun morphology we go onto describe the actual transformation itself. Finally we describe an experiment on our dataset using SWRL rules and queries written in the Semantic Query-Enhanced Rule Web Language (SQWRL).

Keywords: SWRL · Italian nouns · Morphology · Linked open data · SQWRL

1 Introduction

The publication of language resources as Linked (Open) Data is by now a fairly well established practice, with such large-scale resources as WordNet (in English and other languages), Wiktionary, and the Brown Corpus, already available as LOD datasets[1]. The most commonly referenced, and most commonly used, model for the conversion of lexical language resources is the Lexicon Model for Ontologies, lemon [6]. Lemon, however, does not go very far in addressing the complex problem of representing natural language morphology in RDF. Instead, this task has been taken up by the MMoOn (Multilingual Morpheme Ontology) model for encoding morphemic data in RDF, first presented in [5] where it was applied in the case of a Hebrew morpheme inventory. If we broaden our scope to take in lexical representation models that aren't native to RDF, however, then the Lexical Markup Framework (LMF) [3], in particular, boasts a highly comprehensive morphology module taking in both extensional and intensional

[1] http://linguistic-lod.org/llod-cloud.

J. Gracia et al. (Eds.): LDK 2017, LNAI 10318, pp. 134–142, 2017.
DOI: 10.1007/978-3-319-59888-8_11

descriptions of word morphology[2]. LMF allows users to encode morphological rules using a specific formalism[3]; with the limitation that since these patterns are given as strings one would have to use a specialised parser to generate the inflected forms of each lexical entry. We believe, however, that the Semantic Web offers up significant opportunities for using already existing, freely available, and well integrated standards and technologies, in particular the Semantic Web Rule Language (SWRL) and the Semantic Query-enhanced Web Rule Language (SQWRL), to represent such morphological data in a directly machine actionable form, without having to take recourse to specialised parsers or technologies. In this paper we will look at how to use SWRL rules to represent Italian noun morphology, more specifically inflectional morphology, and show how generalisations about Italian nouns based on their inflectional behaviour can be encoded with such rules and used to generate variant noun forms using general purpose rule engines and Semantic Web reasoners[4].

2 The Semantic Web Rule Language

SWRL is a rule language that extends OWL with Horn-like clauses and is based on a subset of Datalog with unary and binary predicates[5]. It was expressly developed as a rule language for the Semantic Web – that is, to realise the "rule" segment of the semantic web stack – thus allowing users to overcome some of the expressive limitations of OWL as a language for Knowledge Engineering. Tool support for the creation of OWL knowledge bases with SWRL rules has become more readily available of late, and the popular ontology design/visualisation tool Protégé now comes with SWRL and SQWRL tabs already pre-installed. SWRL was used by Wilcock to create a context free grammar parser [8], as well as in work on the modelling of rhetoric [7], but aside from these two cases it does not seem to have been utilised all that often in the creation of computational lexical resources; and certainly not in the representation of word morphology. It is our hope that this article will demonstrate the potential usefulness of SWRL in constructing RDF-based lexical resources.

[2] Note that here we intend 'extensional description' to refer to cases in which the inflected forms of a lexeme are explicitly given in a lexicon, and 'intensional' to cases where such forms are represented implicitly through morphological patterns that can be used to generate them.

[3] See for instance the morphological pattern for the inflection of adjectives at http://www.tagmatica.fr/lmf/FrenchLMFTestSuites1.xml.

[4] Note that as we are looking at the use of SWRL explicitly as a Semantic Web-based rule language we will not, in this article, make comparisons between our work and the existing literature on modelling natural language morphology using other logic programming languages like Prolog. Our emphasis here is on making morphological data accessible using Semantic Web technologies.

[5] https://www.w3.org/Submission/SWRL/.

3 Italian Noun Morphology

Italian nouns tend to be assigned, on most morphological treatments, to classes that determine their inflectional behaviour[6]. However, word endings by themselves usually do not suffice to determine which inflectional class a noun belongs to, and this has to be inferred by observing the inflectional behaviour of the noun itself (e.g., its plural form) as well its agreement with other words (e.g., the inflectional behaviour of adjectives or determiners that are controlled by the noun in a phrase). To begin with, the word ending is a weak predictor of a word's morphological gender: although there is a general tendency for masculine words to end in '-o' and feminine words to end in '-a', this rule has several exceptions and a large number of nouns ending in '-e' and other vowels or consonants exist, for which there is an even weaker association with a given gender. So, for instance, words like *crema*, *siepe*, *crisi*, *mano* are all feminine, but this can only be determined by observing their agreement behaviour (e,g., *la crema*, *la crisi*, *la mano*, *la siepe*). In certain rare cases, a word may have one gender in the singular and another in the plural (e.g., *un bell'uovo*, *delle belle uova*). Moreover, the morphological class to which a word is assigned determines the inflection of the noun for number [1]. So the words *poeta* and *casa*, both ending in '-a', are not only distinguished by the fact that they belong to different morphological genders (masculine and feminine) but also because they form the plural in a different way (i.e., *poeti*, *case*).

If we consider only the formation of the plural then six main inflection classes are often recognized. They have a weak association with gender, for instance the 'a/e' class contains feminine nouns. But in other cases the same behaviour in plural formation may be associated with both masculine and feminine nouns. If we create separate classes for each gender, the six classes become more numerous. Moreover, for nouns referring to humans, the formation of the feminine (singular and plural) is also to be considered. Take the words *pittore* and *cantante*; they form the plural in the same way but form the feminine in different ways. *Cantante/i* is invariable for gender, and whereas *pittore/i* becomes *pittrice/i*. In fact all human-referring nouns ending in '-tore' have the same behaviour, thus constituting a separate class. The combination of all these dimensions gives rise to a large set of inflectional classes of Italian that determine both the inflection of the noun itself and that of its accord targets.

4 The Parole-Simple-Clips Morphological Layer

The preceding section will hopefully have served to convince the reader of the complexities inherent in any morphologically driven classification of Italian nouns – as well of the usefulness of lexical resources that render this kind of knowledge accessible to researchers and to language learners. This, then, leads us onto the next topic which we wish to touch upon in this article, and which relates to the publication of legacy lexical resources as Linked Open Data.

[6] For a good introduction to Italian noun morphology see [4].

The legacy resource in this instance, Parole-Simple-Clips (PSC), constitutes a large, wide-coverage, multi-layered computational lexicon for Italian that was built up, and then extended upon, in successive stages through the course of three major, international and national, projects. In previous work we have described the publication of part of the semantic layer of PSC as LOD [2]. However, PSC also contains a rich morphological layer that contains a substantial amount of structured morphological data for 72,001 lemmas, amongst which there are 48,735 nouns, and where 33,362 of these noun lemmas belong to a specific morphological pattern class. We were inspired by the structure and make up of PSC's morphological layer, and in particular the fact that it contained both extensional and intensional morphological data – the latter in the form of representations of morphological patterns – to attempt to publish it, or at least that part of it pertaining to Italian noun morphology, using SWRL rules.

Each lexeme in the original PSC dataset is classified according to its morphological behaviour; in the case of nouns this means that each lexeme is associated with an abstract class, which is described in terms of a set of operations on strings. So that, to take an example, one of these classes with the id number 279, encompasses two different transformation operations, which are as follows:

- (279a) Remove the last two characters from the string; add 'IO' to the string; assign the feature Masculine Singular to the result;
- (279b) Remove the last two characters from the string; add 'II' to the string assign the feature Masculine Plural to the result.

One of the lexical entries belonging to class 279 is the beautiful Italian word *scombussolio*, meaning 'muddle'. In this case the first operation (279a) is redundant when performed on the lemma, in the sense of that it does not alter the original string – although it does give us important information about the endings of the masculine singular forms of this class; the second operation, instead gives us the plural *scombussolii*. In other cases, these class descriptions include rules that enable the derivation of strings giving us both male and female forms of nouns. So for example class 226 allows us, given the lemma form *bischero* of the popular Tuscan word meaning 'fool' or 'prick', to derive the masculine plural *bischeri* as well as the feminine singular *bischera* and the feminine plural *bischere*.

There exist 171 such classes covering the totality of the nouns in PSC; 86 of these classes only have one member and 124 of them contain 10 members or less: instead the top 30 most productive classes together cover around 98% of the nouns in the PSC dataset with a morphological class assigned.

5 Transforming the PSC Nouns' Morphological Layer into Linked Open Data

Although we had originally intended to model the ostensibly more complex morphology of Latin nouns using SWRL rules, we eventually settled on Italian nouns as our first case study, given that we had the PSC morphological data already to hand – a comparable Latin dataset being seemingly much harder to come by – and given the non-trivial challenges that modeling Italian nouns offers in terms of the potential number of rules and exceptions that one has to deal with. The basic idea of the case study was to take the nouns in PSC, arrange them in classes, based in this instance on the classes already given in PSC, and then to create SWRL rules referencing these classes that would then allow us to derive the various different inflected forms of each individual noun. A number of practical issues became immediately apparent on first working with the PSC dataset, the first of which was the fact that, as SWRL does not allow the 'creation' of new OWL individuals representing abstract forms. We had to instead focus on generating new strings to represent the inflected forms of the original lemmas. Consequently, we devised a series of rules where the head of each rule was a clause associating an individual lexical entry with a string instantiating one of the different forms of the noun using an appropriate datatype property. We created a family of datatype properties that related variant forms as strings with lexical entries: such properties as `hasForm`, `hasStem`, `hasLemma`, `hasPlural` etc. This idea can in principle be extended to other lexical categories in Italian, so that for example we can create subproperties of verbal form for different combinations of person, aspect, tense and mood, and indeed we intend to pursue this line of research in future work.

In order to make the noun morphology rules as concise as possible, we decided to assume that the stem for each lexical entry was already in the lexicon. We created these stems by pre-processing the lemma strings contained in the original dataset according to the original class transformation relations, and then associating the resulting strings with members of the class LexicalEntry using the newly created datatype property `hasStem`. This enabled us to create SWRL rules that derived both the lemma and the plural as well as, in appropriate instances, the feminine singular and/or plural of a given lexical entry: for this purpose we created the properties `hasFemaleLemma` and `hasFemalePlural`, siblings of `hasLemma` and `hasPlural`, all of which are collectively children of `hasForm`. For instance the rules 279a and 279b, associated with Class 25 in our classification, are represented respectively by the following two rules in the knowledge base:

```
hasStem(?x, ?y)^swrlb:stringConcat(?z, ?
y,"IO"^^xsd:string)^hasNounClass(?x,Class25)->hasLemma(?x, ?z)

hasStem(?x, ?y)^swrlb:stringConcat(?z, ?y,
"II"^^xsd:string)^hasNounClass(?x,Class25)->hasPlural(?x, ?z)
```

Note here our use of the built-in SWRL string method `stringConcat` which allows for the generation of lemma and plural forms through the classification of these forms as the concatenation of the stem with a string ending. So that given that the lexical entry for *scombussolio* belongs to Class 25 we are able to derive both lemma (singular) and plural forms from the stem *scumbussol*.

In cases where we have an additional female form, such as Class 8 we can have four rules:

```
hasStem(?x, ?y)^swrlb:stringConcat(?z, ?y,
"I"^^xsd:string)^hasNounClass(?x,Class8)->hasPlural(?x, ?z)

hasStem(?x, ?y)^swrlb:stringConcat(?z, ?y,
"O"^^xsd:string)^hasNounClass(?x,Class8)->hasLemma(?x, ?z)

hasStem(?x, ?y)^swrlb:stringConcat(?z, ?y,
"A"^^xsd:string)^hasNounClass(?x,Class8)->hasFemaleLemma(?x, ?z)

hasStem(?x, ?y)^swrlb:stringConcat(?z, ?y,
"E"^^xsd:string)^hasNounClass(?x,Class8)->hasFemalePlural(?x, ?z)
```

In the interests of efficiency, and from a desire to generalise over the levels of detail that we found in the PSC, we decided to encode only the first 30 classes – that is the first 30 classes in terms of number of members – as rules; the rest of the 125 classes have a very low productivity, with 86 of them having only 1 member. Indeed the former 30 classes give us a coverage of over 98% of the nouns in the lexicon belonging to a morphological class (which is 67% of the total number of nouns); in the remaining strongly irregular cases, individual inflectional forms are explicitly associated with the given lexical entries, i.e., we make use of extensional definitions. We believe that these 30 classes offer a comprehensive description of the noun morphology of Italian; each set of rules embodying both a description of the behaviour of Italian morphology and a means of deriving them: a means of deriving these inflectional forms, moreover, that uses general purpose Semantic Web technologies and that therefore renders this description much more accessible than would be otherwise possible. Using a rule engine it is possible to derive new OWL axioms from these rules and to subsequently add these to the morphological knowledge base resulting in a greatly expanded knowledge base. Another possibility would be to not generate new OWL axioms but to instead run SQWRL queries over our hybrid SWRL/OWL knowledge. SQWRL is a powerful query language whose syntax is based on SWRL itself. It can be used to run simple queries such as the following query, Query 1, which counts all the lexical entries in the lexical knowledge base:

```
LexicalEntry(?l) → sqwrl:count(?l).
```

we can also write more complicated queries such as the following query, Query 2, which finds all male Nouns with lemmas ending in ‘O’:

```
hasGender(?l,Male)^hasLemma(?l,?a) ^swrlb:endsWith(?a,"O") → sqwrl:select(?l).
```

The next query, Query 3, instead finds all male Nouns with a Plural ending in ‘A’

```
hasGender(?l, Male)^hasPlural(?l, ?a)^swrlb:endsWith(?a, "A") → sqwrl:select(?l).
```

Query 4 finds all male nouns with a female form and give their female plurals:

```
hasFemalePlural(?l,?f) → sqwrl:select(?l,?f).
```

We can also find all nouns with female forms and give their female plurals, such as in the following query, Query 5:

```
hasFemalePlural(?l,?f) → sqwrl:select(?l,?f).
```

5.1 Practicalities

In order to understand the viability of this approach it was necessary to have some idea of the practicalities of using SWRL and SQWRL on realistically sized lexical knowledge bases such as the PSC morphological layer, especially with regards to time and resource consumption. To this end we used our SWRL rules along with a dataset consisting of the nominal lexical entries in the top 30 noun classes to test rule engine execution using the OWL API and the SWRL Rule Engine API's[7]; in addition we used the same lexical knowledge base to look at the time taken to respond to the SQWRL queries given above using the SQWRL API[8]. We carried out the experiment using two different configurations: the first, Configuration A, consisted of a Mac laptop with an Intel®Core™M3 @1.1 GHz with 8 GB RAM; the second, a PC with an Intel®Core™i7 @3.4 GHZ with 16 GB of RAM. Table 1 gives the results for each of the two configurations on different numbers of nouns where the percentage coverage[9] is also given in each case. The second table, Table 2 gives the execution time for the five queries which we listed above, but only for Configuration B. We tried running the queries on Configuration A but this led to a time out. Time constraints prevented us from carrying out other tests, but the results so far seem to be hopeful, at least to some extent.

Table 1. Generation time of SWRL rules.

		Configuration A	Configuration B
#Nouns	Coverage	Generation time (sec.)	Generation time (sec.)
3,000	9%	6,19	2,92
10,607	31%	15,98	5,21
16,388	49%	19,41	8,94
29,789	89%	34,49	13,47
32,605	98%	53,86	14,18

[7] These API's can be found respectively at http://owlapi.sourceforge.net/ and https://github.com/protegeproject/swrlapi.

[8] https://github.com/protegeproject/swrlapi/wiki.

[9] This percentage is taken over the total number of nouns assigned to a morphological class.

Table 2. Response time of SQWRL queries on configuration B.

Query ID	Execution time (sec.)
Query 1	14.6
Query 2	14.6
Query 3	14.3
Query 4	14.6
Query 5	14.6

6 Further Work

In this article we have presented a method for encoding morphological patterns using the SWRL rule language. We hope that we have been able to demonstrate something of the viability of this approach as a means of providing a directly machine actionable classification and description of the morphology of a language, at least insofar as it pertains to the modeling of Italian noun morphology, and consequently of other languages with a similar nominal morphology. In future work we plan to use SWRL to represent the morphology of other parts of speech in Italian, again using PSC as our foundational dataset, with a view to publishing the whole PSC morphological layer as LOD. We also plan to apply our rule-based approach to Latin, a language whose complex nominal morphology would seem, on first sight, to offer a much greater challenge for this approach, in order to see how well it can carry over. A further challenge would be to see whether we can further generalise the approach to languages with markedly different morphological systems, such as for instance languages with root and pattern morphologies such as Arabic and Hebrew.

References

1. D'Achille, P., Thornton, A.M.: La flessione del nome dall'italiano antico all'italiano contemporaneo (2003)
2. Del Gratta, R., Frontini, F., Khan, F., Monachini, M.: Converting the PAROLE SIMPLE CLIPS Lexicon into RDF with lemon. Semant. Web (Print) **6**, 387–392 (2015)
3. Francopoulo, G.: LMF Lexical Markup Framework. Wiley, New York (2013)
4. Iacobini, C., Thornton, A.M.: Morfologia e formazione delle parole. Manuale di linguistica italiana 13, 190 (2016)
5. Klimek, B., Arndt, N., Krause, S., Arndt, T.: Creating linked data morphological language resources with mmoon - the hebrew morpheme inventory. In: Proceedings of the 10th International Conference on Language Resources and Evaluation (LREC 2016) (2016)
6. McCrae, J., Spohr, D., Cimiano, P.: Linking lexical resources and ontologies on the semantic web with lemon. In: Antoniou, G., Grobelnik, M., Simperl, E., Parsia, B., Plexousakis, D., Leenheer, P., Pan, J. (eds.) ESWC 2011. LNCS, vol. 6643, pp. 245–259. Springer, Heidelberg (2011). doi:10.1007/978-3-642-21034-1_17

7. O'Reilly, C., Paurobally, S.: Lassoing rhetoric with owl and swrl. Unpublished MSc dissertation (2010). http://computationalrhetoricworkshop.uwaterloo.ca/wpcontent/uploads/2016/06/LassoingRhetoricWithOWLAndSWRL.pdf
8. Wilcock, G.: An owl ontology for HPSG. In: Proceedings of the 45th Annual Meeting of the ACL on Interactive Poster and Demonstration Sessions, ACL 2007, Association for Computational Linguistics, Stroudsburg, PA, USA, pp. 169–172 (2007)

Hunger for Contextual Knowledge and a Road Map to Intelligent Entity Linking

Filip Ilievski(✉), Piek Vossen, and Marieke van Erp

Vrije Universiteit Amsterdam, Amsterdam, The Netherlands
{f.ilievski,piek.vossen,marieke.van.erp}@vu.nl

Abstract. The task of entity linking (EL) is often perceived as an algorithmic problem, where the novelty of systems lies in the decision making process, while the knowledge is relatively fixed. As a consequence, we lack an understanding about the importance and the relevance of diverse knowledge types in EL. However, knowledge and relevance are crucial: following the Gricean maxim, an author relies on assumptions about the knowledge of the reader and uses the most efficient and scarce, yet understandable, level of detail when conveying a message. In this paper, we seek to understand the EL task from a knowledge and relevance perspective. We define four categories of contextual knowledge relevant for EL and observe that two of these are systematically absent in existing entity linkers. Consequently, many contextual cases, in particular long-tail entities, can never be interpreted by existing systems. Finally, we present our ideas on developing knowledge-intensive systems and long-tail datasets.

Keywords: Entity linking · Context · Long tail · Knowledge · Reasoning

1 Introduction

The task of Entity Linking (EL) anchors recognized entity mentions in text to their semantic representation, thus establishing identity and facilitating the exploitation of background knowledge, easy integration, and comparison and reuse of systems. Various EL approaches have been introduced in recent years [1,2,10,12,15,17]. These systems optimize the semantic coherence of entities using probabilistic disambiguation. This often revolves around graph optimization over potential entity interpretations within one document with the goal of finding a minimal well-connected graph that contains at most one entity interpretation per mention. Alternatively, machine learning algorithms combine local and global features to score the fit of mention interpretations against mention training data based on popularity, string similarity and the level of association between two entities (cf. [12]). Both graph-based and machine learning methods use common knowledge bases (e.g. Wikidata), and, despite the non-ideal coverage and bias of these sources, the systems yield F_1-scores in the order of 60–70%.[1]

[1] http://gerbil.aksw.org/gerbil/overview.

J. Gracia et al. (Eds.): LDK 2017, LNAI 10318, pp. 143–149, 2017.
DOI: 10.1007/978-3-319-59888-8_12

Recently, we demonstrated that these scores are largely due to the dominance of a limited number of popular entities [3,6]. The accuracy of most probabilistic algorithms is mainly based on test cases for which there is sufficient training data and background knowledge. We refer to these frequently mentioned entities as the *linguistic head*. Besides being frequent news topics, the mentions of head entities are also frequent and the mention-to-entity dominance is very high.

However, at the same time there is a vast amount of *long-tail entities*, each different and with low frequency, that usually remain hard to resolve for any contemporary system. Support for this claim can be found in the related task of Word Sense Disambiguation. Here, the system accuracy on the most frequent word interpretations is close to human performance, while the least frequent words can be disambiguated correctly in at most 1 out of 5 cases [13]. It is our conviction that the linguistic long tail can never be fully tackled with further algorithmic inventions because these long-tail interpretations appear only incidentally and it is unlikely there will ever be sufficient training data. Even if we would increase the training data, it is impossible to guess the a-priori distribution that applies to any actual test set across all the options [13].

Additionally, probabilistic approaches do not employ any mechanisms to exclude anomalous interpretations. This leads to an explosion of potential interpretations which are dominated by the most popular ones even though they often do not make any sense. In the NewsReader project, for example, the most popular detected entity in 2.3 million news articles from 2003–2015 about the car industry was *Abraham Lincoln*, demonstrating how dominance leads to wrong and impossible interpretations [16]. This problem becomes even more substantial when we switch from the popular world represented in Wikipedia to resolving long-tail entities, where the surface form ambiguity becomes too big to handle.[2] For instance, while *Ronaldo* can refer to only a few popular entities according to Wikipedia, the number of people in the world that (have) share(d) this name is many orders of magnitude greater. For current systems, it is extremely hard to deal with this reality, while humans have no problem understanding news mentioning some non-famous *Ronaldo*. As these long-tail interpretations are only relevant within a specific context (time, location, topic, community), we need contextual knowledge and reasoning in order to decide which make sense.[3]

In this position paper, we argue that the extreme ambiguity representing the long tail can only be addressed by robust reasoning over well-targeted, but rich, contextual knowledge. The road to intelligent EL thus requires a revision and extension of contextual knowledge, as well as an approach to dynamically acquire such knowledge for each long-tail case. We summarize the knowledge used by humans when reading, and adapt an existing knowledge classification [9] for a knowledge-intensive EL framework. We compare contemporary systems against

[2] Probabilistic methods are sensitive to even small changes in the background knowledge: only switching to a more recent Wikipedia version causes a drop in performance because of the increased ambiguity and the change in knowledge distribution [12].

[3] These differ from the domain-specific entities, which are defined through a single contextual dimension (of topic) and do not necessarily suffer from knowledge scarcity.

this framework to assess which knowledge aspects are currently left out. We argue that our community should switch focus, away from systems and evaluations that are optimized on the linguistic head, and instead start investigating the use of deeper contextual knowledge and reasoning to perform better on the long tail.

2 The Efficiency of Human Language

Textual documents are surrounded by rich context that is typically leveraged by humans but largely ignored by machines. Ambiguity of language resolves using this context: people optimize their communication to convey maximum information with minimum effort or text given the specific situation. Regardless of the genre (newswire, tweets, fiction, etc.), the Gricean maxim of quantity [4] dictates that an author makes assumptions about the familiarity of the reader with the events and entities that are described in a document at the time of publishing. The author uses this to formulate a message in the most efficient and scarce, yet understandable way. The reader is expected to adequately disambiguate forms and fill in the gaps with presumed knowledge from the current world.

For example, when reading a news item, human readers are aware on which date it was published, the events that occurred around that date, which entities are in the news and recent news articles. Machines, on the contrary, are deprived of such context and expectations. They usually have to deal with individual, isolated news articles, and need to establish identity solely on the basis of a single document in relation to dominant entities in the available resources. To overcome this, we need to build algorithms that can fill contextual knowledge gaps similar to humans with the right assumptions on the familiarity of the entities within a given context. We expect that these considerations are particularly relevant for long-tail entities that are only known within very specific contextual conditions.

3 Types of Knowledge

In [9], four types of contextual knowledge are defined that are essential for humans to interpret text. Here, we relate these four categories to the EL task.

Intratextual knowledge is any knowledge extracted from the text of a document, concerning entity mentions, other word types (e.g. nouns, verbs), and their order and structure in the document. It relates to framing new and given information and notions such as topic and focus. Central entities in the discourse are referred to differently than peripheral ones. Intratextual knowledge is prominent in EL systems: surrounding words (word clouds) [2], entity order [7], co reference [8], substrings [15], abbreviations [7], word senses [10], word relations [1].

Extratextual knowledge concerns any entity-oriented knowledge, found outside the document in (un)structured knowledge bases. Extratextual knowledge can be episodic or conceptual. The former is the knowledge about a concrete entity: its labels, relation to other entities and other facts or experiences. Conceptual knowledge refers to the expectations and knowledge gaps that are filled by an abstract model (i.e. ontology), representing relations between types of entities. Customary extratextual knowledge includes: entity-to-entity links [7,8,10,15], entity labels [7,8,10,15], semantic types [7,8], and textual descriptions [2].

Circumtextual knowledge - Documents are published at a specific time and location, written by a specific author, and released by a certain publisher. We refer to these prefix and suffix items around the text as *circumtextual knowledge.*

Intertextual knowledge - Documents are not self-contained and rely on *intertextual (cross-document) knowledge* distilled by the reader from related documents. They are published in a stream of information and news, assuming knowledge about preceding related documents, which typically share the same topic and community, and may be published around the same time and location. Early documents that introduce a topic typically make more explicit reference than those published later on when both the event and the topic have evolved.[4]

To the best of our knowledge, circumtextual and intertextual knowledge are systematically neglected in current systems. Then it is no surprise that they fail to handle a case such as the *Hobbs murder* that is presented in the next section.

4 Entity Linking in the Long Tail

In the local news article titled "Hobbs man arrested in connection to nephew's murder",[5] a murder is reported that happened in Hobbs, New Mexico in 2016. It involves two long-tail entities: the killer Michael Johnson and its victim Zachariah Fields. Both entities have no representation in Wikipedia, as they are not well-known outside the context of this murder.

Current EL systems perform poorly on this document. For instance, Babelfy [10] links "Michael Johnson" to a retired American sprinter, "Johnson" to an American president, and "Zachariah" to a long-deceased religious clergyman and author from the 19th century. Not only are these interpretations incorrect, they are also highly incoherent from a human perspective: a retired sprinter, a 19th century religious author, and an ex-president are all identified in an article reporting a local murder in New Mexico in 2016.

What makes these interpretations silly to humans, but optimal to EL systems, is the different notion of coherence. Roughly, entity linkers define coherence via a probabilistic optimization over entity and word associations, resulting in interpretations that neither share context among themselves, nor with the document. Unlike machines, people employ rigorous contextual reasoning over time, location, topic, and other circumtextual knowledge about the article. Time would help to decide against the 19th century author as a victim in 2016. Similarly for location and topic: none of the system interpretations is related to Hobbs, New Mexico, or to any violent event. As systems do not use circumtextual knowledge, they have no human-like mechanisms to decide on improbable interpretations.

---

[4] Compare the use of hash tags in Twitter streams once an event becomes trending.

[5] https://goo.gl/Gms7IQ. Last visited: 18 April 2017.

In addition, this document is not self-contained; it provides an update regarding an event that happened and was already reported on earlier. In such cases, its interpretation might benefit from (or even depend on) focused machine reading of earlier documents covering this topic. This is very natural for humans; still, current systems lack ways to obtain and integrate intertextual knowledge.

5 Going Forward

While authors assume that their readers possess knowledge from all four categories, we observe that intertextual and circumtextual knowledge are systematically neglected by current entity linkers. This lack of knowledge prevents EL systems to resolve (long-tail) entities that rely on related documents or on contextual awareness regarding publication time, location, topic, author, etc.

Firstly, resolving documents with context-specific, long-tail entities with the current knowledge is a matter of luck and number-crunching and, considering the vast ambiguity of surface forms, extremely challenging in practice. Systems thus need to incorporate circumtextual and intertextual reasoning to compute the coherence of an interpretation and to discourage interpretations that share no context among themselves or the document. How to best employ this knowledge for EL, and combine it with existing probabilistic methods is to be investigated. One could, for instance, model world expectations based on circumtextual aspects, and inspect if the proposed interpretations in text match these expectations.[6]

Secondly, the knowledge from each type should be used systematically and according to its relevance. For instance, the intratextual knowledge is crucial for fictional stories, but not for epitaphs. Even more importantly, approaches that rely on rich and systematic knowledge would be suitable to detect *hunger for knowledge*,[7] i.e. decide that the accessible knowledge is too scarce for making a well-informed decision and assume that entities may be new or unknown to the knowledge base.[8] Once detected, the system has to decide which strategies can be applied to satisfy the hunger, i.e. obtain this missing knowledge. An example for such a strategy when the intratextual information is incomplete is to find information on the same event from related, more explicit documents (cf. [11]).

Finally, the properties of the EL data sets largely determine the types and depths of knowledge needed. Current datasets tend to focus on head entities, so even context-neutral features such as Page Rank popularity of an entity lead to F_1 scores of over 60% [14]. Moreover, these datasets often consist of self-contained documents (e.g. Wikipedia samples or sports results), thus consistently removing the need for cross-document knowledge. Instead, systems should be evaluated on long-tail entities by either introducing new long-tail data set(s) that deliberately contain entities with low dominance and high ambiguity; or by focusing on the

[6] For instance, we would not expect that a 19th century person is still alive in 2016.

[7] We base our concept of hunger for knowledge on [5].

[8] Most probabilistic systems also decide if an entity is new to a knowledge base. However, they set confidence thresholds to circumvent the complexity of this decision.

few "hard" cases in current datasets. The long-tail cases should also be placed in a broader perspective of the spatio-temporal context by providing documents as a stream of information over time and related to the specific location, thus not only adding documents referring to *Ronaldos* other than the most popular ones, but also the relevant topical stream of documents involving these entities.

We are working on developing datasets that represent long-tail entities better. But considering the complexity and the richness of the long-tail phenomena, this will ultimately need to be a research community effort.

Acknowledgments. The research for this paper was supported by the Netherlands Organisation for Scientific Research (NWO) via the Spinoza fund and the CLARIAH-CORE project. We thank Stefan Schlobach, Frank van Harmelen, Eduard Hovy, and the reviewers for their ideas and input.

References

1. Cheng, X., Roth, D.: Relational inference for wikification. Urbana **51**(61801), 16–58 (2013)
2. Daiber, J., Jakob, M., Hokamp, C., Mendes, P.N.: Improving efficiency and accuracy in multilingual entity extraction. In: Proceedings of SEMANTiCS, pp. 121–124. ACM (2013)
3. van Erp, M., Mendes, P., Paulheim, H., Ilievski, F., Plu, J., Rizzo, G., Waitelonis, J.: Evaluating entity linking: an analysis of current benchmark datasets and a roadmap for doing a better job. In: LREC, ELRA (2016)
4. Grice, P.: Logic and conversation. In: Cole, P., Morgan, J. (eds.) Syntax and Semantics, vol. 3, pp. 41–58. Academic Press, New York (1975)
5. Hovy, E.: Filling the long tail. In: Keynote Slides from the "Looking at the Long Tail" Workshop. VU Amsterdam (2016). https://goo.gl/ieulpF. Accessed 24 June 2016
6. Ilievski, F., Postma, M., Vossen, P.: Semantic overfitting: what world do we consider when evaluating disambiguation of text? In: Proceedings of COLING (2016)
7. Ilievski, F., Rizzo, G., van Erp, M., Plu, J., Troncy, R.: Context-enhanced adaptive entity linking. In: LREC 2016 (2016)
8. Ling, X., Singh, S., Weld, D.S.: Design challenges for entity linking. TACL **3**, 315–328 (2015)
9. MacLachlan, G., Reid, I.: Framing and Interpretation. Melbourne University Press, Portland (1994)
10. Moro, A., Raganato, A., Navigli, R.: Entity linking meets word sense disambiguation: a unified approach. TACL **2**, 231–244 (2014)
11. Narasimhan, K., Yala, A., Barzilay, R.: Improving information extraction by acquiring external evidence with reinforcement learning (2016)
12. Nguyen, T.H., Fauceglia, N., Muro, M.R., Hassanzadeh, O., Gliozzo, A.M., Sadoghi, M.: Joint learning of local and global features for entity linking via neural networks. In: Proceedings of COLING (2016)
13. Postma, M., Izquierdo, R., Agirre, E., Rigau, G., Vossen, P.: Addressing the MFS bias in WSD systems. In: Proceedings of LREC 2016, ELRA, France (2016)
14. Tristram, F., Walter, S., Cimiano, P., Unger, C.: Weasel: a machine learning based approach to entity linking combining different features. In: Proceedings of 3rd International Workshop on NLP and DBpedia, ISWC 2015 (2015)

15. Usbeck, R., Ngonga Ngomo, A.-C., Röder, M., Gerber, D., Coelho, S.A., Auer, S., Both, A.: AGDISTIS - graph-based disambiguation of named entities using linked data. In: Mika, P., et al. (eds.) ISWC 2014. LNCS, vol. 8796, pp. 457–471. Springer, Cham (2014). doi:10.1007/978-3-319-11964-9_29
16. Vossen, P., Agerri, R., Aldabe, I., Cybulska, A., van Erp, M., Fokkens, A., Laparra, E., Minard, A.L., Aprosio, A.P., Rigau, G., Rospocher, M., Segers, R.: NewsReader: using knowledge resources in a cross-lingual reading machine to generate more knowledge from massive streams of news. Special Issue Knowledge-Based Systems, Elsevier (2016)
17. Zwicklbauer, S., Seifert, C., Granitzer, M.: DoSeR - a knowledge-base-agnostic framework for entity disambiguation using semantic embeddings. In: Sack, H., Blomqvist, E., d'Aquin, M., Ghidini, C., Ponzetto, S.P., Lange, C. (eds.) ESWC 2016. LNCS, vol. 9678, pp. 182–198. Springer, Cham (2016). doi:10.1007/978-3-319-34129-3_12

Weak Supervision for Semi-supervised Topic Modeling via Word Embeddings

Gerald Conheady(✉) and Derek Greene

School of Computer Science, University College Dublin, Dublin, Ireland
gerry.conheady@ucdconnect.ie, derek.greene@ucd.ie

Abstract. Semi-supervised algorithms have been shown to improve the results of topic modeling when applied to unstructured text corpora. However, sufficient supervision is not always available. This paper proposes a new process, Weak+, suitable for use in semi-supervised topic modeling via matrix factorization, when limited supervision is available. This process uses word embeddings to provide additional weakly-labeled data, which can result in improved topic modeling performance.

1 Introduction

Unsupervised algorithms, such as Non-Negative Matrix Factorization (NMF) [4], have been used to uncover the underlying topical structure in unlabeled text corpora [1]. Semi-supervised NMF (SS-NMF) algorithms use background information, in the form of word and document constraints, to produce more accurate topic models [5]. In real-world applications it is reasonably easy to obtain a limited sample of labeled data from domain experts. However, when dealing with large corpora, this may not be enough to obtain improved results. We aim to address this issue by using weak supervision automatically generated from a small amount of input provided by an expert.

Recently, word embeddings have been used in a range of domains, where words are represented by vectors in a multi-dimensional space [6]. Words with related meanings will tend to be close together in the vector space. Based on this idea, in Sect. 3 we introduce a new method of **Weak+** supervision for topic modeling, which uses word embeddings to generate additional "weakly-labeled" data. This supervision takes the form of a list of candidate words that are semantically related to a small number of "strong" words supplied by an expert to describe a topic. Our initial experiments in Sect. 4 show that, when this weak supervision is fed to SS-NMF, the results of topic modeling are improved.

2 Related Work

Topic modeling allows for the discovery of themes in an unsupervised manner. While probabilistic approaches have often been used for topic modeling, approaches based on NMF [4] have also been successful [1]. The counts of all the

J. Gracia et al. (Eds.): LDK 2017, LNAI 10318, pp. 150–155, 2017.
DOI: 10.1007/978-3-319-59888-8_13

terms in each document serves as an input to NMF in the form of a non-negative document-term matrix $\mathbf{A}$, corresponding to m documents by n words. NMF seeks to find k topics and starts by randomly initialising an m by k document-topic matrix $\mathbf{W}$ and k by n topic-word matrix $\mathbf{H}$. The algorithm seeks a solution for $\mathbf{W}$ and $\mathbf{H}$ such that $\mathbf{A} \approx \mathbf{WH}$.

SS-NMF typically involves grouping data where limited supervision is available in the form of constraints imposed on pairs of items, provided by a human expert or "oracle" [2]. Methods have been proposed for incorporating constraints into matrix factorization [5]. This paper follows the Utopian approach for weakly-supervised topic modeling [3] which minimises the objective function:

$$||A - WH||_F^2 + ||(W - W_r)M_W||_F^2 + ||(H - H_r D_H)M_H||_F^2$$

Human selected constraints are passed to NMF in the form of reference matrices, $\mathbf{W_r}$ for documents and $\mathbf{H_r}$ for words, whose values are used to initialise the selected documents and words in the $\mathbf{W}$ and $\mathbf{H}$ matrices. The remaining documents and words are initialised randomly. Masking matrices $\mathbf{M_W}$ and $\mathbf{M_H}$ are also used to adjust the effect of the $\mathbf{W_r}$ and $\mathbf{H_r}$ matrices. The diagonal matrix $\mathbf{D_H}$ is used for automatic scaling. The success of such an approach will depend on the availability of useful constraints to populate these matrices [2].

NMF does not directly take into account semantic associations. Related meanings of words, such as between 'computer' and 'data', do not explicitly influence the factorization process. Many applications of word embeddings are based on the original *word2vec* model [6]. Their approach creates distributed representations of words, in the form of dense lower-dimensional vectors, as trained on a large corpus of text using a neural network with one hidden layer. The input and output layers have one entry for each word in the vocabulary n. The hidden layer is considered the dimension layer and has d entries. This allows the output from the hidden layer to be represented by a $n \times d$ matrix. This representation can be used to measure the associations between the words in the corpus vocabulary.

3 Methods

Semi-supervised learning relies on input from domain experts. By definition this input is limited due to the availability of expert time. In this paper, we consider an extreme case, where the expert, referred to as the "oracle", will provide a list of five relevant words and five relevant documents relating to a single topic of interest. An example might be the provision by an auditor of five emails and five words from a health organization's email relating to data privacy breaches.

The Weak+ process uses the Gensim implementation of *word2vec* [7] to produce an embedding representing the corpus being analyzed. It uses this model to extend the list of words provided by the oracle as follows:

1. Construct a skip-gram *word2vec* model for the full corpus.

2. Request the initial list of "strong" supervised words and documents from the oracle for one or more topics.
3. For each of the topic(s) to be supervised:
   - For each supervised word, identify the list of top most similar words in the embedding space based on cosine similarity.
   - Alternate between the lists, adding words to the extended list until a required number of words have been added (This is done to ensure a good balance of similar words relative to the original list).

We then apply the SS-NMF algorithm to the document-term matrix representation $\mathbf{A}$ of the corpus as described in [3], where the reference matrix $\mathbf{H_r}$ is populated from the extended list of supervised words and the reference matrix $\mathbf{W_r}$ is populated from the list of documents originally provided by the oracle.

4 Experimental Evaluation

4.1 Experimental Setup

The aim of our experiments is to investigate whether SS-NMF topic modeling can be improved using the additional words generated by Weak+. The *bbc*, *guardian-2013* and *irishtimes-2013* news corpora are used for the evaluation [2], where the documents in these corpora have been assigned a single human-annotated ground truth topic. The top 100 most relevant words per topic are identified based on these annotations. These documents and words are considered as emanating from the oracle for our experiments. We construct *word2vec* embeddings for each corpus, using a skip-gram model with 100 dimensions and a document frequency threshold of 5.

For each corpus, we identify the least coherent ground truth topic (*i.e.* the topic with the lowest mean within-topic to between-topic cosine similarity ratio). These are 'business' (*bbc*), 'music' (*guardian-2013*), and 'politics' (*irishtimes-2013*). We then examine the extent to which we can improve the identification of these difficult topics. Specifically, we produce supervision in the form of a list of five documents and words for these topics based on the oracle, and then apply the Weak+ supervision process to extend the word list, varying the number of words to be supervised from 0 to 30 in steps of 5. Document supervision is restricted to 0 and 5 documents, as we wish to focus on the effect of word supervision. For each level of supervision, we apply SS-NMF for 50 runs, where the entries in the reference matrices are set to 1 for the supervised words and documents, and 0 otherwise. For the purpose of our experiments, we fix the number of topics k to be the number of ground truth topics in each corpus.

4.2 Results

Firstly, we use Normal Mutual Information (NMI) to measure model accuracy across all topics. For each run of SS-NMF, we compare the disjoint partition produced from the topic-document weights with the ground truth document assignments. The results in Figs. 1a and b show a small improvement in NMI scores with word supervision alone, and a slightly greater improvement when using both word and document supervision.

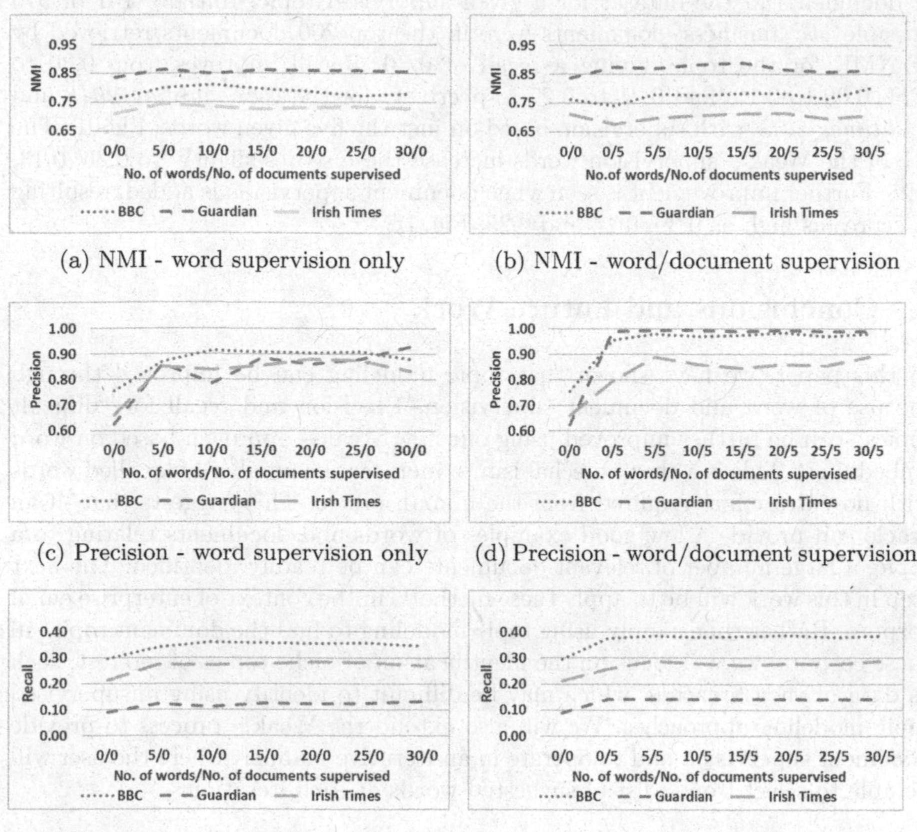

(a) NMI - word supervision only

(b) NMI - word/document supervision

(c) Precision - word supervision only

(d) Precision - word/document supervision

(e) Recall - word supervision only

(f) Recall - word/document supervision

Fig. 1. Plot of NMI, precision, and recall scores for SS-NMF applied on three corpora. The five words and documents provided by the oracle for one topic per corpus are supplemented by words recommended by the Weak+ process.

Since our main interest lies in examining the impact on the "difficult" topics in the three corpora, we next consider precision and recall relative to these supervised topics only. Precision measures the proportion of relevant documents found for a supervised topic – we consider the top 200 documents. Initially 151 of the top 200 documents retrieved by SS-NMF were found for the *bbc* 'business' topic giving a precision of 0.76. Precision shows a bigger improvement than NMI increasing from 0.76 to 0.87, 0.63 to 0.86 and 0.66 to 0.85 respectively for the *bbc*, *guardian-2013* and *irishtimes-2013* topics, with supervision based on just the five words provided by the oracle, Fig. 1c. The use of the Weak+ supervision words increase these scores to as high as 0.92, 0.93, 0.88. Further improvement is seen when supervision of five documents given by the oracle takes place, resulting in scores as high as 0.99, 1.00 and 0.89, Fig. 1d.

Recall measures the ratio of the number of documents found and the number of documents in the dataset for a given supervised topic. Initially 151 of 510 possible *bbc* 'business' documents were in the top 200 documents retrieved by SS-NMF for the topic, giving a recall of 0.30. Recall improves from 0.30 to 0.34, 0.09 to 0.12, and 0.21 to 0.27 respectively for the *bbc*, *guardian-2013* and *irishtimes-2013* with supervision based on just the five given words, Fig. 1e. The use of the Weak+ supervision words increase these scores slightly to 0.36, 0.13, 0.28. Further improvement is seen when document supervision is added, resulting in scores as high as 0.39, 0.14 and 0.29, Fig. 1f.

5 Conclusions and Future Work

In this paper, we have shown that topic modeling can be improved through the use of word and document supervision. Precision and recall for "difficult topics" can be further improved using our new Weak+ approach based on word embeddings. This is a cheap mechanism to increase the number of labelled words with no extra effort required from the human oracle. This suggests that, if an oracle can provide a few good examples of words and documents relating to a topic, a large number of relevant documents can be readily identified. The next step in this work will be to apply these methods in the context of enterprise email corpora. Rather than simply using topic modeling to find the dominant topics in these corpora, we will focus on the identification of niche topics of interest, such as data privacy breaches, which may be difficult to identify using unsupervised topic modeling approaches. We will also extend the Weak+ process to provide document supervision and to operate in an iterative manner, where the user will be able to select from a list of suggested words at each iteration.

Acknowledgement. This research was partly supported by Science Foundation Ireland (SFI) under Grant Number SFI/12/RC/2289.

References

1. Arora, S., Ge, R., Moitra, A.: Learning topic models-going beyond SVD. In: 53rd Annual Symposium on Foundations of Computer Science (FOCS), pp. 1–10 (2012)
2. Greene, D., Cunningham, P.: Constraint selection by committee: an ensemble approach to identifying informative constraints for semi-supervised clustering. In: Kok, J.N., Koronacki, J., Mantaras, R.L., Matwin, S., Mladenič, D., Skowron, A. (eds.) ECML 2007. LNCS, vol. 4701, pp. 140–151. Springer, Heidelberg (2007). doi:10.1007/978-3-540-74958-5_16
3. Kuang, D., Choo, J., Park, H.: Nonnegative matrix factorization for interactive topic modeling and document clustering. In: Partitional Clustering Algorithms, pp. 1–28 (2015)

4. Lee, D.D., Seung, H.S.: Learning the parts of objects by non-negative matrix factorization. Nature **401**(6755), 788–91 (1999)
5. Li, T., Ding, C., Jordan, M.I.: Solving consensus and semi-supervised clustering problems using nonnegative matrix factorization. In: Seventh IEEE International Conference on Data Mining (ICDM 2007), vol. 1, no. 2, pp. 577–582 (2007). https://doi.org/10.1109/ICDM.2007.98
6. Mikolov, T., Corrado, G., Chen, K., Dean, J.: Efficient estimation of word representations in vector space. In: Proceedings of ICLR 2013, pp. 1–12 (2013)
7. Rehurek, R.: gensim 1.0.0rc1: Python Package Index. https://pypi.python.org/pypi/gensim

Towards Interoperability in the European Poetry Community: The Standardization of Philological Concepts

Helena Bermúdez-Sabel[1(✉)], Mariana Curado Malta[1,2], and Elena Gonzalez-Blanco[1]

[1] Laboratorio de Innovación en Humanidades Digitales, Universidad de Educación a Distancia (UNED), Madrid, Spain
{helena.bermudez,mariana.malta,egonzalezblanco}@linhd.uned.es
[2] Polythecnic of Oporto, CEOS.PP, Oporto, Portugal
mariana@iscap.ipp.pt
http://linhd.uned.es
http://iscap.ipp.pt

Abstract. This paper stems from the Poetry Standardization and Linked Open Data project (POSTDATA). As its name reveals, one of the main aims of POSTDATA is to provide a means to publish European poetry (EP) data as Linked Open Data (LOD). Thus, developing a metadata application profile (MAP) as a common semantic model to be used by the EP community is a crucial step of this project. This MAP will enhance interoperability among the community members in particular, and among the EP community and other contexts in general (e.g. bibliographic records). This paper presents the methodology followed in the process of defining the concepts of the domain model of this MAP, as well as some issues that arise when labeling philological terms.

Keywords: Digital humanities · Literary data · Metadata application profile · Terms standardization · Vocabulary encoding scheme · Linked open data · Semantic web

1 Introduction

The need for information exchange has made it necessary to create international standards in most fields. The humanities have evolved independently from other fields [1], as there are important factors such as history, creativity or self-identity that influence each particular tradition with different results. The case of poetry is especially significant, as every country, group and literary genre has followed an independent and idiosyncratic path [2]. As a result of this, online access to poetry collections is highly fragmented [3].

Our challenge as researchers is to reduce the digital gap between the humanities and technology, aiming for interoperable solutions and for an interdisciplinary approach with innovative results that transcend the current state-of-the-art.

J. Gracia et al. (Eds.): LDK 2017, LNAI 10318, pp. 156–165, 2017.
DOI: 10.1007/978-3-319-59888-8_14

Individual literary works have a set of metadata (such as author, title, date of composition or language) that is shared by all literary works. There is also a more limited set of properties that are specific to poetry (such as rhyme, metrical scheme or the number of stanzas). These tags are easy to recognize and would probably fit into any possible classification of any poetic corpus. The problem, however, is that every literary tradition has evolved in a particular way, coining different names and creating different conceptual systems to describe similar phenomena.[1] These differences apply to the way of naming lines, stanzas, poems, rhyme schemes and rhythmical patterns [5].

The first attempts of classification, shaped as metrical repertoires, were published in the late nineteenth century with the aim of gathering the lyrical materials that had been circulating around Europe. During the twentieth century, the number of repertoires and poetic catalogues grew, as also did the criteria and techniques to build them. In the nineteen nineties, some of these books were transformed into digital databases. A good example of this transformation is *Die nicht-lyrischen strophenformen des Altfranzöischen* by Gotthold Naetebus, a poetic repertoire of French Medieval narrative poetry first published in 1891 [6]. This repertoire became the *Nouveau Naetebus* [7]: a digital resource that recovered the original book and incorporated useful information complemented by relevant studies. A very similar and interesting case is *Répertoire de la poésie hongroise ancienne* [9], a repertoire of Hungarian poetry by Horváth [8] already conceived as a digital collection. Further examples of this include the Galician-Portuguese database *MedDB, Base de Datos da Lírica Galego-Portuguesa*, directed by Mercedes Brea [10], which gathers both the secular lyric corpus and the metric and rhyming schemes of the metrical repertoire by Tavani [11], the metrical repertoire by Pillet and Carstens for Occitan lyrics [12], transformed into *BEdT - Bibliografa Elettronica dei Trovatori*, directed by Stefano Asperti [13], or *REMETCA: Repertorio métrico de la poesía medieval castellana* [14]. These, however, are just a few instances of scholarly attempts at metric systematization. Meanwhile, the traditional publications, printed in paper, continued with the repertoires of Antonelli [15], Pagnotta [16], Solimena [17] or Gorni [18] for the Italian lyrics, including, for instance, the Sicilian tradition or the so-called *Dolce Stil Novo*, Betti's repertoire for the *Cantigas de Santa Maria* [19], or a few Spanish examples such as [20] for medieval Catalan metrics or [21] for fifteenth-century Castilian metrics, which has been recently transformed into a online database [22].

Although all of these repertoires and databases focus on the "poem" as their object of study, the way in which they conceptualize the information is very different, and the resulting databases cannot communicate. Thus, interoperability is very complex for two main reasons. First, for technological reasons, as each database is modeled in a different way and may use a different technology, and second, due to the philological tradition, as each literary tradition has followed an independent path to encode its metrical and poetic information. The result is a variety of terminological and classification systems that are very difficult to communicate, especially when it comes to finding equivalences or looking for common models in different traditions.

---

[1] See [4] for a more detailed definition of "literary tradition".

The present article reports a work-in-progress that deals with the standardization of philological concepts and terms. The research for this paper was carried out in the context of POSTDATA, a European Research Council Starting Grant project that aims to reduce the digital gap between the humanities and technology by looking for interoperability solutions. The paper is organized in five sections. The following section briefly explains the technological context of the project. Section 3 presents the methodology followed during the analysis of the databases of the repertoires, and Sect. 4 expounds the issues that arose during the process of concept identification. Section 5 presents our conclusions and briefly explores future work.

2 Linked Open Data and Interoperability

"The classic definition is literal, based on the etymology of the word itself–metadata is 'data about data'" [23, p. 1]; it is data about concepts that represent tangible and non-tangible objects that exist in the real world. This data is published in the Web of Data, a "giant global graph" [24] of data. The Web of Data is not only about publishing data on the Web, it is also about linking this data [25] to enable the access and analysis of data from different sources to final users. This access takes place through the use of software applications that can connect data and and make inferences about it. The data that is linked and open in the Web of Data is called Linked Open Data (LOD).

Publishing data as LOD in the Web of Data is a process that must start with a good data modeling. Linked data must endorse a semantic model before being published. Since this data comes from different sources that incorporate multiple contexts within various cultures and languages, this process of modeling becomes very complex. According to [26], metadata must be modeled as a metadata application profile (MAP) in order to become interoperable. [27] define a MAP as "a generic construct for designing metadata records."

Semantic interoperability is a very important issue in regard to LOD. Interoperability makes it possible for multiple systems with different programs, hardware, and data structures and interfaces to exchange data without previous communication, losing a minimum of content and functionality [23].

As mentioned above (Sect. 1), this work concerns the European Poetry community. It stems from the POSTDATA project, which has as one of its main goals to provide the means for this community of practice to publish data as LOD (for more details about the project see [28]). In the next section, we explain the process whereby POSTDATA is developing a MAP for EP in order to enhance interoperability in the EP community.

3 Methodology

In order to develop a MAP for the European Poetry, the authors are following a systematic set of activities defined by Me4MAP [29]. The issues addressed in this paper are part of the S1 and S2 activities "Defining the Functional Requirements" and "Defining the Domain Model", respectively.

The definition of the domain model, a common conceptual model that should represent the informational needs of the EP community of practice, integrates the data requirements that result from S1, together with the results of the following sub-activities:

- analysis of the data model of a representative sample of EP databases, and
- analysis of a survey addressed to the final users of the repertoires in order to understand the data needs of the users of poetry databases.[2]

The process of developing the domain model is highly iterative: it is made of micro-steps of analysis of data models in which every micro-step might feed a previous analysis, depending on the conclusion of the analysis at hand. The technique used to analyze each data model is described in [30] and is not further explained here, as it is not the object of this paper.

During the process of analysis of a data model (1) every concept of the database, as well as the properties that characterize that concept, are identified and (2) the relationships between concepts are also identified. In what follows, these conceptual elements will be referred to as "Concepts" regardless of whether they are concepts, properties or relationships between concepts.

As it has been mentioned, the analysis is very iterative, which means that similar Concepts that have been already identified in previous analyses are compared with the current analysis, and that those Concepts that are equivalent are given the same description and named in the same way.

Occasionally, the level of abstraction increases and names are changed retroactively; that is, previous analyses are re-evaluated. In the beginning of the process abstraction is low, but it increases with the number of analyses made. As a result, at the end of the procedure the level of abstraction is higher than it was at the start, which decreases the level of granularity of the final model. As in any process of semantic modeling, there is always some tension between interoperability and semantics. The level of semantics is related to the possibilities of data sharing, which means that the researchers look for the highest level of meaning in the definition of the Concepts without compromising interoperability. The same Concepts from different databases will contain data that can be shared, and different Concepts will contain data that cannot be shared. However, if a specific Concept is different but similar to other Concept that has been already identified while analyzing other databases, semantics may be lost in favor of interoperability gain: a new broader Concept is created.

Every Concept analysis integrates the actions presented in Fig. 1. The process begins with the identification of a Concept in a data model analysis. Then a study of similar Concepts in the previous data model analyses is carried out in order to understand if the Concept at hand is new or if it has already been identified. Two possibilities arise:

[2] Survey available at http://postdata.linhd.es/limesurvey/index.php/113575.

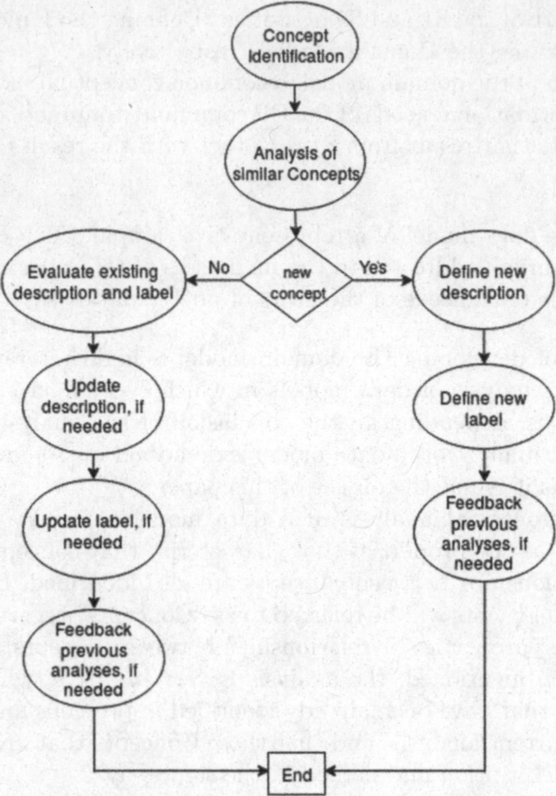

Fig. 1. Diagram with the sequence of actions of a Concept analysis process

- If there is a new Concept: a new description and a new label are defined. If the working group realizes that there are changes to be implemented in previous descriptions or labels during the definition of the description for the new Concept, an update is done in order to re-define preceding data model analyses. The process ends here and the analysis follows the study of a new Concept.
- If there is no new Concept: an evaluation of the description for the same Concept is undertaken, and from that evaluation, there might be an update of the description and label. If this update is required, changes are introduced to the previous analyses, otherwise, the process ends here. The analysis follows the study of a new Concept.

The process of analysis ends when there are no more new Concepts to analyze. The working group moves then to the study of the next data model. The procedure ends when all the data models are analyzed and there are no remaining feedback updates. As it has been explained, the methodology forces the process of analysis to continually reiterate over previous results, so the feedback process is constant. This method avoids any over-representation or bias that could arise due to the order in which the databases are studied.

It is very important to integrate application domain experts since the early stages of development to guarantee the soundness of the foundations on which we keep building the project [29]. Every database has a delegate that verifies the accuracy of the interpretation of the concepts that the working group make. In addition, the aforementioned survey brings a broader sense of the data needs of the community of practice.

4 Concepts Standardization

Some of the fields of study included within the *jurisdiction* of philology have already paid great attention to the construction of standards. For instance, libraries have led the standardization projects in the humanistic field, and as such, the efforts to regularize the metadata of bibliographic records have been remarkably successful [31,32]. The same can be said about other consolidated projects, such as the Text Encoding Initiative, which succeeded at presenting to the research community highly-adopted recommendations for multi-purpose encoding of digital texts [33]. Since these initiatives already convey the means to describe most of the physical artifacts studied by philologists, we make use of the same terminology as much as possible.

On a similar note, much work has been devoted in the last decades[3] to the standardization of linguistic resources (for an updated state-of-the-art see [35]). However, in our study of poetry databases, we could corroborate that the implementation of linguistic standards in projects whose main object of analysis is not purely linguistic seems to be inadequate: none of the analyzed projects that include linguistic information used any existing standard or recommendation, but employed their own model. As a result, we decided that the conceptualization of morphosyntactic and lexical features will be left out during these first stages of the project. Nevertheless, we do model phonetic information when it is recorded due to metrical implications.

The aforementioned context justifies the focus of this paper on literary terms since they are the weakest link of the philological field in terms of standardization. Despite the existence of glossaries and dictionaries that collect information on literary concepts and their denomination, the goal of these works is to be a reference on the subject, to *accumulate* knowledge, not to offer a standardization proposal (least of all, a proposal to be implemented in a digital environment for interoperability purposes).

The aim of this paper is not to expound a taxonomy of literary devices, but to delineate the decision-making process that the authors went through during the selection of concepts and labels. The core points of our criteria are the following:

[3] For instance, the *EAGLES Guidelines*, a set of recommendations for *de facto* standards and for good practice in computational linguistics, was already a consolidated project in 1996. For more information visit its website at http://www.ilc.cnr.it/EAGLES/home.html.

Lingua franca. When establishing a norm, choosing the most widespread label seems like a straightforward criterion. However, our starting point is a multilingual corpus, so the selection of the most common term could not be acknowledged. More so when the same language may present various terms to refer to the same concept. Considering the status of English as a *lingua franca* in science and technology, the most prevalent terminology in the English-speaking scientific community was taken as reference [36,37].
For instance, the concept that defines "the grouping of lines forming the basic recurring metrical unit in a poem or song" receives different names depending on the language (*estrofa*, *strophe*, *strofă* ...). Moreover, certain particularities of a poetic school might determine the existence of various terms for this same concept in one language. In Portuguese, for instance, the term *cobra* is used in relation to the lyric poetic movement, while the more generic term *estrofe* is used in other contexts. In the present standardization proposal, all recurring line groupings were conceptualized as "stanza".

Neutral terms. The selection of "marked" terms is avoided. Although existing terms are hardly ever completely neutral, great care was taken to select labels that do not have special connotations depending on the theoretical approach. For example, this proposal considers the term "apparatus" instead of the more common "critical apparatus" or even *"apparatus criticus"* in order to wrap any recording of textual variants under this label. Hence, we separate the concept from the ecdotic model of critical editions, enabling its use by genetic or synoptic editions without inheriting any theoretical baggage.

Semantic efficiency. The authors' judgments as philologists when facing the materials also play an important role in the decision making process. For instance, our proposal pays great attention to the discerning of textual materials that are previous to the work under analysis (source texts), from those that are contemporary and which may present intertextual relations, and those texts that might have been influenced by the work at hand (derived). Opposite to these concepts, any type of subsequent bibliographical source (including previous editions of the work) is categorized separately. The reason behind these categorial distinctions is that we have identified the potentiality of the application of LOD to map interrelationships between texts. If not explicitly stated in the primary source, these intertextual relations are established by the researchers, which means that they are limited to their knowledge of other literary traditions. Thanks to this method, a researcher in French poetry, with no previous knowledge of Hungarian, can find out which Hungarian poems share the same Latin influences as poems in the corpus s/he is studying. Furthermore, many research questions regarding the existence of intermediary texts in the interrelatedness of literary works could be explored.

Although the level of abstraction in relation to the number of analyzed databases increases (see Sect. 3), the need to further restrain a concept arises sporadically. For instance, most projects include the concept of "metrical scheme". Usually, in the context of a certain tradition the term is unequivocal. However, we decided to establish different categories to define metrical patterns according to the type of meter, that is, syllabic, accentual, accentual-syllabic, and quantitative. Through this course of action, we facilitate that, for instance, a syllabic-verse tradition may find more efficiently similar metrical patterns by taking out the schemes that are not analogous.

Validity check. We evaluate the input of the targeted community of users in order to make decisions regarding the relevance of terms and the quality of their denomination. Our work is always open to be reviewed.

5 Conclusion and Future Work

"There have been great societies that did not use the wheel, but there have been no societies that did not tell stories" [34, p. 22]. If we were to make a comprehensive analysis of how these stories have been built in the European context, we would get a very complex network of relations between the multiple literary traditions developed by the different linguistic communities. As stated by Even-Zohar [38], there are not any European literatures which have not leaned heavily on some other literature [38, p. 48]. As a result, even outside of Comparative Literature, any type of approach that engages with the cultural analysis of a community demands the study of cultural heritages other than the one under study.

Although we can agree on the existing connections among all European literary traditions, and even though the digitalization of cultural heritages facilitates the exploration and retrieval of information, the lack of standards to define the mechanisms employed in the creation of a literary work is a hindrance for complex comparative studies; a hindrance that we aim to surmount, as it has been delineated in this paper. Our solution entails the construction of the required means for literary data to be published as LOD. Due to the relation of this proposal with the POSTDATA (Poetry Standardization and Linked Open Data) project, our object of analysis is data related to European poetics.

The foundation of the POSTDATA work is the development of a MAP, which depends on the definition of a domain model, that is, the common conceptual model that represents the informational needs of the EP community. In order to elicit these informational needs, the authors studied a representative sample of existing resources and consult the EP community as a whole through a survey. In addition, the work undertaken by POSTDATA enables the analysis of poetry within a broader and more complete context. The standardization process overcomes any linguistic barriers and it collocates the cultural products of minoritized communities with major traditions.

After defining the domain model, future work will entail the definition of the RDF vocabulary terms that best describe the concepts of the domain model and the development of vocabulary encoding schemes to constrain certain terms of the model in order to further enhance interoperability. The enrichment of our proposal with this last process will be a major step as regards the standardization of terms in the philological field. It will thus open new lines of inquiry on Literary and Cultural studies and it will enhance the existing ones in order to gain a better understanding of Western cultures.

Acknowledgments. The authors would like to thank the researchers in charge of the analyzed repertoires for their availability and willingness to share information and to discuss issues related to their projects with the POSTDATA team. Mariana Curado Malta thanks the Polytechnic of Oporto for the 3-year leave that granted her the possibility to work in POSTDATA, a wonderful and challenging professional experience in Madrid-UNED. Research for this paper has been achieved thanks to the Starting Grant research project *Poetry Standardization and Linked Open Data: POSTDATA* (ERC-2015-STG-679528), funded by European Research Council (ERC) under the research and innovation program Horizon2020 of the European Union (http://postdata.linhd.es).

References

1. Bod, R.: How a new field could help save the humanities. http://www.chronicle.com/article/How-a-New-Field-Could-Help/239209/
2. Gonzalez-Blanco, E.: Actualidad de las Humanidades Digitales y un ejemplo de ensamblaje poético en la red: ReMetCa. Cuadernos Hispanoamericanos **761**, 53–67 (2013)
3. González-Blanco, E., Selaf, L.: Megarep: A comprehensive research tool in medieval and renaissance poetic and metrical repertoires. In: Humanitats a la xarxa: món medieval/Humanities on the Web: The Medieval World, pp. 321–332. Peter Lang (2014)
4. Literary Articles: Literary tradition (2012). https://literacle.com/literary-tradition
5. Gonzalez-Blanco, E., del Rio Riande, G., Martínez Cantón, C.: Linked open data to represent multilingual poetry collections. A proposal to solve interoperability issues between poetic repertoires. In: Proceedings of the LREC (Tenth International Conference on Language Resources and Evaluation) 2016 Workshop "LDL 2016–5th Workshop on Linked Data in Linguistics: Managing, Building and Using Linked Language Resources" (2016)
6. Naetebus, G.: Die nicht-lyrischen Strophenformen des Altfranzösischen: ein Verzeichnis. Druck von J.B. Hirschfeld, Leipzig (1891)
7. Seláf, L.: Le Nouveau Naetebus. Poémes strophiques non-lyriques en français des origines jusqu'á 1400. http://nouveaunaetebus.elte.hu/
8. Horváth, I.: Répertoire de la poésie hongroise ancienne: Manuel de correction d'erreurs dans la base de données. Editions du Nouvel Objet (1992)
9. Horváth, I.: Répertoire de la poésie hongroise ancienne. http://rpha.elte.hu/
10. Centro Ramón Piñeiro para a Investigación en Humanidades: MedDB - Base de datos da Lírica Profana Galego-Portuguesa. www.cirp.es/meddb
11. Tavani, G.: Repertorio metrico della lirica galego-portoghese. Edizioni dell'Ateneo, Roma (1967)
12. Pillet, A., Carstens, H.: Bibliographie der Troubadours. M. Niemeyer, Halle (Saale) (1933)
13. Asperti, S., De Nigro, L.: Bibliografia Elettronica dei Trovatori. http://www.bedt.it/BEdT_04_25/index.aspx
14. Gonzalez-Blanco, E.: ReMetCa. http://www.remetca.uned.es
15. Antonelli, R.: Repertorio metrico della Scuola poetica siciliana. Centro di Studi Filologici e Linguistici Siciliani (1984)
16. Pagnotta, L.: Repertorio metrico della ballata italiana: secoli XIII e XIV. R. Ricciardi (1995)
17. Solimena, A.: Repertorio metrico dei poeti siculo-toscani. Centro di Studi Filologici e Linguistici Siciliani (2000)

18. Gorni, G.: Repertorio metrico della canzone italiana dalle origini al Cinquecento (REMCI). Franco Cesati, Firenze (2008)
19. Betti, M.P.: Diciassettesimo Repertorio metrico delle Cantigas de santa Maria di Alfonso X di Castiglia. Pacini Editore, Ospedaletto (Pisa) (2005)
20. Parramon i Blasco, J.: Repertori mètric de la poesia catalana medieval. Publicacions de l'Abadia de Montserrat, Barcelona (1992)
21. Gómez-Bravo, A.M.: Repertorio métrico de la poesía cancioneril castellana del siglo XV. University of California, Berkeley (1991)
22. Escribano, J.J., Gonzalez-Blanco, E., del Rio Riande, G.: PoeMetCa—Recursos digitales para el estudio de la Poesía Medieval Castellana (2016). http://poemetca.linhd.es/
23. Riley, J.: Understanding Metadata: What is Metadata, and What is it For?: A Primer. NISO Press, Bethesda (2017)
24. Heath, T., Bizer, C.: Linked data: evolving the web into a global data space. Synth. Lect. Semant. Web Theor. Technol. 1, 1–136 (2011)
25. Berners-Lee, T.: Linked data - design issues. https://www.w3.org/DesignIssues/LinkedData.html
26. Nilsson, M., Baker, T., Johnston, P.: Interoperability levels for Dublin core metadata. http://dublincore.org/documents/interoperability-levels/
27. Coyle, K., Baker, T.: Guidelines for Dublin core application profiles. http://dublincore.org/documents/profile-guidelines/
28. Curado Malta, M., González-Blanco, E., Martínez Cantón, C., del Rio Riande, G.: Digital repertoires of poetry metrics: towards a linked open data ecosystem. In: Proceedings of the First Workshop on Digital Humanities and Digital Curation co-located with the 10th Conference on Metadata and Semantics Research, MTSR 2016, CEUR Workshop Proceedings, pp. 1–11 (2016)
29. Curado Malta, M., Baptista, A.A.: Me4MAP V1.0: a method for the development of metadata application profiles. Submitted for publication (n.d.)
30. Curado Malta, M., Centenera, P., Gonzalez-Blanco, E.: Using reverse engineering to define a domain model: the case of the development of a metadata application profile for European poetry. In: Developing Metadata Application Profiles, pp. 146–180. IGI Global (2017)
31. DCMI Usage Board: DCMI metadata terms. http://dublincore.org/documents/dcmi-terms/
32. IFLA: Functional requirements for bibliographic records (2009). http://archive.ifla.org/VII/s13/frbr/frbr_current_toc.htm
33. TEI Consortium (eds.): TEI P5: guidelines for electronic text encoding and interchange. http://www.tei-c.org/Guidelines/P5/
34. Guin, U.K.L.: The Language of the Night: Essays on Fantasy and Science Fiction. HarperCollins, New York (1992)
35. Herzog, G., Heid, U., Trippel, T., Bański, P., Romary, L., Schmidt, T., Witt, A., Eckart, K.: Recent initiatives towards new standards for language resources. In: Presented at the International Conference of the German Society for Computational Linguistics and Language Technology, 30 September 2015
36. Baldick, C.: The Oxford Dictionary of Literary Terms. Oxford University Press, Oxford (2015)
37. Abrams, M.H.: A Glossary of Literary Terms. Harcourt Brace College Publishers, New York (1999)
38. Even-Zohar, I.: Papers in Historical Poetics. Porter Institute for Poetics and Semiotics, Tel Aviv (1978)

Joint Entity Recognition and Linking in Technical Domains Using Undirected Probabilistic Graphical Models

Hendrik ter Horst(✉), Matthias Hartung, and Philipp Cimiano

Cognitive Interaction Technology Cluster of Excellence (CITEC), Semantic Computing Group, Bielefeld University, Bielefeld, Germany
{hterhors,mhartung,cimiano}@techfak.uni-bielefeld.de

Abstract. The problems of recognizing mentions of entities in texts and linking them to unique knowledge base identifiers have received considerable attention in recent years. In this paper we present a probabilistic system based on undirected graphical models that jointly addresses both the entity recognition and the linking task. Our framework considers the span of mentions of entities as well as the corresponding knowledge base identifier as random variables and models the joint assignment using a factorized distribution. We show that our approach can be easily applied to different technical domains by merely exchanging the underlying ontology. On the task of recognizing and linking disease names, we show that our approach outperforms the state-of-the-art systems *DNorm* and *TaggerOne*, as well as two strong lexicon-based baselines. On the task of recognizing and linking chemical names, our system achieves comparable performance to the state-of-the-art.

Keywords: Joint entity recognition and linking · Undirected probabilistic graphical models · Diseases · Chemicals

1 Introduction

In light of the current proliferation of openly accessible textual data and structured symbolic knowledge in the LOD cloud[1], a versatile approach to the representation of text meaning relies on linking mentions in a text to entities, relations or classes defined in a reference knowledge base such as DBpedia[2] or MeSH[3]. Being coined as named entity disambiguation, entity linking, or wikification, this task has received considerable attention in recent years [7,15,16].

As a subtask in machine reading, i.e., automatically transforming unstructured natural language text into structured knowledge [19], entity linking facilitates various applications such as entity-centric search or predictive analytics

[1] http://lod-cloud.net/.
[2] http://wiki.dbpedia.org.
[3] Medical Subject Headings: https://www.nlm.nih.gov/mesh.

J. Gracia et al. (Eds.): LDK 2017, LNAI 10318, pp. 166–180, 2017.
DOI: 10.1007/978-3-319-59888-8_15

in knowledge graphs. In these tasks, it is advisable to search for the entities involved at the level of unique knowledge base identifiers rather than surface forms mentioned in the text, as the latter are ubiquitously subject to variation (e.g., spelling variants, semantic paraphrases, or abbreviations). Thus, entities at the concept level cannot be reliable retrieved or extracted from text using exact string match techniques.

Prior to linking the surface mentions to their respective concepts, named entity recognition [17] is required in order to identify all sequences of tokens in the input sentence that denote an entity of a particular type (e.g., diseases or chemicals). Until recently, named entity recognition and entity linking have been mostly performed as separate tasks in pipeline architectures ([7,20], inter alia).

In this paper, we present *JLink*[4], a versatile approach to *joint* entity recognition and linking that can be easily applied to different technical domains by exchanging the underlying knowledge base and training data. The approach exploits undirected probabilistic graphical models (factor graphs, in particular) and Markov Chain Monte Carlo methods for inference. Parameter updates are computed using SampleRank [24].

We train and evaluate the system in two experiments focusing on joint entity recognition and linking of diseases and chemical compounds, respectively. In both tasks, the BioCreative V CDR data [23] is used for training and testing. We apply the same model to both problems, only exchanging the underlying reference knowledge base. With an F_1 score of 85.9 in disease linking, we outperform the state-of-the-art systems *DNorm* [12] and *TaggerOne* [11]; in chemical compounds linking, our system achieves an F_1 score of 86.6, which is comparable to the state-of-the-art. Thus, JLink provides high performance on both domains without major need of manual adaptation or system tuning.

2 Related Work

Entity linking approaches have mostly relied on three main sources of information: *Local models* investigate the textual context of a surface entity mention ([15], inter alia), *global models* aim at collective linking of all entities within the same document ([20], inter alia), and *graph-based models* focus on the relation between surface mentions and entity candidates ([16], inter alia).

More recently, these sources have been combined in probabilistic graphical models. The approach by Hakimov et al. [5] incorporates textual and graph-based features in a factor graph model in order to capture compatibilities of pairs of mentions and entities within the same document. Their results show that entity co-occurrences and mention-entity pairs provide complementary information to the model. Based on the same sources of information, Ganea et al. [4] train a Markov network for the entity linking task, using approximate MAP inference by belief propagation. Both Ganea et al. and Hakimov et al. perform entity linking in isolation by relying on gold annotations for the recognition problem.

[4] https://github.com/ag-sc/JLink.

Probabilistic graphical models can be used to couple the tasks of named entity recognition and entity linking in joint models such that mutual dependencies between both problems are exploited. This avenue has recently been explored by Durrett and Klein [2], Luo et al. [14] and Nguyen et al. [18]. Consistently, these approaches extend conditional random fields (CRF; [10]) which constitute the state-of-the-art in named entity recognition. By extending linear-chain CRFs to tree-shaped factor graphs based on syntactic dependency relations between variables, non-local features considering entity-entity pairs or entity-level priors can be incorporated as well [3]. In our work presented here, we adopt an even more flexible model structure which is sufficiently versatile to encode non-local information, while it does not require dependency parsing.

In contrast to the latter approaches which all use Wikipedia as reference knowledge base, there are several domain-specific approaches to entity linking. We focus our discussion on the biomedical domain and disease/chemical recognition and linking, as this is our application scenario in this paper. The DNorm system [12] relies on a learning-to-rank approach in order to induce similarities between disease mentions and concept names directly from training data. However, the system does not include any information about coherence between different entities within the same text. In contrast to DNorm, TaggerOne [11] performs entity recognition and linking simultaneously, using a combination of semi-Markovian sequence labeling (for the recognition problem) and supervised semantic indexing (for the linking problem). These components do not share any parameters, i.e., possible dependencies between the individual problems are not captured in the model. The system by Lee et al. [13], combining disease recognition and linking in a sequential pipeline architecture, obtained the best performance at the BioCreative V Shared Task on disease linking [23]. However, their approach is specifically tailored to the domain as it strongly capitalizes on strategies for expanding the reference knowledge base, which is not our focus in this work. Instead, we aim at a more general model for joint entity recognition and linking that can be flexibly adapted to knowledge bases from various domains. In that respect, our work follows similar goals as the AGDISTIS framework [22], which performs entity linking that is agnostic of the underlying knowledge base, without considering the recognition problem, though.

3 Method

We frame the entity recognition and linking tasks as a joint inference problem in an undirected probabilistic graphical model framework. In such a model, a factor graph representation is used to decompose a joint probability distribution over observed and hidden random variables. In the following, we (i) describe the notion of factor graphs, (ii) show how we use them to represent the problem domain for joint entity recognition and linking, and (iii) how we perform inference over factor graphs using Markov Chain Monte Carlo sampling (Sects. 3.1–3.3). In Sect. 3.4, we describe how the parameters of our model are optimized using SampleRank. Section 3.5 presents the methods used in order to retrieve candidate concepts from a reference knowledge base. The features of our model are described in Sect. 3.6.

3.1 Factor Graphs

Following Kschischang et al. [9] and Hakimov et al. [5], we define a factor graph $\mathcal{G}$ as a bipartite graph that consists of variables V and factors Ψ. Variables can further be divided into *observed* variables $\boldsymbol{x}$ and *hidden* variables $\boldsymbol{y}$. A factor Ψ_i connects subsets of observed variables $\boldsymbol{x}_i$ and hidden variables $\boldsymbol{y}_i$. Each factor computes a scalar score based on the exponential of the scalar product of a feature vector $f_i(\boldsymbol{x}_i, \boldsymbol{y}_i)$ to be determined from the corresponding subset of variables and a set of parameters θ_i: $\Psi_i = e^{f_i(\boldsymbol{x}_i,\boldsymbol{y}_i)\cdot\theta_i}$. Based on these definitions, the inference problem in factor graphs, i.e., computing the posterior distribution of the hidden variables given the observed ones, can be formulated in terms of the product of the individual factors:

$$p(\boldsymbol{y}|\boldsymbol{x};\theta) = \frac{1}{Z(\boldsymbol{x})} \prod_{\Psi_i \in \mathcal{G}} e^{\Psi_i} = \frac{1}{Z(\boldsymbol{x})} \prod_{\Psi_i \in \mathcal{G}} e^{f_i(\boldsymbol{x}_i,\boldsymbol{y}_i)\cdot\theta_i} \tag{1}$$

where $Z(\boldsymbol{x})$ is the normalization function.

For a given set of observed variables, we generate a factor graph automatically making use of factor templates $\mathcal{T}$. Each template $T_j \in \mathcal{T}$ defines (i) the subsets of observed and hidden variables $(\boldsymbol{x}_j, \boldsymbol{y}_j)$ for which it can generate factors and (ii) a function $f_j(\boldsymbol{x}_j, \boldsymbol{y}_j)$ to generate features for these variables. All factors generated by a given template T_j share the same parameters θ_j. With this definition, we can reformulate the conditional probability from Eq. (1) as follows:

$$p(\boldsymbol{y}|\boldsymbol{x};\theta) = \frac{1}{Z(\boldsymbol{x})} \prod_{T_j \in \mathcal{T}} \prod_{(\boldsymbol{x}_j,\boldsymbol{y}_j) \in T_j} e^{f_j(\boldsymbol{x}_j,\boldsymbol{y}_j)\cdot\theta_j} \tag{2}$$

Thus, we define a probability distribution over possible configurations of observed and hidden variables, which enables us to explore the joint space of variable assignments in a probabilistic fashion.

3.2 Model Structure

Each document d is defined as a tuple $d = \langle \boldsymbol{w}, \boldsymbol{t}, \boldsymbol{m}, \boldsymbol{c} \rangle$ comprising an observed sequence of tokens $\boldsymbol{w}$ together with hidden sequences of non-overlapping entity mentions $\boldsymbol{m}$ and corresponding concepts $\boldsymbol{c}$. Further, we capture possible semantic transformations $\boldsymbol{t}$ as hidden variables that are intended to capture (near-) synonymy of individual tokens. Semantic transformations can be applied to observed input words in order to facilitate the normalization step in cases where a surface mention and a concept name differ by one synonymous token (e.g., "kidney dysfunction" vs. "kidney disease"). Each annotation span can have only one semantic transformation and must have at least one token that was not

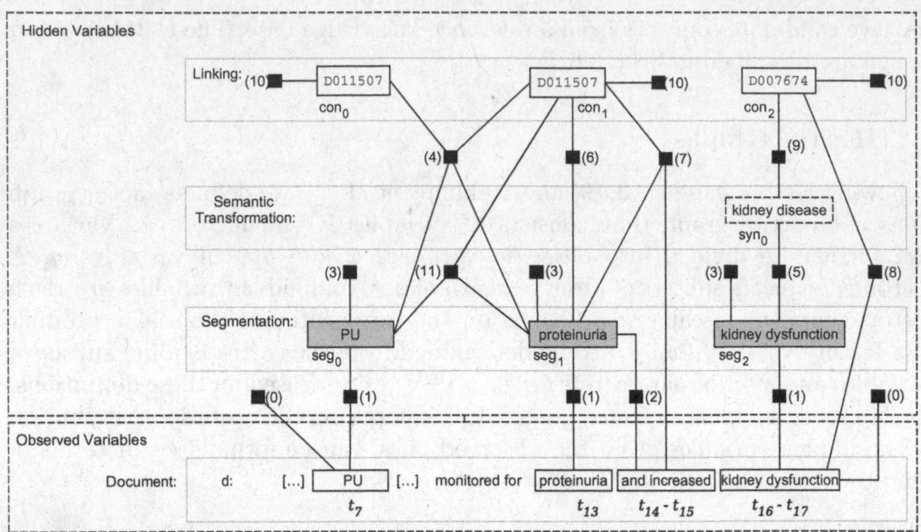

Fig. 1. Simplified factor graph for a correctly annotated document. The figure shows all different types of factors (small black boxes) that are used in order to link observed and hidden variables. Hidden variables comprise concept variables (nodes labeled as con_i), semantic transformation variables (syn_i), and segmentation (recognition) variables (seg_i). Individual factor types are numbered to be referenceable (cf. Sect. 3.6). The approach tackles both tasks, recognition and linking, thus the only observed variables are the tokens from the pre-tokenized document content marked as t_i.

semantically transformed. Figure 1 shows a (simplified) factor graph representation of our model for an example document.

We define one specific assignment of values to these variables in a document as a *state*. By applying Eq. (2), we can compute the probability of each state, which will be exploited during inference and learning.

3.3 Inference

In order to assign values to the hidden variables in the model, i.e., recognize token spans corresponding to entity types of interest and link them to knowledge base identifiers, we perform approximate inference following a Markov Chain Monte Carlo (MCMC) sampling scheme [21]. In MCMC sampling, the goal is to construct an approximation that is maximally close to the posterior distribution of interest, while sharing the factorization properties as defined by the factor graph [8]. This is achieved by generating a sequence of *states*, each of which corresponds to an assignment of a value to all (or a subset of) the variables in the model (cf. Sect. 3.2). Thus, by performing a local search, this procedure successively explores the search space of variable assignments for a given document.

Exploring the Search Space. Initially, an empty state s_0 is generated for each document, which can be modified in subsequent sampling steps. In each iteration, an annotation span explorer and a concept assignment explorer are consecutively applied in order to generate a set of proposal states which differ from the current state in one atomic change. The annotation span explorer is able to add a new non-overlapping (empty) annotation, remove an existing annotation, or apply a semantic transformation to one token. We do not extend or shrink existing spans. Instead, new annotations can be of different length, spanning 1 to 10 tokens. The concept assignment explorer can assign a concept to an empty annotation, or change or remove one from an non-empty annotation.

Applying these explorers in an alternating consecutive manner effectively guarantees that all variable assignments are mutually guided by several sources of information: (i) Possible concept assignments can inform the annotation span explorer in proposing valid spans over observed input tokens, while (ii) proposing different annotation spans together with semantic transformations on these may facilitate concept linking. Thus, this intertwined sampling strategy effectively enables joint inference on the recognition and the linking task. In order to illustrate the sampling procedure, Fig. 2 shows a subset of proposal states as generated by the annotation span explorer.

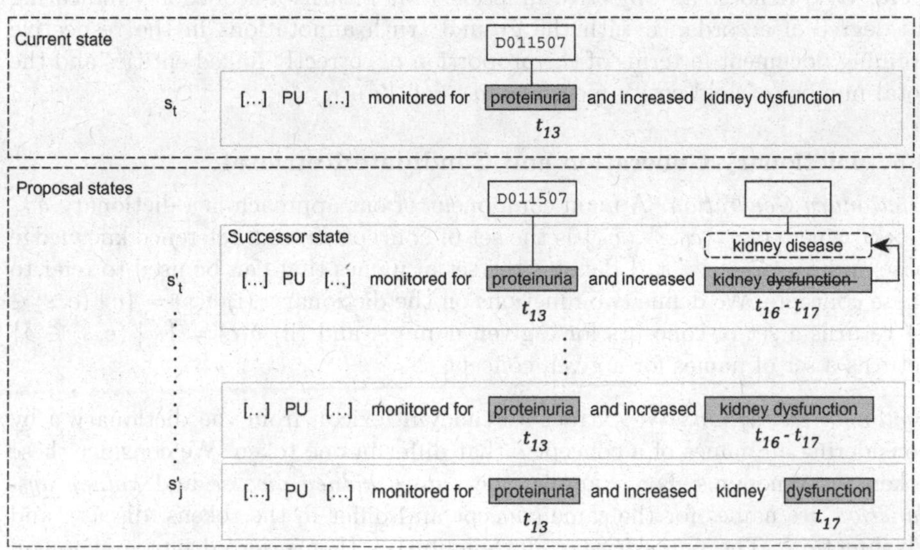

Fig. 2. Subset of proposal states generated by the annotation span explorer, originating from the current state s_t which has already one annotated span on token t_{13}. Each proposal state has a new non-overlapping segment annotation (marked in grey). Proposal states may include semantic transformations (depicted as dashed boxes). As shown for s'_t, new annotations have an empty concept assigned. Semantic transformations in a successor state are accepted for all subsequent sampling steps.

Evaluating States. From the set of all generated proposal states, we select one state s_{t+1} to be used as the successor state in the subsequent sampling step, following Hakimov et al. [5]. States are evaluated according to their individual probability (cf. Eq. 2). But, the possible successor state s'_t is only accepted if its probability is higher than the probability of the current state s_t[5]:

$$s_{t+1} = \begin{cases} s'_t, & \text{if } p(s'_t) \geq p(s_t) \\ s_t, & \text{otherwise} \end{cases} \tag{3}$$

3.4 Parameter Learning

The learning problem consists in finding the optimal weight matrix θ that maximizes the probability of a sequence of assigned entity labels given observed training sequences (cf. Eq. 2). We use SampleRank [24] to learn these parameters based on gradient descent on pairs of states (s_t, s'_t) that are investigated in individual steps of the inference procedure. Two states are compared according to the following preference function $\mathbb{P} : S \times S \rightarrow \{0, 1\}$:

$$\mathbb{P}(s', s) = \begin{cases} 1, & \text{if } \mathbb{O}(s') > \mathbb{O}(s) \\ 0, & \text{otherwise} \end{cases} \tag{4}$$

Here, $\mathbb{O}(s)$ denotes an objective function that returns a score for s indicating its degree of accordance with the ground truth annotations in the respective training document in terms of the proportion of correctly linked entities and the total number of gold entity mentions in s (cf. [5]).

3.5 Dictionary Generation and Candidate Retrieval

Dictionary Generation. A main component of our approach is a dictionary $\delta \subseteq C \times S$, where $C = \{c_0, \ldots, c_n\}$ is the set of concepts from a reference knowledge base and $S = \{s_0, \ldots, s_m\}$ denotes the set of names that can be used to refer to these concepts. We define two functions on the dictionary: (i) $\delta(s) = \{c \mid (c, s) \in \delta\}$ returns a set of concepts for a given name s, and (ii) $\delta(c) = \{s \mid (c, s) \in \delta\}$ returns a set of names for a given concept c.

Synonym Extraction. We extract a synonym lexicon from the dictionary δ by considering all names of a concept c that differ in one token. We consider these tokens as synonyms. For example, the names *kidney disease* and *kidney dysfunction* are names for the same concept and differ in the tokens 'disease' and 'dysfunction'. The pair (*disease*, *dysfunction*) is then inserted into a synonym lexicon denoted as σ provided that the pair occurs in at least two concepts.

Concept Candidate Retrieval. Candidate retrieval identifies, for each annotated segment, a number of concept candidates that the segment can denote. We implement the candidate retrieval using an index for the dictionary δ that maps names to concepts. The index is implemented using Lucene[6]; results are ranked using

[5] We stop the inference procedure if the state does not change for 3 times in a row.
[6] https://lucene.apache.org/.

the built-in Lucene similarity score. We retrieve the top k candidates with a similarity of at least λ.

3.6 Templates and Feature Generation

As shown in Fig. 1, our model is designed by 12 individual types of factors (henceforth numbered between 0 and 11). We distinguish factors by their scope, i.e., whether they are used for the recognition or the linking task or jointly for both. Recognition factors are either connected to a single observed variable (type 0), or connect two variables of type *segmentation* or *synonym* (1, 2, 3 and 5). All these factors contribute features for the recognition task. Being connected to a single hidden variable of type *concept*, factor (10) has a scope that is limited to the linking task. Joint factors (4, 6, 7, 8 and 11) connect at least one variable of type *concept* with at least one variable of a different type.

Although factors can be grouped by their scope, we decide to apply a more semantic grouping of factors in our implementation. In the following, we describe our design of templates capturing the semantic relatedness of factors. All described features are of boolean type. Henceforth, we use d to denote the current document, s_i to denote the ith annotation span in d and c_i to denote the concept assigned to s_i. Further, the templates make use of the dictionary δ, and the semantic lexicon σ as previously described in Sect. 3.5. For readability, we introduce the abbreviations *seg*, *sem* and *con* for the three types of hidden variables: segmentation, semantic transformation, and concept, respectively.

Dictionary Lookup. This template adds factors of type 1, 5, 6 and 9 to the factor graph. A feature of this template indicates whether s_i corresponds to an entry in the dictionary δ, i.e., whether $(s_i, c') \in \delta$ for some c'. A further set of features specific for each concept c_i indicates whether the span of an annotated entity mention refers to concept c_i according to the dictionary, i.e. $(s_i, c_i) \in \delta$. A further set of features indicate whether the semantically transformed version of s_i is in the dictionary or denotes concept c_i according to the dictionary.

Semantic Transformation. The semantic transformation template adds a new factor of type 5 connecting a variable of type *sem* with a *seg* variable. The feature indicates for a given synonym pair (t_j, t'_j) whether *seg* corresponds to the semantically transformed version *sem* modulo the fact that some token t_j in *seg* is replaced by t'_j in *sem*.

Token Length. This template connects a factor of type 3 to a *seg* variable. The factor defines n_i features indicating whether the number of tokens in *seg* is lower or equal than n_i where n_i is the number of tokens in s_i.

Token Context. This template extends the factor graph by factors 2 and 7. It introduces three types of context features indicating if a span (i) is preceded by a certain n-gram, (ii) is followed by a certain n-gram, and (iii) whether it is preceded and followed by a pair of n-grams ($1 \leq n \leq 4$). In addition, each of these features is conjoined with a specific concept c_i that the span is linked to.

Annotation Prior. This template extends the factor graph by factor types 0, 8 and 10. The features provide a context-independent prior derived from training data indicating whether a segment s_i appearing in the training data represents a mention of an entity. Another set of features are concept-specific and indicate whether a segment s_i appearing in the training data represents a mention of an entity denoting concept c_i. In addition to considering the whole segment, we also consider n-grams ($1 \leq n \leq |s_i| - 1$).

Coherence. This template adds a factor of type 4 which measures the coherence of annotations. Given all *seg* variables with the same mention text, we record whether all these variables are annotated with the same concept.

Abbreviation. In this template, we address the problem of abbreviations (cf. [6]) in the task of entity linking. The template adds three types of factors 3, 6 and 11, where each factor has exactly one feature. Factor 3 is connected to a segmentation variable. The corresponding feature indicates whether the mention text represents an abbreviation[7] that occurs in the training data. Factor 6 connects segmentation variables with concept variables. Its feature indicates whether the given mention text is an abbreviation for the given concept according to the training data. Factor 11 connects two or more segmentation variables with a concept variable. Its feature measures whether there is a longform annotated that has the same concept assigned as the annotation s_i.

4 Experiments

We state our problem as joint sequence labeling and resolution comprising named entity recognition and linking. The objective is to recognize segments in text denoting an entity of a specific type and linking them to a reference knowledge base by assigning a unique concept identifier. In this section, we describe our experiments on two types of biomedical entities. The first experiment evaluates our system in disease recognition and linking. The second experiment is conducted on chemicals. Both experiments use the same data set described below.

4.1 Data Sets and Resources

Data Sets. All experiments were conducted on data from the BioCreative V Shared Task for Chemical Disease Relations (BC5CDR) [23]. The data set was

[7] We define an abbreviation as a single token which is solely in uppercase and has at most 5 characters.

designed to solve the tasks of entity recognition and linking for disease and chemicals and further to find relations between both. However, the latter task is not yet considered in our approach. Each annotation contains information about its span in terms of character offsets and a unique concept identifier. Annotated entities are linked to the Comparative Taxicogenomics Database[8] for diseases (CTD_{dis}) or chemicals (CTD_{chem}), respectively. The data set consists of 1,500 annotated Pubmed abstracts equally distributed into training, development and test set with about 4,300 unique annotations each.

Reference Knowledge Base. CTD_{dis} is derived from the disease branch of MeSH and the Online Mendelian Inheritance in Man (OMIM)[9] data base. CTD_{dis} contains 11,864 unique disease concept identifiers and 75,883 disease names. CTD_{chem} is solely derived from the chemical branch of MeSH. It comprises 163,362 unique chemical concept identifiers and 366,000 chemical names.

Cleaning Procedure. In order to remove simple spelling variations, we implement a text cleaning procedure which is applied to all textual resources and data sets. The strategy uses six manually created regular expressions like replacing *'s* by *s*. Further, we convert all tokens into lowercase if they are not solely in uppercase, we remove all special characters including punctuation and brackets, and replace multiple whitespace characters by a single blank. We apply the same strategy to both diseases and chemicals.

Resources Used in the Experiments. In the experiments for disease recognition and linking, we initialize the dictionary δ with CTD_{dis} and enhance it with the disease annotations from the training data. We then apply the text cleaning procedure as described above to all entries, as well as to all documents in training and test set. Due to the cleaning, the size of the dictionary reduces to 73,773 unique names (−2,113), while the number of concepts remains the same. The resulting synonym lexicon σ stores 2,366 entries.

In the experiments for chemicals, the dictionary δ is initialized with CTD_{chem} and enhanced with the chemical annotations from the training data. After the cleaning procedure, the size of the dictionary reduces to 359,564 unique names (−8.186), while the number of concepts remains the same. The resulting synonym lexicon σ stores 4,912 entries.

The system's overall performance depends on the two parameters k and λ that influence the candidate retrieval procedure (cf. Sect. 3.5), as they determine the maximum recall that can be achieved. We empirically set the best parameter values using a two-dimensional grid search on the development set, assuming perfect entity recognition. Best performance is achieved with $k = 20$ and $\lambda = 0.7$. Given these parameters, a maximum recall of 90.4 for diseases, and 91.5 for chemicals can be obtained by our system on the BC5CDR test set.

[8] http://ctdbase.org, version from 2016.
[9] http://www.omim.org.

4.2 Baselines

We compare our approach to the two state-of-the-art systems *DNorm* [12] and *TaggerOne* [11], as well as against two simple baselines (*LMB* and *LMB*$^{+}$). The latter baselines are based on non-overlapping longest matches, using the dictionary as described in Sect. 3.5. While in *LMB*$^{+}$ all resources (including the dictionary and documents) were cleaned, resources in *LMB* remain as they are. Due to the cleaning, we lose track of the real character offset position. Thus, these baselines are not applicable to the entity recognition subtask.

4.3 Experimental Settings

Evaluation Metrics. We use the official evaluation script as provided by the BioCreative V Shared Task organizers [23]. The script uses Precision, Recall and F_1 score on micro level. In the recognition task the measure is on mention level comparing annotation spans including character positions and the annotated text. Experiments on the linking task are evaluated on concept level by comparing *sets* of concepts as predicted by the system and annotated in the gold standard, i.e., multiple occurrences of the same concept and their exact positions in the text are disregarded.

Hyper-parameter Settings. During development, the learning rate α and the number of training epochs ϵ as hyper-parameters of SampleRank were empirically optimized by varying them on the development set. Best results could be achieved with $\alpha = 0.06$. The results reached a stable convergence at $\epsilon = 130$.

4.4 Results

We report results on the BC5CDR test set in Table 1. Results on the disease and chemicals subtasks are shown in the left and right part of the table, respectively. For both tasks, we assess the performance of our system on end-to-end entity linking (columns labeled with "Linking"), as well as the entity recognition problem in isolation ("Recognition").

Table 1. Evaluation results on BC5CDR test set for recognition and linking on diseases (left part) and chemicals (right part).

	Diseases						Chemicals					
	Recognition			Linking			Recognition			Linking		
	P	R	F_1	P	R	F_1	P	R	F_1	P	R	F_1
JLink	84.6	**81.9**	**83.2**	**86.3**	**85.5**	**85.9**	90.0	86.6	88.3	85.9	**91.0**	88.4
TaggerOne	**85.2**	80.2	82.6	84.6	82.7	83.7	**94.2**	**88.8**	**91.4**	88.8	90.3	**89.5**
DNorm	82.0	79.5	80.7	81.2	80.1	80.6	93.2	84.0	88.4	**95.0**	80.8	87.3
LMB^{+}	n/a	n/a	n/a	80.5	80.9	80.7	n/a	n/a	n/a	80.4	82.7	81.5
LMB	n/a	n/a	n/a	82.3	58.5	68.3	n/a	n/a	n/a	84.0	58.8	69.2

Disease Recognition and Linking. In disease recognition, our approach exhibits the best F_1 score of all systems compared here ($F_1 = 83.2$). Only in terms of Precision, TaggerOne has slight advantages.

In the linking task, our system clearly outperforms both lexicon-based baselines as well as both state-of-the-art systems. In particular, JLink exceeds TaggerOne by 2.2 and DNorm by 5.3 points in F_1 score, respectively.

Comparing these results to the baselines, we observe that a simple lexicon lookup (LMB) already achieves robust precision levels that cannot be met by the DNorm system. More than 22 points in recall can be gained by simply applying a cleaning step to the dictionary and documents (LMB^+). However, the increasing recall comes with a drop in precision of 1.8 points. This shows that preprocessing the investigated data can be helpful to find more diseases, while aggravating the linking task. Obviously, our system (in contrast to DNorm and to a greater extent than TaggerOne) benefits from a number of features that provide strong generalization capacities beyond mere lexicon matching. A more detailed feature analysis is deferred until Sect. 4.5.

Chemicals Recognition and Linking. In the second experiment, we are interested in assessing the domain adaptivity of our model. Therefore, we apply the same factor model to a different reference knowledge base, without changing any system parameters or engineering any additional domain-specific features.

The evaluation (cf. Table 1, right part) shows promising results regarding the adaptation to chemicals, particularly in the linking task. Our approach is competitive to DNorm and TaggerOne, while clearly outperforming both lexicon baselines. Compared to DNorm, our approach lacks in precision (−9.1), but shows better results in recall (+10.2), which results in a slightly higher F_1 score (+1.1). Overall, TaggerOne obtains the best performance in this experiment, due to the best precision/recall trade-off. However, the superior recall of our system is remarkable ($R = 91.0$), given that the dictionary for chemicals as used in TaggerOne was augmented in order to ensure that all chemical element names and symbols are included [11].

4.5 Discussion

Comparison to Previous Work. To our knowledge, the best performance in previous work on disease linking has been obtained by Lee et al. [13] who report an F_1 score of 86.5 ($P = 89.6$; $R = 83.5$) on the BC5CDR test set. While these results are slightly higher than the ones we report in Table 1, their system benefits from two design choices that are highly task-specific: First, the authors extend their lexicon annotations from the NCBI Disease corpus [1]. Further, they manually extend the dictionary underlying their system to account for synonym variations in the corpus. We apply automatically learned semantic transformations to this problem. Third, their dictionary lookup follows a fixed sequential order in which the lexical resources are consulted. This order is optimized to the disease linking task on BC5CDR data. In contrast, we aim at a general model for joint entity recognition and linking that can be flexibly applied to existing knowledge bases of various domains, without the need of manual adaptations.

Upper Bounds. The upper bound of our approach is determined by the maximum recall of the candidate retrieval. Given the optimized parameters $k = 20$ and $\lambda = 0.7$ (cf. Sect. 4.3), our upper bound is limited to $R = 90.4$ for disease linking. Compared to our observed recall performance in the linking task, there are 4.9 points left for improvement. Keeping k and λ for the chemical linking task, we reach the upper bound in recall with a delta of only 0.5 points. Thus, a further increase in recall can only be obtained by varying the candidate retrieval at the cost of generating a larger amount of spurious candidates.

Template Ablation. We investigated the impact of the individual templates in an ablation test. The resulting Δ in F_1 (in comparison to the full model) is shown in Table 2. All evaluations were done on the development set for diseases, using the previously described settings.

As can be seen from the table, the relative impact of templates on recognition and linking follows a largely consistent pattern. As for disease recognition, the strongest increase in F_1 is due to the *Lexicon* template ($\Delta F_1 = -22.3$). In disease linking, this template heavily increases recall but leads to slight drop in precision ($\Delta F_1 = -15.5$). The *Token Length* template equally increases recall and precision in both tasks. Its impact is the second highest, which can be explained by its broad scope. Although the *Annotation Prior* has a similarly broad scope, its impact is smaller as we added the training data to the dictionary, which leads to a partial subsumption of this template by the *Lexicon* template. *Abbreviation*, *Coherence* and *Semantic Transformation* templates have a rather restricted scope in that they address very specific phenomena. Our evaluation shows that adding these templates does not negatively interfere with other templates, but increases either recall, precision, or both.

Table 2. Impact of individual templates to overall performance in disease recognition and linking, according to an ablation test on the development set.

Configuration	Recognition				Linking			
	Prec.	Recall	F_1	ΔF_1	Prec.	Recall	F_1	ΔF_1
All Templates	83.9	76.9	80.2		85.6	80.7	83.1	
−Annotation Prior	81.5	77.0	79.2	−1.0	81.6	80.8	81.2	−1.9
−Abbreviation	83.3	76.8	79.9	−0.3	85.3	80.9	83.0	−0.1
−Coherence	84.2	76.3	80.0	−0.2	85.1	80.4	82.6	−0.5
−Token Context	84.2	74.4	79.0	−1.2	86.3	79.2	82.6	−0.5
−Token Length	81.3	72.7	76.8	−3.4	83.9	76.5	80.0	−3.1
−Lexicon	76.2	46.6	57.9	−22.3	87.2	55.1	67.6	−15.5
−Sem. Transform.	84.0	75.4	79.5	−0.7	85.7	79.1	82.3	−0.8

Error Analysis. Typical errors of our system are due to incorrectly resolved abbreviations, erroneous span detection during recognition (e.g., *infection by hepatitis B virus* vs. *infection*), fine-grained semantic distinctions during linking (e.g., (i) terms such as *seizures* or *shock* which exactly match an entry in the dictionary, but are not annotated as diseases in the data, or (ii) distinctions between *psychological* or *physiological* diseases, or *substance-induced*, *acute*, or *chronic* diseases), and discrepancies in the annotated training and testing data.

5 Conclusion

We have presented a probabilistic system that jointly addresses both the entity recognition and linking task using a probabilistic framework. The framework builds on an undirected probabilistic graphical model that considers the span of mentions of entities as well as the corresponding knowledge base identifier as random variables and models the joint assignment using a factorized distribution. We have shown that our approach can be easily applied to different domains by merely exchanging the underlying ontology and training data. On the task of recognizing and linking disease names, we show that our approach outperforms the state-of-the-art systems *DNorm* [12] and *TaggerOne* [11], as well as two lexicon-based baselines. On the task of recognizing and linking chemical names, our system achieves comparable performance to the state-of-the-art.

In future work, we plan to corroborate the domain adaptivity of our system by investigating different entity types beyond diseases and chemicals. Moreover, applying JLink to *simultaneously* linking entities of *multiple* types (as demonstrated by [11] for the two types of diseases and chemicals) would be a promising avenue towards semantic representation of large heterogeneous text collections.

Acknowledgments. This work has been funded by the Federal Ministry of Education and Research (BMBF, Germany) in the PSINK project (project number 031L0028A).

References

1. Doğan, R.I., Leaman, R., Lu, Z.: NCBI disease corpus. A resource for disease name recognition and concept normalization. J. Biomed. Inform. **47**, 1–10 (2014)
2. Durrett, G., Klein, D.: A joint model for entity analysis. Coreference, typing, and linking. TACL **2**, 477–490 (2014)
3. Finkel, J.R., Grenager, T., Manning, C.: Incorporating non-local information into information extraction systems by Gibbs sampling. In: Proceedings of ACL, pp. 363–370 (2005)
4. Ganea, O.E., Ganea, M., Lucchi, A., Eickhoff, C., Hofmann, T.: Probabilistic bag-of-hyperlinks model for entity linking. In: Proceedings of WWW, pp. 927–938 (2016)
5. Hakimov, S., Horst, H., Jebbara, S., Hartung, M., Cimiano, P.: Combining textual and graph-based features for named entity disambiguation using undirected probabilistic graphical models. In: Blomqvist, E., Ciancarini, P., Poggi, F., Vitali, F. (eds.) EKAW 2016. LNCS, vol. 10024, pp. 288–302. Springer, Cham (2016). doi:10.1007/978-3-319-49004-5_19

6. Hartung, M., Klinger, R., Zwick, M., Cimiano, P.: Towards gene recognition from rare and ambiguous abbreviations using a filtering approach. In: Proceedings of BioNLP 2014, pp. 118–127 (2014)
7. Hoffart, J., Yosef, M.A., Bordino, I., Fürstenau, H., Pinkal, M., Spaniol, M., Taneva, B., Thater, S., Weikum, G.: Robust disambiguation of named entities in text. In: Proceedings of EMNLP, pp. 782–792 (2011)
8. Koller, D., Friedman, N.: Probabilistic Graphical Models. Principles and Techniques. MIT Press, Cambridge (2009)
9. Kschischang, F.R., Frey, B.J., Loeliger, H.A.: Factor graphs and sum product algorithm. IEEE Trans. Inf. Theory **47**(2), 498–519 (2001)
10. Lafferty, J., McCallum, A., Pereira, F.: Conditional random fields. Probabilistic models for segmenting and labeling sequence data. In: Proceedings of ICML, pp. 282–289 (2001)
11. Leaman, R., Lu, Z.: TaggerOne. Joint named entity recognition and normalization with semi-Markov models. Bioinformatics **32**, 2839–2846 (2016)
12. Leaman, R., Dogan, R.I., Lu, Z.: DNorm. Disease name normalization with pairwise learning to rank. Bioinformatics **29**, 2909–2917 (2013)
13. Lee, H.C., Hsu, Y.Y., Kao, H.Y.: An enhanced CRF-based system for disease name entity recognition and normalization on BioCreative V DNER task. In: Proceedings of the BioCreative V Workshop, pp. 226–233 (2015)
14. Luo, G., Huang, X., Lin, C.Y., Nie, Z.: Joint entity recognition and disambiguation. In: Proceedings of EMNLP, pp. 879–888 (2015)
15. Mihalcea, R., Csomai, A.: Wikify! Linking documents to encyclopedic knowledge. In: Proceedings of CIKM, pp. 233–242 (2007)
16. Moro, A., Raganato, A., Navigli, R.: Entity linking meets word sense disambiguation. A unified approach. TACL **2**, 231–244 (2014)
17. Nadeau, D., Sekine, S.: A survey of named entity recognition and classification. Lingvisticae Investigationes **30**(1), 3–26 (2007)
18. Nguyen, D., Theobald, M., Weikum, G.: J-NERD. Joint named entity recognition and disambiguation with rich linguistic features. TACL **4**, 215–229 (2016)
19. Poon, H., Domingos, P.: Machine reading: a "Killer App" for statistical relational AI. In: Proceedings of StarAI, pp. 76–81 (2010)
20. Ratinov, L., Roth, D., Downey, D., Anderson, M.: Local and global algorithms for disambiguation to wikipedia. In: Proceedings of ACL: HLT, pp. 1375–1384 (2011)
21. Singh, S., Wick, M., McCallum, A.: Monte Carlo MCMC. Efficient inference by approximate sampling. In: Proceedings of EMNLP, pp. 1104–1113 (2012)
22. Usbeck, R., Ngomo, A.C.N., Röder, M., Gerber, D., Coelho, S.A., Auer, S., Both, A.: AGDISTIS. Graph-based disambiguation of named entities using linked data. In: The Semantic Web-ISWC 2014, pp. 457–471 (2014)
23. Wei, C.H., Peng, Y., Leaman, R., Davis, A.P., Mattingly, C.J., Li, J., Wiegers, T.C., Lu, Z.: Overview of the BioCreative V Chemical Disease Relation (CDR) task. In: Proceedings of the BioCreative V Evaluation Workshop, pp. 154–166 (2015)
24. Wick, M., Rohanimanesh, K., Culotta, A., McCallum, A.: SampleRank. learning preferences from atomic gradients. In: Proceedings of the NIPS Workshop on Advances in Ranking, pp. 1–5 (2009)

Neural Induction of a Lexicon for Fast and Interpretable Stance Classification

Jérémie Clos(✉) and Nirmalie Wiratunga

Robert Gordon University, Garthdee Road, Aberdeen, UK
{j.clos,n.wiratunga}@rgu.ac.uk

Abstract. Large-scale social media classification faces the following two challenges: algorithms can be hard to adapt to Web-scale data, and the predictions that they provide are difficult for humans to understand. Those two challenges are solved at the cost of some accuracy by lexicon-based classifiers, which offer a white-box approach to text mining by using a trivially interpretable additive model. However current techniques for lexicon-based classification limit themselves to using hand-crafted lexicons, which suffer from human bias and are difficult to extend, or automatically generated lexicons, which are induced using point-estimates of some predefined probabilistic measure on a corpus of interest. In this work we propose a new approach to learn robust lexicons, using the backpropagation algorithm to ensure generalization power without sacrificing model readability. We evaluate our approach on a stance detection task, on two different datasets, and find that our lexicon outperforms standard lexicon approaches.

1 Introduction

Text classification is a core task in natural language processing, with applications ranging from web search to opinion mining. For instance, being able to perform this task on large amounts of social media data enables businesses to know in real time how the public perceives them, talks about them, which has repercussions in key areas such as predictions of the stock market prices for a given company.

Large-scale social media classification faces the challenges of scaling algorithms and producing predictions that can be explained and interpreted. Those two challenges are solved at the cost of some accuracy by lexicon-based classifiers, which offer a white-box approach to text mining by using a trivially interpretable additive model, where the probability of an instance belonging to a class is a weighted sum of the probabilities of each term belonging to that class. However, current techniques used to create those lexicons fall short in many ways compared to more traditional black-box machine learning models. That difference in performance is easily explained by the fact that, unlike lexicon-based classifiers, those models are trained in a black-box way, with no regard to their interpretability. This paper attempts to conciliate lexicon-based classification and traditional text classification by designing a simple and efficient training procedure that can generate

J. Gracia et al. (Eds.): LDK 2017, LNAI 10318, pp. 181–193, 2017.
DOI: 10.1007/978-3-319-59888-8_16

domain-specific lexicons with a high degree of interpretability and a high classification performance.

We first formalize the concept of lexicons and explore the state of the art in the domain of lexicon-based classification. We then detail our contribution, formalizing lexicon-based classification as a form of computational graph. We then detail our evaluation protocol on a stance detection task and on two different datasets. We perform an evaluation against standard lexicons and baselines found in the literature and report that our approach significantly outperforms standard techniques for generating lexicons. Finally, we analyze and discuss our results, before concluding on the next steps of our work.

2 Related Works

The literature on text classification is rich in approaches of varying degree of complexity, but there has been scarce research done on approaches which are both interpretable [11] and accurate.

2.1 Lexicon-Based Classification

Lexicons are early tools adopted by the computational linguistics community to automatically classify text. They can take many forms, the most common of which being either a simple list of terms associated to a certain class of interest, or a $T \times C$ matrix where each pair (t, c) where $t \in T$ is one of the T terms and $c \in C$ is one of the C classes is mapped to a strength of association score $s = l(t, c)$. Several lexicons also contain additional contextual information in order to help their users build more complex models, but they all share the same core architecture, which we formalize as follows:

Definition 1 (formal lexicon). *A lexicon Lex is a tuple* $Lex = \langle \mathcal{L}, \mathcal{A}, \mathcal{D} \rangle$ *where:*

$$\mathcal{L} : T \times C \mapsto \mathbb{R}$$
$$\mathcal{A} : \mathbb{R}^n \mapsto \mathbb{R}$$
$$\mathcal{D} : \mathbb{R}^n \mapsto \mathbb{R}$$

In this definition, $\mathcal{L}$ is a mapping function that assigns an unbounded value to each pair (t, c) where term $t \in T$ and class $c \in C$, $\mathcal{A}$ is an aggregation function that aggregates the accumulated scores into one value, and $\mathcal{D}$ is a decision function that selects one of these aggregated values.

Concretely, the mapping determines an evidence value for each term using a look-up list, propagates it to the aggregation function which aggregates the set of evidence values from the terms contained within one instance into multiple stacks of evidence (one for each class). Finally, the decision function evaluates each stack of evidence to select the one that is the most likely. Using this formal definition we can reformulate previous lexicons using the same format.

Simple lists of terms fit under this definition by having the decision function be ArgMax, the aggregation function be a simple sum, and the mapping function be the indicator function where $L(t) = 1$ if t is in the Lexicon and 0 otherwise.

Traditional matrix-shaped lexicons fit under this definition by having the decision function be ArgMax, the aggregation function be a simple sum, and the mapping function be a simple look-up in the Lexicon which defaults to 0 if the term is not in the Lexicon.

This leads us to define the challenge of lexicon-based classification: the lexicon induction problem. The remaining parts of the section review techniques traditionally used to solve the lexicon induction problem.

Definition 2 (lexicon induction problem). ***The lexicon induction problem*** *is the estimation, given aggregation function $\mathcal{A}$ and decision function $\mathcal{D}$, of the optimal function $\mathcal{L}$ so that the resulting lexicon $Lex = \langle \mathcal{L}, \mathcal{A}, \mathcal{D} \rangle$ minimizes its classification errors on unseen data.*

2.2 Traditional Hand-Crafted Lexicons

The first lexicons were not obtained using computational means but rather hand-crafted by domain experts. This is due to the computational cost of building a lexicon and the fact that it is only recently that we have had access to the computational resources to parse the amount of data necessary to the generation of useful lexicons. Traditional lexicons were usually either a hand-crafted list of words with a numerical or categorical value associated to each class or a simple list of words that are known to be associated to a class (with no quantification of that association). This comprises sentiment lexicons as well as more complex linguistic patterns such as emotion lexicons, argument lexicons, etc.

Two different aggregation/decision mechanisms appear in the literature using these lexicons. In the case of non-quantified lexicons, a counting of the number of lexicon terms appearing in the text produces an appropriate aggregated value. The class which has the most terms appearing in the text is then chosen as part of the decision function. In the case of quantified lexicons, a sum of the weights of the lexicon terms appearing in the text produces an aggregated weight. The class which has the highest weight is then chosen as part of the decision function.

The strength of these approaches is twofold: firstly in how well they generalize, because they were consciously created by subject domain experts, and secondly in their human-interpretability, because they were formed by human users assigning scores to each term. To this day, hand-crafted lexicons such as the LIWC lexicon [10] are still sold for commercial computational linguistics applications. Conversely their weakness are that they tend to be small, due to the human labor involved in generating them, and less effective than other methods, due to their focus on human interpretability.

2.3 Lexicon Induction Techniques

In order to attend to the issues inherent to hand-crafted lexicons, research in computational linguistics evolved towards computing lexicon scores from external data sources, rather than being generated by a set of experts with domain knowledge. In this section we will review learning techniques of existing approaches as well as the challenges that they face. Research in lexicon induction outlines multiple families of techniques that can be used in order to produce a computational lexicon. Those techniques are either built on an extensive lexical resource such as an ontology, or on an estimation of strength of association between each term and a class.

Graph Propagation Based Lexicons (GPBL). GPBL learning techniques use a few human-provided seed words for which the class is known, and leverage some external relationship (typically synonyms, antonyms and hypernyms) in a semantic graph such as WordNet [7] to propagate class values along that graph [3]. For example, if the term "agreement" was deemed fully associated to a class, its synonym "accord" would be associated to the same class while its antonym "disagreement" would be associated to its opposite class. Because this family of techniques is extremely foreign to the one we are proposing, we do not evaluate against it and only refer to it for the sake of exhaustiveness.

Conditional Probability-Based Lexicons (CPBL). CPBL learning techniques are the baseline against which we evaluate our lexicon induction algorithm. They operate by computing the conditional probability of observing each lexicon entry under each class [1]. The value for each pair (t, c) where term $t \in T$ and class $c \in C$ is computed as indicated in Eq. 1. The main flaw of this technique is that it overestimates strength of association based on coincidences, which means that it would be easy to build a completely correct dataset to trick the algorithm in learning a lexicon full of spurious association scores.

$$\mathrm{Lex}(t, c) = \frac{p(t|c)}{\sum_{i=0}^{|C|} p(t|c_i)} \tag{1}$$

Mutual Information Based Lexicons. Mutual information-based lexicon learning techniques attempt to fix the issues of previous approaches by estimating the pointwise mutual information (PMI) between a term and a class [12] using the formula described in Eq. 2. Mutual information being inherently more robust to coincidences because of its denominator, is chosen as a strength of association measure. Some works [2] have shown that NPMI, a normalized version of the standard PMI metric described in Eq. 3, slightly improves classification performance. While this approach is sensible to create a general purpose lexicon, it suffers some flaws in the following cases: (1) if none of the terms used in the child post has an argumentative value or is present within the lexicon, no classification is possible, and (2) some terms might end up with an undeserved score because they accidentally appear more frequently within comments of one class. For example if non-argumentative terms such as "Monday" accidentally co-occur too often within one class, they will be misconstrued as being indicative of that class.

$$\mathrm{PMI}(x;y) = \frac{\log(p(x;y))}{p(x)p(y)} \tag{2}$$

$$\mathrm{NPMI}(x;y) = \frac{\frac{\log(p(x;y))}{p(x)p(y)}}{-\log\left[p(x,y)\right]} \tag{3}$$

Hybrid Lexicons. Recent work [9] has attempted to hybridize handcrafted and automatically generated lexicons, based on the assumption that the coverage of the former would help the specialization of the latter as a fallback option, and that a hybrid lexicon would thus be able to deal with domain-specific and general knowledge. Hybrid lexicons tend to improve classification accuracy as shown in [9] but have the drawback of requiring a handcrafted lexicon and are thus beyond the scope of this work as of now.

3 Building a Neural Lexicon

Traditional ways of learning a lexicon from a corpus of data either use point estimates of some statistical values, such as pointwise mutual information, or semantic values directly derived from human expertise. However, we can observe in Fig. 1 that a standard lexicon can be expressed in the form of a computational graph, where the lexicon is described as a composition of functions as seen in Eq. 4. That graphical form gives us the possibility of using gradient-based learning techniques such as backpropagation in order to learn both the lexicon and the strength of association scores.

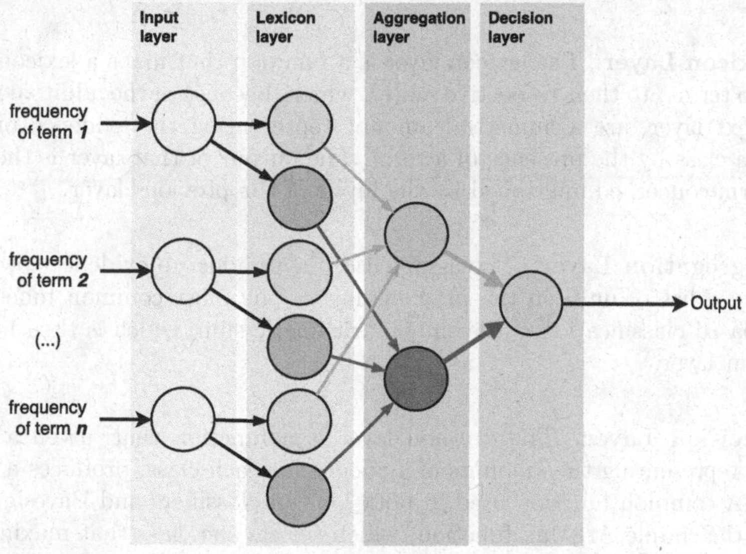

Fig. 1. Lexicon computational graph

$$\text{Class}(i) = \text{ArgMax}_c \left(\sum_{t \in i} [s_c(t)] \right) \tag{4}$$

Traditional lexicons are thus considered as a specific network topology that do not have sigmoid activation functions but instead a simple aggregation layer with one aggregation unit per class and a output layer of one single unit that transforms the aggregated evidence into the relevant format. The details of the network topology and the training protocol are explained in the following sections.

3.1 The Lexicon Network Topology

The lexicon follows a specific network topology where each vocabulary input is mapped to one unit, which is linked to as many hidden units as there are classes, which are then aggregated by the following layer into a sum of evidence towards that class. Finally, the last layer uses this sum of evidence to produce a decision which is the output of the classifier. In this section we review each layer of the neural lexicon and their precise function.

The First Layer: Vocabulary Input. The first layer is the input layer, which maps a term to its matching unit. The input signal coming to this layer is some measure of frequency of occurrences of each term in the text that is being classified. We can apply a scaling function such as $scaledFrequency = log(1 + frequency)$ in order to smooth out the differences between long and short comments, or just take the raw frequency and communicate it to the next layer.

The Lexicon Layer. The lexicon layer is a function that maps a lexicon entry (linked to terms) to their respective scores, which, because of the additive nature of the next layer, are a numerical amount representing the evidence brought towards a class by the presence of a term. The output of that layer is the score of the term concerned multiplied by the input of the previous layer.

The Aggregation Layer. The aggregation layer adds up evidence towards a class from a list of units in the previous layer. The most common function in lexicon-based classification is the simple arithmetic sum, which is then fed into the output layer.

The Decision Layer. The decision layer is a function that, given a set of numbers representing the amounts of evidence for each class, produces a classification. A common function used in both lexicon classifiers and Bayesian classifiers is the simple ArgMax function, which selects the class that maximizes a numerical amount. However, because it is impossible to differentiate the ArgMax function, a proxy function is used during the training phase of the algorithm.

3.2 Lexicon Network Training

In this section we detail the process of training the lexicon network.

Cost Function and Regularization. The backpropagation algorithm relies on reverse-mode differentiation in order to train the network in a computationally efficient way, by updating the weight of local units based on the error partial derivative with respect to those units. This process requires that the network be differentiable in order to compute the error properly. We use a proxy decision function during the training process because the original ArgMax function is not differentiable.

Because the only thing the ArgMax relies on is the proportion of evidence in favor of one class versus another, we can use the cross-entropy error function E:

$$E(C,\hat{C}) = -\sum_{i=1}^{|C|}\left(C_i \times log(\hat{C}_i) + (1 - C_i) \times log(1 - \hat{C}_i)\right) \tag{5}$$

Here, the optimal class distribution is $\left[\hat{C}_1, \hat{C}_2, ..., \hat{C}_n\right]$ and the predicted class distribution is $[C_1, C_2, ..., C_n]$ where each prediction is normalized from the aggregated evidence using the Softmax function $C_i = \frac{\exp a_i}{\sum_{j=0}^{|a|} \exp a_j}$ where a_i is the aggregated weight for a class i. However, optimizing over a direct function of the error with a large amount of free parameters (numbers of classes × number of lexicon entries) will lead to overfitting on the training data and poor performance on the test data, which emphasizes the need to regularize our training process. We selected L_2 regularization, which is a minimization of the L_2 *norm* of the parameters, because it is differentiable and minimizes weights without pushing them completely to 0 (unlike L_1 regularization). This property is desirable for learning a lexicon because pushing a weight to 0 would just remove many terms observed only in the training data and thus increase overfitting. The resulting cost function J is shown in Eq. 6.

$$J(C,\hat{C}) = E(C,\hat{C}) + \lambda * \sqrt{\sum_{j=0}^{m} w_j^2} \tag{6}$$

Here λ corresponds to a regularization parameter, which modulates the importance that we are putting on obtaining a generalizable lexicon against having a low error in the training set and is selected empirically, w_i corresponds to the weight of unit i in the lexicon layer.

Optimization. The backpropagation algorithm trains the network by propagating the error gradient backwards through the computational graph and applying a local update rule based on its value. Using the chain rule, the partial derivative of the error with respect to each lexicon input can be decomposed in a set of simpler partial derivatives. Equation 7 shows the update rule for a lexicon weight w from the error J.

$$w_i = w_i - \gamma \times \frac{\partial J}{\partial w_i} \tag{7}$$

Here J corresponds to the cost (Eq. 6) of the current iteration over the dataset and γ represents the learning rate, a parameter that we manually set to a very small value. Since our datasets are small, we train our network using the Conjugate Gradient Descent algorithm [6], updating the weights of the network after each iteration over the dataset. It is however important to note that since the goal of the network is only to generate a lexicon, the update rule is only applied to the weight of the edges coming from the lexical layer and all others are held constant.

4 Evaluation

We evaluate our approach on an argument stance classification task, which is a type of text classification specializing on argumentative discourse. Argument stance classification is the classification of textual content coming from an agent, e.g., user comments extracted from a discussion forum, into multiple classes representing the stance of those comments with respect to the comments they are responding to. We study argument stance classification on a binary scale, where neutral responses are removed and only rebutting/disagreeing or supporting/agreeing statements are conserved. Using Fig. 2 as an example, we can see a debate on the social discussion website Reddit[1] where user 1 (in green) is in complete agreement with the parent comment, while user 2 (in red) is in complete agreement with user 1 while being in complete disagreement with the core topic of the discussion. This difference differentiates stance classification from sentiment analysis and makes it a harder problem.

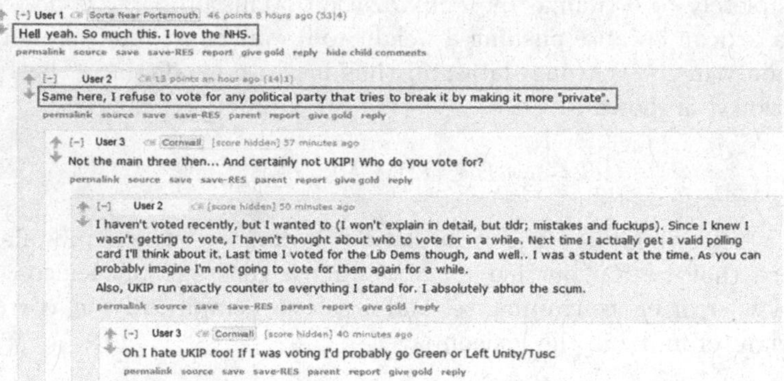

Fig. 2. Local stance classification in context: a debate on Reddit (Color figure online)

[1] http://www.reddit.com.

4.1 Datasets

We performed our experiments on two social media datasets. The first one is the Internet Argument Corpus [13] (further referred to as IAC). It is a subset of a publicly available dataset collected on a discussion forum and manually labeled. The second one is the Reddit Noisy-Labeled Corpus (further referred to as RNLC). It was created by collecting data from a discussion forum and automatically labeling it using distant supervision learning [4,8]. Statistics on the corpora can be found in Table 1 and show that the two datasets are similar with the exception that the RNLC was collected on comments which were on average twice as long as the IAC. This has an important impact on lexicon-based methods because of the risk of inserting more noise into the system.

The Internet Argument Corpus (IAC). The IAC [13] is a corpus of forum comments manually labeled by 5 annotators that contain (among other things) degree of agreement/disagreement with their immediate parent comment. A subset of this dataset was used for our experiment, by selecting the comments that ensured disjoint class membership (meaning filtering out comments with an average score close to 0). For instance, a comment such as "*For the same reasons that I do not agree with the first conclusion of your statement, I feel that your second conclusion is correct*" would technically belong to both classes as the user both supports and attacks the previous comment and it would thus be filtered out.

The Reddit Noisy-Labeled Corpus (RNLC). The RNLC is a newly formed corpus of comments extracted from the Reddit[2] website and automatically labeled with a binary class using evidence contained in the comment. A list of explicit expressions such as "*I [positive adverb] agree*" and "*I [positive adverb] disagree*" (and variations) were used to detect strong evidence of a user comment belonging to a class. In the case of the presence of conflicting evidence, i. e., expressions acting as strong evidence towards both classes, the comments were not considered. Otherwise, comments were automatically assigned to their respective class and the corresponding sentences were deleted from the comments in order to avoid an advantage due to class bias. The data is labeled using a noisy labeling approach inspired from distant supervision

Table 1. Descriptive statistics on IAC and RNLC

Dataset	IAC	RNLC
Number of comments	8,000	100,000
Average terms/sentence	39.8	33.7
Average sentences/comment	3.1	12.2
Instances of agreement	4,000	50,000
Instances of disagreement	4,000	50,000

[2] http://www.reddit.com.

learning [8] whereby highly discriminative expressions such as "*I agree*" and "*you are wrong*" are used as cues to class labels agreement and disagreement. A minimum comment length was also added as a requirement in order to remove uninformative data points. The complete dataset, spanning posts from a year of crawling, was then randomly subsampled for computational efficiency.

4.2 Baselines

We contextualize our approach by comparing it to Naive Bayes (NaiveBayes), a strong baseline in text classification that allows the user to manually inspect the parameters of its model in the form of word probabilities, thus allowing predictions to be interpreted and corrected. We will also compare our approach to two existing approaches for lexicon induction from text data: the Conditional Probability-Based Lexicon (CPBLex) which models each term score as the conditional probability of observing that term in that particular class, and both the Pointwise Mutual Information Lexicon (PMILex) which models each term score as the pointwise mutual information between that term and that particular class and its variation using normalized pointwise mutual information NPMILex. Both lexicons then use the classification rule described in Eq. 8, which classifies a user comment x on the basis of maximizing the sum of associations between each of its terms t and each class c. Lexicon size is always kept to 400 to avoid overfitting after removal of stopwords[3] and non-alphanumerical characters.

$$\text{ClassLabel}(x) = \text{ArgMax}_c \left[\sum_{t \in x} \text{TermScore}(t, c) \right] \tag{8}$$

CPBLex *baseline.* We compute this lexicon using the conditional probability of observing each term in each class, as referred in Eq. 1.

PMILex *baseline.* We compute this lexicon using normalized pointwise mutual information (NPMI, referred in Eq. 3) as a way to measure strength of association between terms and their class.

5 Results and Discussion

We present the results of our experiment in Tables 2 and 3. Two approaches are tested: LexicNet_1 uses a raw term frequencies as input, while LexicNet_2 uses a logarithmically scaled frequency. A 10 fold cross-validation was done, the accuracy results were averaged over the 10 folds and a 2-tailed paired T test was performed, with a 95% confidence threshold (i. e., a p-value < 0.05). In Tables 2 and 3, the best approach is highlighted in bold.

We can observe that the $\text{Log}(tf)$ scaling yields a higher accuracy (+0.704%), which can be explained by the difference in comment length that we can see

[3] Using the stopword list from http://www.ranks.nl/stopwords.

Table 2. Results on IAC

	Method	Accuracy
Baseline lexicons	CPBLEX	0.604
	PMILEX	0.647
	NPMILEX	0.679
Baseline ML	NAIVEBAYES	0.655
Approaches	LEXICNET$_1$	0.695
	LexicNet$_2$	**0.701**

Table 3. Results on RNLC

	Method	Accuracy
Baseline lexicons	CPBLEX	0.538
	PMILEX	0.577
	NPMILEX	0.609
Baseline ML	NAIVEBAYES	0.590
Approaches	LEXICNET$_1$	0.595
	LexicNet$_2$	**0.627**

in Table 1. A logarithmic scaling of the input scores make sure that there is no large difference between two user comments based only on their length and as such would have a higher impact where there is great variation in comment length. It is evident from the results that LEXICNET$_2$ performs significantly better than standard lexicons approaches (CPBLEX and PMILEX) as well as simple but traditional machine learning approaches (NAIVEBAYES), which can be explained by the lack of a typical training phase in the latter approaches. Having an optimization phase on the set of training examples allows our approach to outperform mere point estimates, while keeping the attractive simplicity of their additive model. Statistical significance ($p < 0.05$) was achieved on the two tailed paired T test between LEXICNET$_2$ and the rest of the lexicon-based approaches, thus showing that our approach is a significant improvement over traditional techniques for lexicon induction from text.

Finally, a significant gap between the accuracy obtained in the IAC and the RNLC datasets can be observed, due to the noisy nature of the latter leading potentially to wrongly labeled data from the start. Further study will see the use of these larger amounts of unreliable data as a source of background information to enrich an existing manually labeled dataset, but it is beyond the scope of this work.

6 Conclusion and Future Work

In this work we showed the viability of modeling classification lexicons as generic computational graphs in order to compute the lexical scores in an efficient manner. There has been research done on finding faster alternatives to the more complex models [5] while maximizing performance but none so far focusing on human interpretability of the models that are produced. Our future works will thus focus on two different aspects that were not presently developed.

Firstly, the first layer of the graph described in this work can be seen as analogous to a one dimensional convolution on text. It then stands to reason that we should be able to learn that layer as well instead of providing an existing list of terms, thus producing an end-to-end neural algorithm for lexicon induction. Learning it from the data would allow us to generalize the lexicon from unigrams to n-grams.

Secondly, our current solution, while competitive with simple learners that are used for their efficiency and interpretability, is not competitive with the more complex algorithms such as deep neural networks or kernel methods. The main reason for this is that we force a fixed structure on the learning of our model so that each word class association can be inspected and changed a posteriori if necessary. However, there are ways to work around that while keeping this simplicity using more complex inference schemes and taking into account for example sequences of terms rather than unordered bag of words, taking inspiration from techniques such as backpropagation-through-time [14] to detect special terms such as valence modifiers or valence shifters.

References

1. Bandhakavi, A., Wiratunga, N., Deepak, P., Massie, S.: Generating a word-emotion lexicon from# emotional tweets. In: Proceedings of the Third Joint Conference on Lexical and Computational Semantics (*SEM 2014), pp. 12–21 (2014)
2. Clos, J., Wiratunga, N., Massie, S., Cabanac, G.: Shallow techniques for argument mining. In: Proceedings of the 1st European Conference on Argumentation: Argumentation and Reasoned Action, ECA 2015, vol. 63, p. 2 (2016)
3. Esuli, A., Sebastiani, F.: SentiWordNet: a publicly available lexical resource for opinion mining. In: Proceedings of LREC, vol. 6, pp. 417–422. Citeseer (2006)
4. Go, A., Bhayani, R., Huang, L.: Twitter sentiment classification using distant supervision. CS224N Project Report, Stanford, vol. 1, no. 12 (2009)
5. Joulin, A., Grave, E., Bojanowski, P., Mikolov, T.: Bag of tricks for efficient text classification. arXiv preprint, arXiv:1607.01759 (2016)
6. Luenberger, D.G.: Introduction to Linear and Nonlinear Programming, vol. 28. Addison-Wesley, Reading (1973)
7. Miller, G.A.: WordNet: a lexical database for English. Commun. ACM **38**(11), 39–41 (1995)
8. Mintz, M., Bills, S., Snow, R., Jurafsky, D.: Distant supervision for relation extraction without labeled data. In: Proceedings of the Joint Conference of the 47th Annual Meeting of the ACL and the 4th International Joint Conference on Natural Language Processing of the AFNLP, vol. 2, pp. 1003–1011. Association for Computational Linguistics (2009)

9. Muhammad, A., Wiratunga, N., Lothian, R.: A hybrid sentiment lexicon for social media mining. In: 2014 IEEE 26th International Conference on Tools with Artificial Intelligence (ICTAI), pp. 461–468. IEEE (2014)
10. Pennebaker, J.W., Francis, M.E., Booth, R.J.: Linguistic Inquiry and Word Count: LIWC 2001, vol. 71. Lawrence Erlbaum Associates, Mahway (2001)
11. Ribeiro, M.T., Singh, S., Guestrin, C.: Why should i trust you?: explaining the predictions of any classifier. In: Proceedings of the 22nd ACM SIGKDD International Conference on Knowledge Discovery and Data Mining, pp. 1135–1144. ACM (2016)
12. Turney, P.D.: Thumbs up or thumbs down?: semantic orientation applied to unsupervised classification of reviews. In: Proceedings of the 40th Annual Meeting on Association for Computational Linguistics, pp. 417–424. Association for Computational Linguistics (2002)
13. Walker, M.A., Tree, J.E.F., Anand, P., Abbott, R., King, J.: A corpus for research on deliberation and debate. In: LREC, pp. 812–817 (2012)
14. Werbos, P.J.: Backpropagation through time: what it does and how to do it. Proc. IEEE **78**(10), 1550–1560 (1990)

The Colloquial WordNet: Extending Princeton WordNet with Neologisms

John P. McCrae[1(✉)], Ian Wood[1], and Amanda Hicks[2]

[1] Insight Center for Data Analytics, National University of Ireland, Galway, Galway, Ireland
john@mccr.ae, ian.wood@insight-centre.org
[2] Department of Health Outcomes and Policy, University of Florida, Gainesville, USA
aehicks@ufl.edu

Abstract. Princeton WordNet is one of the most important resources for natural language processing, but has not been updated for over ten years and is not suitable for analyzing the fast moving language as used on social media. We propose an extension to WordNet, with new terms that have been found from Twitter and Reddit, and cover language usage that is emergent or vulgar. In addition to our methodology for extraction, we analyze new terms to provide information about how new words are entering the English language. Finally, we discuss publishing this resource both as linguistic linked open data and as part of the Global WordNet Association's Interlingual Index.

Keywords: WordNet · Neologisms · Slang · Linked data · Lexicography

1 Introduction

Princeton WordNet (PWN) [9] is the most widely used lexical resource in natural language processing. However, it has not been updated significantly since the release of Version 3.0 in 2006. As such, there are many new terms that have entered the English language, which are not covered by this resource. Yet many applications, especially in sentiment analysis, base their analysis on texts extracted from social media platforms, where the use of language is often quite distinct from the general language that is covered by WordNet. Moreover, social media has allowed communities to gather around specific topics of interest [11] and often the language exhibits distinct features [10] and a vocabulary that is not captured by WordNet.

In this paper, we present the initial version of a new resource we call the Colloquial WordNet, which extends Princeton WordNet to work better in new domains, especially those such as internet forums and messaging services such as Twitter. Furthermore, we extend on some of the challenges in this domain and provide not only traditional lexical entries, but also lists of misspellings, abbreviations and common errors. Furthermore, we investigate the construction of neologisms in social media in comparison to language used in general and technical domains.

J. Gracia et al. (Eds.): LDK 2017, LNAI 10318, pp. 194–202, 2017.
DOI: 10.1007/978-3-319-59888-8_17

2 Methodology

2.1 Corpus Preparation

We extracted a corpus from two social media websites: Twitter, where text was gathered using the Twitter sample API endpoint[1] between February 2nd and 22nd 2016; and Reddit, where we extracted data from the top 1000 most popular forums ('subreddits') using a webpage crawler[2]. In total, we collected 255,908 Reddit posts (3.4 million tokens) and 3,018,180 Twitter posts (29.8 million tokens).

Our approach for selecting terms was based on the ratio of the frequency of terms in the Reddit or Twitter corpus relative to a background corpus, in particular, the *Google Web Trillion Word Corpus*[3]. To improve the ranking of this ratio, we discarded all terms that did not occur at least 10 times in the Reddit or Twitter corpus and set the frequency of terms not found in the background corpus or in the lowest decile to the highest value in the lowest decile. We then filtered terms to only those that occurred in Urban Dictionary[4], that occur in all lowercases more frequently than otherwise and other filters to remove simple non-terms (such as phrases starting with 'a' or 'the'). This gave us the ability to find terms that would be relevant with high precision, and our annotators accepted 61.3% of terms as worthy of inclusion in the lexicon, among the 500 highest scoring terms.

2.2 Annotation Procedure

Using the terms selected as potentially relevant, the annotators were asked to create entries using the interface shown in Fig. 1. The first decision made by the annotator was the status of the term, which could be one of the following:

General. A term that is generally used in the language and would be suitable for inclusion in PWN. This covers some new terms such as 'steampunk' or 'hoverboard' that cover novel concepts. A few times surprising gaps in PWN were found for example a sense of the verb 'pick' in 'lock picking'. This can mean that novel senses are added to existing Princeton WordNet entries.

Novel. This is for terms that the annotators believed may not be stable in the language, in that they are extremely colloquial, e.g., 'bestie' (best friend) or they refer to a current cultural phenomenon, e.g., 'twerk' and 'dab' (popular dance moves). As such terms may not remain in the language for long they are tagged in the data as novel terms.

Vulgar. This covers both terms that use vulgar language, refer to sexual acts or are defamatory (racist, sexist, etc.). A significant number of the tweets in our corpus were advertising pornography or sexual services, resulting in many vulgar terms in the output.

[1] This end point provides a sample of approximately 1% of all tweets.
[2] https://github.com/lucasdnd/simple-reddit-crawler.
[3] Compiled at http://norvig.com/ngrams/.
[4] http://www.urbandictionary.com.

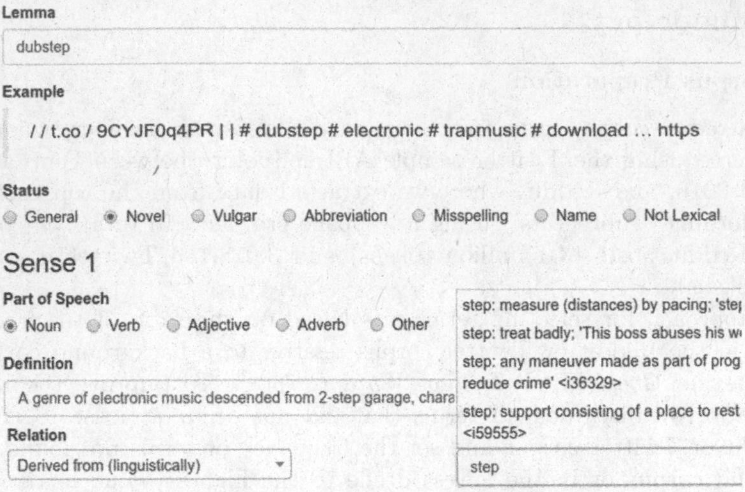

Fig. 1. An example entry, 'dubstep', showing the status definition and one link being created

Abbreviation. The term is an abbreviation.

Misspelling. The term is a misspelled version of a standard English word or phrase.

Name. The term is a name of a person, organization or place. Note we classed terms derived from names, e.g., 'belieber' (a fan of Justin Bieber) as novel words.

Not Idiomatic. The algorithm detected some short expressions as new terms when they were in fact just collocations, e.g., 'can i get'.

Error. This was used for technical errors, e.g., 'nbsp' (the HTML entity for non-breaking space).

The next step of the annotation involved either selecting an existing synset in PWN to which the word referred or writing a novel English definition for the term as well as deciding the part of speech. Note that following Morgado da Costa and Bond [6] we also allow the annotation of interjection expressions such as 'oh' or 'haha' as these are useful for understanding emotion and meaning in social media texts. If the word had multiple meanings the annotator could create multiple senses, each with their own definition and part-of-speech. The final step for the annotator was to add links from the new synset to any other synsets in PWN. This was supported by an interactive selection tool (see Fig. 1) and all the standard relations could be selected. In addition, we included two new relations that were useful, firstly a 'loanword' as many of our neologisms were words from other languages and secondly an 'emotion' property to indicate what feeling is expressed by the meaning of a word.

Table 1. The size of the resource in terms of elements it contains

	Size		Size
Entries	428	Non-entries	1340
– General	83	– Non-Idiomatic	392
– Novel	181	– Errors	83
– Vulgar	46	– Proper nouns	336
– Interjections	117	– Abbreviations	484
		– Misspellings	345
Synsets	430		
Sense relations	408		
Synset relations	365		

3 Results

3.1 Resource Creation

The overall statistics for the resource are presented in Table 1, where we describe the number of new entries found, broken down into the categories (General, Novel, Vulgar) described above as well as the number of synsets and relations between synsets in the new graph. In addition, we provide the non-lexical items that we found during the construction of the resource, which represent one of the major forms of the elements found. While we see that very few of the forms are true errors, there are a large number of items in the categories of non-idiomatic phrases, misspellings and proper nouns. This is slightly surprising given that a lexicon (Urban Dictionary) was used to filter out terms that were not suitable for inclusion in the dictionary and this demonstrates the unreliability of Urban Dictionary as a base resource.

3.2 An Analysis of Neologisms

In addition, we collected information during the annotation procedure about the origin of neologisms that have been defined. We did this by classifying neologisms into the following groups:

Novel Sense. This describes a novel meaning that a word has acquired recently. For example the noun 'post' in the sense of a 'forum post' is a sense that does not match the existing senses of the noun in PWN 3.1[5]. In addition, we also count cases where a word has changed part-of-speech as new senses, such as the verb 'favorite', which is only listed as an adjective in PWN 3.1.

Multiword Expression. The standard method of constructing new terms is the combination of two or more words to describe a novel concept. For example 'social media' is a new concept to PWN 3.1.

[5] See http://wordnetweb.princeton.edu/perl/webwn?s=post.

Compounding. Similar to above it is often common to create new words by combining two existing words into a new word, for example the combination of a 'hash' and 'tag' to make 'hashtag'. This is distinct from the previous category as it creates a single new word.

Affixation. Many words are derived by adding a suffix or prefix to the word, in particular adding a prefix such as 're-', e.g., 'repost' or the affix '-ie' such as in 'selfie'.

Portmanteau. The blending of two words to create a novel term, resulting in a word that contains phonetic characteristics of both words, such as 'cosplayer' (from 'costume' and 'player') or 'bromance' (from 'brother' and 'romance').

Loanwords. Many novel words are loaned from other languages, examples include 'oppa' (from Korean) and 'waifu' (from Japanese).

Shortening. Some novel words are created by shortening existing words, for example 'notif' (from 'notification') or 'sesh' (from 'session').

Phonetic spelling. This is when neologisms are created by intentionally misspelling a word frequently for effect, for example 'smol' (from 'small') or 'bruv' (from 'brother'). It is also particularly common to see this in words that are associated with African-American Vernacular English, e.g., 'shawty' (from 'short').

Unknown. For some words the derivation was not clear or could not be conclusively established, an example of this is 'twerk', whose etymology is unclear[6].

We classified the words into each of the categories and the results are presented in Table 2.

Table 2. Breakdown of neologism construction methods for colloquial terms not in Princeton WordNet

Neologism type	Twitter	Reddit
Portmanteau	16(14.8%)	4(3.1%)
Novel Sense	18(16.7%)	25(19.2%)
Affixation	17(15.7%)	16(12.3%)
Phonetic	8(7.4%)	9(6.9%)
Loanwords	9(8.3%)	7(5.4%)
Compounds	15(13.9%)	25(19.2%)
Multiword Expression	12(11.1%)	29(22.3%)
Abbreviation	7(6.5%)	5(3.9%)
Other	6(5.5%)	10(7.7%)

[6] http://blog.oxforddictionaries.com/2013/08/what-is-the-origin-of-twerk/.

4 Publishing the Resource

We have made the data available under an open license, namely the Creative Commons Attribution (CC-BY 4.0) License in order to ensure that it can be reused as widely as possibly. In addition, we have integrated our resource with two best practices in the area of WordNet data, namely with the Linguistic Linked Open Data Cloud and the Collaborative Interlingual Index from our website.[7]

4.1 Publishing the Resource as Linked Data

The Linguistic Linked Open Data cloud [4] has been proposed as a method for linking data between different resources and across modalities and these technologies promise to improve the interoperability and reusability of language resources on the Web. The OntoLex-Lemon model [5,14] has been proposed as a model for the representation of lexical data on the Semantic Web and while its initial goal was to expand ontologies with lexical information it has recently been used for all kinds of lexical resources. We published the data using the Yuzu [15] system for linked data publishing and we link to the Polylingual WordNet [1], which has further links to the Interlingual Index. Using the Yuzu interface allows the data to be made available in RDF formats including Turtle, RDF/XML and N-Triples as well as JSON-LD [18].

4.2 Integrating the Resource with Collaborative Interlingual Index

The Collaborative Interlingual Index [2,19] has been proposed as a method to enable cross-lingual development of wordnets. One of the major goals of this project has been defining a procedure by which new synsets can be defined and this goal overlaps with the objective of the Colloquial WordNet. Moreover, it is the case that non-English WordNets have not just introduced new concepts for words that are not directly lexicalisable in English, but have also introduced new synsets for novel concepts, often even when the term is a loanword from English. A notable example of this is the Polish plWordNet [13], which is significantly larger than any existing resource.

In order to facilitate the integration of Colloquial WordNet with the Collaborative Interlingual Index, we have made the full version of the resource available in the Global WordNet Association's recommended formats[8] and made it available under an open and permissive license. Furthermore, the Colloquial WordNet is participating in a pilot program to introduce the first set of new terms in the interlingual index and one term from the Colloquial WordNet, the verb 'to tweet', is a special test case as we believe this meaning is found in all major world languages.

[7] http://colloqwn.linguistic-lod.org/.
[8] http://globalwordnet.github.io/schemas/.

5 Related Work

A previous project [7], called SlangNet, has already attempted to create a wordnet of slang for English, however this project has not released any version of the resource yet and appears to be inactive[9]. A certain number of our terms are also included in large-scale resources such as BabelNet [16] and we find that some of the terms added by our resource are already defined in BabelNet, however this is primarily only terms that are derived from Wiktionary and represents, 72.5% of our entries, which still means many terms would not be found in such resources. Similarly, the CROWN project [12] extended WordNet by means of automatically adding terms from Wiktionary.

The issue of detecting Neologisms has received some attention but approaches still have significant weaknesses. Neologism are of interest in traditional lexicography and major publishers work to detect neologisms [17] however these still rely significantly on manual work. Semi-automated detection has been attempted such as by extracting relevant features and classifying them using an SVM [8] or by relying on language-specific features [3]. We plan to use the training data we have collected in the first development round to improve the accuracy of the neologism collection procedure, using such supervised machine learning.

6 Conclusion

We have presented a method for development of a new extension to Princeton WordNet that covers the kind of language used in Twitter, Reddit and similar social media. Our resource relies on few annotators and as such we hope to encourage crowd validation by making the tool available online. Our extraction method relies on a mixture of corpus statistics and the usage of a crowd-sourced dictionary, Urban Dictionary, which we found to be of too poor quality to be used directly. While our method finds neologisms with high precision, we are not yet sure on the recall and as we cast a wider net this will become more critical. We analyzed the neologisms introduced and found that these terms are introduced not only by conventional methods such as affixation and sense extension, but also saw that a large number of words are entering as loanwords and in particular that portmanteaus are becoming much more common in colloquial English.

Acknowledgements. This work was supported in part by the Science Foundation Ireland under Grant Number SFI/12/RC/2289 (Insight) and NIH/NCATS Clinical and Translational Science Awards to the University of Florida UL1 TR000064/UL1 TR001427. The content is solely the responsibility of the authors and does not necessarily represent the official views of NIH/NCATS.

[9] We have aimed to combine this resource with our data, but discussions with the authors on licensing have been inconclusive.

References

1. Arcan, M., McCrae, J.P., Buitelaar, P.: Expanding wordnets to new languages with multilingual sense disambiguation. In: Proceedings of The 26th International Conference on Computational Linguistics (2016)
2. Bond, F., Vossen, P., McCrae, J.P., Fellbaum, C.: CILI: the collaborative interlingual index. In: Proceedings of the Global WordNet Conference (2016)
3. Breen, J.: Identification of neologisms in Japanese by corpus analysis. In: Proceedings of the E-lexicography in the 21st Century: New Challenges, New Applications, ELex 2009, Louvain-la Neuve, pp. 13–21 (2010)
4. Chiarcos, C., McCrae, J., Cimiano, P., Fellbaum, C.: Towards open data for linguistics: linguistic linked data. In: Oltramari, A., Vossen, P., Qin, L., Hovy, E. (eds.) New Trends of Research in Ontologies and Lexical Resources, pp. 7–25. Springer, Heidelberg (2013)
5. Cimiano, P., McCrae, J.P., Buitelaar, P.: Lexicon model for ontologies: community report. Final Community Group Report, World Wide Web Consortium (2016)
6. Morgado da Costa, L., Bond, F.: Wow! what a useful extension! introducing non-referential concepts to WordNet. In: Proceedings of the 10th International Conference on Language Resources and Evaluation (LREC 2016), Portorož, Slovenia. (2016)
7. Dhuliawala, S., Kanojia, D., Bhattacharyya, P.: SlangNet: a WordNet like resource for English slang. In: Proceedings of the Tenth International Conference on Language Resources and Evaluation, pp. 4329–4332 (2016)
8. Falk, I., Bernhard, D., Gérard, C.: From non word to new word: automatically identifying neologisms in French newspapers. In: The 9th Language Resources and Evaluation Conference, LREC (2014)
9. Fellbaum, C.: WordNet. Blackwell Publishing Ltd., Hoboken (1998)
10. Grant, H.: Tumblinguistics: innovation and variation in new forms of written CMC. Master's thesis, University of Glasgow (2015)
11. Hicks, A., Rutherford, M., Fellbaum, C., Bian, J.: An analysis of WordNet's coverage of gender identity using Twitter and the national transgender discrimination survey. In: Global WordNet Conference (2016)
12. Jurgens, D., Pilehvar, M.T.: Reserating the awesometastic: an automatic extension of the WordNet taxonomy for novel terms. In: HLT-NAACL, pp. 1459–1465 (2015)
13. Maziarz, M., Piasecki, M., Rudnicka, E., Szpakowicz, S., Kedzia, P.: plWordNet 3.0-a comprehensive lexical-semantic resource. In: Proceedings of the 26th International Conference on Computational Linguistics, COLING 2016: Technical Papers, pp. 2259–2268 (2016)
14. McCrae, J., Aguado-de-Cea, G., Buitelaar, P., Cimiano, P., Declerck, T., Gómez-Pérez, A., Gracia, J., Hollink, L., Montiel-Ponsoda, E., Spohr, D., et al.: Interchanging lexical resources on the semantic web. Lang. Resour. Eval. **46**(4), 701–719 (2012)
15. McCrae, J.P.: Yuzu: publishing any data as linked data. In: ISWC 2016 Posters and Demonstrations Track (2016)
16. Navigli, R., Ponzetto, S.P.: BabelNet: the automatic construction, evaluation and application of a wide-coverage multilingual semantic network. Artif. Intell. **193**, 217–250 (2012)
17. O'Donovan, R., O'Neill, M.: A systematic approach to the selection of neologisms for inclusion in a large monolingual dictionary. In: Proceedings of the 13th Euralex International Congress, pp. 571–579 (2008)

18. Sporny, M., Longley, D., Kellogg, G., Lanthaler, M., Lindström, N.: JSON-LD 1.1: a JSON-based serialization for linked data. Community Group Report, World Wide Web Consortium (2017)
19. Vossen, P., Bond, F., McCrae, J.P.: Toward a truly multilingual global WordNet grid. In: Proceedings of the Global WordNet Conference (2016)

Shifting Complexity from Text to Data Model

Adding Machine-Oriented Features to a Human-Oriented Terminology Resource

Karolina Suchowolec(✉), Christian Lang(✉), Roman Schneider, and Horst Schwinn

Institut für Deutsche Sprache (IDS), Mannheim, Germany
{suchowolec,lang,schneider,schwinn}@ids-mannheim.de

Abstract. *Grammis* is a web-based information system on German grammar, hosted by the Institute for the German Language (IDS). It is human-oriented and features different theoretical perspectives on grammar. Currently, the terminology component of *grammis* is being redesigned for this theoretical diversity to play a more prominent role in the data model. This also opens opportunities for implementing some machine-oriented features. In this paper, we present the re-design of both data model and knowledge base. We explore how the addition of machine-oriented features to the data model impacts the knowledge base; in particular, how this addition shifts some of the textual complexity into the data model. We show that our resource can easily be ported to a SKOS-XL representation, which makes it available for data science, knowledge-based NLP applications, and LOD in the context of digital humanities.

1 Introduction

Grammis[1] is an online resource on German grammar, hosted by the Institute for the German Language (IDS) in Mannheim, Germany. As described in [1, p. 622], 'it combines traditional description of grammatical structures with the results of corpus-based studies [...]'. The resource is modular, and each module has a different function—for instance, *Systematische Grammatik* is a comprehensive reference, which describes grammatical phenomena of German in great detail. In this paper, we deal with the terminology module of *grammis*, which serves as a short reference and points to the corresponding entries in *Systematische Grammatik* for further reading. Currently, the resource is being re-designed in terms of data model, technology, and knowledge base.

The group of *grammis'* target users is heterogeneous, ranging from expert grammarians to students of linguistics and interested laymen. However, the basic principle of *grammis* is to give a non-reductionist view on the diversity of grammatical theories and standpoints. This diversity of standpoints is typical to

[1] http://www.ids-mannheim.de/grammis/.

J. Gracia et al. (Eds.): LDK 2017, LNAI 10318, pp. 203–212, 2017.
DOI: 10.1007/978-3-319-59888-8_18

humanities and needs to be accounted for scholarly reasons, because knowledge often proliferates in the theoretical discourse.

By re-applying a conceptualization by Huijsen from the field of Controlled Natural Language, we regard *grammis* as a predominantly human-oriented resource [6]. Redesigning the process does not mean altering this orientation. However, we see potential for implementing some machine-oriented features, opening up the new resource for data science and knowledge-based applications. In this paper we present our approach to include these machine-oriented features. The first section introduces the new data model and shows a proof of concept that the new terminological resource can be easily ported to a SKOS-XL representation. Subsequently, we relate our future resource to existing terminological resources in the domain of linguistics. In the second part of the paper, we exemplify some challenges regarding the knowledge base. These challenges result from the combination of the above-mentioned non-reductionist principle and machine readability. In particular, we show how we shift some of the textual complexity into the data model of our new resource. We conclude with some general ideas on practical applications in the context of NLP and Linked (Open) Data.

2 Data Model and Machine-Oriented Representation

As described in [9], terminological resources at IDS are heterogeneous. On the one hand, there are several traditional, human-oriented, and semasiological (term-oriented) dictionaries which are results of different research projects, '[...] with different goals, scopes, scholarly traditions [...]' [9, p. 60]. On the other hand, there is an onomasiological (concept-oriented) thesaurus, which can be used for manual browsing by humans, but also for automatic full-text search and query expansion. Our re-designed Terminology Management System (TMS) combines these various resources into one powerful, state-of-the-art resource. The data model for this new TMS is onomasiological and based on incorporating hybrid best practices from the fields of terminology management, thesaurus management, and online lexicography [10]. The new data model is shown in Fig. 1.

Our new data model uses several well-known elements such as *concepts* and *terms*, as well as standard relations between those elements. However, it also introduces a unique notion of *concept rings* as a container for concepts from different grammatical theories that are similar enough to be treated as a unit [10]. *Concept rings* can also be seen as an implementation of prototypical units of understanding as described by Temmerman [11].

Based on this data model, we implemented our new unified TMS in a generic object-relational database management system (ORDMS) by Oracle. In order to see if we can add a machine-oriented level to our predominantly human-oriented resource, we used the D2RQ Platform[2] in a test environment. D2RQ Platform provides an instantaneous virtual RDF representation of relational data '[...] without having to replicate it into an RDF store' (http://d2rq.org/). Our data

[2] http://d2rq.org/.

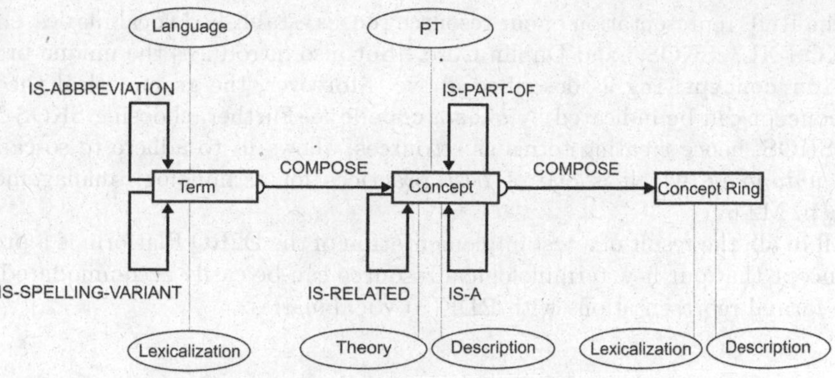

Fig. 1. Data model of the re-designed *grammis'* terminological resource [10]

Description of http://localhost:2020/resource/TB_KONZEPT/123:

property	hasValue	isValueOf
ids:conceptRing	db:TB_KONZEPTRING/123	-
dc:identifier	123	-
rdf:type	skos:Concept	-
skos:broader	db:TB_KONZEPT/1897	-
skos:definition	"Kommunikanten-Pronomina sind eine Subklasse der Pronomina. Ihre Funktion ist der Verweis auf den aktuellen Sprecher bzw. die Sprechergruppe oder den aktuellen Hörer bzw. die Hörergruppe."	-
skos:narrower	db:TB_KONZEPT/103	-
skos:narrower	db:TB_KONZEPT/246	-
skos:related	db:TB_KONZEPT/317	-
skos:scopeNote	"Systematische Grammatik"	-
skosxl:altLabel	db:TB_TERM/619	-
skosxl:altLabel	db:TB_TERM/8587	-
skosxl:altLabel	db:TB_TERM/8710	-
skosxl:altLabel	db:TB_TERM/8711	-
skosxl:altLabel	db:TB_TERM/8712	-
skosxl:altLabel	db:TB_TERM/8713	-
skosxl:altLabel	db:TB_TERM/8714	-
skosxl:altLabel	db:TB_TERM/8715	-
skosxl:altLabel	db:TB_TERM/8716	-
skosxl:altLabel	db:TB_TERM/9836	-
skosxl:altLabel	db:TB_TERM/9837	-
skosxl:prefLabel	db:TB_TERM/615	-
skos:related	-	db:TB_KONZEPT/185
skos:related	-	db:TB_KONZEPT/394
skos:related	-	db:TB_KONZEPT/577
skos:related	-	db:TB_KONZEPT/717

Powered by D2R Server

Fig. 2. SKOS-XL representation of *grammis'* terminological resource in a test D2RQ environment. Concept: *Kommunikanten-Pronomen*

allows for a straightforward customization of the *mapping.ttl* file to a SKOS-XL[3] representation and the result is exemplified in Fig. 2.

[3] https://www.w3.org/TR/skos-reference/skos-xl.html.

The RDF representation of our resource reuses established vocabularies, such as SKOS-XL,[4] SKOS,[5] and Dublin Core,[6] but also introduces the unique property `ids:conceptRing` as described above. Moreover, the grammatical theory of a concept can be indicated by `skos:scopeNote`. Further, choosing SKOS-XL over SKOS, hence treating terms as resources, allows us to adhere to so-called *term autonomy*, which is one of best practices for terminology management [cf. 3, p. M2-6] .

All in all, the result of a test implementation of the D2RQ Platform is a proof of concept that our new terminological resource can be easily accommodated to more formal representations with RDF(S) vocabularies.

3 Related Work

There are different language resources and repositories in the domain of linguistics that can be used for knowledge-based applications. In the context of the Linguistic Linked Open Data (LLOD) cloud [8] distinguishes between (1) lexical-semantic resources, (2) metadata and terminological repositories, and (3) annotated corpora and schemes for annotated corpora [cf. 2, p. 4465]. We consider terminological repositories the most relevant group for our new resource. Within this group, GOLD,[7] ISOcat,[8] and OLiA[9] share a common, although a non-exclusive, focus on morphosyntax, i.e. grammar; however, there are some major differences to our project.

Although those three repositories can be also used by individuals, they are mostly designed to be used by the machines. As a primarily human-oriented resource, our terminology repository is modeled in a less formal fashion, just as other SKOS resources. Moreover, the primary goal of these three repositories is to serve as a common representation of grammar, ensuring interoperability of different resources in and for different languages. As such, they each propose one common view on morphosyntax with regard to concepts and terms; by contrast, our goal is to reflect the conceptual and linguistic diversity in grammar description, which we exemplify by the concepts *Pronomen* ('*pronoun*') and *Artikel* ('*article*') in the next section. Finally, our resource is in German and predominantly for German language, while the above-mentioned repositories use English as a common language.

There is also a recent SKOS representation of grammatical terminology in English and German[10] as an intermediate result of linking the Thesaurus for the Bibliography of Linguistic Literature (BLL) with the OLiA repository [2].

---

[4] Namespace URI: http://www.w3.org/2008/05/skos-xl.
[5] Namespace URI: http://www.w3.org/2004/02/skos/core.
[6] Namespace URI: http://purl.org/dc/elements/1.1/.
[7] http://linguistics-ontology.org/gold.
[8] http://www.isocat.org.
[9] http://www.acoli.informatik.uni-frankfurt.de/resources/olia/.
[10] https://datahub.io/de/dataset/bll-thesaurus/resource/0f991247-64a6-4b99-bbc7-2b2626f6636e.

Because of the machine-oriented goal of this representation and the use of only index terms of the BLL thesaurus as source data, this resource significantly differs from our resource in terms of diversity coverage.

The *Glossary of Linguistic Terms & Bibliography*[11] by Christian Lehmann is a human-oriented resource on linguistic terminology. Although it is called a glossary, it offers more than an alphabetical list of terms—it models different types of relations between linguistic concepts, e.g. hierarchical relations, but also non-hierarchical relations such as *is a result of* or *manifests*, which are not covered by our resource. There are strong similarities to our resource in terms of general descriptive information, such as definition or history note on a concept, and synonyms and foreign-language equivalents to its preferred term. However, the *Glossary* does not address the issue of different theoretical viewpoints on grammar, which is a crucial part of our project.

Finally, the subject of the project *EcoLexicon* [e.g. 4,5] is not directly related to our work because it deals with environmental terminology. However, just as our project, *EcoLexicon* accommodates different contextual perspectives on certain concepts, especially so-called *versatile concepts* such as *water*, because their conceptual behavior might differ depending on the sub-domain [7]. Therefore, the conceptual model is split according to these sub-domains. Similarly, our project uses theory tags to label and alert to theory-specific conceptualizations of a fragment of grammar; in this regard, concept rings serve as generalizing units. However, while we use the traditional concept-oriented approach to terminology, *EcoLexicon* uses the frame-based approach to structure its concepts as environmental events. The use of frames results in rich conceptual relation types that are not covered by our predominantly hierarchical thesaurus.

4 Revision of the Knowledge Base

It appears that displaying diversity of theoretical viewpoints is the key feature that distinguishes our project from related projects in the domain of linguistics. So far in our dictionaries, this complexity was addressed merely textually—a single dictionary entry discussed competing conceptualizations. However, these competing conceptualizations were not implemented on the data model level of the dictionaries and could not be addressed and retrieved individually by machine applications. On the other hand, the model of the thesaurus was different. While it is generally feasible for a thesaurus to implement competing conceptualizations, our thesaurus was theory-neutral and modeled one common view on grammar, in which it resembled the related projects mentioned above. To sum it up, while the dictionaries covered theoretical complexity, the thesaurus had the means to render it machine accessible. Hence, re-designing the existing resources puts the thesaurus at the center of our system and thereby requires the dictionaries' entries to follow its onomasiological approach [10]. We intend to shift some textual complexity from the dictionary entries, i.e., our knowledge base, to the data model of the new resource.

[11] http://linguistik.uni-regensburg.de:8080/lido/Lido.

As the first step we review the current knowledge base and evaluate in which cases the existing textual complexity can be implemented on the data model level. This revision is qualitative and performed manually on a case-by-case basis. Moreover, it is iterative and might lead to a conceptual re-evaluation of already reviewed data in a later stage of the process. In the following sections we discuss some of the challenges during this process based on two examples. The first example—*Pronomen*—illustrates the issue of deciding what constitutes a concept for a grammarian. It can also be interpreted as our approach to ambiguity in terminology. The second example—*Artikel*—deals with synonymy, but also illustrates another case of ambiguity.

4.1 Pronomen

Most people are familiar with the part of speech *Personalpronomen* (‘*personal pronoun*’) as a subclass of *pronoun* that represents people or things and is closely related to the grammatical category of *person*. Similar definitions can be found in the repositories mentioned in Sect. 3. A grammarian's view on *Personalpronomen* is, however, more multifaceted and depends on the conceptualization approach in a given theoretical framework. For example, there is no concept *Personalpronomen* within the framework of *Systematische Grammatik*; instead, the inventory of what is commonly known as *Personalpronomen* is split into two separate concepts—*Kommunikanten-Pronomen* (‘*communicant pronoun*’) and *anaphorisches Personalpronomen* (‘*anaphoric pronoun*’).[12]

To a non-grammarian, these conceptual differences in the presence or absence of the concept *Personalpronomen* are negligible and contribute to neither their understanding of the phenomenon, nor the use of the inventory, especially because there is a significant tacit overlap in both conceptualizations; however, while too granular to the layman, these conceptual differences matter to a grammarian for several reasons. Functional considerations are at the very heart of *Systematische Grammatik*, therefore, the distinction between *Kommunikanten-Pronomen* and *anaphorisches Personalpronomen* introduces a more specialized perspective on the function of the phenomenon (*anaphorisches Personalpronomen*: anaphoric, *Kommunikanten-Pronomen*: deictic). In the more general view of *Personalpronomen* this functional specialization is lost. In our redesigned resource we want to represent this kind of theoretical diversity. Instead of choosing one common perspective, multiple perspectives on the same inventory should be accounted for side by side.

Prior to the revision, this theoretical diversity was addressed non-uniformly by our terminological resources. The texts of the dictionaries mainly discussed the view of *Systematische Grammatik* and only briefly mentioned the alternative views; by contrast, the old thesaurus included multiple perspectives. However, in our *Pronomen* example the hierarchical structure of hyponyms was not clear-cut,

---

[12] *Kommunikanten-Pronomen* refers to the speaker or the person being addressed (*I*, *you*, *we*), whereas *anaphorisches Personalpronomen* refers to third parties other than speaker or the person being addressed (*he*, *she*, *it*, *they*).

see Fig. 3. As a consequence, theoretical diversity was accessible only to human, but not to machine interpretation. However, even for humans identifying, sorting, and organizing various perspectives already required advanced expertise. The revision of our knowledge base renders explicit the relations between various perspectives. While our primary focus remains human accessibility, the functionality extends to machine processing as an added value.

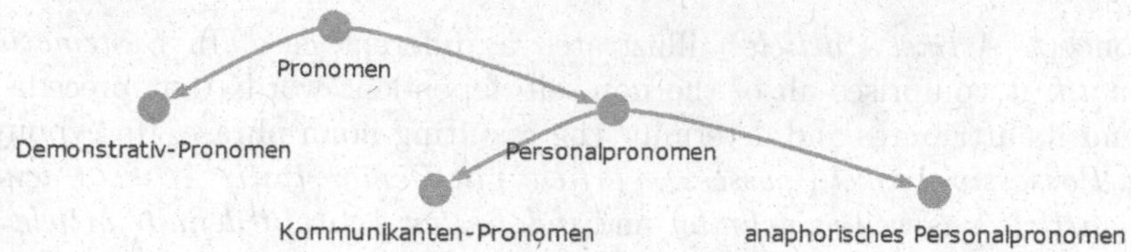

Fig. 3. Pre-revision model of *Pronomen* in the thesaurus, relation displayed: IS-A

In order to do so, we decided to treat *Personalpronomen* on the one hand and *Kommunikanten-Pronomen* and *anaphorisches Pronomen* on the other hand as subclasses of two separate concepts of *Pronomen.* In other words, we split one theory-neutral concept of *Pronomen* into two theory-sensitive concepts of *Pronomen.* On the one hand, this improves accessibility and allows for a theory-sensitive attachment of hyponyms. On the other hand, having two different *Pronomen* concepts is also motivated by our observation that in humanities, the choice and scope of hyponyms seem to be crucial for the notion of the hypernym. However, this way we introduce ambiguity as two (or more) concepts share the same preferred term *Pronomen.* Therefore, we attach a theory tag to improve retrieval; only concepts that can unequivocally be identified as belonging to a particular linguistic framework receive an explicit theory tag whereas, all other cases are unmarked.

This handling of theory tags can be explained using the examples in Fig. 4: the concept *Pronomen* with the hyponyms *Kommunikantenpronomen* and *anaphorisches Personalpronomen* receives a *Systematische Grammatik* theory tag as it is limited to a particular framework. By contrast, *Pronomen ()* with the hyponym *Personalpronomen ()* is generally used in multiple conceptualizations and theories and, therefore, receives an empty default tag. In addition, note that the concept of *Demonstrativpronomen ()* is polyhierarchical and a hyponym of

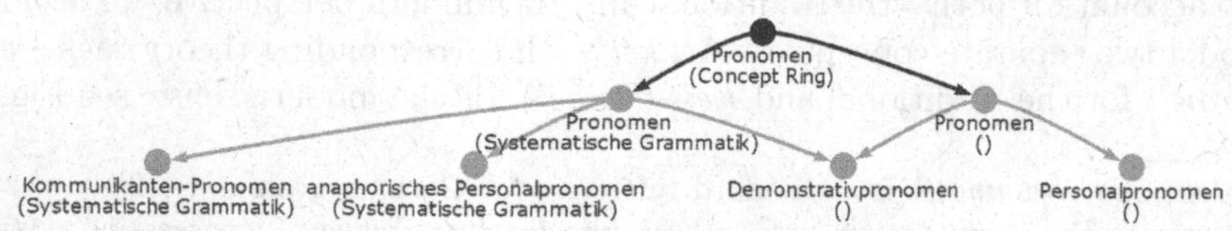

Fig. 4. Revised model of *Pronomen* in the thesaurus, relation displayed: IS-A

both—*Pronomen ()* and *Pronomen (Systematische Grammatik)*. Due to the fact that it is identical in the *Systematische Grammatik* and the default conceptualization of *Pronomen* and, therefore, not limited to a certain framework, it receives the empty default tag. Finally, the close proximity of both *Pronomen* concepts is modeled by uniting them into a *concept ring*.

4.2 Artikel

The concept *Artikel* (‘*article*’) illustrates a different case. In *Systematische Grammatik* it comprises all of the non-self-dependent words that precede the noun and its attributes and determine the resulting noun phrase. Its hyponyms are e.g. *Possessiv-Artikel* (‘*possessive article*’) or *Demonstrativ-Artikel* (‘*demonstrative article*’) as well as *definiter* and *indefiniter Artikel* (‘*definite article* and *indefinite article*’).

The view of *Systematische Grammatik* corresponds to the perspective of *Duden*[13] regarding the concept's structure, i.e. hyponyms and their scope. However, the two perspectives differ in term usage—*Systematische Grammatik* refers to all hyponyms with a compound including *Artikel* (see above); in *Duden*, there are only *definiter Artikel* and *indefiniter Artikel*; the other hyponyms are referred to with a compound including *Artikelwort.*[14] Therefore, in our view, theory-sensitive concept splitting seems to be unjustified and we treat these differences in perspective as an instance of synonymy.

Interestingly, the concept of *Artikel* bears another case of ambiguity. In contrast to the modern perspective outlined above, traditionally only *definiter Artikel* and *indefiniter Artikel* were considered *Artikel*, whereas the other hyponyms of the modern view (e.g. *Possessiv-Artikel* or *Demonstrativ-Artikel*) were considered adjectively used pronouns. Prior to the revision of our knowledge base, only the modern view was represented in our thesaurus, see Fig. 5. Again, the dictionary texts only briefly mentioned alternative perspectives.

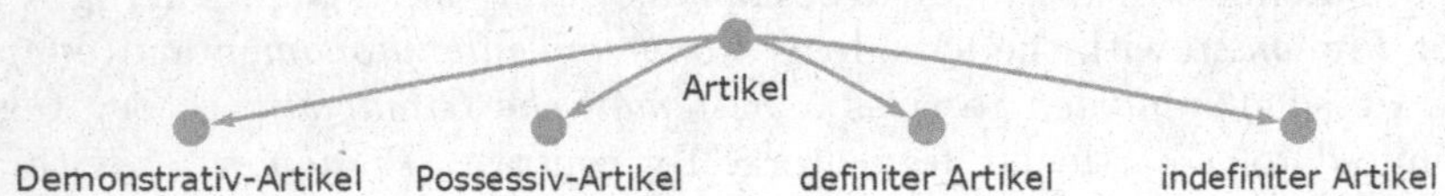

Fig. 5. Pre-revision model of *Artikel* in the thesaurus, relation displayed: IS-A

To account for both—the traditional and the modern perspective, we decided to model two separate concepts of *Artikel* with corresponding theory tags—*eng* (‘*narrow*’) for the traditional and *weit* (‘*wide*’) for the modern sense, see Fig. 6.

[13] *Duden. Die Grammatik* is a standard reference for German grammar [12].

[14] Compare: *Possessiv-Artikel* vs. *possessivisches Artikelwort* (‘*possessive article word*’); *Demonstrativ-Artikel* vs. *demonstrativisches Artikelwort* (‘*demonstrative article word*’).

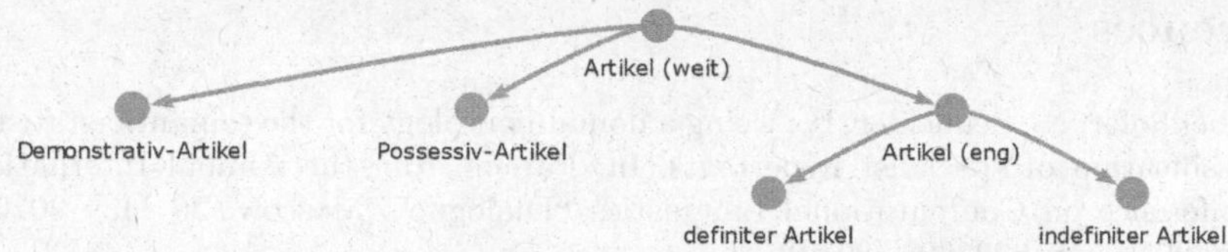

Fig. 6. Revised model of *Artikel* in the thesaurus, relation displayed: IS-A

Note that in the case of *Pronomen* we use a *concept ring* to bundle two cohyponyms of *Pronomen*. Here we refrain from the use of *concept ring* because *Artikel (eng)* and *Artikel (weit)* are not cohyponyms but the former is a proper subset of the latter.

5 Conclusion

In this paper we reported on the ongoing project of re-designing terminological resources at IDS. We covered the re-design of both the data model and the knowledge base. As for the chosen data model and its technical implementation, we provided a proof of concept that it can be easily represented as a SKOS-XL resource. However, adding these machine-oriented options has far-reaching consequences for the knowledge base; in order to make the theory-driven complexity machine accessible, it needs to be partially shifted from the knowledge base to the data model. We discussed the challenges arising from this shift using two examples.

So far, we have revised approx. one third of the knowledge base. However, because the revision is an ongoing and iterative process, we expect that a re-evaluation of some modeling decisions will be necessary. After the revision is completed, we intend to extract some generalized principles from the modeling decisions. Yet, our resource and approach remain mainly qualitative and human-oriented with only a certain degree of formalization.

Once completed, the application scenarios of our resource are similar to those of other onomasiological, semi-formal resources such as WordNet,[15] yet focused on a specialized rather than the general domain. Hence, it can support semantic NLP tasks such as topic modeling, word-sense disambiguation, or automatic document indexing in the domain of grammar. Moreover, we are also interested in applications in the context of Linguistic Linked Open Data, but the details regarding implementation and licensing have yet to be specified. Due to the high granularity of theoretical perspectives reflected, our future resource can function as a hub for other predominantly single-perspective resources on grammar.

To conclude, although our resource remains predominantly human-oriented, we believe that it is a valuable contribution in the context of digital humanities.

[15] https://wordnet.princeton.edu/.

References

1. Bubenhofer, N., Schneider, R.: Using a domain ontology for the semantic-statistical classification of specialist hypertexts. In: Papers from the Annual International Conference on Computational Linguistics "Dialogue", Moscow, 26 May 2010/30 May 2010, pp. 622–628 (2010)
2. Chiarcos, C., Fäth, C., Renner-Westermann, H., Abromeit, F., Dimitrova, V.: Lin|gu|is|tik: building the linguist's pathway to bibliographies, libraries, language resources and Linked Open Data. In: Calzolari, N., Choukri, K., Declerck, T., Goggi, S., Grobelnik, M., Maegaard, B., Mariani, J., Mazo, H., Moreno, A., Odijk, J., Piperidis, S. (eds.) Proceedings of LREC 2016, Tenth International Conference on Language Resources and Evaluation, Portorož, Slovenia, 23 May 2016/28 May 2016 (2016)
3. Deutscher Terminologie-Tag e.V.: Terminologiearbeit-Best Practices, 2.0 edn. DTT, Köln, Ordner (2014)
4. Faber, P.: Frames as framework for terminology. In: Kockaert, H.J., Steurs, F. (eds.) Handbook of Terminology, pp. 14–33. John Benjamins Publishing Company, Amsterdam/Philadelphia (2015)
5. Faber, P., Martínez, S.M., Prieto, M.R.C., Ruiz, J.S., Velasco, J.A.P., León-Araúz, P., Linares, C.M., Expósito, M.V.: Process-oriented terminology management in the domain of coastal engineering. Terminology **12**(2), 189–213 (2006)
6. Huijsen, W.O.: Controlled language–an introduction. In: Proceedings of the Second International Workshop on Controlled Language Application, CLAW 1998, Pittsburgh, Pennsylvania, 21 May 1998/22 May 1998, pp. 1–15 (1998)
7. León Araúz, P., Magaña Redondo, P.J.: Ecolexicon: contextualizing an environmental ontology. In: Proceedings of the Terminology and Knowledge Engineering (TKE) Conference, pp. 341–355 (2010)
8. Pareja-Lora, A., Brümmer, M., Chiarcos, C.: General introduction to Open Data, Linked Data, Linked Open Data, and Linked Open Data in linguistics. In: Workshop on Development of Linguistic Linked Open Data (LLOD). Resources for Collaborative Data-intensive Research in the Language Sciences, Chicago, 25 July 2015/26 July 2015. Presentation Slides. LSA Summer Institute (2015)
9. Suchowolec, K., Lang, C., Schneider, R.: Re-designing online terminology resources for German grammar. In: Mayr, P., Tudhope, D., Golub, K., Wartena, C., Luca, E.W.D. (eds.) Proceedings of the 15th European Networked Knowledge Organization Systems Workshop (NKOS 2016), Hannover, 09 September 2016, pp. 59–63 (2016)
10. Suchowolec, K., Lang, C., Schneider, R.: Grammar and its terminology. Re-designing terminology management system according to best practices (forthcoming)
11. Temmerman, R.: Towards New Ways of Terminology Description. The Sociocognitive Approach. John Benjamins Publishing Company, Amsterdam/Philadelphia (2000)
12. Wöllstein, A., Dudenredaktion (eds.): Duden. Die Grammatik, 9th edn. Dudenverlag, Berlin (2016)

Comparison of Word Embeddings from Different Knowledge Graphs

Kiril Simov(✉), Petya Osenova, and Alexander Popov

Institute of Information and Communication Technologies, BAS, Akad. G. Bonchev. 25A, 1113 Sofia, Bulgaria
{kivs,petya,alex.popov}@bultreebank.org

Abstract. The paper focuses on the manipulation of a WordNet-based knowledge graph by adding, changing and combining various semantic relations. This is done in the context of measuring similarity and relatedness between words, based on word embedding representations trained on a pseudo corpus generated from the knowledge graph. The UKB tool is used for generating pseudo corpora that are then used for learning word embeddings. The results from the performed experiments show that the addition of more relations generally improves performance along both dimensions – similarity and relatedness. In line with previous research, our survey confirms that paradigmatic relations predominantly improve similarity, while syntagmatic relations benefit relatedness scores.

Keywords: Knowledge-based word embedding · Semantic relations · Similarity · Association

1 Introduction

Recent research in NLP has focused on distributional semantic models that incorporate linguistic information from various resources. Such models are trained with different algorithms, among them: Neural Network Language Models, Latent Semantic Analysis (LSA), etc. Word embeddings are among those popular distributed representations. Word vectors with varying dimensionalities and produced by different algorithms have been extensively discussed in the literature. The corpora that the algorithms are trained on can contain either natural language text (e.g. Wikipedia or newswire articles) or artificially generated pseudo corpora, such as the output of the Random Walk algorithm, when run to select sequences of nodes from a knowledge graph (KG)—see [5] for generation of pseudo corpora from WordNet knowledge graph and [13] for generation of pseudo corpora from RDF knowledge graphs such as DBPedia, GeoNames, FreeBase. Here we report results only for knowledge graphs based on WordNet and its extensions. Thus the paper discusses the impact of various knowledge graph extensions on the quality of the word embeddings that are trained on the pseudo corpora generated from these knowledge graphs. The main knowledge graph in the experiments is the English WordNet (WN) [3]. It is represented as nodes

J. Gracia et al. (Eds.): LDK 2017, LNAI 10318, pp. 213–221, 2017.
DOI: 10.1007/978-3-319-59888-8_19

corresponding to synsets in WN and arcs corresponding to relations encoded in WN, such as hypernymy, meronymy, entailment, etc. The extensions of the main knowledge graph are in the form of additional relations between synsets (i.e. additional arcs in the graph). These new relations come from sources outside WordNet, such as relations extracted from semantically annotated corpora or explication of implicit knowledge in WordNet on the basis of inference procedures (e.g. transitive closure over the relations). Our goal in this work is to demonstrate the impact of the extensions of WordNet main knowledge on the training of word embeddings, but not to provide the best word embeddings. Thus, in our experiments we fixed the size of the vectors for the word embeddings to 300 and the method used for the training—Skip-gram model of [10]. In this way we are able to compare to work done by others researchers within the same way.

Previous work has shown that enriching the knowledge graph can lead to accuracy improvement in the Word Sense Disambiguation (WSD) task. For example, [12] introduce the idea that the transfer of new relations from Wikipedia to WordNet can make the knowledge-based WSD systems comparable in performance to the supervised ones. Our own experimental work has shown that combining paradigmatic information and syntagmatic information also improves WSD results [15,17]. We aim to explore whether similar effects are achieved with relation to word embedding models.

Here we report experiments on improving the contribution of the knowledge graph as measured on the following datasets: WordSim-353 Similarity, WordSim-353 Relatedness (WS353) and SimLex-999 (SL999). Generally, the addition of new relations improves the results. These improvements confirm some of the previously stated assumptions, such as: the inclusion of syntactic dependencies improves similarity scores; a wider context window improves association scores; the inclusion of glosses in the training corpora improves association scores, etc.

In the paper we adopt the following understanding of the notions of similarity and relatedness from [14]: "Semantic similarity and semantic relatedness are sometimes used interchangeable in the literature. These terms however, are not identical. Semantic relatedness indicates degree to which words are associated via any type (such as synonymy, meronymy, hyponymy, hypernymy, functional, associative and other types) of semantic relationships. Semantic similarity is a special case of relatedness and takes into consideration only hyponymy/hypernymy relations."

The structure of the paper is as follows: the next section discusses related work; Sect. 3 describes the experimental setups, including the knowledge graphs used, tools and evaluation datasets; Sect. 4 presents the results from the experiments; Sect. 5 concludes the paper.

2 Related Work

The content as well as the relation distribution within the knowledge graph play an important role for the successful performance of systems on various

NLP tasks. One such task is Knowledge-based Word Sense Disambiguation (KWSD)—see [1]. Our own experiments have shown that the manipulation of the knowledge graph with respect to adding new relations, combining various lexical relations or combining syntagmatic (corpus-based) and paradigmatic (lexicon-based) relations can improve results on this task. For example, in [17] we experiment with lexical relations from WN, with relations extracted from glosses of extended WN, as well as with semantic relations derived from a syntactic annotation of SemCor [11]. These extensions have improved the results for KWSD for Bulgarian and English. The experiments for WSD are described in a number of papers: [15–17]. We reuse the sets of relations developed in these works to check whether the addition of new relations has an impact on the word embeddings trained on pseudo corpora generated using these knowledge graphs.

Many researchers have come lately to differentiate between the similarity and relatedness tasks. Even though the two may seem similar, they involve different types of semantic relations. Therefore, the two should be used separately in the evaluation of semantic models (by scoring them on different datasets). Research has also been published on which relations and contexts are better suited when modeling similarity or relatedness. Although it is apparent that no categorically clear borderline can be traced between these two sets of relations, similarity is usually expressed through synonymy and hypernymy, while association – through gloss relations and syntactic relations.

Goikoetxea et al. 2015 [5] describe an architecture in which a run of the Random Walk algorithm [1] produces an artificial corpus from WordNet. The graph that is fed to the algorithm is composed of WordNet synsets (the graph vertices) and of different types of relations between them (the graph arcs; some relation types are antonymy, hypernymy, derivation, etc.). This corpus is then fed into a shallow neural net which creates distributed word representations. The authors use the CBOW and Skip-gram algorithms as introduced in [10]. They show that training on the artificial corpus gives improvements over text-trained models, on some datasets (SL999 and WS353). They also conclude that all explored methods are complementary to each other. In Goikoetxea et al. 2016 [4], the idea described above is further developed with the inclusion of a text corpus in addition to the corpus generated from WordNet. Learning is first performed on each of the two resources, and then various combination methods are introduced. The combined system outperforms the other systems on similarity, equals in relatedness, showing the advantages of simple combinations (like concatenation of independently learned embeddings) to the more complex ones.

Hill et al. 2015 [6] describes in detail the SimLex-999 dataset, which was specially designed to reflect similarity. The golden resource takes into account parts-of-speech as well as the difference between concreteness and abstractness. Two hypotheses have been explicated in that paper: (a) dependency-based models handle similarity better than text-based ones; and (b) models with narrower context windows handle similarity better than such with larger windows. The authors report that Mikolov's NLM performs better on the similarity task on this dataset in comparison to other methods (LSA, VSM). The authors also claim that modeling similarity is more difficult than modeling relatedness.

It bears mentioning that there have been other methods proposed, dealing with similarity/relatedness and using embedding techniques that rely on knowledge graph information. For instance, [8] train sense embeddings on a natural language text corpus, in their case a Wikipedia dump. They use the knowledge-based WSD system Babelfy[1] to tag words in the corpus with senses from BabelNet[2] and then use the enriched resource to train the sense embeddings, using the Word2Vec CBOW architecture. Subsequently, the sense embeddings are used to calculate various distance measures between words in the similarity/relatedness task. In the present study, however, we focus rather on using various extensions of the knowledge graph itself for producing word embeddings, not so much on the embedding of senses or on the joint embedding of words and senses.

3 Experimental Setup

The experimental setup takes as input pseudo corpora generated by the UKB[3] tool, which was designed for the task of WSD as well as for measuring lexical similarity. The tool uses a set of random-walk-on-graph algorithms described in [2]. For the WSD task, the tool creates a knowledge graph over a set of relations that can be induced from different types of resources, such as WordNet; then it selects a context window of open class words and runs the algorithm over the graph, until it obtains the relative ranks for the nodes (synsets) in the context window. The tool requires a lexicon that maps lemmas to synsets; a graph generated from the lexicon, and a set of relations that hold between the synsets. UKB can also be used [5] to generate random paths of varying length along the graph. These random paths constitute a pseudo corpus that can be used in different learning architectures for producing word representations. Here is an example of a sequence of lemmas produced in this way: *goldbrick dupery take_in gull dupe person laugh_at*. The generated sequences list semantically related lemmas in a random manner. Thus, the context of each lemma is determined by these semantically similar lemmas. The idea behind this approach is that the word embeddings over such a pseudo corpus would encode the relational knowledge information represented in the knowledge graph. Changing the relations in the knowledge graphs the system will generate different pseudo corpora. In this way the trained word embeddings reflects the differences in the semantic relations in the corresponding knowledge graphs. For the generation of the pseudo corpora the following UKB settings have been explored: taking into account the lemma weights in synsets (based on word counts in a corpus); the number of the generated examples (between 100M and 500M pseudo sentences).

In this paper we measure the difference between the different word embeddings on the task of measuring word similarity and relatedness. The evaluation

[1] http://www.babelfy.org/.
[2] http://www.babelnet.org/.
[3] http://ixa2.si.ehu.es/ukb/.

is done over the following datasets: *WordSim353 Similarity*, *WordSim353 Relatedness*[4], and *SimLex999*[5]. Each of the datasets consists of pairs of words and numeric values of their similarity (*WordSim353 Similarity* and *SimLex999*) or their relatedness (*WordSim353 Relatedness*). The numerical values were established on the basis of a consultation with a number of human subjects. The evaluation was done in the following manner: first, the distance between the words in each pair was calculated on the basis of the corresponding word embedding using cosine similarity; then, Spearman's rank correlation between the predicted distances and the gold standard values from the datasets was calculated. The pseudo corpora generated on the basis of WordNet Knowledge Graphs contain only lemmas aligned to synsets in WordNet. Some of the pairs of words in the datasets *WordSim353 Similarity* and *WordSim353 Relatedness* include word forms different from lemmas (street children 4.94, for example) or named entities (Arafat Jackson 2.50, for example). Such pairs of missing in WN words were deleted from the datasets—for dataset *WordSim353 Similarity* there are 11 such pairs from 203 and for dataset *WordSim353 Relatedness* there are 19 pairs from 252. This was done in order that the comparison between ranks for different word embeddings be over the same pairs of words.

In the experiments we are using the following knowledge graphs. The knowledge graph **WN** is based on WordNet 3.0. **WNG** and **WNGL** contain relations extracted from WN3.0 glosses, as the glosses are annotated with synset ids in eXtended WordNet (XWN)—[9]. Each gloss in WordNet defines the corresponding synset. In XWN the open class words in glosses are annotated with senses from WordNet. The relations in **WNG** are constructed as co-occurrences of a particular synset and the synsets for open class words in its gloss. **WNGL** is also formed of relations extracted from the annotation of glosses in XWN, but reflecting the predicate structure of the logical form of the glosses.

For example, the multiword expression *ice-cream cone* is defined by the gloss *ice cream in a crisp conical wafer*. In WordNet there is just one sense of *ice-cream cone* forming one synset for it. It is related to one another synset for the multiword expression *frozen dessert* by the hyperonymy relation and *frozen dessert* is connected by hyperonymy relation to *dessert*. From the annotation of the gloss in the graph **WNG** relation between the senses for *ice-cream cone* and em wafer is added—the cooccurrences between the synset and each annotated word in its gloss. In the graph **WNGL** are added relations on the basis of the logical form. For the example, a relation between *crisp* and em wafer is added. Most of these new relations are not presented in the original WordNet graph.

The graph **GrRelSC** contains relations constructed on the basis of dependency analyses of about 15000 sentences in SemCor. Each dependency tree is represented in the knowledge graph via a set of non-WordNet nodes (NWN nodes). The relations between NWN nodes represent the structure of the dependency trees. The NWN nodes that correspond to open class words in the sentences are connected via relations to WordNet nodes (WN nodes) in the knowledge graph.

[4] Downloaded from http://alfonseca.org/eng/research/wordsim353.html.

[5] Downloaded from https://www.cl.cam.ac.uk/~fh295/simlex.html.

The graph **WN30glCon** is similar to **GrRelSC** in the sense that the relations are formed using the whole sentence for each gloss. Again, there are NWN nodes which represent the structure of the sentence and relations from NWN nodes to WN nodes in the knowledge graph. A detailed description of the creation of **WNGL**, **GrRelSC**, and **WN30glCon** can be found in [15].

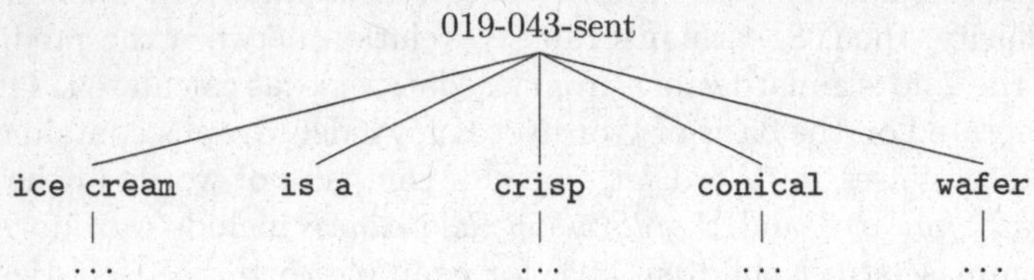

Fig. 1. The graph for the sequence of words in the gloss. Node 019-043-sen is a non-WordNet node. The ... nodes are the nodes for the synsets from WordNet.

The NWN nodes do not correspond to synsets in WordNet and thus there are no lemmas aligned to them. Thus, in the process of generating the pseudo corpus there are no lemmas stored in this corpus for them. In order to minimize these nodes, we collapse the structure of each sentence into one NWN node. The new knowledge graphs are named **GrRelSCOne** and **WN30glConOne**. An example of a sentence represented in this is given in Fig. 1.

In addition to the knowledge graph extensions created on the basis of sources external for WordNet, we also exploited a knowledge graph extension created by performing inference over the **WN** knowledge graph. This knowledge graph extension represents the transitive closure of the hypernymy relation of WordNet. We named it **HypInf**. For example, from the two hypernymy relations mentioned above the relation between *ice-cream cone* and *dessert* is inferred.

The generated corpora are then fed into the Word2Vec tool[6] in order to train the models. Initially we performed experiments with different settings of the parameters of the system: context window size varying from 1 to 19 words, with the best results in most cases being for context window of 5 and context window of 15 words (reported below); iterations from 1 to 9, with best results for 7 iterations; negative examples set to 5; and frequency cut sampling set to 7.

The pseudo-corpus-based embeddings have been compared also with text-based embeddings. We have selected two text-based sets of word vectors[7]: Google News trained over 100 billion running words—named **GoogleNews**; and Wikipedia dependency trained over context extracted from a dependency analysis of Wikipedia articles—named **Dependency**.

[6] https://code.google.com/archive/p/word2vec/.
[7] The models are downloaded from here https://github.com/3Top/word2vec-api.

4 Experiment Results

We have performed a number of experiments through the combination of different knowledge graphs. As baselines, we have evaluated two sets of text-corpus-based word embeddings that are freely available on the web, as well as the best result of Goikoetxea et al. [5], available from the UKB web page[8]. The results for these baselines are presented in Table 1.

Table 1. The first two embeddings are text-corpus based. The third line is the best pseudo corpus based result of [5]. We consider these three embeddings as baselines for the two tasks. Results from experiments with different extensions of the WordNet knowledge graph are presented in the rest of the table. With *C5* and *C15* we denote the size of the context used by word2vec.

Embedding	*WordSim353 Similarity*	*WordSim353 Relatedness*	*SimLex999*
GoogleNews	0.77145	**0.61988**	0.44196
Dependency	0.76699	0.46764	0.44730
WN+WNG$_{best}$	**0.78670**	**0.61316**	**0.52479**
WN30+WN30G+HypInf *C5*	0.77730	0.54419	**0.55192**
WN30+WN30G+HypInf *C15*	0.77205	0.55955	**0.55868**
WN30+WN30glConOne *C5*	0.77761	**0.64747**	**0.53242**
WN30+WN30glConOne *C15*	**0.79659**	**0.65548**	**0.52632**
WN30+WN30G+WN30GL+ GrRelSC *C5*	**0.79847**	**0.63587**	0.51974
WN30+WN30G+WN30GL+ GrRelSC *C15*	**0.81862**	0.61455	0.52350

The main experiments are divided into two groups: (1) experiments with graphs enriched predominantly with paradigmatic relations; and (2) experiments with graphs enriched predominantly with syntagmatic relations. In Table 1 we present some results for each type of the experiments. In the knowledge graph **WN30+WN30G+HypInf** we combined the basic knowledge graph **WN**, the co-occurrence gloss knowledge graph and the knowledge graph defined by the transitive closure over the hypernymy relation. We consider the additional knowledge to be predominantly paradigmatic. These experiments proved our expectation that the corresponding word embeddings will be better on the similarity task. In this case the improvement is significant for the *SimLex999* dataset. In the knowledge graph **WN30+WN30glConOne** we have added predominantly syntagmatic relations from glosses as text. The experiments demonstrated significant improvement for the *WordSim353 Relatedness*

[8] http://ixa2.si.ehu.es/ukb/.

dataset. The improvements for the other two datasets show that the knowledge graph **WN30glConOne** contains a considerable quantity of paradigmatic knowledge because of the nature of the gloss texts. In the case of the **WN30+WN30G+WN30GL+GrRelSC** knowledge graph, combining several knowledge graphs demonstrates the possibility for improving mainly on the *WordSim353 Similarity* dataset.

5 Conclusion

This paper has focused on ways of manipulating a WordNet-based knowledge graph in order to produce models for measuring word similarity and relatedness. The presented experiments include various combinations of relations, such as: only WN, WN plus glosses, WN plus syntactic relations, etc. In this setting the UKB tool has been used for generating pseudo corpora from lexical resources that were then fed into learning architectures for producing word embeddings.

The results show improvements over the baselines. Generally, the addition of new relations leads to better figures in both dimensions - similarity and relatedness. Our findings support the assumptions from previous research, namely, that adding more paradigmatic relations helps in improving similarity, while adding more structural information (such as syntactic analyses) benefits relatedness. In some cases it is apparent that all test sets improve. This suggests that the issue with the specific roles played by the separate relation sets remains open and subject to future investigation. Also, for the pseudo corpus generation task, it would be useful to define linguistically motivated meaningful paths in addition to the random ones. Under linguistically motivated paths we consider paths that corresponds to lexical chains as defined in [7].

Our observations show that the more relations are added, the more generated examples are needed in order to accommodate the expansion of the graph information. For that reason, in some of the knowledge graph combinations the results are suboptimal. The differences in the improvements over the two datasets for similarity: *WordSim353 Similarity* and *SimLex999* show that evaluation on these relatively small datasets reflect only partially the knowledge encoded in the corresponding word embeddings. Thus in future we need to define a better evaluation setup which would include also extrinsic evaluation.

Acknowledgements. This research has received partial support by the grant 02/12—*Deep Models of Semantic Knowledge (DemoSem)*, funded by the Bulgarian National Science Fund in 2017–2019. We are grateful to the anonymous reviewers for their remarks, comments, and suggestions. All errors remain our own responsibility.

References

1. Agirre, E., López de Lacalle, O., Soroa, A.: Random walks for knowledge-based word sense disambiguation. Comput. Linguist. **40**(1), 57–84 (2014). http://dx.doi.org/10.1162/COLI_a_00164

2. Agirre, E., Soroa, A.: Personalizing PageRank for word sense disambiguation. In: Proceedings of the 12th Conference of the European Chapter of the ACL, EACL 2009, pp. 33–41 (2009). http://www.aclweb.org/anthology/E09-1005
3. Fellbaum, C. (ed.): WordNet An Electronic Lexical Database. The MIT Press, Cambridge (1998). http://mitpress.mit.edu/catalog/item/default.asp?ttype=2&tid=8106
4. Goikoetxea, J., Agirre, E., Soroa, A.: Single or multiple? Combining word representations independently learned from text and WordNet. In: AAAI, pp. 2608–2614. AAAI Press (2016)
5. Goikoetxea, J., Soroa, A., Agirre, E.: Random walks and neural network language models on knowledge bases. In: HLT-NAACL, The Association for Computational Linguistics, pp. 1434–1439 (2015)
6. Hill, F., Reichart, R., Korhonen, A.: Simlex-999: evaluating semantic models with (genuine) similarity estimation. In: Computational Linguistics (2015)
7. Hirst, G., St-Onge, D.: Lexical chains as representations of context for the detection and correction of malapropisms. In: Fellbaum, C. (ed.) WordNet: An Electronic Lexical Database, pp. 305–332. MIT Press, Cambridge (1998)
8. Iacobacci, I., Pilehvar, M.T., Navigli, R.: Sensembed: learning sense embeddings for word and relational similarity. In: ACL, vol. 1, pp. 95–105 (2015)
9. Mihalcea, R., Moldovan, D.I.: Extended WordNet: progress report. In: Proceedings of NAACL Workshop on WordNet and Other Lexical Resources, pp. 95–100 (2001)
10. Mikolov, T., Chen, K., Corrado, G., Dean, J.: Efficient estimation of word representations in vector space. CoRR abs/1301.3781 (2013). http://arxiv.org/abs/1301.3781
11. Miller, G.A., Leacock, C., Tengi, R., Bunker, R.T.: A semantic concordance. In: Proceedings of HLT 1993, pp. 303–308 (1993). http://dx.doi.org/10.3115/1075671.1075742
12. Ponzetto, S.P., Navigli, R.: Knowledge-rich word sense disambiguation rivaling supervised systems. In: Proceedings of the 48th Annual Meeting of the Association for Computational Linguistics, ACL 2010, Association for Computational Linguistics, Stroudsburg, PA, USA, pp. 1522–1531 (2010). http://dl.acm.org/citation.cfm?id=1858681.1858835
13. Ristoski, P., Paulheim, H.: RDF2Vec: RDF Graph Embeddings for Data Mining. Springer, Cham (2016). http://dx.doi.org/10.1007/978-3-319-46523-4_30
14. Salahli, M.A.: An approach for measuring semantic relatedness between words via related terms. Math. Comput. Appl. **14**(1), 55–63 (2009). http://www.mcajournal.org/volume14/Vol14No1p.55.pdf
15. Simov, K., Osenova, P., Popov, A.: Using Context Information for Knowledge-Based Word Sense Disambiguation. Springer, Cham (2016). http://dx.doi.org/10.1007/978-3-319-44748-3_13
16. Simov, K., Popov, A., Osenova, P.: Improving word sense disambiguation with linguistic knowledge from a sense annotated treebank. Proc. RANLP **2015**, 596–603 (2015)
17. Simov, K., Popov, A., Osenova, P.: The role of the WordNet relations in the knowledge-based word sense disambiguation task. In: Proceedings of Eighth Global WordNet Conference, pp. 391–398 (2016)

Multi-pass Sieve Coreference Resolution System for Polish

Bartłomiej Nitoń and Maciej Ogrodniczuk(✉)

Institute of Computer Science, Polish Academy of Sciences,
ul. Jana Kazimierza 5, 01-248 Warsaw, Poland
bartek.niton@gmail.com, maciej.ogrodniczuk@ipipan.waw.pl

Abstract. This paper examines the portability of Stanford's multi-pass rule-based sieve coreference resolution system to inflectional language (Polish) with a different annotation scheme. The presented system is implemented in BART, a modular toolkit later adapted to the sieve architecture by Baumann et al. The sieves for Polish include processing of zero subjects and experimental knowledge-intensive sieve using the newly created database of periphrastic expressions. Evaluation shows that the results for Polish are higher than those seen on the CoNLL-2011/2012 data.

Keywords: Coreference resolution · BART · The Stanford's multi-pass sieve architecture · Polish language · Knowledge-based resources

1 Introduction

Coreference resolution, the task of grouping textual fragments that refer to the same entity in the discourse world, has been at the core of natural language understanding since the 1960s. Proper decoding of reference is important for various applications such as question answering, information extraction and retrieval, machine translation and text summarization.

Owing in large part to the public availability of several coreference-annotated corpora since the 1990s, such as MUC, ACE, and OntoNotes, significant progress has been made in the development of corpus-based approaches to coreference resolution. After a shift from heuristics to machine learning in the 2000s, recorded e.g. in Ng's survey paper [14], the beginning of the current decade brought reversal of these tendencies, with the most prominent multi-pass sieve approach [11], the winner of the CoNLL-2011 shared task on English coreference resolution, followed by several extensions such as Ratinov and Roth's learning-based sieves [25]. Application of this approach to other languages also showed considerable improvements in the resolution results [4,10].

Former coreference resolution systems for Polish [16,17] did not take into account the new advances brought to the field with multi-pass sieve models. In the current paper we adapt BART [27] and its Polish Language Plugin [9] to the sieve architecture following the approach of Baumann et al. [3] and investigate

J. Gracia et al. (Eds.): LDK 2017, LNAI 10318, pp. 222–236, 2017.
DOI: 10.1007/978-3-319-59888-8_20

both how it improves coreference resolution score for Polish and how features specific to inflectional languages (lemmatization, zero pronouns and lack of definite articles) are reflected in a sieve-based resolver.

As a separate step we perform the experiment with a knowledge-intensive periphrastic sieve based on a newly created resource combining data from dictionary definitions, plWordNet, Wikidata and common clues found in crossword puzzles linked with potential answer words.

2 Polish Coreference Resolution Sieves

Sieve architecture relies on a sequence of hand-written rules (sieves), ordered from most to least precise. It is more or less a cascade of simple rule based coreference resolvers where the output of one is the input of the next. Thanks to that following sieves can use entity information gathered by previous ones, which makes sieve architecture entity-based. Decisions can be made, not about mentions in the text, but about entities–clusters of mentions in the system's model of the world—allowing the system to reason about the properties of entities as a whole. The system's precision ordering allows it to first link high-confidence mention-pairs, and only later consider lower-confidence sources of information. In our approach we are using both pair (antecedent-anaphora) and entity based features using those which perform better for specific sieve.

Our final system uses eight sieves for Polish coreference resolution. They are described in the next subsections in order of execution. We have also experimented with periphrastic sieve (see Sect. 4.3), but because of small score improvement, with high memory and time complexity we decided not to include it in our final system. Types of mentions matched by each sieve are shown in Table 1.

Table 1. Sieves precisions and matched types of mentions

Sieve	Matched mentions	Links	Correct links	Precision [%]
1. ExactStringMatch	*nominal*	12930	11004	85.10
2. BaseStringMatch	*nominal*	7804	5873	75.26
3. PreciseConstructs	*nominal*	197	145	73.60
4. HeadMatchB	*nominal*	9273	5214	56.23
5. ZeroMatch	*zero*	13228	8632	65.26
6. PronounMatch	*pronominal*	3601	2153	59.79
7. ZeroToNP	*zero with nominal*	3595	1507	41.92
8. PronounToNP	*pronominal with nominal*	3508	1399	39.88

Sieves are evaluated with *MUC* [28], B^3 [2], and *CEAFE* [12] metrics calculated using *Scoreference*[1], a mention detection and coreference resolution evaluation tool [16, Chap. 15]. Following i.a. CoNLL-2011 approach [20], for the final

[1] http://zil.ipipan.waw.pl/Scoreference.

evaluation we used average score of the above metrics which tracked influence on different coreference dimensions (the B^3 measure being based on mentions, *MUC* on links, and *CEAFE* on entities).

All experiments were carried out on the Polish Coreference Corpus[2] [16] version 0.92 (all texts).

2.1 Polish Coreference Corpus

Polish Coreference Corpus (PCC) is a large corpus of Polish general nominal coreference built upon the National Corpus of Polish (NKJP)[3] [21]. Each text of the corpus is a 250–350-word sample consisting of full subsequent paragraphs extracted from longer texts. With its 1900 documents from 14 genres, containing about 540,000 tokens, 180,000 mentions and 128,000 coreference clusters, the PCC is among the largest manually annotated coreference corpora in the international community.

Mentions in PCC are understood as broadly as possible, with such complex components as relative clauses, coordinated phrases or prepositional-nominal phrases attached to semantic heads and included in respective nominal phrases. PCC also features annotation of zero anaphora, clitic pronouns attached to verbs, multi-level nested and discontinuous mentions. Appositions are attached (not linked) to respective mention and referential nominal groups are distinguished from attributive ones.

Coreference clusters group mentions with the same reference regardless of linguistic means used to invoke the referent in text.

2.2 Mention Types

During sieve preparation we decided to divide mentions into three types: *nominal*, *pronominal*, and *zero*. The idea was to match mentions within each group with high-precision sieves which would also have a positive impact on overall recall.

Nominal mentions are all nominal phrases whose syntactic head is a noun marked with a *subst* (general noun) or *ger* (gerund) tags[4] while pronominal mentions are first-, second- (annotated as *ppron12*) or third-person pronouns (*ppron3*).

The last group are zero mentions as defined in [8]. For Polish (also all Balto-Slavic languages and most Romance languages) it is possible for an independent clause to lack an explicit subject; its role is maintained by the predicate. Due to its rich morphology, value of person, number and/or gender category of the verb can be used to maintain agreement with referent, as in example below:

(1) Maria wróciła już z Francji. Ø Spędziła tam miesiąc.
'Maria came back from France. She had$_{sg:f}$ spent a month there.'

[2] http://zil.ipipan.waw.pl/PCC.
[3] http://nkjp.pl.
[4] See http://nkjp.pl/poliqarp/help/en.html for a concise tag descriptions.

Zero mentions are marked with tags corresponding to verbal forms (*fin*, *praet*, *bedzie*, *winien* and *aglt*). Moreover, we take into account also verbs tagged as *impt* (imperative; it is omitted in [8]). We can clearly imagine texts representing dialogues or instructions using imperatives as zero mentions:

(2) Ø Upewnij się, że SZBD PostgreSQL został pomyślnie uruchomiony. Ø Zaloguj się na konto użytkownika postgres.
'Ø Make sure that PostgreSQL DBMS was successfully launched. Ø Log into postgres user account.'

2.3 Pass 1 and 2 – Exact and Base String Match

Exact String Match Sieve links two nominal mentions only if they contain exactly the same text, without any modification. As expected, this model is extremely precise, see Table 1.

Base String Match Sieve is working in the same way except that it is matching lemmatized forms of mention strings, obtained with Morfeusz morphological analyser[5] [30] and Pantera tagger[6] [1]. This sieve is also highly precise and is also working only on nominal mentions.

Surprisingly, the system is matching more mentions and gets better score when both *Exact* and *Base* sieves are used (see Table 2). We expected that *Base String Match Sieve* would cover all cases covered by *Exact String Match Sieve* but it seems that the setting can correct errors introduced by the tagger, supposedly assigning wrong base forms to some of analysed tokens. The configuration with both sieves obtains better score in every presented measure (see Table 2), so finally we decided to use both *Exact* and *Base* sieves in our system.

Table 2. *String Match* sieves comparison

Sieves	Precision			F-score [%]			
	Links	Correct links	Precision [%]	MUC	B^3	CEAFE	CoNLL
Exact	12930	11004	**85.10**	34.17	85.45	80.91	66.84
Base	19072	15462	81.07	44.18	86.51	82.27	70.99
Base+Exact	20734	16877	81.40	**44.43**	**86.54**	**82.31**	**71.09**

2.4 Pass 3 – Precise Constructs Sieve

Initially this sieve was intended to mimic the original Precise Constructs Sieve described by [23] which linked two mentions if one of the following rules is fulfilled:

- the two nominal mentions are in an appositive construction
- the two mentions are in copulative subject-object relation

[5] http://sgjp.pl/morfeusz/.
[6] http://zil.ipipan.waw.pl/PANTERA.

- the candidate antecedent is headed by a noun and appears as a modifier in an NP whose head is the current mention
- the mention is a relative pronoun that modifies the head of the antecedent NP
- one mention is an acronym of the other
- one of the mentions is a demonym of the other.

Eventually we decided to link acronyms only due to decisions taken in the PCC annotation where appositive constructions are marked as single mention, copula constructions are not marked at all and intersecting mentions are never marked as being in the same cluster.

The acronym rule occurred to be highly precise even though it does not cover many cases in real text (only 197 matched links in full corpora, with 73.6% precision). For the rule we use a simple acronym detection algorithm which marks a mention as an acronym of another if its text equals the sequence of uppercase characters in the other mention.

Demonym case was also tested but it did not affect coreference score in a positive way.

2.5 Pass 4 – Strict Head Matching

Similarly to *Precise Constructs Sieve* this one was also inspired by [23]. It is responsible for matching nominal mentions and is the first one to use cluster information gathered by previous sieves.

Originally the sieve was passed three times with match rules relaxation after each pass. The most orthodox pass (*HeadMatchA*) links two mentions only if they match all of the following rules:

- *Cluster head match* – the mention head word matches any head word in the antecedent cluster
- *Word inclusion* – all the non-stopwords[7] in the mention cluster are included in the set of non-stopwords in the cluster of the antecedent candidate
- *Compatible modifiers only*—the mention's modifiers are all included in the modifiers of the antecedent candidate, with only nouns and adjectives taken into account
- *Not i-within-i* – the two mentions are not in an i-within-i construct [7].

The second (*HeadMatchB*) and more relaxed sieve removes *Compatible modifiers* rule, while the third one (*HeadMatchC*) removes also the *Word inclusion* constraint.

Because in *PCC* appositive phrases are marked as a single mention in *not i-within-i* rule, we are simply checking if one mention string is not embedded in another mention string.

[7] Polish stop-words list was taken from the Polish Wikipedia stop-words list https://pl.wikipedia.org/wiki/Wikipedia:Stopwords.

Table 3. Different *Head Match* sieves configurations comparison

Sieves: Base+Exact +Precise+...	Precision			F-score [%]			
	Links	Correct links	Precision [%]	MUC	B^3	CEAFE	CoNLL
HeadMatchA	1359	771	**56.73**	45.50	86.58	**82.39**	71.49
HeadMatchB	9273	5214	56.23	**48.99**	**86.61**	82.31	**72.64**
HeadMatchC	23049	7305	31.69	47.49	84.42	77.95	69.95
HeadMatchAB	9499	5339	56.21	48.97	**86.61**	82.30	72.63
HeadMatchAC	23621	7640	32.34	47.49	84.41	77.94	69.95
HeadMatchBC	27192	9655	35.51	47.49	84.41	77.94	69.95
HeadMatchABC	27247	9708	35.63	47.49	84.41	77.94	69.95

In Table 3 we present *Strict Head Match* sieves configurations precision. Precision is calculated only for specified configuration, but all of the preceding sieves are used (*Exact String Match*, *Base String Match*, *Precise Constructs*).

As expected, the most precise configuration is the one using only *HeadMatchA* sieve. Unfortunately, it matches a small number of links as compared to other configurations. The biggest recall is acquired, as expected, by the *HeadMatchC* sieve, but in this case precision is very low.

As we can see in Table 3, the highest score is obtained for the first relaxation of *Head Match* sieve (B). Therefore, we choose *HeadMatchB* relaxation as our next sieve.

2.6 Pass 5 – Zero Mentions Match

This pass is matching zero mentions within their group. First of all it is checking whether both mentions are zero mentions and their numbers match. If both constraints are met, based on the part of speech tag we are then checking person (for *fin*, *bedzie*, *impt*, *aglt* tags) or gender (for *praet*, *winien*) match. If all conditions are met, mentions are marked as coreferent.

As we can see in Table 1, precision of this sieve is not very high (65.26%). It can be easily increased by matching only mentions in the same paragraph, which is in accordance with intuition: new object is brought into the discourse mostly at the beginning of the paragraph and then we are mentioning it with zero mentions. Bringing up the same paragraph constraint raises sieve precision to 79.72% (8409 total links, with 6704 out of them correct), but at the same time overall coreference score is decreasing (see Table 4). Because of that we decided not to use this constraint in the current version of the system.

2.7 Pass 6 – Pronoun Match Sieve

This pass is matching personal pronouns within their group. Pronouns are matched when their person, gender, and number agree.

Table 4. Overall system score with or without same paragraph constraint for *Zero* and *Pronoun* sieves

Configuration	F-score [%]			
	MUC	B^3	CEAFE	CoNLL
No SameP	**67.77**	86.58	**87.53**	**80.63**
Zero+SameP	65.33	86.81	86.67	79.60
Pronoun+SameP	67.00	**86.83**	87.28	80.37

Similarly to *Zero* sieve, precision of *Pronoun* sieve is not very high (59.79%). It can be also easily increased by matching only mentions in the same paragraph: a new object is brought into the discourse mostly at the beginning of the paragraph and then we are mentioning it by pronouns. Bringing up same paragraph constraint raises sieve precision to 78.9% (1673 total links, with 1320 out of them correct), but the correct ones cover half of the links added without this constraint so at the same time the overall coreference score is decreasing (see Table 4). So as for *Zero Mentions Sieve* we decided not to use the same paragraph constraint at this time.

2.8 Pass 7 – Zero to Nominal Mention Sieve

This sieve is matching zero mentions against nominal mentions. This sieve and the next one are currently very simple and have low precision but at the same time offer a positive impact on overall *CoNLL* system score (see Table 5).

In this sieve we are simply checking if the antecedent is a nominal mention tagged as *subst* and is the first mention in the sentence. If previous constraints are met we are checking if the number and gender of mentions match.

Table 5. Coreference resolution score changes after adding new sieves to the system

System	F-score [%]			
	MUC	B^3	CEAFE	CoNLL
Exact	34.17	85.45	80.91	66.84
...+Base	44.43	86.54	82.31	71.09
...+Precise	44.59	86.56	82.32	71.16
...+HeadMatchB	48.99	86.61	82.31	72.64
...+Zero	63.60	**87.05**	86.19	78.95
...+Pronoun	66.14	86.90	87.32	80.12
...+ZeroToNP	66.78	86.78	87.31	80.29
...+PronounToNP	**67.77**	86.58	**87.53**	**80.63**

2.9 Pass 8 – Pronoun to Nominal Mention Sieve

This sieve is matching personal pronouns against nominal mentions. The link is created when the antecedent is a nominal mention and anaphor is a personal pronoun, they are in the same paragraph, and their number match. If previous constraints are met we are checking if pronoun gender and person are matching gender and person of any mention in the nominal mention cluster. Unknown gender and person is treated as a wildcard.

3 Results

Table 6 presents comparison of *Bartek-S1*, our sieve-based solution described in this article and two existing coreference resolution systems for Polish described in detail in [16]. *Ruler* is simple rule-based tool with design following [6] and *Bartek-3* is an adaptation of the BART system for Polish, being at the moment the best machine learning based system for coreference resolution for Polish.

Table 6. Coreference resolution systems for Polish; scores for *Bartek-S1* were counted on the same subset of 530 texts from *PCC 0.92* as scores of *Ruler* and *Bartek-3* taken from [16].

System	F-score [%]			
	MUC	B^3	CEAFE	CoNLL
Ruler	58.21	81.94	80.04	73.40
Bartek-3	64.68	85.31	85.24	78.41
Bartek-S1	**67.16**	**86.66**	**87.57**	**80.47**

The comparison shows that even without using complex statistical mechanisms our system performs slightly better than previous systems for Polish (more than 2% *CoNLL* score increase over state-of-the-art *Bartek-3* system). The reason for that is twofold: firstly we explicitly divide mentions by types and match them within each group, which was not present in previous systems (specially for zero mentions, not treated as separate problem at all); secondly using sieve architecture provide us with the whole entity information. In conclusion, sieve architecture outperforms previous systems because it gives us a mechanism to divide coreference resolution into subproblems making information flow very natural: use highly precise general sieves first, match mentions within each mention type, try to match mentions of different types using cluster (entity) information.

4 Experiments with a Periphrastic Sieve

After completion of the sieve system additional experiment was performed to verify whether knowledge-intensive resources could be used as input for a high-precision sieve. Even though the results did not meet our expectation, we present them below.

4.1 Related Work

Ponzetto and Strube [18, 19] describe use of Wikipedia, WordNet and semantic role tagging in computing semantic relatedness between anaphor and antecedent to achieve 2.7 points MUC F_1 score improvement on ACE 2003 data.

Rahman and Ng [24] labelled nominal phrases with FrameNet semantic roles achieving 0.5 points B^3 and CEAF F_1 score improvement and used YAGO type and means relations achieving 0.7 to 2.8 points improvement on OntoNotes-2 and ACE 2004/2005 data.

Durrett and Klein [5] incorporated in their system shallow semantics by using WordNet hypernymy and synonymy, number and gender data for nominals and propers, named entity types and latent clusters computer from English Gigaword corpus, reaching 1.6 points improvement on gold data and 0.36 points on system data.

For Polish, WordNet and Wikipedia-related features were used to improve verification of semantic compatibility for common nouns and named entities in *Bartek-3* coreference resolution system [16, Sect. 12.3] resulting in improvement of approx. 0.5 points MUC F_1 score. Experiments with integration of external vocabulary resources coming from websites registering the newest linguistic trends in Polish, fresh loan words and neologisms not yet covered by traditional dictionaries have been also performed showing low coverage of new constructs in evaluation data [15].

All these results showed challenges regarding knowledge-based resources, mainly concerning the memory and time complexity of the task as well as low coverage of complex features in the test data, but at the same time brought some (sometimes tiny) improvements to coreference resolution scores. In this article we describe if this 'tiny' improvements can be also acquired using the new knowledge database for Polish *Periphraser*.

4.2 Periphraser

Periphraser is a newly created knowledge base of conventionalized periphrastic nominal expressions (i.e. phrases headed by a noun) together with their textually attested realizations. For instance, the database entry for the phrase "Lewandowski" will include the phrase "the Polish international" while "pediatrics" will be featured as "medical care for children". The database is still expanding and at this moment contains over:

- 78,000 meanings and 193,000 expressions from *SJP*[8], a community-built dictionary of Polish
- 72,000 meanings and 183,000 expressions from *plWordNet*[9] [13], the largest WordNet of Polish
- 157,000 meanings and 384,000 expressions from *Wikidata*[10]

[8] http://sjp.pl/.

[9] http://plwordnet.pwr.wroc.pl/.

[10] https://www.wikidata.org/.

– 239,000 meanings and 497,000 expressions from the crosswords portal *Szarada.net*[11].

4.3 Periphrastic Sieve

The periphrastic sieve is intended to link mentions which are hard to match using syntactic features only but which are attested by the knowledge sources included in *Periphraser*. The match can be achieved by:

- *heads matching* – checking if mentions heads are connected in *Periphraser*
- *whole expressions matching* – checking if the whole mentions strings are connected in *Periphraser*
- *head to expression matching* – checking if the head of one mention is connected to the other mention string in *Periphraser*.

In our experiments we used lemmatized forms of strings, both on the side of *Periphraser* with strings tagged by *Concraft-pl* [29] and on the *PCC* side with texts tagged during preanotation by *Pantera* [1] tagger. Scores are counted on the subcorpus of 1250 short PCC texts using *Scoreference* tool. *Periphraser* sieve follows *Strict Head Matching* sieve (see Sect. 2.5) in our experiments.

Table 7. *Periphraser* – possible ways of matching (head or expression)

Matching	Precision			F-score [%]			
	Links	Correct links	Precision [%]	MUC	B^3	CEAFE	CoNLL
Heads	**7905**	**641**	8.1	63.59	84.28	83.47	77.11
Expressions	1606	292	**18.2**	**67.51**	**86.53**	**87.21**	**80.42**
Head to expression	4102	472	11.5	65.98	85.67	85.86	79.17
Heads (descr ana)	**4733**	**219**	4.6	64.64	85.13	84.84	78.20
Expressions (descr ana)	107	48	**44.9**	**68.06**	**86.92**	**87.82**	**80.93**
Head to expression (descr ana)	1540	115	7.5	67.03	86.36	86.97	80.12

From the previous experiments we know that matching mentions by their heads without any additional constraints is not sufficiently effective. In fact, matching them using *Periphraser* is even more error prone because we are using, more or less, synonyms (cf. first part of Table 7). In *Periphraser* the mentioned *whole expression* can be in fact a single mention, in which case again mention matching will be brought to synonymous head matching problem.

[11] http://szarada.net/.

Because in the text (usually) we are using simple entity name before we are writing about it, to avoid repetition, in a more descriptive way, thus it will be natural that anaphor should consist of more than one significant word (see the second part of Table 7).

As we can see in Table 7, matching periphrastic expressions without any constraints is very imprecise. It is getting more promising when we assume that anaphora should consist of more than one word, but it is still far from being satisfying and does not cover many cases in real texts. One more conclusion from this experiment is that it is best to match whole mentions instead of using their heads only.

Another problem is whether it is better to use pair or entity information while linking possibly periphrastic mentions. In general, entity information should help, but in our system nominal sieves preceding periphrastic ones are not very precise (see Sect. 2.5), match small number of mentions (see Sect. 2.4) and exact/base strings (which is not bringing too much new data to the entity). In Table 8 we can see that sieve based on the entity and mention pair features gives more or less the same results.

Table 8. *Periphraser* – possible ways of matching 'whole expressions' (pair or entity)

Matching	Precision			F-score [%]			
	Links	Correct links	Precision [%]	MUC	B3	CEAFE	CoNLL
Pairs	**1606**	292	18.2	**67.51**	**86.53**	**87.21**	**80.42**
Entities	1582	**422**	**26.7**	**67.51**	86.52	**87.21**	80.41
Pairs (descr ana)	107	**48**	**44.9**	**68.06**	**86.92**	**87.82**	**80.93**
Entities (descr ana)	**111**	**48**	43.2	**68.06**	**86.92**	**87.82**	**80.93**

As we can see simple matching is not very precise, especially when we are matching mentions by heads. Thus we must add some constraints to minimize error rate.

4.4 Error Analysis

Analyzing sieve errors we discovered that a lot of them can be filtered out by grammatical number match rule, e.g.:

- *ślimaka 'snail' – winniczków 'pomatia snails'*
- *słońcem 'sun' – gwiazdy 'stars'*
- *Szczecinie – miasta 'cities'*.

Other common errors come from imperfections of *Periphraser* database. It is still under construction and requires some data cleaning which is especially visible while matching mentions by heads coming from crossword-related part of the data, e.g.:

- *minus 'minus' – plus 'plus'*, crossword answers can be based on antonyms
- *tajemnica 'secret' – film 'movie'*, because there is a French movie titled 'Un Secret'
- *liga 'league' – mistrza 'champion'*, crossword answers can be also based on associations, here with *Liga Mistrzów 'the Champions League'*.

Other possible constraints are: full grammatical agreement (person, gender, number match) or simple semantic class agreement. Table 9 presents best results acquired by *Periphraser* sieve using various types of constraints:

- *Base* – the system scores without using *Periphraser* sieve
- *Exp1* – a pair based matching of whole expressions with grammatical number match rule and descriptive anaphora rule
- *Exp2* – an entity based matching of whole expressions using grammatical agreement, basic semantic classes agreement and descriptive anaphora rule.

To conclude, using *Periphraser* in coreference resolution system for Polish does not bring significant improvements. To make periphrastic sieve precision satisfying we must use a lot of constraints and at the same time recall is dropping very quickly. Even then we get some errors hard to recognise without knowing wider text context, e.g.:

- *prezydenta 'president' – głowę państwa 'head of state'*
- *telewizją kablową 'cable television' – sieci kablowej 'cable network'*
- *narkotyków 'drugs' – środków odurzających 'intoxicants'*
- *prezydent Rosji 'president of Russia' – Borys Jelcyn 'Boris Yeltsin'*.

Table 9. The most precise *Periphraser* sieve configurations

Matching	Precision			F-score [%]			
	Links	Correct links	Precision [%]	MUC	B3	CEAFE	CoNLL
Base	N/A	N/A	N/A	68.03	**86.93**	**87.83**	80.93
Exp1	**94**	**47**	50	**68.07**	**86.93**	**87.83**	**80.94**
Exp2	24	17	**70.8**	68.04	**86.93**	**87.83**	80.93

5 Conclusion and Future Work

In this article we described adaptation of a multi-pass sieve approach to coreference resolution for Polish showing its good adaptability and advantage of using inflectional properties, reflected in the resolution score, higher than those seen on the CoNLL-2011/2012 data.

On the other hand, we were testing *Periphraser* database usage for coreference resolution. Summarizing *Periphraser* sieve is matching what it meant to match, but in real texts it is not always correct match. For example, in text about

Russian politicians, both Boris Yeltsin and Vladimir Putin can be referred as president or prime minister of Russia. Moreover, such knowledge has low coverage in the test data. *Periphraser* is still under development so one of the next steps will be data verification. More complex machine learning algorithms can also be applied (initial experiments with *C4.5* algorithm used to generate a decision tree [22] resulted in insignificant improvement of 0.03% *CoNLL* score).

Currently the system offers rule-based sieves only, so the most immediate step would be testing whether combination of rule-based and machine-learning sieves could improve resolution results as seen in the work of [25, 26]. The most promising candidates for adoption of statistical methods seem to be sieves matching mentions of different types (*nominal*, *pronominal*, and *zero*), preceded by rule-based highly precise sieves clustering mentions within a single type.

Acknowledgements. The work reported here was carried out within the research project financed by the Polish National Science Centre (contract number 2014/15/B/HS2/03435) and as part of the investment in the CLARIN-PL research infrastructure funded by the Polish Ministry of Science and Higher Education.

References

1. Acedański, S.: A morphosyntactic Brill Tagger for inflectional languages. In: Loftsson, H., Rögnvaldsson, E., Helgadóttir, S. (eds.) NLP 2010. LNCS, vol. 6233, pp. 3–14. Springer, Heidelberg (2010). doi:10.1007/978-3-642-14770-8_3
2. Bagga, A., Baldwin, B.: Algorithms for scoring coreference chains. In: Proceedings of the 1st International Conference on Language Resources and Evaluation Workshop on Linguistics Coreference, pp. 563–566 (1998)
3. Baumann, J., Kühling, X., Ruder, S.: Rule-based coreference resolution with BART, Technical poster (2014). http://www.cl.uni-heidelberg.de/studies/projects/poster/baumann_kuehling_ruder_poster.pdf
4. Chen, C., Ng, V.: Combining the best of two worlds: a hybrid approach to multilingual coreference resolution. In: Proceedings of the Shared Task on Joint Conference on EMNLP and CoNLL, pp. 56–63 (2012)
5. Durrett, G., Klein, D.: Easy victories and uphill battles in coreference resolution. In: Proceedings of the 2013 Conference on Empirical Methods in Natural Language Processing, pp. 1971–1982. Association for Computational Linguistics, Seattle (2013). http://www.aclweb.org/anthology/D13-1203
6. Haghighi, A., Klein, D.: Unsupervised coreference resolution in a nonparametric Bayesian model. In: Carroll, J.A., van den Bosch, A., Zaenen, A. (eds.) Proceedings of the 45th Annual Meeting of the Association of Computational Linguistics, pp. 848–855. The Association for Computational Linguistics (2007)
7. Haghighi, A., Klein, D.: Simple coreference resolution with rich syntactic and semantic features. In: Proceedings of the 2009 Conference on Empirical Methods in Natural Language Processing (EMNLP 2009), vol. 3, pp. 1152–1161. Association for Computational Linguistics (2009)
8. Kopeć, M.: Zero subject detection for Polish. In: Proceedings of the 14th Conference of the European Chapter of the Association for Computational Linguistics, Short Papers, vol. 2, pp. 221–225. Association for Computational Linguistics, Gothenburg (2014)

9. Kopeć, M., Ogrodniczuk, M.: Creating a coreference resolution system for Polish. In: Proceedings of the 8th International Conference on Language Resources and Evaluation, LREC 2012, pp. 192–195. ELRA, Istanbul (2012)
10. Krug, M., Puppe, F., Jannidis, F., Macharowsky, L., Reger, I., Weimar, L.: Rule-based coreference resolution in German historic novels. In: Proceedings of the 4th Workshop on Computational Linguistics for Literature, pp. 98–104. Association for Computational Linguistics, Denver, June 2015. http://www.aclweb.org/anthology/W15-0711
11. Lee, H., Peirsman, Y., Chang, A., Chambers, N., Surdeanu, M., Jurafsky, D.: Stanford's multi-pass sieve coreference resolution system at the CoNLL-2011 shared task. In: Proceedings of the 15th Conference on Computational Natural Language Learning: Shared Task, pp. 28–34. Association for Computational Linguistics (2011)
12. Luo, X.: On coreference resolution performance metrics. In: Proceedings of the Conference on Human Language Technology and Empirical Methods in Natural Language Processing, HLT 2005, pp. 25–32. Association for Computational Linguistics, Vancouver (2005). http://dx.doi.org/10.3115/1220575.1220579
13. Maziarz, M., Piasecki, M., Szpakowicz, S.: Approaching plWordNet 2.0. In: Proceedings of the 6th Global Wordnet Conference, Matsue, Japan, January 2012
14. Ng, V.: Supervised noun phrase coreference research: the first fifteen years. In: Proceedings of the 48th Annual Meeting of the Association for Computational Linguistics, ACL 2010, pp. 1396–1411. Association for Computational Linguistics, Stroudsburg (2010)
15. Ogrodniczuk, M.: Discovery of common nominal facts for coreference resolution: proof of concept. In: Prasath, R., Kathirvalavakumar, T. (eds.) MIKE 2013. LNCS, vol. 8284, pp. 709–716. Springer, Cham (2013). doi:10.1007/978-3-319-03844-5_69
16. Ogrodniczuk, M., Głowińska, K., Kopeć, M., Savary, A., Zawisławska, M.: Coreference in Polish: Annotation, Resolution and Evaluation. Walter De Gruyter (2015). http://www.degruyter.com/view/product/428667
17. Ogrodniczuk, M., Kopeć, M.: Rule-based coreference resolution module for Polish. In: Proceedings of the 8th Discourse Anaphora and Anaphor Resolution Colloquium (DAARC 2011), Faro, Portugal, pp. 191–200 (2011)
18. Ponzetto, S.P., Strube, M.: Exploiting semantic role labeling, WordNet and wikipedia for coreference resolution. In: Proceedings of the Human Language Technology Conference of the NAACL, Main Conference, pp. 192–199. Association for Computational Linguistics, New York (2006). http://www.aclweb.org/anthology/N06-1025
19. Ponzetto, S.P., Strube, M.: Knowledge derived from wikipedia for computing semantic relatedness. J. Artif. Intell. Res. **30**(1), 181–212 (2007)
20. Pradhan, S., Ramshaw, L., Marcus, M., Palmer, M., Weischedel, R., Xue, N.: CoNLL-2011 shared task: modeling unrestricted coreference in ontonotes. In: Proceedings of the 15th Conference on Computational Natural Language Learning: Shared Task, CONLL Shared Task 2011, pp. 1–27. Association for Computational Linguistics, Stroudsburg (2011). http://dl.acm.org/citation.cfm?id=2132936.2132937
21. Przepiórkowski, A., Bańko, M., Górski, R.L., Lewandowska-Tomaszczyk, B. (eds.): Narodowy Korpus Języka Polskiego [Eng.: National Corpus of Polish]. Wydawnictwo Naukowe PWN, Warsaw (2012)
22. Quinlan, J.R.: C4.5: Programs for Machine Learning. Morgan Kaufmann Publishers Inc., San Francisco (1993)

23. Raghunathan, K., Lee, H., Rangarajan, S., Chambers, N., Surdeanu, M., Jurafsky, D., Manning, C.: A multi-pass sieve for coreference resolution. In: Proceedings of the 2010 Conference on Empirical Methods in Natural Language Processing, pp. 492–501. Association for Computational Linguistics (2010)
24. Rahman, A., Ng, V.: Coreference resolution with world knowledge. In: Proceedings of the 49th Annual Meeting of the Association for Computational Linguistics: Human Language Technologies, pp. 814–824 (2011)
25. Ratinov, L., Roth, D.: Learning-based multi-sieve co-reference resolution with knowledge. In: Proceedings of the 2012 Joint Conference on Empirical Methods in Natural Language Processing and Computational Natural Language Learning, EMNLP-CoNLL 2012, pp. 1234–1244. Association for Computational Linguistics, Stroudsburg (2012). http://dl.acm.org/citation.cfm?id=2390948.2391088
26. Stoyanov, V., Eisner, J.: Easy-first coreference resolution. In: Proceedings of the 24th International Conference on Computational Linguistics (COLING 2012), Mumbai, India, pp. 2519–2534 (2012)
27. Versley, Y., Ponzetto, S.P., Poesio, M., Eidelman, V., Jern, A., Smith, J., Yang, X., Moschitti, A.: BART: a modular toolkit for coreference resolution. In: Association for Computational Linguistics (ACL) Demo Session (2008)
28. Vilain, M., Burger, J., Aberdeen, J., Connolly, D., Hirschman, L.: A model-theoretic coreference scoring scheme. In: Proceedings of the 6th Message Understanding Conference (MUC-6), pp. 45–52 (1995)
29. Waszczuk, J.: Harnessing the CRF complexity with domain-specific constraints. The case of morphosyntactic tagging of a highly inflected language. In: Proceedings of the 24th International Conference on Computational Linguistics (COLING 2012), Mumbai, India, pp. 2789–2804 (2012)
30. Woliéski, M.: Morfeusz reloaded. In: Calzolari, N., Choukri, K., Declerck, T., Loftsson, H., Maegaard, B., Mariani, J., Moreno, A., Odijk, J., Piperidis, S. (eds.) Proceedings of the 9th International Conference on Language Resources and Evaluation, LREC 2014, pp. 1106–1111. ELRA, Reykjavík (2014). http://www.lrec-conf.org/proceedings/lrec2014/index.html

Assessing VocBench Custom Forms in Supporting Editing of Lemon Datasets

Manuel Fiorelli, Tiziano Lorenzetti, Maria Teresa Pazienza, and Armando Stellato(✉)

ART Research Group, Department of Enterprise Engineering (DII), University of Rome Tor Vergata, Via Del Politecnico, 1, 00133 Rome, Italy
{fiorelli,pazienza}@info.uniroma2.it, tiziano.lorenzetti@gmail.com, stellato@uniroma2.it

Abstract. The lexicon model for ontologies OntoLex/*lemon* has been released in May, 2016, following more than 2 years of work of the Ontology-Lexicon (OntoLex) W3C Community Group. *Lemon* provides rich linguistic grounding for ontologies, including the representation of morphological and syntactic properties of lexical entries as well as the syntax-semantics interface. The rich expressivity of *lemon* requires however non-trivial modeling, with complex patterns characterized by indirections and reifications, indeed very difficult to handle by general-purpose ontology editing tools providing triple-grained manipulation. Extending such tools with *lemon*-tailored editing primitives would enable agile editing of lexicons and ontology-lexicon interfaces, while still benefiting from the wider modeling spectrum provided by RDF. In this paper, we assess the potential of VocBench Custom Forms, a flexible data-driven form definition mechanism being developed for the VocBench 3 collaborative editing platform, by evaluating their ability to assist the creation of *lemon* entities, disburdening the user from low-level modeling details and letting them focus on the content being edited.

Keywords: Lemon · OntoLex · Human-computer interaction · Lexicon · VocBench · Ontology engineering

1 Introduction

The W3C Community Group Ontology-Lexicon (OntoLex) published its final report [1] at the beginning of May 2016, describing *lemon*, a lexicon model for ontologies. The main purpose of *lemon* is to define a common vocabulary (actually a suite of vocabularies, called *lemon* modules) for the representation of lexicons and their interfacing with ontologies in a manner compatible with current Semantic Web practices. The core model offers a set of entities describing the basic elements of a lexicon and of its interface with ontologies, thesauri and datasets in general. Through its various modules, *lemon* supports a richer linguistic characterization of ontologies than it is possible with vocabularies currently established in the Semantic Web (e.g. in RDFS, through `rdfs:labels`, or in SKOS through `skos:{pref,alt,hidden}Labels`), by supporting morphological and syntactical information, as well as the

J. Gracia et al. (Eds.): LDK 2017, LNAI 10318, pp. 237–252, 2017.
DOI: 10.1007/978-3-319-59888-8_21

representation of variations and translations of lexicons in different languages. Beyond its original scope, the *lemon* model has found application in the context of the construction of the Linguistic Linked Open Data (LLOD) cloud, since it provides a principled and agreed upon model to represent and interlink lexicons and lexical-semantic resources (e.g. *wordnets* [2]). Therefore, there is a large community interested in editing *lemon* lexicons and, in some cases, interact with Semantic Web ontologies as well.

The rich expressivity of *lemon* requires however non-trivial modeling, with complex patterns characterized by indirections and reifications. These intrinsic characteristics make editing of *lemon* data highly inconvenient with traditional ontology editing tools, as the user is required to express *lemon* complex patterns resource by resource, triple by triple, lacking the overall view and the required abstraction over the model. On the other hand, dedicated editors, such as [3], would lack all the richness in expressivity and the possibilities offered by the underlying RDF model. Losing the connection to these standards may result in a siloed experience: the editor may not support the load and use of arbitrary ontologies, by defeating the ability of RDF to support an arbitrary mix of vocabularies. In addition, the user might not benefit from standardized query and manipulation languages (e.g. SPARQL) or other RDF-OWL specific technologies.

A third way, consisting in extending available ontology editing tools with *lemon-tailored* editing primitives, seems to catch the best of both worlds: it enables agile editing of lexicons and ontology-lexicon interfaces, while still benefiting from the wider modeling spectrum provided by RDF. Indeed, the exploitation of the existing *ecosystem* was advocated [4] as an important benefit of Linked Data adoption in Linguistics.

As contributors to the *lemon* community group, and in our role of developers of VocBench 3, a new collaborative editing platform funded by the ISA^2 programme, we considered *lemon* a much valuable and complete use case for assessing the potential of Custom Forms: a flexible data-driven form definition mechanism that we devised for the above platform.

In this paper, we will evaluate the ability of VocBench Custom Forms to assist the management of *lemon* constructs; specifically, we will consider if and to which extent Custom Forms support the creation and visualization of *lemon* entities at the proper level of abstraction, while offering a ductile environment for low-level refinements.

The paper is structured as follows: Sects. 2, 3 and 4 introduce *lemon* and the modeling and technological background behind the realization of Custom Forms. Section 5 details the application of Custom Forms to *lemon*. Section 6 discusses the approach, highlighting benefits, flaws and lessons learned for future improvements. Section 7 informs on related approaches, while Sect. 8 concludes the paper.

2 VocBench

VocBench [5] is a web-based collaborative thesaurus editing and workflow system. It natively supports Semantic Web standards such as RDF, OWL and SKOS(-XL), and is thought as a Web Interface for the Knowledge Management and Acquisition platform Semantic Turkey [6].

At the time of writing, we are developing – in the context of an action funded by the ISA^2 work programme – the third version of VocBench, slated for general availability after summer 2017. The main goal of this new incarnation of VocBench is to provide an even more general-purpose and powerful RDF editing platform than its predecessor – focused on SKOS-XL thesauri – was, while keeping (and improving) the characteristics that made it much appreciated, such as collaboration, validation and its publication workflow.

In the context of empowering the platform with advanced RDF editing capabilities that would guarantee expressive power and flexibility, we introduced into the system a mechanism for defining *Custom Forms* (that is customizable forms associable to the creation of new resources, such as concepts, classes, properties and instances).

3 Custom Forms

The mechanism behind the realization of *custom forms* is based on the declarative specification of the key elements that concur to the creation of a complex RDF resource. In particular, *custom forms* rely on the combination of the following four key elements:

- a declaration of the data that is expected to be prompted by the user
- the transformation of the prompted data into valid RDF entities to be stored
- the organization of the produced RDF entities into meaningful graph patterns, instantiating the template of the resource to be created
- the automatic production of a form layout based on the above declarations

This declarative specification is expressed through PEARL (ProjEction of Annotations Rule Language [7]), a transformation language thought for producing RDF content from feature structures. A processor for the PEARL language is already available in our platform CODA (Computer-aided Ontology Development Architecture, [8]).

In our approach, we repurposed the above technologies – originally thought for the acquisition of structured information from unstructured content – by applying them to the creation of a form-based interface for ontology development.

Our approach is best illustrated by first studying the architecture of a typical information extraction (IE) system based on CODA (see Fig. 1). An *information extraction component*, fed with a source (usually a document, though not limited in the kind of media, if not by the capabilities of the specific IE component) containing unstructured content, produces structured data by filling the slots of an extraction template. For example, if the goal is to recognize events (e.g. meetings), the template may contain slots for the name of the event, its location, date and time. In CODA, this first part is orchestrated by UIMA (Unstructured Information Management Architecture [9]), an architecture and a framework for analyzing large volumes of unstructured information in order to discover relevant knowledge. The information extracted through UIMA is organized in the form of Feature Structures [10] and the extraction template is expressed in terms of a Type System for these feature structures. Though being structured, the extracted data are not yet RDF triples nor do they match the structure and the vocabulary for the target *knowledge base*. In short, they lack the

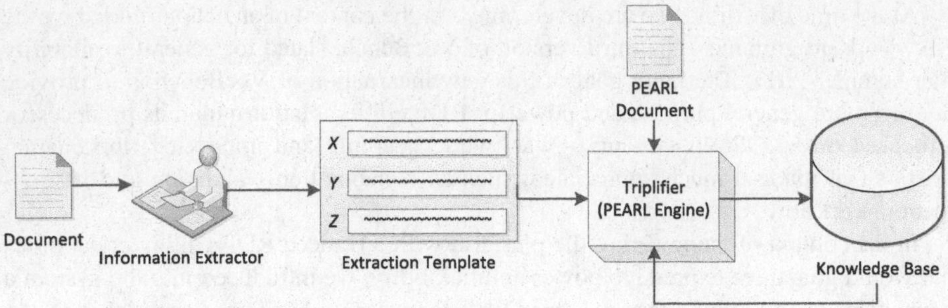

Fig. 1. Architecture of a typical IE application based on CODA

semantics that would make this knowledge universally understandable by humans and machines on the Semantic Web. This gap is filled by a *triplification component,* which translates the populated template into RDF triples. In our system, CODA extends UIMA with triplification capabilities and in particular, it uses PEARL for the declarative specification of these transformations.

Our intuition for the repurposing of CODA is that the extraction template can be understood as a specification of a form for entering data (see Fig. 2). Additionally, we observed that the other characteristics of a *custom form* can be inferred from the PEARL rules that convert this data to RDF. Therefore, we introduced a *form generator* that automates the generation of forms for creating new RDF resources.

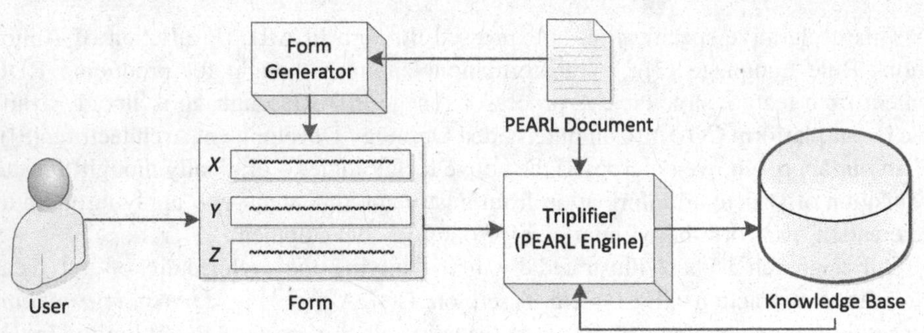

Fig. 2. Architecture of custom forms

This description of custom forms does not mention how *custom forms* are presented to the users of VocBench. In fact, custom forms are a building block for the development of higher-level abstractions such as *custom range* and *custom constructor*.

Custom constructors can be associated to specific RDFS or OWL classes in order to override the standard initialization of an instance of that class, and prompt instead a *custom form* to the user. The *custom forms* can be defined in order to realize the complex resources mentioned above, or simply to present a series of suggested/mandatory fields to the user that are expected to be filled when the resource is being introduced.

A *custom range* is a mechanism to customize the range of a *property* beyond what is axiomatically expressed in the underlying ontology. For instance, `skos:note` is defined as an `owl:AnnotationProperty`, which in principle can hold any value. In practice, however, this property is used either with a language tagged literal (e.g. `:aConcept skos:note "this is a note"@en`) or with a reified note (e.g. `:aConcept skos:note :aNote . :aNote rdf:value "this is a note"@en`). Reification is necessary to overcome the RDF constraint for which literals may not appear as the subject of a triple, thus preventing the description of the note itself. Unfortunately, the creation of these reified notes would be unpleasant, since the user should first create a resource for the note together with its description, and then attach that resource to a concept as a note. A rather ad hoc solution is the development of a dedicated functionality for the creation of reified notes, as we did in [11] for supporting development of SKOS-XL thesauri. However, this rather specific solution would fail to address similar problems with different vocabularies, especially in the case of domain vocabularies, which cannot be foreseen a-priori by a general-purpose editing platform. Instead of accumulating a number of ad hoc services, *custom ranges* allow to solve all these problems uniformly. The idea is that in the situation above one may associate with the property `skos:note` a *custom range*, containing a *custom form* for the reified note. Currently, *custom forms* add up on ranges recognized by VocBench because of the axiomatization of a property. In the example above, that means the possibility to create a reified note or a simple literal.

In addition to their support for the creation of resources, *custom ranges* enhance the visualization of data as well. When visualizing the property values of a resource (e.g. a SKOS concept), reified notes are rendered by default via their URIs, which can be completely unrelated to the textual content of the notes themselves. *Custom ranges* improve the situation, since a *form* can define a *show property chain*, that is to say a sequence of properties that locate a suitable label to render a resource. In our case, the chain for reified notes is represented by the sole property `rdf:value`, so that notes can be rendered via their associated content. Beyond this single value preview of a resource, *custom ranges* ease the interpretation of data, through the generation of a form-based preview of a property value. That preview is computed by reversing the process described so far. Firstly, the system tries to identify a *form* that could have generated that value, by matching the associated graph pattern against the data. Then, if a match is found, the variable bindings are used to fill the corresponding form.

In this article, we will mainly show examples with *custom ranges*, since *custom constructors* are in an earlier development stage. However, all considerations done for the *ranges* hold, without any loss of generality, for the *constructors* as well.

4 The Lemon Model

The Lexicon Model for Ontologies (*lemon*) is the result of the conjoint effort of several researchers participating in the OntoLex W3C Community Group. Realization of the model started from a previous version of *lemon* [12], later development has then been informed by other models realized by the members of the community [13–16]. In fact, *lemon* consists of a core module (*ontolex*) together with a number of modules covering different aspects of an ontology lexicon.

The list below includes existing modules and their description:

- Core (ontolex): defines the main vocabulary to represent the correspondence between lexical entries and ontology elements;
- Syntax and Semantics (synsem): defines the vocabulary for the representation of the syntax-semantics interface, i.e. the mapping between syntactic arguments of a lexical entry and the semantic arguments of the corresponding predicate in the ontology;
- Decomposition (decomp): defines the vocabulary for describing how compound or multiword lexical entries are decomposed into their constituent parts;
- Variation and Translation (vartrans): defines the vocabulary to represent relations between lexical entries or lexical senses, such as variant or translation;
- Metadata (*lime* [17]): is an extension of the VoID vocabulary [18], representing metadata pertaining to the ontology-lexicon interface.

Figure 3 illustrates a lexical entry for the word "actor" which is said to denote the class `dbo:Actor` from the DBpedia ontology [19]. An entry has a number of forms (`ontolex:Form`) representing different grammatical realizations of the entry. Each form has a number of surface realizations (`ontolex:writtenRep`), corresponding to different orthographies (e.g. "colour" vs. "color"). The relation between a lexical entry and a form is expressed via the property `ontolex:lexicalForm`, or more informatively via its subproperties `ontolex:canonicalForm` and `ontolex:otherForm` indicating the lemma and inflected forms, respectively. The example uses LexInfo [13] as a source of linguistics annotations, to represent the difference between those forms. Additionally, LexInfo represents the part of speech of the lexical entry. The meaning of the lexical entry is represented through a reference to the class `dbo:Actor`. An instance of the class `ontolex:LexicalSense` is intended to be unique for a given pair of lexical entry and ontology reference. A `synsem:OntoMap` (linked to the

```
ex:actor_entry a ontolex:LexicalEntry ;
 lexinfo:partOfSpeech lexinfo:commonNoun ;
 ontolex:canonicalForm ex:actor_entry-form1 ;
 ontolex:otherForm ex:actor_entry-form2 ;
 ontolex:sense ex:actor_entry-sense ;
 synsem:synBehavior ex:actor_entry-frame .
ex:actor_entry-form1 a ontolex:Form ;
 lexinfo:number lexinfo:singular ;
 ontolex:writtenRep "actor"@en .
ex:actor_entry-form2 a ontolex:Form ;
 lexinfo:number lexinfo:plural ;
 ontolex:writtenRep "actors"@en .
ex:actor_entry-sense a ontolex:LexicalSense, synsem:OntoMap ;
 synsem:ontoMapping ex:actor_entry-sense ;
 ontolex:reference dbo:Actor ;
 synsem:isA ex:actor_frame_arg1.
ex:actor_entry-frame a lexinfo:NounPredicateFrame ;
 lexinfo:copulativeArg ex:actor_frame_arg1 .
lexinfo:copulativeArg rdfs:subPropertyOf synsem:synArg.
```

Fig. 3. A lexical entry for the class `dbo:Actor`

sense) maps syntactic and semantic arguments. When both a sense and an ontomap are required, the OntoLex *lemon* specification suggests to use same URI for both. In the example, the reference is a class, and thus it has one semantic argument, the unbound variable of the predicate associated with the class (represented in the example via the property `synsem:isA`). The synsem module allows to represent the syntactic behavior of the lexical entry, through the use of the property `synsem:synBehavior`, which relates an entry to a syntactic frame. A syntactic frame represents a stereotypical occurrence of a lexical entry together with its syntactic arguments. Our example entry is associated with a `lexinfo:NounPredicateFrame` that represents a copulative construction: the use of `lexinfo:copulativeArg` encompasses both *X is an actor* and *the actor is X*. The core of the syntax-semantic interface is a mapping between syntactic and semantic arguments, which is realized technically by unifying them to a single distinguished resource (i.e. `ex:actor_frame_arg1`).

5 Custom Forms for Lemon

The *lemon* model is a perfect candidate for the use of *custom forms* (and thus an interesting use case for their evaluation), because of the following:

- Instances of its classes (e.g. `ontolex:LexicalEntry`) need to be arranged into complex graph structures;
- These graphs conform to recurring patterns, which are determined by the nature of the lexical entry we aim to represent and its reference in the ontology;
- There is a number of different patterns.

In our experimentation, we consider the use case related to the construction of an OntoLex *lemon* lexicon for an existing ontology. With this regard, we considered the *lemon* Design Patterns [20] as a reference, attempting to implement them as faithfully as possible with *custom forms* (published here: https://bitbucket.org/art-uniroma2/lemon-vb-customforms).

In our experiment, by defining a set of *custom ranges*, we associated the implemented *custom forms* with the property `lime:entry`, which relates an instance of the class `lime:Lexicon` to a set of lexical entries. A `lime:Lexicon` becomes thus the entry point through which creating new lexical entries. Similarly, it is possible to associate the forms above to the class `ontolex:LexicalEntry` as *custom constructors* in order to enable creation of new instances mediated by the forms directly from the class. In the following sections, we discuss how the different patterns have been implemented by use of *custom forms*. We skip discussion on verbs and adjectives, as their associated patterns bear a similar complexity to the presented ones.

5.1 Names

A *name* denotes an individual in the ontology. It is not associated with an explicit syntactic frame, nor is it necessary to use the synsem module to map syntactic and semantic arguments. We will skip a detailed discussion of this pattern, since from the perspective of evaluating the adequacy of custom forms it is subsumed by all other patterns.

5.2 Class Nouns

A *class noun* denotes the set of individuals sharing a given characteristic: it is therefore associated with a class, either defined by the ontology or defined locally in the lexicon. The latter is required when the relevant concept is not named in the ontology, nonetheless it can be described through the vocabulary already defined.

A *custom form* for a *class noun* is associated with the PEARL rule below:

```
rule it.[…].ClassNounOntoLexLexicalEntry id:ClassNounOntoLexLex-
icalEntry {
  nodes = {
    cfWrittenRepLang literal userPrompt/canonicalFormLang .
    cfWrittenRep literal(coda:langString(
      $cfWrittenRepLang)) userPrompt/canonicalForm .
    referenceResource uri userPrompt/reference .
    lexicalEntry uri(coda:randIdGen("ontolexLexicalEntry",
      {canonicalForm = $cfWrittenRep})) .
    canonicalForm uri(coda:randIdGen("ontolexForm",
      {entry = $lexicalEntry, writtenRep = $cfWrittenRep})) .
    synFrame uri(coda:randIdGen("synsemSyntacticFrame", {
      entry = $lexicalEntry, type = lexinfo:NounPredicate-
      Frame})) .
    arg uri(coda:randIdGen("synsemSyntacticArgument",
      {entry = $lexicalEntry, type = lexinfo:copulativeArg})) .
    lexSense uri(coda:randIdGen("synsemOntoMap",
      {entry = $lexicalEntry, reference = $referenceResource}))
  }
  graph = {
    $lexicalEntry a ontolex:LexicalEntry .
    $lexicalEntry lexinfo:partOfSpeech lexinfo:commonNoun .
    $lexicalEntry ontolex:canonicalForm $canonicalForm.
    $canonicalForm ontolex:writtenRep $cfWrittenRep.
    $lexicalEntry synsem:synBehavior $synFrame .
    $synFrame a lexinfo:NounPredicateFrame .
    $synFrame lexinfo:copulativeArg $arg .
    $lexicalEntry ontolex:sense $lexSense .
    $lexSense a ontolex:LexicalSense .
    $lexSense a synsem:OntoMapping .
    $lexSense synsem:ontoMapping $lexSense .
    $lexSense ontolex:reference $referenceResource .
    $lexSense synsem:isA $arg .
  }
}
```

The definition of the rule begins with the keyword `rule` followed by the name of the template form and a rule identifier. The definition of the rule consists of two main parts, the `nodes` section and the `graph` section. The `nodes` section contains the definition of a number of placeholders for RDF names (e.g. URI or literals), while the `graph` section contains a graph pattern that will be instantiated into a set of triples for each assignment of values to placeholders.

The declaration of each node placeholder consists of three parts:

- The placeholder name
- Either the keyword `uri` or `literal` (optionally associated with a language tag or datatype) and an optional *converter* with parameters
- An optional *feature path* for the extraction of information from the source form (which is modeled as a *feature structure* [10])

The third component (the *feature path*) is crucial to understand how the form is constructed. Indeed, for each feature path of the form `userPrompt/XYZ` a field labeled `XYZ` is added to the form.

The value retrieved via the feature path (e.g. the content of the form field) is then used to construct the RDF name to be stored by the placeholder. The nature of the name is determined by the second component (i.e. `uri` or `literal`), which can additionally specify a *converter* to carry out the transformation. A *converter* is a pluggable function transforming the input into a valid RDF name according to a given *contract* (which can be resolved as a URI). In lack of the mention of an explicit *converter*, a default *converter* will be invoked. The default *converter* copies the input as-is for the creation of a literal or, in case of a URI, assembles one by concatenating the default namespace with the value of the feature path as local name (an appropriate *sanitization* is in order to generate a valid URI). In the example, we define a placeholder for the *canonical form* and the *ontological reference* based on the user input. Other placeholders will hold the resources associated with the *lexical entry*, the *syntactic frame*, its sole *argument* and the *lexical sense*. In the latter case, there is no feature path, since the *converter* `coda:randIdGen` generates a random URI. That converter has two parameters: a *role* (identifying the nature of the considered resource) and a map of role-dependent arguments. For example, we associated with the role `ontolexLexicalEntry` the parameter `canonicalForm`, to which we assign the value bound to the placeholder `$cfWrittenRep`. In VocBench 3, the generation of URIs is configurable, and can be influenced by these additional parameters.

Figure 4 shows the form that is prompted to the user for the creation of a new lexical entry, in which we can recognize the fields for the canonical form and the ontology reference. Concerning the canonical form, the fields for its written representation and its language tag have been rendered as a single combined field (because of the tight binding determined by the converter `coda:langString`). Concerning the ontology reference, the user may enter the URI manually. More effectively, the user can click the button on the right of the field, opening a dialog in which existing classes in the ontology can be found either by browsing a hierarchical visualization or by text search.

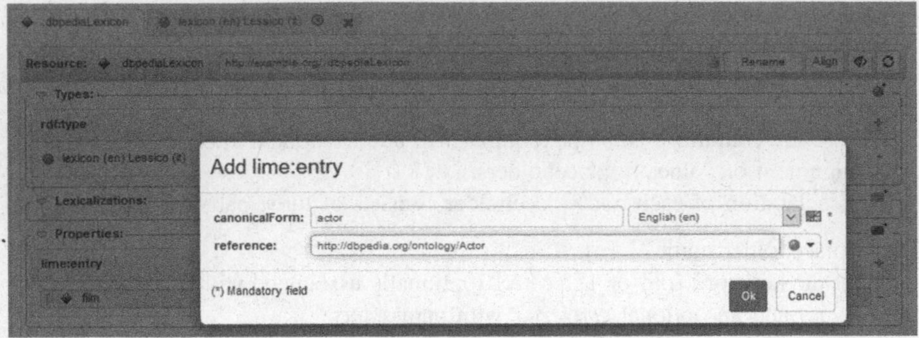

Fig. 4. Custom form the creation of a class noun

5.3 Data and Object Property Nouns

A *data/object property noun* is a class noun the meaning of which is defined as a restriction on a data/object property. There is no substantial difference with respect to the case above, except for the fact that now the user is requested to enter a property and the desired value, instead of a class. The graph pattern associated with the rule will generate the triples representing the restriction using `owl:Restriction`, `owl:onProperty` and `owl:hasValue`.

5.4 Relational Nouns

A *relational noun* expresses a relation rather than a class or an individual. Therefore, it is usually associated with a property in the ontology. The properties `synsem:subjOfProp` and `synsem:objOfProp` can be attached to the lexical sense (actually, a `synsem:OntoMap`) to represent the subject and the object of the property, respectively. The syntactic behavior of a relational noun is still a `lexinfo:NounPredicateFrame` or its subclass `lexinfo:NounPossessiveFrame`, when a possessive adjunct is considered such as in "Berlin is the capital of Germany" or "Berlin is Germany's capital". In this case we have two possible mappings between syntactic and semantic arguments, depending on whether the semantic subject is mapped to the copulative argument or the possessive adjunct (prepositional object).

Two possible solutions are to define *custom forms* for each mapping, or to have one subsuming both mappings. The critical part of the latter lies in the portion of the graph section reported below (we assume an intuitive interpretation of placeholders)

```
$lexicalEntry synsem:synBehavior $synFrame .
$synFrame a lexinfo:NounPredicateFrame .
$synFrame $subjMapping $subjArg .
$synFrame $objMapping $objArg .
$lexicalEntry ontolex:sense $lexSense .
$lexSense a synsem:OntoMapping .
$lexSense ontolex:reference $referenceResource .
$lexSense synsem:subjOfProp $subjArg .
$lexSense synsem:objOfProp $objArg .
```

In the pattern, the properties differentiating between the syntactic arguments are represented via placeholders that correspond (in the `nodes` section) to distinct fields in the *custom form*: the user can fill them with suitable properties from the LexInfo ontology, effectively establishing which syntactic argument is bound to the semantic subject and the semantic object, respectively. Since prepositional objects require a prepositional marker, we introduce for both `$subjArg` and `$objArg` an optional graph pattern like the following:

```
OPTIONAL {
  $subjArg synsem:marker $subjMarker .
  $subjMarker a ontolex:LexicalEntry .
  $subjMarker lexinfo:partOfSpeech lexinfo:preposition .
  $subjMarker ontolex:canonicalForm $subjMarkerForm .
  $subjMarkerForm a ontolex:Form .
  $subjMarkerForm ontolex:writtenRep $subjMarkerWrittenRep .
}
```

Figure 5 depicts the *custom form* described so far, and already filled with the details of the relational noun "director", denoting the property `dbo:director` in the DBpedia ontology: the semantic subject (a `dbo:Film`) is mapped to the prepositional object.

As already said in Sect. 3, *custom ranges* not only deal with the creation of resources, but also on their appropriate visualization inside VocBench 3. Figure 6 depicts the view showing an instance of `lime:Lexicon`, focusing on the section enumerating the entries contained in the lexicon (i.e. the values of the property `lime:entry`). Without any customization, VocBench would show such entries via their URIs (possibly abbreviated as qnames). Since URIs may be completely arbitrary (e.g. an alphanumeric code), the resulting representation would be completely uninformative, forcing the user to explicitly request (as a separate view) the description of each entry. Conversely, the figure depicts a much better situation in which lexical entries are displayed via their lemma. That has been made possible by a suitable *show property chain* (i.e. `ontolex:canonicalForm/ontolex:writtenRep`). In addition to this *single value preview*, *custom ranges* make it possible to construct a *multi-value preview* for property values, when they match the pattern of a *custom form* associated

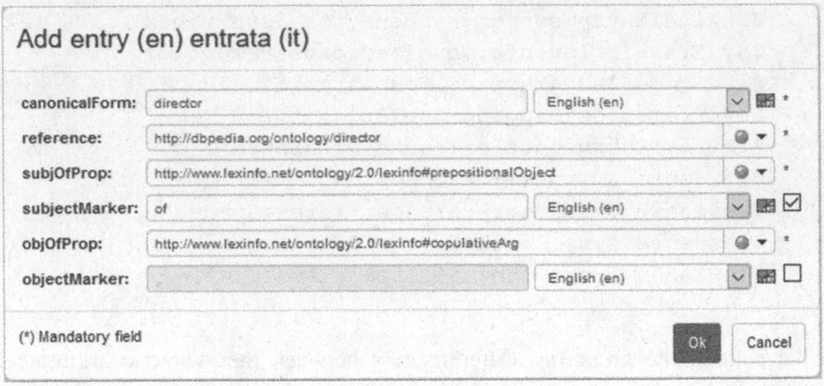

Fig. 5. Custom form for a relational noun

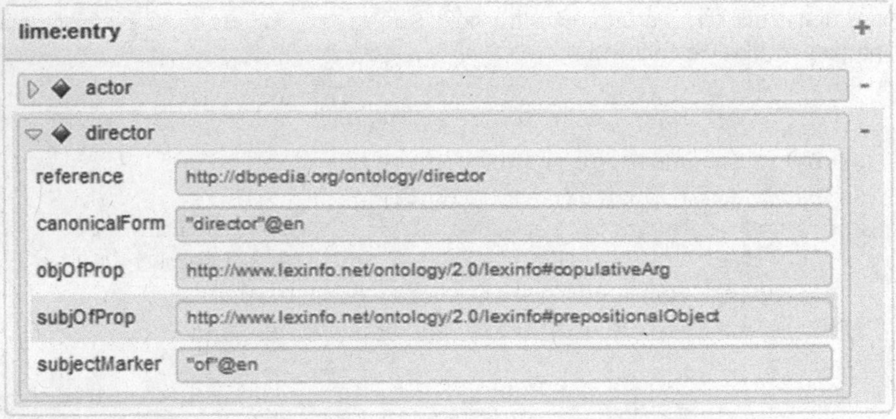

Fig. 6. Multi-value preview of a property value

with the property. In Fig. 6, we expanded the preview of a lexical entry into a *multi-value* one, matching the *custom form* for a relational noun: the form shows the lemma and the correspondence between syntactic and semantic arguments (implicitly represented in RDF as the unification of the mapped arguments).

6 Discussion

In the previous sections, we showed the adequacy of *custom forms* for the representation of diverse *lemon* Design Patterns. Their use effectively allows to customize VocBench for the creation of an ontology lexicon, relieving the user from the burden of creating and then relating the numerous resources necessary to represent even the simplest lexical entries. Additionally, we showed how custom forms can be used the other way around for previewing property values (e.g. held by `lime:entry`).

Actually, a faithful implementation of the *lemon* Design Patterns is hampered by some contingent limitations of *custom forms*. For example, it is difficult to guarantee that every lexical entry added to a lexicon shares the same language (though it is possible to block all the language tags to a certain language). Another difficulty is determined by patterns with a variable number of components, such as non-canonical forms (i.e. inflected forms), linguistic annotations, and syntactic/semantic arguments (e.g. in case of multivalent relational nouns and the most verbs). The PEARL language could handle all these cases via its implicit support for lists: each value of a feature is used to assign a different RDF name to a placeholder, and each possible assignment is used transparently for instantiating the pattern in the `graph` section. Consequently, the *custom form generator* has no syntactic clue suggesting that a feature is supposed to hold a list. We worked around this limitation by introducing optional fields in the form, up to a reasonable number. In the future, we will define some *annotations* (already supported by PEARL) to explicitly drive the generation of multi-valued fields.

7 Related Work

CODA was initially aimed at knowledge acquisition from unstructured content. For instance, the AgroIE [21] system exploited CODA to extract relationships for the enrichment of the AGROVOC [22] thesaurus. Still bound to the core objective of knowledge acquisition, but targeted to a very specific application domain, Sheet2RDF [23] was built on top of CODA for triplifying tabular data. *Custom forms* have reinterpreted CODA to further level of exploitation, by generating a form (i.e. a row in a table) that fits the desired graph pattern. Though the approaches differ in many aspects, the result appears similar to the one of Populous [24], which supports the population of ontologies through a tabular interface, possibly constrained by the input ontology.

TopBraid Composer (TBC) [25] and Protégé [26] (in version 3.x, which influenced WebProtégé [27]) also support form customization to some extent. Their customization mainly focuses on dedicated widgets (e.g. table widgets, map widgets) and form layout. In this aspect, they surpass VocBench, although *custom forms* already feature dedicated components for some datatypes and others will be added in the near future.

However, the main value of *custom forms* in VocBench lies in the specification of arbitrary graph patterns for creating complex resources. TBC also supports the specification of graphs for resource creation, by means of *constructors*, i.e. associations of SPIN (http://www.spinrdf.org/) rules to the creation of a new resource. This is however limited to data that can be inferred from available information (e.g. the SPARQL function `now()` returning the current time, or other existing information) and does not bind dedicated form fields.

Concerning the views, we could not find an equivalent of single/multi value preview in Protégé nor in TBC. Both Protégé and TBC provide some customization for rendering resources. This is however limited to simple operations such as reading pre-configured properties (e.g. `rdfs:label`) or concatenating user-defined series of strings and property values, whereas *custom forms* single-value preview allow for the traversal of arbitrary property chains. Additionally, TBC supports nested descriptions of resources, which may appear similar to the *multi-value preview* of *custom ranges*. However, TBC merely presents the available triples, while the latter builds the preview based on the available *custom forms*, looking ahead even various levels in the graph describing the previewed resource, in order to provide the best resuming information. Specifically for this case, that means recognizing a Lemon Design pattern, and organizing the available information according to its prescriptions. In this sense, *custom forms* recall more the approach of Fresnel [28], where the forms may be bound to arbitrary long property paths by means of SPARQL queries (Fresnel was for visualization only).

8 Conclusion

In the context of the development of VocBench 3, we designed the mechanism of *custom forms* to ease the creation and visualization of resources arranged into complex graph patterns. In this paper, we evaluated the adequacy of this mechanism in the context of the OntoLex Lemon model, which heavily depends on reification and indirection to support a rich linguistic characterization of ontologies and RDF datasets, in general. An overall positive result was accompanied by the identification of some weak points, which dot not indicate theoretical flaws in our approach, but rather the direction for polishing the implementation of *custom forms* before the final release of VocBench 3.

Conventions. The RDF examples in the paper are expressed in the Turtle syntax (https://www.w3.org/TR/turtle/) and use the prefix declarations adopted in [1].

Acknowledgments. This work has been partially funded by the ISA^2 Work Programme, action for the realization of the VocBench 3 collaborative editing platform for ontologies and thesauri: https://ec.europa.eu/isa2/solutions/vocbench3.

References

1. Cimiano, P., McCrae, J.P., Buitelaar, P.: Lexicon model for ontologies: community report, 10 May 2016. Community report, W3C (2016). https://www.w3.org/2016/05/ontolex/
2. Bond, F., Paik, K.: A survey of wordnets and their licenses. In: Proceedings of the 6th Global WordNet Conference (GWC 2012), Matsue, pp. 64–71 (2012)
3. Rico, M., Unger, C.: Lemonade: a web assistant for creating and debugging ontology lexica. In: Biemann, C., Handschuh, S., Freitas, A., Meziane, F., Métais, E. (eds.) NLDB 2015. LNCS, vol. 9103, pp. 448–452. Springer, Cham (2015). doi:10.1007/978-3-319-19581-0_45
4. Chiarcos, C., McCrae, J., Cimiano, P., Fellbaum, C.: Towards open data for linguistics: linguistic linked data. In: Oltramari, A., Vossen, P., Qin, L., Hovy, E. (eds.) New Trends of Research in Ontologies and Lexical Resources, pp. 7–25. Springer, Heidelberg (2013). doi:10.1007/978-3-642-31782-8_2
5. Stellato, A., Rajbhandari, S., Turbati, A., Fiorelli, M., Caracciolo, C., Lorenzetti, T., Keizer, J., Pazienza, M.T.: VocBench: a web application for collaborative development of multilingual thesauri. In: Gandon, F., Sabou, M., Sack, H., d'Amato, C., Cudré-Mauroux, P., Zimmermann, A. (eds.) ESWC 2015. LNCS, vol. 9088, pp. 38–53. Springer, Cham (2015). doi:10.1007/978-3-319-18818-8_3

6. Pazienza, M.T., Scarpato, N., Stellato, A., Turbati, A.: Semantic Turkey: a browser-integrated environment for knowledge acquisition and management. Semant. Web J. **3**(3), 279–292 (2012)
7. Pazienza, M.T., Stellato, A., Turbati, A.: PEARL: ProjEction of Annotations Rule Language, a language for projecting (UIMA) annotations over RDF knowledge bases. In: LREC, Istanbul (2012)
8. Fiorelli, M., Pazienza, M.T., Stellato, A., Turbati, A.: CODA: computer-aided ontology development architecture. IBM J. Res. Dev. **58**(2/3), 14:1–14:12 (2014)
9. Ferrucci, D., Lally, A.: UIMA: an architectural approach to unstructured information processing in the corporate research environment. Natl. Lang. Eng. **10**(3–4), 327–348 (2004)
10. Carpenter, B.: The Logic of Typed Feature Structures. Cambridge Tracts in Theoretical Computer Science, vol. 32, (hardback) edn. Cambridge University Press, Cambridge (1992)
11. Fiorelli, M., Pazienza, M.T., Stellato, A.: Semantic Turkey goes SKOS managing knowledge organization systems. In: I-SEMANTICS 2012 Proceedings of the 8th International Conference on Semantic Systems, Graz, Austria, pp. 64–71 (2012)
12. McCrae, J., Spohr, D., Cimiano, P.: Linking lexical resources and ontologies on the semantic web with lemon. In: Antoniou, G., Grobelnik, M., Simperl, E., Parsia, B., Plexousakis, D., Leenheer, P., Pan, J. (eds.) ESWC 2011. LNCS, vol. 6643, pp. 245–259. Springer, Heidelberg (2011). doi:10.1007/978-3-642-21034-1_17
13. Cimiano, P., Buitelaar, P., McCrae, J., Sintek, M.: LexInfo: a declarative model for the lexicon-ontology interface. Web Semant. Sci. Serv. Agents World Wide Web **9**(1), 29–51 (2011)
14. Pazienza, M.T., Stellato, A., Turbati, A.: Linguistic watermark 3.0: an RDF framework and a software library for bridging language and ontologies in the semantic web. In: 5th Workshop on Semantic Web Applications and Perspectives (SWAP2008), Rome, Italy, 15–17 December 2008, CEUR, FAO-UN, vol. 426, p. 11 (2008)
15. Montiel-Ponsoda, E., de Cea, G.A., Gómez-Pérez, A., Peters, W.: Enriching ontologies with multilingual information. Natl. Lang. Eng. **17**(3), 283–309 (2011)
16. Francopoulo, G., George, M., Calzolari, N., Monachini, M., Bel, N., Pet, M., Soria, C.: Lexical Markup Framework (LMF). In: LREC 2006, Genoa, Italy (2006)
17. Fiorelli, M., Stellato, A., McCrae, J.P., Cimiano, P., Pazienza, M.T.: LIME: the metadata module for OntoLex. In: Gandon, F., Sabou, M., Sack, H., d'Amato, C., Cudré-Mauroux, P., Zimmermann, A. (eds.) ESWC 2015. LNCS, vol. 9088, pp. 321–336. Springer, Cham (2015). doi:10.1007/978-3-319-18818-8_20
18. Alexander, K., Cyganiak, R., Hausenblas, M., Zhao, J.: Describing linked datasets with the VoID vocabulary (W3C interest group note). In: World Wide Web Consortium (W3C). http://www.w3.org/TR/void/. Accessed 3 Mar 2011
19. Bizer, C., Lehmann, J., Kobilarov, G., Auer, S., Becker, C., Cyganiak, R., Hellmann, S.: DBpedia - a crystallization point for the web of data. Web Semant. Sci. Serv. Agents World Wide Web **7**(3), 154–165 (2009)
20. McCrae, J.P., Unger, C.: Design patterns for engineering the ontology-lexicon interface. In: Buitelaar, P., Cimiano, P. (eds.) Towards the Multilingual Semantic Web: Principles, Methods and Applications, pp. 15–30. Springer, Heidelberg (2014)
21. Pazienza, M.T., Stellato, A., Tudorache, A.G., Turbati, A., Vagnoni, F.: An architecture for data and knowledge acquisition for the semantic web: the AGROVOC use case. In: Herrero, P., Panetto, H., Meersman, R., Dillon, T. (eds.) OTM 2012. LNCS, vol. 7567, pp. 426–433. Springer, Heidelberg (2012). doi:10.1007/978-3-642-33618-8_58
22. Caracciolo, C., Stellato, A., Morshed, A., Johannsen, G., Rajbhandari, S., Jaques, Y., Keizer, J.: The AGROVOC linked dataset. Semant. Web J. **4**(3), 341–348 (2013)

23. Fiorelli, M., Lorenzetti, T., Pazienza, M.T., Stellato, A., Turbati, A.: Sheet2RDF: a flexible and dynamic spreadsheet import and lifting framework for RDF. In: Ali, M., Kwon, Y., Lee, C.H., Kim, Y. (eds.) IEA/AIE 2015. LNCS, vol. 9101, pp. 131–140. Springer, Cham (2015). doi:10.1007/978-3-319-19066-2_13
24. Jupp, S., Horridge, M., Iannone, L., Klein, J., Owen, S., Schanstra, J., Wolstencroft, K., Stevens, R.: Populous: a tool for building OWL ontologies from templates. BMC Bioinf. **13**(Suppl 1) (2012)
25. TopBraid Composer. http://www.topquadrant.com/tools/ide-topbraid-composer-maestro-edition/
26. Gennari, J., Musen, M., Fergerson, R., Grosso, W., Crubézy, M., Eriksson, H., Noy, N., Tu, S.: The evolution of Protégé-2000: an environment for knowledge-based systems development. Int. J. Hum Comput Stud. **58**(1), 89–123 (2003)
27. Tudorache, T., Nyulas, C., Noy, N.F., Musen, M.A.: WebProtégé: a collaborative ontology editor and knowledge acquisition tool for the web. Semant. Web **4**(1), 89–99 (2013)
28. Pietriga, E., Bizer, C., Karger, D., Lee, R.: Fresnel: a browser-independent presentation vocabulary for RDF. In: Cruz, I., Decker, S., Allemang, D., Preist, C., Schwabe, D., Mika, P., Uschold, M., Aroyo, L.M. (eds.) ISWC 2006. LNCS, vol. 4273, pp. 158–171. Springer, Heidelberg (2006). doi:10.1007/11926078_12

Answering the Hard Questions

Maria Khvalchik(✉), Chanin Pithyaachariyakul, and Anagha Kulkarni

Computer Science Department, San Francisco State University,
1600 Holloway Ave, San Francisco, CA 94132, USA
{mkhvalch,cpithyaa}@mail.sfsu.edu, ak@sfsu.edu

Abstract. We present an end-to-end system for open-domain non-factoid question-answering. To accomplish this we leverage the information on the ever-growing World Wide Web, and the capabilities of commercial search engines to find the relevant information. Our QA system is composed of three components: (i) query formulation module (QFM) (ii) candidate answer generation module (CAGM) and (iii) answer selection module (ASM). A thorough empirical evaluation using two datasets demonstrates that the proposed approach is highly competitive.

1 Introduction

The popularity of QA websites such as Quora, and Yahoo! Answers highlights users' preference to express certain information needs as natural language questions (e.g. "What is the best way to cook fish?"), rather than keyword based queries. Currently, the person who posts the question has to wait for the answer until someone responds with the correct answer. As a result, there is a latency as well as scalability problem. Often the answer to the posted question is already out there on the World Wide Web (WWW), either as an answer to a similar question, or embedded in the content of one or more web pages. This observation was inspired evaluation forums such as the TREC LiveQA Track[1], and QALD Challenge[2] that are facilitating the research on the automated QA problem.

Developing an automated QA system that is capable of answering factoid or non-factoid questions from any domain (e.g. health, sports, cooking, etc.) is a challenging problem. In this paper we present our take on this problem. The end-to-end system that we have developed consists of three modules: (i) QFM converts the free-text question into a boolean query that can be processed by a commercial search engine; (ii) CAGM extracts all the promising candidate answers from the top ranked web pages returned by the search engine and (iii) ASM employs different ranking and classification approaches to select the best answer from the set of candidates. In the subsequent sections we describe our approach and provide its detailed empirical evaluation.

The subproblem of answering factoid questions using a static collection of documents (e.g. "What is the capital of France?") has been researched for a

[1] https://sites.google.com/site/trecliveqa2015/.
[2] https://project-hobbit.eu/challenges/qald2017/.

J. Gracia et al. (Eds.): LDK 2017, LNAI 10318, pp. 253–261, 2017.
DOI: 10.1007/978-3-319-59888-8_22

long time since late 1960s [4,8,16]. One of the recent examples is work by Bian et al. [3] where they built a framework which allows to extract facts from the data source and rank them. Their work defines a set of textual features some of which we use in our work. Suryanto et al. [14] propose a similar method using the reputation of the question asker and the answerer to determine the relevance of the answer. Both papers are focused on factoid question answering and they use Yahoo! Answers as the source data. While our method is focused on non-factoid questions with using the entire Web as the data source.

Soricut and Brill [12] published one of the first papers on non-factoid question answering, and many others have followed [9,11,13]. As a training set they used a corpus of 1 million question-answer pairs from FAQ collected on the Web. To search for the answer candidates they used MSNSearch and Google. Our work uses different algorithm for QFM, is trained using Yahoo! Answers dataset and uses learning to rank techniques which started to advance in mid-00s. In recent years the advancements in NLP/ML techniques, and availability of large QA datasets has propelled research and contests on answering open-domain non-factoid questions [2]. Wang et al. [17,18] works were the winner of two subsequent TREC LiveQA competitions. In the first paper they trained an answer prediction model using BLSTM Neural Network. In the second one, they used Neural Machine Translation techniques to train the model which generates the answer itself given only a question. In our work we will investigate whether a comparable performance is achievable using only statistical text features.

2 Open Domain Factoid/Non-factoid QA System

Our QA system consists of three main phases. The first phase transforms the natural language question to a keyword based boolean query. A commercial search engine, Bing is then used to obtain the most relevant web pages to the boolean query, and these web pages are mined for candidate answers. Finally, the best answer from all the candidates is identified, and presented to the user. Next we describe each of these phases in detail.

Query Formulation Module (QFM): The QFM transforms the natural language question to a well-formed boolean conjunctive query that can be evaluated by a search engine. This is a challenging problem as questions are often verbose. They contain information that is useful for a human but is superfluous, or even misleading, if included in the query. We address this verbosity problem at multiple levels. First, not every sentence in the question contributes to the query. Only sentences that start with WH-words (e.g. Who, When, Where, Why) and end with a question mark do [15]. Second, within a sentence only certain parts of the question are included in the query. Also, the length of these parts, individual words or phrases, is selected carefully. For example, transforming the following question *Why's juice from orange peel supposed to be good for eyes?* into a boolean query: *(orange) AND (peel) AND (juice) AND (good) AND (eyes)* is not effective because most of the retrieved web pages are about *orange juice* and not about *orange peel juice.* To achieve this, QFM performs grammatical analysis using the Stanford Dependency Parser [6] to obtain the grammatical structure of the sentence and then apply a recursive logic to identify important phrases rather than just individual words. For the above question this approach selects a noun phrase *orange peel*, an adjective phrase *good for eyes*, and a single word *juice*. The final boolean conjunctive query is as follows: *(juice) AND (orange peel) AND (good for eyes)*. This query is successful at retrieving web pages about *orange peel juice*.

The English *closed class* terms (pronouns, determiners, prepositions) in the question are often ignored since they do not capture the central topic of the question. However, in certain situations the prepositions should be included in the query. In case of the following question *How much should I pay for a round trip direct flight from NYC to Chicago in early November?*, if the preposition words, *from* and *to*, are ignored then the information about the travel direction is lost. To address this issue, the grammatical tree structure of the sentence is leveraged to identify the preposition phrases, such as, *from NYC* and *to Chicago*, and these are included as-is in the boolean query.

The verb phrases are also important because the verb alone is too broad to be a standalone keyword in the query. For question *What should I have in my disaster emergency kit stored outside my house?*, without the verb phrase detection, the system generates *(disaster emergency kit) AND (outside house) AND (store)*. Some of the web pages retrieved by this query are about stores that sell disaster emergency kit. Whereas with verb phrase detection logic, a better query is generated: *(disaster emergency kit) AND (store outside house)*.

Candidate Answer Generation Module (CAGM): The boolean query created by QFM is executed against the commercial search engine, Bing. The top 20 web pages returned for the query are downloaded. Each of the web pages is passed through the following text processing pipeline, where the first step extracts ASCII text from the web page using an html2text library[3]. We refer to the extracted text as a document. This document is next split into passages, where each passage consists of five consecutive sentences. A sliding span of five consecutive sentences is used to generate the passages. Thus a document containing 6 sentences would generate two passages. This approach generates many passages, specifically, $1 + (n-5)$, where n is the total number of sentences in the document. Passages that do not contain any of the query terms, or that contain more than 2 line breaks, or more than 10 punctuation marks, or non-printable symbols are eliminated. Also, passages that are not in English are filtered out. The langdetect library[4] is employed for language identification. All the passages that survive the filtering step are considered as *candidate answers*.

Answer Selection Module (ASM): In this final step of the QA pipeline, the best answer from all the candidate answers is chosen. We experiment with three algorithms for this task: Okapi BM25, Binary Support Vector Machine (BSVM), and LambdaMart Learning To Rank (LLTR) [5]. Okapi BM25 is a widely used

[3] https://pypi.python.org/pypi/html2text.
[4] https://pypi.python.org/pypi/langdetect.

ranking approach that assigns a score to each candidate based on which terms occur in both, query and the candidate answer. BSVM is trained to classify a candidate answer as either being relevant or non-relevant to the query. If none of the candidate answers from a document are classified as relevant or if there are multiple relevant candidates, then the candidate with the highest Okapi BM25 score is selected as the best answer. LLTR is trained to rank the passages based on their relevance to the query. The highest ranking candidate is chosen as the answer by LLTR approach.

The BSVM classification model, and the LLTR ranking model were trained using a subset of Webscope Yahoo! Answers L6 dataset[5] which contains questions and answers provided by users. For many questions one of the answers is identified as the best answer. For training BSVM the best answer for each question is assigned the positive label (i.e. relevant) and all other answers receive negative label. When compiling the labeled data for LLTR, the best answer is assigned the highest rank label, and the remaining answers were assigned a rank label proportional to their BM25 score with the best answer.

For both, the BSVM classification algorithm, and LLTR ranking algorithm, the labeled data has to be represented as a set of features. We used the following feature set: Okapi BM25 score, cosine similarity, number of overlapping terms, number of punctuation marks in the passage, number of words in the answer, number of characters in the answer, query likelihood probability (using the multinomial unigram language model[6]), largest distance between two terms in the answer, average distance between two terms, number of terms in longest continuous span, maximum number of terms matched in a single sentence, maximum number of terms in order. Before computing each of these features, all terms from query and passages were stemmed using Porter.

3 Experimental Setup, Results and Analysis

A subset of 60,000 question-answers from the L6 dataset is used to train the BSVM classification model. For training the LLTR ranking model a subset of 1000 questions was used. The small size of data was necessitated by the computational cost of training the models. We used 5-fold cross validation to evaluate the effectiveness of both models. To evaluate the ASM we employed the TREC 2015 data[7] which contains the answers from all participant systems for approximately 1000 questions where each answer is rated by human judges on the scale from 1 (poor) to 4 (excellent). The three answer selection approaches employed by our system are applied to the above data. Their effectiveness at selecting the best answer is quantified using the metrics that are commonly used for this task: NDCG (Normalized Discounted Cumulative Gain), MAP (Mean average precision), and MRR (Mean Reciprocal Rank).

[5] http://webscope.sandbox.yahoo.com.
[6] https://nlp.stanford.edu/IR-book/.
[7] https://sites.google.com/site/trecliveqa2015/trec-liveqa-2015--qrels.

Evaluating the end-to-end QA system is challenging because the generated answer might change if the search engine results change, and thus manual assessment of answer relevance cannot be a one-time activity. As a compromise, we attempt to provide quantitative evaluation by using similarity metrics (Jaccard, Cosine, and Symmetric KL Divergence). The similarity between the answer generated by our system and the best-quality answer for each question of TREC Live QA 2015 dataset is computed using one of these metrics. The intuition being that higher the similarity score the more effective the system is. The absolute similarity scores are not the focus, but the relative difference in scores for the different systems is worth analyzing. We define a baseline QA system that treats the original question as a query (stopwords excluded), downloads the top web page by Bing, and selects the passage with highest BM25 score as the answer.

Table 1 provides the results for the evaluation of the ASM. BM25 was used as the baseline where each candidate answer is ranked based on its BM25 score with the query, and the top ranked candidate is selected as the best answer. BSVM does not have a significant improvement over the baseline. It happens because BSVM fails to predict the relevance order of the passages and falls back on BM25 when it has to select the best passage. LLTR has far better performance because it predicts the order and never falls back to BM25.

Table 1. Results of answer ranking

	NDCG	MAP@			MRR@		
		2	3	4	2	3	4
Lower bound	0.3924	0.2225	0.1232	0.0519	0.0800	0.0524	0.0274
Upper bound	1.0000	1.0000	0.7977	0.4668	1.0000	0.7977	0.4668
BM25	0.5636	0.4307	0.2631	0.1205	0.4303	0.2555	0.1174
Encoder-Decoder	0.6346	0.5124	0.3390	0.1657	0.5645	0.3672	0.1779
BSVM	0.5749	0.4465	0.2805	0.1302	0.4812	0.2732	0.1185
LLTR	0.6222	0.4843	0.3162	0.1551	0.5490	0.3522	0.1562

The results for MAP suggest that in 48% of the cases our system selects the answer with at least fair quality (2+), and in 15% of the cases the quality is excellent. For reference, Table 1 provides the performance of the TREC 2015 LiveQA winning system – Encoder-Decoder [18]. This approach is superior to LLTR, but we should note that our approach relies only on statistical text features. We do not use any semantical features and it leaves us a margin to improve our model in future. We believe that we can further improve the quality of the model by sanitizing the training dataset. Currently, two main problems are: (i) presence of

Table 2. Overall system quality results

Metric name	Jaccard			Cosine			KL divergence		
Question length (in tokens)	[0;10]	[11;32]	[33;)	[0;10]	[11;32]	[33;)	[0;10]	[11;32]	[33;)
Number of questions	134	152	148	134	152	148	134	152	148
BM25 QA system	0.05 ± 0.01	0.05 ± 0.01	0.06 ± 0.01	0.07 ± 0.01	0.08 ± 0.02	0.07 ± 0.01	0.43 ± 0.05	0.48 ± 0.05	0.44 ± 0.06
BSVM QA system	0.10 + 0.02	0.11 ± 0.02	0.12 ± 0.02	0.18 ± 0.03	0.20 ± 0.03	0.20 ± 0.03	0.59 ± 0.06	0.60 ± 0.05	0.62 ± 0.07
LLTR QA system	0.12 ± 0.02	0.11 ± 0.01	0.11 ± 0.02	0.23 ± 0.03	0.25 ± 0.02	0.25 ± 0.03	0.64 ± 0.04	0.65 ± 0.05	0.67 ± 0.06

words with misspellings which make computations of statistical features imprecise; (ii) quality of the best answers manually selected by voters. There exist a few approaches to diminish impact of both issues such as [7] for misspellings and [1] for keeping only high-quality answers.

Table 2 reports the overall system evaluation results where the similarity between the answer generated by our system and the assessed answers is computed. The presented results are also binned based on question-length, so as to analyze the effects of question-length on the system's performance. As compared to the baseline system (BM25-based QA system), both the versions of our system (with BSVM, and with LLTR), perform better. However, our system struggles with shorter questions. Indicating that the system is better at eliminating noise than it is with data sparsity. Although we might expect that longer questions will produce long conjunctive boolean queries that retrieve very few web pages, clearly that is not the case. The short questions are doubly hard because many of them are poorly worded (e.g. "What should I do?").

We should note that using the described similarity measures does not show the accurate picture. Two high-quality answers to a question may be expressed in different terms and may look different with regards to our metrics. For instance, none of the described metrics takes synonyms into account. This drawback is partially alleviated by fact that each of the questions in TREC dataset has several high-quality answers. It increases the probability of our answer partially matching at least one of the provided. The disadvantage of our metrics paves a way for using of contextual similarity, such as METEOR[8] or doc2vec[9] in future.

In Table 3 we present examples of the answers given by our system for some of the dataset questions. In some cases, such as a question about dog allergies the QA system produces more comprehensive answer than humans. Also, it is worth noting that the quality of the questions varies dramatically (e.g. questions about Windows 10 key lock) which is one of the big challenges for this problem.

[8] http://www.cs.cmu.edu/~alavie/METEOR/.
[9] https://radimrehurek.com/gensim/models/doc2vec.html.

Table 3. Answers returned by the System compared to Best Human Answers

---

Question: Can dogs be allergic to dust? And what are the symptoms?
System's Answer: Dogs with dust mite allergies can be misdiagnosed because the symptoms are very similar to other conditions. The scratching and inflammation may be mistaken for fleas, dry skin, or chronic dermatitis when it is actually the dust mite causing the reaction. Dust mites are microscopic organisms that live in every home no matter how much you clean. In fact, it is during or after vacuuming or dusting that the allergy seems to get much worse. The main difference between dust mite allergy and other causes of itchy skin (dermatitis, dry skin, fleas) is that with dust mite allergy your dog will also have sneezing, runny eyes and nose, a cough, and possible wheezing.
Best Human Answer: Yes. The symptoms might be sneezing, itchy ears, or red itchy skin.

Question: How do I change the background color in Windows10?
System's Answer: Select the Start symbol button, then select Settings > Personalization to choose a picture worthy of gracing your desktop background, and to change the accent color for Start, the taskbar, and other items. The preview window gives you a sneak peek of your changes as you make them. In Background, select a picture or solid color, or create a slideshow of pictures. In Colors, let Windows pull an accent color from your background, or choose your own color adventure. After you've selected an accent color, decide where you want to see it show up, and whether it looks better in a dark or light setting.
Best Human Answer: Change Desktop Background. How to change the Windows 10 desktop background. ... something that almost all of us will do when we create a new account.

Question: Any DPS in Dallas area that accepts walk-in and schedule road test on the same day?
System's Answer: Update on centers that accepts walk-in: The Mega Center in Fort Worth does not accept walk-in. The Hurst center do take walk-ins but you will have to get there between 6.30–7am. Getting there early does not guarantee you a spot however if they do have any spots open(same day) they will add you on the schedule but this opportunity is only available in morning so anything after the time stated above has a low chance of success. Rate this post positively.
Best Human Answer: After the state reduced the number of offices it is a very long wait if you walk in, so maybe or maybe not.

Question: Windows 10 key lock? Hello, I couldn't find help on google so I might as well ask here.
System's Answer: The Toggle Keys can emit a beep when the Lock keys are pressed. The Sticky Keys function can emit a beep when the Ctrl, Alt, Shift, and Lock keys are pressed. Use the following steps to disable Toggle Keys: 1. Type Ease into the Start Search field and select Ease of access from the populated list. 2. Scroll down the page and select Make the keyboard easier to use.
Best Human Answer: If you are still running a technical preview, that is not a release version of Windows. Hope you have a backup to revert to since that Windows 10 is not downgradable.

Question: How can I open up a win.dat file?
System's Answer: The best way to open a .DAT file is to use the program that created it. Obviously, that's easy if you knew which program created it, right? So how does one go about figuring this out? Well, there are a couple of ways. Firstly, you can try opening the file in something like Notepad. You should know that Notepad can open anything, even image and video files and display them as text.
Best Human Answer: Open with in notepad.

---

4 Conclusions and Future Work

In this paper we presented our attempt at tackling the challenging problem of answering open-domain non-factoid questions. The empirical evaluation illustrates that our simply but intuitive approach is on par with state-of-the-art system, and clearly better than the baseline. The qualitative evaluation shows that the system is capable of producing high-quality answers. To further improve our approach we are currently working on integrating neural network model with word2vec embeddings [10]. We also plan to investigate summarization techniques to transform questions to queries, and to generate more concise answers[10].

References

1. Agichtein, E., et al.: Finding high-quality content in social media. In: Proceedings of WSDM (2008)
2. Agichtein, E., et al.: Overview of the TREC 2015 LiveQA track. In: Proceedings of TREC (2015)
3. Bian, J., et al.: Finding the right facts in the crowd: factoid question answering over social media. In: Proceedings of WWW (2008)
4. Bobrow, D.G.: A question-answering system for high school algebra word problems. In: Proceedings of FJCC (1964)
5. Burges, C.: From ranknet to lambdarank to lambdamart: an overview. Learning **11**, 23–581 (2010)
6. Chen, D., Manning, C.: A fast and accurate dependency parser using neural networks. In: Proceedings of EMNLP (2014)
7. Chen, Q., Li, M., Zhou, M.: Improving query spelling correction using web search results. In: Proceedings of EMNLP-CoNLL (2007)
8. Green, C.: Theorem proving by resolution as a basis for question-answering systems. In: Machine Intelligence (1969)
9. Higashinaka, R., Isozaki, H.: Corpus-based question answering for why-questions. In: Proceedings of IJCNLP (2008)
10. Mikolov, T., et al.: Efficient estimation of word representations in vector space. In: Proceedings of ICLR (2013)
11. Oh, J.H., et al.: Why question answering using sentiment analysis and word classes. In: Proceedings of EMNLP-CoNLL (2012)
12. Soricut, R., Brill, E.: Automatic question answering using the web: beyond the factoid. Inf. Retrieval **9**, 191–206 (2006)
13. Surdeanu, M., Ciaramita, M., Zaragoza, H.: Learning to rank answers to non-factoid questions from web collections. Comput. Linguist. **37**, 351–383 (2011)
14. Suryanto, M.A., et al.: Quality-aware collaborative question answering: methods and evaluation. In: Proceedings of WSDM (2009)
15. Varanasi, S., Neumann, G.: Question/answer matching for Yahoo! Answers using a corpus-based extracted Ngram-based mapping. In: Proceedings of TREC (2015)

[10] https://research.googleblog.com/2016/08/text-summarization-with-tensorflow.html.

16. Waltz, D.L.: An English language question answering system for a large relational database. Commun. ACM **21**, 526–539 (1978)
17. Wang, D., Nyberg, E.: CMU OAQA at TREC 2015 LiveQA: discovering the right answer with clues. In: Proceedings of TREC (2015)
18. Wang, D., Nyberg, E.: CMU OAQA at TREC 2016 LiveQA: an attentional neural encoder-decoder approach for answer ranking. In: Proceedings of TREC (2016)

Multilingual Fine-Grained Entity Typing

Marieke van Erp(✉) and Piek Vossen

Computational Lexicology and Terminology Lab, The Network Institute,
Vrije Universiteit Amsterdam, Amsterdam, The Netherlands
{marieke.van.erp,piek.vossen}@vu.nl

Abstract. Many entity recognition approaches classify recognised entities into a limited set of coarse-grained entity types. However, for deeper natural language analysis and end-user tasks, fine-grained entity types are more useful. For example, while standard named entity recognition may determine that an entity is a person knowing whether that entity is a politician or an actor is important for determining whether, in a subsequent relation extraction task, a relation should be acts or governs. Currently, fine-grained entity typing has only been investigated for English. In this paper, we present a fine-grained entity typing system for Dutch and Spanish using training data extracted from Wikipedia and DBpedia. Our system achieves comparable performance to English with an F_1 measure of .90 on over 40 types for both Dutch and Spanish.

1 Introduction

Entity typing is the task of assigning types (also called classes) to previously recognised entity mentions in text. Traditionally, a limited set of types is employed (e.g. Person, Location, Organisation, Miscellaneous) [12] but for many NLP tasks more fine-grained types have been proven useful [16,23]. Fine-grained entity typing can support, coreference resolution, relation extraction, entity linking (e.g. distinguishing between Douglas Adams the author or the American Football Player) and dark entity classification (i.e. determining the class of those entities not described in a knowledge base). For English, the task of fine-grained entity typing has received some attention (cf. [3,5,9,24]), but to the best of our knowledge, other languages such as Spanish and Dutch have thus far not been addressed.

One of the main issues in fine-grained entity typing is noise in the training data, as training samples are usually generated automatically [5] by assigning Freebase types to entity mentions extracted from news or Wikipedia. [17] seek a solution to this problem by proposing a cleaning method. We mitigate this issue by choosing a more restrictive, but cleaner type hierarchy for generating our training samples, namely DBpedia [1].

In this paper, we present a distantly supervised approach to fine-grained entity typing for Dutch and Spanish based on Wikipedia and DBpedia. Our approach is inspired by [9] (further explained in Sect. 3) who also generate training data from Wikipedia, but instead of using Freebase types, we use the DBpedia

J. Gracia et al. (Eds.): LDK 2017, LNAI 10318, pp. 262–275, 2017.
DOI: 10.1007/978-3-319-59888-8_23

type hierarchy. There are three advantages to this: (1) as DBpedia is derived from Wikipedia, there is a direct link between the two sources leading directly to the entity type, and (2) DBpedia only assigns one type to an entity, thus leading to less noise in the training data, and (3) DBpedia contains language and cultural specific data that can be leveraged for training and testing. Furthermore, we are the first to employ the Fasttext algorithm [2,8] to the task of entity typing and to apply it to morphologically richer languages than English.

To compare our approach to previous work, we report results on a subset of DBpedia's 685 types mapped to the types reported on in [5]. As well as on the full DBpedia class hierarchy. Our code and experimental setup are available at https://github.com/cltl/multilingual-finegrained-entity-typing.

The contributions of this work are threefold:

1. state-of-the-art fine-grained entity typing models for Dutch and Spanish;
2. an extensible system for entity typing for other languages using Wikipedia and DBpedia; and
3. an analysis of the DBpedia entity type system for this task.

The remainder of this paper is organised as follows. In Sect. 2, we discuss related work. In Sect. 3, we detail our data preparation and algorithm used. In Sect. 4, our experiments and results are presented, followed by a discussion in Sect. 5. We conclude with conclusions and future work in Sect. 6.

2 Related Work

Entity recognition and classification (NERC) has been a long-standing and popular task in the natural language processing community [12]. However, most work has focused on a limited set of entity types, for example, four in the CoNLL NER campaigns (Person, Location, Organisation and Miscellaneous) [19] and seven main types in the ACE campaigns (Person, Organization, Location, Facility, Weapon, Vehicle and Geo-Political Entity) [10]. Several extensions to these were proposed such as hierarchy of 150 entity types [18] and unsupervised approaches that could infer new entity types from text [4,6,7,13]. The increase in external knowledge bases such as DBpedia and Freebase has allowed research into fine-grained entity typing gained to expand.

In the FIGER system [9], a two-level hierarchy consisting of 112 entity types is proposed. The training data is generated using Wikipedia, where the wikilink anchor text is extracted as an entity mention which map it to its corresponding Freebase entity types, following [15]. For each entity mention, a feature vector is generated that contains information about the entity tokens, the word shape (capitalisation patterns), part-of-speech tags, its length, and words before and after the entity mention. They then train a perceptron algorithm which is evaluated on a manually annotated test set of 18 articles taken from a student newspaper. Their system achieves an F_1 score of .70.

The FIGER hierarchy initially consisted of two levels, but was extended to three levels by [5]. They also use an automated method to generate training data but use news articles instead of Wikipedia. In follow-up work [24], their best system achieves an F_1 of .72 in classifying 86 entity types using an embedding method. The features used are loosely based on [9] and they evaluate on 77 manually annotated news articles from the OntoNotes corpus [20]. In the approach presented in [24], an embedding is learnt for each label and feature which allows for information sharing between labels.

The HYENA system [25] also employs Wikipedia to gather training data. They use a type hierarchy consisting of 505 types, up to 9 levels deep that is induced from YAGO[1] and WordNet.[2] For each type, an SVM classifier is trained, after which the results of the individual classifiers are put through a meta-classifier to define the final top-n types for an entity mention. Their system achieves a macro F_1 score of .93 on the 5 top-level types and .87 on the full 505 types.

Word embeddings and the FIGER hierarchy are also used by the FIGMENT system [21,22]. In this system, the 112 FIGER types are learnt through different character, word and entity level models using a training and test dataset generated from a web crawl. They also analyse their system's performance for dark entities, where they achieve an F_1 of around .51. Related to this is the PEARL system [14] which explicitly tries to detect entity types for emerging entities using integer linear programming (ILP). They use the YAGO2 type system, which is derived from WordNet.

The FINET system [3] generates training data from WordNet. Their system uses various patterns on parsed text to determine types. Their type system consists of more than 16,000 types, which are mapped to two other type system consisting of 505 and 200 types to determine the first three levels in the type hierarchy (coarse-grained types, fine-grained types and super fine-grained types).

In Table 1 we summarise the characteristics of previous approaches to fine-grained entity typing.

Table 1. Characteristics of previous approaches to fine-grained entity typing.

System	Type system	# Types	Depth	Global/Contextual	Approach	Training data
FIGER	Freebase	112	2	Global	Perceptron	Wikipedia
FINET	WordNet	1,000+	9	Contextual	Patterns	WordNet
FIGMENT	Freebase	86	3	Both	Embeddings	Websites
GFT	Freebase	86	3	Contextual	Embeddings	News
HYENA	YAGO	505	9	Contextual	SVM	Wikipedia
PEARL	YAGO2	NA	NA	Contextual	ILP	News
Hovy 2014 [7]	Induced	1,000+	NA	Contextual	HMM	News

[1] https://www.mpi-inf.mpg.de/departments/databases-and-information-systems/research/yago-naga/yago/.

[2] https://wordnet.princeton.edu/.

An important distinction to be made is whether the system is aimed at global entity typing or contextual entity typing. In global entity typing, multiple types can be assigned to an entity. This is generally used to generate entity type information for knowledge bases where the goal is to describe an entity in the most detailed fashion possible. In contextual entity typing, usually fewer types are assigned, and the goal is to decide for a particular sentence what entity type is meant. FIGER and [5] are aimed at global entity typing, FINET at contextual typing and FIGMENT can do both.

However, none of these systems has been applied to languages other than English.

3 System Description

In Fig. 1, a systematic overview is given of our system. As in [9], we generate labelled training instances from Wikipedia, but where they gather the entity types from Freebase, we use the DBpedia type system to obtain associated types for each entity. Then, feature vectors are generated that contain information about the word shape of the entity and its context (a detailed overview of the features is given in Table 2) which is used to train a model. The model is then applied to a new instance, for which it is to predict a type. In the remainder of this section, each step is explained in more detail.

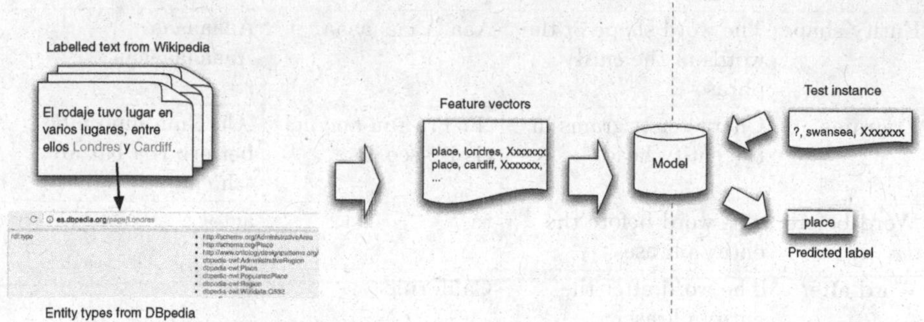

Fig. 1. System overview

3.1 Data Preparation

We use the Dutch and Spanish 2017-02-01 Wikipedia XML dumps.[3] The text was extracted from each dump using the Wikiextractor tool[4] while preserving the wikilinks. For each wikilink, we extract the anchor as our entity mention,

[3] https://dumps.wikimedia.org/backup-index.html.
[4] https://github.com/attardi/wikiextractor.

and we look up the corresponding DBpedia type through a Wikipedia-DBpedia mapping.[5]

There are three main reasons for using the DBpedia type hierarchy: (1) we presume that a single type per entity results in cleaner training data, (2) whilst some other type hierarchies such as yago, umbel and schema.org are well connected to the English DBpedia, they are less commonly used in the Dutch and Spanish DBpedias, limiting their use to generate training examples from such data, (3) as DBpedia is derived from Wikipedia, there is a direct link through which the entity type can be retrieved.

For each entity, we generate a feature vector containing the mention, the head, and some context, following [5]. We leave out the dependency and topic related features due to processing constraints. A sample of the features for both Dutch and Spanish is presented in Table 2.

Table 2. Description of the extracted features.

Feature	Description	Dutch example	Spanish example
Mention	The entity phrase	San Francisco	Benedict Cumberbatch
Head	The syntactic head of the entity phrase	Francisco	Cumberbatch
Non-head	The non-head tokens in the entity phrase	San	Benedict
Entity shape	The word shape of the words in the entity phrase	Aaa Aaaaaaaaa	Aaaaaaaa Aaaaaaaaaaa
Trigrams	Character trigrams in the entity head	_Fr Fra ran anc nci cis isc sco co_	_Cu Cum umb mbe ber erb rba bat atc tch ch_
Word before	The word before the entity phrase	te	actor
Word after	The word after the entity phrase	Californië	fue

To compare our results to those in previous work, we mapped the DBpedia type hierarchy to the entity typing hierarchy used in [5,24]. Out of the 86 types that were present, 9 types could not be mapped to the DBpedia type hierarchy.[6]

[5] Using the wikilinks and instance types dumps from the latest DBpedia, version 2016-04 http://wiki.dbpedia.org/downloads-2016-04.

[6] The types we could not map were the following: `location/structure/government`, `organization/stock_exchange`, `other/health`, `other/living_thing`, `other/product/car`, `other/product/computer`, `person/education`, `person/education/student`, `person/education/teacher`.

To check the mappings, we compared some of the entity mentions and their types from the GFT dataset [5] to entity mentions and their respective DBpedia types.

As there are currently no fine-grained entity type gold standard datasets available for Dutch and Spanish, we split the generated data into training and test sets by random stratified sampling, i.e. in both the training and test sets the class distribution is proportionally equal. We chose the test sample as 1/3 of the total dataset. In Table 3, we present some statistics of our datasets. On average, each entity mention occurs about 5 times in the Spanish dataset and about 7 times in the Dutch dataset.[7]

Table 3. Dataset statistics

	Dutch		Spanish	
	Instances	Unique mentions	Instances	Unique mentions
Training GFT types	1,011,810	143,793	561,249	104,174
Test GFT types	498,355	93,735	276,437	69,137
Training DBpedia types	2,088,381	256,502	1,066,644	209,653
Test DBpedia types	1,028,607	166,001	525,363	138,482

3.2 Model Construction

We use the fastText [2,8][8] algorithm in our classification experiments. The fastText algorithm is a linear algorithm inspired by the word2vec cbow model [11] that utilises a hierarchical softmax function to speed up computations as it represents more frequent classes in the dataset at a lower depth than more infrequent ones. Representations are learnt for character n-grams, and words are represented as the sum of the n-gram vectors, which helps in covering morphologically rich languages, words that do not occur often and potentially entity mentions that do not occur in the training corpus. As in the algorithm used by [24], fastText can share information between features, which can be particularly useful for classes with few examples.

4 Experiments and Results

We ran two sets of experiments for each language: in the first, we only take the GFT types into account, in the second, we consider all DBpedia types present in our datasets.

[7] Although there is more text in the Spanish DBpedia, we only included a sample here to showcase the adaptability of the approach to other languages.

[8] https://github.com/facebookresearch/fastText.

4.1 GFT Types

There are some differences between our setup and the setup of [5,24]. First, their gold standard dataset is manually labelled and entities can contain multiple labels, which, if they follow [5] are separated into different instances.[9]

We only assign a single type to an entity, and we take a sample from the automatically generated data from Wikipedia for testing. The single type per entity premise does mean that we do not generate global type information for entities (i.e. multiple types per entity which would be useful for knowledge base creation), but we do only focus on the 'main' type of an entity according to our training dataset. How much this overlaps with the contextual types that are generated in [5,24] can only be investigated with a gold standard dataset for Dutch and Spanish. [24] report a micro-averaged F_1 of 72.98 for their best system using 86 fine-grained types.

In Table 4, we present our scores per level of depth in the hierarchy. The results for the coarse-grained entity types (depth 1) are near perfect, reaching scores in the high 90s, but the fine-grained (depth 2) and super fine-grained (depth 3) are also quite high.[10] Not all GFT types are covered in our datasets. We could determine various causes for this. The first is that the type information in the Dutch and Spanish DBpedias seems to be less extensive than for the English DBpedia, and the types file only contains the most specific entity type assigned to a resource, not its supertypes. We will delve deeper into these issues in Sect. 5.

Table 4. Macro-averaged Precision (P), Recall (R) and F_1 scores

Types	Dutch			Spanish		
	P	R	F_1	P	R	F_1
1 (4 types)	.98	.98	.98	.97	.97	.97
2 (33/24 types)	.92	.90	.91	.91	.90	.90
3 (24/20 types)	.89	.91	.90	.87	.90	.88
Overall (59/41 types)	.93	.88	.90	.92	.88	.90
Only dark entities (59/41 types)	.67	.56	.60	.74	.63	.66
All DBpedia types overall (269/143 types)	.68	.52	.57	.83	.75	.78
All DBpedia types only dark entities (266/143 types)	.50	.41	.44	.44	.37	.39

Whilst the test set is a separate set that is held out from the training set, some entity mentions may overlap between the two, for example for popular entities that occur with a high frequency in Wikipedia. To gain an insight into how our

[9] If an entity X has types `location/structure` and `organisation/education` assigned to it, two instances are generated namely X, `location/structure` and X, `organisation/education`.

[10] The number of types from levels 1–3 do not add up to the total number of types as some of the higher level types are not present on their own, such as `other`.

approach performs on unknown, or dark, entities, we removed all entity mentions from the test set that also occurred in the training dataset and evaluated our models on only those. This results in an F_1 score of .60 for Dutch and .66 for Spanish. This does leave major room for improvement, but these results are a bit higher than those reported for dark entities in [21] (F_1.51). Furthermore, it is unlikely that all entities in a task are unknown.

Table 5 in the Appendix presents the results of our system per class for Dutch and Spanish. The results in this table highlights differences in the type distribution between Dutch and Spanish, and ensuing differences in performance (cf. `other/art/stage`). For most types, despite there not being that much training data, the performance is still quite reasonable. The performance on `person/doctor`, for example, is quite reasonable with an F_1 score of .81, but other types seem much less well defined (for example `person/legal` for which more training examples were available). Further analysis of the entity types is needed to determine how this could be improved.

4.2 DBpedia Types

As the training data contains more types than those defined in the GFT hierarchy, we also ran an experiment using those types. In total, the DBpedia ontology contains 685 types, but these were not all present in our data. Upon inspecting the Dutch DBpedia types file, we found that only 274 types are present there. For Spanish, we only find 147 in the DBpedia types file. One reason for this is that the typing file only contains the most specific type that is assigned to an instance, for example for http://nl.dbpedia.org/resource/Old_Amsterdam, the most specific type is `cheese`, but the mapping only goes only to its parent node `Food`. Furthermore, the Dutch and Spanish DBpedias are less likely to report on entities of type `AustralianRulesFootballPlayer` or `NationalCollegiateAthleticAssociationAthlete`.

The last two rows of Table 4 presents the results of the DBpedia types experiments. The first DBpedia results row is on the full test set, the second reports results only on the dark entities. For Spanish, the experiments with the DBpedia types still perform quite well, but for Dutch they drop dramatically compared to the experiments using the GFT types. This can partially be explained by the fact that for Dutch there are twice as many types in the dataset, making the typing problem more complex. The drop is less steep for the dark entities for Dutch though, indicating that the approach somehow captures information about unknown entities better for Dutch than for Spanish.

5 Discussion

Whilst the results, in particular for the smaller GFT hierarchy, are comparable to English, there is room for improvement on typing using more extended hierarchies such as the DBpedia type hierarchy. In this section, we discuss causes for the lower scores using the DBpedia typing and possible solutions.

Dataset Extension

As mentioned in the previous section, the DBpedia entity types file only lists the most specific type for a given entity. The availability of this file allows for quick adaptation to another language without having to download the entire DBpedia version, but it does have limitations in that its coverage is lower. In future work, we aim to investigate including more super- and sub-types in generating the training and test samples to increase the coverage of types.

DBpedia has other type information available besides the DBpedia type hierarchy. We chose to utilise the DBpedia type hierarchy because each DBpedia resource has only one set of types possible subtypes assigned to it. For example, `dbpedia:Arnold_Schwarzenegger`[11] has only `dbo:Agent`[12] `dbo:Person` `dbo:OfficeHolder` assigned through the DBpedia type hierarchy, for which we would choose the most specific type to include in our training data. The 108 yago[13] type categories assigned to him vary from `Actor` to `BodyBuilder` to `Emigrant` and `Traveler`. Whilst this does provide a richer representation of the entity, it may also introduce additional noise in the training dataset as the majority of `dbo:OfficeHolders` are not (former) body builders or actors.

If our approach is applied to running text instead of Wikipedia, the system could apply different types per document or mention. Nevertheless, it is better to use clear cases with single types for training and allow multiple types for applying/testing, either per data set or per document/mention.

Coverage of Types

The type information in the Spanish DBpedia dataset is less complete than for the Dutch and English DBpedias. This holds in particular if we look at the number of DBpedia types associated with each instance. Upon analysing the instance_type dumps from DBpedia 2016-04, we find that only 80.92% of the Spanish DBpedia instances have a DBpedia type associated with them versus 96.70% of the Dutch DBpedia instances. The coverage of the latter is similar to the English DBpedia (95.72%). But both Spanish and Dutch DBpedia datasets have fewer types associated with them than the English DBpedia. If we compare for example the English http://dbpedia.org/resource/San_Francisco,

[11] `dbpedia:` is shorthand for http://dbpedia.org/resource.

[12] `dbo:` is shorthand for http://dbpedia.org/ontology/.

[13] http://www.mpi-inf.mpg.de/departments/databases-and-information-systems/research/yago-naga/yago/downloads/.

then there are in total 45 types assigned, of which 30 come from yago, 4 from umbel, 2 from schema.org, 2 from wikidata, 1 from w3c Basic Geo Vocabulary and 6 from the DBpedia ontology (including the top level node `owl:Thing`). The Dutch http://nl.dbpedia.org/resource/San_Francisco has 11 types associated with it in total, of which 7 are from the DBpedia ontology, 2 from schema.org types and two from wikidata. The Spanish http://es.dbpedia.org/resource/San_Francisco_(California) has nine types associated with it, 4 from the DBpedia hierarchy, 2 from schema.org, 1 from ontologydesignpatterns and one from Open Geospatial Consortium. The resource http://es.dbpedia.org/resource/Europa only has `skos:Concept` associated with it as its type. This limits the number of different type hierarchies that can be exploited for training a type classifier and the number of instances that can be included. However, we are looking into leveraging the type information in the English DBpedia and its links to other language DBpedias to experiment with different type hierarchies.

6 Conclusion and Future Work

We have presented a system and experiments for fine-grained entity typing for Dutch and Spanish. We show that our system performs comparable to systems presented previously for English. Furthermore, our approach is easily extensible to other languages for which Wikipedia and DBpedias exist. The trained models, as well as the code to extend the approach to other languages are available from GitHub.

Whilst using DBpedia as the typing system is a strength of the system in that it provides us with high quality typing information, it also has its limitations, in particular when certain types are not or insufficiently referenced in the dataset. We observe that the DBpedia types are better covered in the English DBpedia (which is no surprise as the type hierarchy was originally developed for English) and we intend to leverage this to provide DBpedia types to Dutch and Spanish entities that lack these.

Furthermore, we found that certain entity types used in prior work such as `car` and `person/education` have no equivalent in the DBpedia hierarchy. We therefore aim to experiment with different entity type hierarchies, whilst still preserving our 'clean' approach to generating training samples. This is particular interesting for domain-specific applications in which certain types that are less well defined in the current DBpedia hierarchy are more important.

Looking further, we aim to develop our system so that it can expand to hundreds of entity types in tens of languages.

Acknowledgements. The research for this paper was made possible by the CLARIAH-CORE project financed by NWO.

Appendix A: Results

Table 5. Precision, recall and F_1 scores on the overall datasets (macro-averaged) and per class.

Type	Dutch				Spanish			
	P	R	F_1	# instances	P	R	F_1	# instances
location/celestial	.99	.98	.98	1,895	.98	.93	.95	690
location/city	.98	.99	.99	179,919	.95	.98	.96	35,036
location/country	.99	.99	.99	142,240	.99	.99	.99	79,091
location/geography/island	.93	.84	.88	5,310	.94	.92	.93	3,473
location/geography/mountain	.97	.90	.93	2,940	.92	.83	.87	832
location/park	.94	.87	.91	253	.94	.89	.91	453
location/structure	.92	.88	.90	1,693	.92	.86	.89	1148
location/structure/airport	.96	.87	.91	575	.97	.85	.91	459
location/structure/hotel	.86	.83	.84	46	.79	.71	.75	31
location/structure/restaurant	.83	.42	.56	60	-	-	-	-
location/structure/sports_facility	.96	.72	.83	36	-	-	-	-
location/transit/bridge	.95	.92	.94	460	.97	.89	.93	149
location/transit/railway	.96	.96	.96	2,100	-	-	-	-
location/transit/road	.99	.98	.99	2,392	.93	.97	.95	286
organization	.98	.96	.97	1,895	.96	.96	.96	13,308
organization/company	.97	.96	.97	9,529	.94	.80	.86	55
organization/company/broadcast	.99	.99	.99	1,975	-	-	-	-
organization/company/news	.98	.98	.98	1,316	.97	.97	.97	2,058
organization/government	.97	.98	.97	419	-	-	-	-
organization/military	.98	.97	.97	1,025	-	-	-	-
organization/political_party	.98	.97	.97	2,714	.98	.97	.98	5,149
organization/sports_league	.99	.99	.99	1,485	-	-	-	-
organization/sports_team	.97	.87	.92	39	-	-	-	-
organization/transit	.97	.94	.96	1,285	-	-	-	-
other/art	-	-	-	-	.63	.70	.66	90
other/art/broadcast	.95	.93	.94	6,071	.91	.88	.89	5,972
other/art/film	.91	.86	.89	4,697	.81	.79	.80	4,637
other/art/music	.87	.66	.75	304	1.00	.56	.71	27
other/art/stage	.50	.20	.29	5	.88	.75	.81	838
other/art/writing	1.00	.91	.95	57	-	-	-	-
other/award	.93	.97	.95	70	.97	.97	.97	1,321
other/body_part	.95	.96	.96	1,298	-	-	-	-
other/currency	.98	.96	.97	898	.98	.91	.94	583
other/event	.92	.87	.90	305	-	-	-	-
other/event/election	.97	.98	.98	1,092	-	-	-	-
other/event/holiday	-	-	-	-	.94	.93	.94	665
other/event/protest	.97	.93	.95	61	-	-	-	-
other/event/sports_event	1.00	.98	.99	1,493	-	-	-	-
other/event/violent_conflict	.99	.98	.99	15,128	.97	.96	.97	9,238
other/health/malady	.98	.98	.98	4,964	.95	.97	.96	4,197
other/heritage	.90	.85	.88	2,167	-	-	-	-

(continued)

Table 5. (*continued*)

Type	Dutch				Spanish			
	P	R	F_1	# instances	P	R	F_1	# instances
other/internet	.97	.94	.95	891	.99	.97	.98	1,693
other/language	.98	.98	.98	25,781	.96	.96	.96	12,227
other/language/programming_ language	-	-	-	-	.91	.84	.88	186
other/legal	.99	.92	.95	148	-	-	-	-
other/living_thing/animal	-	-	-	-	.95	.89	.92	650
other/product	.96	.89	.93	76	-	-	-	-
other/product/software	.96	.94	.95	1,881	.91	.88	.89	1,022
other/religion	1.00	.99	.99	1,491	-	-	-	-
other/product/weapon	-	-	-	-	.92	.83	.87	471
other/scientific	.94	.90	.92	3,012	.90	.86	.88	4,512
other/sports_and_leisure	.99	.99	.99	6,696	1.00	1.00	1.00	5,082
other/supernatural	.89	.86	.87	1,947	.88	.87	.87	4,497
person	.90	.90	.90	10,821	.86	.86	.86	14,818
person/artist	.93	.88	.90	3,712	.90	.81	.85	2,723
person/artist/actor	.87	.87	.87	6,985	.89	.92	.90	18,428
person/artist/author	.93	.93	.93	6,538	.92	.89	.91	7,534
person/artist/music	.91	.93	.92	15,308	.91	.92	.92	24,234
person/athlete	.77	.73	.75	2,961	.80	.76	.78	6,544
person/doctor	1.00	.60	.75	10	-	-	-	-
person/legal	.31	.31	.31	36	-	-	-	-
person/political_figure	.89	.87	.88	5,088	-	-	-	-
person/title	.96	.94	.95	4,500	-	-	-	-
person/religious_leader	-	-	-	-	.96	.92	.94	2,030
Total	.94	.87	.90	498,355	.92	.88	.90	276,437

References

1. Bizer, C., Lehmann, J., Kobilarov, G., Auer, S., Becker, C., Cyganiak, R., Hellmann, S.: DBpedia - a crystallization point for the web of data. Web Semant. Sci. Serv. Agents World Wide Web **7**(3), 154–165 (2009)
2. Bojanowski, P., Grave, E., Joulin, A., Mikolov, T.: Enriching word vectors with subword information. Technical report, Archiv (2016). https://arxiv.org/abs/1607.04606
3. Corro, L.D., Abujabal, A., Gemulla, R., Weikum, G.: FINET: context-aware fine-grained named entity typing. In: Proceedings of the 2015 Conference on Empirical Methods in Natural Language Processing, Lisbon, Portugal, 17–21 September 2015, pp. 868–878 (2015)
4. Ekbal, A., Sourjikova, E., Frank, A., Ponzetto, S.P.: Assessing the challenge of fine-grained named entity recognition and classification. In: Proceedings of the 2010 Named Entities Workshop at ACL 2010, Uppsala, Sweden, July 2010, pp. 93–101 (2010)
5. Gillick, D., Lazic, N., Ganchev, K., Kirchner, J., Huynh, D.: Context-dependent fine-grained entity type tagging. arXiv (2014)
6. Giuliano, C.: Fine-grained classification of named entities exploiting latent semantic Kernels. In: Proceedings of the Thirteenth Conference on Computational Natural Language Learning, CNLL, Boulder, Colorado, USA, pp. 201–209 (2009)

7. Hovy, D.: How well can we learn interpretable entity types from text? In: Proceedings of the 52nd Annual Meeting of the Association for Computational Linguistics (Short papers), Baltimore, Maryland, USA, 23–25 June 2014, pp. 482–487. Association for Computational Linguistics (2014)
8. Joulin, A., Grave, E., Bojanowski, P., Mikolov, T.: Bag of tricks for efficient text classification. Technical report, arXiv (2016). https://arxiv.org/abs/1607.01759
9. Ling, X., Weld, D.S.: Fine-grained entity recognition. In: AAAI (2012)
10. Linguistic Data Consortium: ACE (automatic content extraction) english annotation guidelines for entities. Technical report, Linguistic Data Consortium, version 5.6.6 2006.08.01 (2006)
11. Mikolov, T., Chen, K., Corrado, G., Dean, J.: Efficient estimation of word representations in vector space. arXiv preprint arXiv:1301.3781 (2013)
12. Nadeau, D., Sekine, S.: A survey of named entity recognition and classification. Lingvisticae Investigationes **30**(1), 3–26 (2007)
13. Nadeau, D., Turney, P.D., Matwin, S.: Unsupervised named-entity recognition: generating gazetteers and resolving ambiguity. In: Lamontagne, L., Marchand, M. (eds.) AI 2006. LNCS, vol. 4013, pp. 266–277. Springer, Heidelberg (2006). doi:10.1007/11766247_23
14. Nakashole, N., Tylenda, T., Weikum, G.: Fine-grained semantic typing of emerging entities. In: Proceedings of the 51st Annual Meeting of the Association for Computational Linguistics, Sofia, Bulgaria, 4–9 August 2013, pp. 1488–1497. Association for Computational Linguistics (2013)
15. Nothman, J., Curran, J., Murphy, T.: Transforming wikipedia into named entity training data. In: Proceedings of the Australasian Language Technology Association Workshop, pp. 124–132 (2008)
16. Recasens, M., de Marneffe, M.C., Potts, C.: The life and death of discourse entities: identifying singleton mentions. In: Proceedings of NAACL (2013)
17. Ren, X., He, W., Qu, M., Hang, L., Ji, H., Han, J.: AFET: automatic fine-grained entity typing by hierarchical partial-label embedding. In: Proceedings of the 2016 Conference on Empirical Methods in Natural Language Processing (EMNLP), Austin, TX, USA, 1–5 November 2016
18. Sekine, S., Sudo, K., Nobata, C.: Extended named entity hierarchy. In: LREC (2002)
19. Tjong Kim Sang, E.F., De Meulder, F.: Introduction to the CoNLL-2003 shared task: language-independent named entity recognition. In: Proceedings of the Seventh Conference on Natural Language Learning at HLT-NAACL 2003, vol. 4, pp. 142–147. Association for Computational Linguistics (2003)
20. Weischedel, R., Hovy, E., Marcus, M., Palmer, M., Belvin, R., Pradhan, S., Ramshaw, L., Xue, N.: Ontonotes: a large training corpus for enhanced processing. In: Olive, J., Christianson, C., McCary, J. (eds.) Handbook of Natural Language Processing and Machine Translation: DARPA Global Autonomous Language Exploitation, pp. 54–63. Springer, New York (2011)
21. Yaghoobzadeh, Y., Schütze, H.: Corpus-level fine-grained entity typing using contextual information. In: Proceedings of the 2015 Conference on Empirical Methods in Natural Language Processing, Lisbon, Portugal, 17–21 September 2015, pp. 715–725. Association for Computational Linguistics (2015)
22. Yaghoobzadeh, Y., Schütze, H.: Multi-level representations for fine-grained typing of knowledge base entities. In: Proceedings of the European Chapter of the Association for Computational Linguistics (EACL), 3–7 April 2017. https://arxiv.org/abs/1701.02025 (2017, to appear)

23. Yao, L., Riedel, S., McCallum, A.: Collective cross-document relation extraction without labelled data. In: Proceedings of EMNLP (2010)
24. Yogatama, D., Gillick, D., Lazic, N.: Embedding methods for fine grained entity type classification. In: Proceedings of the 53rd Annual Meeting of the Association for Computational Linguistics and the 7th International Joint Conference on Natural Language Processing (ACL-IJCNLP 2015), Short papers, Bejing, China, 26–31 July 2015, pp. 291–296. Association for Computational Linguistics (2015)
25. Yosef, M.A., Bauer, S., Hoffart, J., Spaniol, M., Weikum, G.: HYENA: hierarchical types classification for entity names. In: Proceedings of COLING 2012: Posters, Mumbai, India, December 2012, pp. 1361–1370 (2012)

AATOS – A Configurable Tool for Automatic Annotation

Minna Tamper[1,2](✉), Petri Leskinen[1,2], Esko Ikkala[1,2], Arttu Oksanen[1,2], Eetu Mäkelä[1,2], Erkki Heino[1,2], Jouni Tuominen[1,2], Mikko Koho[1,2], and Eero Hyvönen[1,2]

[1] Semantic Computing Research Group (SeCo), Aalto University, Espoo, Finland
{minna.tamper,petri.leskinen,esko.ikkala,arttu.oksanen,eetu.makela, erkki.heino,jouni.tuominen,mikko.koho,eero.hyvonen}@aalto.fi

[2] HELDIG – Helsinki Centre for Digital Humanities, University of Helsinki, Helsinki, Finland
http://seco.cs.aalto.fi, http://heldig.fi

Abstract. This paper presents an automatic annotation tool AATOS for providing documents with semantic annotations. The tool links entities found from the texts to ontologies defined by the user. The application is highly configurable and can be used with different natural language Finnish texts. The application was developed as a part of the WarSampo (http://seco.cs.aalto.fi/projects/sotasampo/en/) and Semantic Finlex (http://seco.cs.aalto.fi/projects/lawlod/en/) projects and tested using Kansa Taisteli magazine articles and consolidated Finnish legislation of Semantic Finlex. The quality of the automatic annotation was evaluated by measuring precision and recall against existing manual annotations. The results showed that the quality of the input text, as well as the selection and configuration of the ontologies impacted the results.

1 Introduction

Document databases are explored by users on a daily basis. The databases can be searched for different documents but it can be difficult to obtain satisfactory results easily. To improve the search results, search engines can utilize document metadata that contains descriptive keywords among other descriptive data about the document [4]. One way to enrich document metadata is by using Semantic Web technologies where relevant keywords would be identified from each document and linked to existing controlled vocabularies, giving the keywords semantic meanings. In the context of the Semantic Web this can be also called annotating.

Manually annotating or subject indexing each document is, however, laborious, costly, and time consuming work [3,15]. On the other hand, this is not a simple task for the computer either. Identification of terms from texts by extracting words can be inefficient and inaccurate. One word can mean many things. For example, it might be difficult to distinguish whether a word refers for

J. Gracia et al. (Eds.): LDK 2017, LNAI 10318, pp. 276–289, 2017.
DOI: 10.1007/978-3-319-59888-8_24

example a person's name or a place. Futhermore, a referring expression may consist of multiple words; it can be difficult to identify a term if different chunks of words form a term separately and together. These tasks would require dedicated algorithms and possibly domain specific information extraction (IE) methods combined with Natural Language Processing (NLP) approach to identify terms with satisfactory precision.

This paper presents a generic tool for automatic annotation that has been developed as part of the WarSampo and Semantic Finlex projects in the Semantic Computing Research Group (SeCo)[1]. The tool is used to annotate Finnish documents and is tested in two use cases: Kansa Taisteli magazine articles and the consolidated legislation of Semantic Finlex[2]. Kansa Taisteli magazine articles can be searched and explored in the WarSampo portal, which models the Second World War in Finland as Linked Open Data (LOD) [12]. Kansa Taisteli is a magazine published by Sanoma Ltd and Sotamuisto association between 1957 and 1986 [24]. The magazine articles cover the memoirs of WW2 from the point of view of Finnish military personnel and civilians. Semantic Finlex, on the other hand, is a service that offers the Finnish legislation and case law as Linked Open Data [7]. The results of the annotation process for both projects have been published in the Linked Data Finland service[3] [13].

2 The Annotation Model

Due to the monotonous and costly nature of manual annotation, it is important to design annotation tools where the annotation process can be performed as swiftly as possible. The entrance barrier to annotation can be lowered with a generic annotation tool because it would reduce development costs and preparatory work [26].

One example of an automatic annotation system is the DBpedia Spotlight service[4]. DBpedia Spotlight is an open source service that recognizes DBpedia resources in natural language text. It is a solution to linking unstructured information sources to the Linked Open Data cloud [6]. In a generic automatic annotation tool, the text can ideally be linked to multiple ontologies. In addition to linking documents, the application needs to be able to select the best describing keywords for a document. This is not a simple task and it needs natural language processing methods in addition to linking text correctly to ontologies.

In natural language processing, *named entity linking (NEL)* [2,9] is the task of determining the identity of named entities mentioned in a text, by linking found named entity mentions to strongly identified entries in a structured knowledge base. In general, NEL consists of *named entity recognition (NER)*, followed by *named entity disambiguation (NED)* [9,16]. NER [8,20] recognizes the occurrence or mention of a named entity (e.g., people's names, organizations, locations) in a

[1] http://seco.cs.aalto.fi.
[2] http://data.finlex.fi.
[3] http://www.ldf.fi.
[4] https://github.com/dbpedia-spotlight/dbpedia-spotlight/wiki/Introduction.

text and NED [2,5,25] identifies which specific entity it is. A further refinement to this formulation is suggested by Hachey et al. [9], which divides NEL into *extraction*, *searching* and *disambiguation* steps.

The automatic annotation tool (AATOS)[5] presented in this paper has been designed by taking into consideration the use cases and the background of the field. In order to annotate Finnish texts, it requires specific tools designed for the Finnish language. In addition to the NLP approach, it needs to identify relevant concepts and named entities and link them to controlled vocabularies with matching terms. Based on both of the requirements mentioned, a general model for annotation has been created and implemented using Python.

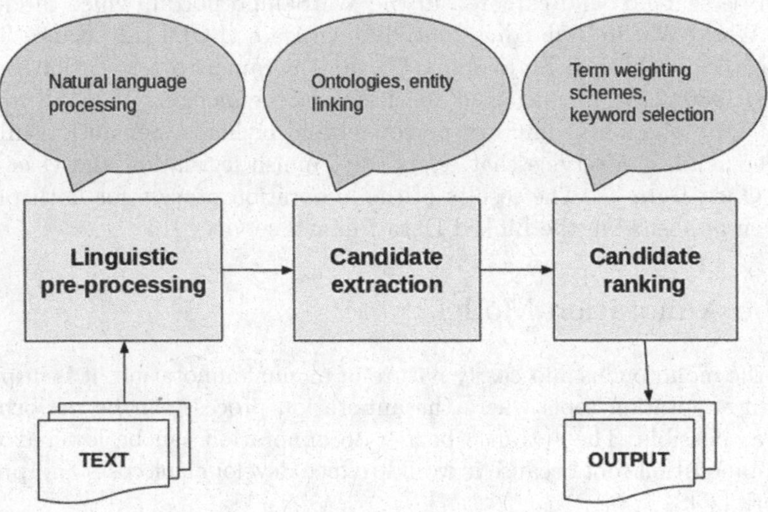

Fig. 1. Model of annotation.

As shown in Fig. 1, AATOS consists of the following components or phases: (1) linguistic preprocessing, (2) candidate extraction, and (3) candidate ranking. These components process the input in the given order and produce an output.

The application needs by default its input in text format. It is possible to give the input in HTML format and the application is able to extract all text from the body element to use as an input. The user needs to define input and output formats, their locations (URL or file path), file extensions, an output file, and possible a source file in RDF format that can be populated with the results. The input text is written in a natural language that can be processed using linguistic tools and methods. The linguistic preprocessing transforms words on the textual data into their base form (lemma), and extracts textual entities that can be linked to ontologies in the next phase. The candidate extraction component, given vocabularies, can link the text with other resources and identify

[5] https://github.com/SemanticComputing/aatos.

keyword candidates to create more accurate descriptions of the documents. For these purposes the SPARQL ARPA tool can be used. ARPA is a configurable automatic annotation tool that uses LAS (Lexical Analysis Services), SPARQL, and ontologies to identify entities from a text document, and in return gives suggestions for annotating texts [18].

In order to use ARPA the user needs to define ARPA configurations file that can be given to the annotation tool from command line. Each ARPA configuration is defined separately and the set of configurations are shown in Table 1. The tool executes the given ARPA configurations and produces a list of concepts (URI references). Disambiguation strategies are utilized to identify the best concepts from the result list (Primary, Second, Third) and they can be used to identify the best property for linking. In addition, the list can be filtered to contain only the most frequent terms. A stop word list can be used to remove terms that the user is not interested in. Such terms could be terms in documents that do not describe the content but give structure to it such as form labels like name, address, and country.

Table 1. ARPA specific configuration options for AATOS.

#	Configuration name	Values	Description
1	Name	Text	Name of the ARPA query or ontology
2	URL	URL	URL to the ARPA query
3	Map Property Type	URL	Map results to a given property
4	Map Graph	URL	Map results to a given graph
5	Frequency Limit	Number	Lowest accepted term frequency
6	Stop Word List	File name	File that contains a list of used stop words
7	Ranked	True/false	Set ranking on/off
8	Top N	Number	If ranking is on, this setting can be used to create a top n listing of keywords per document
9	Primary	URL	Disambiguation strategy: the best target property for linking
10	Second	URL	Disambiguation strategy: 2nd best target property for linking
11	Third	URL	Disambiguation strategy: 3rd best target property for linking

In the last phase, the application has acquired the linked data and the keyword candidates. The data and the text are analyzed to determine which keyword candidates are useful in describing the content and to function as keywords for the given document. For this purpose, term relevance and different weighting schemes are required. Using weights, the extracted candidates can be ranked and the top candidates picked. In addition, the application has support for keyword density calibrations and it allows the user to pick top n candidates.

The user can define whether to limit or a range for the keywords in the ontology configurations.

Finally, the application needs to produce an output after the candidate selection. The output contains the results in a user specified format such as RDF or CSV that can be defined in the tool configuration.

3 Use Case 1: Kansa Taisteli Magazine Articles

The first case for automatic annotation is the Kansa Taisteli magazine articles. The magazine articles are publicly available in PDF format via a website of The Association for Military History in Finland[6] in collaboration with Bonnier Publishing.

The magazine articles were accompanied with manually collected metadata for 3,385 articles [24]. The metadata contains information regarding the article (author, title, issue, volume, and pages) in addition to annotations describing the content (war, arms of service, a military unit, place, and comments). The articles can be browsed according to their metadata via a faceted search demo application[7]. The metadata is available at the WarSampo data service[8].

3.1 Extraction of Text

In order to perform automatic annotation for the Kansa Taisteli magazine articles, AATOS requires the articles in text format. For extracting texts from the PDF files, two tools were used: ABBYY FineReader[9] and Tesseract[10].

During the evaluation of the OCR tools, it was noted that Tesseract consistently produced solid results that contained a few errors. ABBYY FineReader, on the other hand, seemed to fare better with the Finnish texts as the error rates were much lower than with Tesseract. However, during testing it was noted that, unlike with Tesseract, ABBYY seems to mix up paragraphs for unidentified reasons. Therefore, it was decided that both tools needed to be used to get the best results from the OCR process. Both tools would be used to extract text and the results would be combined.

The process of combining the results was semiautomatic, using both, comparing the results, and merging them into one result in the end. In addition, occasionally some errors (such as problems with paragraphs) needed to be fixed manually. The preprocessing and post-processing of the articles was laborious and could not eliminate all the errors. Therefore only a small sample of 433 articles was annotated for evaluation. From each decade a year was selected randomly and all magazine issues of that year were selected for processing.

6 http://kansataisteli.sshs.fi.
7 http://www.ldf.fi/dataset/kata/faceted-search/.
8 http://www.ldf.fi/dataset/warsa.
9 http://www.abbyy.com.
10 https://github.com/tesseract-ocr.

3.2 Automatic Annotation Process

In order to annotate the articles, AATOS requires a set of ontologies and their configuration in the ARPA annotation service. The chosen ontologies come from the WarSampo project: people, military units, Karelian places, and municipalities. External ontologies, such as KOKO ontology and DBpedia, were also used to enrich the annotations with more general concepts. The order of ontologies impacts the annotations and aids in disambiguation; the first ontologies match most of the terms from their vocabularies and this can impact the ability to match terms into other ontologies. In this case the order of ontologies was the following: people, military units, Karelian places and municipalities, DBpedia, and lastly the KOKO[11] ontology.

The ARPA tool configurations[12] for military unit, DBpedia, and KOKO ontologies included the filtering of forenames and surnames. In place ontologies the filtering of forenames and surnames cannot be used because Finnish names for places and villages are similar to surnames [17], such as "Kestilä" which can be a name of a place or to a person's surname. The military personnel (people) ontology had the highest N-Gram (5) in order to include a full name and a title whereas others had a lower n-gram length (2 to 3) to target words and open compound words.

In place ontology configurations, places such as water formations and buildings were ignored and only villages, towns, and municipalities were targeted for linking. In most cases most of the smaller places are never mentioned in the Kansa Taisteli articles. Often times a village may be carrying the same name as a building or a lake. Therefore, it was seen as useful to rule out all but municipalities, towns, and villages to minimize confusion. All ontologies include extraction of terms that have been POS tagged as nouns or proper nouns, base forming of the words and setting the default language to Finnish. Nouns and proper nouns were selected as keyword candidates because nouns are preferred parts of speech for terms [1]. In addition, selected ontologies mainly have the terms in the form of nouns (e.g., the KOKO ontology) [22] and proper nouns (e.g., the ontologies of the WarSampo project).

For the Kansa Taisteli magazine articles, the application was configured to produce the output in Turtle format and add the annotations into their corresponding properties. These properties are defined in the configuration along with the output format and target file. In the case Kansa Taisteli magazine articles, all found and linked annotations were added into the dataset without candidate filtering based on term relevancy.

3.3 Evaluation

The automatic annotation results were evaluated by calculating precision, recall, and F-measure for 50 randomly selected articles. The evaluation is laborious

[11] https://finto.fi/koko/en/.
[12] https://github.com/SemanticComputing/aatos-arpa-configurations.

and therefore not all 433 articles could be used. In contrast to original manual annotations, the results were richer. This also became visible when calculating and inspecting the precision and recall results.

The measures were calculated by comparing the automatic annotations with the original manual annotations. In addition, three different executions of the application for three different sets of inputs that have been produced by the OCR process: untouched OCR output text from the Tesseract OCR tool, automatically fixed text using regular expression patterns, and semi-automatically fixed text. The automatically fixed text utilizes the regular expression created while combining the results of two OCR tools. The regular expression patterns were created based on systematic and frequently occurring OCR errors. For example, a military unit name in inflected form *JR 35:n* contains a colon that was often transformed into i or z in the OCR output.

In addition to comparing these different versions of the articles, different annotation methods were used to calculate the precision and recall: exact matches (method 1), accepting also direct meronyms (method 2), and all correctly linked terms (method 3). Method 1 accepts only the exact matches of terms. In method 2, exact matches and meronyms are also counted as positive matches because original annotations sometimes use municipalities instead of villages that are part of the municipality. For example, sometimes in the manual annotations the articles have been annotated with specific municipalities. For example, the text itself may mention the villages of that municipality and they were counted as positive matches for the municipality in method 2. In method 1, the villages are negative matches and only the municipality is a positive match. In addition, a third method was also used to calculate the measures in comparison to what is found from the article texts. It interprets all correctly extracted and linked matches as true positives.

The difference between the results of unfixed, automatically fixed, and semi-automatically fixed results, shown in Tables 2, 3, and 4, are notable. Depending on the method the results vary. The precision is poor for all but method 3. The precision for methods 1 and 2 depends on the interpretation of original annotations and their correctness. Whereas the method 3 measures how well the mentioned military units and places were found and linked correctly from the article texts.

Table 2. Evaluation of the annotations produced from the unfixed Tesseract output of Kansa Taisteli magazine articles. P is the precision, R is the recall, and F is the F-measure.

	Method 1		Method 2		Method 3	
	M. units	Places	M. units	Places	M. units	Places
P	26.14%	6.78%	30.26%	10.47%	82.02%	61.69%
R	69.70%	38.46%	67.65%	51.92%	54.89%	44.28%
F	38.02%	11.53%	41.82%	17.42%	65.77%	51.56%

Table 3. Evaluation of the annotations produced from the automatically fixed Kansa Taisteli magazine articles. P is the precision, R is the recall, and F is the F-measure.

	Method 1		Method 2		Method 3	
	M. units	Places	M. units	Places	M. units	Places
P	25.26%	6.78%	30.38%	10.47%	79.17%	61.69%
R	72.73%	38.46%	72.73%	51.92%	57.14%	44.28%
F	37.50%	11.53%	42.86%	17.42%	66.38%	51.56%

Table 4. Evaluation of the annotations produced from the semi-automatically fixed Kansa Taisteli magazine articles.

	Method 1		Method 2		Method 3	
	M. units	Places	M. units	Places	M. units	Places
P	25.77%	6.80%	30.77%	10.55%	80.61%	61.82%
R	75.76%	38.46%	75.00%	51.92%	59.40%	44.42%
F	38.46%	11.56%	43.64%	17.53%	68.40%	51.69%

The difference between precision and recall for places and military units is notable. The precision is lower for the places mainly because of the regular expression fixes concentrating on military units. In comparison to a study by Kettunen et al. [14], AATOS produces similar results. It performed somewhat better in finding correct matches. OCR post-processing had a positive impact on the results and it is visible that the recall was impacted by the amount of OCR post-processing, especially in the case of military units. However, the military unit results are weighted down by a few remaining irregular OCR errors whereas the issue. The issues that impacted the linking of places are presented in Table 5.

Table 5. The breakdown of the error types found when the place annotations for semi-automatically texts were analyzed.

#	Error type	Amount	Percentage
1	Wrong place	32	12.12%
2	Ambiguous	14	5.30%
3	Confusion between places and people's names	16	6.06%
4	Noise from other articles	9	3.41%
5	Clutter (for example advertisements)	7	2.65%
6	ARPA/LAS error	1	0.38%
7	Misidentified POS	9	3.41%
	Total	88	36.07%

The errors encountered can be divided into three groups: firstly, the most numerous category is that of disambiguation errors, further divided based on if they arise from ambiguity in the place data itself, or from the extractor confusing the people's names' with place names. The second category contains errors arising from the faulty article segmentation in the magazine data. Finally, there are errors relating to the tool itself, arising for example from faulty inflection handling or incorrect part of speech filtering. From these results it is apparent that more robust disambiguation of the places would be needed. Luckily, this is a well-researched area, so ready choices for this are available for future work, e.g. [10,11,21].

3.4 Application: Semantic Search and Recommending

The purpose of the faceted search application[13] is to help a user to find Kansa Taisteli articles and to provide context to the found articles by showing links to related WarSampo data. Contextual Reader (CORE) [19] was integrated into the application, to highlight found concepts and offering additional information about them, when viewing the PDF format article.

The updated Kansa Taisteli magazine article perspective is shown in Fig. 2. In the perspective, the user can find articles by using the author, magazine, a related place, army units, or mentioned terms facets. The facet will show a list of mentioned terms and names that can be used to filter the article list. The mentioned terms facet adds diversity into the article search. By adding the mentions of terms and names as a facet into the web application, the user can find articles that contain certain terms, army units, people, or places. For example, a user can search for articles that mention a person or the term *lice*.

Fig. 2. The faceted search browser targeting the Kansa Taisteli magazine articles.

[13] http://sotasampo.fi/articles.

4 Use Case 2: Semantic Finlex

Semantic Finlex is a service that offers the Finnish legislation and case law as Linked Open Data. The purpose of automatic annotation in the Semantic Finlex project was to make it easier to read, find, and browse statutes and case laws. To achieve this, the metadata had to be enriched by linking it to ontologies [7]. The goal of automatic annotation is to describe the contents of each document accurately and plentifully using keywords.

4.1 Automatic Annotation Process

The ontologies used for the law documents were: Combined Legal Concept Ontology, Original Finlex Vocabulary (FinlexVoc), EuroVoc[14] ontology, KOKO ontology, and Finnish DBpedia. The general ARPA configurations for all cases included the filtering out all but nouns and proper nouns and base forming of terms, and the default language is set to Finnish. The typical n-gram length for these ontologies is set to 3. The SPARQL query is set to exclude numbers and the length of the terms is calculated to enable the selecting of the longest match for the terms. For example, when linking the text *European Union* the ARPA can find, depending on the ontology, matches such as *Europe* and *European Union*. It is important that the tool picks the longest option out of the two as it is the correct one and therefore it was implemented into the application.

In the EuroVoc ontology, the used SPARQL query was set to match strings into synonyms to maximize the amount of found links. In addition, the Combined Legal Concept Ontology, EuroVoc, FinlexVoc, DBpedia, and KOKO ontologies are set to target only Finnish terminology. Also, DBpedia is restricted to law terminology in SPARQL and the matches to category names or properties are ignored whereas KOKO ontology targets general-purpose terminology.

The results were set to be filtered based on the relevancy of the concept to the text. The application was set to produce the results in RDF format and to add selected annotations (based on the linked ontology) into their corresponding properties. The unidentified textual entities are filtered out respectively.

The initial results, however, were not satisfactory as there were problems with word recognition and ambiguity. A stopword list was required to filter out the most common terms such as *article*, *Finland* or *law*. The need to add term relevancy analysis or weighing schemes arose, as the purpose of the task is to identify the relevant concepts and not all named entities like in the Kansa Taisteli case. In the annotation process, a simple TF-IDF measure was used to rank each term found in the text.

4.2 Evaluation

The annotation process was executed for 2,803 law documents. The evaluation of AATOS was done by using the R-precision measure. R-precision expresses the

[14] http://eurovoc.europa.eu/.

precision for the top n keywords where n is the number of keywords in the original annotations. In order to measure the R-precision of the annotation for the law documents, AATOS was configured to use the same controlled vocabulary FinlexVoc with the same keyword density that was used in the original material. After the automatic annotation, 30 documents were selected randomly and their keywords compared with the original annotations.

The calculations for R-precision were done by selecting the same amount of keywords from the automatically produced keywords as in the original keywords and comparing them. The keywords from the annotation tool result set were selected by picking the keywords that were evaluated by the weighting scheme as the most relevant to the document. The R-precision result is equal to the precision and recall measures when the amount of keywords for both sets used in the calculations is the same. The result of the R-precision calculation is 45.45% for this result set.

The low amount of keywords in the original annotations has impacted the result of the R-precision calculations. For example, sometimes a keyword was found by the annotation tool but it was evaluated not relevant enough for the document. If the amount of keywords for a document would have been 5 instead of 1 in the original annotations, the keyword would have been included in the list of generated keywords. The results are, however, similar but not fully comparable to the results of Sinkkilä et al. [23] for different Finnish texts. AATOS performed well in contrast to the tools and strategies used in the study. The precision and recall are higher than the produced precision 27.00% and recall 24.40% using TF-IDF, FDG[15] and other tools by the earlier study by Sinkkilä et al.

Table 6. Error types found from the result set of the Semantic Finlex.

#	Error type	Amount	Percentage
1	Keyword found but evaluated not relevant enough	20	29.85%
2	Keywords not found in the document	14	20.90%
3	Configuration error (language detection)	1	1.49%
4	Source material error	1	1.49%
5	Tool error	1	1.49%
	Total	37	55.22%

The evaluation results are presented in Table 6. The encountered errors can be divided into three groups: firstly, the most numerous category is that of low keyword relevancy. The second category contains configuration errors, tool errors, or errors related to the source materials. From these results it is apparent that more robust method of evaluation for the keywords would be needed.

[15] http://www.connexor.com.

5 Conclusions, Discussion, and Future Work

This paper presents a new highly configurable and generic tool for annotating and subject indexing documents. It can be configured in multiple ways to produce semantic annotations for different Finnish texts. It links textual entities to matching concepts in controlled vocabularies of the user's choice and produces output in RDF and CSV formats. For subject indexing, the application supports adding different evaluation methods such as TF-IDF that was added into the application during the project. It also supports multiple ways to define keyword density.

This paper presented two use cases for AATOS: Kansa Taisteli magazine articles and Semantic Finlex. In both cases the success of the tool depended on the interpretation of the results. Compared with a human annotator the tool provides a richer amount of annotations.

Disambiguation of the annotations proved to be a challenging task. The selection and the order of ontologies can be used to remove ambiguity. For example, in Kansa Taisteli magazine articles the issue was approached by prioritizing the context specific ontologies. In addition, there are ontology specific configurations for determining if some concepts are better than others and need to be prioritized. These actions helped to minimize the amount of issues regarding the ambiguity of terms. In case Kansa Taisteli, there remain challenges such as differentiating between places with the same names, last names, and place names.

The OCR quality impacted the results for Kansa Taisteli magazine articles. A semi-automatic handling of the results was required and as a byproduct a list of regular expressions was constructed to aid in the correction of the errors. During the evaluation it was noticed that the post-processing of the OCR output improved the annotations and prevented erroneous annotations. However, there is still a need for improvement and further developing an automatic set of rules could speed up the process of post-processing of OCR output.

In case Semantic Finlex, the challenge was the estimation of relevancy and keyword density. It would be interesting to try other strategies for selecting the keyword amount. In addition, a few new terms should be added to the stopword list to see how it would impact the results. All this is fine-tuning of the application configurations. In general, the application manages to produce satisfactory results.

In addition to improvements mentioned above, the application can benefit from future development. It requires more fine-tuning and optimization. In order to utilize the application more efficiently it needs to be possible to run as a compact command line tool. Also a graphical user interface could be useful for the users and for testing purposes. In addition to these improvements, large scale testing is needed.

Acknowledgements. Our work was funded by the Ministry of Education and Culture and Finnish Cultural Foundation and Ministry of Justice. The Association for Military History in Finland and Bonnier Publications provided the project with resources and published the Kansa Taisteli magazine articles for public usage. Kasper Apajalahti originally converted the metadata into an RDF format. Timo Hakala provided the manual annotations for the Kansa Taisteli magazine articles.

References

1. Anderson, J.D.: Guidelines for Indexes and Related Information Retrieval Devices. NISO Press, Bethesda (1997)
2. Bunescu, R.C., Pasca, M.: Using encyclopedic knowledge for named entity disambiguation. EACL **6**, 9–16 (2006)
3. Chung, Y.M., Pottenger, W.M., Schatz, B.R.: Automatic subject indexing using an associative neural network. In: Proceedings of the Third ACM Conference on Digital Libraries, pp. 59–68. ACM (1998)
4. Committee on Cataloging: Task force on metadata. Final report. Technical report, June 2000. http://libraries.psu.edu/tas/jca/ccda/tf-meta6.html
5. Cucerzan, S.: Large-scale named entity disambiguation based on Wikipedia data. In: EMNLP-CoNLL, vol. 7, pp. 708–716 (2007)
6. Daiber, J., Jakob, M., Hokamp, C., Mendes, P.N.: Improving efficiency and accuracy in multilingual entity extraction. In: Proceedings of the 9th International Conference on Semantic Systems (I-Semantics) (2013)
7. Frosterus, M., Tuominen, J., Hyvönen, E.: Facilitating re-use of legal data in applications - finnish law as a linked open data service. In: Proceedings of the 27th International Conference on Legal Knowledge and Information Systems (JURIX 2014), pp. 115–124. IOS Press, December 2014
8. Grishman, R., Sundheim, B.: Message understanding conference-6: a brief history. In: Coling, vol. 96, pp. 466–471 (1996)
9. Hachey, B., Radford, W., Nothman, J., Honnibal, M., Curran, J.R.: Evaluating entity linking with Wikipedia. Artif. Intell. **194**, 130–150 (2013). http://dx.doi.org/10.1016/j.artint.2012.04.005
10. Hoffart, J., Yosef, M.A., Bordino, I., Fürstenau, H., Pinkal, M., Spaniol, M., Taneva, B., Thater, S., Weikum, G.: Robust disambiguation of named entities in text. In: Proceedings of the Conference on Empirical Methods in Natural Language Processing, EMNLP 2011 pp. 782–792. Association for Computational Linguistics, Stroudsburg (2011). http://dl.acm.org/citation.cfm?id=2145432.2145521
11. Hu, Y., Janowicz, K., Prasad, S.: Improving Wikipedia-based place name disambiguation in short texts using structured data from DBpedia. In: Proceedings of the 8th Workshop on Geographic Information Retrieval, GIR 2014, pp. 8:1–8:8. ACM, New York (2014). http://doi.acm.org/10.1145/2675354.2675356
12. Hyvönen, E., Heino, E., Leskinen, P., Ikkala, E., Koho, M., Tamper, M., Tuominen, J., Mäkelä, E.: WarSampo data service and semantic portal for publishing linked open data about the second world war history. In: Sack, H., Blomqvist, E., d'Aquin, M., Ghidini, C., Ponzetto, S.P., Lange, C. (eds.) ESWC 2016. LNCS, vol. 9678, pp. 758–773. Springer, Cham (2016). doi:10.1007/978-3-319-34129-3_46
13. Hyvönen, E., Tuominen, J., Alonen, M., Mäkelä, E.: Linked data Finland: a 7-star model and platform for publishing and re-using linked datasets. In: Presutti, V., Blomqvist, E., Troncy, R., Sack, H., Papadakis, I., Tordai, A. (eds.) ESWC 2014. LNCS, vol. 8798, pp. 226–230. Springer, Cham (2014). doi:10.1007/978-3-319-11955-7_24
14. Kettunen, K., Kunttu, T., Järvelin, K.: To stem or lemmatize a highly inflectional language in a probabilistic IR environment? J. Doc. **61**(4), 476–496 (2005)

15. Lauser, B., Hotho, A.: Automatic multi-label subject indexing in a multilingual environment. In: Koch, T., Sølvberg, I.T. (eds.) ECDL 2003. LNCS, vol. 2769, pp. 140–151. Springer, Heidelberg (2003). doi:10.1007/978-3-540-45175-4_14
16. Mendes, P.N., Jakob, M., García-Silva, A., Bizer, C.: Dbpedia spotlight: shedding light on the web of documents. In: Proceedings of the 7th International Conference on Semantic Systems, pp. 1–8. ACM (2011)
17. Mikkonen, P., Paikkala, S.: Sukunimet. Otavan kirjapaino Oy (2000)
18. Mäkelä, E.: Combining a REST lexical analysis web service with SPARQL for mashup semantic annotation from text. In: Presutti, V., Blomqvist, E., Troncy, R., Sack, H., Papadakis, I., Tordai, A. (eds.) ESWC 2014. LNCS, vol. 8798, pp. 424–428. Springer, Cham (2014). doi:10.1007/978-3-319-11955-7_60
19. Mäkelä, E., Lindquist, T., Hyvönen, E.: CORE - a contextual reader based on linked data. In: Proceedings of Digital Humanities 2016, Long Papers, pp. 267–269, July 2016. http://dh2016.adho.org/abstracts/2580
20. Nadeau, D., Sekine, S.: A survey of named entity recognition and classification. Lingvisticae Investigationes **30**(1), 3–26 (2007)
21. Overell, S., Rüger, S.: Using co-occurrence models for placename disambiguation. Int. J. Geogr. Inf. Sci. **22**(3), 265–287 (2008)
22. SFS 5471: Guidelines for the establisment and maintenance of Finnish language thesauri. SFS standard. Finnish Standards Association (1988)
23. Sinkkilä, R., Suominen, O., Hyvönen, E.: Automatic semantic subject indexing of web documents in highly inflected languages. In: Antoniou, G., Grobelnik, M., Simperl, E., Parsia, B., Plexousakis, D., Leenheer, P., Pan, J. (eds.) ESWC 2011. LNCS, vol. 6643, pp. 215–229. Springer, Heidelberg (2011). doi:10.1007/978-3-642-21034-1_15
24. The Association for Military History in Finland: Kansa taisteli magazines 1957–1986 (2014). http://www.sshs.fi/sitenews/view/-/nid/92/ngid/1
25. Wentland, W., Knopp, J., Silberer, C., Hartung, M.: Building a multilingual lexical resource for named entity disambiguation, translation and transliteration. In: Proceedings of the Sixth International Conference on Language Resources and Evaluation (LREC 2008). European Language Resources Association (ELRA), Marrakech, May 2008. http://www.lrec-conf.org/proceedings/lrec2008/
26. Yimam, S.M., Biemann, C., Eckart de Castilho, R., Gurevych, I.: Automatic annotation suggestions and custom annotation layers in WebAnno. In: Proceedings of 52nd Annual Meeting of the Association for Computational Linguistics: System Demonstrations, pp. 91–96. Association for Computational Linguistics, Baltimore, June 2014. https://www.aclweb.org/anthology/P/P14/pp.14-5016.pdf

Deep Text Generation – Using Hierarchical Decomposition to Mitigate the Effect of Rare Data Points

Nina Dethlefs(✉) and Alexander Turner

School of Engineering and Computer Science, University of Hull,
Cottingham Road, Hull HU7 6RX, UK
{n.dethlefs,alexander.turner}@hull.ac.uk

Abstract. Deep learning has recently been adopted for the task of natural language generation (NLG) and shown remarkable results. However, learning can go awry when the input dataset is too small or not well balanced with regards to the examples it contains for various input sequences. This is relevant to naturally occurring datasets such as many that were not prepared for the task of natural language processing but scraped off the web and originally prepared for a different purpose. As a mitigation to the problem of unbalanced training data, we therefore propose to decompose a large natural language dataset into several subsets that "talk about" the same thing. We show that the decomposition helps to focus each learner's attention during training. Results from a proof-of-concept study show 73% times faster learning over a flat model and better results.

Keywords: Artificial intelligence · Natural language processing · Deep learning

1 Introduction

Language data for almost all domains can be scraped off the web with relative ease and in large quantities. As more data becomes available, research is needed into methods that facilitate access to this data, including the generation of natural language text from non-linguistic data input. Many NLG techniques are available to generate high-quality outputs from annotated datasets [6,8,13,23], aligned corpora [1,12] or annotated databases [11,19]. More work is also done recently on generating language from unaligned input data [5,16], where it is the learner's task to work out the mapping between non-linguistic data points and sequences of words. Nonetheless, most state-of-the-art techniques in statistical NLG still do not readily transfer to language datasets that were scraped off the web and are unaligned and thus in some respects "messy".

The most promising method for such messy tasks is probably deep learning. Recurrent neural networks (RNNs) have made important advances in natural language processing, including NLG. Results have been particularly impressive

J. Gracia et al. (Eds.): LDK 2017, LNAI 10318, pp. 290–298, 2017.
DOI: 10.1007/978-3-319-59888-8_25

for deep learning models that are trained from large datasets and that contain a well-balanced distribution of the linguistic target phenomena. For applications in NLG, the sequence-to-sequence encoder-decoder model by [9,24] has been shown to successfully learn to map an input sequence $\mathbf{x}$ of symbolic inputs, such as any form of non-linguistic data, to an output sequence $\mathbf{y}$ of words expressing the data in natural language. Again however, this technique works best when a sufficiently large, and well-balanced, dataset is available. For many natural language processing tasks, datasets are smaller due to the time and effort involved in preparing them. In such cases, it can be challenging to learn good feature representations. This is the problem we focus on in this short paper.

We present an approach that decomposes a large NLG task into a set of subtasks, each of which can be represented by an individual neural network that focuses on a subset of the training data. The idea is to automatically identify partitions of the training data that focus on the same semantics. Intuitively, the words and syntactic phrases used to forecast "rain" might be different from those used to forecast "wind"—even though overlaps are possible. Our idea is that focusing on a subset of relevant training instances will help a deep learning agent perform better on infrequent data points that would otherwise "get lost" in the large input dataset in a flat learning setup. Experiments in the weather forecast domain show that our approach substantially increases performance on outputs that occur infrequently in the dataset. We find that the divide-and-conquer approach is also much faster to train and achieves higher than state-of-the-art performance in a comparison with previous work.

2 Background

The sequence-to-sequence model that underlies much work on deep learning for NLG was first presented by [4,20], who use an RNN Encoder-Decoder model to learn a mapping from an input sequence to an output sequence for machine translation. By training both models jointly, a mapping from the source to the target language is learnt. This model was first applied to NLG by [24], who use an LSTM to do sentence planning and surface realisation in an application to information-seeking dialogue, and show that their model outperforms other approaches to the same domain. [9] apply a similar model to generate output sequences alongside dependency trees, and show that additional benefits can be gained from the use of an attention mechanism during training.

The idea of learning a direct mapping from inputs to outputs without intermediate annotation is related to work on NLG from unaligned datasets. Two popular approaches to do this are the use of parallel corpora or annotated databases. [1] define the generation process as a sequence of hierarchically-organised local decisions, and [11] generate language from weighted hypergraphs.

A practical limitation of deep learning algorithms is that they rely on large datasets to learn good representations. This can be problematic in domains like NLG or other NLP tasks that rely on a paired set of inputs and outputs—which are not available in large quantities. Previous work on hierarchical reinforcement

Algorithm 1. Finding a hierarchy.

function FINDSUBTASKS(forecast texts f, alignments a, weather events e) **return** *subtasks*
  subtasks = list []
  for each sentence s in f **do**
    Get alignments a_s with weather events e_s
    event_combination = the types of all weather events expressed in s as identified from alignments a
    if *event_combination* is **not** in *subtasks* **then**
      add *event_combination* to *subtasks* as an object with input and output examples
    end if
  end for
  for each element in subtasks **do**
    Create a separate subtask (neural net).
  end for
end function

learning for NLG has shown that when using a divide-and-conquer approach to decompose a complex task into a hierarchical set of subtasks, it becomes feasible to solve the problem in a scalable way without significant loss in performance [7]. Similar results have been observed for the hierarchical decomposition of neural language models [15].

3 Deep learning model

A neural network, such as a *multi-layer perceptron*, learns a hidden representation $\mathbf{h}$ of an input sequence $\mathbf{x} = (x_1, \ldots, x_N)$ by learning an increasingly abstract encoding of the inputs, and a mapping from $\mathbf{h}$ to either a single output (for classification tasks) or an output sequence $\mathbf{y} = (y_1, \ldots, y_M)$ (in a sequence-to-sequence learning task). The hidden representation $\mathbf{h}$ can be computed as $\mathbf{h} = f(x)$, where f is an activation function, such as sigmoid, tangent or relu. During training, the goal is to minimise the loss L between the input and output, e.g. using cross entropy.

In a *recurrent neural net*, we follow the same procedure, except that $\mathbf{h}$ is learnt as an increasingly abstract representation through recursive updates at each time step t: $\mathbf{h}_t = f(\mathbf{h}_{t-1}, x_t)$. As conventional RNNs are associated with the problem of vanishing or exploding gradients [3], we use an LSTM and follow the definition of [10].

4 Data and Learning Task

As we aim mainly for a proof-of-concept study in this paper, we will focus our experiments on a single domain: weather forecast generation. We use the

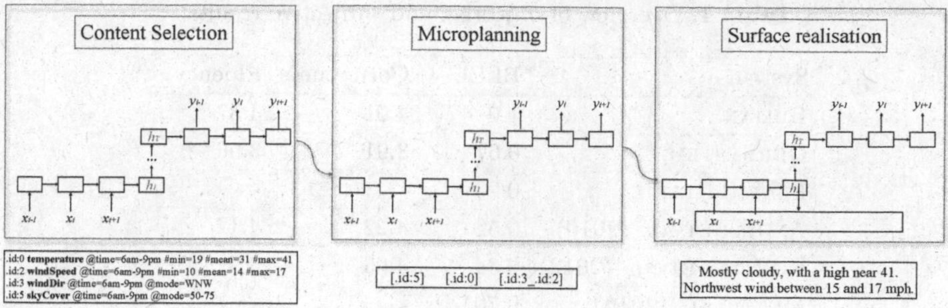

Fig. 1. Illustration of the NLG task as a pipeline [18]: *content selection* decides which weather events to include in the forecast; *microplanning* produces an ordered list of these events, and *surface realisation* produces a string of words. Example representations are shown for each stage.

WEATHERGOV dataset from [12], which contains 29,528 weather scenarios. It contains 12 different weather events, such as *temperature*, *skyCover*, etc. We use this existing dataset for ease of availability and also to allow for a comparison of our model's performance with previous work on the same dataset. Given that the dataset was originally collected from the web[1], we argue that our technique will be transferable to other such collected datasets. Future work will endeavour to demonstrate this.

Each of the weather events can be seen as a collection of lexical-syntactic constructions that describe the same semantic concepts. In other words, we can identify a subset of words and syntactic phrases that are reused in the datasets to describe a certain group of weather events. However, not all weather events map neatly onto a single sentence. Instead, we find cases of sentences that express more than one weather record and we find weather records that get described across multiple sentences.

4.1 Hierarchical Decomposition

Algorithm 1 shows the heuristics we used to identify a hierarchy of weather events from [12]'s WEATHERGOV dataset, which provides alignments between weather events and sentences. From these alignments, it is possible find out exactly which weather events are expressed in which sentence. To find a hierarchy, we loop over each sentence in the human forecasts, find the weather events that it expresses and create one generation subtask for each unique combination of aggregated weather events. This led to 22 subtasks overall, which can be seen as subtasks of a single large task "weather forecast".

Subtask generators can be seen as sentence generators that are associated with their own portion of the dataset including input examples (weather events) and output examples (word sequences). To generate a forecast, we obtain individual sentences from their respective generators and then concatenate them into a single text.

[1] http://www.weather.gov/.

Table 1. Overview of objective and subjective results.

System	BLEU-4	Correctness	Fluency
HUMAN	1.0	4.01	4.37
OURSYSTEM	0.67	3.91	3.96[a]
FLAT BASELINE	0.23	-	-
ANGELI ET AL. (2010)	0.52	4.22	4.12
KONSTAS ET AL. (2012)	0.34	4.03	3.92
MEI ET AL. (2016)	0.70	-	-

[a]indicates statistically different from HUMAN using a 2-tailed Wilcoxon signed-rank test.

4.2 Natural Language Generation Tasks

Figure 1 shows our NLG pipeline with the representations used at each stage. The outputs of each generation stage are fed as inputs to the next stage. This is important in order not to generate fragmented and isolated sequences of words but a coherent output text. The first stage, *content selection* decides for each weather record whether it should be included in the final forecast or not. We learn a binary classification value: 1 if the record is used in the forecast and 0 if it is not used. An LSTM with 2 layers and 20 hidden units does not find this task very challenging and achieves an accuracy of 98% for WEATHERGOV after 100 training epochs. All events chosen for inclusion at the content selection stage are passed on to the *microplanning* module in the second stage. The aim of this stage is to rank and order the weather events that were selected for inclusion. Part of this problem is also to decide whether to present weather events individually in a single sentence or to aggregate several events into the same sentence. We treated the microplanning task as a sequence-to-sequence learning task, e.g. [.id:0, .id:2, .id:3, .id:5] is mapped to [.id:5 .id:0 .id:3_.id:2] in Fig. 1, representing a new order of events and the fact that .id:3 and .id:2 should be aggregated into one sentence. We train an LSTM with 4 layers and 20 hidden units for 2000 epochs, and obtained an accuracy of 87% for WEATHERGOV. The *surface realisation* stage finally is also implemented as an LSTM with 4 layers and 50 hidden units. The input sequence corresponds to an ordered set of non-linguistic measurements $\mathbf{x} = (x_1, \ldots, x_N)$, and the output sequence is a sequence of words $\mathbf{y} = (y_1, \ldots, y_M)$. All models are trained with 32 batches over 2,000 epochs. To facilitate training, we use a `BOS` and an `EOS` symbol to denote the beginning and end of a sequence. All results use the same data split as previous work [1,11]: 25,000 for training, 1,000 for validation and 3,528 for testing.

5 Experiments and Evaluation

Our experiments evaluate the final outputs generated by the generator illustrated in Fig. 1. A future evaluation could investigate the errors made at individual generation stages and quantify their contribution to the overall objective and subjective assessment; see Table 1. In this paper, we focus on evaluating the overall output quality.

5.1 Objective Evaluation

Table 1 (left) shows results in terms of the BLEU modified precision score [17] measuring similarity with human examples. We compare against a human upper-bound and previous work on the same domain by [1,11,14]. Our system reaches higher BLEU scores than the former two studies, 22% and 49%, respectively, but a slightly lower score than [14], 4.3%. Table 2 shows an example of one of our generated forecasts and a human equivalent. We chose to present a non-perfect example, as the type of error shown is representative for our system's outputs. The LSTM policy learns the correct word sequences and mappings from semantic inputs, but occasionally duplicates phrases. We were able to train our hierarchical model in 45 h on a GPU (Tesla K40)—73% faster than we observed for a flat setup.

Table 2. Generated example outputs.

	Generated output
Human	A 30% chance of showers and thunderstorms after noon. Mostly cloudy, with a high near 69. South wind between 10 and 20 mph, with gusts as high as 30 mph
WeatherGov	A 30% chance of showers and thunderstorms after noon. Mostly cloudy, Mostly cloudy, with a high near 69. With a south wind 10 to 20 mph, with gusts as high as 30 mph

We also present results from a flat baseline model that learns from the whole training set without hierarchical decomposition. This model skips the steps shown in Fig. 1 and maps (the redundant set of) weather records directly to words. As can be seen in Table 1, the results are not strong. We believe that this is due to some examples being too rare in the training data in the flat case for the LSTM to learn good representations for them. For example, while *temperature* occurs in over 90% of weather forecasts across both datasets, *snow* occurs in only 1%, thus "getting lost" in the training data in the flat setup. Given the low BLEU score (and manual inspection) we decided not to evaluate the flat model with human raters.

5.2 Subjective Evaluation

Table 1 (right) shows results from a human rating study. To allow for a comparison with previous work, we asked human raters the same questions as [1,11]: "Does the meaning conveyed by the text correspond to the database input?" to determine *semantic correctness* and "Is the text grammatical and overall understandable?" to determine *English fluency*. *Semantic correctness* is evaluated on a 1–5 scale with values mapping to "perfect", "near perfect", "minor errors", "major errors" and "completely wrong". *English fluency* also uses 5 values "flawless", "good", "non-native", "disfluent" and "gibberish". 43 human raters were recruited from Amazon Mechanical Turk (www.mturk.com) to rate altogether 800 weather forecasts (400 system-generated, 400 human) on a scale of 1–5. The human-authored forecasts were rated better than our system-generated ones for both categories. The difference is statistically significant at $p < 0.01$ for *fluency*, according to a 2-tailed Wilcoxon ranked sum test. OURSYSTEM forecasts receive scores comparable to earlier work by [11]. [14] do not report a subjective evaluation, which is unfortunate for our comparison given the low correlation between BLEU scores and human quality assessment [2].

The difference for *semantic correctness* is not significant between OURSYSTEM and HUMAN. We believe that rounding of measurements played a role in the correctness ratings. The human forecasts might round a windSpeed of "max:78" to "up to 80 mph". This is frequent in the data and our system learnt to do this too. Some raters penalised this phenomenon more severely than others, but it occurred in both our human and system-generated data. We are surprised to see that Angeli's and Konstas' systems achieve better results than our human examples in the correctness case.

6 Conclusion and Future Work

We have presented a proof-of-concept study on using hierarchical decomposition for large NLG tasks into subsets of smaller tasks within a deep learning framework. The divide-and-conquer approach to learning can (a) lead to much faster learning (up to 73%), and (b) allow us to learn good generation policies for a dataset that is not ideally balanced with some examples occurring much more frequently than others. We believe that this work is relevant to language datasets that are scraped off the web. While language data is available in abundance on the web, directly scraped data is often less clean and structured as required for many state-of-the-art techniques in NLP, including deep learning. We observed that the latter can particularly struggle to learn good representations for infrequent data points in large training sets.

Future work needs to find ways to decompose datasets of examples automatically in a more principled way than based on heuristics, e.g. using genetic algorithms [21,22]. Also, we have applied our technique to a vanilla LSTM model only and could explore more sophisticated deep learning models including e.g. such with attention mechanism. Also, we plan to test our approach on additional language datasets scraped off the web.

Acknowledgements. We acknowledge the VIPER high-performance computing facility of the University of Hull and its support team. We are also grateful for Nvidia's donation of a Titan X Pascal graphics card for our work on deep learning.

References

1. Angeli, G., Liang, P., Klein, D.: A simple domain-independent probabilistic approach to generation. In: Proceedings of the Conference on Empirical Methods in Natural Language Processing (EMNLP), Cambridge, Massachusetts (2010)
2. Belz, A., Gatt, A.: Intrinsic vs. extrinsic evaluation measures for referring expression generation. In: Proceedings of the 46th Annual Meeting of the Association for Computational Linguistics (ACL), Columbus, OH, USA (2008)
3. Bengio, Y., Simard, P., Frasconi, P.: Learning long-term dependencies with gradient descent is difficult. IEEE Trans. Neural Netw. **5**(2), 157–166 (1994)
4. Cho, K., van Merrienboer, B., Gülçehre, Ç., Bougares, F., Schwenk, H., Bengio, Y.: Learning phrase representations using RNN encoder-decoder for statistical machine translation. In: Proceedings of the 2014 Conference on Empirical Methods in Natural Language Processing (EMNLP), Doha, Qatar (2014)
5. Cuayáhuitl, H., Dethlefs, N., Hastie, H., Liu, X.: Training a statistical surface realiser from automatic slot labelling. In: Proceedings of the IEEE Workshop on Spoken Language Technology (SLT), South Lake Tahoe, USA (2014)
6. Dethlefs, N., Cuayáhuitl, H.: Hierarchical reinforcement learning and hidden markov models for task-oriented natural language generation. In: Proceedings of the 49th Annual Conference of the Association for Computational Linguistics (ACL-HLT), Short Papers, Portland, OR, USA (2011)
7. Dethlefs, N., Cuayáhuitl, H.: Hierarchical reinforcement learning for situated natural language generation. Natl. Lang. Eng. **21**, 391–435 (2015)
8. Dethlefs, N., Hastie, H., Cuayáhuitl, H., Lemon, O.: Conditional random fields for responsive surface realisation. In: Proceedings of the 51st Annual Meeting of the Association for Computational Linguistics (ACL), Sofia, Bulgaria (2013)
9. Dusek, O., Jurcicek, F.: Sequence-to-sequence generation for spoken dialogue via deep syntax trees and strings. In: Proceedings of the Annual Meeting of the Association for Computational Linguistics (ACL), Berlin, Germany (2016)
10. Graves, A.: Generating sequences with recurrent neural networks. CoRR abs/1308.0850 (2013). http://arxiv.org/abs/1308.0850
11. Konstas, I., Lapata, M.: Unsupervised concept-to-text generation with hypergraphs. In: Proceedings of the North American Chapter of the Association for Computational Linguistics (NAACL), Montreal, Canada (2012)
12. Liang, P., Jordan, M., Klein, D.: Learning semantic correspondences with less supervision. In: Proceedings of the 47th Annual Meeting of the Association for Computational Linguistics (ACL), Singapore (2009)
13. Mairesse, F., Jurčíček, F., Keizer, S., Thomson, B., Yu, K., Young, S.: Phrase-based statistical language generation using graphical models and active learning. In: Proceedings of the 48th Annual Meeting of the Association of Computational Linguistics (ACL), Uppsala, Sweden (2010)
14. Mei, H., Bansal, M., Walker, M.: What to talk about and how? Selective Generation using LSTMs with coarse-to-fine alignment. In: Proceedings of the North American Chapter of the Association for Computational Linguistics (NAACL), San Diego, CA, USA (2016)
15. Morin, F., Bengio, Y.: Hierarchical probabilistic neural network language model. In: Proceedings of the International Conference on Artificial Intelligence and Statistics (AISTATS), pp. 246–252 (2005)
16. Novikova, J., Rieser, V.: The aNALoGuE Challenge: Non Aligned Language GEneration. In: Proceedings of the 9th International Natural Language Generation Conference (INLG) (2016)

17. Papineni, K., Roukos, S., Ward, T., Zhu, W.J.: BLEU: a method for automatic evaluation of machine translation. In: Proceedings of the 40th Annual Meeting on Association for Computational Linguistics (ACL), Association for Computational Linguistics, pp. 311–318 (2001)
18. Reiter, E., Dale, R.: Building Natural Language Generation Systems. Cambridge University Press, New York (2000)
19. Snyder, B., Barzilay, R.: Database-text alignment via structured multilabel classification. In: Proceedings of 20th International Joint Conference on Artificial Intelligence (IJCAI), Hyderabad, India (2007)
20. Sutskever, I., Vinyals, O., Le, Q.V.: Sequence to sequence learning with neural networks. Adv. Neural Inf. Process. Syst. (NIPS) **27**, 3104–3112 (2014)
21. Turner, A.P., Caves, L.S., Stepney, S., Tyrrell, A.M., Lones, M.A.: Artificial epigenetic networks: automatic decomposition of dynamical control tasks using topological self-modification. IEEE Trans. Neural Netw. Learn. Syst. (2016)
22. Turner, A.P., Lones, M.A., Fuente, L.A., Stepney, S., Caves, L.S., Tyrrell, A.M.: The artificial epigenetic network. In: 2013 IEEE International Conference on Evolvable Systems (ICES), pp. 66–72. IEEE (2013)
23. Walker, M., Stent, A., Mairesse, F., Prasad, R.: Individual and domain adaptation in sentence planning for dialogue. J. Artif. Intell. Res. **30**(1), 413–456 (2007)
24. Wen, T.H., Gašić, M., Mrkšić, N., Su, P.H., Vandyke, D., Young, S.: Semantically conditioned LSTM-based natural language generation for spoken dialogue systems. In: Proceedings of the 2015 Conference on Empirical Methods in Natural Language Processing (EMNLP) (2015)

Identifying Equivalent Relation Paths in Knowledge Graphs

Sameh K. Mohamed[1], Emir Muñoz[1,2(✉)], Vít Nováček[1], and Pierre-Yves Vandenbussche[2]

[1] Insight Centre for Data Analytics at NUI, Galway, Ireland
{sameh.kamal,emir.munoz}@insight-centre.org
[2] Fujitsu Ireland Limited, Dublin, Ireland

Abstract. Relation paths are sequences of relations with inverse that allow for complete exploration of knowledge graphs in a two-way unconstrained manner. They are powerful enough to encode complex relationships between entities and are crucial in several contexts, such as knowledge base verification, rule mining, and link prediction. However, fundamental forms of reasoning such as containment and equivalence of relation paths have hitherto been ignored. Intuitively, two relation paths are equivalent if they share the same extension, i.e., set of source and target entity pairs. In this paper, we study the problem of containment as a means to find equivalent relation paths and show that it is very expensive in practice to enumerate paths between entities. We characterize the complexity of containment and equivalence of relation paths and propose a domain-independent and unsupervised method to obtain approximate equivalences ranked by a tri-criteria ranking function. We evaluate our algorithm using test cases over real-world data and show that we are able to find semantically meaningful equivalences efficiently.

1 Introduction

Knowledge graphs (KGs) are graph-structured knowledge bases (KBs), consisting of facts encoded in the form of (subject, relation, object) triples, indicating that *subject* and *object* entities hold the relationship *relation*, e.g., (*Bob*, hasPartner, *Alice*). Popular KGs such as NELL, DBpedia, Freebase, or YAGO, have been developed in both academia and industry environments, attracting lot of attention due to their usefulness for many applications such as search, analytics, recommendations, and data integration. Relation paths with inverse are convenient means for complete exploration of KGs as they allow for unconstrained navigation that will not get stuck in sink nodes with no outgoing edges. However, there has been little study of their reasoning in comparison to single relations.

S.K. Mohamed and E. Muñoz—Contributed equally to this work.

This work has been supported by the TOMOE project funded by Fujitsu Laboratories Ltd., Japan and Insight Centre for Data Analytics at National University of Ireland Galway, Ireland (supported by the Science Foundation Ireland grant 12/RC/2289).

J. Gracia et al. (Eds.): LDK 2017, LNAI 10318, pp. 299–314, 2017.
DOI: 10.1007/978-3-319-59888-8_26

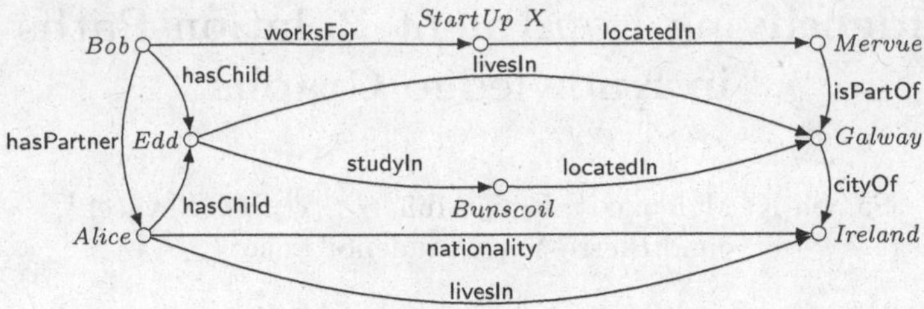

Fig. 1. Example knowledge graph of a family living in Ireland.

In this paper we study two fundamental forms of reasoning on relation paths, namely, containment and equivalence, and show how they can be used in the analysis of selected popular KGs. Intuitively, two relation paths P and Q are equivalent if they share the same extension, i.e., set of pairs (u, v), where nodes u and v are connected by P and Q. Recently, [20,23] have addressed the problem of determining whether two relations are equivalent or synonymous, using inductive approaches based on similarity and frequent itemsets, respectively. We generalize this task and compute equivalence between relation paths instead of single relations, which is a computationally more challenging problem. Relation paths in KGs have been mainly used in inference systems [11,12], and the link prediction task [14,15]. For instance, a relation path is able to encode complex relationships between entities, e.g., $Bob \xrightarrow{\mathsf{hasChild}} Edd \xrightarrow{\mathsf{hasChild}^{-1}} Alice$ in Fig. 1, can guide the inference that Bob is partner of Alice because they have a child in common, even if there was no direct relation between them. Also, $Bob \xrightarrow{\mathsf{livesIn}} Galway$ does not exists in Fig. 1, indicating possible missing information, which can be inferred by knowing that *Bob* works for a company located in *Mervue* which is part of *Galway* city, and he has a child living and studying in that city.

Reasoning on relation paths can be a computational challenge, especially when dealing with large KGs and considering inverse relations as well, and has hitherto been ignored. Given a fixed relation path, finding paths equivalent to it requires testing equivalence with all possible paths in the KG. Enumerating all simple paths between two entities is generally intractable, as their number can be in $\mathcal{O}(n!)$ for complete graphs (with n nodes) and tends to be quite large even for relatively sparse undirected graphs. We argue that despite of the challenges, a proper analysis of their reasoning is needed to unlock further applications in tasks such as knowledge graph completion, rule mining, and link prediction.

We propose to reduce the problem of finding equivalences to path containment. We map the problem to the well-studied regular path queries with inverse (2RPQs) in graph databases (see [2–4], among others). In graph databases, the notion of equivalence is defined in terms of containment, more specifically, query containment, which consists of determining whether the evaluation of a query Q_1 is a subset of the evaluation of a query Q_2. Checking containment of queries in databases is crucial in several contexts, such as query optimization, query reformulation, knowledge base verification, information integration, integrity checking, and cooperative answering [1]. Whether a relation paths and its reasoning in KGs can play a similar crucial role, and bring similar benefits is an open question. We hope that this work shed light on this topic.

More formally, the problem of interest in this paper is as follows:

SEARCH OF EQUIVALENT RELATION PATHS PROBLEM
Given: a knowledge graph $\mathcal{G}$, relation path query Q, integer k, depth d **Find:** top-k equivalent relation paths of max. length $2d$ for Q in $\mathcal{G}$ according to a ranking function $Rank_Q(P)$, for all $P \in \mathcal{C}$ set of candidates.

In this paper, we formulate an approximate solution to this problem, and illustrate it using four real-world knowledge graphs under different test cases from different domains of knowledge.

Example 1. Let us consider the KG in Fig. 1 with eight entities and nine different relationships. A query $Q = \langle \mathsf{livesIn}, \mathsf{cityOf}^{-1} \rangle$ asks for equivalent relation paths to *"a person living in a country which has a city"*. Valid answers will contain: (a) $\langle \mathsf{nationality}, \mathsf{cityOf}^{-1} \rangle$, (b) $\langle \mathsf{hasChild}, \mathsf{studyIn}, \mathsf{locatedIn} \rangle$, (c) $\langle \mathsf{hasChild}, \mathsf{livesIn} \rangle$, (d) $\langle \mathsf{hasPartner}^{-1}, \mathsf{hasChild}, \mathsf{livesIn} \rangle$. Interestingly, these results can be translated into insights about the person: (a) she has the *nationality* of the *country* where *city* is, (b) she has a *child* who study in a *school* located in *city*, (c) she has a *child* who lives in *city*, and (d) she has a *partner* whose child lives in *city*.

Organization. The rest of the paper is organized as follows. Section 2 presents background definitions for knowledge graphs, subgraphs, and connecting paths. In Sect. 3 we study the properties of containment and equivalence of relation paths. Section 4 presents our algorithm for efficient search for equivalent relation paths in a knowledge graph. Experimental results of our approach over four real-world knowledge graphs are presented in Sect. 5. We discuss related work in Sect. 6. Conclusions and future work are summarised in Sect. 7.

2 Preliminaries

In the following, we give definitions and examples supporting the two key notions of our approach – knowledge graph and query relation path.

Knowledge Graphs. We define a *knowledge graph* $\mathcal{G} = (V, E, \Sigma_V, \Sigma_E, \ell)$ as an edge-labeled directed multigraph, where V is the set of nodes, $E \subseteq V \times \Sigma_E \times V$ is the set of directed, labeled edges between two nodes, $\Sigma_V \subseteq \Sigma^*$ is a finite set denoted as the *node vocabulary*, $\Sigma_E \subseteq \Sigma^*$ is a finite set denoted as the *edge vocabulary*, and ℓ is a labeling function that assigns a label in Σ_V to a node in V, and a label in Σ_E to an edge in E. Each node $v \in V$ represents an entity, and each edge $e = (v, a, v') \in E$ represents a a-labeled relationship between entities v and v' (endpoints), where v is the domain of e, and v' is the range of e, denoted $Dom(e)$ and $Ran(e)$, respectively. Here, for simplicity, we omit the node and edge vocabularies, and use $\mathcal{G} = (V, E, \ell)$ to refer to a knowledge graph.

Example 2. Figure 1 shows a fragment of a knowledge graph. Each entity (e.g., *Edd*) has a label name, and connects to other entities (e.g., *Galway*) via labeled relationships (e.g., livesIn).

Paths. A *path* P in graph $\mathcal{G}$ is a sequence of edges $\langle e_1, e_2, \ldots, e_k \rangle$, where for $1 \leq i \leq k$, $e_i = (v_{i-1}, a_i, v_i)$ is an edge in $\mathcal{G}$ with label a_i and endpoints v_{i-1} and v_i. The integer k is called the *length* of P, denoted by $|P|$. We use $P(u \rightsquigarrow v)$ to denote a variable-length path with first node u and last node v, where u and v are known as the endpoints. We define the functions domain and range of a path P, $Dom(P) = Dom(e_1)$ and $Ran(P) = Ran(e_k)$. We define the binary associative operator $\oplus$ that concatenates two paths, $P_1 \oplus P_2$, by adding the edges in P_2 to the back of P_1 iff $Ran(P_1) = Dom(P_2)$. A *path label* $\ell(P)$ is defined as $\ell(v_0)\ell(e_1)\ldots\ell(v_{k-1})\ell(e_k)\ell(v_k)$, i.e., the concatenation of all node and edge labels on the path P. For instance, in our running example, we can have the paths $P_1 = \langle Edd, \mathsf{livesIn}, Galway \rangle$, and $P_2 = \langle Ireland, \mathsf{cityOf}^{-1}, Galway \rangle$. Notice that $\mathcal{G}$ is a directed graph, and we would like to walk through the graph in a *two-way unconstrained* manner, meaning that an edge can be walked in its opposite direction. This is to avoid the problem of getting stuck in sink nodes with no outgoing edges. This allows for complete exploration of the graph structure. To preserve the semantics of the original directed relations, we consider auxiliary *inverse* relations in the traversal, which is considered as a different relation, and equivalent to following a directed edge in its opposite direction. We use the '−1' superscript to denote the inverse relations.

Relation Paths. We introduce the use of the wildcard symbol '_' in paths to replace any node in the path. The use of a wildcard or "don't care" character in a path means that the position where the wildcard is used can take any value, i.e., any node label in Σ_V can be put in that place. For instance, we can have $P_1' = \langle \_, \mathsf{livesIn}, Galway \rangle$, which can serve to match all people (nodes) that live in Galway. We call a path *relation path* when all its nodes are replaced by wildcards, and wildcard symbols are omitted from the path.

Subgraph. Let $\mathsf{Graph}^d(\mathcal{G}, v)$ be the subgraph function that extracts $\mathcal{G}' = (V', E', \ell')$ around a node $v \in V$ from $\mathcal{G}$ up to depth d. The set of nodes $V' \subseteq V$ in $\mathcal{G}'$ contains all nodes that are reachable in $\mathcal{G}$ from v following paths of length $\leq d$. Similarly, the set of edges $E' \subseteq E$, where if $(v_1, a, v_2) \in E'$ then $v_1, v_2 \in V'$. Note that when $d = 0$, $\mathsf{Graph}^d(\mathcal{G}, v)$ extracts only the node v with no edges.

Intuitively, a subgraph allows us to generate a neighborhood for node v, which contains all reachable nodes from v following paths of a variable length.

Connecting Paths. If we relax the definition of path in such a way that the edges still carry a label, but the non-endpoint nodes do not (i.e., they are replaced by wildcards), then the path degenerates into a so-called *connecting path* anchored by its starting and ending nodes (endpoints). Formally, a node u is said to be *connected* to a node v in $\mathcal{G}$ via P if there is a $P(u \rightsquigarrow v)$ path.

Example 3. Considering the KG in Fig. 1, one can extract $\mathsf{Graph}^1(\mathcal{G}, Alice)$ and $\mathsf{Graph}^1(\mathcal{G}, Galway)$, which are the subgraphs of depth 1 around nodes *Alice* and

Galway, respectively. Considering the overlapping nodes, i.e., *Edd*, and *Ireland*, we can identify the following connecting paths:

(a) $\langle$*Alice*,hasChild,livesIn,*Galway*$\rangle$
(b) $\langle$*Alice*,livesIn,cityOf^{-1},*Galway*$\rangle$
(c) $\langle$*Alice*,nationality,cityOf^{-1},*Galway*$\rangle$
(d) $\langle$*Alice*,hasChild,studyIn,locatedIn,*Galway*$\rangle$.

Moreover, by replacing the endpoint nodes in connecting path (a) by wildcards, we get a relation path $P_k = \langle \mathsf{hasChild}, \mathsf{livesIn} \rangle$ of length 2.

3 Equivalence of Relation Paths

With the definitions of knowledge graph and relation paths, in this section, we present our study on the reasoning of relation paths.

Every relation path has an associated path extension in $\mathcal{G}$, that consists of pairs of entities: from node u we can reach node v following a relation path P if the pair (u, v) is a member of the *relation path extension* $\mathsf{PEXT}_{\mathcal{G}}(P)$. Therefore, the size of a relation path extension, correspond to the number of valid connecting paths we can generate for any pair of nodes in the graph. Formally, given $\mathcal{G} = (V, E, \ell)$ we define the relation path extension of a relation path P as:

$$\mathsf{PEXT}_{\mathcal{G}}(P) = \{(u, v) \mid u, v \in V \wedge \mathbf{I}_{\mathcal{G}}(P(u \rightsquigarrow v))\}, \quad (1)$$

where $\mathbf{I}_{\mathcal{G}}(P(u \rightsquigarrow v))$ is an indicator function that takes value True if there is a $P(u \rightsquigarrow v)$ path in $\mathcal{G}$, and False otherwise. Syntactically, relation paths can be seen as *2-way regular path queries* (2RPQs) [3], the default core navigational language for graph databases, where inverse relations are allowed. Then, the problem of deciding whether a pair of nodes is connected via a relation path P over a knowledge graph $\mathcal{G}$ (i.e., $P(u \rightsquigarrow v)$?) can be translated into computing the answer of 2RPQs, which is in low polynomial time [2,17]. The problem of determining whether a path P with inverse relations exists between nodes $u, v \in V$ can be easily reduced to the evaluation of *regular path queries* (RPQs) by extending the underlying KG with inverse edges (cf. [2]). Next, we define the notion of *symmetric closure* of a knowledge graph $\mathcal{G}$, denoted by $\mathcal{G}^{\pm}$. Let $\mathcal{G}^{\pm}$ be the knowledge graph obtained from $\mathcal{G} = (V, E, \ell)$ by adding the edge (u, a^{-1}, v), for each $(v, a, u) \in E$.

Proposition 1. *For every relation path P and knowledge graph $\mathcal{G}$ the problem of deciding whether a pair (u, v) of nodes belongs to $\mathsf{PEXT}_{\mathcal{G}}(P)$ can be solved in time $\mathcal{O}(|E| \cdot |P|)$.*

Proposition 2. *(See e.g., [6]). Let P be a relation path. There is a* NLOGSPACE *procedure that computes $\mathsf{PEXT}_{\mathcal{G}}(P)$ for each knowledge graph $\mathcal{G}$.*

Proof (Sketch). Given a knowledge graph $\mathcal{G}$ and its symmetric closure $\mathcal{G}^{\pm}$. For each pair (u, v) of nodes in V, we check whether it belongs to $\mathsf{PEXT}_{\mathcal{G}}(P)$ over $\mathcal{G}$ as a simple evaluation of a regular path query over $\mathcal{G}^{\pm}$ [17]. Clearly, $\mathcal{G}^{\pm}$

can be constructed in LOGSPACE from $\mathcal{G}$ [1]. Non-emptiness of $P(u \rightsquigarrow v)$ in $\mathcal{G}^{\pm}$ can be checked in NLOGSPACE in $|E|$ using a standard "on-the-fly" algorithm. We conclude that the whole process can be computed in NLOGSPACE for each relation path P.

With the relation path extension definition in place, two interesting and basic analysis tasks that arise are the containment and equivalence problem, defined in databases query languages (see, e.g., [5] for details of a relational database context, and [3,10,21] for a graph database context). In a query scenario, if a relation path (i.e., 2RPQ) is equivalent to other with better computational properties (e.g., shorter, faster evaluation), then the initial relation path can be replaced for optimization purposes. In other words, we can search for a simpler relation path that is *contained* in the original one. Indeed, the containment and equivalence problems have been always very related and played a prominent role in the analysis of query languages in databases. In the following, we build upon these ideas, and use the containment problem as a building block for the equivalence of relation paths.

Definition 1 (Path Extension Containment). *Let P_1 and P_2 be two relation paths, and $\mathcal{G}$ a knowledge graph. We say that P_1 is* contained *in P_2, denoted $P_1 \sqsubseteq P_2$, if $\mathsf{PEXT}_{\mathcal{G}}(P_1) \subseteq \mathsf{PEXT}_{\mathcal{G}}(P_2)$.*

Theorem 1 ([4], Theorem 5). *The path extension containment problem is* PSPACE*-complete.*

We can reduce the path extension containment problem to the well-studied 2RPQ containment. A proof of Theorem 1 considering 2RPQs is given in Calvanese et al. [4], where is shown that for 2RPQs the problem of containment has a PSPACE-complete upper bound. The proof uses two-way automata techniques, where the containment problem is reduced to determine whether there is a path from start state to final state in a two-way automata.

Definition 2 (Path Extension Equivalence). *Let P_1 and P_2 be two relation paths. We say that P_1 and P_2 are* extension equivalent *(or* PEXT*-*equivalent*), denoted by $P_1 \equiv P_2$, iff $P_1 \sqsubseteq P_2$ and $P_2 \sqsubseteq P_1$. While when only $P_1 \sqsubseteq P_2$ (resp. $P_2 \sqsubseteq P_1$) is true, we say that P_1 and P_2 are* approximate equivalent *(or Δ-*equivalent*), denoted as $P_1 \preceq_{\Delta} P_2$ (resp. $P_2 \preceq_{\Delta} P_1$).*

It is easy to see, that path extension equivalences are in PSPACE-complete complexity given Theorem 1 and Definition 2.

Corollary 1. *The PEXT-equivalence problem is* PSPACE*-complete.*

Example 4. Using the KG in Fig. 1, the following are two PEXT-equivalences: (a) ⟨livesIn⟩ ≡ ⟨studyIn,locatedIn⟩, and (b) ⟨hasPartner⟩ ≡ ⟨hasChild,hasChild^{-1}⟩,

[1] Given a two-way automaton with n states, we can construct a one-way automaton with $\mathcal{O}(2^{n \log n})$ states accepting the same language [22].

which could be interpreted as: (a) people who lives in *city* also study in *school* located in *city*, and (b) people that has *partner* also has a *child* who is children of *partner*. Whilst one can consider $\langle \mathsf{hasChild}, \mathsf{livesIn}, \mathsf{isPartOf}^{-1} \rangle \preceq_\Delta \langle \mathsf{worksFor}, \mathsf{locatedIn} \rangle$ to be a Δ-equivalence, because the PEXT of the r.h.s. path is a superset of the l.h.s. one. In other words, not everybody works for a company located in the same neighborhood where their children live.

Theorem 2. *PEXT-equivalence is an equivalence relation.*

Proof. We need to show that PEXT-equivalence is reflexive, symmetric, and transitive. This follows from the $\sqsubseteq$ relation (path extension containment) definition. Two paths P_1, P_2 are PEXT-equivalent iff $P_1 \sqsubseteq P_2 \wedge P_2 \sqsubseteq P_1$ where $\sqsubseteq$ is defined using a standard set inclusion operation $\subseteq$ on the path extensions. *(Reflexivity)* $P \equiv P$ for all P, because $\mathsf{PEXT}(P) \subseteq \mathsf{PEXT}(P)$. *(Symmetry)* If $P_1 \equiv P_2$, then $\mathsf{PEXT}(P_1) \subseteq \mathsf{PEXT}(P_2) \wedge \mathsf{PEXT}(P_2) \subseteq \mathsf{PEXT}(P_1)$, therefore also $P_2 \equiv P_1$ for all P_1, P_2. *(Transitivity)* If $P_1 \equiv P_2$ and $P_2 \equiv P_3$ then $\mathsf{PEXT}(P_1) \subseteq \mathsf{PEXT}(P_2) \wedge \mathsf{PEXT}(P_2) \subseteq \mathsf{PEXT}(P_1) \wedge \mathsf{PEXT}(P_2) \subseteq \mathsf{PEXT}(P_3) \wedge \mathsf{PEXT}(P_3) \subseteq \mathsf{PEXT}(P_2)$, which means that $\mathsf{PEXT}(P_1) = \mathsf{PEXT}(P_2) = \mathsf{PEXT}(P_3)$, i.e., $\mathsf{PEXT}(P_1) \subseteq \mathsf{PEXT}(P_3) \wedge \mathsf{PEXT}(P_3) \subseteq \mathsf{PEXT}(P_1)$, and therefore also $P_1 \equiv P_3$ for all P_1, P_2, and P_3. □

Theorem 3. *Δ-equivalence is a partial order.*

Proof. This comes as straightforward from Definition 2 – the $\subseteq$ relation used in the definition is a partial order (on path extensions) and therefore $\sqsubseteq$ is also a partial order (on relation paths).

4 Search of Δ-Equivalences

In the following, we mainly focus on the extraction of Δ-equivalences for two reasons: (a) extracting Δ-equivalences from large-scale KGs is cheaper than PEXT-equivalences, and (b) we argue that because of the incompleteness of knowledge graphs[2], PEXT-equivalences are harder to find in real-world KGs, than instances of its more relaxed version (Δ-equivalence), which we believe are more abundant. Point (a) is justified by our theoretical discussion in Sect. 3, while point (b) will be later justified for our experimental results in Sect. 5.

We present Algorithm 1 as an implementation of our method for finding Δ-equivalences of a query path relying on connecting paths between pairs of entities in $\mathsf{PEXT}_\mathcal{G}(Q)$. All steps of our method are shown in Fig. 2, along the data structures that each step takes as input an returns as output.

Next, we describe in details the four steps of our method:

(1) Extracting the extension of query path Q. This step corresponds to line 1 in Algorithm 1. In this step we extract the pairs of nodes in $\mathsf{PEXT}_\mathcal{G}(Q)$.

[2] Dong et al. (2014) [7] report that 71% of the people described in Freebase have unknown place of birth, 75% have unknown nationality, and the coverage for less used relations can be even lower.

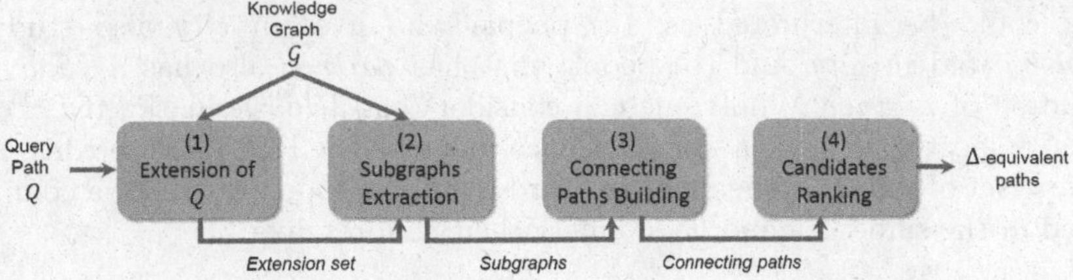

Fig. 2. Flow diagram of the process of retrieving Δ-equivalent paths for Q.

Algorithm 1. (SearchEquiv: SEARCH OF Δ-EQUIVALENT PATHS)

Input: Knowledge graph $\mathcal{G}$, query relation path Q, depth d
Output: Ranked list of Δ-equivalent paths of Q

$\mathcal{E} \leftarrow \mathsf{PEXT}_{\mathcal{G}}(Q)$
$\mathcal{C} \leftarrow set()$
for $(v_1, v_2) \in \mathcal{E}$ **do**
  $\mathcal{C} \leftarrow \mathcal{C} \cup \mathsf{ConnectingPaths}(v_1, v_2, d, \mathcal{G})$
return $\mathsf{RankFunc}(\mathcal{C})$

Despite being a NLOGSPACE procedure, in practice this computation is very expensive for large-scale KGs, therefore, here we take a divide-and-conquer strategy to obtain this set. Let $Q = \langle \mathsf{e}_1, \mathsf{e}_2, \ldots, \mathsf{e}_k \rangle$ be the query relation path. First, we find the m-th relation with $m = \lfloor k/2 \rfloor$, and divide Q into two relation paths, $Q_1 = \langle \mathsf{e}_1, \mathsf{e}_2, \ldots, \mathsf{e}_m \rangle$ and $Q_2 = \langle \mathsf{e}_{m+1}, \mathsf{e}_{m+2}, \ldots, \mathsf{e}_k \rangle$. Second, we compute the set $\mathcal{Q} = \{u \mid Ran(\mathsf{e}_m) = u \wedge Dom(\mathsf{e}_{m+1}) = u\}$ of *witness nodes*, which are nodes that are range of Q_1 and domain of Q_2. For each node $u \in \mathcal{Q}$, we walk backwards through Q_1 and forwards through Q_2 in $\mathcal{G}$, saving all final endpoint nodes on both sides, i.e., all nodes which are $Dom(\mathsf{e}_1)$ and $Ran(\mathsf{e}_k)$. Considering that we followed Q_1 and Q_2 from the witness nodes, we know that the destination nodes which are $Dom(\mathsf{e}_1)$ and/or $Ran(\mathsf{e}_k)$ are indeed connected by Q. Thus, the $\mathsf{PEXT}_{\mathcal{G}}(Q)$ is obtained from generating pairs between the found endpoints.

It is worth to mention, that some nodes in $\mathcal{G}$ can be densely connected, and paths passing through them are prone to outnumber the true facts in $\mathcal{G}$, because they usually contain many-to-many relations. For example, the relation path $\langle \mathsf{hasGender}, \mathsf{hasGender}^{-1} \rangle$ in most knowledge graphs will have more instances than the total count of fact triples, as it represents all possible combinations of instances of people with same gender in the graph. Because of that, we consider here a random sample of 1000 path instances, thus $\mathsf{PEXT}_{\mathcal{G}}(Q)$ is a sample rather than the full set. This constraint can be seen as a limitation of our method; however, it is a parameter that users can set accordingly, at a cost in the throughput. Further study and optimization of this part are left for future work.

(2) Subgraphs extraction. This step correspond to line 2 in Algorithm 2, where the subgraph generation routine is called twice. For each pair of nodes (u, v) in $\mathsf{PEXT}_{\mathcal{G}}(Q)$, we generate $\mathsf{Graph}^d(\mathcal{G}, u)$ and $\mathsf{Graph}^d(\mathcal{G}, v)$. A subgraph of depth d is generated using a mix between Depth-first search (DFS) and Breath-

Algorithm 2. (ConnectingPaths: CONNECTING PATHS EXTRACTION)

Input: v_1, v_2 nodes, depth d, knowledge graph $\mathcal{G}$
Output: $\mathcal{C}$ list of connecting paths between v_1 and v_2
1: $\mathcal{G}_1, \mathcal{G}_2 \leftarrow \mathsf{Graph}^d(\mathcal{G}, v_1),\ \mathsf{Graph}^d(\mathcal{G}, v_2)$
2: $T_1, T_2 \leftarrow \{v \mid u, v \in V_{\mathcal{G}_1} \wedge \mathbf{I}_{\mathcal{G}_1}(P(u \rightsquigarrow v))\}, \{w \mid y, w \in V_{\mathcal{G}_2} \wedge \mathbf{I}_{\mathcal{G}_2}(P(y \rightsquigarrow w))\}$
3: **for** $t \in T_1 \cap T_2$ **do**
4:     **for** $P_1 \in \{P \mid u \in V_{\mathcal{G}_1} \wedge \mathbf{I}_{\mathcal{G}_1}(P(u \rightsquigarrow t))\}$ **do**
5:         **for** $P_2 \in \{P \mid v \in V_{\mathcal{G}_2} \wedge \mathbf{I}_{\mathcal{G}_2}(P(v \rightsquigarrow t))\}$ **do**
6:             $\mathcal{C}.append(P_1 \oplus \mathsf{Inverse}(P_2))$
7: **return** $\mathcal{C}$

first search (BFS) from a node. It is easy to see that the subgraph generation step also suffers of scalability issues on large-scale KGs, where a simple DFS or BFS search can become very expensive, and return non-representative subgraphs if taken separately. Applying only DFS would lead to very deep subgraphs which might not consider all neighbor relations; and applying only BFS would lead to very wide subgraphs with not enough depth. To cope with this, we apply a DFS with BFS flavor by considering the following two restrictions: (1) from a given node, we extract a maximum of 50 instances of a same relation, to avoid neglecting under represented relations in nodes with highly common relations; and (2) in each iteration of DFS, we take a sample of 200 edges, to keep a manageable final size for a subgraph. Again, such decisions are implementation parameters that can be tuned by users. In this way, we try to keep instances for all neighbor relations (even the underrepresented ones, such as one-to-one relations that otherwise could be discarded), and we try to keep a representative enough subgraph while keeping an adequate size.

(3) Connecting paths building. This step is used in line 4 of Algorithm 1, and fully expanded in Algorithm 2. In this step we use subgraphs extracted in step (2) to build connecting paths, which are considered as Δ-equivalent to Q. For clarity, we depict the process in Fig. 3. For a given pair of nodes (v_1, v_2) in $\mathsf{PEXT}_{\mathcal{G}}(Q)$, we consider their corresponding subgraphs (line 1, Algorithm 2), and identify those nodes that are endpoints of paths in both subgraphs (lines 2–3, Algorithm 2). In other words, we find the so-called *target nodes* in which the subgraphs intersect. A target node is a connecting point which allows us to connect nodes from the domain and range of a query Q. Thus, we build connecting path around them as shown in Fig. 3. Notice that when creating a connecting path from a target node, we must append the inverse of the path from the right subgraph to the one on the left (line 6, Algorithm 2). This is because paths on the right subgraph originally considers v_2 as starting point, while now v_2 becomes the final point. The $\mathsf{Inverse}(\cdot)$ function in line 6 of Algorithm 2 inverts a path walking backwards: Let $P = \langle v_0, \mathsf{e}_1, \ldots, v_{k-1}, \mathsf{e}_k, v_k\rangle$, then $\mathsf{Inverse}(P) = \langle v_k, {\mathsf{e}_k}^{-1}, v_{k-1}, \ldots, {\mathsf{e}_1}^{-1}, v_0\rangle$, and $({\mathsf{e}_i}^{-1})^{-1} = \mathsf{e}_i$. The output of this step is a set of connecting paths which are ranked in the next step.

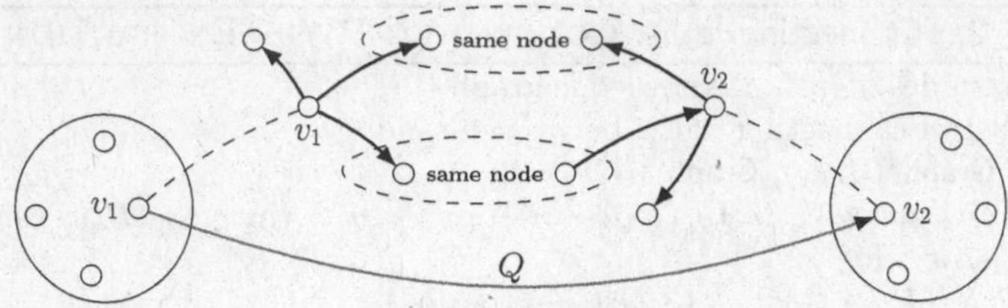

Fig. 3. Generation of connecting paths from the path extension of query Q.

(4) Candidate Path Ranking. This is the last step and line 5 of Algorithm 1. After extracting connecting paths between nodes of the $\mathsf{PEXT}_{\mathcal{G}}(Q)$, we can design a ranking function in order to get the most relevant Δ-equivalences. We argue that such a ranking function should consider three criteria to rank candidates $P \in \mathcal{C}$: (Cr-1) if $P \preceq_{\Delta} Q$, then the size of the $\mathsf{PEXT}_{\mathcal{G}}(P)$ set could be big but always smaller than the size of $\mathsf{PEXT}_{\mathcal{G}}(Q)$; (Cr-2) the number of instances of P among the candidates should be normalized to avoid ranking first the more frequent paths; and (Cr-3) users can specify whether they would like longer or shorter paths on top of the ranking. To satisfy all requirements enumerated above, we designed the following ranking function:

$$Rank_Q(P) = \alpha \underbrace{\frac{|\mathsf{PEXT}_{\mathcal{G}}(P)|}{|\mathsf{PEXT}_{\mathcal{G}}(Q)|}}_{\text{Cr-1}} + \beta \underbrace{\frac{\sigma(P)}{max\{\sigma(P_i) : P_i \in \mathcal{C}\}}}_{\text{Cr-2}} + \gamma \underbrace{\frac{|Q| - |P|}{max\{|Q|, |P|\}}}_{\text{Cr3}}, \quad (2)$$

where each criterion is weighted using constants α, β, and γ; and σ(P) returns the total count of instances of path P in $\mathcal{C}$. The parameters α, β, and γ can be defined by a user to match her expectations of the rank, and are set to 1 in our experiments. In Eq. 2, we implement Cr-1 using the Jaccard index to find those paths whose PEXT is similar enough to the query one. Remember that we only compute $\mathsf{PEXT}(Q)$ extensively, while $\mathsf{PEXT}(P)$ is obtained from the former, and will always be a subset of it. Therefore, the Jaccard index is reduced to the simple ratio in Cr-1.

Using this tri-criteria function users are allowed to tune the ranking in order to favor, e.g., shorter paths setting $\gamma = +1$, or longer ones using $\gamma = -1$. Similarly, the other two criteria can be highlighted or decreased tuning α and β.

5 Experimental Evaluation

In this section, we present the set up of our experiments considering four different KGs, and discuss results that are encouraging for further research in this area.

5.1 Experimental Setup

We design a set of test cases using four large and well-known KGs, generated from different sources and tailored to different domains. To the best of our knowl-

Table 1. Statistics of knowledge graphs used in our experiments.

	NELL	DBpedia	YAGO3	WordNet
#Entities - $\|V\|$	1.2M	1.2M	2.6M	10K
#Relations - Σ_E	520	644	36	18
#Triples - $\|E\|$	3.8M	4M	5.5M	141K

edge, there is no benchmark to evaluate equivalence between relation paths. Zhang et al. [23] have a crowd-sourced gold standard for single relations not covering complex relation paths, so it does not meet our requirements. We consider the generation of a gold standard for relation paths as future work, and here our goal is to examine the capabilities of our proposed approach for finding Δ-equivalences. For each dataset we propose two queries that are evaluated and the Δ-equivalent paths are ranked. Furthermore, for the top-5 results of each query, we present the values of the three criteria, and the ranking score.

Dataset. Our proposed method relies on KG exploration to search for equivalences. We noticed that more interesting results arise from KGs with a rich set of interconnected entities and relation paths. A possible reason is that in KGs with low depth relation paths are rather short and more prone to contain loops with inverse relations. Here, we use four commonly used and general human knowledge KGs of different size and domain (Table 1 shows their characteristics): (A) Never Ending Learning (NELL) [19] is a knowledge base generated continuously by a never-ending machine learning system that crawls web pages and extracts facts from a pre-defined set of categories and relations; (B) YAGO3 [16] applies similar techniques to NELL, but it limits its sources to Wikipedia and WordNet [18]; (C) DBpedia [13] is a crowd-sourced knowledge base extracted from Wikipedia and Geonames as sources; and (D) WordNet [18] is a large lexical database of English, linking words and concepts using cognitive synonyms.

Queries. To date, there is no publicly available gold standard for relation paths equivalence. The generation of such a gold standard requires a deep understanding of the structure and semantics of a knowledge graph, which is not always available, showing the importance of having methods as the one described here. Therefore, we evaluate our method by using a set of eight manually generated queries, and leave as future work the generation of such a gold standard. For each knowledge graph in Table 1, we manually generated two relation paths that are used as queries. The queries are of different length, include inverse relations when possible, and cover different topics according to the domain of the KGs.

Implementation. In general, we implemented our approach using *Python* 3.5. We use *adjacency lists* (which provides a time complexity $\mathcal{O}(1)$ to find neighbors of a node) as data structure for storing the knowledge graphs in memory. Because our method considers inverse relations, we include the symmetric closure $\mathcal{G}^{\pm}$ of the KG for easy traversal. As an optimization, the discovery of connecting paths can be performed in parallel, giving one pair of nodes to a thread/process which computes connecting paths between them, and stores the results in a shared variable among threads. All experiments are executed in a Linux virtual machine configured with 40 GB of RAM and 10 processing cores of 2.20 GHz.

5.2 Results

As shown in Table 2, the running time of the algorithm varies between 35 and 193 min when considering 1000 elements in the relation path extensions. We noticed that such limit is reached in queries B.1, B.2, and C.1 only, while for all other cases a size of 500 should be sufficient. To put the running time in contrast, we also ran the same experiments using a limit size of 100 in the relation path extensions, and got running times between 4 and 60 min. Running time values depend on the size of the KG (see Table 1) and on the cardinality of the relations included in the relation paths. Table 2 shows the queries for the first three dataset with the ranked equivalences. For each relation path answer, we report the values of each criterion, and the final ranking score w.r.t. Eq. 2.

Remember that what we extract are Δ-equivalences, and in order to identify PEXT-equivalences from them, we try to determine whether $Q \equiv P$ for a given path P in the results of Q. We capture this comparison by using the Jaccard similarity between the full PEXT of a query and its Δ-equivalent paths. If the Jaccard similarity is 1, we can safely state that $Q \equiv P$; otherwise, the similarity value gives us a relative indication of how similar they are. We noticed that checking whether $Q \equiv P$ for the top results of queries over NELL, DBpedia and YAGO3 quickly becomes infeasible, and we stopped our processes after 24 h. We associate this high computation time to the existence of relations with many-to-many cardinality and large number of instances which, as mentioned earlier, directly affects the computation of PEXT.

On the other hand, we have WordNet queries $\langle$_hypernym$\rangle$ and $\langle$_part_of$\rangle$, which are composed of single relations that usually do not contain many range values for a given entity. In these cases, it was easy to compute the full PEXT and generate a score for the equivalences. We found that $\langle$_hypernym$\rangle \equiv \langle$_hyponym$^{-1}\rangle$ and $\langle$_part_of$\rangle \equiv \langle$_has_part$^{-1}\rangle$ are 87.7% and 87.5% similar, respectively, according to the KG. In theory they are strictly equivalent, indicating the effectiveness of our ranking function. Because of the characteristics of our method, we cannot tell if these numbers should be higher, but could be considered as a sign that the KG is incomplete.

We also observed that some query results differ from the query in length and building relations. A clear example of it is given by the path $P = \langle$cityLiesOnRiver^{-1},generalizations,generalizations$^{-1}\rangle$, which ranks higher for query A.1, and contains new and different relations from the query. Also, its semantics "*a city has a river, and city has a generalization*" is different from the original relation path query semantics. In NELL [19], the relation generalizations is common and acts as a meta relation for classes of entities, e.g., the generalization of a city is *Location*. So, the second part of P is a loop decoded as "*a city is a location, and location is a generalization of a city*". A deeper study is required to analyze other possible equivalences between individual relations

Table 2. Top-5 best ranked Δ-equivalent paths for example queries.

Query	$Rank_Q(P)$	CR-1	CR-2	CR-3
Query A.1: ⟨riverEmptiesIntoRiver,riverFlowsThroughCity⟩	Time ca. 53.2 min.		519 instances	
⟨cityLiesOnRiver^{-1},generalizations,generalizations^{-1}⟩	1.342	0.688	0.987	-0.333
⟨riverFlowsThroughCity,generalizations,generalizations^{-1}⟩	1.337	0.688	0.982	-0.333
⟨cityLiesOnRiver^{-1},generalizations,generalizations^{-1},generalizations^{-1}⟩	1.192	0.692	1.000	-0.500
⟨riverFlowsThroughCity,generalizations,generalizations^{-1},generalizations^{-1}⟩	1.189	0.692	0.997	-0.500
⟨riverEmptiesIntoRiver,cityLiesOnRiver^{-1}⟩	1.015	0.996	0.019	0.000
Query A.2: ⟨athletePlaysForTeam,teamHomeStadium,stadiumLocatedInCity⟩	Time ca. 35 min.		326 instances	
⟨athletePlaysForTeam,generalizations,generalizations^{-1},citySportsTeams^{-1}⟩	1.404	0.770	0.884	-0.250
⟨athletePlaysForTeam,generalizations,generalizations^{-1},teamPlaysInCity⟩	1.353	0.764	0.839	-0.250
⟨teamMember^{-1},generalizations,generalizations^{-1},citySportsTeams^{-1}⟩	1.264	0.739	0.775	-0.250
⟨athletePlaysForTeam,teamPlaysAgainstTeam^{-1},teamPlaysAgainstTeam^{-1}, citySportsTeams^{-1}⟩	1.249	0.531	0.969	-0.250
⟨teamMember^{-1},generalizations,generalizations^{-1},teamPlaysInCity⟩	1.244	0.733	0.761	-0.250
Query B.1: ⟨wasBornIn,isLocatedIn⟩	Time ca. 118 min.		1000[b] instances	
⟨wasBornIn,isLocatedIn,isLocatedIn^{-1},isLocatedIn⟩	1.276	0.776	1.000	-0.500
⟨isCitizenOf⟩	1.025	0.016	0.001	0.500
⟨isPoliticianOf⟩	0.517	0.013	0.001	0.500
⟨livesIn⟩	0.514	0.007	0.000	0.500
⟨hasGender,hasGender^{-1},isPoliticianOf⟩	0.507	0.332	0.243	-0.333
Query B.2: ⟨actedIn,directed^{-1}⟩	Time ca. 193 min.		1000[b] instances	
⟨actedIn,isLocatedIn,isLocatedIn^{-1},directed^{-1}⟩	1.360	0.860	1.000	-0.500
⟨hasGender,hasGender^{-1}⟩	0.587	0.583	0.004	0.000
⟨actedIn,actedIn^{-1},actedIn,directed^{-1}⟩	0.524	0.674	0.350	-0.500
⟨ϵ⟩[a]	0.518	0.018	0.000	0.500
⟨isMarriedTo⟩	0.503	0.003	0.000	0.500
Query C.1: ⟨artist,bandMember⟩	Time ca. 58 min.		1000[b] instances	
⟨artist,associatedMusicalArtist^{-1},associatedBand,bandMember⟩	1.435	0.935	1.000	-0.500
⟨artist,associatedBand^{-1},associatedMusicalArtist,bandMember⟩	1.429	0.935	0.994	-0.500
⟨artist,associatedBand^{-1},associatedMusicalArtist,associatedBand^{-1}⟩	0.953	0.524	0.929	-0.500
⟨artist,associatedMusicalArtist^{-1},associatedBand,associatedMusicalArtist^{-1}⟩	0.952	0.524	0.928	-0.500
⟨genre,instrument,instrument^{-1},genre^{-1}⟩	0.736	0.432	0.804	-0.500
Query C.2: ⟨academicAdvisor,almaMater⟩	Time ca. 80 min.		335 instances	
⟨academicAdvisor,birthPlace,birthPlace^{-1},almaMater⟩	1.080	0.580	1.000	-0.500
⟨academicAdvisor,deathPlace,birthPlace^{-1},almaMater⟩	0.846	0.575	0.771	-0.500
⟨almaMater⟩	0.641	0.121	0.020	0.500
⟨academicAdvisor,deathPlace,deathPlace^{-1},almaMater⟩	0.587	0.620	0.467	-0.500
⟨notableStudent^{-1},almaMater⟩	0.540	0.459	0.081	0.000

(*a*) ϵ denotes the empty path
(*b*) maximum size of the PEXT set reached

that appear in the results, such as cityLiesOnRiver and riverFlowsThroughCity, or athletePlaysForTeam and teamMember, or citySportsTeams and teamPlaysInCity.

YAGO query results are also interesting. First result for query B.1 is a loop around wasBornIn, while the 2nd, 3rd and 4th results show Δ-equivalence to a single relation, having a high CR-3. Interestingly, for query B.2, we get an empty path as result, which indicates that actors are also directors of movies where they perform. And that some actors are married to the directors of the movies.

Results for DBpedia queries C.1 and C.2 are usually high in CR-2, meaning that the data are relatively complete. For C.1 we get an interesting results using a relation path between songs and their artists (band members) as query. Equivalent paths usually include bands associated to the artists, and even genres and instruments of the artists. In query C.2, we can see that the relation path ⟨academicAdvisor,almaMater⟩ can be Δ-equivalent to ⟨almaMater⟩, i.e., people usually graduate from the university where their supervisor studied. We also get that they usually were a notableStudent for their supervisor.

6 Related Work

Research on equivalences in knowledge graphs (bases) has been mainly focused on single relations, which are emulated by our approach as paths of unitary length. In [23], authors address the problem of mining equivalent relations from Linked Data datasets as a clustering problem using an equivalence score. Similarly, [20] deals with the problem of finding synonymous relations in Linked Data using an itemset mining approach on the domain and range types of a relation instance. Both [20,23] require the notion of typed entities and do not consider inverse relations, which are significant shortcomings for mining knowledge graphs. Here, we consider variable-length relation paths with inverse relations, and although we do not require any kind of schema knowledge, our method can benefit from it, e.g., in the interpretation of paths. [8] used distributional semantics to find semantically related class type paths, i.e. meta paths, using latent feature space. Our work is also related to AMIE+ [9], a system for mining Horn rules in knowledge bases, where in each rule the body is a path and the head is a relation. Our work is orthogonal to [9] since we do not focus on mining rules, but rather on ranking the most prominent equivalences for a given relation path. The application of our method for rule mining, considering more generic rules than Horn rules, is part of our future work. Last but not least, [23] describes an annotation process that could be used for generating a gold standard applicable to evaluation of the presented approach and other similar experiments.

7 Conclusions and Future Work

We explored the problem of identifying relation path equivalences in KGs using a data-driven, unsupervised and domain independent method. We addressed several practical and theoretical issues regarding finding strict equivalences, and proposed a more efficient, approximate approach that is still able to bring valuable insights. Using different test queries, we show that our approach can efficiently rank candidates that are Δ-equivalent. In our experiments, we achieved results consistent with our initial assumptions, as our method retrieved intuitively similar relation paths that were, however, of different length and contained different relations when compared to the input query.

As a part of our future work, we intend to perform a user evaluation of the ranking results to: (1) come up with a universally applicable gold standard for relation paths equivalence, and (2) determine the influence of particular weights in the tri-criteria function on the performance of the method across different use cases. We are also interested in using the Δ-equivalences between relation paths to improve embedding and prediction methods that require a deeper knowledge of the KG structure. An example could be generating similar embeddings for entities that have equivalent relation paths.

References

1. Abiteboul, S., Hull, R., Vianu, V. (eds.): Foundations of Databases: The Logical Level, 1st edn. Addison-Wesley Longman Publishing Co., Inc., Boston (1995)
2. Baeza, P.B.: Querying graph databases. In: PODS, pp. 175–188. ACM (2013)
3. Calvanese, D., De Giacomo, G., Lenzerini, M., Vardi, M.Y.: Containment of conjunctive regular path queries with inverse. In: KR, pp. 176–185. Morgan Kaufmann (2000)
4. Calvanese, D., De Giacomo, G., Lenzerini, M., Vardi, M.Y.: Reasoning on regular path queries. SIGMOD Rec. **32**(4), 83–92 (2003)
5. Chandra, A.K., Merlin, P.M.: Optimal implementation of conjunctive queries in relational data bases. In: STOC, pp. 77–90. ACM (1977)
6. Consens, M.P., Mendelzon, A.O.: GraphLog: a visual formalism for real life recursion. In: PODS, pp. 404–416. ACM Press (1990)
7. Dong, X., Gabrilovich, E., Heitz, G., Horn, W., Lao, N., Murphy, K., Strohmann, T., Sun, S., Zhang, W.: Knowledge vault: a web-scale approach to probabilistic knowledge fusion. In: KDD, pp. 601–610. ACM (2014)
8. Freitas, A., da Silva, J.C.P., Curry, E., Buitelaar, P.: A distributional semantics approach for selective reasoning on commonsense graph knowledge bases. In: NLDB, Montpellier, France, 18–20 June 2014, pp. 21–32 (2014)
9. Galárraga, L., Teflioudi, C., Hose, K., Suchanek, F.M.: Fast rule mining in ontological knowledge bases with AMIE+. VLDB J. **24**(6), 707–730 (2015)
10. Kostylev, E.V., Reutter, J.L., Romero, M., Vrgoč, D.: SPARQL with property paths. In: Arenas, M., et al. (eds.) ISWC 2015. LNCS, vol. 9366, pp. 3–18. Springer, Cham (2015). doi:10.1007/978-3-319-25007-6_1
11. Lao, N., Cohen, W.W.: Relational retrieval using a combination of path-constrained random walks. Mach. Learn. **81**(1), 53–67 (2010)
12. Lao, N., Subramanya, A., Pereira, F.C.N., Cohen, W.W.: Reading the web with learned syntactic-semantic inference rules. In: EMNLP-CoNLL, pp. 1017–1026. ACL (2012)
13. Lehmann, J., Isele, R., Jakob, M., Jentzsch, A., Kontokostas, D., Mendes, P.N., Hellmann, S., Morsey, M., van Kleef, P., Auer, S., Bizer, C.: DBpedia - a large-scale, multilingual knowledge base extracted from Wikipedia. Seman. Web **6**(2), 167–195 (2015)
14. Lin, X., Liang, Y., Guan, R.: Compositional learning of relation paths embedding for knowledge base completion. CoRR abs/1611.07232 (2016)
15. Lin, Y., Liu, Z., Sun, M.: Modeling relation paths for representation learning of knowledge bases. CoRR abs/1506.00379 (2015)
16. Mahdisoltani, F., Biega, J., Suchanek, F.M.: YAGO3: a knowledge base from multilingual wikipedias. In: CIDR (2015). www.cidrdb.org
17. Mendelzon, A.O., Wood, P.T.: Finding regular simple paths in graph databases. SIAM J. Comput. **24**(6), 1235–1258 (1995)
18. Miller, G.A.: WordNet: a lexical database for English. Commun. ACM **38**(11), 39–41 (1995)

19. Mitchell, T.M., Cohen Jr., W.W., Hruschka, E.R., Talukdar, P.P., Betteridge, J., Carlson, A., Mishra, B.D., Gardner, M., Kisiel, B., Krishnamurthy, J., Lao, N., Mazaitis, K., Mohamed, T., Nakashole, N., Platanios, E.A., Ritter, A., Samadi, M., Settles, B., Wang, R.C., Wijaya, D.T., Gupta, A., Chen, X., Saparov, A., Greaves, M., Welling, J.: Never-ending learning. In: AAAI, pp. 2302–2310. AAAI Press (2015)
20. Morzy, M., Ławrynowicz, A., Zozuliński, M.: Using substitutive itemset mining framework for finding synonymous properties in linked data. In: Bassiliades, N., Gottlob, G., Sadri, F., Paschke, A., Roman, D. (eds.) RuleML 2015. LNCS, vol. 9202, pp. 422–430. Springer, Cham (2015). doi:10.1007/978-3-319-21542-6_27
21. Pichler, R., Skritek, S.: Containment and equivalence of well-designed SPARQL. In: PODS, pp. 39–50. ACM (2014)
22. Vardi, M.Y.: A note on the reduction of two-way automata to one-way automata. Inf. Process. Lett. **30**(5), 261–264 (1989)
23. Zhang, Z., Gentile, A.L., Augenstein, I., Blomqvist, E., Ciravegna, F.: Mining equivalent relations from linked data. In: ACL, vol. 2, pp. 289–293. The Association for Computer Linguistics (2013)

SRDF: A Novel Lexical Knowledge Graph for Whole Sentence Knowledge Extraction

Sangha Nam, GyuHyeon Choi, and Key-Sun Choi(✉)

Machine Reading Lab, School of Computing, Semantic Web Research Center, KAIST, Daejeon, Republic of Korea
{nam.sangha,wiany11,kschoi}@kaist.ac.kr

Abstract. In this paper, we present a novel lexical knowledge graph called SRDF and describe an extraction system that automatically generates a SRDF graph from the Korean natural language sentence. In the semantic web, knowledge is expressed in the RDF triple form but natural language sentences consist of multiple relationships between the predicates and arguments. For this reason, we design a SRDF graph structure that combines open information extraction method with reification for the whole sentence knowledge extraction. In addition, to add semantics to a SRDF graph, we establish a link between the lexical argument and entity in ontological knowledge base using the Entity Linking system. The proposed knowledge graph is adaptable for many existing semantic web applications. We present the results of an experimental evaluation and demonstrate the use of SRDF graph in developing a Korean SPARQL template generation module in the OKBQA platform.

Keywords: Open Information Extraction · Semantic web · Lexical knowledge graph · Natural language processing · Question answering

1 Introduction

The recent victory of IBMs Watson [1] and Exobrain [2] systems over human competitors in a quiz show has renewed interest in almost all fields of artificial intelligence, such as natural language processing, question answering, knowledge representation, extraction, and reasoning. In order to answer questions effectively, a knowledge base is required to have the necessary clues needed to answer the question. To implement this, numerous information extraction schemes that extract structured knowledge in the form of RDF triple from unstructured text are being studied.

Information extraction approaches can be divided into three major categories. The first one is ontological information extraction [3]. In this method, only knowledge that matches a predefined ontology and schema can be learnt and extracted. Traditional approaches rely heavily on human intervention in the form of manually designed rules and training data about pre-specified relations. The distant supervision [4] technique was proposed to overcome this problem. In this approach, training data is automatically collected using knowledge and an associated sentence pair. Many of the proposed schemes could expand target relations and reduce the cost of constructing manual

J. Gracia et al. (Eds.): LDK 2017, LNAI 10318, pp. 315–329, 2017.
DOI: 10.1007/978-3-319-59888-8_27

training data using the distant supervision approach. However, distantly supervised training data is noisy, and an additional effort to refine [5] this is necessary. Moreover, it is impossible to extract all the knowledge from a human-written text and categorize it into only one ontology.

To overcome the limitations of ontological information extraction approaches, Open Information Extraction (Open IE) systems were proposed. It is possible to process massive text corpora without having to expend much human effort using these systems. Moreover, Open IE only takes the corpus as input, and can extract the knowledge ontology independently. Reverb [6], OLLIE [7], ClausIE [8] are representative Open IE systems. These are knowledge extraction systems based on the dependency parsing of input sentence that outputs lexical-level knowledge in the ternary or N-ary form. Based on this, an Open QA system was studied in [9]. In Open QA, an attempt was made to improve performance by adding the question paraphrase module to overcome the limitation of lexical level knowledge representation. However, this is not easy because of the absence of semantic relations. Although the existing Open IE system has the advantage of wider extraction scope over traditional IE, it has a disadvantage that it cannot extract the knowledge of the whole sentence.

Recently, the Abstraction Meaning Representation (AMR) [10] graph was proposed to describe the semantics of whole sentences as rooted, labeled, directed, acyclic graphs (DAGs). They are intended to abstract away from syntactic representations, in the sense that sentences that are similar in meaning should be assigned the same AMR, even if they are not identically worded. For example, the two sentences, "`he described her as a genius`" and "`his description of her: genius`" resulted in the same AMR graph. AMR defines the general semantics, quantities, date, and list relations, and includes framesets of PropBank [11] so that the AMR graph can have semantics. As in the above example, in order to arrive at the same AMR graph for input statements that have different expressions but the same meaning, a human annotator generates an AMR graph for English sentences. As a result, about 50,000 AMR graphs were manually constructed over The Little Prince Corpus, Bio-related corpus, and other documents such as newswire, discussion forum, and web logs. Using this AMR data, AMR-LD [12] has been researched to generate RDF triples using an Entity Linking system and mapping table between the AMR relation and ontology relation. Moreover, efforts have been undertaken to design automatic AMR parsing systems [13]. Thus, the demand for research on extracting knowledge of the whole sentence is useful for many natural language processing applications such as machine translation. AMR has a disadvantage in that it is dependent on framesets of PropBank. For example, "`History teacher`" and "`History professor`" have different AMR graphs since the frameset contains teacher but not professor, and AMR is biased towards English. This illustrates the need for an integrated approach toward creating the AMR for other languages or to make a graph similar to AMR for each language.

In this paper, we propose a new lexical level knowledge graph called SentenceRDF (SRDF) and a SRDF extraction system that automatically generates SRDF graphs from unstructured Korean texts. SRDF differs from other Open IE systems in terms of the whole-sentence extraction and knowledge representation in reified triple form. In semantic web, knowledge is commonly expressed in RDF triple form that consists of a subject, predicate, and object. However, multiple relationships exist between arguments within a sentence in many cases. The goal of SRDF is to make a graph about a whole sentence like AMR. In other words, we put all the predicates and arguments in a sentence into one SRDF graph and make a large-scale lexical level knowledge graph that merges these graphs. The SRDF graph is generated by a transition of the predicate-argument structure on dependency parsing, and the structure of SRDF is simple. Therefore, a system that automatically extracts SRDF graphs in various languages can be easily designed. We describe the specification of SRDF in Sect. 2, an extraction system in Sect. 3, experimental results in Sect. 4, and an example application using the SRDF graph in Sect. 5.

2 SentenceRDF

2.1 Definition

SentenceRDF is a rooted, undirected, acyclic, and ontology independent lexical knowledge graph. SRDF is generated by a transition of the predicate-argument structure on dependency parsing of a sentence into RDF triple form. One SRDF graph is generated per input sentence. SRDF has the RDF form that consists of a subject, predicate, and object to make it compatible with existing knowledge base and semantic web applications such as the SPARQL [14] query language. A common feature of the SRDF graph and syntactic tree is that they can be searched by concatenating all the words in the input sentence into a single graph, and the difference is that the SRDF graph is represented by a reified RDF triple form, a kind of knowledge representation. In other words, SRDF graph is a bridge between sentence and RDF triple.

Figure 1 shows a SRDF graph generation scenario and Fig. 2 depicts an example SRDF graph in reified triple form. To generate the SRDF graph, the noun phrases and verbs are first extracted from the input sentences. In this example, there are two noun

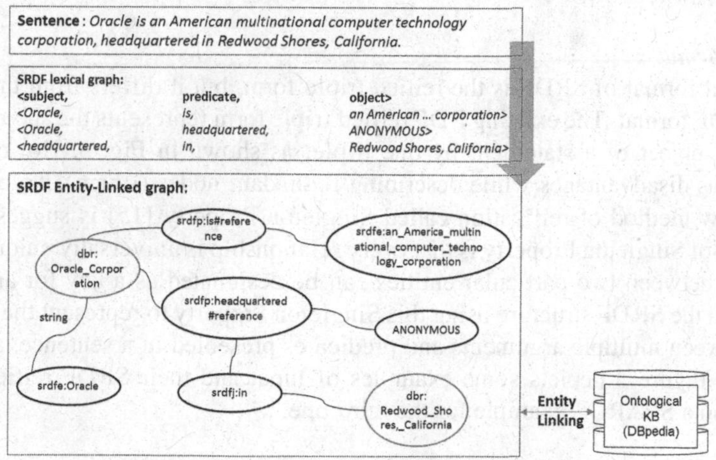

Fig. 1. SRDF graph generation process

phrases; “`Oracle`” and “`Redwood Shores, California`” and two verbs “`is`” and “`headquartered`”. Next, a lexical knowledge graph is created from the perspective of Open IE using these noun phrases and verbs. Then, the link between the lexical argument and entity in ontological knowledge base is established to add semantics using the Entity Linking system. SRDF graph is a combination of entity and lexical factors, so it can express additional information in a single graph that the ontological knowledge base cannot represent.

```
<dbr:Oracle_Corporation, srdf:string, srdfe:Oracle>
<dbr:Oracle_Corporation, srdfp:is#reference,
srdfe:an_America_..._corporation>
<dbr:Oracle_Corporation, srdfp:headquartered#reference,
ANONMOUS>
<srdfep:headquartered#reference, srdfj:in,
dbr:Redwood_Shores, California>
```

Fig. 2. Example of SRDF graph in reified triple form

2.2 Specification

Input and Output Format

Input Format

SRDF takes a natural language sentence as input if it (1) has a subject, and (2) there is a verb for the subject. The subject and the predicate are mandatory among the key elements of a sentence such as subject, predicate, object, and complement. The object, adjective, and idiom are optional. While extracting ontological knowledge requires at least two arguments, SRDF can extract a triple when the input has subject and predicate. For example, the SRDF of a sentence “`The sun rises.`” would be `<The sun, rises, ANONYMOUS>`.

Output Format

The output format of SRDF is the reified triple form, but it differs from the typical reified RDF format. The existing RDF reified triple form represents the subject, predicate, and object of a statement by one triple, as shown in Fig. 3. However, this method has disadvantages while describing redundant nodes (`stmt`). To overcome this, a new method of reification called Singleton Property [15] is suggested. The main idea of Singleton Property is that every relationship is universally unique, so the predicate between two particular entities can be designated as a key for any triple. We design the SRDF structure using this Singleton Property to represent the relationships between multiple arguments and predicates presented in a sentence, as shown in Fig. 4. Figure 5 depicts some examples of input and their SRDF reified triples output, and a SPARQL example for the third one.

```
<stmt, rdf:type, rdf:statement>
<stmt, rdf:subject, subj>
<stmt, rdf:predicate, pred>
<stmt, rdf:object, object>
```

Fig. 3. RDF reified triple form

```
<Subject, OneProperty, object>
<OneProperty, AnotherProperty | Pre/Post-position, Object>
<One | AnotherProperty, OtherProperty | Pre/Post-position, Object>
… (cont.)
```

Fig. 4. SRDF reified triple form

```
I1: "The earth rotates."
O11: <dbr:Earth, srdfp:rotates, ANONYMOUS>

I2: "Obama was reelected defeating Romney"
O21: <dbr:Barack_Obama, srdfp:was_reelected, ANONYMOUS>
O22: <srdfp:was_reelected, srdfp:defeating, dbr:Mitt_Romney>

I3: "Steve Jobs founded Apple in 1976"
O31: <dbr:Steve_Jobs, srdfp:founded, dbr:Apple_Inc.>
O32: <srdfp:founded, srdfj:in, dbr:1976.>

"When Steve Jobs founded Apple?"
SPARQL SELECT ?x WHERE {
  dbr:Steve_Jobs   ?p                  dbr:Apple_(Inc) .
  ?p               srdf:abstraction    srdfp:founded .
  ?p               ?j                  ?x .
  ?x               rdf:type            xsd:YEAR
}
```

Fig. 5. Examples of SRDF reified triples

Structure

The structure of SRDF is a graph represented in the reified triple form. For a single input statement, a small graph is created that includes all the arguments and predicates. Many such small graphs are combined to form a large graph. In this chapter, we describe the structure of a SRDF graph in terms of a small graph. Each node in the SRDF graph consists of a lexicalized argument, a lexicalized predicate, and a pre/post-position.

Lexicalized Argument

In the SRDF structure, a lexicalized argument can be placed in the subject and the object position. Lexicalized argument is a noun phrase presented in a sentence, and the term "ANONYMOUS". However, "ANONYMOUS" can only be placed in the object position when there is no object corresponding to the property. Moreover, a lexicalized argument is replaced by the entity of ontological knowledge base only when they are linkable. Figure 6 shows examples of lexicalized arguments and linked entities in a SRDF graph.

```
I1: "Steve Jobs shows great performance."
O11: <dbr:Steve_Jobs(KB-entity), srdfp:shows,
srdfe:great_performance(Lexicalized Argument)>

I2: "The earth rotates."
O21: <dbr:Earth, srdfp:rotates, ANONYMOUS(Lexicalized Argument)>
```

Fig. 6. Examples of lexicalized argument and linked entity in SRDF

```
I1: "Steve Jobs shows great performance."
O11: <dbr:Steve_Jobs, srdfp:shows#reference(Lexicalized Predicate),
srdfe:great_performance>

I2: "Barack Obama was reelected defeating Mitt Romney."
O21: <dbr:Barack_Obama,
srdfp:was_reelected#reference(Lexicalized Predicate), ANONYMOUS>
O22: <srdfp:was_reelected#reference(Lexicalized Predicate),
srdfp:defeating#reference(Lexicalized Predicate),
dbr:Mitt_Romney>
```

Fig. 7. Examples of lexicalized predicate in SRDF

Lexicalized Predicate In the SRDF structure, a lexicalized predicate generated by attaching the verb and its reference can be placed in the subject and the predicate positions. The reason for attaching reference is to reveal the source of this knowledge and provide a way to identify each lexicalized predicate. The same verb can be used in different meanings in different knowledge. There is a chance for confusion if a lexicalized predicate is constructed using only the verb. Therefore, lexicalized predicate must be associated with a reference to distinguish them.

Pre/Post-position

Pre or post-position in a sentence can sometimes serve as a key feature that determines the meaning of the sentence. Especially, in agglutinative languages such as Korean, the meaning of the sentence changes according to the postpositions. Besides, preposition is also important to identify the types of argument such as location, time, etc. Thus, we designate pre or post-positions as nodes in the SRDF graph. The position of pre or post-position is predicate on reified triple. Figure 8 shows an example of pre or post-position in the SRDF. We assume that pre or post-position is useful while performing natural language generation using the SRDF graph, or providing semantics to the SRDF graph.

I_1: "Sun-sin Yi was born in Geoncheon-dong at 1545."
O_{11}: <dbr:Yi_Sun-sin, srdfp:was_born#reference, ANONYMOUS>
O_{12}: <srdfp:was_born#reference, **srdfj:at**$_{\textbf{(preposition)}}$, dbr:1545>
O_{13}: <srdfp:was_born#reference, **srdfj:in**$_{\textbf{(preposition)}}$, srdfe:Geoncheon-dong>

Fig. 8. Examples of pre/post-position in SRDF

Reification

SRDF triple applies reification for knowledge representation while maintaining RDF triple form and whole sentence extraction. As mentioned before, there are often multiple relationships between predicates and arguments in a sentence, making it difficult to represent all of these using the simple RDF triple form. In Fig. 7, the first input sentence is "Steve Jobs shows great performance". Here, there are only two arguments, "Steve Jobs", and "great performance", and only one predicate, "shows". Hence, the output SRDF triple is also simple <Steve Jobs, shows, great performance> with no reification like the Open IE style. The second input sentence is "Barack Obama was reelected defeating Mitt Romney". In this case, there are two arguments, "Barack Obama", and "Mitt Romney", and two predicates, "was reelected", and "defeating". We cannot represent these relationships using the simple RDF triple form. Therefore, as shown in O_{21} and O_{22}, we construct a SRDF graph in the form of a reified triple. The algorithm of reification is described in Sect. 3.3.

Reference

Since the SRDF graph is generated using the text available on the web as input data, it is desirable to reveal the reference of the source text. This is because lexicalized arguments and predicates may have different meanings even if they are in the same lexical form. In the SRDF structure, the reference consists of the document id, sentence id, and last modified date of document. In AMR, the same AMR graph is generated manually for sentences that have different expressions but the same meaning using semantic

I_1: "Jimmy carter was born on October 1, 1924."
O_{11}: <dbr:Jimmy_Carter,
srdfp:was_born#5$_{\textbf{(docid)}}$**#27**$_{\textbf{(stcid)}}$**#20170205**$_{\textbf{(date)}}$, ANONYMOUS>
O_{12}: <**srdfp:was_born#5**$_{\textbf{(docid)}}$**#27**$_{\textbf{(stcid)}}$**#20170205**$_{\textbf{(date)}}$, srdfj:on, srdfe:October 1, 1924>

Fig. 9. Examples of reference in SRDF

relations such as the framesets of PropBank. However, we assume that the SRDF graph is generated by a computer automatically from web-scale text, and so we have no semantic relations. Assigning semantics to a SRDF graph is postponed until the SRDF graph is created, so we attach a reference to the lexicalized predicate (Fig. 9).

Abstraction

As mentioned before, we attach a reference to each lexicalized predicate to distinguish lexicalized predicates that have the same surface form but different meaning. Thus, to increase the usability of the SRDF graph, abstraction is necessary. For example, as shown in Fig. 10, although two lexicalized predicates have different references associated with "`led`" in the Korean War and "`led`" in the Second World War, they should be abstracted to the upper expression to increase the usability of the SRDF graph. In this example, "`srdfp:led#31#15#20170325`" and "`srdfp:led#98#85#-20160514`" are abstracted to "`srdfp:led`". By using the abstraction, the SPARQL query can be answered by the SRDF graph itself as shown by the example in Fig. 10.

I_1: "MacArthur led the Korean War."
O_{11}: <dbr:Douglas_MacArthur, srdfp:led#31#15#20170325, dbr:Korean_War>

I_2: "Winston Churchill led the Second World War."
O_{21}: <dbr:Winston_Churchill, srdfp:led#98#85#20160514, dbr:World_War_II>

Abstracted Triples_{11}: <srdfp:led#31#15#20170325, srdf:abstraction, srdfp:led>
Abstracted Triples_{21}: <srdfp:led#98#85#20160514, srdf:abstraction, srdfp:led>

"Who led the Korean War?"
SPARQL SELECT ?x **WHERE** {
  ?x ?abstraction dbr:Korean_War.
  ?abstraction srdf:abstraction srdfp:led .
}

Fig. 10. Examples of abstraction in SRDF

3 Korean SRDF Extraction System Architecture

In this chapter, we describe the design and implementation of a system that automatically generates the SRDF graph for Korean input sentences based on the SRDF structure described so far. The SRDF extraction system simply receives input as a text and outputs an extracted set of reified triples. The system operation procedure consists of four steps: Preprocessor, Basic Skeleton Tree (BST) generator, SRDF generator, and Entity Linker. The details are shown in Fig. 11. All the examples that follow have been translated to

English to facilitate understanding, but the system architecture and algorithm are not specific to the Korean language. The contents of Chaps. 3.1 to 3.3 have been previously published [16] by the author. However, these are included here for completeness to help understand further discussions in this paper.

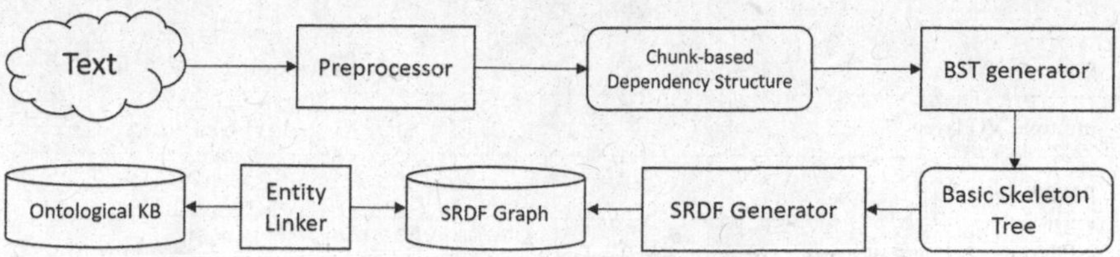

Fig. 11. System architecture of Korean SRDF extraction module

3.1 Preprocessing

The Preprocessor consists of three sub-modules: Sentence segmentor, Chunker, and Dependency parser. The Sentence segmentor divides a sentence into its component sentences and attaches the subject to the divided sentences. The Chunker returns only noun phrases and verb groups. Noun phrases can contain adnominal phrase and verb groups could contain adverb phrase. Finally, the Dependency parser outputs a chunk-based dependency structure as shown in Fig. 12.

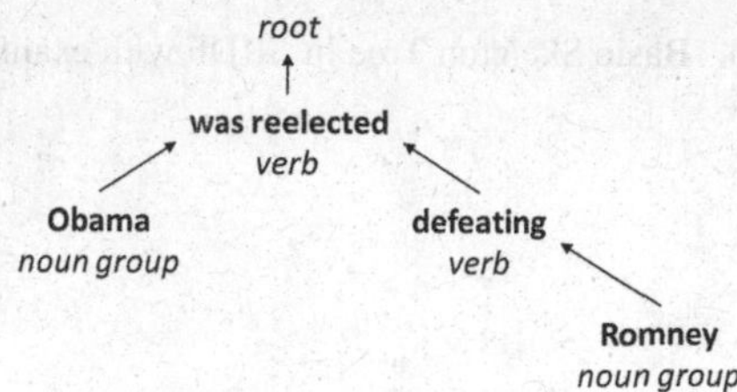

Fig. 12. Example of chunk-based dependency structure

3.2 Basic Skeleton Tree Generator

The BST generator takes a chunk-based dependency structure as input and outputs a BST. The chunk-based dependency structure strongly depends on the language characteristics. For example, the dependency structure of English, Korean, and Chinese are different from one another. Therefore, we create an intermediate structure between the chunk-based dependency structure and SRDF graph. The BST maintains almost the same structure for any language and can be adapted to SRDF generation rules as well. Figure 13 illustrates a Basic Skeleton Tree example. The BST has five layers: root-Verb Group (VG), VG, Noun Phrase (NP), preposition, and recursion layer. The root-VG layer is the top layer and has only one node that is the root verb group on dependency structure. The NP layer contains all noun phrases including the subject of the sentence.

The VG layer is placed between the root-VG and the NP layer. There could be numerous VG layers depending on the depth of corresponding verb groups in chunk-based dependency structures. The preposition layer contains only preposition of its noun phrase and is located over the NP layer. The recursion layer decomposes noun phrases that have more details such as an adnominal phrase.

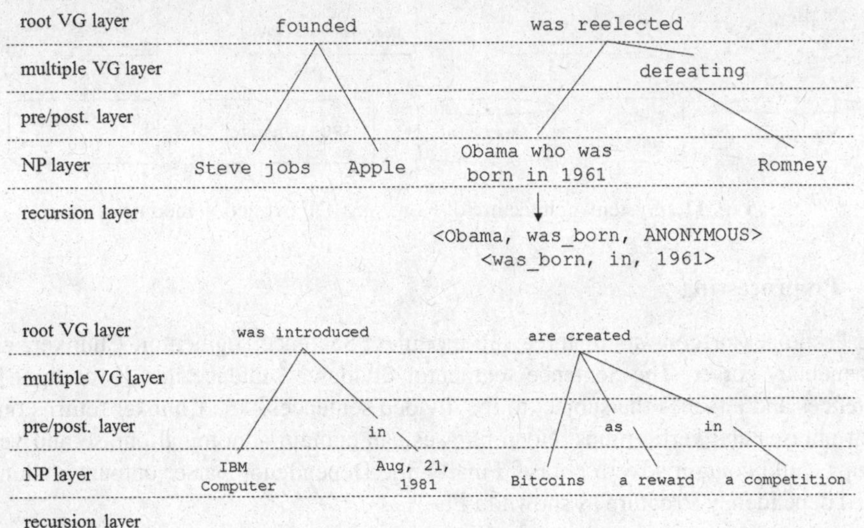

Fig. 13. Basic Skeleton Tree in SRDF with examples

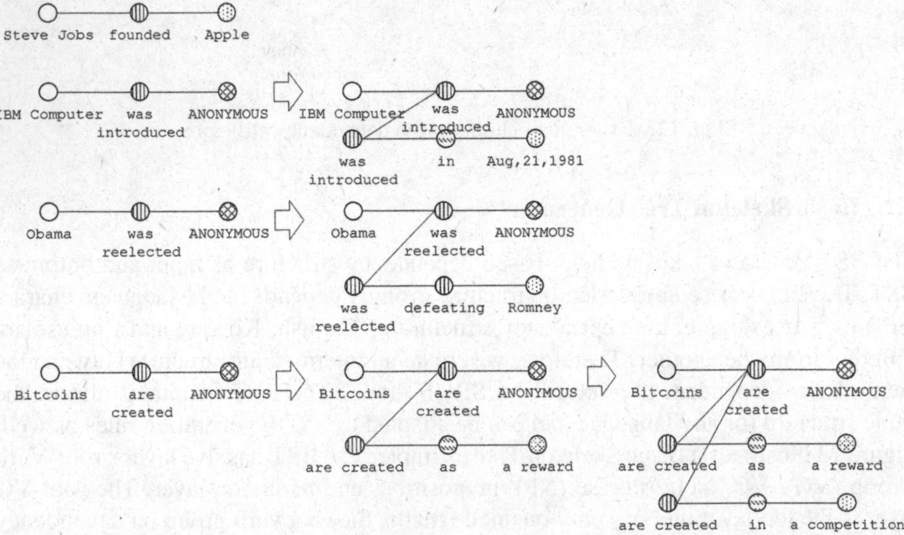

Fig. 14. Examples of SRDF reified triple generation algorithm

3.3 SRDF Triple Generator

SRDF generator takes a BST as the input and outputs a lexical knowledge graph in the reified triple for musing the simple and concise algorithm shown in Algorithm 1. The input to the algorithm consist of a graph `G`, a subject of sentence `sbj`, a root verb group `pred`, and child nodes of root verb group `objQueue` and the output is returned in `G`. Each `obj` in the `objQueue` is checked to verify if it is in NP layer or not. If the `obj` is in the NP layer, a triple is created and inserted into the graph `G` (Line 4). If not, an `ANONYMOUS` triple is created and inserted into `G`. Then, the `sbj` and `pred` are changed for reification (Line 6 to 8). Finally, the `generateSRDF` function is called recursively (Line 9). Figure 14 shows an example of our algorithm for the third BST in Fig. 13.

Algorithm 1 SRDF reified triple generation algorithm

```
1: procedure generateSRDF(G, sbj, pred, objQueue)
2:     for obj in objQueue do
3:         if obj is in NP layer then
4:             G <- G ∪ {<sbj, pred, obj>} ▷ Overwrite
ANONYMOUS object with the same sbj and pred
5:         else
6:             G <- G ∪ {<sbj, pred, ANONYMOUS>}
7:             sbj <- pred
8:             pred <- obj
9:             generateSRDF(G, sbj, pred, obj.child)
10:    return G
```

3.4 Entity Linker

Entity Linker takes a SRDF graph and the entities in an input text as input. Entities are recognized by using the Korean Entity Linking system (ELU) [17]. The output of ELU consists of an array of entities, where each entity contains a word token, entity URI, score, and position of sentence. The Entity Linker matches the lexicalized argument nodes and linked entities, and replaces the lexicalized argument with an entity if they are exactly matched. Figure 15 shows an example of Entity Linker. In this example, the Entity Linking system outputs that "`Bitcoins`" is "`DBR:Bitcoin`," but "`a reward`," and "`a competition`" are not entities. Thus, the node "`Bitcoins`" is replaced with "`DBR:Bitcoin`" and the nodes "`a reward`" and "`a competition`" remain as lexicalized arguments.

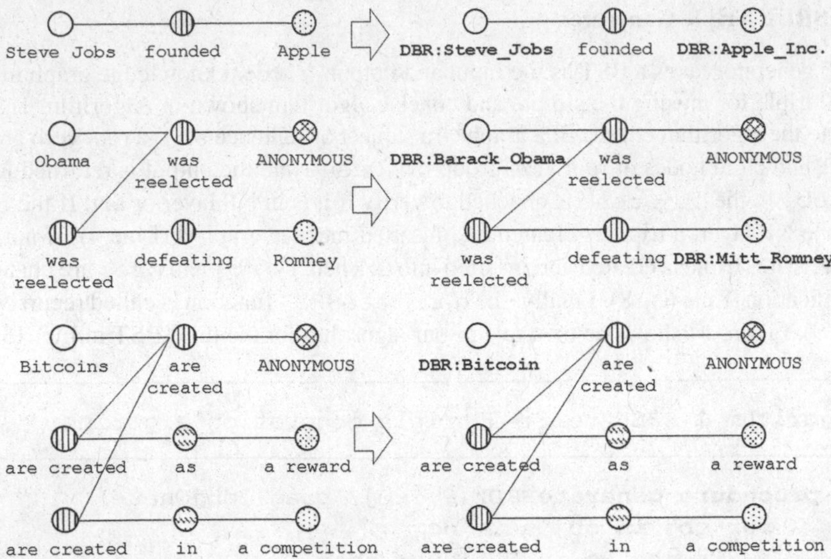

Fig. 15. Examples of entity linker

4 Experiments

The performance of the SRDF system was evaluated using randomly sampled sentences from featured articles in the Korean Wikipedia. This evaluation was based only on the extracted SRDF graph itself, except Entity Linker. The evaluation results were assessed by two human evaluators based on the precision, recall, completeness, and the number of extractions. As shown in Table 1, our system extracted 407 triples from 137 sentences. The precision was 77% and the recall was 79%. Completeness indicates whether all the information was extracted as reified triples from an input sentence or not. The overall completeness was observed to be 93%. We found that the 7% of incomplete extractions was caused by the Korean Analyzer[1], specifically a problem related to correctly finding the subject in a given sentence.

Table 1. Evaluation results

Precision	Recall	F1-score	Completeness
0.77 (314/407)	0.79 (251/320)	0.78	0.93 (127/137)

On analyzing the errors of the SRDF extraction system, we found three error types: dependency parsing, sentence segmentor, and chunking. The error count and ratio of each are shown in Table 2. The dependency parsing error occurs in the Korean Analyzer, and so we cannot handle it. The sentence segmentor error usually occurs in sentences that contain quotes and narrative phrases. While creating a chunking module, it would

[1] Specifically, we used ETRI Korean NLP tool.

be good to use a CRF-based learning approach, but there was not enough training data in Korean. Hence, we created a rule-based chunking module that has intermediate performance. If we implement a preprocessing module with higher performance, the overall performance will increase. The Korean SRDF extraction system was implemented on a server[2] using REST API. The input format is application/json like `{"text": "input_sentence"}`.

Table 2. Error ratio

Dependency parsing	Sentence segmentor	Chunking
36 (39.6%)	35 (38.5%)	20 (22%)

5 Application of SRDF

5.1 SenTGM

Open Knowledge Base and Question Answering (OKBQA) [18] is a community that focuses on advanced technology for developing a question answering system. The virtue of OKBQA is open collaboration that harmonizes resources developed by different groups scattered around the world. We design SenTGM for Template Generation, the first step of OKBQA, using our SRDF system. SenTGM takes a Korean natural language question and produces a pseudo SPARQL query defined in Templator [19]. It is a fully functional system capable of processing the Korean natural language question in OKBQA framework properly. The architecture and an example of SenTGM is shown in Fig. 16.

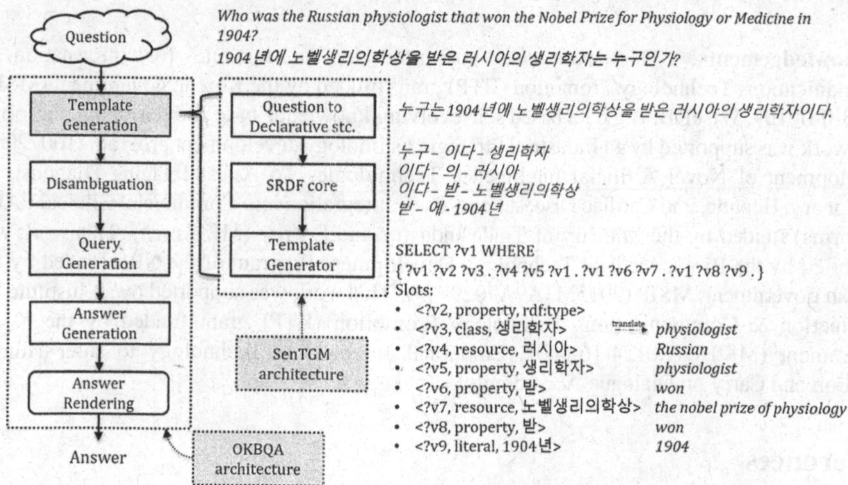

Fig. 16. Architecture and example of SenTGM

[2] http://wisekb.kaist.ac.kr:8832/el_srdf.

SenTGM starts by converting the natural language question into a declarative sentence. Then, the SRDF triple including the question target, such as who, whom, where, and what, is generated in the SRDF core. Finally, in the Template Generator, the SRARQL template is generated based on the SRDF graph created in the previous step. The advantage of SenTGM is that the generated SPARQL includes all the clues given in the question since SRDF is a whole sentence extraction method. This approach works well with the Question Generation at the middle of the OKBQA pipeline, because the Question Generation module generates SPARQL with various options using clues from the Template Generation module. Measuring the performance of the Template Generation module is a hard problem, so we can only say that SenTGM works well in the OKBQA 4[3] official test suite of 10 questions reasonably. In the future, if a Question to Declarative sentence module is expanded and improved the overall performance will increase.

6 Conclusion

In this paper, we proposed a new lexical knowledge graph called SRDF and the SRDF graph extraction algorithm. Our approach is a novel method that combines aspects of the Open IE approach with reification, singleton property, and method for whole sentence knowledge extraction. Furthermore, the SRDF graph represents the extracted knowledge in a reified triple form for it to be compatible with existing semantic web applications such as the question answering system. We demonstrated that our SRDF graph could be used in the OKBQA framework. In the future, we will analyze approaches to add more semantic factors to the SRDF graph to resolve the ambiguity in terms of predicate linking, and implement a question answering method over the SRDF graph.

Acknowledgements. This work was supported by an Institute for Information & communications Technology Promotion (IITP) grant funded by the Korean government (MSIP) (2013-0-00109, WiseKB: Big data based self-evolving knowledge base and reasoning platform). This work was supported by an Industrial Strategic technology development program (10072064, Development of Novel Artificial Intelligence Technologies To Assist Imaging Diagnosis of Pulmonary, Hepatic, and Cardiac Diseases and Their Integration into Commercial Clinical PACS Platforms) funded by the Ministry of Trade Industry and Energy (MI, Korea). This work was supported by the Bio & Medical Technology Development Program of the NRF funded by the Korean government, MSIP (2015M3A9A7029735). This work was supported by an Institute for Information & Communications Technology Promotion (IITP) grant funded by the Korea government (MSIP) (R0124-16-0002, Emotional Intelligence Technology to Infer Human Emotion and Carry on Dialogue Accordingly).

References

1. Ferrucci, D.A.: Introduction to "This is Watson". IBM J. Res. Dev. **56**(3.4), 1 (2012)
2. Exobrain. http://www.exobrain.kr/exointro

[3] http://4.okbqa.org.

3. Wimalasuriya, D.C., Dou, D.: Ontology-based information extraction: an introduction and a survey of current approaches. J. Inf. Sci. **36**, 306–323 (2012)
4. Mintz, M., Bills, S., Snow, R., Jurafsky, D.: Distant supervision for relation extraction without labeled data. In: Proceedings of the Joint Conference of the 47th Annual Meeting of the ACL and the 4th International Joint Conference on Natural Language Processing of the AFNLP, vol. 2, pp. 1003–1011 (2009)
5. Xu, W., Hoffmann, R., Zhao, L., Grishman, R.: Filling knowledge base gaps for distant supervision of relation extraction, vol. 2, pp. 665–670. ACL (2013)
6. Banko, M., Cafarella, M.J., Soderland, S., Broadhead, M., Etzioni, O.: Open information extraction from the web. In: International Joint Conference on Artificial Intelligence, pp. 2670–2676 (2007)
7. Schmitz, M., Bart, R., Soderland, S., Etzioni, O.: Open language learning for information extraction. In: Proceedings of the 2012 Joint Conference on Empirical Methods in Natural Language Processing and Computational Natural Language Learning, pp. 523–534. Association for Computational Linguistics (2012)
8. Del Corro, L., Gemulla, R.: Clausie: clause-based open information extraction. In: Proceedings of the 22nd International Conference on World Wide Web, pp. 355–366. ACM (2013)
9. Fader, A., Zettlemoyer, L., Etzoini, O.: Open question answering over curated and extracted knowledge bases. In: Proceedings of the 20th ACM SIGKDD International Conference on Knowledge Discovery and Data Mining, pp. 1156–1165. ACM (2014)
10. Banarescu, L., Bonial, C., Cai, S., Georgescu, M., Griffitt, K., Hermjakob, U., Knight, K., Palmer, M., Schneider, N.: Abstract meaning representation for sembanking. In: Proceedings of the 7th Linguistic Annotation Workshop and Interoperability with Discourse, pp. 178–186 (2013)
11. Martha, P., Dan, G., Paul, K.: The Proposition Bank: a corpus annotated with semantic roles. Comput. Linguist. J. **31**, 71–106 (2005)
12. Burns, G.A., Hermjakob, U., Ambite, J.L.: Abstràct meaning representations as linked data. In: Groth, P., Simperl, E., Gray, A., Sabou, M., Krötzsch, M., Lecue, F., Flöck, F., Gil, Y. (eds.) ISWC 2016. LNCS, vol. 9982, pp. 12–20. Springer, Cham (2016). doi: 10.1007/978-3-319-46547-0_2
13. Wang, C., Xue, N., Pradhan, S., Pradhan, S.: A transition-based algorithm for AMR parsing. In: HLT-NAACL, pp. 366–375 (2015)
14. Prud, E., Seaborne, A.: SPARQL Query Language for RDF (2006)
15. Nguyen, V., Bodenreider, O., Sheth, A.: Don't like RDF reification?: Making statements about statements using singleton property. In: Proceedings of the 23rd International Conference on World Wide Web, pp. 759–770. ACM (2014)
16. Nam, S., Choi, G., Hahm, Y., Choi, K.: SRDF: extracting lexical knowledge graph for preserving sentence meaning. In: OKBQA 2016 (2016)
17. Kim, J., Choi, K.: KoEL: Korean entity linking system using sentence features and extended entity relations. Master's thesis, KAIST, Daejeon, Korea, p. 40 (2017, in Korean)
18. OKBQA. http://www.okbqa.org
19. Unger, C., Bühmann, L., Lehmann, J., Ngonga Ngomo, A.C., Gerber, D., Cimiano, P.: Template-based question answering over RDF data. In: Proceedings of the 21st International Conference on World Wide Web, pp. 639–648. ACM (2012)

Letting the Genie Out of the Lamp: Using Natural Language Processing Tools to Predict Math Performance

Scott Crossley[1(✉)] and Victor Kostyuk[2(✉)]

[1] Applied Linguistics and ESL, Georgia State University, Atlanta, GA, USA
scrossley@gsu.edu
[2] Reasoning Mind, Houston, TX, USA
vak@reasoningmind.org

Abstract. This study examines links between natural language processing and its application in math education. Specifically, the study examines language production and math success in an on-line, blended learning math program. Unlike previous studies that have relied on correlational analyses between linguistic knowledge tests and standardized math tests or compared math success between proficient and non-proficient speakers of English, this study examines the linguistic features of students' language production while e-mailing a virtual pedagogical agent. In addition, the study examines a number of non-linguistic features such as grade and objective met within the program. The findings indicate that linguistic features related to the use of standardized language use explain around 8% of math success. These linguistic features outperform non-linguistic features.

Keywords: Natural language processing · Online tutoring systems · Math education · Text analytics

1 Introduction

A number of cognitive skills are necessary for young students to be successful in the math classroom. Primarily, research has focused on skills that strongly overlap with math knowledge including spatial attention and quantitative ability [1]. Less attention has been paid to supporting cognitive skills such as language ability. However, some researchers argue that language skills are needed to transfer cognitive operations between math and language domains.

In support of this notion, researchers have begun to examine links between language skills and math success with the understanding that student with greater language abilities are likely able to better engage with math concepts and problems. More specifically, this research is premised on the notion that success in the math classroom is at least partially explained through language development that allows students to constructively participate in math discussions, understand and solve word problems, as well as quantitatively engage with math problems that arise outside of the classroom [2, 3]. In a similar fashion, it is argued that math literacy is not just having knowledge of numbers and symbols, but also having the language skills to understand the discourse of math

J. Gracia et al. (Eds.): LDK 2017, LNAI 10318, pp. 330–342, 2017.
DOI: 10.1007/978-3-319-59888-8_28

(i.e., the words surrounding the numbers and symbols) [4]. While other cognitive skills are also critical to math success.

Until recently, studies linking language skills to math success in the classroom generally relied on correlational analyses among standardized tests of math and linguistic knowledge. For instance, several studies have examined links between tests of language proficiency (e.g., syntax, knowledge, verbal ability, and phonological skills) and success on tests of math knowledge (e.g. algebraic notation, procedural arithmetic, and arithmetic word problems [2, 5]. Other studies have compared success on standardized math tests between first language (L1) speakers of English and second language speakers of English, who have lower linguistic ability [6–8]. However, the majority of studies have not examined the actual language produced by students and the relationship between the complexity of this language and success on math assessments (see [9] for an exception).

This study builds on the work of Crossley et al. [9] by examining links between the affect and complexity of language produced by students in an e-mail system used within a math intelligent tutoring system and students' math success within the system. To do so, we examine students' emails within the systems for a number of linguistic features related to text cohesion, lexical sophistication, and affect derived from natural language processing (NLP) tools. The goal of this study is to examine the extent to which the language features produced by students are predictive of their math success within the tutoring system. In addition to the linguistic features, we also examine a number of non-linguistic factors that are potentially predictive of math success including grade, number of messages sent and received by the students, hours spent on-line, and number of objective met within the platform.

1.1 Linking Language and Math

Previous studies have examined links between language proficiency and math skills in native speakers (NS) of English. These studies generally demonstrate strong links between math ability and language ability. As an example, Macgregor and Price [5] analyzed relations between three cognitive indicators of language proficiency (syntax, metalinguistic awareness of symbols, and language ambiguity) and understanding of algebraic notation. Those students who scored high on the algebra test also scored well on language tests. A follow-up study using more difficult algebra found a stronger relationship between algebraic notation and language ability. The authors concluded that low metalinguistic awareness was negatively related to algebra learning. Similarly, Vukovic and Lesaux [2] examined links among arithmetic knowledge (arithmetic word problems and procedural arithmetic), symbolic number skills, and linguistic skills (i.e., phonological skills and general verbal ability) in NS students. They also included control variables consisting of visual–spatial ability and working memory. The participants comprised 287 third graders using the same math curriculum from five different schools. Their results showed links between linguistic and math skills, but that the linguistic skills differed in their degree of relation with arithmetic knowledge. For example, general verbal ability was indirectly related through symbolic number skills while phonological skills were found to be directly related to arithmetic knowledge. Vukovic and Lesaux argued that general verbal ability was related to how children reason numerically but that phonological skills were related to executing arithmetic problems.

Other research has investigated indirect links between math and language skills. Hernandez [10] examined relationships between reading ability and math achievement levels under the presumption that there was a positive correlation between math scores and reading skills. In his study, he analyzed 652 ninth-grade students' scores from the reading and math sections of the *Texas Assessment of Knowledge and Skills*. Correlations between the math scores and the reading scores were calculated for tests taken in sixth, seventh, and eighth grades. The results demonstrated significant positive correlations between reading ability and math achievement. These findings led Hernandez to recommend that students' reading skills should factored to provide more effective math instruction, especially for poor readers.

Not all studies have found significant links between math knowledge and language skills. For instance, LeFevre et al. [1] conducted a longitudinal study of 182 NS children ages 4 to 8 (37 in preschool and 145 in kindergarten) that followed the children's math progress. Data collection from a year including non-linguistic skills such as spatial attention, early numeracy skills (nonlinguistic arithmetic and number naming) quantitative knowledge and linguistics skills (phonological awareness and receptive vocabulary). Dependent variables included research-based and standardized tests of math ability. The results indicated that linguistic skills were significantly related to number naming, that quantitative abilities were related to processing numerical magnitudes, and that spatial attention was related to a variety of numerical and math tests. However, the quantitative abilities and spatial attention results reported that non-linguistic features were stronger predictors of math ability.

In terms of language production, only one study to our knowledge has examined links between the language produced by NS students and their success in the math classroom. Crossley et al. [9] examined the linguistic and affective features of student discourse while students were engaged in collaborative problem solving within an online math tutoring system. Student speech was transcribed and natural language processing tools were used to extract linguistic information related to text cohesion, lexical sophistication, and affect. They examined links between the linguistic features and pretest and posttest math performance scores as well as links with a number of non-linguistic factors including gender, age, grade, school, and content focus (procedural versus conceptual). The results indicated that non-linguistic factors are not predictive of math scores but that linguistic features related to cohesion, affect, and lexical proficiency explained around 30% of the variance in the math scores such that higher scoring students produced more cohesive texts that were more linguistically sophisticated.

Beyond studies examining NS math students, a rich source of evidence for connecting language and math abilities are non-native speakers (NNS) of English who are learning math skills in an English classroom. NNS, unlike NS, generally have lower language skills in English and it is argued that these lower language skills will result in lower math skills. The general notion behind this theory is that most NNS have not reached a threshold of language proficiency that allows them the resources to perform on par with NS [11]. This notion is supported by the US Department of Education [7], which reports that over a five-year period (from 1st to 5th grade), NS report higher math scores than proficient NNS who report higher math scores lower proficiency NNS.

A number of studies have supported the findings reported by the US Department of Education report. For instance, Alt et al. [6] investigated relations between language achievement and math among school-age children (ages 7–10) who were grouped into NS, NNS who spoke Spanish as a first language (L1), and students with specific language impairment (SLI). Data included two standardized math tests (one in Spanish and the other in English) and three experimental tasks (quantity comparison, number comparison, and concept mapping games). The tests and tasks were categorized in terms of language, symbol, and visual working memory as either heavy processing (the English math test for the NNS) or light processing (the visual working memory for the NNS). The results indicated that SLI students performed significantly worse than NS in all tests and tasks and that NS significantly outperformed the NNS only in language-heavy tests and games. From these results, Alt et al. concluded that language proficiency is a key component of math success for NNS.

Martinello [8] analyzed item difficulty differences across math tests between NS and NNS by examining pictures and schemas for different levels of linguistic complexity (grammatical and lexical complexity) and contextual support. The items examined comprised 39 questions that assessed knowledge of patterns and relations, algebra, measurement, geometry, probabilities, and number sense and operations. The results indicated that the non-linguistic representations and linguistic complexity of the items accounted for around 66% of the variation in scores between native and non-native students. The findings demonstrated that items with complex grammatical structures and low frequency non-math words were more difficult for NNS. Non-linguistic representations (especially schemas) were found to decrease the difficulty of more linguistically complex items for NNS. Similar findings have been reported in a number of studies [12–14], all of which indicate that NNS are at a disadvantage in math performance when compared to NS, providing support for the threshold hypothesis [11] that proficiency in English is necessary for achievement in other academic disciplines such as math. These results may hold across NNS of different proficiency levels as well [15].

1.2 Current Study

A number of studies have demonstrated strong links between linguistic knowledge and success in math. Studies examining these links in L1 speakers have traditionally relied on correlational analyses between linguistic knowledge tests and standardized math tests [1, 4, 5]. For L2 speakers, the majority of studies have compared math success between proficient and non-proficient speakers of English [6, 7, 12–14]. In this study, we take a novel approach and examine the language features of students' language production while e-mailing a virtual pedagogical agent in an on-line math intelligent tutoring system (Reasoning Mind). To derive our language features of interest, we analyzed the language produced by the students using a number of natural language processing tools to extract linguistic information related to text cohesion, lexical sophistication, and sentiment. Thus, in contrast to most previous studies (see [9] for an exception), our interest is not on language performance as measured by standardized tests, but on language performance as a function of language production in student e-mails.

Our criterion variables are students' accuracy on beginning level math problems within the Reasoning Mind system. In addition to examining relations between linguistic features of student language production and math scores, we also control for a number of non-linguistic factors, including grade level, number of messages sent by the student to the avatar, number of messages sent to the teacher and number received by the teacher, hours spent online in the Reasoning Mind platform, and number of objectives met within the Reasoning Mind platform. Thus, in this study, we address two research questions:

1. Are non-linguistic factors significant predictors of math performance in the Reasoning Mind on-line tutoring environment?
2. Are linguistic factors related to lexical sophistication, cohesion, and affect significant predictors of math performance in the Reasoning Mind on-line tutoring environment?

2 Method

2.1 Reasoning Mind

Data was collected from Reasoning Mind *Foundations*, which is a blended learning math program used primarily in grades 2–5. In Foundations classrooms, teachers facilitate the class, while students study on computers, allowing the teacher to conduct both one-on-one and small-group interventions. *Foundations* includes a sequenced main curriculum divided into objectives, each of which introduces a new topic (e.g., the distributive property) using interactive explanations, presents problems of increasing difficulty on the topic, and reviews previously studied topics. (The algorithms and pedagogical logic underlying *Foundations* are described in detail by Khachatryan et al. [16]) All students complete first difficulty level ("Level A") problems – these problems address the basic knowledge and skills in the objective. Students who do well progress to problems of greater difficulty. Other modes in *Foundations* allow students to play math games against classmates, tackle challenging problems and puzzles, and use points earned by solving math problems to buy virtual prizes.

Foundations uses many animated characters to provide a backstory to the mathematics being learned and to deliver emotional support. The main character is the Genie, who helps students when they struggle with independent problem solving by guiding them through the solution and provides praise when they get many problems right in a row. The Genie, who appears in many of the animated stories in the *Foundations* system, has a virtual house where students can play games, and students have the option to send email messages to the Genie. These messages are answered in character by Reasoning Mind employees (Student Mentors) who project an empathetic persona (i.e., consistent, warm, and encouraging), model a positive attitude toward learning, and emphasize the importance of practice and hard work for success. Messages reflect an extensive Genie biography, which includes political beliefs (fractions over factions), educational interests (mathematics, physics, disappearing & reappearing, literature, flying, and musicology), and other facts about the Genie. The Genie email system is popular. For instance, the Genie received 157,346 messages from about 40,000 different students in 2014–2015.

2.2 Participants and Corpus

The students sampled in this study consists of all *Foundations* students in two academic years, who had written at least 50 words to the Genie through the email system from August 1, 2013 to July 1, 2015. We used the messages sent from the students to the Genie as our language sample for this analysis. Because many of the samples contained few words, we aggregated all e-mails sent by each student to create a representation of individual student's linguistic knowledge. The 50-word threshold provides a sample with enough linguistic coverage for normal distribution of most linguistic features reported by the natural language processing tools used in this study. All samples were cleaned of non-ASCII characters. Misspellings were kept in the data. There were a total of 13,983 such students, in grades 1 through 6 with the majority of students in grades 2 through 5. The students were from 546 different schools located in 107 different districts. Most districts were located in Texas.

2.3 Natural Language Processing Tools

Each transcript was run through a number of natural language processing tools including the Tool for the Automatic Analysis of Lexical Sophistication (TAALES) [17], the Tool for the Automatic Analysis of Cohesion (TAACO) [18] and the SEntiment ANalysis and Cognition Engine (SEANCE) [19]. The selected tools reported on language features related to lexical sophistication, text cohesion, and sentiment analysis respectively. The tools are discussed in greater detail below.

TAALES. TAALES [17] is a computational tool that is freely available and easy to use, works on most operating systems (Windows, Mac, Linux), allows for batch processing of text files, and incorporates over 150 classic and recently developed indices of lexical sophistication. These indices measure word frequency, lexical range, n-gram frequency and proportion, academic words and phrases, word information, lexical and phrasal sophistication, and age of exposure. In terms of word frequency, TAALES reports frequency counts retrieved from Thondike-Lorge [20], Kucera-Francis [21], Brown [22], and SUBTLexus databases [23]. In addition, TAALES derives frequency counts from the British National Corpus (BNC) [24] and the Corpus of Contemporary American English (COCA) [25]. TAALES calculates scores for all words (AW), content words (CW), and function words (FW). In addition to frequency information, TAALES includes a number of range indices which calculate how many texts within a corpus a word appears (i.e., specificity). Range indices are calculated for the spoken (574 texts) and written (3,083 texts) subsets of the BNC, SUBTLEXus (8,388 texts) and Kucera-Francis (500 texts).

TAALES also calculates a number of phrasal indices. These include bigram and trigram frequencies and proportion scores (i.e., the proportion of n-grams in a text that are common in a reference corpus) from BNC and COCA. TAALES also computes strength of association indices between words to measure the conditional probability that words will occur together. These include mutual information scores, *T* values, Delta P, and approximate Colexeme Strength.

Lastly, TAALES reports on a number word information and psycholinguistic scores. The word information scores are derived from the MRC Psycholinguistic Database [26], Kuperman norms [27], Brysbaert norms [28], WordNet [29], the Edinburgh Associative Thesaurus (EAT) [30], the University of South Florida (USF) norms [31], and the English Lexicon Project (ELP) [32]. Word information scores are calculated for word familiarity, concreteness, imageability, meaningfulness, age of acquisition, word association norms, polysemy, hypernymy, orthographic, phonographic, and phonologic neighborhoods.

TAACO. TAACO [18] incorporates over 150 classic and recently developed indices related to text cohesion. For a number of indices, the tool incorporates a part of speech (POS) tagger from the Natural Language Tool Kit [33] and synonym sets from the WordNet lexical database [29]. The POS tagger affords the opportunity to look at content words (i.e., nouns, verbs, adjectives, adverbs) as well as function words (i.e., determiners, propositions). TAACO provides linguistic counts for both sentence and paragraph markers of cohesion and incorporates WordNet synonym sets. Specifically, TAACO calculates type token ratio (TTR) indices (for all words, content words, function words, and n-grams), sentence overlap indices that assess local cohesion for all words, content words, function words, POS tags, and synonyms, paragraph overlap indices that assess global cohesion for all words, content words, function words, POS tags, and synonyms, and a variety of connective indices such as logical connectives (e.g., *moreover, nevertheless*), causal connectives (*because, consequently, only if*), sentence linking connectives (e.g., *nonetheless, therefore, however*), and order connectives (e.g., *first, before, after*).

SEANCE. SEANCE [19] is a sentiment analysis tools that relies on a number of pre-existing sentiment, social positioning, and cognition dictionaries. SEANCE contains a number of pre-developed word vectors to measure sentiment, cognition, and social order. These vectors are taken from freely available source databases. For many of these vectors, SEANCE also provides a negation feature (i.e., a contextual valence shifter) that ignores positive terms that are negated (e.g., not happy). SEANCE also includes a part of speech (POS) tagger.

2.4 Statistical Analysis

We calculated linear models to determine if linguistic features in the students' language output along with other fixed effects (grade, number of messages sent and received, hours online, and objectives met) could be used to predict the students' math scores. In this study, we use accuracy on first difficulty level problems as a proxy to student mastery of the taught curriculum. Prior to LME analysis, we first checked that the linguistic variables were normally distributed. We also controlled for multicollinearity between all the linguistic variables ($r \geq .900$). We used R [34] for our statistical analysis and the package *relaimpo* [35] to report the importance of the individual features in the linear models. Final model selection and interpretation was based on *t* and *p* values for fixed effects and visual inspection of residuals distribution. To obtain a measure of effect sizes, we computed correlations between fitted and observed values, resulting in an overall R^2 value for the fixed factors. We first developed a baseline linear model that included non-linguistic fixed effects (e.g., grade, number of messages, objectives met). We next developed a second model that included only linguistic factors (e.g., frequency, word neighborhood effects, number of determiners). We then created a final model that include both linguistic and non-linguistic effects. We compared the strength of each model using Analyses of Variance (ANOVAs) to examine which models were most predictive.

3 Results

3.1 Non-linguistic Linear Model

A linear model considering all non-linguistic fixed effects revealed significant effects for grade level, number of messages sent to Genie, number of messages received from Genie, number of messages from the teacher, and the number of objectives met on math scores. Table 1 displays the coefficients, standard error, *t* values, *p* values, and relative importance for each of the non-linguistic fixed effects. The overall model was significant, $F(4, 13597) = 220.80$, $p < .001$, $R^2 = .061$. Inspection of residuals suggested the model was not influenced by homoscedasticity. The non-linguistic variables explained around 6% of the variance of the math scores and indicated that students in lower grades who sent more messages to the Genie and received more messages from their teachers had low math proficiency. In addition, students who met a greater number of objectives, had higher math proficiency.

Table 1. Non-linguistic model for predicting math scores

Fixed effect	Coefficient	Std. error	*t*	*r*
(Intercept)	77.796	0.340	228.87**	
Grade level	−0.423	0.086	−4.942**	0.001
Number of messages to Genie	−0.082	0.01	−9.964**	0.004
Number of messages from teacher	0.217	0.030	7.184**	0.006
Objectives met	0.145	0.005	27.607**	0.051

**p < .001

3.2 Linguistic Linear Model

A linear model including linguistic fixed effects revealed significant effects for a number of features related to proportion of n-grams used, phonographic and orthographic neighborhoods, number of unique function words, word frequency, incidence of determiners, strength of word associations, and term certainty. Table 2 displays the coefficients, standard error, *t* values, *p* values, and relative importance for each of the linguistic fixed effects. The overall model was significant, F(11, 13590) = 112.70, $p < .001$, $r = .290$, $R^2 = .084$. Inspection of residuals suggested the model was not influenced by homoscedasticity. The linguistic variables explained around 8% of the variance of the math scores and indicated that students that used more common n-grams with stronger associations and used words with fewer orthographic and phonological neighbors that were more frequent had higher math proficiency. In addition, students that used more unique function words, more determiners, and were more certain also had higher math proficiency scores. An ANOVA comparison between the non-linguistic model and the linguistic found a significant difference between the models, ($F = 47.867$, $p < .001$), indicating that linguistic features contributed to a better model fit than non-linguistic features.

Table 2. Linguistic model for predicting math scores

Fixed effect	Coefficient	Std. error	*t*	*r*
(Intercept)	88.656	3.710	23.894**	
Bigram proportion (COCA news)	3.447	1.261	2.734*	0.01
Phonological neighbors	−0.244	0.039	−6.255**	0.014
Average Levenshtein distance of closest orthographic neighbors	13.437	1.221	11.005**	0.013
Trigram proportion (BNC spoken)	5.533	1.913	2.892*	0.006
Unique function words	0.07	0.012	6.066**	0.007
Content word frequency (BNC written)	2.062	0.409	5.044**	0.006
Average frequency of closest orthographic neighbors	−3.549	0.428	−8.29**	0.009
Incidence of determiners	14.674	3.75	3.913**	0.004
Trigram association strength (COCA spoken MI)	0.381	0.072	5.293**	0.005
Certainty words	4.312	1.431	3.013*	0.003
Bigram association strength (COCA spoken T)	0.022	0.004	5.803**	0.005

*p < .010, **p < .001

3.3 Full Linear Model

A linear model considering non-linguistic and linguistic fixed effects revealed significant effects for all the non-linguistic features in the first model and all the linguistic features in the second model. Table 3 displays the coefficients, standard error, *t* values, *p* values, and relative importance for each of the fixed effects. The overall model was significant, F(15, 13586) = 154.60, $p < .001$, $r = .381$, $R^2 = .145$. Inspection of residuals suggested the model was not influenced by homoscedasticity. The non-linguistic and linguistic variables explained around 15% of the variance of the math scores and followed the same trends as reported in the first two models. An ANOVA comparison between the full model and the linguistic model found a significant difference between the models,

(F = 122.65, $p < .001$), indicating that a combination of non-linguistic and linguistic features contributed to a better model fit than linguistic features alone.

Table 3. Full model for predicting math scores

Fixed effect	Coefficient	Std. error	*t*	*r*
(Intercept)	88.436	3.704	23.877**	
Bigram proportion (COCA news)	2.387	1.261	1.894	0.010
Phonological neighbors	−0.237	0.038	−6.293**	0.014
Average Levenshtein distance of closest orthographic neighbors	13.680	1.185	11.543**	0.013
Trigram proportion (BNC spoken)	4.539	1.851	2.453*	0.006
Unique function words	0.126	0.013	9.394**	0.008
Content word frequency (BNC written)	2.357	0.396	5.950**	0.006
Average frequency of closest orthographic neighbors	−3.401	0.414	−8.207**	0.009
Incidence of determiners	13.300	3.633	3.661**	0.004
Trigram association strength (COCA spoken MI)	0.393	0.070	5.647**	0.005
Certainty words	5.317	1.397	3.805**	0.004
Bigram association strength (COCA spoken T)	0.021	0.004	5.811**	0.005
Grade level	−1.277	0.086	−14.823**	0.007
Number of messages from Genie	−0.103	0.009	−10.909**	0.005
Number of messages from teachers	0.182	0.029	6.316**	0.004
Objectives met	0.133	0.005	26.470**	0.046

*p < .010, **p < .001

4 Discussion

Cognitive skills are important indicators of math success. Most previous studies have examined indicators related to spatial attention and quantitative ability. In this study, we take an innovative approach and examine links between math success and language production. This approach is unlike many previous studies examining math success and language skills in that we did not examine standardized assessment of language ability or differences in math success between native and non-native speakers of English. In addition to language production, we also co-varied a number of non-linguistic factors to better assess the relationships between language production and math success. We found that a linguistic features model was a stronger predictor of math success than a model based on non-linguistic features. A blended model containing both linguistic and non-linguistic features outperformed both models.

The linguistic linear model showed that about 8% of the variation in math scores was accounted for by linguistic features. The results indicated that students who used more common n-grams (words and phrases), phrased in which the words were more strongly associated, more difficult words (e.g., words with fewer neighbors), a greater number of unique function words, more determiners, and more certainty words received higher math scores. These findings indicate that students with more conventional language production (i.e., students that follow standardized language patterns) scored higher in math assessments. In addition, students that expressed more certainty scored higher. These findings likely indicate that students that have acquired greater standardized patterns of language (i.e., academic language) perform better in math because those types of language skills allow for greater transfer of cognitive operations between language and academic domains such as math.

These findings differ from those reported by [9] in that greater cohesion and linguistic complexity were strong predictors of math success their study. In addition, the previous analysis indicated that linguistic features predicted about 30% of the variance in math scores. These differences likely stem from context in that student language production in [9] was recorded in the context of mathematics problem solving, while in the current study the context of language production was personal communication with an emphatic avatar. A qualitative analysis of the Genie data indicated that much of this communication was non-mathematical in nature and informal. As verbalized reasoning in the process of problem solving is a closer reflection of the mental processes of mathematical problem solving than informal communication, it's not surprising that the linguistic features of that communication were more strongly associated with language complexity and explained a greater percentage of mathematics performance.

The covariates used in the non-linguistic linear model, with the exception of Objectives Met, accounted for very little of the variation in math scores, despite the statistical significance of their coefficients. However, they did indicate that students in higher grades scored better and that students who wrote fewer messages to the Genie and received more messages from their teacher scored better. The negative co-efficient reported between math success and messages to Genie may relate to the number of off topic messages sent to the Genie and the informal nature of those messages. In terms of objectives met, the strength of the relation to math scores is not surprising: students who have higher accuracy in answering problems are generally able to complete objectives faster, even though, due to the adaptive logic of *Foundations*, they are presented with harder problems [16].

5 Conclusions and Future Work

In conclusion, we present additional evidence that linguistic features in language production can predict math success such that students with more standardized language perform better on math assessments. Future iterations of this work will use a wider range of outcomes, both more proximal to language production and semantic content – like student self-efficacy, topic knowledge interest in mathematics, and mastery orientation – and more distal – like scores on summative assessment of mathematics, scores on standardized state tests, and academic outcomes (graduation, placement in advanced courses, etc.). In addition, future studies will use additional covariates related to language exposure in the models, like geographic location, ELL status, ethnicity, socio-economic status, to investigate how those factors interact with language production features to account for variation in attitudinal and achievement outcomes. Such studies will strengthen the analyses presented here and extend our knowledge of how language skills can transfer cognitive operations between math and language domains.

Acknowledgements. This research was supported in part by NSF 1623730. Opinions, conclusions, or recommendations do not necessarily reflect the views of the NSF.

References

1. LeFevre, J.A., Fast, L., Skwarchuk, S.L., Smith-Chant, B.L., Bisanz, J., Kamawar, D., Penner-Wilger, M.: Pathways to math: longitudinal predictors of performance. Child Dev. **81**(6), 1753–1767 (2010). doi:10.1111/j.1467-8624.2010.01508.x
2. Vukovic, R.K., Lesaux, N.K.: The relationship between linguistic skills and arithmetic knowledge. Learn. Individ. Diff. **23**, 87–91 (2013). doi:10.1016/j.lindif.2012.10.007
3. Martiniello, M.: Language and the performance of English-language learners in math word problems. Harv. Educ. Rev. **78**(2), 333–368 (2008)
4. Adams, T.L.: Reading math: more than words can say. Read. Teach. **56**(8), 786–795 (2003)
5. MacGregor, M., Price, E.: An exploration of aspects of language proficiency and algebra learning. J. Res. Math. Educ. **30**, 449–467 (1999). doi:10.2307/749709
6. Alt, M., Arizmendi, G.D., Beal, C.R.: The relationship between math and language: academic implications for children with specific language impairment and English language learners. Lang. Speech Hear. Serv. Sch. **45**(3), 220–233 (2014). doi:10.1044/2014_LSHSS-13-0003
7. Hampden-Thompson, G., Mulligan, G., Kinukawa, A., Halle, T.: Math Achievement of Language-Minority Students During the Elementary Years. U.S. Department of Education, National Center for Education Statistics, Washington, DC (2008)
8. Martiniello, M.: Linguistic complexity, schematic representations, and differential item functioning for English language learners in math tests. Educ. Assess. **14**(3–4), 160–179 (2009). doi:10.1080/10627190903422906
9. Crossley, S.A., Liu, R., McNamara, D.: Predicting math performance using natural language processing tools. In: Proceedings of the 7th International Learning Analytics and Knowledge (LAK) Conference. ACM, New York (2017)
10. Hernandez, F.: The relationship between reading and math achievement of middle school students as measured by the Texas assessment of knowledge and skills. Doctoral dissertation (2013)
11. Cummins, J.: Linguistic interdependence and the educational development of bilingual children. Rev. Educ. Res. **49**(2), 222–251 (1979)
12. Ardasheva, Y., Tretter, T.R., Kinny, M.: English language learners and academic achievement: revisiting the threshold hypothesis. Lang. Learn. **62**(3), 769–812 (2012). doi: 10.1111/j.1467-9922.2011.00652.x
13. Mosqueda, E., Maldonado, S.I.: The effects of English language proficiency and curricular pathways: Latina/os' math achievement in secondary schools. Equity Excell. Educ. **46**(2), 202–219 (2013). doi:10.1080/10665684.2013.780647
14. Wang, J., Goldschmidt, P.: Opportunity to learn, language proficiency, and immigrant status effects on math achievement. J. Educ. Res. **93**(2), 101–111 (1999). doi: 10.1080/00220679909597634
15. Chen, F., Chalhoub-Deville, M.: Differential and long-term language impact on math. Lang. Test. **33**(4), 577–605 (2015)

16. Khachatryan, G.A., Romashov, A.V., Khachatryan, A.R., Gaudino, S.J., Khachatryan, J.M., Guarian, K.R., Yufa, N.V.: Reasoning Mind Genie 2: an intelligent tutoring system as a vehicle for international transfer of instructional methods in mathematics. Int. J. Artif. Intell. Educ. **24**(3), 333–382 (2014). doi:10.1007/s40593-014-0019-7
17. Kyle, K., Crossley, S.A.: Automatically assessing lexical sophistication: indices, tools, findings, and application. TESOL Q. **49**(4), 757–786 (2015). doi:10.1002/tesq.194
18. Crossley, S.A., Kyle, K., McNamara, D.S.: The tool for the automatic analysis of text cohesion (TAACO): automatic assessment of local, global, and text cohesion. Behav. Res. Methods **48**(4), 1227–1237 (2016)
19. Crossley, S.A., Kyle, K., McNamara, D.S.: Sentiment analysis and social cognition engine (SEANCE): an automatic tool for sentiment, social cognition, and social order analysis. Behav. Res. Methods (in press). doi:10.3758/s13428-016-0743-z
20. Thorndike, E.L., Lorge, I.: The Teacher's Wordbook of 30,000 Words. Teachers College: Bureau of Publications: Columbia University, New York (1944)
21. Kučera, H., Francis, N.: Computational Analysis of Present-Day American English. Brown University Press, Providence (1967)
22. Brown, G.D.: A frequency count of 190,000 words in the London-Lund Corpus of English conversation. Behav. Res. Methods Instr. Comput. **16**(6), 502–532 (1984). doi:10.3758/BF03200836
23. Brysbaert, M., New, B.: Subtlexus: American word frequencies (2009). http://subtlexus.lexique.org
24. The British National Corpus, Version 3 (BNC XML Edition) 2007 Distributed by Oxford University Computing Services on Behalf of the BNC Consortium. http://www.natcorp.ox.ac.uk/
25. Davies, M.: The 385+ million word Corpus of Contemporary American English (1990–2008+): design, architecture, and linguistic insights. Int. J. Corpus Linguist. **14**, 159–190 (2009). doi:10.1075/ijcl.14.2.02dav
26. Coltheart, M.: The MRC psycholinguistic database. Q. J. Exp. Psychol. **33**(4), 497–505 (1981)
27. Kuperman, V., Stadthagen-Gonzalez, H., Brysbaert, M.: Age-of-acquisition ratings for 30,000 English words. Behav. Res. Methods **44**(4), 978–990 (2012). doi:10.3758/s13428-012-0210-4
28. Brysbaert, M., Warriner, A.B., Kuperman, V.: Concreteness ratings for 40 thousand generally known English word lemmas. Behav. Res. Methods **46**(3), 904–911 (2014). doi:10.3758/s13428-013-0403-5
29. Miller, G.A.: WordNet: a lexical database for English. Commun. ACM **38**(11), 39–41 (1995). doi:10.1145/219717.219748
30. Kiss, G.R., Armstrong, C., Milroy, R., Piper, J.: An associative thesaurus of English and its computer analysis. In: Aitken, A.J., Bailey, R.W., Hamilton-Smith, N. (eds.) The Computer and Literary Studies, pp. 153–165. Edinburgh University Press, Edinburgh (1973)
31. Nelson, D.L., McEvoy, C. L., Schreiber, T.A.: The University of South Florida word association, rhyme, and word fragment norms (1998). http://www.usf.edu/FreeAssociation/
32. Balota, D.A., Yap, M.J., Cortese, M.J., Hutchison, K.I., Kessler, B., Loftis, B., et al.: The English lexicon project. Behav. Res. Methods **39**, 445–459 (2007)
33. Bird, S., Klein, E., Loper, E.: Natural Language Processing with Python. O'Reilly Media, Inc., Sebastopol (2009)
34. R Core Team: R: A language and environment for statistical computing. R Foundation for Statistical Computing, Vienna, Austria. (2014). http://www.R-project.org/
35. Grömping, U.: Relative importance for linear regression in R: the package relaimpo. J. Stat. Softw. **1**(1) (2006)

Measuring Accuracy of Triples in Knowledge Graphs

Shuangyan Liu(✉), Mathieu d'Aquin, and Enrico Motta

Knowledge Media Institute, The Open University, Milton Keynes, UK
{shuangyan.liu,mathieu.daquin,enrico.motta}@open.ac.uk

Abstract. An increasing amount of large-scale knowledge graphs have been constructed in recent years. Those graphs are often created from text-based extraction, which could be very noisy. So far, cleaning knowledge graphs are often carried out by human experts and thus very inefficient. It is necessary to explore automatic methods for identifying and eliminating erroneous information. In order to achieve this, previous approaches primarily rely on internal information i.e. the knowledge graph itself. In this paper, we introduce an automatic approach, Triples Accuracy Assessment (TAA), for validating RDF triples (source triples) in a knowledge graph by finding consensus of matched triples (among target triples) from other knowledge graphs. TAA uses knowledge graph interlinks to find identical resources and apply different matching methods between the predicates of source triples and target triples. Then based on the matched triples, TAA calculates a confidence score to indicate the correctness of a source triple. In addition, we present an evaluation of our approach using the FactBench dataset for fact validation. Our findings show promising results for distinguishing between correct and wrong triples.

Keywords: Data quality · Triple matching · Predicate semantic similarity · Knowledge graphs · Algorithm configuration optimisation

1 Introduction

The concept of Knowledge Graph (KG) was introduced by Google in 2012, to refer to a knowledge base used for enhancing its web-based search results. It is now often used to describe semantic web knowledge bases, i.e. RDF-based representation of some wide domains. Such an RDF representation is known as an RDF triple (subject, predicate, object). An example of RDF triples is (*dbr:Birmingham dbo:populationTotal "1123000"^^xsd:integer*), which represents the fact that the city of Birmingham has a total population of 1123000 (*dbr* and *dbo* are the namespace prefixes of DBpedia repositories).[1] In recent years,

[1] *dbr* refers to http://dbpedia.org/resource, *dbo* points to http://dbpedia.org/ontology, *xsd* refers to http://www.w3.org/2001/XMLSchema#.

J. Gracia et al. (Eds.): LDK 2017, LNAI 10318, pp. 343–357, 2017.
DOI: 10.1007/978-3-319-59888-8_29

several large-scale knowledge graphs have been constructed such as DBpedia[2], YAGO[3], Freebase[4], Wikidata[5], and others.

Many of these knowledge graphs were created by extracting Web contents or through crowdsourcing. These processes could be very noisy, and the created knowledge graphs are unlikely to be fully correct. There is an increasing interest in quality assessment for knowledge graphs [1,4,6,8,17,20]. Some approaches focus on completing or correcting entity type information, while others target towards relations between entities, or interlinks between different knowledge graphs. However, research in identifying erroneous literal values automatically is very rare [16]. Proposing a generic approach for measuring the accuracy of triples can identify erroneous information and thus improve the quality of knowledge graphs.

In this paper, we propose the Triples Accuracy Assessment (TAA), an approach for automatically validating RDF triples in a KG (source triples) by collecting consensus of matched triples (among target triples) from other knowledge graphs. A confidence score is assigned to a source triple that is validated to represent the accuracy of this triple. Our approach searches external information for assessing the correctness of triples, which is similar to [6,8]. The main difference is that we explore other semantic web knowledge bases to find evidence while [6] searches proofs from the Web for validating facts. The main contributions of this paper are presented as follows:

(1) we present an automatic approach that finds consensus from other knowledge graphs for validating the correctness of RDF triples;
(2) we propose a predicate semantic similarity metric based on word-to-word similarity and corpus-based information content;
(3) we enrich our triple validation model to support different types of data including numerical, date and string;
(4) we apply the iterated racing algorithm for tuning the parameters of our system, which finds the best configuration of the parameters of our system.
(5) we evaluate the performance of our approach using gold standard data extracted from a benchmark dataset for fact validation. The findings show that we achieve a competitive F-measure of 95.2% on a train set and 96.1% on a test set.

The initial description of our approach was presented in a workshop paper [12]. The main additions include that we present a new method to compute predicate semantic similarity based on word-to-word similarity and corpus-based information content; we apply the iterated racing algorithm for tuning the parameters of our system, which finds the best configuration of our system; and we also report a systematic evaluation of our approach using a benchmark dataset in this paper.

[2] http://wiki.dbpedia.org/.
[3] http://yago-knowledge.org/.
[4] https://developers.google.com/freebase/.
[5] http://www.wikidata.org.

2 Related Work

There is a growing body of work on fact validation [5,6,10,20]. This literature can be categorised into two groups in terms of the sources utilised: (1) approaches such as [10,20] using internal information (i.e. the knowledge graph itself) for proofs; and (2) approaches such as [6] exploring external information as sources for evidences. Our approach is similar to methods of the second kind, which validate triples using external sources. The main difference from them is that we match evidence triples from other knowledge graphs, not from web documents.

Different methods have been adopted for the fact validation tasks. The approach DeFacto [6,8] transforms statements into natural language sentences, and retrieves web pages in a web search engine that contain these sentences. A low confidence score is assigned to statements if no or only a few web pages support these sentences. The approaches [5,20] apply outlier detection methods to identify errors in numerical property values that are extracted from a data repository. The work [5] improves the prior work by lowering the influence of natural outliers. In more details, [5] performs a second outlier detection on the same property values from equivalent instances to confirm or reject the assessment of a wrong value. However, the work [5] did not address the identification of the same properties of an additional instance for a given instance. Our approach proposes a predicate matching algorithm for finding similar properties of triples.

For predicate matching, we intend to find properties of two different triples which are semantically equivalent but not necessarily syntactically the same. In this paper, we combine a predicate semantic similarity metric and outlier detection techniques for predicate matching, which is different from [3]. The work [3] adopts a string-based similarity method for measuring the similarity between properties.

3 The Proposed Approach

TAA is composed of five components (Fig. 1). The first two components identify equivalent subject links for a set of source triples, while the middle two components find target triples having matching predicates to the source triples. The last component generates a confidence score for each source triple, representing the level of accuracy of the source triple.

The first component, *Subject Link Fetching* (SLFetching), is used to obtain equivalent links of the subject of a source triple (i.e. equivalent subject links). Since non-resolvable and duplicate subject links might be retrieved from the first step, the *Subject Link Filtering* component (SLFiltering) tries to filter out these subject links to achieve an overall efficiency of the subsequent components. Then the *Predicate Object Retrieving* component (POR) collects target triples from external knowledge graphs which contain the identified subject links. In addition, the *Target Triple Matching* component (TTM) combines a set of functions for identifying matched triples among the target triples which have predicates semantically similar to the source triple. Finally, the *Confidence Calculation*

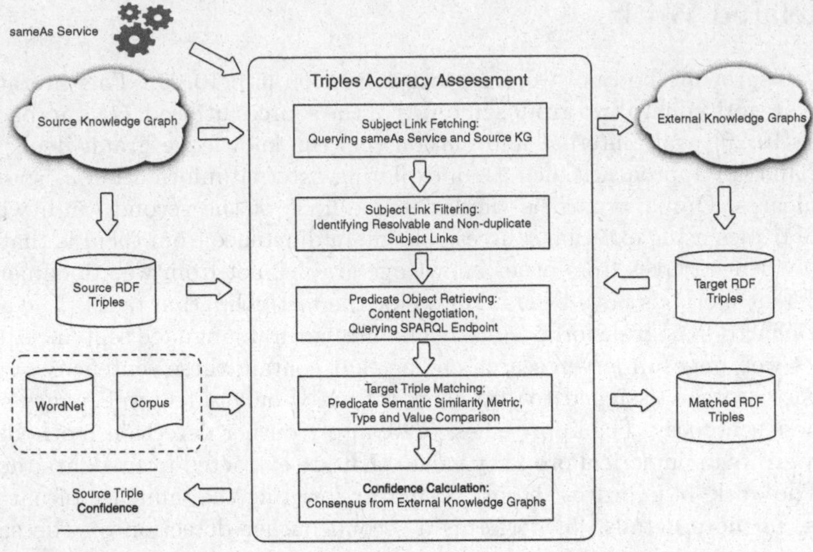

Fig. 1. The TAA approach.

component (CC) generates the confidence score for the source triple based on agreement among matched triples from different knowledge graphs.

3.1 Fetching and Filtering Equivalent Subject Links

The SLFetching component takes the subject of a source triple as input and query the sameAs service[6] and the source knowledge graph to fetch equivalent links for the subject link. The sameAs service can provide equivalent links to arbitrary URIs, and currently serves 200 million URIs. We use the SameAs4J API[7] to fetch equivalent subject links that are provided by the sameAs service. In addition, according to a recent analysis of the LOD cloud datasets [19], *owl:sameAs*[8] is the most commonly used predicate for linking. Hence, we also try to query the source KG using the *owl:sameAs* property. This provides us an alternative way to fetch equivalent subject links when they might not be covered in the sameAs service. Suppose SPARQL query language is implemented in the source KG management system and *subject_uri* denotes the URI link of the subject of the source triple, then the equivalent subject links can be obtained using the following SPARQL query.

```
SELECT ?e WHERE { <subject_uri> owl:sameAs ?e . }
```

[6] sameAs service, http://sameas.org.
[7] SameAs4J API, http://99soft.github.io/sameas4j/.
[8] owl is a namespace prefix referring to http://www.w3.org/2002/07/owl#.

Different techniques are combined in the SLFiltering component for filtering the fetched subject links. For identifying a non-resolvable subject link, an HTTP HEAD request is sent to the host where the resource is stored, and the SLFiltering component checks whether a success or redirection HTTP status code can be returned from the host within a given time limit. If not, the subject link is treated as non-resolvable. Meanwhile, an URI equality comparison method is used to clean duplicate subject links.

3.2 Retrieving Predicates and Objects

The clean set of subject links come from different sources which serve data in their own formats and provide different access methods. There are different ways of accessing a data repository. Many knowledge repositories e.g. DBpedia, GeoNames[9], LinkedGeoData[10] support content negotiation. Another widely acceptable way is querying SPARQL endpoint. We combine these different data access methods in the POR component for providing a more resilient predicate and object retrieving mechanism. To enable the POR component to handle requests to different SPARQL repositories, we maintain a mapping between common repositories and their SPARQL endpoints. This mapping is provided in a configuration file, which is easy to modify and update.

3.3 Matching Target Triples

We combine a predicate semantic similarity metric which is introduced in the following subsection and a predicate type and value comparison algorithm to identify target triples having matching predicates to a source triple. First, we select target triples with predicate similarity that are higher than a given predicate matching threshold (α) and remove the target triples which are lower than the given threshold value from the collection of target triples. We then use the selected triples as inputs for the property type comparison procedure, and filter out target triples that have mismatched property types. Then we continue the matching process by applying the predicate value comparison algorithm to remove anomaly triples from the set of target triples. Finally, we obtain the set of matched triples that can be used to examine the accuracy of source triples.

Predicate Semantic Similarity. We present a method to compute the semantic similarity between two predicates based on word-to-word similarity and corpus-based information content of words. Information Content (IC) is a measure of concept specificity. More specific concepts (e.g. dog) have higher values of IC than more general concepts (e.g. animal).

We use a matrix to represent the word-to-word similarity of all pairwise combinations of words which constitute the two input predicates. The word-to-word similarity in the matrix is converted from concept-to-concept semantic

[9] http://www.geonames.org/.
[10] http://linkedgeodata.org/.

similarity by taking over the maximal similarity score over all the concepts of the words [18,22]. Metrics such as [7,11,18,22] can be used to compute the concept-to-concept similarity. In the implementation of TAA, the Wu and Palmer (WUP) method [21] is adopted which measures the depths of the Least Common Subsumer (LCS) of two concepts in the semantic network WordNet [15]. In terms of the concept-to-concept similarity metrics such as the WUP method, WordNet is applied as a concept taxonomy where nodes represent the WordNet concepts or synsets and edges denote hierarchical relations of hypernym and hyponymy between concepts.

We choose the maximal similarity score in a row to represent the similarity of a word in the predicate that the row stands for. Then, we apply the corpus-based information content of the word as the weighting factor to compute the predicate similarity. The definition of corpus-based IC proposed in [18] is presented in Definition 1.

Definition 1. *The* IC_{corpus} *(c) of a concept c is defined as:* $IC_{corpus}(c) = -logP(c)$*, where* $P(c)$ *is the probability of encountering the set of instances subsumed by concept c. Let* $freq(c) = \sum_{n \in words(c)} count(n)$ *be the frequency of concept c occurs in corpus and words(c) is the set of words subsumed by concept c, then* $P(c) = \frac{freq(c)}{N}$ *where N is the total number of concepts observed in corpus.*

Then the similarity of two predicates is calculated using the predicate similarity metric defined in Eq. (1), which takes the average of the weighted word similarity in either predicate.

$$sim(P_1, P_2) = \frac{1}{2}\left(\frac{\sum_{w \in P_1} maxSim(w, P_2) * IC(c)}{\sum_{w \in P_1} IC(c)} + \frac{\sum_{w \in P_2} maxSim(w, P_1) * IC(c)}{\sum_{w \in P_2} IC(c)}\right), \tag{1}$$

where $maxSim(w, P_2), w \in P_1$ is the maximal word-to-word similarity of a word in the first predicate; $maxSim(w, P_1), w \in P_2$ is the maximal word similarity of a word in the second predicate; and $IC(c)$ is the corpus-based information content of the sense of a word represented by concept c.

In Eq. (1), a word sense disambiguation (WSD) method can be used to find a concept c in a lexicon to represent the sense of a word. In the implementation of the TAA system, we adopted the Lesk algorithm [9] for word sense disambiguation. The Lesk algorithm determines the sense of a ambiguous word by selecting the concept or synset with the highest number of overlapping words between the context sentence and different definitions from each synset. To determine the concept that represents the sense of a word in a given predicate, the predicate that contains the word is applied as the context information in the Lesk algorithm.

Predicate Type and Value Comparison. The predicate type and value comparison is intended for filtering out target triples which could be assigned a high predicate similarity score but actually are mismatching. For example, the triples (*dbr:Milton_Keynes dbp:latitude "52.04"*) and (*geodata:2642465 geonames:locationMap http://www.geonames.org/2642465/milton-keynes.html*) have different types of predicates but the two predicates have a high predicate similarity score.[11]

In order to identify the mismatched predicate types, we use a heuristic method. That is, given the predicate type of a source triple, we will first resolve the predicate type that a target triple belongs to and then check whether it matches the format of the source predicate. For numerical type, we check whether the target predicate values conform to a numerical format. In terms of date type, we check whether the target predicate values follow a date pattern (e.g. "yyyy-MM-dd", "yyyy-MM-dd'T'HH:mm:ss'Z'"). For string type, we treat a target predicate as a string type if it does not conform to the numerical type or the date type.

Furthermore, we define a predicate value comparison algorithm (Algorithm 1) to identify mismatched predicates by determining whether there are outliers in the predicate values. We define two procedures for achieving this.

The first procedure which we call *IRange* uses Interquartile Range (IQR) for selecting outliers in a set of predicate values. Many outlier detection methods assume a specific distribution of the datasets to be validated, and the distribution of target predicate values is unknown. Hence, we apply the IQR method here since it is designed for data drawn from a wide range of probability distributions, especially for distributions that are not normal. The concept of the *IRange* procedure is that we first generate the interquartile range, the upper and lower limits of outliers for a set of predicate values, and then determine the outliers in target predicate values if a predicate value is out of the range of $(Q_1 - \varphi * IQR, Q_3 + \varphi * IQR)$. In the implementation of the TAA system, the outlier factor φ is set to the value of 1.5 by convention.

The second procedure which we call *SDeviation* is provided to complement the *IRange* procedure for identifying outliers in small sets of data values ($N \leq 4$). The idea of the *SDeviation* procedure is that we first calculate the mean (m) and standard deviation (s) of a small set of predicate values (A), then we consider a data value as an outlier if it is a certain number of standard deviations away from the mean (noted as $\theta \cdot s$). The standard deviation threshold θ is set to one in the implementation of the TAA system.

3.4 Confidence Calculation

The Confidence Calculation component is intended to generate a confidence score based on multiple different matched triples for each source triple to represent its level of accuracy. For triples that have numerical property values, we

[11] *geodata* and *geonames* refer to http://sws.geonames.org/ and http://www.geonames.org/ontology# respectively.

Algorithm 1. Predicate Value Comparison

Precondition: A is an array containing the property values of a source triple and its target triples

```
procedure IRange(A)                ▷ Find outliers in A based on Interquartile Range
    Sort(A)
    CalculateQuartiles(A)
    n ← A.length − 1
    for i ← 0, n do
        if isOutlier(A[i]) then
            Mark(A[i], true)
        else
            Mark(A[i], false)
        end if
    end for
end procedure
procedure SDeviation(A)            ▷ Identify outliers for a small A using Standard Deviation
    if A.length > 2 and A.length ≤ 4 then
        m ← Mean(A)
        s ← Std(A)                 ▷ s is the standard deviation of all property values in A
        n ← A.length − 1
        for i ← 0, n do
            if |A[i] − m| ≤ θ · s then        ▷ θ is the predefined threshold
                Mark(A[i], false)
            else
                Mark(A[i], true)
            end if
        end for
    end if
end procedure
```

calculate the confidence score based on a ratio of the difference in property values between a source triple and its matched triples and the weighted average of the matched triples. While for triples that have string property values, we represent the confidence score using a weighted average of the string similarity of the property values between a source triple and its matched triples. We treat date properties as a special case of numerical properties. This is because we can convert a date value into a numerical value representing the number of seconds counted from January 1, 1970, 00:00:00 GMT.

The method to calculate the confidence score for triples having numerical or date type predicate is formulated in Eq. (2):

$$C_{num/date}(x) = 1 - \frac{|x - \gamma|}{|\gamma|} \text{ with } \gamma = \frac{\sum_{i=1}^{m} \omega_i \cdot \nu_i}{\sum_{j=1}^{m} \omega_j}, \tag{2}$$

where x is the property value of a source triple; γ is the weighted average of the property values of its matched triples; ω refers to the product of weighting factors

Table 1. Rating scale for reliability of subject links

Rating score	Definition
1	Very unreliable
2	Unreliable
3	Neutral
4	Reliable
5	Very reliable

including the reliability of the subject link of a matched triple and the predicate similarity between a source triple and a matched triple; ν_i is the property value of the ith matched triple; and m represents the total number of matched triples obtained.

Furthermore, the method to calculate the confidence score of a triple with a string property value is formulated in Eq. (3):

$$C_{string}(y) = \frac{\sum_{i=1}^{m} \omega_i \cdot y_i}{\sum_{j=1}^{m} \omega_j}, \tag{3}$$

where y_i is the string similarity of property values between a source triple and the ith matched triple; ω refers to the product of weighting factors including the reliability of the subject link of a source triple and the predicate similarity between a source triple and a matched triple; and m is the total number of matched triples obtained.

In Eqs. (2) and (3), the reliability of the subject link of a target triple is rated based on the type of service that is used to fetch the subject link. We define a five-level Likert-scale to represent the reliability of the subject link of a target triple (Table 1). The larger the rating score, the more reliable a subject link is. Two types of services are used in our method: the sameAs service and the source knowledge graph which provides the *owl:sameAs* interlinks. In the implementation of the TAA system, the reliability of the subject link of a target triple which was retrieved from the source knowledge graph was set to be 4 and the equivalent subject links retrieved from the sameAs service was set to be 3. This rating method can also be applied to other services for obtaining equivalent subject links of a source triple.

The confidence score provided by our approach is an indicator for the correctness of triples. A larger value can indicate a higher possibility that a triple is correct. To classify a triple to be correct or wrong, we use a given confidence threshold (β) to apply to the confidence score.

4 Evaluation Methods, Datasets and Experimental Setting

TAA is a parameterised approach since pre-defined values should be provided for the predicate matching threshold (α) and confidence threshold (β) for the system to distinguish between correct and wrong triples. Thus, the performance (evaluated in F_1 measure) of TAA can be strongly affected by the specific values taken for the parameters. The goal of the evaluation presented in this paper included: (a) find elite configuration of the parameters that can generate the best performance measured in F_1; (b) evaluate the best configuration on a test set which is different from the training set.

We adopted a racing algorithm called iRace [13] to find an appropriate setting of the parameters for TAA. The racing methods for algorithm configuration optimisation were inspired from racing algorithms in machine learning, particularly Hoeffding races [14]. The essential idea of racing algorithms is to evaluate a given set of potential configurations on provided instances, the poor candidate configurations are eliminated as soon as sufficient statistical evidence is gathered, and the race continues only with the surviving ones. The iRace algorithm is an iterative application of F-Race algorithm [2] biasing the sampling of new configurations towards the better candidate solutions at each iteration.

We chose the iterated racing method for our algorithm configuration for three reasons. First, the dependence of TAA's performance on parameter settings is unknown and no explicit model exist to describe the dependence. The iRace method as a model-free algorithm configuration method, can be applied straightaway. Second, the iterated racing methods have been used successfully to automatically configure a variety of state-of-the-art algorithms. Finally, compared with the brute-force approach, the iterated racing approach is more efficient since it does not require repeating the cost evaluation steps for each candidate configuration and poor performing configurations will be discarded as soon as enough statistical evidence is gathered.

To carry out the configuration tuning and validation procedures, we collected gold standard data from the FactBench 2016 benchmark dataset[12]. The collected data are comprised of two subsets: a train set and a test set. The description of the datasets used in experiment is listed below.

- Train set was used in the racing procedure for finding the best configuration for TAA.
  - It consists of 750 triples that were extracted from DBpedia: 150 correct triples and 600 wrong triples.
  - These triples represent two types of relations: date when a person was born and date when a person died. Each triple has either dbo:birthDate or dbo:deathDate as its predicate.
- Test set was applied in the validation procedure for testing the performance of TAA using the best configuration found in the racing procedure.
  - It consists of 748 triples that were extracted from DBpedia: 150 correct triples and 598 wrong triples.
  - Each triple in the test set has either dbo:birthDate or dbo:deathDate as its predicate.

[12] https://github.com/SmartDataAnalytics/FactBench.

The racing and validation procedures were carried out using the irace package[13], which implements the iterated racing procedure [13]. The irace package option maxExperiments was set to 1000 as the budget of the experiments for both the tuning and the validation processes. The Friedman test (*F-test*) was used to identify statistically poor performing configurations that can be discarded from the race. The confidence level for the elimination test was set to 0.95. An implementation of TAA was developed and used as the target algorithm to be tuned for irace. An auxiliary program was also implemented for the evaluation, which is called from irace to execute TAA with a specific configuration and instance and return an evaluation value to irace. The evaluation value is the additive inverse of F_1 score i.e. $-1 * F_1$. This is because the objective of irace is to minimise the obtained evaluation values, we had to invert the F_1 score to maximise the performance of TAA. For predicate matching, we implemented the predicate similarity metric in Eq. (1) based on WordNet version 3.0[14] and NLTK interface.[15] We use the implementation of the word-to-word similarity method in the Sematch framework[16] which adopts the default implementation of the concept-to-concept similarity methods in the WordNet NLTK interface. All the implementations of TAA and resources are available publicly.[17]

5 Evaluation Results

For the experiment on the train set, the racing procedure finished after 19 iterations and executed the evaluations for 458 configurations for finding the best configuration. The evaluation results for all the configurations on the train set are plotted in Fig. 2.

The results in Fig. 2 are grouped by the candidate configuration identifier. For each configuration, the bottom and top of the rectangle represent the minimum and maximum values of evaluation respectively. The middle segment stands for the mean of evaluation values across the instances in the race. Note that the F_1 score ranges between 0 and 1, hence, the performance of the TAA system is maximised when the evaluation value equals to -1. It is shown that the evaluation values $(-1 * F_1)$ have been greatly decreased (dropped below -0.5 in general) after the first iteration of the racing procedure which ended at configuration 55. This demonstrates that the performance of TAA have been largely increased after the first iteration.

The best configuration obtained from the racing procedure is the configuration that demonstrates the minimum average evaluation value (i.e. the maximum average F_1 score) across different instances. For the racing procedure on the train set, the best configuration *(id = 180, $\alpha = 0.812$, $\beta = 0.999$, mean = -0.952)* was obtained. For the test set, the best configuration has obtained a mean evaluation

[13] http://iridia.ulb.ac.be/irace/.
[14] https://wordnet.princeton.edu/.
[15] http://www.nltk.org/.
[16] https://github.com/gsi-upm/sematch.
[17] https://github.com/TriplesAccuracyAssessment.

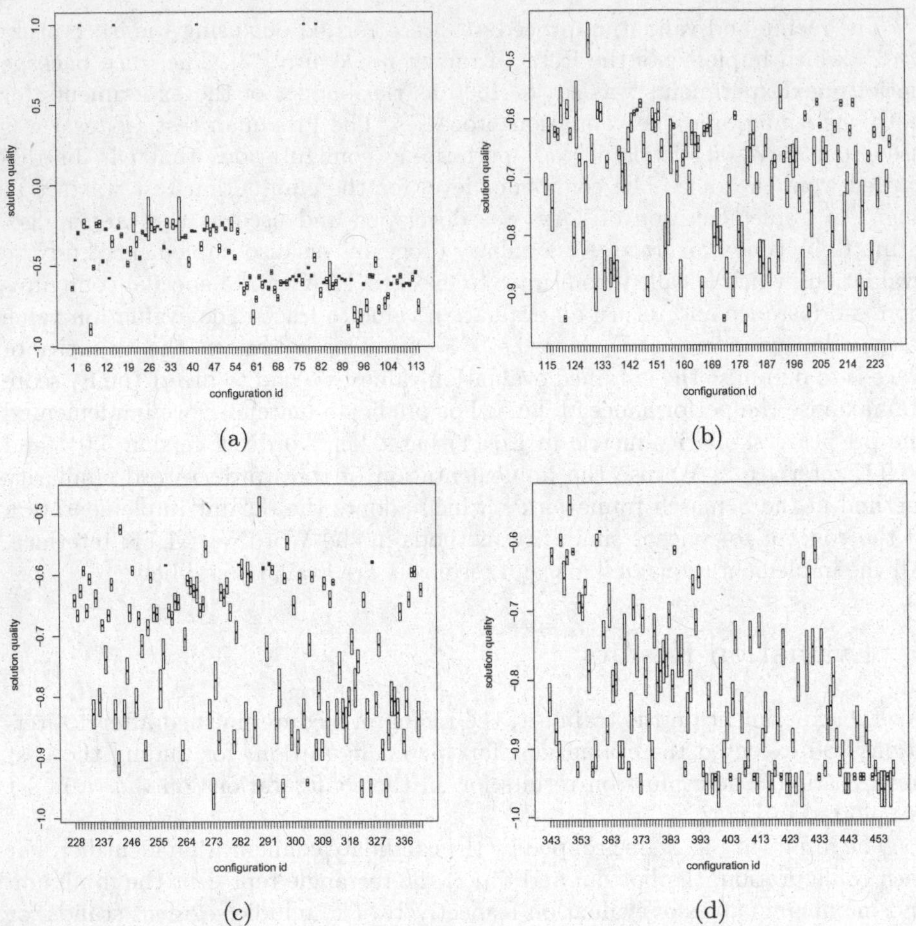

Fig. 2. Training results of all configurations in the racing procedure

value of −0.961. The Friedman test results showed that the best configuration is statistically significant different from all the other configurations in the race on both data sets.

During the racing procedure, irace iteratively updated the sampling models of the parameters which enabled the tuning process to focus on the best regions of the parameter search space. The frequency of the sampled configurations is presented in Fig. 3. It shows that the configurations with a value between 0.8 and 0.9 for the parameter α have the largest density, and are approximately five times as big as the configurations with a value in between 0.6 and 0.7. For the parameter β, the configurations with a value in between 0.9 and 1.0 have the largest density, and are eight times as big as the configurations with a value between 0.8 and 0.9.

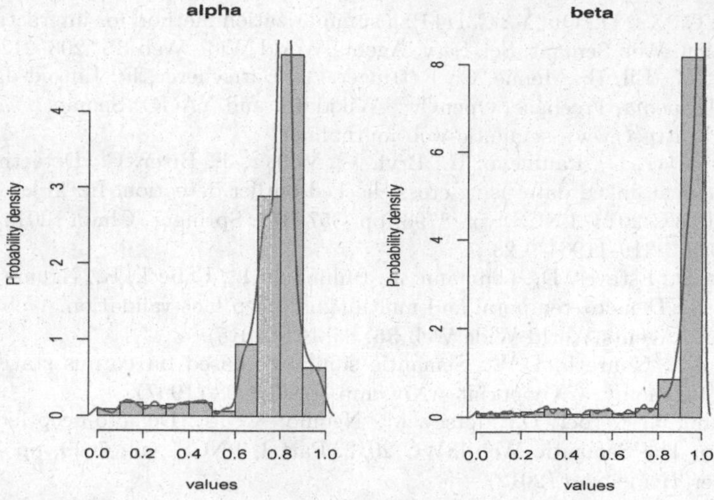

Fig. 3. Parameters sampling frequency.

6 Conclusions and Future Work

In this paper, we presented an automatic approach, Triples Accuracy Assessment (TAA), for measuring accuracy of RDF triples by checking consensus from different knowledge graphs. We exploit knowledge graph interlinks for discovering equivalent resources, and perform different functions to identify target triples having matching predicates to source triples. This approach supports checking the accuracy of fact triples that have numerical, date or string type properties. The evaluation of the TAA system showed that the best configuration that was identified by the iterated racing procedure is ($\alpha = 0.812, \beta = 0.999$), which demonstrates an F-measure of 95.2% on a train set containing 750 triples from DBpedia and 96.1% on a test set containing 748 triples from DBpedia. The evaluation values obtained for the best configuration is statistically significant different from other candidate configurations on both the train set and the test set.

In the future, we hope to explore how multi-lingual knowledge graph interlinks can be used for fact validation. We also plan to carry out an efficiency evaluation of our approach on large-scale linked data repositories to investigate the scalability of our approach on large-scale linked data.

References

1. Acosta, M., Zaveri, A., Simperl, E., Kontokostas, D., Flöck, F., Lehmann, J.: Detecting linked data quality issues via crowdsourcing: a DBpedia study. Semant. Web J. (to appear). http://www.semantic-web-journal.net/
2. Birattari, M., Yuan, Z., Balaprakash, P., Stützle, T.: F-race and iterated F-race: an overview. In: Bartz-Beielstein, T., Chiarandini, M., Paquete, L., Preuss, M. (eds.) Experimental Methods for the Analysis of Optimization Algorithms, pp. 311–336. Springer, Heidelberg (2010)

3. Cheng, G., Xu, D., Qu, Y.: C3D+P: a summarization method for interactive entity resolution. Web Semant. Sci. Serv. Agents World Wide Web **35**, 203–213 (2015)
4. Färber, M., Ell, B., Menne, C., Rettinger, A., Bartscherer, F.: Linked data quality of DBpedia, Freebase, OpenCyc, Wikidata, and YAGO. Semant. Web J. (to appear). http://www.semantic-web-journal.net/
5. Fleischhacker, D., Paulheim, H., Bryl, V., Völker, J., Bizer, C.: Detecting errors in numerical linked data using cross-checked outlier detection. In: Mika, P., et al. (eds.) ISWC 2014. LNCS, vol. 8796, pp. 357–372. Springer, Cham (2014). doi:10.1007/978-3-319-11964-9_23
6. Gerber, D., Esteves, D., Lehmann, J., Bühmann, L., Usbeck, R., Ngomo, A.C.N., Speck, R.: Defacto–temporal and multilingual deep fact validation. Web Semant. Sci. Serv. Agents World Wide Web **35**, 85–101 (2015)
7. Jiang, J.J., Conrath, D.W.: Semantic similarity based on corpus statistics and lexical taxonomy. arXiv eprint arXiv:cmp-lg/9709008 (1997)
8. Lehmann, J., Gerber, D., Morsey, M., Ngomo, A.C.N.: Defacto-deep fact validation. In: The Semantic Web-ISWC 2012, Part I. LNCS, vol. 7649, pp. 312–327. Springer, Heidelberg (2012)
9. Lesk, M.: Automatic sense disambiguation using machine readable dictionaries: how to tell a pine cone from an ice cream cone. In: Proceedings of the 5th Annual International Conference on Systems Documentation, pp. 24–26. ACM (1986)
10. Li, H., Li, Y., Xu, F., Zhong, X.: Probabilistic error detecting in numerical linked data. In: Chen, Q., Hameurlain, A., Toumani, F., Wagner, R., Decker, H. (eds.) DEXA 2015. LNCS, vol. 9261, pp. 61–75. Springer, Cham (2015). doi:10.1007/978-3-319-22849-5_5
11. Lin, D.: An information-theoretic definition of similarity. In: ICML, vol. 98, pp. 296–304 (1998)
12. Liu, S., d'Aquin, M., Motta, E.: Towards linked data fact validation through measuring consensus. In: 2nd Workshop on Linked Data Quality, CEUR Workshop Proceedings, vol. 1376 (2015)
13. López-Ibáñez, M., Dubois-Lacoste, J., Cáceres, L.P., Birattari, M., Stützle, T.: The irace package: iterated racing for automatic algorithm configuration. Oper. Res. Perspect. **3**, 43–58 (2016)
14. Maron, O., Moore, A.W.: Hoeffding races: accelerating model selection search for classification and function approximation. Adv. Neural Inform. Proc. Syst. **6**, 59–66 (1994)
15. Miller, G.A.: Wordnet: a lexical database for english. Commun. ACM **38**(11), 39–41 (1995)
16. Paulheim, H.: Knowledge graph refinement: a survey of approaches and evaluation methods. Semant. Web J. **8**(3), 489–508 (2017)
17. Paulheim, H., Bizer, C.: Improving the quality of linked data using statistical distributions. Int. J. Semant. Web Inform. Syst. (IJSWIS) **10**(2), 63–86 (2014)
18. Resnik, P.: Using information content to evaluate semantic similarity in a taxonomy. In: 14th International Joint Conference on AI (IJCAI), pp. 448–453. IJCAI/AAAI (1995)
19. Schmachtenberg, M., Bizer, C., Paulheim, H.: Adoption of the linked data best practices in different topical domains. In: Mika, P., et al. (eds.) ISWC 2014. LNCS, vol. 8796, pp. 245–260. Springer, Cham (2014). doi:10.1007/978-3-319-11964-9_16
20. Wienand, D., Paulheim, H.: Detecting incorrect numerical data in DBpedia. In: Presutti, V., d'Amato, C., Gandon, F., d'Aquin, M., Staab, S., Tordai, A. (eds.) ESWC 2014. LNCS, vol. 8465, pp. 504–518. Springer, Cham (2014). doi:10.1007/978-3-319-11964-9_23

21. Wu, Z., Palmer, M.: Verbs semantics and lexical selection. In: 32nd Annual Meeting on Association for Computational Linguistics, pp. 133–138. Association for Computational Linguistics (1994)
22. Zhu, G., Iglesias, C.A.: Computing semantic similarity of concepts in knowledge graphs. IEEE Trans. Knowl. Data Eng. **29**(1), 72–85 (2017)

Exploring the Role of Gender in 19th Century Fiction Through the Lens of Word Embeddings

Siobhán Grayson[1](✉), Maria Mulvany[2], Karen Wade[2], Gerardine Meaney[2], and Derek Greene[1]

[1] School of Computer Science, University College Dublin, Dublin, Ireland
{siobhan.grayson,derek.greene}@insight-centre.org
[2] Humanities Institute, University College Dublin, Dublin, Ireland
{maria.mulvany,karen.wade,gerardine.meaney}@ucd.ie

Abstract. Within the last decade, substantial advances have been made in the field of computational linguistics, due in part to the evolution of word embedding algorithms inspired by neural network models. These algorithms attempt to derive a set of vectors which represent the vocabulary of a textual corpus in a new embedded space. This new representation can then be used to measure the underlying similarity between words. In this paper, we explore the role an author's gender may play in the selection of words that they choose to construct their narratives. Using a curated corpus of forty-eight 19th century novels, we generate, visualise, and investigate word embedding representations using a list of gender-encoded words. This allows us to explore the different ways in which male and female authors of this corpus use terms relating to contemporary understandings of gender and gender roles.

1 Introduction

In the fields of natural language processing and text mining, the study of word co-occurrences has often been used to identify the linkages between words in unstructured texts. The motivation for this type of analysis comes from the distributional hypothesis in linguistics, which states that "a word is characterised by the company it keeps" [4]. One of the most popular approaches in the literature has been *word2vec* [10], which uses a two-layer neural network model to capture word contexts in a corpus, translating words into d-dimensional *word vectors*. This allows for the detection of contextually similar words without human intervention, as vectors for words with similar semantic meanings tend to be located close to one another. One interesting corollary to this is that biases such as gender stereotypes that may be implicitly present within a corpora, can be identified and studied from a quantitative perspective [3]. Such insights are beneficial to wide range of fields, including humanities, where an increasing number of scholars are seeking to complement their literary research by incorporating computational techniques to provide alternative perspectives [7].

This particularly benefits scholars who are interested in 'distant reading' [11], the practice of understanding literature from a macro-level viewpoint, as opposed

J. Gracia et al. (Eds.): LDK 2017, LNAI 10318, pp. 358–364, 2017.
DOI: 10.1007/978-3-319-59888-8_30

to exclusively from a traditional micro-level 'close reading' standpoint. So far, a number of different computational methods have been applied to quantitatively study literature from a macro perspective. Jockers and Mimno [8] apply topic modelling to a large corpus of 19th-century fiction to identify broad themes. Whilst Reagan *et al.* [12] use sentiment analysis to understand the emotional arcs of 1,700 works of fiction from Project Gutenberg. More recently, Grayson *et al.* [5] applied word embeddings to explore 19th century fiction and investigate differences in characterisation between novels. While Heuser[1] analyses word associations produced by a *word2vec* model built on 18th-century texts, and Cherny[2] creates a visualisation of the nouns appearing in Jane Austen's *Pride and Prejudice*, generated using *word2vec* and the t-SNE visualisation method.

The most similar work to this paper is perhaps that of Schmidt [13], who uses embeddings to identify gender bias present within 'Rate My Professors' reviews and then proposes a *vector rejection* method for de-biasing embeddings by eliminating gender effects. However, unlike Schmidt, we do not seek to eliminate gender bias. Here we analyse word embeddings generated using a curated corpus of forty-eight British and Irish 19th century novels that have been manually annotated to include definitive character names[3]. We focus on uncovering the different contexts in which female and male authors of the 19th century engage with gender specific words, by compiling a list of gender-encoded unigrams, such as 'she' and 'he', and then annotating each of their occurrences within our corpus to reflect the author's gender of the text they appear in ('she_female', 'he_female'). We subsequently find differences which tally with those identified previously [1], where pronouns and nouns appear in different semantic spaces, depending on the gender of the author.

2 Methods

In this paper we consider a collection of forty-eight novels from twenty-nine 19th century novelists sourced from Project Gutenberg, summarised by author gender in Table 1. Initial data preparation involves the manual annotation of the novels, where literary scholars identify all character references in the text of each novel as described in [5]. The corpus was then further annotated using a list of gender encoded unigrams, see Fig. 1(a), where each of their occurrences within our corpus was labelled to reflect the author's gender of the text they appear in. Afterwards, part-of-speech tagging (POS tagging) was applied using the Natural Language Toolkit (NLTK) [2] PerceptronTagger implementation. For the purposes of converting our textual datasets into vector word embeddings, we employ a skipgram word2vec model [10].

Based on [5], word embeddings were generated using a skipgram model with 300 dimensions, a context window size of 5 words, and a minimum word frequency of 50. All other parameters were left at their default settings. We then

[1] http://ryanheuser.org/word-vectors-1.

[2] http://www.ghostweather.com/files/word2vecpride.

[3] The annotated texts were created as part of the "Nation, Gender, Genre" project. See http://www.nggprojectucd.ie.

visualised the resulting embeddings by reducing the dimension of each vector into a 2D space using t-Distributed Stochastic Neighbour Embedding (t-SNE) [9]. Finally, to analyse the semantic differences in how female and male authors incorporated our list of gender encoded words, we computed the cosine similarity between each of the resulting *female* and *male* labelled word embeddings to measure how similarly these words are used by authors of different genders.

Table 1. Summary of the corpus used in this work, by author gender.

Gender	#Authors	#Novels	#Characters	#Chapters	#Sentences	#Words	%Words
Female	11	22	4005	816	111,102	2,707,884	46%
Male	18	26	6436	983	136,023	3,130,090	54%
Total	29	48	10,441	1,799	247,125	5,837,974	

3 Results

The word frequency of the initial list of gender-encoded words is displayed in Fig. 1(a), where bar lengths correspond to log frequency values, while the actual word frequency is displayed within the bars. The top four words are pronouns {he, her, she, him} where 'he' is the most frequently used word by both female and male authors, with male authors using 'he' almost double the number of times they use the second most frequent word 'she'. As described in Sect. 3, a minimum word frequency 50 was applied when training the word2vec model. Therefore, words highlighted in yellow do not appear in our final embeddings, as either one or both genders did not use these words more than 50 times within our corpus. In Fig. 1(b), the resulting cosine similarity of the remaining female and male annotated embeddings are displayed: higher scores equate to greater semantic similarity whilst lower scores indicate lower semantic similarity. In this case, 'fellow' is the word that appears to be used in the most semantically similar contexts for both female and male authors, while 'husband' appears to be used in the most semantically dissimilar contexts by both genders.

As well as calculating the cosine similarity between gender annotated embeddings, we have visualised all embeddings in Fig. 2. Gender-encoded unigrams by female authors are depicted as large, pink circles while the corresponding male authored unigrams are depicted as large, grey circles. In particular, we found gender-encoded embeddings to occupy four different spaces within our embeddings projection. These spaces have been annotated A–D in Fig. 2. Group A consists of both female- and male-authored plural nouns {*fellows, women, men, ...*} from our gender-encoded list, see Fig. 1(b), nested within a pocket of past-participles verbs. However, no family related nouns such as {*daughters, sisters, brothers*} by female authors are contained despite the presence of their male-authored counterparts. Group B is the largest of our clusters and consists of singular gender-encoded nouns by both genders surrounded by nouns referring primarily to (typically male) occupations, such as "priest", "clerk", "magistrate", and "farmer". However, it also contains all the male-authored pronouns

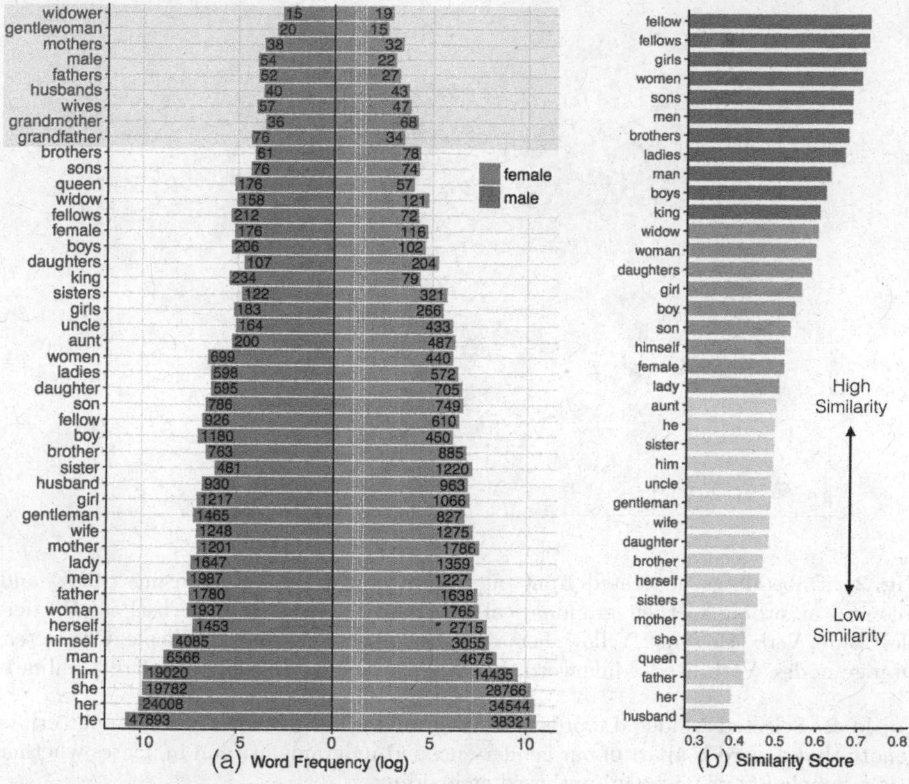

Fig. 1. (a) Word frequencies for our initial list of gender-encoded words. (b) The cosine similarity scores between female and male authored words in our gender-encoded list. (Color figure online)

within our list, again see Fig. 1(b), but only one female authored pronoun, "himself". The rest of our female authored pronouns are found within Group D, next to a mixture of past-participles (blue) and past verbs (purple). This provides and interesting counterpoint to Argamon *et al.* [1] who found differences in how women and men used words, particularly personal pronouns. Meanwhile, Group C consists of family related nouns (singular and plural) by only female authors, nested within a cluster of characters predominately from Jane Austen's novels.

Finally, we have analysed the nearest neighbours for each gender-encoded unigram. The differences between male and female authors' use of the word "her" are particularly striking. In works by female authors, "her" is frequently found alongside terms pertaining to emotional experiences, including "shrinking", "sobs", "trembling", and "flutter". By contrast, the pronoun's nearest neighbours in male-authored texts include "she", "him", and "his". Further details of the nearest neighbouring words after filtering out character names for a subset of our gender-encoded unigrams are included in Table 2. Where we observe similar behaviour in how the pronoun "he" is used differently depending

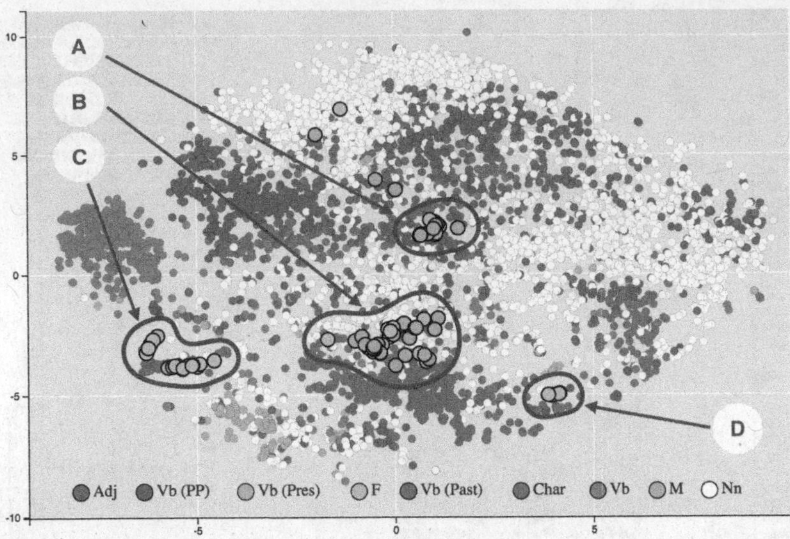

Fig. 2. Embeddings generated from our entire corpus visualised using t-SNE and coloured according to their grammatical class. Adjective: Green, Verb (Past Participle): Blue, Verb (Present): Yellow, Female: Large pink, Verb (Past): Purple, Character: Orange nodes, Verb: Red, Male word: Large grey, Noun: White. (Color figure online)

Table 2. Selected gendered words and their nearest neighbours where superscripts denote that a word is apart of our gender-encoded unigrams list and indicates whether it is a female (f) or male (m) authored embedding.

Word	Gender	8 nearest neighbours
He	F	she^f, him^f, her^f, he^m, himself^f, vaguely, nervously, trembling
	M	she^m, him^m, himself^m, his, he^f, her^m, it, that
Lady	F	gentleman^f, woman^f, girl^f, ladies^f, heiress, lady^m, widow^f, maid
	M	woman^m, gentleman^m, girl^m, aunt^m, widow^m, major, maid, friend
Gentleman	F	lady^f, man^f, farmer, clergyman, bachelor, barrister, nobleman, lawyer
	M	soldier, man^m, lady^m, officer, magistrate, farmer, nobleman, colonel

on the gender of the author. Again this tallies with what has previously been found by Argamon *et al.* [1] with respect to pronouns. The second observation is that both female and male authors tend to use the word "gentleman" in similar spaces as occupation, whilst we see the word "girl" make an appearance in both gendered neighbour lists for "lady", although the converse is not true for "boy" which is absent from both lists for "gentleman".

4 Conclusion

In this paper, we explored the differences between word use by male and female authors in a corpus of 19th century novels. Having generated, visualised and analysed word embedding representations using a list of gender-encoded word pairs, we found that there are differences in the ways in which the male and female authors of this corpus use terms relating to contemporary understandings of gender and gender roles (such as “she”, “lady”, “gentleman” and occupations/professions). Our results correspond with those of Argamon *et al.* [1], who identified significant differences in the use of personal pronouns in the writing of men and women. Although identifying the meaning of these gendered differences is beyond the scope of this preliminary survey, our analysis of word embeddings (as shown in Fig. 2) shows marked differences in the use of gendered pronouns by male and female authors. In future work, we hope to extend the size of our corpus to allow for diachronic word embedding analysis [6], in order to explore potential differences arising as a result of the era in which a novel was written and to clarify how this interacts with the gender differences we have identified.

Acknowledgments. This research was partly supported by Science Foundation Ireland (SFI) under Grant Number SFI/12/RC/2289, in collaboration with the Nation, Genre and Gender project funded by the Irish Research Council.

References

1. Argamon, S., Koppel, M., Fine, J., Shimoni, A.R.: Gender, genre, and writing style in formal written texts. Text **23**, 321–346 (2003)
2. Bird, S., Klein, E., Loper, E.: Natural Language Processing with Python. O’Reilly Media, Inc., Sebastopol (2009)
3. Bolukbasi, T., Chang, K.W., Zou, J.Y., Saligrama, V., Kalai, A.T.: Man is to computer programmer as woman is to homemaker? Debiasing word embeddings. In: Advances in Neural Information Processing Systems, pp. 4349–4357 (2016)
4. Firth, J.R.: A synopsis of linguistic theory 1930–55. In: Selected papers of J.R. Firth, 1952–59, pp. 1–32 (1957)
5. Grayson, S., Mulvany, M., Wade, K., Meaney, G., Greene, D.: Novel2Vec: characterising 19th century fiction via word embeddings. In: Proceedings of the 24 Irish AICS (2016)
6. Hamilton, W.L., Leskovec, J., Jurafsky, D.: Diachronic word embeddings reveal statistical laws of semantic change. In: Proceedings of the 54th ACL (2016)
7. Jockers, M.L.: Macroanalysis: Digital Methods and Literary History. University of Illinois Press, Urbana (2013)
8. Jockers, M.L., Mimno, D.: Significant themes in 19th-century literature. Poetics **41**(6), 750–769 (2013)
9. van der Maaten, L., Hinton, G.: Visualizing data using t-SNE. J. Mach. Learn. Res. **9**, 2579–2605 (2008)
10. Mikolov, T., Chen, K., Corrado, G., Dean, J.: Efficient estimation of word representations in vector space. In: Proceedings of the Workshop on ICLR (2013)

11. Moretti, F.: Network theory, plot analysis. New Left Rev. **68**, 80–102 (2011)
12. Reagan, A.J., Mitchell, L., Kiley, D., Danforth, C.M., Dodds, P.S.: The emotional arcs of stories are dominated by six basic shapes. arXiv e-prints (2016)
13. Schmidt, B.: Rejecting the gender binary: a vector-space operation (2015). http://bookworm.benschmidt.org/posts/2015-10-30-rejecting-the-gender-binary.html

Scalable Disambiguation System Capturing Individualities of Mentions

Tiep Mai[1], Bichen Shi[2](✉), Patrick K. Nicholson[1], Deepak Ajwani[1], and Alessandra Sala[1]

[1] Nokia Bell Labs, Dublin, Ireland
{tiep.mai,patrick.nicholson, deepak.ajwani,alessandra.sala}@nokia-bell-labs.com

[2] University College Dublin, Dublin, Ireland
bichen.shi@insight-centre.org

Abstract. Entity disambiguation, or mapping a phrase to its canonical representation in a knowledge base, is a fundamental step in many natural language processing applications. Existing techniques based on global ranking models fail to capture the individual peculiarities of the words and hence, struggle to meet the accuracy-time requirements of many real-world applications. In this paper, we propose a new system that learns specialized features and models for disambiguating each ambiguous phrase in the English language. We train and validate the hundreds of thousands of learning models for this purpose using a Wikipedia hyperlink dataset with more than 170 million labelled annotations. The computationally intensive training required for this approach can be distributed over a cluster. In addition, our approach supports fast queries, efficient updates and its accuracy compares favorably with respect to other state-of-the-art disambiguation systems.

Keywords: Entity linking · Entity disambiguation · Wikification · Word-sense disambiguation

1 Introduction

Many fundamental problems in natural language processing, such as text understanding, automatic summarization, semantic search, machine translation and linking information from heterogeneous sources, rely on entity disambiguation [6,22]. The goal of entity disambiguation and more generally, word-sense disambiguation is to map potentially ambiguous words and phrases in the text to their canonical representation in an external knowledge base (e.g., Wikipedia, Freebase entries). This involves resolving the word ambiguities inherent to natural language, such as homonymy (phrases with multiple meanings) and synonymy (different phrases with similar meanings), thereby, revealing the underlying semantics of the text.

T. Mai—Now at TrustingSocial (tiep@trustingsocial.com).

J. Gracia et al. (Eds.): LDK 2017, LNAI 10318, pp. 365–379, 2017.
DOI: 10.1007/978-3-319-59888-8_31

Challenges: This problem has been well-studied for well over a decade and has seen significant advances. However, existing disambiguation approaches still struggle to achieve the required *accuracy-time trade-off* for supporting real-world applications, particularly those that involve streaming text such as tweets, chats, emails, blogs and news articles.

A major reason behind the *accuracy* limitations of the existing approaches is that they rely on a single global ranking model (unsupervised or supervised) to map all entities. In a sense, such inflexible methods use a single rule set (a single trained/unsupervised model) for the disambiguation of all text phrases. Apart from their meanings, the phrases also differ in their origins, emotional images they evoke, their general popularity, their usage by demographic groups as well as in how they relate to the local culture. Hence, even synonymous phrases can have very different probability distribution of being mapped to different nodes in the knowledge base. However, global ranking models do not customize disambiguation rules per text phrase, fail to capture the subtle nuances of individual words and phrases in the language, and are, thus, more prone to mistakes in entity disambiguation.

Some systems perform joint disambiguation on multiple text phrases together for accuracy improvement. However, due to the utilization of pairwise word-entity, entity-entity interactions or even combinatorial interactions, many joint disambiguation approaches suffer from slow *query time*.

Our Approach: We propose a novel approach to address all of these issues in word-sense disambiguation. Our approach aims at learning the individual peculiarities of entities (words and phrases) in the English language and learns a specialized classifier for each ambiguous phrase. This allows us to find and leverage features that best differentiate the different meanings of each phrase.

To train the hundreds of thousands of classifiers for this purpose, we use the publicly available Wikipedia hyperlink dataset. This dataset contains about 170 million annotations. Since training each classifier is an independent task, our approach can be easily parallelized and we use a distributed Spark cluster for this purpose. The small number of features used in these classifiers are based on text overlap and are, therefore, light-weight enough for its usage in real-time systems. We consider this parallelization to be an important advantage of our approach of learning specialized and independent classifier for each mention (as most global supervised and unsupervised approaches are non-trivial to parallelize, if they can be parallelized at all).

Updating our system for new entities (e.g., "Ebola crisis", "Panama papers", "Migrant crisis") as well as for changing meanings of existing entities (e.g., the phrase "US President" has a higher prior of referring to "Donald Trump" after Jan. 20, 2017 and to "Barack Obama" for the previous eight years) simply requires learning the models for those entities, and does not affect the other classifiers. In contrast, existing state-of-the-art approaches would either fail to capture such changes in semantics of individual entities or require significant amount of time to update their global models.

Furthermore, unlike the increasingly popular deep learning architectures, our approach is interpretable: it is easy to understand why our models chose a particular mapping for a phrase.

We provide an extensive experimental evaluation to show that even though our system was designed to support fast disambiguation queries (average less than 3 ms) and enable efficient updates, the accuracy of our approach is comparable to many state-of-the-art disambiguation systems.

Outline: The rest of the paper is organized as follows. Section 2 presents related disambiguation techniques. Section 3 gives an overview of the Wikipedia hyperlink data used in the training of our disambiguation system. In Sect. 4, we present the details of our novel disambiguation approach. Sections 5, 6 and 7 present the experimental results of comparing with other disambiguation systems, using both Wikipedia data and the benchmark framework GERBIL [24].

2 Related Work

There is a substantial body of work focussing on the task of disambiguating entities to Wikipedia entries. The existing techniques can be roughly categorized into unsupervised approaches that are mostly graph-based and supervised approaches that learn a global ranking model for disambiguating all entities.

Graph-Based Approaches: In these approaches, a weighted graph is generally constructed with two types of nodes: phrases (mentions) from the text and the candidate entries (senses) for that phrase. For the mention-sense edges, the weights represent the likelihood of the sense for the mention in the text context. For the sense-sense edges, the weights capture their relatedness, e.g. the similarity between two Wikipedia articles in terms of categories, in-links, out-links. A scoring function is designed and then optimized on the target document so that a single sense is associated with one mention. Depending on the scoring function, this optimization can be solved using one of the following algorithms:

- Densest subgraph algorithms on an appropriately defined semantic graph and selecting the candidate sense with maximum score [11,18]
- Random walk techniques and choosing the candidate senses by the final state probability [8,10]
- Some path-based metrics for joint disambiguation [13]
- A centrality measure based on HITS algorithm on a DBpedia subgraph containing all the candidate senses (AGDISTIS approach) [23]
- PageRank on the mention-entity graph where the transition probabilities are evaluated by Word2Vec semantic embeddings and Doc2Vec context embeddings [25]
- Other centrality measures such as variant of Betweenness, Closeness, Eigenvector and Degree centrality [1]
- A probabilistic graphical model that addresses collective entity disambiguation through the loopy belief propagation [7]

Since these graph-based solutions are mostly unsupervised, there is no parameter estimation or training during the design of the scoring function to guarantee the compatibility between the proposed scoring function and the observed errors in any trained data [10,11,20]. Some disambiguation systems do apply a training phase on the final scoring function (e.g., TAGME [5]), but even here, the learning is done with a global binary ranking classifier. An alternative system uses a statistical graphical model where the unknown senses are treated as latent variables of a Markov random field [14]. In this system, the relevance between mentions and senses is modeled by a node potential and trained with max-margin method. The trained potential is combined with a non-trained measure of sense-sense relatedness, to form the final scoring function. However, maximizing this scoring function is NP-hard and computationally intensive [5].

Supervised Global Ranking Models: On the other hand, non-graph-based solutions [4,9,15–17,19] are mostly supervised in the linking phase. Milne and Witten [17] assumed that there exists unambiguous mentions associated with a single sense, and evaluated the relatedness between candidate senses and unambiguous mentions (senses). Then, a global ranking classifier is applied on the relatedness and commonness features. Not relying on the assumption of existing unambiguous mentions, Cucerzan [2] constructed document attribute vector as an attribute aggregation of all candidate senses and used scalar product to measure different similarity metrics between document and candidate senses. While the original method selected the best candidate by an unsupervised scoring function, it was later modified to use a global logistic regression model [3].

Han and Sun [9] proposed a generative probabilistic model, using the frequency of mentions and context words given a candidate sense, as independent generative features; this statistical model is also the core module of the public disambiguation service DBpedia Spotlight [4]. Olieman et al. [19] proposed various adjustments (calibrating parameters, preprocessing text input, merging normal and capitalized results) to adapt Spotlight to both short and long texts. They also used a global binary classifier with several similarity metrics to prune off uncertain Spotlight results. Houlsby and Ciaramita [12] employed a probabilistic model based upon Latent Dirichlet Allocation (LDA), and proposed a scalable Gibbs sampling scheme that exploits sparsity in the Wikipedia-LDA model.

In contrast to these approaches that learn a global ranking model for disambiguation, our approach constructs specialized features by contrasting the Wikipedia contexts of candidate senses, and learns a specialized model for each unique mention. This specialization is the main factor that enables our proposed system to achieve high accuracy, fast queries and efficient updates.

Per-mention Disambiguation: In terms of per-mention disambiguation learning on the Wikipedia knowledge base, the method by Qureshi et al. [21] is the most similar to our proposed method. However, as their method only uses Wikipedia links and categories for feature design and is trained with a small Twitter annotation dataset (60 mentions), it does not fully leverage the significantly larger Wikipedia annotation data to obtain highly accurate per-mention trained models. Also, while our feature extraction procedure is light and tuned to contrast different candidate senses per mention, their method extracts related categories, sub-categories and articles up to two depth level for each candidate sense, and requires pairwise relatedness scores between candidate sense and context senses. All these high cost features are computed on-the-fly due to the dependency on the context, potentially slowing down the disambiguation process.

3 Annotation Data and Disambiguation Problem

We begin with an example to illustrate terminology. Consider the sentence, "Java is a language understood by my computer," and focus on the underlined phrase, "Java". A human can easily link this phrase to its corresponding *entity*, `Java_(programming_language)`, by understanding that the *context* (i.e., the sentence) refers to a programming language. However, this is a non-trivial task, as there are numerous other *senses* of this phrase, such as, `Java_(island)` and `Java_(coffee)`.

Since the senses of phrases are subjective, the first task is to fix a knowledge base and produce a mapping between phrases and senses. For this purpose, we use Wikipedia as our knowledge base.[1] From Wikipedia, we extract the text bodies from Wikipedia entities (i.e., articles) e. In each entity's text body, there are hyperlink texts, linking text phrases to other Wikipedia entities. These hyperlink texts are called *annotations*; their associated text phrases and Wikipedia entities are called *mentions* and *senses*, respectively. In terms of the example above, if the example sentence appeared on some Wikipedia page in which the phrase Java was linked to the Wikipedia page `Java_(programming_language)`, we would refer to the combination of the hyperlink and phrase as an annotation: "Java" would be the mention, and `Java_(programming_language)` would be the sense.

We extract all such annotations a, linking mentions m to Wikipedia senses e[2]. Each annotation includes an annotation context, which is a number of sentences extracted from both sides of the annotation, such that the number of words on each side exceeds a predefined threshold. This threshold is set to 50 in this paper. During the extraction, text elements such as text bodies, mentions, annotation contexts are lemmatized using the python package nltk[3] for the purpose of grouping different forms of the same term. This extracted dataset is denoted by $\mathcal{A}$ in the sequel.

Formal Problem Statement: The extracted annotations are grouped by their mentions. For a single unique mention m such as "Java", we obtain the list of distinct candidate senses $E(m)$ from the annotation group of mention m, e.g. `Java_(programming_language)`, `Java_(island)`, `Java_(coffee)`. In the *disambiguation problem*, given a new unlinked annotation a with its mention m and context, one wants to find correct destination sense e among all candidate senses $E(m)$.

[1] We used WikiExtractor (http://medialab.di.unipi.it/wiki/Wikipedia_Extractor) on the 2015-07-29 dump.

[2] In our notation, a sense is a Wikipedia entity and is coupled with a specific mention.

[3] http://www.nltk.org/.

4 Disambiguation Method

Disambiguation: We use a big data approach with supervised discriminative machine learning models for the disambiguation problem. In our approach, all annotations with the same lemmatized mention are grouped together and one multi-class classifier is learnt for each lemmatized mention only using the annotations corresponding to it.

We use the light-weight and robust word-based similarity features between annotation context and sense text body, and show that coupling the specialized per-mention classifier with these features, which are tuned to contrast candidate senses, can deliver a very accurate and fast disambiguation solution. We also tried other more complex features, but they turned out to be either too costly or not as good as similarity features.

For each unique mention m, we first construct a local tf-idf matrix for the text bodies of all candidate senses $E(m)$. For each candidate sense e in $E(m)$, we consider the top n_1 words, ranked by tf-idf values. We then evaluate the similarity between an annotation context and a candidate sense by measuring the overlap between the set of annotation-context-words and the set of sense-text-body-words.

The overlap metrics are weighted in 4 different ways: *(a)* the overlap between context-words and text-body-words (number of common words in the two sets); *(b)* the overlap weighted by the tf-idf of the sense text body; *(c)* the overlap weighted by the word count of the annotation context; *(d)* the overlap weighted by the product of tf-idf and the word count. For standardization, the metrics are scaled by logarithm of the context length, which can be different for different annotations.

To further improve the accuracy, the n_1 words in the annotation context are divided, in order of their tf-idf values, into n_2 parts. In the classification model, the various overlap metrics for each part are treated as separate features, thus enabling the different tf-idf value-bands to play different roles in measuring the overall similarity.

We then group all weighted metrics of all candidate senses together as a single feature vector and learn a different multinomial logistic regression model for each mention. The size of the feature vector for a mention m is $4 * length(E(m)) * n_2$. After the learning process, the estimated model can be used to disambiguate new unlinked annotations. The complexity for each disambiguation of unlinked annotations is linear with respect to the context length and the number of candidate senses.

The key point in the above process is the per-mention learning. By doing so, we can leverage the local tf-idf construction among candidate senses to learn highly discriminative words specific to each mention. For instance, for the mention "Java", we can extract words such as "code", "machine", "drink", "delicious", that best discriminate between its different senses like "Java_(programming_language)", "Java_(coffee)". This is different from constructing features from a single global tf-idf of all Wikipedia articles, which suffers from noisy and unrelated Wikipedia articles. Furthermore, this procedure allows flexible weighting of words and features among different unique mentions, capturing the individual nuances of mentions to improve the disambiguation accuracy. The idea of this procedure is analogous to the localization property of kernel method and smoothing spline in machine learning.

Pruning: Like other annotation systems, our system has a pruner which can be enabled to remove uncertain annotations and balance the trade-off between precision and recall. However, our pruning is performed on the per-sense level.

The output of the previous multinomial logistic regression model includes both the predicted senses and the probability. Annotations with same predicted sense are grouped together. By comparing the predicted probabilities with the ground-truth, we obtain, for each sense, a list of probability scores for the correct and a list for incorrect annotations. Then, for each sense, we adjust its probability threshold to maximize the precision, subject to the constraint that the F1 should be higher than a predefined value. Thus, for each sense, we get a threshold value specific to it and we use these thresholds to prune at a per-sense level. This procedure can be easily modified to optimize F1-measure or any predefined criteria. Due to the space constraint, the pruning experiments for tuning the constraint of F1-measure and precision are omitted.

5 Experimental Set-up

One of the numerical challenges for this approach is the required computation power needed for the processing of more than 700K of unique ambiguous mentions and 170 million labelled annotations. Fortunately, as the feature construction and classification learning is per-mention, the disambiguation system is highly compatible with a data-parallel computation system. So, in order to deal with the numerical computation, we use Apache Spark[4], a distributed processing system based on Map-Reduce framework, for all data processing, feature extraction and model learning. Our Spark cluster consists of three 16×2.6 GHz 96 GB-RAM machines. All the algorithms and procedures are implemented in Python with PySpark API. For machine learning methods, we use the standard open source library scikit-learn[5].

Training and Validation Set-up: For the purposes of training and validation, the annotation dataset $\mathcal{A}$ in Sect. 3 is split by ratio (90%, 10%) per-mention. The 90% training dataset is denoted by $\mathcal{A}_1$ and the other is by $\mathcal{A}_2$. In order to validate the disambiguation system in different data scenarios such as short-text and noisy-text, we use the following transformation on the original annotation dataset $\mathcal{A}$ and create different validation sets (aside from the original validation set $\mathcal{A}_2$).

For a mention m and its candidate senses, we construct a noisy vocabulary by the unique words of the text bodies of the candidate senses. Then, for every original annotation of m in $\mathcal{A}$, we form a new annotation by sampling a fraction of

[4] http://spark.apache.org/.
[5] http://scikit-learn.org/stable/.

Table 1. Data transformation parameters

Dataset	$\mathcal{B}$	$\mathcal{C}$	$\mathcal{D}$	$\mathcal{E}$
p_1	80%	60%	40%	20%
p_2	20%	0%	0%	0%

original context-words with ratio p_1, and a fraction of noisy vocabulary with ratio p_2. For instance, given $p_1 = 80\%$, $p_2 = 20\%$, the new annotation contains 80% of the original content (randomly sampled) with 20% noisy. Four such datasets are constructed with parameters p_1, p_2 specified in Table 1 and are only used for validation purpose. We would like to see how the disambiguation system performs in short text environemnt (small values of p_1) or in the case where the real context words are contaminated by random context words (non-zero value of p_2).

Metrics: We use the standard metrics, precision $\mathcal{P}$ and recall $\mathcal{R}$, for evaluating our system. As the above metrics may be biased to mentions with a large number of labelled annotations in Wikipedia dataset, we also use a slightly different precision $\underline{\mathcal{P}}$ and recall $\underline{\mathcal{R}}$, which are averaged by per-mention precision and recall metrics across all mentions.

6 Analysis on Learning Settings

In this section, we explore and analyze the accuracy of the proposed disambiguation system.

In the feature extraction step, n_1 defines the number of unique words, ranked by tf-idf values, in each candidate sense context, used for matching with an annotation context. In the case of using a large value of n_1, we may expect the effect of high ranking words to the disambiguation classifier is different from the ones of low ranking words, and hence divide them in a number of parts n_2, as described in Sect. 4. In terms of computation, n_1 affects the cost of matching the annotation context with the top-ranked words of candidate context while n_2 affects the number of training features.

Another variable that affects the system performance is the classifier. Through preliminary experiments which are omitted from this paper due to the page limit, we find multinomial logistic regression to be the best in terms of accuracy and time complexity for this problem.

For this analysis of configurable system variables, the system is trained and evaluated on 3.4 million random annotations of 8834 randomly selected unique mentions. The validation results are provided for both the original validation dataset $\mathcal{A}_2$ and the scrambled datasets described in Sect. 5

Performance results by varying n_1 and n_2 with multinomial logistic regression are given in Table 2. The validation on $\mathcal{A}_2$ follows the holdout approach while the other validation results are evaluated on modified test sets (with shrinked contexts and random context words). $\mathcal{T}_{\text{total}}$ is the total time of feature construction, training and validation of all datasets and $\mathcal{T}_{\text{pred}}$ is the prediction time

Table 2. Performance results of different settings (n_1, n_2) with multinomial logistic regression. The best results are in bold.

n_1	n_2	$\mathcal{P}^{\mathcal{A}_2}$	$\underline{\mathcal{P}}^{\mathcal{A}_2}$	$\mathcal{P}^{\mathcal{B}}$	$\underline{\mathcal{P}}^{\mathcal{B}}$	$\mathcal{P}^{\mathcal{C}}$	$\underline{\mathcal{P}}^{\mathcal{C}}$	$\mathcal{P}^{\mathcal{D}}$	$\underline{\mathcal{P}}^{\mathcal{D}}$	$\mathcal{P}^{\mathcal{E}}$	$\underline{\mathcal{P}}^{\mathcal{E}}$	$\mathcal{T}_{\text{total}}(\times 10^3\text{s})$	$\mathcal{T}_{\text{pred}}(\text{ms})$
400	8	**.9186**	.9206	**.9325**	**.9274**	**.9351**	**.9529**	**.9053**	**.9260**	**.8550**	**.8787**	47.56	5.69
100	2	.9157	.9163	.9243	.9203	.9225	.9347	.8947	.9098	.8487	.8686	2.55	3.00
400	1	.9152	**.9215**	.9213	.9186	.9182	.9296	.8951	.9106	.8532	.8754	24.32	3.91
100	1	.9138	.9188	.9193	.9163	.9160	.9263	.8916	.9063	.8491	.8701	**18.13**	**2.81**

Table 3. Results of setting $(n_1 = 100, n_2 = 1)$ for entire Wikipedia

$\mathcal{P}^{\mathcal{A}_2}$	$\underline{\mathcal{P}}^{\mathcal{A}_2}$	$\mathcal{P}^{\mathcal{B}}$	$\underline{\mathcal{P}}^{\mathcal{B}}$	$\mathcal{P}^{\mathcal{C}}$	$\underline{\mathcal{P}}^{\mathcal{C}}$	$\mathcal{P}^{\mathcal{D}}$	$\underline{\mathcal{P}}^{\mathcal{D}}$	$\mathcal{P}^{\mathcal{E}}$	$\underline{\mathcal{P}}^{\mathcal{E}}$	$\mathcal{T}_{\text{total}}(\times 10^3\text{s})$	$\mathcal{T}_{\text{pred}}(\text{ms})$
.9188	.9220	.9261	.9172	.9238	.9265	.9012	.9067	.8617	.8712	1400.77	2.82

per-annotation (including the feature construction time); both are measured in a sequential manner as the running time of all mentions in all Spark executor instances is summed up before the evaluation.

As we want to validate purely the disambiguation process, we do not prune off uncertain predictions in this section and the disambiguation always returns a non-NIL candidate for any annotation. Consequently, precision, recall and F1-measure are all equivalent and only precision values are reported. We make the following observations about Table 2:

- Increasing n_1 and n_2 raises the precision but the increment magnitude is diminishing.
- There is a trade off between precision and running time/prediction time. If more top-ranked candidate context words and number of features are considered, the result is higher precision but slower training per-mention/prediction time per-annotation.
- The precision decreases when the context length is reduced between validation datasets $\mathcal{C}$ and $\mathcal{E}$.
- Between dataset $\mathcal{B}$ and $\mathcal{C}$, $\mathcal{B}$ has a longer but noisier context than $\mathcal{C}$, resulting in a lower precision.

The trends are clear without any random fluctuation, indicating experiment stability.

Our last experiment in this section extends to all Wikipedia mentions of more than one candidate senses. Due to the long processing time of more than 170 million annotations, we only run the system with one setting $(n_1 = 100, n_2 = 1)$. The precision results and time statistics are presented in Table 3, and it can be seen that the full performance results are stable and comparable to the ones of the corresponding settings in Table 2.

7 Comparison to Other Systems

A big advantage of our system *Per-Mention Learning* (*PML*) is that it has very fast sequential query time (less than 3ms on average). The only other system

Table 4. Comparison of DBpedia Spotlight (DS) and our proposed system (PML)

DS instance (γ)	$\lvert\mathcal{G}'\rvert$	$\mathcal{P}_{DS}$	$\underline{\mathcal{P}}_{DS}$	$\mathcal{P}_{PML}$	$\underline{\mathcal{P}}_{PML}$
0.0	65k	.8781	.8169	.9035	.8985
0.5	64k	.8822	.8201	.9051	.8989

Table 5. Comparison of TAGME (TM) and our proposed system (PML)

$\lvert\mathcal{G}'\rvert$	$\mathcal{P}_{TM}$	$\underline{\mathcal{P}}_{TM}$	$\mathcal{P}_{PML}$	$\underline{\mathcal{P}}_{PML}$
37872	.8752	.8244	.9077	.8950

Table 6. GERBIL v.1.2.2 comparison of different systems. The micro-F1 (top) and macro-F1 (bottom) scores of each system on each dataset are reported. Each column displays the best micro/macro-F1 score in red (marking the row with †), and the second best micro/macro-F1 score in blue (marking the row with ‡). An archived version of the GERBIL experiment (for all systems except for PML) can be found at http://gerbil.aksw.org/gerbil/experiment?id=201604050003.

	ACE2004	AIDA-CoNLL	AQUAINT	DBSpotlight	IITB	KORE50	Micropost	MSNBC	N3-Reuters-128	N3-RSS-500	OKE-2015	Macro-Average
PML	.637 †.793	‡.545 ‡.571	.685 .683	†.806 †.812	.460 ‡.459	.403 .376	.527 .729	.573 †.648	‡.553 ‡.592	†.677 †.676	.737 .742	‡.600 †.644
AGDISTIS	.618 .752	.498 .491	.508 .495	.263 .273	‡.467 †.480	.323 .290	.323 .593	‡.621 .569	†.642 †.699	‡.607 ‡.607	.615 .629	.499 .534
AIDA	.076 .410	.416 .384	.071 .072	.210 .184	.166 .173	‡.623 ‡.563	.331 .556	.069 .077	.353 .294	.404 .347	.617 .607	.303 .333
Babelfy	.517 .685	.543 .496	.668 .667	.520 .512	.364 .348	†.731 †.696	.471 .621	.600 .538	.439 .378	.441 .379	.684 .663	.543 .544
DBSpotlight	.471 .664	.426 .436	.520 .502	.701 .675	.296 .279	.439 .401	.495 .660	.351 .333	.325 .255	.200 .161	.244 .200	.406 .415
Dexter	.507 .667	.407 .387	.513 .502	.284 .251	.204 .204	.183 .123	.404 .587	.293 .298	.354 .302	.369 .293	.580 .510	.373 .375
EC-NER	.488 .656	.439 .420	.403 .369	.244 .194	.137 .150	.290 .252	.412 .594	.429 .407	.365 .335	.331 .320	.192 .160	.339 .351
Kea	.634 .755	.539 .524	†.763 †.753	‡.733 ‡.725	†.472 .453	.588 .527	†.631 †.758	†.662 ‡.615	.501 .447	.435 .387	‡.761 ‡.753	†.611 ‡.609
NERD-ML	.558 .714	.465 .427	.575 .554	.548 .528	.422 .411	.312 .252	.478 .629	.513 .502	.402 .340	.367 .297	.740 .719	.489 .488
TAGME 2	†.660 ‡.776	.513 .481	‡.723 .708	.661 .642	.385 .372	.590 .532	.578 .712	.590 .556	.445 .380	.470 .391	†.832 †.814	.586 .579
WAT	‡.643 .758	†.597 †.581	.714 ‡.714	.653 .666	.401 .385	.593 .491	‡.601 ‡.740	.601 .542	.504 .427	.433 .364	.697 .648	.585 .574
Macro-Average	.528 .694	.490 .473	.558 .547	.511 .497	.343 .338	.461 .409	.477 .653	.482 .462	.444 .404	.430 .384	.609 .586	

with comparable query time is TAGME. Nonetheless in this section, we show the accuracy comparison results of PML with 10 other disambiguation systems (including the ones with significantly slower query time) for the sake of completeness.

Comparison using Wikipedia as Ground Truth: In this section, we compare the proposed disambiguation system with DBpedia Spotlight[6] and TAGME[7].

An annotation set $\mathcal{G} \subset \mathcal{A}_2$ is used as an input of two Spotlight instances of different confidence values $\gamma = 0.0$ and $\gamma = 0.5$. We note that as Spotlight may not return disambiguation results for intended target mentions in annotations input due to pruning, Spotlight outputs are only for a subset $\mathcal{G}' \subset \mathcal{G}$. We then use the proposed PML disambiguation system of setting $(n_1 = 100, n_2 = 1)$ without pruning. For fairness, we only compare precision results on the subset $\mathcal{G}'$. The results are shown in Table 4, indicating that our proposed system has a higher accuracy of between 2.2% and 8.2% depending on the metric. The precision drop from $\mathcal{P}_{DS}$ to $\underline{\mathcal{P}}_{DS}$ implies that Spotlight disambiguation does not work as well as PML across distinct mentions.

For TAGME, a similar methodology is employed, but with a minor difference: the TAGME web API does not allow the user to specify the annotation for disambiguation. As a result, we rely on the TAGME spotter, and only include results where TAGME annotated exactly the same mention as the ground truth data. The precision results are shown in Table 5, indicating that our proposed system has a higher accuracy from 3.3% to 7.1%.

Comparison using GERBIL: To provide convincing evidence that our system works well on more than just Wikipedia text, we also compared our system to 10 other disambiguation systems over 11 different datasets. This was done by implementing a web-based API for our system that is compatible with GERBIL 1.2.2. [24]. Due to space constraints, we refer the interested reader to the GERBIL website[8] and paper [24] for a complete description of these systems and datasets. The task we considered is the *strong annotation task* (D2KB). In this task, we are given an input text containing a number of marked phrases, and in the output, marked phrases are associated with entities from the knowledge base. Note that the systems AGDISTIS, Babelfy, KEA, Spotlight, and WAT support D2KB directly, whereas other systems only support a *weak annotation task* (A2KB). However, GERBIL has a built-in methodology to allow these annotators to take part in the experiment[9].

We tested our system using all datasets available by default in GERBIL, which are primarily based on news articles, RSS feeds, and tweets. In Table 6, we report, for each combination of system and dataset, the micro-F1 (top) and

---

[6] We used Spotlight 0.7 [4] (statistical model en_2+2 with the SpotXmlParser.

[7] We used the TAGME version 1.8 web API http://tagme.di.unipi.it/tag in January, 2016.

[8] http://aksw.org/Projects/GERBIL.html.

[9] See the main Gerbil website as well as https://github.com/AKSW/gerbil/wiki/D2KB#handling-of-higher-order-annotators for more details. To quote the GERBIL documentation, "The response of these annotators is filtered using a strong annotation match filter. Thus, all entities that do not exactly match one of the marked entities in the gold standard are removed from the response of the annotator before it is evaluated.".

macro-F1 (bottom) scores. The micro-F1 score is the F1-measure aggregated across annotations, while the macro-F1 score is aggregated across documents. Even though not being trained on such datasets, our system is very competitive to the others.

Firstly, we observe that our system achieves very high macro-F1 scores. These macro-F1 scores are the highest in terms of average (c.f. Fig. 1), .644, and lowest in terms of the average of the ranking among 11 systems (c.f. Fig. 2), 2.45; Kea comes in second with .609 and 2.64 respectively. In terms of micro-F1, we fall slightly short of Kea in terms of average and ranking-average, .611 vs. .600 and 2.72 vs. 3.36, respectively.

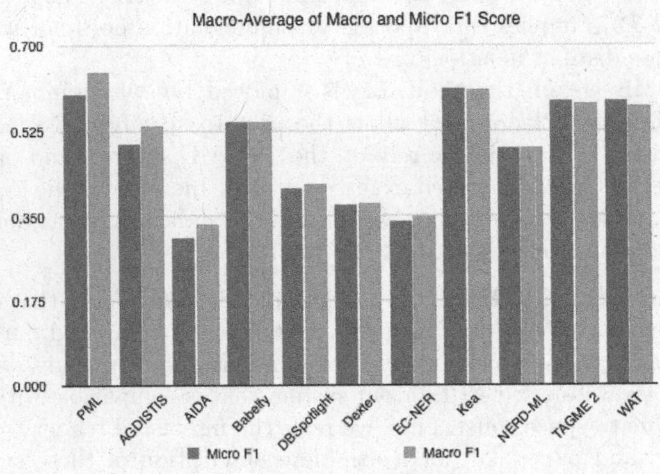

Fig. 1. The average of Micro and Macro F1 for different techniques across different data sets in Table 6

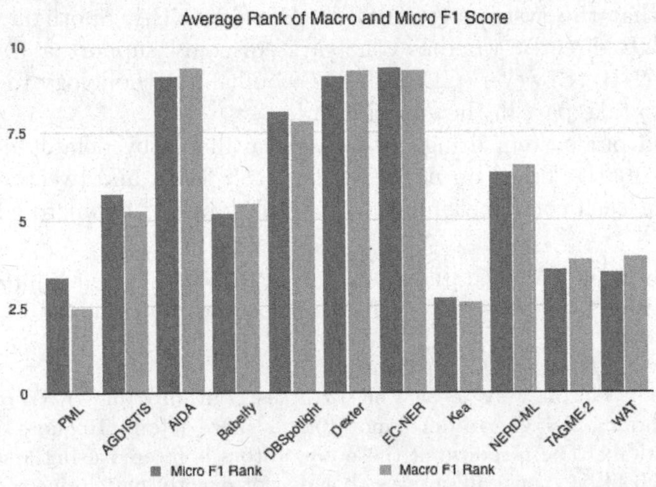

Fig. 2. Average rank of Micro and Macro F1 for different techniques (across different data sets in Table 6)

Secondly, our system does very well on news. If we restrict ourselves to the news datasets (ACE2004, AIDA/CoNLL, AQUAINT, MSNBC, N3-Reuters-128, N3-RSS-500), then we achieve the highest average and lowest rank-average scores in terms of both micro-F1 and macro-F1: .661/1.83 and .612/3.

However, our system performs quite poorly on the KORE50 dataset, which is significantly different from the training environment of Wikipedia dataset. Many entries in KORE50 dataset are single sentences involving very ambiguous entities: since our system does not perform joint disambiguation, these highly ambiguous entities are problematic, resulting in a performance drop[10].

8 Conclusions

This paper proposes a new per-mention learning (PML) disambiguation system, in which the feature engineering and model training is done per unique mention. The most significant advantage of this approach lies in the specialized learning that is highly parallelizable, supports fast queries and efficient updates. Furthermore, this per-mention disambiguation approach can be easily calibrated or tuned for specific mentions with new datasets, without affecting the results of other mentions.

In a pairwise direct comparison over 30–60 thousands of samples, our system clearly outperforms Dbpedia Spotlight and TAGME. Moreover, under the public benchmark system GERBIL, we have shown that our PML system is very competitive with 10 state-of-the-art disambiguation systems over 11 different datasets, and, for the case of disambiguating news, consistently outperforms other systems. In terms of macro-F1, PML achieves the highest average-score and the lowest average-ranking across all datasets.

References

1. Brando, C., Frontini, F., Ganascia, J.: REDEN: named entity linking in digital literary editions using linked data sets. CSIMQ **7**, 60–80 (2016)
2. Cucerzan, S.: Large-scale named entity disambiguation based on wikipedia data. In: Proceedings of the EMNLP-CoNLL, pp. 708–716, June 2007
3. Cucerzan, S.: Name entities made obvious: the participation in the ERD 2014 evaluation. In: Proceedings of the ERD, pp. 95–100. ACM, New York (2014)
4. Daiber, J., Jakob, M., Hokamp, C., Mendes, P.N.: Improving efficiency and accuracy in multilingual entity extraction. In: Proceedings of the I-SEMANTICS (2013)
5. Ferragina, P., Scaiella, U.: TAGME: on-the-fly annotation of short text fragments (by Wikipedia entities). In: Proceedings of the CIKM, pp. 1625–1628 (2010)

[10] Ideally, to achieve better performance, one would need to adapt and retrain supervised models for scenarios with short and dynamic contexts such as KORE50 dataset. One potential issue of such retraining is the lack of big labelled data. This issue could be solved by integrating the target labelled dataset with Wikipedia dataset and adjusting the sample weights to balance the training cost of the target and Wikipedia datasets. However, we decided not to do so to maintain the fairness of this comparison.

6. Ferrucci, D.A.: Introduction to "This is Watson". IBM J. Res. Dev. **56**(3), 235–249 (2012)
7. Ganea, O., Ganea, M., Lucchi, A., Eickhoff, C., Hofmann, T.: Probabilistic bag-of-hyperlinks model for entity linking. In: Proceedings of the WWW, pp. 927–938 (2016)
8. Guo, Z., Barbosa, D.: Robust entity linking via random walks. In: Proceedings of the CIKM, pp. 499–508 (2014)
9. Han, X., Sun, L.: A generative entity-mention model for linking entities with knowledge base. In: Proceedings of the HLT, pp. 945–954 (2011)
10. Han, X., Sun, L., Zhao, J.: Collective entity linking in web text: a graph-based method. In: Proceedings of the SIGIR, pp. 765–774 (2011)
11. Hoffart, J.: Discovering and disambiguating named entities in text. In: Proceedings of the SIGMOD/PODS Ph.D. Symposium, pp. 43–48 (2013)
12. Houlsby, N., Ciaramita, M.: A scalable Gibbs sampler for probabilistic entity linking. In: Rijke, M., Kenter, T., Vries, A.P., Zhai, C.X., Jong, F., Radinsky, K., Hofmann, K. (eds.) ECIR 2014. LNCS, vol. 8416, pp. 335–346. Springer, Cham (2014). doi:10.1007/978-3-319-06028-6_28
13. Hulpuş, I., Prangnawarat, N., Hayes, C.: Path-based semantic relatedness on linked data and its use to word and entity disambiguation. In: Arenas, M., Corcho, O., Simperl, E., Strohmaier, M., d'Aquin, M., Srinivas, K., Groth, P., Dumontier, M., Heflin, J., Thirunarayan, K., Staab, S. (eds.) ISWC 2015. LNCS, vol. 9366, pp. 442–457. Springer, Cham (2015). doi:10.1007/978-3-319-25007-6_26
14. Kulkarni, S., Singh, A., Ramakrishnan, G., Chakrabarti, S.: Collective annotation of Wikipedia entities in web text. In: Proceedings of the KDD, pp. 457–466 (2009)
15. McNamee, P.: HLTCOE efforts in entity linking at TAC KBP 2010. In: Proceedings of the TAC (2010)
16. Meij, E., Weerkamp, W., de Rijke, M.: Adding semantics to microblog posts. In: Proceedings of the WSDM, pp. 563–572 (2012)
17. Milne, D., Witten, I.H.: Learning to link with Wikipedia. In: Proceedings of the CIKM, pp. 509–518 (2008)
18. Moro, A., Raganato, A., Navigli, R.: Entity linking meets word sense disambiguation: a unified approach. TACL **2**, 231–244 (2014)
19. Olieman, A., Azarbonyad, H., Dehghani, M., Kamps, J., Marx, M.: Entity linking by focusing DBpedia candidate entities. In: Proceedings of the ERD, pp. 13–24 (2014)
20. Piccinno, F., Ferragina, P.: From TAGME to WAT: a new entity annotator. In: Proceedings of the ERD, pp. 55–62 (2014)
21. Qureshi, M.A., O'Riordan, C., Pasi, G.: Exploiting wikipedia for entity name disambiguation in tweets. In: Proceedings of the NLDB, pp. 184–195 (2014)
22. Suchanek, F., Weikum, G.: Knowledge harvesting in the big-data era. In: Proceedings of the SIGMOD, pp. 933–938. ACM, New York
23. Usbeck, R., Ngomo, A.N., Röder, M., Gerber, D., Coelho, S.A., Auer, S., Both, A.: AGDISTIS - agnostic disambiguation of named entities using linked open data. In: Proceedings of the ECAI, pp. 1113–1114 (2014)

24. Usbeck, R., Röder, M., Ngonga Ngomo, A.-C., Baron, C., Both, A., Brümmer, M., Ceccarelli, D., Cornolti, M., Cherix, D., Eickmann, B., Ferragina, P., Lemke, C., Moro, A., Navigli, R., Piccinno, F., Rizzo, G., Sack, H., Speck, R., Troncy, R., Waitelonis, J., Wesemann, L.: GERBIL: general entity annotator benchmarking framework. In: Proceedings of the WWW, pp. 1133–1143 (2015)
25. Zwicklbauer, S., Seifert, C., Granitzer, M.: Robust and collective entity disambiguation through semantic embeddings. In: Proceedings of the 39th International ACM SIGIR Conference on Research and Development in Information Retrieval, pp. 425–434. ACM (2016)

Multi-label Text Classification Using Semantic Features and Dimensionality Reduction with Autoencoders

Wael Alkhatib(✉), Christoph Rensing, and Johannes Silberbauer

Fachgebiet Multimedia Kommunikation, Technische Universität Darmstadt, S3/20, Rundeturmstr. 10, 64283 Darmstadt, Germany
{wael.alkhatib,christoph.rensing}@kom.tu-darmstadt.de,
johannes_david.silberbauer@stud.tu-darmstadt.de

Abstract. Feature selection is of vital concern in text classification to reduce the high dimensionality of feature space. The wide range of statistical techniques which have been proposed for weighting and selecting features suffer from loss of semantic relationship among concepts and ignoring of dependencies and ordering between adjacent words. In this work we propose two techniques for incorporating semantics in feature selection. Furthermore, we use autoencoders to transform the features into a reduced feature space in order to analyse the performance penalty of feature extraction. Our intensive experiments, using the EUR-lex dataset, showed that semantic-based feature selection techniques significantly outperform the Bag-of-Word (BOW) frequency based feature selection method with term frequency/inverse document frequency (TF-IDF) for features weighting. In addition, after an aggressive dimensionality reduction of original features with a factor of 10, the autoencoders are still capable of producing better features compared to BOW with TF-IDF.

Keywords: Semantics · Feature selection · Dimensionality reduction · Text classification · Semantic relations · Autoencoders

1 Introduction

Text classification applications have become widespread as a result of the tremendous growth in the amount of data, most of which are unstructured [1]. Popularised by search engines like Google, searching through large amounts of natural language text has become a key research topic. Since most users search for documents using concepts describing a conceptual topic, techniques based on literal word matching are often not good enough to produce relevant results [2]. The need for machine learning techniques for text classification has emerged as a result of the fact that, the amount of data to be searched and classified is too large to rely on classification by human subject matter experts outside very limited high value application fields.

J. Gracia et al. (Eds.): LDK 2017, LNAI 10318, pp. 380–394, 2017.
DOI: 10.1007/978-3-319-59888-8_32

Classification problems deal with the task of assigning a number of classes C out of a predefined set of classes L to an input. Such problems can either be binary, multi-class or multi label [3]. Binary classification is the problem of assigning one out of two labels meaning that $|C| = 1$ and $|L| = 2$. A problem where the task is to assign exactly one class C out of $|L|$ mutually exclusive classes to an input is called multi-class, while a classification problem is called a multi-label classification problem when the task is to classify the input into $m = |C|$ out of the set of classes L where $m \leq |L|$.

Text representation is an essential preprocessing step in text classification where documents are transformed into a format consumable by machine learning models. This involves representing each document as a vector with the size of the vocabulary where each dimension corresponds to the relevance of a concept to the document [4]. Relevance can for example be computed using weighting schema i.e. TF-IDF. In general this method produces high dimensional, sparse vectors which are extremely challenging for learning algorithms [5]. To increase the manageability of the problem, machine learning techniques apply a process called dimensionality reduction which aims at reducing redundancy and noise in the data set by mapping it into a lower dimensional space using a wide range of feature selection and extraction techniques. The potential of such techniques to improve computational efficiency and result accuracy has been demonstrated as well [6].

In this work, we propose a new method for incorporating semantic knowledge into feature selection for dimensionality reduction. Using linguistic filters we extract all noun phrases to provide a terminology of basic and extended concepts. Then we extract semantic relations between the noun phrases in order to build an acyclic directed graph as a basic shallow ontology of the documents. Using the directed graph of concepts, we propose different techniques to select the features based on the relationship between concepts. Further, aiming to a reduced feature space, we investigate the trade-off between the dimensionality reduction factor and the performance penalty using autoencoders. The empirical evaluation results showed that two of our proposed methods significantly outperform the baseline approach of BOW with TF-IDF weighting method using different multi-label classifiers.

The paper is organized as follow: An overview of related work in feature selection and extraction is provided in Sect. 2. We introduce our concept for the semantic-based feature extraction in Sect. 3. Section 4 presents the evaluation metrics while Sect. 5 demonstrates the comparative analysis and evaluation of the proposed methods against TF-IDF as a baseline. Finally, Sect. 6 summarizes the paper and discusses future work.

2 Related Work

Dimensionality reduction can be achieved by feature selection and feature extraction [7]. In the following, we introduce a variety of methods which fall into these two categories and we relate them to our methodology.

2.1 Feature Selection

Feature selection handles the problem of selecting a subset of features that is most effective for building a good predictor. This can be done by statistical or semantic-based measures [8]. The more widely used feature selection approaches are the statistical-based [9–11]. The most common methods include Information Gain (IG) and Chi-Square (Chi2). Information Gain (IG) makes use of the presence and absence of a concept in a document to select its features, while Chi2 measures the degree of dependence between a concept and a category as a base to select the features. The major drawback of the earliest statistical-based feature selection is ignoring textual features dependencies, structure and ordering.

Incorporating text semantics can provide better performance with regard to the used feature selection techniques. Masuyama et al. analysed the impact of selecting terms as features based on their part-of-speech (POS) specifically nouns, verbs, adjectives and adverbs. By analysing the different combinations of these four categories, they found out that a much smaller feature set of nouns is able to perform better than other POS combined [12]. D.D. Lewis used all noun phrases that occurred at least twice as feature phrases in text categorization [13]. After applying clustering of phrases and words, he concluded that phrases produce less effective representation than single words. Y. Liu et al. showed that using bi-gram and tri-gram to leverage context information of word depending on previous or next words can improve the performance, however, word sequence of more than 3 decreases the performance [14,15]. A. Khan et al. used frequent sequence (MSF) for extracting of associated frequent sentences and co-occurring terms. Also, they used WordNet [16], a lexical database, as a domain ontology to convert these terms to concepts and update the SVM with new feature weights [17] which also leads to a better performance. Other researchers incorporate the ontological knowledge for training-less ontology-based text classification or to provide meta-information for feature selection [18–20].

2.2 Feature Extraction

Feature extraction attempts to build a new optimised set of features from the original dataset i.e. the text documents or the selected features. One of the most widely used and well known statistical-based methods for reducing the dimensionality is principal component analysis (PCA) [21]. The aim of this technique is to find the directions of greatest variance in the data. The data set is then represented as a linear combination of those directions. This presumes that the data is located in a low-dimensional linear space and discards class information [22]. Similar to PCA, linear discriminant analysis (LDA) tries to find a linear combination of variables to represent the data but takes class assignment information into account. Another technique relying on linear combinations is local linear embedding (LLE) [23]. This technique attempts to represent each data point through a linear combination of its neighbours. A further technique introduced by L. Maaten et al. t-distributed stochastic neighbour embedding (t-SNE) is particularly useful for reducing the feature space to two or three dimensions for visualisation [24]. It strives to preserve similarity between data points and has been successfully applied not only to documents [25] but also to other fields like malicious software [26]. The algorithm scales quadratically with the number of samples making the technique computationally expensive [27]. There are a multitude of extensions and variations to the algorithms described above as well as further different approaches [28–30].

Previously, researchers have incorporated text semantics in feature selection by selecting noun phrases or n-grams as features, others tried to leverage external lexical databases mainly WodNet to enhance the performance more. However, extracting ontological associations using external lexical resources has shortcomings due to the small coverage of concepts for particular domains and thus less ontological entities can be acquired. In our work, we improve on previous research by considering words context and dependencies to extract single and multi-word noun phrases as candidate features. Later on, instead of relying on external thesaurus, we extract semantic associations between concept pairs from the unstructured text using lexico syntactic patterns. Finally, based on the semantic relations between concepts in the taxonomic hierarchy of relationships, we propose four methods for selecting features based on semantics. Moreover, we analyse the performance penalty of using autoencoders for constructing reduced feature space from the original feature set.

3 Methodology

In the proposed method, we incorporate text semantics by taking context information and dependencies of words in consideration to select new features. Later on, we analyse the trade-off between dimensionality reduction factor and performance penalty using autoencoders. As shown in Fig. 1, the proposed approach consists of the following steps:

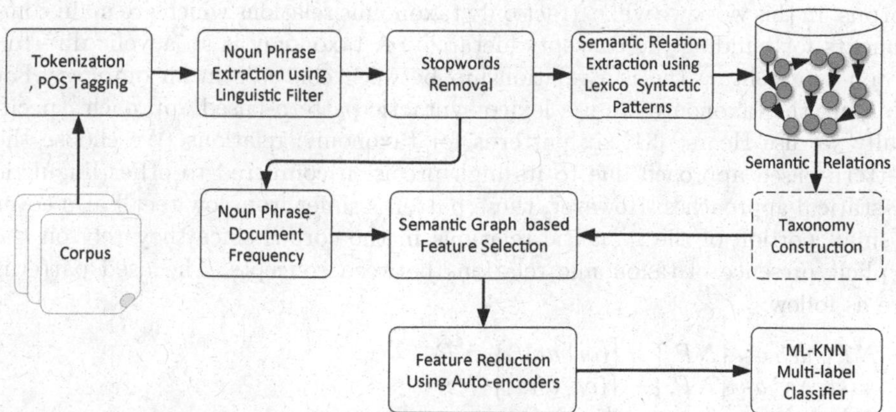

Fig. 1. Block diagram of the proposed semantic-based feature selection method

3.1 Linguistic Filter

In the first step we identify the domain terminology by extracting all noun phrases in order to form the basis for our semantic relation extraction phase. The role of the linguistic filter is to recognize essential concepts and filter out sequence of words that are unlikely to be concepts using linguistic information. In the linguistic component, the text documents need to be preprocessed by a part-of-speech tagger for marking up the words in a text (corpus), based on their context, as corresponding to a particular part of speech i.e. noun, preposition, verb, etc. Multi-word NP like Supervised Machine Learning will be considered as one feature and concatenated as supervised_machine_learning. A combination of 3 linguistic filters is used to extract multi-word noun phrases NPs that can reflect essential concepts.

- $Noun\,Noun+$
- $Adj\ Noun+$
- $(Adj|\,Noun)+\ Noun$

3.2 Stop-Word Removal

In this phase, words that are unlikely to be part of concepts are excluded using stop-words list. A stop-word is a word that frequently appears with no strong association to a particular domain terminology and thus it is not expected to occur as concept word i.e. "regularly", "followed", "mostly", "everywhere", etc.

3.3 Semantic Relation Extraction

The aim here is to identify noun phrases which represent a concept or an instance of a concept, through extracting both explicit and implicit semantic relations i.e. Hypernym *(Is-A)* or Meronymy *(Part-Whole)* from all documents in the used corpus. In this work we will extract only taxonomic relations which are main components for building the concepts hierarchy. A taxonomy is an acyclic directed graph representing the is-a relationship between concepts in an ontology. For building the taxonomy, we use lexico syntactic pattern-based approach, specifically we use Hearst [31] six patterns for taxonomic relations. We choose the pattern-based approach due to its high precision compared to other linguistic or statical approaches. However, these patterns suffer from low recall also cover a small portion of the semantic relations in the corpus since they rely on the explicit presence of taxonomic relations between concepts. The used patterns are as follow:

- $NP\ such\,as\ \{NP,\}*\ \{(or|\ and)\}\ NP$
- $sush\ NP\,as\ \{NP,\}*\ \{(or|\ and)\}\ NP$
- $NP\ \{,NP\}*\{,\}\ or\ other\ NP$
- $NP\ \{,NP\}*\{,\}\ and\,other\ NP$
- $NP\ \{,\}\ including\ \{NP,\}*\ \{(or|\ and)\}\ NP$
- $NP\ \{,\}\ especially\ \{NP,\}*\ \{(or|\ and)\}\ NP$

3.4 Semantic-Based Feature Selection

We propose four different feature selection techniques based on the associations between the extracted concepts using the linguistic filter and the taxonomic relations as shown in Fig. 2. Based on the graph theory we can identify candidate features using the concept position in the hierarchy and the associated sub-concepts.

- ***Concept-Document Frequency (C-DF):*** The number of documents where this concept occurs.
- ***Associated Concepts:*** The number of sub-concepts underneath in the taxonomic hierarchy.
- ***Concept Height:*** The degree is the number of edges connected to the concept, in other words, direct sub-concepts.
- ***Concept Degree:*** The height is the number of edges on the longest downward path between that concept and a sub-concept.

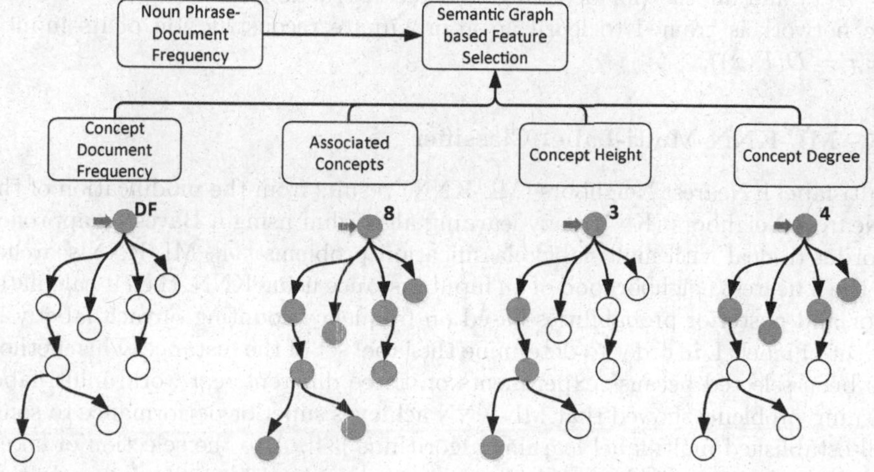

Fig. 2. Semantic feature selection based on concept associations to the underneath sub-concepts.

3.5 Feature Transformation with Autoencoders

A basic autoencoder is a feedforward, non-recurrent neural network trained to learn a reconstruction of its input. It consists of input layer and output layer with several hidden layers in between. The key element is a bottleneck in the middle that forces the network to learn an encoded version of its data [32]. This concept is illustrated in Fig. 3. This approach has been shown to outperform

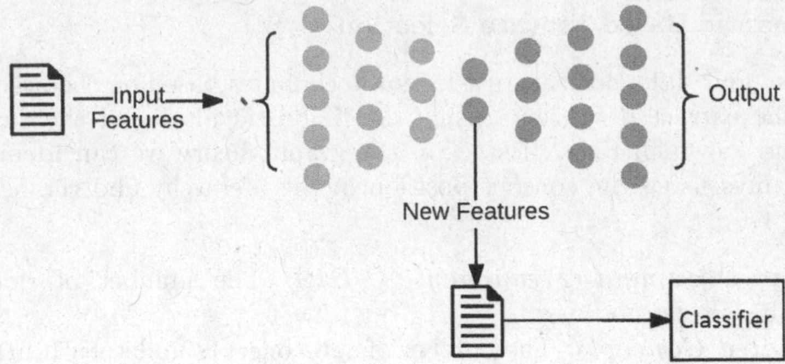

Fig. 3. Feature transformation using autoencoders

linear approaches for dimensionality reduction i.e. PCA or LDA Sect. 2 as well as more recent algorithms [33].

The network can be looked upon as a two part function: One for encoding $e = E(x)$ and another for decoding to a reconstruction of the input $r = D(e)$. The network is trained to learn an approximate reconstruction of its input : $x \approx r = D(E(x))$.

3.6 ML-KNN Multi-Label Classifier

Multi-label k Nearest Neighbors (ML-KNN) results from the modification of the k Nearest Neighbors (KNN) lazy learning algorithm using a Bayesian approach in order to deal with multi-label classification problems [34]. ML-KNN searches for the k nearest neighborhood of an input instance using KNN, then it calculates prior and posterior probabilities based on frequency counting of each label y in the set of labels L in order to determine the label set of the instance. This method has been selected because experiments on three different real-world multi-label learning problems showed that ML-KNN achieves superior performance to some well-established multi-label learning algorithms [34]. Also the selection of labels based on nearest neighborhood is more convenient with our feature selection technique which consider features order and dependencies.

4 Evaluation Metrics

A classifier can either be evaluated by examining each label separately and then averaging the results. Such schemes are called *label-based.* Another approach is by considering the average difference between the expected and the predicted sets of labels over all test examples, such metrics are called *example-based.*

For a number of classifier predictions, we have the number of *true positive (TP), false positive (FP), true negative (TN)* and *false negative (FN)* predictions respectively. From those numbers we can calculate the evaluation metrics mentioned below:

$$Precision = \frac{TP}{TP + FP} \tag{1}$$

$$Recall = \frac{TP}{TP + FN} \tag{2}$$

$$F - Measure = 2 * \frac{Precision * Recall}{Precision + Recall} \tag{3}$$

The total label-based evaluation measures for a multi-label problem where TP_j, FP_j, TN_j, FN_j are the predictions for the *j-th* label. A micro-averaged metric M_{micro} is defined as:

$$M_{micro} = M(\sum_{j=1}^{q} TP_j, \sum_{j=1}^{q} FP_j, \sum_{j=1}^{q} TN_j, \sum_{j=1}^{q} FN_j) \tag{4}$$

While macro-averaged metric M_{micro} is defined as:

$$M_{macro} = \frac{1}{q} \sum_{j=1}^{q} M(TP_j, FP_j, TN_j, FN_j) \tag{5}$$

In addition, one example based metric, the Hamming Loss, is used in our evaluation:

$$HammingLoss(h, D) = \frac{1}{|D|} \sum_{i=1}^{|D|} \frac{xor(Y_i, Z_i)}{|L|} \tag{6}$$

D is the set of examples (x_i, Y_i) with $Y_i \subseteq L$ and Z_i is the predicted set of labels for x_i.

5 Evaluation

In the context of our comparative analysis, the EUR-lex dataset has been used [35]. It is a text dataset containing European Union laws, treaties, international agreements, preparatory acts and other public documents. It contains 19.348 text documents, which are published in 24 official languages of the European Union. The EUR-Lex repository readily contains three different labelling schemes - *directory-codes, subject-matters* and *eurovoc-descriptors* - for its documents. However, for the evaluation we used only *subject-matters.* A detailed description of parsing and obtaining the documents, the TF-IDF features as well as the dataset properties can be found here [36]. Table 1 provides a summary of the characteristics of the subject-matters labelling scheme.

Stanford CoreNLP toolkit [37] was used in this work for performing the different natural language processing tasks (POS, linguistic filter and taxonomic

Table 1. Data-Set statistics

	Unique labels	Label cardinality	Label density
Subject matters	201	2.21	1.10

relations extraction). It combines machine learning and probabilistic approaches to NLP with sophisticated, deep linguistic modelling techniques. This toolkit provides state-of-the-art technology for wide range of natural-language processing tasks. Also it is quite widely used, both in the research NLP community, industry, and government.

The used linguistic filter to extract single and multi-word concepts resulted in 940685 distinct features. Then lexico syntactic pattern-based approach for extracting semantic relations between different features was applied using Hearst patterns for taxonomic relation extraction. Thus only taxonomic *(Is-A)* relationships were extracted, this phase resulted in 26333 is-a relationships. By incorporating other patterns from [38] in addition to Hearst patterns, we managed to retrieve 47500 relations but with significantly lower precision. For that, in the next steps we used the taxonomic relations extracted only from Hearst six patterns due to their higher precision. The extracted relations resulted in an acyclic directed graph representing the is-a relationships in the dataset.

5.1 Semantic-Based Feature Selection

The carried out experiments aimed to compare the effectiveness of using semantic-based feature selection techniques against the BOW model of TF-IDF as a baseline. Four different feature selection techniques were evaluated *Concept Height*, *Concept Degree*, *Associated concepts* and *Concept-Document Frequency* with binary weighting of the features. TF-IDF with BOW feature selection was used for comparison since this approach was successfully implemented as statistical feature selection method [36]. For multi-label classification we used ML-KNN with the number of nearest neighbours $K = 10$ as fixed parameter during the experiments. In addition the number of features was fixed to 5000 features for the comparative analysis with the original TF-IDF feature set provided by EL Mencía et al. [36]. The used ML-KNN classifier for the evaluation was implemented using the MULAN open-source library for multi-label classification [39].

Figure 4 shows the cross-validation evaluation results of the different performance metrics namely, Macro/Micro-averaged F-Measure, Subset Accuracy and Average Precision. The figure compares the proposed semantic-based feature selection techniques against the baseline using ML-KNN with same configurations. Higher values indicate better performance for these metrics while lower values indicate better performance for Hamming Loss in Fig. 5. The results indicate that *Associated Concepts* and *Concept-Document Frequency (C-DF)* significantly outperformed the baseline over all performance metrics, while the baseline performed better compared to *Concept Degree* and *Concept Height. Associated Concepts* and *C-DF* had relative reduction in Hamming Loss of 15.38% and

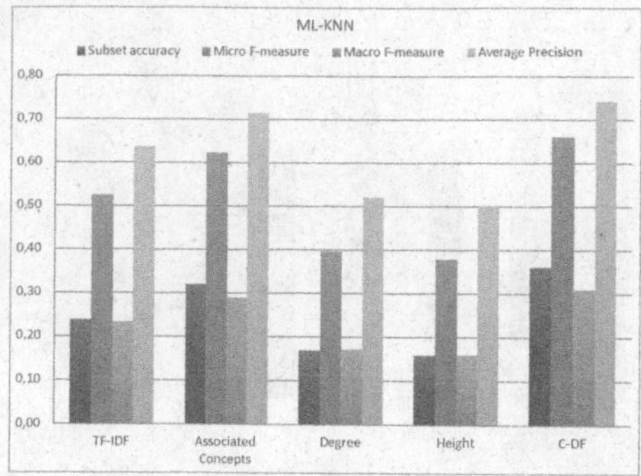

Fig. 4. Evaluation metrics of using ML-KNN with TF-IDF and BOW feature selection against different semantic-based feature selection techniques.

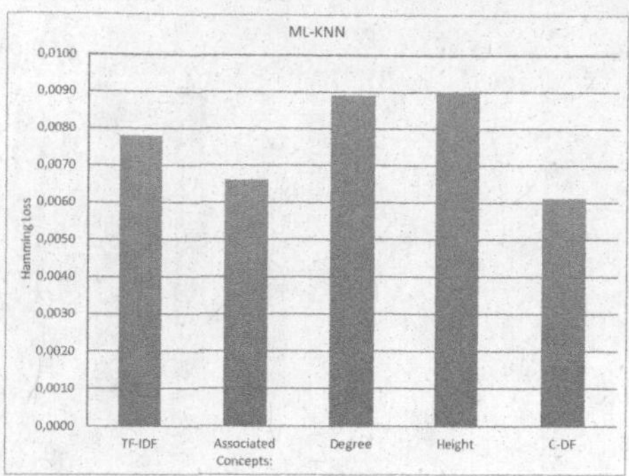

Fig. 5. Hamming Loss of using ML-KNN with TF-IDF and BOW feature selection against different semantic-based feature selection techniques.

21.79% respectively over TF-IDF with BOW feature selection Fig. 5, which indicates lower probability of an incorrect prediction of the relevance of an example to a class label.

For more comprehensive evaluation, we compared ML-KNN using *C-DF* as feature selection techniques with a set of multi-label classifiers of the two main classifier categories namely, transformation and adaptation approaches using TF-IDF with BOW for feature selection and weighting. The used methods are Binary Relevance, Clustering Based, HOMER, BPMLL, HMC, BRKNN and Pruned Sets. We selected these methods because they have very distinct classification procedures. Figure 6 shows that ML-KNN with *C-DF* as feature selection technique had the best performance with the lowest Hamming Loss value.

The significant improvement in performance using *Associated Concepts* and *C-DF* aligns with previous researches which proved the importance of considering text semantics for feature selection. However, *C-DF* also outperformed *Associated Concepts* technique which can be justified by the relatively low number of extracted semantic relations using Hearst patterns. Based on that, further improvement is possible by integrating other techniques for associating different concepts based on their taxonomic and none-taxonomic relations. Also the lower performance of *Concept Degree* and *Concept Height* is roughly related to the low document frequency for concepts with less number of associated concepts underneath in the hierarchy.

5.2 Feature Transformation with Autoencoders

In this evaluation phase, we analysed the trade-off between dimensionality reduction factor and performance penalty. The input for the autoencoders network were the top 5000 *C-DF* features. Also ML-KNN was used with the number of nearest neighbours $K = 10$.

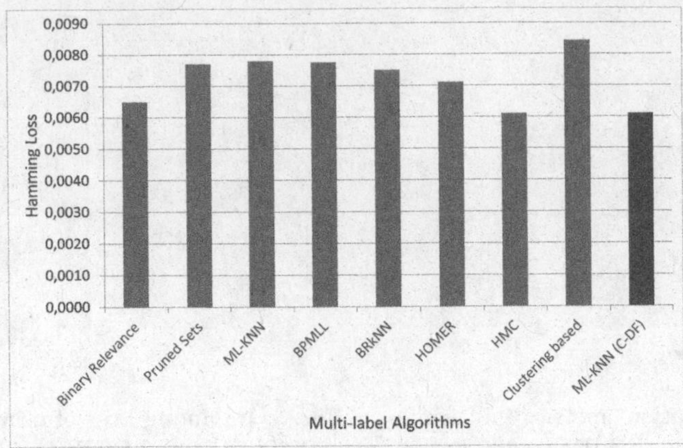

Fig. 6. Comparative analysis of ML-KNN using *C-DF* as feature selection techniques against a set of multi-label classifiers with TF-IDF features.

During the experiments, different layers configuration for the network have been evaluated as shown in Table 2. The resulted feature set of *C-DF* was directly fed into the autoencoder network. The autoencoder were configured with a network of 5 hidden layers. To analyse the effect of layer sizes on the classification results, we applied the evaluation multiple times for the different layers configurations. The outer layer size remained fixed since those have to be the size of the original *C-DF* features. We trained the network for one iteration using a batch size of 1000. The autoencoder network was implemented using the open-source Deeplearning4j framework.

Table 2. The autoencoder layers configuration for each experiment

Experiment #	Layers configurations
1	10-250-1000-5000
2	30-500-1500-5000
3	50-800-2000-5000
4	100-800-2500-5000
5	150-800-3000-5000
6	250-800-3500-5000
7	500-800-4000-5000
8	750-2000-4500-5000
9	1000-2500-4800-5000
10	1500-2800-4800-5000
11	2000-3000-4800-5000
12	3000-3500-4800-5000

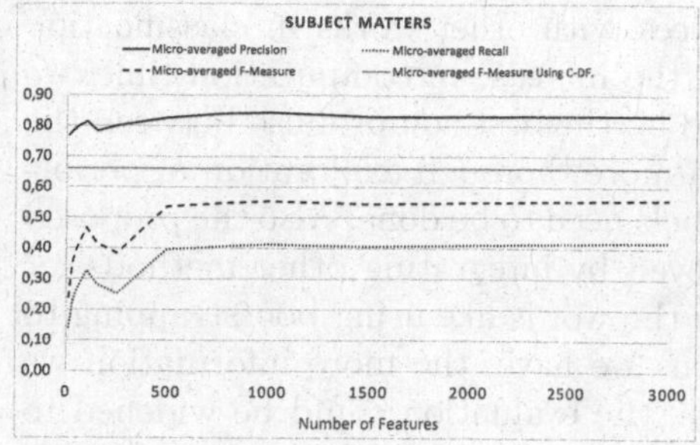

Fig. 7. Performance evaluation of ML-KNN with different number of reduced features from the original *C-DF* set using autoencoders as feature extraction technique.

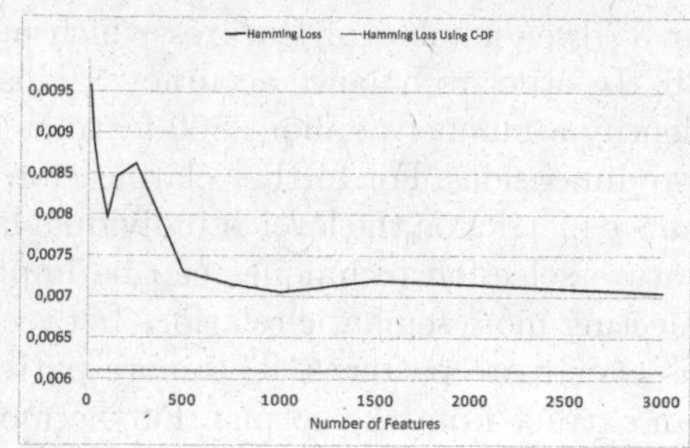

Fig. 8. Hamming Loss of ML-KNN with different number of reduced features from the original *C-DF* set using autoencoders as feature extraction technique.

Here we considered the performance of ML-KNN with *C-DF* as feature selection method with no further feature extraction as a baseline. Figure 7 shows that the classification performance based on the micro-averaged metrics, namely recall, precision and F-Measure was significantly improving when the number of encoded features increased till 500 features. However, the performance slightly improved or was almost flat with higher number of features than 500. The micro-averaged F-measure converged towards a common value of $0,56$ which still better than the performance of ML-KNN using TF-IDF with micro-averaged F-measure equals $0,52$. This means using semantic-based features with feature transformation using the autoencoder of factor 10 (transforming the original 5000 features into 500) can still provide better performance compared to the baseline statistical approach. However, Fig. 7 shows a drop in the performance when the number of used features equals 250 then it increased again for 500, this give us insights about the quality of the features and that more effort should be paid on configuring the autoencoders hybrid parameters. Same conclusion can be applied on Hamming Loss Fig. 8, which changed more drastically till 500 features and then slightly improved when the number of features increased above 500.

6 Discussion

In this work we proposed four methods to select semantic-based features without relying on any external lexical databases or dictionaries. The *Associated Concepts* and *C-DF* significantly outperformed the statistical-based approach of TF-IDF with BOW feature selection over different multi-label classifiers. The different techniques proved that taking in consideration the structure, order and dependencies between words can provide better performance with regard to the statistical-based approaches. Furthermore, using autoencoders we showed that even aggressive dimensionality reduction up to a factor of 10 produced better results compared to the baseline. We also found that classification works better for a lower number of features which agrees with other works in classification [36]. In order to balance accuracy against the increase in computation time, we identify a number of about 500 features to be the best compromise between the two dimensions. For further clarification a more thorough exploration of performance metrics on the level of individual labels need to be done. Also the proposed feature selection techniques can be improved by integrating other methods for selecting more semantic relations between the words like using bootstrapping to discover more patterns. The more patterns we have, the more information we can extract from the corpus. Furthermore, the evaluation could be widened to include other types of autoencoders, e.g. denoising autoencoders.

References

1. Witten, I.H., Frank, E., Hall, M.A., Pal, C.J.: Data Mining: Practical Machine Learning Tools and Techniques. Morgan Kaufmann, San Francisco (2016)
2. Deerwester, S., Dumais, S.T., Furnas, G.W., Landauer, T.K., Harshman, R.: Indexing by latent semantic analysis. J. Am. Soc. Inf. Sci. **41**(6), 391 (1990)
3. Sokolova, M., Lapalme, G.: A systematic analysis of performance measures for classification tasks. Inf. Process. Manage. **45**(4), 427–437 (2009)
4. Sebastiani, F.: Text categorization. In: Encyclopedia of Database Technologies and Applications, pp. 683–687. IGI Global (2005)
5. Fodor, I.K.: A survey of dimension reduction techniques, Center for Applied Scientific Computing, Lawrence Livermore National Laboratory, vol. 9, pp. 1–18 (2002)
6. Cunningham, P.: Dimension reduction. In: Cord, M., Cunningham, P. (eds.) Machine Learning Techniques for Multimedia, pp. 91–112. Springer, Heidelberg (2008)
7. Pudil, P., Novovičová, J.: Novel methods for feature subset selection with respect to problem knowledge. In: Liu, H., Motoda, H. (eds.) Feature Extraction, Construction and Selection, vol. 453, pp. 101–116. Springer, New York (1998)
8. Guyon, I., Elisseeff, A.: An introduction to variable and feature selection. J. Mach. Learn. Res. **3**, 1157–1182 (2003)
9. Ogura, H., Amano, H., Kondo, M.: Feature selection with a measure of deviations from poisson in text categorization. Expert Syst. Appl. **36**(3), 6826–6832 (2009)
10. Soucy, P., Mineau, G.W.: Beyond TFIDF weighting for text categorization in the vector space model. In: IJCAI, vol. 5, pp. 1130–1135 (2005)
11. Yang, Y., Pedersen, J.O.: A comparative study on feature selection in text categorization. In: ICML, vol. 97, pp. 412–420 (1997)
12. Masuyama, T., Nakagawa, H.: Cascaded feature selection in SVMs text categorization. In: Gelbukh, A. (ed.) CICLing 2003. LNCS, vol. 2588, pp. 588–591. Springer, Heidelberg (2003). doi:10.1007/3-540-36456-0_65
13. Lewis, D.D.: Feature selection and feature extraction for text categorization. In: Proceedings of the Workshop on Speech and Natural Language, pp. 212–217. Association for Computational Linguistics (1992)
14. Liu, Y., Loh, H.T., Lu, W.F.: Deriving taxonomy from documents at sentence level. In: Prado, H.A.D., Ferneda, E. (eds.) Emerging Technologies of Text Mining: Techniques and Applications, Idea, Hershey, PA, pp. 99–119 (2007)
15. Fürnkranz, J.: A study using n-gram features for text categorization. Austrian Res. Inst. Artif. Intell. **3**, 1–10 (1998)

16. Miller, G.A.: Wordnet: a lexical database for english. Commun. ACM **38**(11), 39–41 (1995)
17. Khan, A., Baharudin, B., Khan, K.: Semantic based features selection and weighting method for text classification. In: 2010 International Symposium in Information Technology (ITSim), vol. 2, pp. 850–855. IEEE (2010)
18. Janik, M., Kochut, K.: Training-less ontology-based text categorization. In: Workshop on Exploiting Semantic Annotations in Information Retrieval (ESAIR 2008) at the 30th European Conference on Information Retrieval, ECIR, vol. 20 (2008)
19. Chang, Y.-H., Huang, H.-Y.: An automatic document classifier system based on Naive Bayes classifier and ontology. In: 2008 International Conference on Machine Learning and Cybernetics, vol. 6, pp. 3144–3149. IEEE (2008)
20. Chua, S., Kulathuramaiyer, N.: Feature selection based on semantics. In: Elleithy, K. (ed.) Innovations and Advanced Techniques in Systems, Computing Sciences and Software Engineering, pp. 471–476. Springer, Dordrecht (2008)
21. Wold, S., Esbensen, K., Geladi, P.: Principal component analysis. Chemom. Intell. Lab. Syst. **2**(1–3), 37–52 (1987)
22. Jolliffe, I.: Principal Component Analysis. Wiley Online Library, Aberdeen (2002)
23. Roweis, S.T., Saul, L.K.: Nonlinear dimensionality reduction by locally linear embedding. Science **290**(5500), 2323–2326 (2000)
24. Maaten, L., Hinton, G.: Visualizing data using t-SNE. J. Mach. Learn. Res. **9**, 2579–2605 (2008)
25. Lacoste-Julien, S., Sha, F., Jordan, M.I.: DiscLDA: discriminative learning for dimensionality reduction and classification. In: Advances in Neural Information Processing Systems, pp. 897–904 (2009)
26. Thonnard, O., Mees, W., Dacier, M.: Addressing the attack attribution problem using knowledge discovery and multi-criteria fuzzy decision-making. In: Proceedings of the ACM SIGKDD Workshop on CyberSecurity and Intelligence Informatics, pp. 11–21. ACM (2009)
27. Van Der Maaten, L.: Fast optimization for t-SNE. In: 2010 Workshop on Challenges in Data Visualization Neural Information Processing Systems (NIPS), vol. 100 (2010)
28. Bengio, Y., Paiement, J.-F., Vincent, P., Delalleau, O., Le Roux, N., Ouimet, M.: Out-of-sample extensions for LLE, Isomap, MDS, Eigenmaps, and spectral clustering. MIJ **1**, 2 (2003)
29. Belkin, M., Niyogi, P.: Laplacian eigenmaps and spectral techniques for embedding and clustering. NIPS **14**(14), 585–591 (2001)
30. Tenenbaum, J.B., De Silva, V., Langford, J.C.: A global geometric framework for nonlinear dimensionality reduction. Science **290**(5500), 2319–2323 (2000)
31. Hearst, M.A.: Automatic acquisition of hyponyms from large text corpora. In: Proceedings of the 14th Conference on Computational linguistics, vol. 2, pp. 539–545. Association for Computational Linguistics (1992)
32. Vincent, P., Larochelle, H., Lajoie, I., Bengio, Y., Manzagol, P.-A.: Stacked denoising autoencoders: learning useful representations in a deep network with a local denoising criterion. J. Mach. Learn. Res. **11**, 3371–3408 (2010)
33. Hinton, G.E., Salakhutdinov, R.R.: Reducing the dimensionality of data with neural networks. Science **313**(5786), 504–507 (2006)
34. Zhang, M.-L., Zhou, Z.-H.: ML-KNN: a lazy learning approach to multi-label learning. Pattern Recogn. **40**(7), 2038–2048 (2007)
35. (01, 2017). http://www.ke.tu-darmstadt.de/resources/eurlex

36. Loza Mencía, E., Fürnkranz, J.: Efficient multilabel classification algorithms for large-scale problems in the legal domain. In: Francesconi, E., Montemagni, S., Peters, W., Tiscornia, D. (eds.) Semantic Processing of Legal Texts. LNCS, vol. 6036, pp. 192–215. Springer, Heidelberg (2010). doi:10.1007/978-3-642-12837-0_11
37. Manning, C.D., Surdeanu, M., Bauer, J., Finkel, J.R., Bethard, S., McClosky, D.: The stanford coreNLP natural language processing toolkit. In: ACL (System Demonstrations), pp. 55–60 (2014)
38. Seitner, J., Bizer, C., Eckert, K., Faralli, S., Meusel, R., Paulheim, H., Ponzetto, S.: A large database of hypernymy relations extracted from the web. In: Proceedings of the Language Resources and Evaluation Conference, Portoroz, Slovenia, 10th edn. (2016)
39. Tsoumakas, G., Katakis, I., Vlahavas, I.: Mining multi-label data. In: Maimon, O., Rokach, L. (eds.) Data Mining and Knowledge Discovery Handbook, pp. 667–685. Springer, New York (2009)

Author Index

Printed in the United States
By Bookmasters